COLLECTING FIRST DAY COVERS

26th Edition 2007

The complete guide to the variety of first day covers and postmarks available for each Royal Mail stamp issue.

Compiled, designed & edited by

ADRIAN BRADBURY

A.G. BRADBURY FIRST DAY COVERS

BFDC

Published by A G BRADBURY
3 Link Road Stoneygate Leicester LE2 3RA
Telephone: 0116 2705367 email brad@bfdc.co.uk www.bfdc.co.uk

1st Edition - Dec 1980
2nd (revised) Edition - Oct 1981
3rd (revised) Edition - Oct 1982
4th (revised) Edition - Oct 1983
5th (revised) Edition - Oct 1984
6th (revised) Edition - Oct 1985
7th (revised) Edition - Oct 1986
8th (revised) Edition - Oct 1987
9th (revised) Edition - Oct 1988
10th (revised) Edition - Oct 1989
11th (revised) Edition - Oct 1990
12th (revised) Edition - Oct 1991
13th (revised) Edition - Oct 1992
14th (revised) Edition - Oct 1993
15th (revised) Edition - Oct 1994
16th (revised) Edition - Oct 1995
17th (revised) Edition - Oct 1996
18th (revised) Edition - Oct 1997
19th (revised) Edition - Oct 1998
20th (revised) Edition - Oct 1999
21st (revised) Edition - Dec 2000
22nd (revised) Edition - Oct 2001
23rd (revised) Edition - Oct 2002
24th (revised) Edition - Oct 2004
25th (revised) Edition - Oct 2005
26th (revised) Edition - Nov 2006

ISBN 0-9540710-5-0

Origination by A G Bradbury
Printed by A. T. Shelley (Printers) Ltd., Leicester.

The original work of 1980 was compiled by Norman C. Porter.
His contribution is gratefully acknowledged.

FOREWORD

I am delighted to have been asked by Adrian Bradbury (Brad to his many friends, acquaintances and customers) to write the foreword to this catalogue.

Now in its 26th year, Collecting British First Day Covers has become the standard reference work for British first day cover collectors, due to the sheer volume and accuracy of the information contained and the clarity of the layout. A useful addition to this year's catalogue is the pricing of all official covers from the 1999 Millennium issues onwards, though it has to be said that the pricing of all recently issued collectables is far from an exact science and prices should only be taken as a guide. As a cover gets older and examples are traded and auctioned more frequently, then an established price tends to develop.

Over the last two or three years there has been, in my opinion, a considerable improvement in the subject matter and quality of design of Royal Mail stamps. This has made for a vibrant collecting market, with many fine covers being produced. The cover market remains strong, but there is evidence that collectors are increasingly seeking, and prepared to pay high prices for, covers that they find to be well designed and with strong subject matter. My own view is that, in the case of modern covers, it is now less important to collectors in general whether or not a cover is technically an official cover, that is where the cover has been designed by the person or organisation who sponsored the handstamp. Equally, the number of covers issued, whilst naturally of some importance, is not necessarily a key factor. Many covers have been produced over the last ten years in quantities of less than 100, but unless the cover has been well produced and is historically or thematically interesting, it may not be exceptionally collectable in the long term.

Prices in this catalogue should be taken only as a guide, and undoubtedly there are some covers priced in this catalogue at £20.00 which would fetch £50.00 at auction tomorrow and vice versa; but though a cover fetches £50.00 at auction, if it is auctioned a month later, it might only fetch half that. At the end of the day, as in all markets, price is determined by what the collector is prepared to pay and what the vendor is prepared to accept, but Brad's expertise and years of experience in the First Day Cover business, combined with peer review by others closely associated with the trade, means that the prices quoted will give all collectors as good an idea as possible of the relative scarcity of material.

Antony Grodecki
Managing Director, The Benham Group

CONTENTS

GENERAL NOTES

The first day covers illustrated below are good examples of what to look for when buying:
(1) Clean covers with stamps positioned in a neat manner.
(2) Postmarks clearly legible and relevant to the stamp issue.
(3) No hand written addresses.

Now look at the cover below which has almost everything wrong:
(1) Untidy hand written address.
(2) Postmark bears no relevance to the stamp issue.
(3) Stamps are overlapping and too close to the edge of the cover.

1. Introduction

The General Notes set out at the beginning of this catalogue should answer most of the questions concerning the hobby of *Collecting British First Day Covers*. After studying these notes and the body of the catalogue, it will become apparent that this fascinating subject can prove to be a very worthwhile and absorbing hobby. There is a wide variety of covers and postmarks available for each stamp issue, giving plenty of choice for the collector.

2. What is a first day cover?

First Day Covers (FDCs) are essentially envelopes with newly issued postage stamps affixed and postmarked on the first day that those stamps are placed on sale by Royal Mail. Early examples are usually only available on plain envelopes with specially designed envelopes appearing regularly in the 1950s. All first day of issue dates are listed alongside the title of each stamp issue in the catalogue.

First day covers should not be confused with souvenir or commemorative covers. These are usually issued to coincide with the date of a special event or anniversary, whereas first day covers are issued on the first day of sale of new stamps.

3. Scope

All first day covers for both British commemorative and definitive stamp issues are listed in this catalogue. The publisher makes no judgements as to the suitability of particular makes of cover or types of postmark - this is a decision solely for the collector. Sections 6 and 7 of these General Notes will guide the collector through the vast array of postmarks and covers available.

It should be remembered, that like many collectables, certain types of cover or postmark which are popular now, may, or may not be, sought after in the future.

4. Format

First day covers for **commemorative** stamp issues are divided into the following four sections:

4.1 1924 Wembley - 1961 Parliament
Prices for these issues have been set out in two columns - the first for illustrated covers and the second for plain (i.e. non-illustrated covers).

4.2 1962 National Productivity Year - 1967 Flowers
During this period commemorative stamps were issued both with and without phosphor bands. The two columns reflect prices for both types of cover. All prices from 1962 are for illustrated covers. Plain covers are often available for this period but not generally collected - being worth very little compared to illustrated covers.

4.3 1967 British Paintings - 1998 Christmas
With effect from the 1967 Paintings issue all commemorative stamps were phosphor-coated. Prices are now shown for *ordinary* and *official/sponsored* covers (see Section 7).

First day covers for **definitive** stamp issues are listed in an easy to follow section at the end of the catalogue.

5. Values and Condition

This catalogue has been compiled as a work of reference and is NOT A G Bradbury's own price list.

The prices quoted should be treated as a guide, and are for clean, undamaged covers and unless otherwise stated, with the full set of stamps. Many factors affect the price of first day covers, e.g:

5.1 Condition

The following are important in determining the value of a cover:

(a) the proper siting of stamps.
(b) the neatness of the address on older covers, more recent covers should be unaddressed.
(c) the quality and legibility of the postmarks.
(d) the relevance of the postmarks to the stamp issue.

Invariably older covers will be of inferior quality when compared to more recent issues and allowance should be made for this when buying such covers. **As a general guide** the prices quoted in the catalogue are for unaddressed covers or with a small address label or small printed or rubber stamped address. Covers from before the mid 60s are acceptable with neat hand-written addresses whilst covers from the mid 60s to early 70s are acceptable with typed addresses.

Very scarce covers may well retail at full catalogue value even if they do not conform to the above guidelines. Condition is everything - a scruffy cover in poor condition will only be worth a small fraction of its pristine counterpart.

5.2 Supply and Demand

The market in first day covers is no different to any other commodity and is subject to the same economic forces.

5.3 VAT

Check whether your supplier is charging VAT. Values quoted in this catalogue include VAT at the standard rate.

In the final analysis, the value of a cover is determined at a price which both dealer and collector feel is acceptable.

Values quoted with **(s)** appended or where this appears after the official cover description, indicates that the covers are only known with a single stamp or incomplete set. The initials **'n.k.'** in the price column indicates that as far as the editor is aware the covers do not exist. My thanks go to **Benhams** who have assisted with the prices of their own covers and for covers from 1999 onwards.

6. Types of Postmarks

Each commemorative stamp issue has been classified according to the type of postmarks available. These fall into four distinct categories: special handstamps, ordinary first day of issue postmarks, counter date stamps and slogan postmarks.

6.1 Special Handstamps

These are specially designed postmarks which are by far the most popular with most collectors - see examples alongside. Until the 1990s special handstamps were applied with hand held machines and the quality of impressions varied considerably. However, today's covers are serviced with more sophisticated *pad canceller* machines which give consistently good impressions, and allow for more intricate postmark designs.

Any member of the public is permitted to sponsor a special handstamp - at a current cost of £195 (plus VAT) - provided that they adhere to certain Royal Mail guidelines. The special handstamp remains the property of Royal Mail and is applied to philatelic items by trained Royal Mail staff. All special

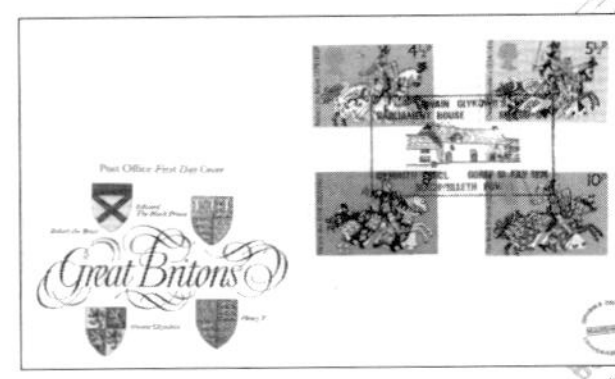

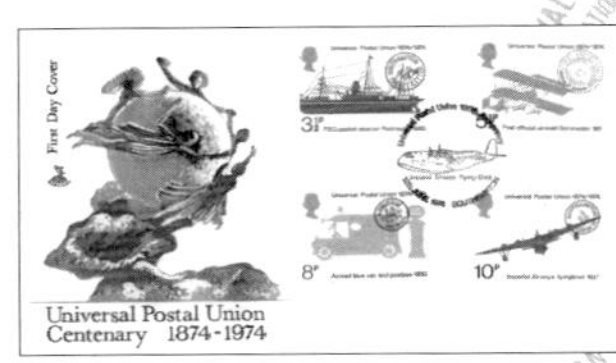

SPECIAL HANDSTAMPS

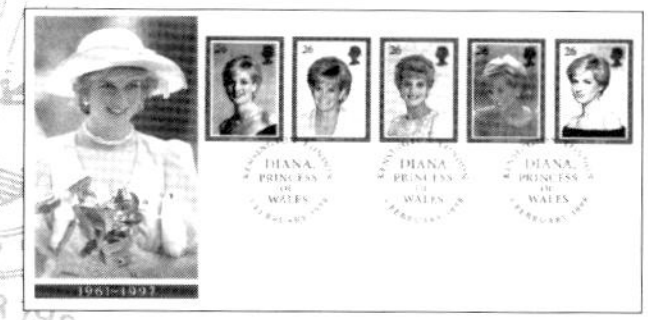

ORDINARY FDI POSTMARK

CDS PMKS: NAME ASSOCIATION

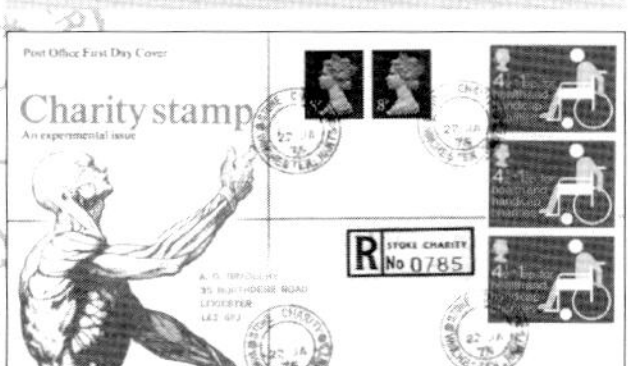

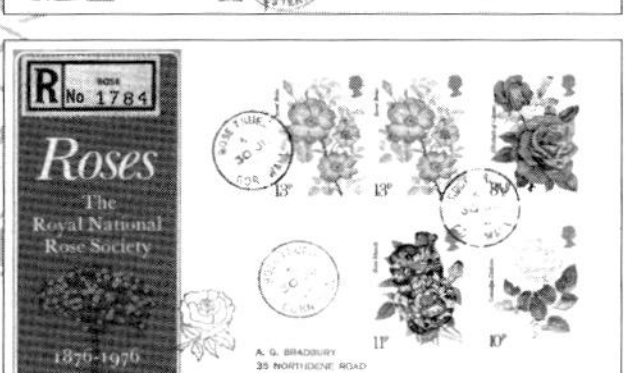

handstamps are advertised in advance in the ***British Postmark Bulletin*** - a fortnightly newsletter issued by Royal Mail (see page 14). By subscribing to the Bulletin collectors can find out before the stamp issue date which postmarks will be available. They can then send in to the appropriate Special Handstamp Centres requesting that particular special handstamps be applied to their first day covers. This is known as the *re-posting facility*.

Royal Mail operates five Special Handstamp Centres which provide an excellent service for dealers and collectors. These centres employ staff working full-time on philatelic items. All special handstamps are now applied at these Centres, each of which covers a specific area of the country, viz:

Royal Mail London	for London & SE England
Royal Mail Cardiff	for Wales & SW England
Royal Mail Birmingham	for Midland & East to the Wash
Royal Mail Newcastle	for Northern England
Royal Mail Glasgow	for Scotland & Northern Ireland

All special handstamps in use on the first day of issue of a set of commemorative stamps are included in the catalogue whether relevant to an issue or not. Some covers serviced with handstamps which are not relevant may be priced higher than others with more appropriate handstamps. This is because past issues are often more difficult to obtain, as fewer were serviced - especially with the full set of stamps.

Over the years Royal Mail (and some sponsors) have provided special handstamps which are available on every first day of issue. Except where relevant to an issue these have been omitted. Please refer to Section 8 for more details.

6.2 Ordinary First Day of Issue (FDI) postmarks 1964 - 1998

These postmarks were introduced with the 1964 Shakespeare issue when the then GPO realised that there was a need for proper philatelic postmarking. They are circular in design, incorporating the town name and date of stamp issue and were used in many towns and cities throughout the UK. In use for all commemorative issues and many definitive stamp issues, FDI postmarks were applied by Royal Mail staff using hand held machines. They were also available to collectors under the *re-posting facility*.

These postmarks are listed from their introduction up to the 1970 Christmas issue. The start of the decimal period saw much wider use of special handstamps. However there are numerous examples of where no special handstamps were available at places with an obvious connection with the stamp issues. In such cases, where a FDI postmark was available, these have been listed. FDI postmarks were withdrawn after the 1998 Christmas issue.

6.3 Counter Date Stamp (CDS) postmarks

Sometimes known as circular date stamps, these are standard everyday cancellations available at all Post Office counters. In most cases the only way to obtain these operational postmarks is to use Royal Mail's **Special Delivery Service**, although some Post Offices will cancel ordinary mail.

During the early years, first day covers were generally only available with CDS postmarks and most had no relevance to the stamp issue.

During the 1960s and up to the present day, the collecting of relevant CDS postmarks has become a specialist interest. The criterion used for the inclusion of these postmarks is that they should have a bearing on the stamp issue. Items which are 'one-off' or have a dubious connection with the issue are not listed. The items included were available in reasonable quantities - i.e. twenty or more covers. The CDS postmarks

6. Types of Postmarks (contd)

are included even if there is a special handstamp or ordinary FDI postmark available for the same area because often the CDS postmarks are more valid. For example on the 2002 Airliners issue all Heathrow special handstamps were applied by the London Special Handstamp Centre; the only covers to be actually postmarked at Heathrow are the CDS postmarks of Terminal 2 & 4.

The proliferation of CDS postmarks (from the 1979 Christmas issue) necessitated their classification into main and ancillary listings. Those postmarks which have a more direct connection to an issue are given a full listing. Other CDS postmarks are listed in italics below the main listing. From 1999 only the more relevant CDS postmarks are listed.

It should be noted that it is not always possible to get perfect postmark impressions. Post Office counter staff who agree to frank covers in this way do so for little or no reward. Quite often the metal counter date stamps are old or worn, or the ink pad may be under or over inked causing faint or smudged postmarks. The general rule is that at least one of the postmarks should provide a legible place name and date.

Broadly speaking, the criteria used to for determining whether a postmark is included in the main listing are as follows:

(a) Name association
The name of a Post Office has a strong link with the stamp issue, e.g. 1991 Roses postmaked at Rose, Cornwall.

(b) Place association
A Post Office is located in, or near to, a place which is commemorated on the stamp issue, e.g. 2002 Bridges of London issue postmarked at London Bridge Post Office. Where the connection is not obvious, better covers will have an explanatory cachet.

(c) House of Commons & House of Lords
These CDS postmarks are not usually available to members of the public, and are only listed where relevant, e.g.:

- (i) Where an issue commemorates the passing of legislation, e.g. the 1980 Birds issue celebrates the centenary of the Wild Bird Protection Act.
- (ii) Parliamentary issues, e.g. 1973 and 1975
- (iii) Where a featured individual has a strong connection with parliament, e.g. 1965 and 1974 Churchill issues.
- (iv) Royalty issues.

(d) Royal households
Postal facilities at Buckingham Palace, Windsor Castle, Balmoral Castle, and Sandringham House are only available to members of the Royal Family or staff of the Royal Household. Whilst these postmarks on first day covers are extremely scarce, especially Balmoral and Sandringham, these are only listed where the stamp issue involves a royal theme, e.g. Royal Weddings.

(e) Travelling Post Offices
e.g. 1975, 1980, 1985 and 1994 train issues.

(f) Paquebots
European issues, e.g. 1973 EEC, 1979 European Elections.

6.4 Slogan Postmarks 1924 -1996
These were machine cancellations applied to the vast majority of British mail. A slogan postmark consists of two parts, viz: a circle showing the time, date and sorting office; and more often than not, an advertising 'slogan'. The dates the slogans were to be used were advertised in advance in the ***British***

CDS PMKS: PLACE ASSOCIATION

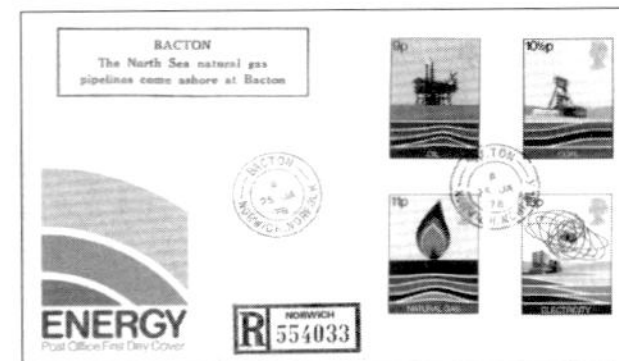

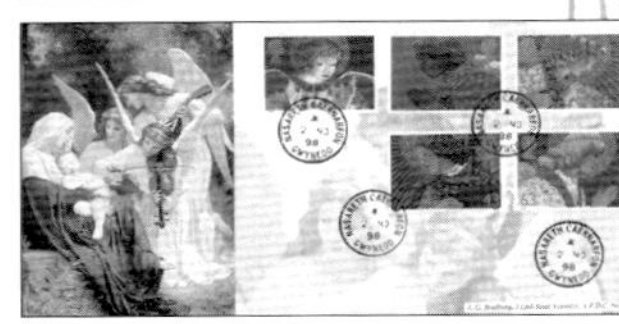

CDS PMKS: HOUSE of COMMONS

CDS PMKS: HOUSE of LORDS

CDS PMKS: BUCKINGHAM PALACE

CDS PMKS: TPOs

SLOGAN POSTMARKS

COVER PRODUCERS

Postmark Bulletin. The *re-posting facility* for this service was withdrawn after the 1996 Christmas issue. Three types of slogan have been available to the collector, viz:

(a) First Day of Issue Slogans
First introduced in 1963 (Paris Postal Conference issue), these were used on covers posted in special posting boxes at selected Post Offices. These were mostly replaced by the ordinary FDI handstamps (see Section 6.2).

(b) 'Wavy-line' machine postmarks
These have only been listed if the location at which they were used was connected to the stamp issue.

(c) Advertising slogans
The criterion used to determine whether a slogan should be included depends on its relevance to the stamp issue. Unlike CDS postmarks, the location of the Post Office at which a slogan was used was not as important as the wording or illustration of the slogan, which should have a good connection with the stamp issue. The proliferation of slogan postmarks (from 1979 Christmas issue) necessitated their classification into main and ancillary listings. Those postmarks which, in the opinion of the publisher, have a close or direct connection to an issue are given a full listing. Other slogan postmarks are listed in italics below the main listing.

Late use of slogans
Slogan postmark campaigns were booked to run for a specified period and were advertised as such in the *Postmark Bulletin*. Sometimes slogans ran over their allotted time because there was no alternative available. This sometimes resulted in a slogan being in use at the time of the first day of issue of a new set of stamps where the subject of the stamps and slogan were closely linked. This situation produced some very collectable covers.

Proper siting of stamps
Earlier covers are usually only available with a slogan which obliterates the stamps which often makes the slogan difficult to read. However with effect from 1974 most covers were available with the stamps positioned in such a way as to make the slogan clearly legible. To achieve this the stamps had to be sited so that the slogan or its date slug only cancelled one stamp, the remaining stamps being franked with a CDS or FDI postmark. Once again, it should be stressed that it was not always possible to get good clean impressions. To obtain these postmarks the covers were fed through automatic franking machines which handled thousands of items per day.
Royal Mail ceased to provide a re-posting facility for slogans after the 1996 Christmas issue, and now no longer accepts advertising slogans from firms or organisations.

7. Types of Cover

First day cover envelopes fall into two categories: 'ordinary' (or commercial) covers and 'official' (or sponsored) covers.

7.1 Ordinary/Commercial Covers
These are produced primarily for the general FDC collector and are usually sold as 'blanks' (i.e. with no stamps affixed). They are available from most good stamp shops before the day of issue of the postage stamps. Collectors purchase the 'blanks', affix the stamps and arrange to have their covers

7. Types of Cover (contd)

postmarked. Royal Mail produce their own FDC which is available through Post Offices prior to the issue date. Only three makes are currently available for collectors, viz: *Royal Mail, Cotswold* and *Stuart*. The list below is a summary of the different covers which have been available since first day cover collecting became an active hobby.

Abbey: Produced from 1969 until 1982 and sold fully serviced. All numbered limited editions and recognisable by their 'Abbey' logo.

Artcraft: Based in America - covers produced from 1948 Olympic Games until Battle of Hastings issue of 1966.

Benham small 'silks': These are only available fully serviced - usually sets of single stamp covers. They commenced with 1980 Birds issue. See also entries in 'official' covers section.

Benham 'woodcut': The only Benham covers which were available as blanks were first produced for the 1968 Bridges issue and continued through to the 1978 Historic Buildings issue.

Cameo: The Cameo Stamp Centre produced a few covers in 1970 and 1971 bearing the 'Cameo' logo.

Colorano 'silk': These were first produced for the 1974 Horse Chestnut issue and appeared for most issues up to the early 1980s.

Connoisseur: Published between 1963–1970 and bearing an Old English 'C' logo, these were marketed by R F Grover of Fareham, Hants.

Cotswold: Cotswold die-stamped covers first appeared with the 1970 Christmas issue and are still in production. A large square 'C' border is common to all their designs.

Heyden: At least three designs for each issue. Published by Jeffrey Booth (Stamp Searchers) since 1990. These are not available as blanks.

Fourpenny Post: From 1996 Burns until 2003.

Mercury: Published from 1972 to 1993 by Harry Allen of Rickmansworth, these die-stamped covers bear a 'Mercury' logo.

Philart: Produced from 1964 Geographical issue through to 1990. Philart 'Luxury' die-stamped covers were available from the 1969 Ships issues until the early 1980s.

Newlands Rd Philatelic Society: An all junior stamp club which produced covers between 1957 Scouts - 1983 Christmas.

PPS: Presentation Philatelic Services produced their first blank for the 1981 Butterflies issue. Christmas 1981 saw their first 'silk' cover which continued through to Christmas 1983. The Sotheby's 'silk' series ran from 1984 Heraldry to 1995 Christmas, with the Cigarette Cards 'silk' series from 1988 Linnean through to 1994 Christmas.

PTS/BPA: The Philatelic Traders Society and the British Philatelic Association jointly produced a number of covers from the 1948 Olympics issue through to the 1966 World Cup.

Peter Scot: Covers from 1978 Energy and ceasing in 1988.

Royal Mail: The first PO cover appeared for the 1964 Shakespeare issue and for all issues to date with the exception of 1965 Salvation Army, Joseph Lister, Arts, UN, ITU and 1966 England Winners.

Save the Childen Fund: These were produced for the earlier

BENHAM SMALL SILK

BENHAM WOODCUT

COTSWOLD

FOURPENNY POST

MERCURY

PHILART

SAVE THE CHILDREN FUND

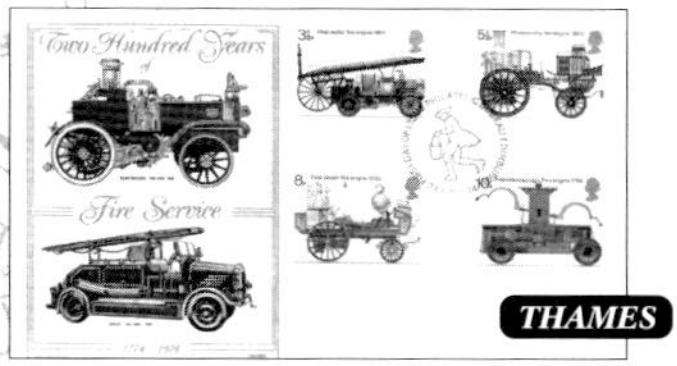

'OFFICIAL' COVER PRODUCERS

Benham BLCS Series

Benham Special Gold Series

Leicester First Day Cover Series

Victorian Prints Series

decimal issues commencing with the 1973 Royal Wedding.

Stuart: First produced for the 1965 Churchill issue, this series is still available and now published by Cotswold covers. The envelopes are die-stamped and feature a 'thistle' logo.

Thames: First issued for the 1968 Bridges set and continuing through to the 1974 Christmas issue, the covers had a similar appearance to die-stamping. The earlier issues were printed with a 'Thames estuary' logo on the envelope flap.

Trident: Produced for some 1969/70 issues and bearing a 'Trident' logo.

Wessex: Printed with a 'wyvern' logo, these were first produced for the 1967 EFTA issue and then regularly until 1975. A few have been produced since, most notably the 1977 Silver Jubilee.

7.2 Official/Sponsored Covers

In the context of this catalogue, 'official' covers are defined as covers produced by private organisations or cover producers, who at the same time sponsor a special handstamp to accompany their cover. Some official/sponsored covers are produced in small quantities and in some cases may not be available to collectors. Such covers are therefore rarer than the 'ordinary' covers with the same handstamp.

Sometimes an organisation will not affix the full set of stamps to their covers because not all of the stamps may be relevant. It may be possible in such cases to obtain the blank envelopes from the sponsor and affix your own stamps, thus creating a full set cover. However, where covers are only known to exist with an incomplete set, the official cover description in italics is suffixed with **(s)**.

Since the mid 1980s the rules governing the sponsorship of special handstamps has been relaxed with the result that there are now far more sponsored - mostly by first day cover producers. Anyone can sponsor handstamps depicting places such as Westminster Abbey or Windsor Castle. The covers used to accompany these handstamps are only 'official' in the context of this catalogue, i.e. in most cases no special sanction has been received from the places depicted. Therefore with effect from 1997 I have referred to such covers as 'sponsored' - a more meaningful description.

(a) Covers published by First Day Cover Producers

(i) those forming a FDC series

BL	- British Library (1976-82) - with BL pmks
BLCS	- Benham luxury cover series (1985 to date)
BLS	- Benham large 'silk' (1982-1984)
BenL	- Benham limited edition (1981 to date)
BenSG	- Benham Special Gold (1986 to date)
Ben500	- Benham 500 series (1985 to date)
BOCS	- Benham official cover series (1978-84)
Bletchley PO	- Bletchley Park PO (1994 to date)
P Barrett	- Southern Cover Series (1998 to date)
M Brazier	- Public Houses Series (1999 to date)
Britannia	- Bradbury Britannia Series (2001 to date)
BritHerCollect	- British Heritage Collectables (1999-2002)
Buckingham	- Buckingham Covers of Folkestone (2001 to date)
FDP Co	- First Day Publishing Co. (1994-98)
Fine Art	- Fine Art Covers, Brentwood (1984-86)
FourpennyPost	- Fourpenny Post of Wallsend (1999-2001)
GBFDC	- Assoc. GB FDC Collectors (1995 to date)
Gem Covers	- Gem Covers, Bletchley (1996)
Havering	- Havering Covers, Romford (1980-84)
Hawkwood	- Hawkwood Covers, Chingford (1980-86)
T Hurlstone	- Terry Hurlstone, Romford (1997 to date)
LFDC	- Bradbury Leicester FDC Series (1980-2000)
S. Petty	- Stewart Petty, Weybridge (1981-84)
RAF FDC	- Forces Charities (1992-1998)
RAF (P&P)	- Planes & Places (1997-2000)
RN Cvrs Gp	- Royal Naval Covers (1997 to date)
B. Reeve	- Brian Reeve (1992)

RFDC - Forces first day covers (1981-92)
Phil Stamp Cvrs - Phil Stamp Covers of Dartford (2002 to date)
P Sheridan - P Sheridan of Widnes (1999 to date)
Sovereign - Bradbury Sovereign Series (2001 to date)
Stamp Searchers - Stamp Searchers, Lewes (RNLI)
Steven Scott - Steven Scott, London (1996 to date)
VP - Bradbury Victorian Prints Series (1985-2000)
Windsor - Bradbury Windsor Series (2001 to date)
(f) - denotes forerunner to the series

Official covers forming a numbered series are normally listed with the appropriate number after the abbreviation, e.g. *BOCS(2)3* indicates the third cover in the second series of the Benham official cover series.

Benham of Folkestone were the first cover producer to promote the concept of 'official' covers. The idea of being able to purchase fully serviced first day covers for each stamp issue quickly caught on with collectors as a trouble free way of collecting covers. Furthermore, most of the covers were linked to organisations connected with the stamp issue.

(ii) some of those not forming a FDC series
Arlington - J & M Arlington of London
Benham - Benham of Folkestone
BFPS/Forces - British Forces Postal Services
Bradbury - A G Bradbury of Leicester
Cam S.C. - Cambridge Stamp Centre
CoverCraft - CoverCraft (R.deSwarte)
Dawn - Dawn Covers of Stockport
F.A.A. - Fleet Air Arm Museum
FourPennyPost - FourPenny Post of Wallsend
H.R. - Historic Relics
NYMoorsRly - North York Moors Railway
NVRly - Nene Valley Railway
Pilgrim - Pilgrim Philatelics of Canterbury
P.P.S. - Presentation Philatelic Services
RH/RHDR - Rly History/Romney, Hythe & Dym. Rly
S.P. - Stamp Publicity, Worthing
D.G.T. - D. G. Taylor of Harrow
W & W - Warwick & Warwick
Westminster - Westminster Collection, Watford

Other abbreviations used in the official covers column:
n.o.c./n.s.c. - no official cover/no sponsored cover
Post Office/Royal Mail - Handstamp sponsored by Royal Mail with no 'official' covers produced

(b) Covers produced by private organisations
Many organisations/companies have produced their own first day covers to raise funds or as a public relations exercise where their work/activity is related to the theme of the stamp issue. The abbreviations used in the official covers column should be easy to interpret once you view the cover. The value of a cover can differ dramatically depending whether it is the official cover or not. If in doubt, seek the advice of an expert.

(c) Other categories
There are many so called 'official' covers produced which bear special handstamps sponsored by other organisations or handstamps provided by Royal Mail. A classic example is the 1971 Christmas cover published by Canterbury Cathedral. Whilst the cover bears the legend *Stained Glass Official First Day Cover,* the stamps are franked with the Canterbury special first day of issue postmark provided free of charge by Royal Mail, i.e. the Cathedral did not sponsor the handstamp. Such covers have been excluded from the catalogue. These would however command a premium on say a normal Post Office cover with the same postmark.

(d) CDS and slogan postmarks used on official covers
Some official cover producers service their covers with alternative postmarks - CDS or alternative special handstamps. It would be impossible to list all these variations. Such covers usually command a premium over, say the same postmark on an ordinary cover. This is especially so where there is a direct link between the cover and postmark.

British Library Series

CoverCraft

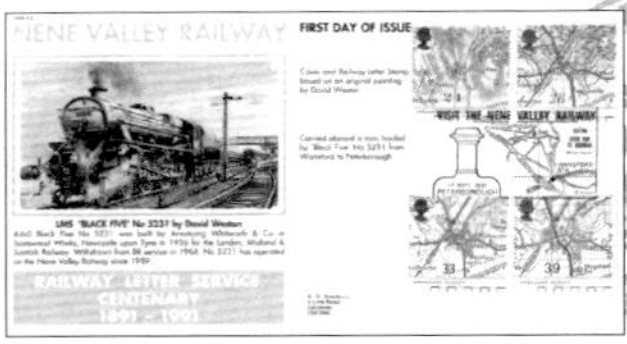

Nene Valley Railway

Cambridge Stamp Centre

Steven Scott

Benham Coin Cover

8. Permanent Handstamps

There are now numerous special handstamps available to the collector which are in use on each first day of issue of new postage stamps. These have not been listed under each stamp issue except where relevant to the particular issue, e.g. the Buckingham Palace and Windsor Castle postmarks are listed for royal issues - see example alongside. All of these handstamps are available under the 're-posting' facility from the Special Handstamp Centres as described in Section 6.1.

These handstamps can be divided in seven sections, viz:

- 8.1 Royal Mail Permanent Philatelic handstamps
- 8.2 Tourist and other Royal Mail sponsored handstamps
- 8.3 Other long-running handstamps
- 8.4 Semi-permanent handstamps in use on first day of issues
- 8.5 Operational style handstamps
- 8.6 Philatelic Counter handstamps (now ceased)
- 8.7 British Forces BFPS 1000 postmark

8.1 Royal Mail Permanent Philatelic handstamps

These depict notable landmarks or symbols and bear the legend *Royal Mail.* These handstamps were introduced on 18th March 1997 (except where stated) to replace the existing Philatelic Counter handstamps and were currently in use at the time of publication - these are all illustrated alongside.

Bath	Abbey
Belfast	City Hall
Birmingham	Cathedral
Brighton	Pavilion
Bristol	Clifton Bridge
Cambridge	Trinity Fountain
Canterbury	Cathedral
Cardiff	Castle Clock
changed to bilingual 8 Dec 97	
Chester	Eastgate Clock
Colchester	St. John's Abbey
Coventry	Cathedral
Croydon	Clock Tower
Durham	Cathedral
Edinburgh	St. Giles
Exeter	Cathedral
Gatwick	Airliner
Glasgow	City Chambers
Gloucester	Cathedral
Grimsby	Dock Tower
Guildford	Cathedral
Harrogate	Pump Rooms
Leeds	Town Hall
Leicester	Clock Tower
Liverpool	Liver Building
London EC	St. Paul's
London EC3	Tower
London SW	Palace
London WC	Nelson's Column
Manchester	Town Hall
Newcastle	Cathedral
Norwich	Castle
Nottingham	City Hall
Oxford	Tom Tower
Plymouth	Smeaton's Tower
Portsmouth	Mary Rose
Romford	Havering Town Hall
Southampton	Bargate
Southend	The Kursaal
Stevenage (8/12/97)	Town Sq
Stratford	Swan Theatre
Truro	Cathedral
Windsor	Castle
York	Minster

8.2 Tourist and other Royal Mail handstamps.

The first long-running changeable date handstamp was introduced at the National Postal Museum (NPM) in 1969. Since then a number of Royal Mail changeable date postmarks have come and gone. These are listed below:

(1)	NPM (maltese cross in circle)	19 Feb 69 -	30 Sep 72
(2)	NPM (maltese cross)	2 Oct 72 -	30 Jun 80
(3)	NPM (maltese cross & circle)	1 Jul 80 -	13 Apr 01
	excluding 10 Jan -31 Dec 1990 (see No.36)		
(4)	Windsor (small circle)	8 Oct 73 -	10 May 75
(5)	Windsor (rectangle - castle)	12 May 75 -	9 Jul 77
(6)	Windsor (rectangle - castle & oak)*	11 Jul 77 -	19 Feb 83
(7)	Branch Office, Trafalgar Square*	14 Aug 72 -	22 Sep 81
(8)	Chief Office, London EC1*	14 Aug 72 -	22 Sep 81
(9)	Cardiff (Welsh dragon & buildings) *	1 Mar 76 -	22 Sep 81
(10)	Edinburgh (Castle)*	1 Mar 76 -	22 Sep 81
(11)	Belfast (shipyard crane)*	1 Mar 76 -	22 Sep 81
	**replaced by Philatelic Counter handstamps*		
(12)	Haroldswick (rectangle)	1 Jul 72 -	1 Dec 93

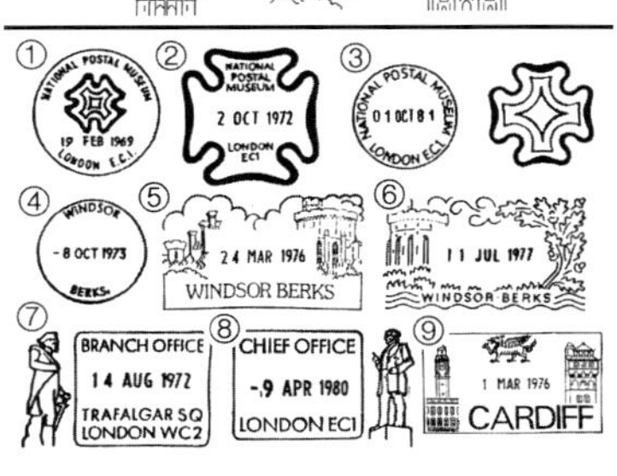

Thames Barrier cover produced by CoverCraft with Thames Barrier permanent handstamp - this is not included in the body of the catalogue because the handstamp is not relevant to the Queen's 60th Birthday stamp issue.

(13) Haroldswick PO (oval) .... 2 Dec 93 - 30 Nov 99
(14) Heathrow Airport (large circle) .... 1 Oct 74 - 21 Nov 79
(15) Heathrow Airport (smaller circle) .... 22 Nov 79 - early 2000
(16) Codesort Manchester .... 6 Jun 79 - 31 Dec 91
(17) Codesort Liverpool (two styles) .... 6 Jun 79 - 12 Nov 90
(18) Shakespeare (birthplace)† .... 7 May 80 - 30 Sep 81
(19) Shakespeare (masks)† .... 23 Apr 82 - 30 Sep 84
(20) Shakespeare (swan)† .... 23 Apr 82 - 30 Sep 87
(21) Shakespeare (book & quill)† .... 23 Apr 89 - 9 Nov 92
(22) Shakespeare (bust, masks & swan) .... 10 Nov 92 - 17 Mar 97
(23) Holmfirth, Land of Summer Wine† .... 21 Aug 83 - 1 Oct 90
†used for the tourist season only
(24) NE Parcel Centre, Washington .... 30 May 84 - 31 Dec 89
(25) London SW1 (Palace & guards) .... 17 Jan 84 - 5 May 86
(26) London SW1 (Buckingham Palace) .... 6 May 86 - 17 Mar 97
(27) Dorchester Philatelic Sales .... 22 Jan 85 - 31 Dec 91
(28) Taunton Philatelic Sales .... 22 Jan 85 - 6 Jun 90
(29) Salisbury Philatelic Sales .... 22 Jan 85 - 31 Dec 91
(30) Hastings, East Sussex .... 6 Jan 86 - 7 Apr 92
(31) Battle, East Sussex .... 6 Jan 86 - 31 Dec 91
(32) Rye, East Sussex .... 6 Jan 86 - 7 Dec 88
(33) Wish You Were Here - Holmfirth .... 6 Jan 86 - 31 Aug 91
(34) Tower Hill, London EC3 .... 21 Apr 86 - 17 Mar 97
(35) Carlisle First Roadside Pillar-Box .... 15 Dec 89 - 17 Sep 91
(36) National Postal Museum 1840-1990 .... 10 Jan 90 - 31 Dec 90
(37) Queen Eleanor's Cross Northampton .... 20 Aug 90 - 31 Aug 91
(38) Romford .... 21 Jul 92 - 17 Mar 97
(39) New Lanark Visitor Centre .... 19 Jul 93 - 1 Nov 94
(40) The Comet 1812, Port Glasgow .... 19 Jul 93 - 1 Nov 94
(41) McCaig Tower, Oban .... 19 Jul 93 - 1 Nov 94
(42) National Exhibition Centre, B'ham .... 12 Oct 93 - 28 Feb 99
(43) Burns Monument, Ayr .... 25 Jan 94 - 21 Jul 95
(44) St. Paul's, City of London EC4 .... 17 Mar 94 - 17 Mar 97
(45) Robin Hood, Nottingham .... 2 Aug 94 - 17 Mar 97
(46) York Post Shop .... 27 Sep 94 - 17 Mar 97
(47) Robert Burns, Kilmarnock .... 25 Jan 96 - 25 Jan 97
(48) Robert Burns, Alloway .... 25 Jan 96 - 25 Jan 97
(49) Robert Burns, Dumfries .... 25 Jan 96 - 25 Jan 97
(50) Robert Burns, Ayr .... 25 Jan 96 - 25 Jan 97
(51) Giant's Causeway, Bushmills .... 31 May 96 - to date
(52) Post Impressions, British Library .... 3 Aug 99 - 18 Jan 00

8.3 Other long-running handstamps

(1) Kelloggs, Manchester .... 13 Mar 80 - 18 Nov 82
(2) WRU Cardiff Arms Park .... 10 Oct 80 - 30 Apr 81
(3) Caldey Island Museum† .... 11 May 81 - 31 Aug 82
(4) Port Sunlight (Persil promotion) .... 22 Jul 81 - 30 Apr 82
(5) Travelling Tram, Blackpool† .... 12 Sep 81 - 31 Jul 84
(6) Army Bag NPMuseum .... 21 Apr 82 - 21 Jul 82
(7) Centenary Forces Postal Service .... 28 Apr 82 - 31 Dec 82
(8) Open Days, Broadlands, Romsey† .... 4 Aug 82 - 30 Sep 87
†used for the tourist season only
(9) IEW NPMuseum .... 6 Jan 83 - 1 Jul 83
(10) London FS Air Mail NPMuseum .... 5 Jan 84 - 25 May 84
(11) Colchester Castle Restoration .... 23 Jan 84 - 29 Sep 84
(12) International Gdn Festival Liverpool .... 2 May 84 - 14 Oct 84
(13) Wembley Exhib. Grange Museum .... 29 May 84 - 31 Jul 84
(14) UPU Exhibition NPMuseum .... 5 Jun 84 - 27 Jul 84
(15) North Norfolk Railway .... 1 Apr 85 - 30 Sep 85
(16) 350 Years of Service NPMuseum .... 30 Jul 85 - 25 Apr 86
(17) Thames Barrier Visitor Centre .... 24 Mar 86 - 19 Jul 88
(18) National Gdn Festival Stoke .... 1 May 86 - 26 Oct 86
(19) England v. India Tour Match .... 10 May 86 - 2 Aug 86
(20) Commonwealth Games 1986 MAC .... 9 Jun 86 - 4 Aug 86
(21) England v. NZ Tour Match .... 21 Jun 86 - 20 Sep 86
(22) High Wycombe Bucks .... 28 Aug 86 - 28 Feb 87
(23) Queen Victoria's Jubilee NPMuseum .... 6 Jan 87 - 3 Jul 87
(24) Age of Chivalry Royal Academy .... 6 Nov 87 - 5 Mar 88
(25) Railways & the Post NPMuseum .... 11 Jan 88 - 30 Dec 88
(26) Garden Festival Glasgow .... 28 Apr 88 - 26 Sep 88
(27) W. Indian Tour .... 1 May 88 - 9 Aug 88
(28) K (Kelloggs) Blackburn .... 19 Jul 88 - 30 Sep 88
(29) Italian Art in 20th Century .... 9 Jan 89 - 8 Apr 89
(30) Stampway to the World Newcastle .... 24 Aug 89 - 13 Jan 90

(31) National Garden Festival Gateshead ... 18 May 90 - 21 Oct 90
(32) Bluebell Railway ... 25 Jan 96 - 31 Dec 96
(33) Bluebell Railway making tracks ... 29 Mar 97 - 28 Mar 00
(34) Historic Channel Tunnel (*Style 1*) ... 25 Jan 96 - 19 Jan 98
(35) Historic Channel Tunnel (*Style 2*) ... 20 Jan 98 - 20 May 06
(36) 25 Years Football Covers ... various 96 - 31 Dec 96
Birmingham, Leeds, Manchester, Nottingham, Wembley, Liverpool, Newcastle, Sheffield
(37) AmEx Old England XI (Bowler) ... 22 Jun 97 - 21 Jun 98
(38) AmEx Old England XI (Batsman) ... 14 Jun 98 - 13 Jun 99
(39) St. Andrews Fife ... 19 May 97 - 31 May 03
(40) Noak Hill Chimaera Production ... 13 Feb 98 - 31 Dec 98
(41) The Heraldic City, City of London ... 13 Feb 98 - 31 Dec 98
(42) Manchester United (various designs) ... 13 Sep 97 - 19 Apr 00
(43) Arsenal Cup Winners 1998 ... 17 Aug 98 - 17 May 99
(44) Variety Club ... 21 Jul 98 - 20 Jul 99
(45) CDT 20 Design Inspiration ... 1 Jan 99 - 31 Dec 99
(46) Millennium Dome Greenwich ... 12 Jan 99 - 31 Dec 99
(47) N.Y.M.R. Celebrates Millennium ... 2 Feb 99 - 6 Jun 00
(48) Millennium Commemorative Covers ... 2 Mar 99 - 1 Mar 00
(49) Royal Yacht Britannia Edinburgh ... 1 May 99 - 31 May 03
(50) 900th Anniv. Westminster Hall ... 24 May 99 - 30 Sep 99
(51) Leighton Buzzard Railway ... 26 Jun 99 - 31 Dec 99
(52) Post Impressions British Library ... 1 Aug 99 - 18 Jan 00
(53) Sunderland (Football) ... 10 Aug 99 - 6 Jun 00
(54) Tottenham Hotspur ... 28 Aug 99 - 20 Jun 00
(55) Peterborough Cathedral City ... 1 Sep 99 - 31 Aug 02
(56) Millennium Definitives Windsor ... 21 Sep 99 - 31 Mar 00
(57) National Postal Museum ... 2 Nov 99 - 1 Nov 00
(58) Century Rd London E17 ... 1 Dec 99 - 31 Mar 00
(59) Isle of Pabay ... 1 Jan 00 - 31 Dec 00
(60) Leighton Buzzard Rly 2000 ... 1 Jan 00 - 31 Dec 00
(61) The Dome Greenwich ... 1 Jan 00 - 31 Dec 00
(62) Year 2000 Definitives Windsor ... 21 Mar 00 - 30 Jun 00
(63) Christ Church Rd, London SW14 ... 21 Mar 00 - 30 Jun 00
(64) Bluebell Rly, East Grinstead ... 22 Apr 00 - 21 Apr 01
(65) London Art Centre ... 1 May 00 - 31 Dec 00
(66) Year 2000 Definitives Windsor ... 30 Jun 00 - 30 Sep 00
(67) Queen Mother, London N14 ... 30 Jun 00 - 30 Sep 00
(68) Battle of Britain ... 1 Jul 00 - 31 Oct 00
(69) Leonard Cheshire ... 21 Jul 00 - 7 Sep 00
(70) Liverpool Football Club ... 19 Aug 00 - 22 Aug 01
(71) Manchester United Football Club ... 20 Aug 00 - 17 Aug 01
(72) The Dambusters ... 1 Dec 00 - 31 May 01
(73) English Heritage Blue Plaque Coll'n ... 8 Dec 00 - 7 Dec 01
(74) Isle of Pabay ... 1 Jan 01 - 31 Dec 01
(75) RN Submarine Service Gosport ... 1 Jan 01 - 31 Dec 01
(76) Flowergirl Harold Hill Romford ... 16 Jan 01 - 15 Jan 02
(77) Concorde Supersonic Flight ... 21 Jan 01 - 20 Jan 02
(78) Cosmo Place Reach for the Sky ... 22 Jan 01 - 24 Apr 06
(79) HMS Petard Portsmouth ... 12 Feb 01 - 31 Dec 01
(80) HM The Queen's 75th Birthday ... 13 Mar 01 - 13 Jun 01
(81) RN Submarine Service Faslane ... 10 Apr 01 - 31 Dec 01
(82) Nobel Prize Centenary ... 14 Jun 01 - 6 Nov 01
(83) NEXPOWA, Whitehall ... 28 May 01 - 28 May 06
(84) Battle of Britain ... 1 Jul 01 - 31 Oct 01
(85) Manchester United Museum ... 18 Aug 01 - 18 Aug 02
(86) Liverpool FC ... 18 Aug 01 - 18 Aug 02
(87) Guy Gibson - Dambusters ... 19 Sep 01 - 18 Sep 02
(88) Apollo Place - Lunar Landings ... 1 Oct 01 - 30 Sep 02
(89) Most Northerly PO - Baltasound ... 1 Nov 01 - to date
(90) Columbia Road, London E2 ... 1 Dec 01 - 30 Nov 02
(91) Norwich City FC Centenary ... 8 Dec 01 - 7 Dec 02
(92) Blue Plaque Collection, Savile Row ... 8 Dec 01 - 7 Dec 02
(93) 2002 Anniversaries, Jubilee Way ... 1 Jan 02 - 31 Mar 02
(94) The Malta Convoys, Whitehall ... 14 Jan 02 - 11 Nov 02
(95) Maryhill Writers Group, Glasgow ... 15 Jan 02 - 14 Jan 03
(96) First Commercial Supersonic Flight ... 21 Jan 02 - 20 Jan 03

For the latest information on special handstamps: collectors can subscribe to Royal Mail's *British Postmark Bulletin* apply to:
TALLENT'S HOUSE 21 SOUTH GYLE CRESCENT
EDINBURGH EH12 9PB

8.3 Other long-running handstamps (contd)

(1)	Bath Postal Museum	1 Feb 02 - 31 Dec 03
(2)	The Falklands Conflict, Reading	19 Mar 02 - 20 Jun 02
(3)	Stoneleigh Abbey, Kenilworth	24 Mar 02 - 24 Mar 03
(4)	Britain's Last Trolleybus, Bradford	26 Mar 02 - 31 Dec 02
(5)	Anniversaries 2002, Games Road	1 Apr 02 - 31 Jul 02
(6)	Battle for the Falklands, Portsmouth	25 Apr 02 - 14 Jun 02
(7)	St Kilda, Western Isles	10 May 02 - 10 May 03
(8)	Coventry Cathedral	1 May 02 - 31 Dec 02
(9)	2002 Anniversaries, London SE2	20 Aug 02 - 5 Dec 02
(10)	Bluebell Railway, East Grinstead	3 Aug 02 - 2 Aug 03
(11)	Liverpool European Trophies	10 Sep 02 - 11 May 03
(12)	Arsenal Double into Europe	10 Sep 02 - 17 May 03
(13)	Westminster Cathedral, London SW1	1 Jan 03 - 31 Dec 03
(14)	Centenary Old Post Office, Tintagel	1 Jan 03 - 31 Dec 03
(15)	Classic British Films, Ealing	14 Jan 03 - 13 Jan 04
(16)	Centenary Powered Flight, Heathrow	14 Jan 03 - 31 Dec 03
(17)	Brecknock Museum	1 Mar 03 - 13 Apr 03
(18)	Dambusters, Scampton Lincoln	21 Mar 03 - 20 Mar 04
(19)	Lord's Cricket Ground, London NW8	1 Apr 03 - 1 Apr 04
(20)	Isle of Pabay	1 May 03 - 30 Apr 04
(21)	Mount Pleasant (style 1)	5 May 03 - 4 May 06
(22)	Mount Pleasant (style 2)	5 May 03 - 4 May 06
(23)	St Kilda, Western Isles	20 May 03 - 19 May 04
(24)	The Big Match, Manchester	12 Aug 03 - 11 Aug 04
(25)	Arsenal FA Cup Winners	16 Aug 03 - 15 Aug 04
(26)	Liverpool FC League Cup	12 Aug 03 - 11 Aug 04
(27)	WWII Operations Cenotaph London	22 Sep 03 - 21 Sep 04
(28)	2004 Payne Official Covers	13 Jan 04 - 30 Nov 04
(29)	First Flight Concorde Anniversary	13 Feb 04 - 21 Jan 05
(30)	First British Talking Film	13 Feb 04 - 31 Dec 04
(31)	Dambusters, Scampton	21 Mar 04 - 12 Nov 04
(32)	Dambusters, Scampton	21 Mar 04 - 12 Nov 04
(33)	Bluebell Railway, East Grinstead	10 Apr 04 - 9 Apr 05
(34)	Ocean Liners to Welsh History	13 Apr 04 - 13 July 04
(35)	Isle of Pabay	1 May 04 - 30 Apr 05
(36)	RAF Scampton	14 May 04 - 26 Sep 04
(37)	St Kilda, Western Isles	20 May 04 - 19 May 05
(38)	Route to Victory, Trafalgar Square	1 Aug 04 - 31 July 05
(39)	Norwich City Football Club	14 Aug 04 - 12 Feb 05
(40)	Liverpool Football Club	14 Aug 04 - 12 Feb 05
(41)	Manchester a city United in Football	14 Aug 04 - 13 Aug 05
(42)	Arsenal Premiership Champions	22 Aug 04 - 21 Aug 05
(43)	World War II 65th Anniversary	3 Sep 04 - 2 Sep 05
(44)	Millwall Football Club	16 Sep 04 - 17 Mar 05
(45)	Middlesbrough, Carling Cup Winners	16 Sep 04 - 17 Mar 05
(46)	Concorde Final Flight	23 Oct 04 - 26 Nov 05
(47)	617 Squadron, Scampton	12 Nov 04 - 25 Apr 05
(48)	Concorde Anniversary	26 Nov 04 - 25 Nov 05
(49)	British Films, Leicester Square	1 Jan 05 - 31 Dec 05
(50)	The Age of Steam, London Victoria	1 Feb 05 - 31 Jan 06
(51)	South West England	8 Feb 05 - 13 July 05
(52)	Legends of the Beautiful Game	25 Feb 05 - 24 Feb 06
(53)	Bluebell Railway	26 Mar 05 - 23 Sep 05
(54)	John's Classic Cars	5 Apr 05 - 30 Jun 05
(55)	British Postal Museum & Archive	6 May 05 - to date
(56)	Op. Chastise to Op. Exodus	16 May 05 - 8 May 06
(57)	St. Kilda, Western Isles	20 May 05 - 19 May 06
(58)	Happy Birthday, Mount Pleasant	12 May 05 - 9 May 06
(59)	Phil Stamp - Laughterton	7 Jun 05 - 6 Jun 06
(60)	Liverpool FC - 5 Times European	12 Jul 05 - 11 Jul 06
(61)	Football in Greater Manchester	13 Aug 05 - 12 Aug 06
(62)	Sunderland AFC	13 Aug 05 - 12 Aug 06
(63)	Football in Greater Manchester	13 Aug 05 - 12 Aug 06
(64)	Liverpool & Manchester Railway	15 Sep 05 - 17 Mar 06

8.3 Other long-running handstamps (contd)

(1)	British Films, Leicester Square	1 Jan 06 -	31 Dec 06
(2)	Concorde 1969-2003	1 Jan 06 -	31 Dec 06
(3)	Scott Official Covers	1 Mar 06 -	28 Feb 07
(4)	Legends of the Beautiful Game	11 May 06 -	10 May 07
(5)	The Mount, London EC1	8 May 06 -	to date
(6)	St. Kilda - World Heritage Site	21 May 06 -	20 May 07
(7)	Dawn Covers Football	6 Jun 06 -	5 Jun 07
(8)	A Glorious Past, Wembley	6 Jun 06 -	5 Jun 07
(9)	The Great Britons	1 Jul 06 -	30 Jun 07
(10)	The Cenotaph, Whitehall	1 Aug 06 -	31 Jul 07
(11)	Reading FC Premier League	1 Aug 06 -	31 Jul 07
(12)	Liverpool FC Cup Winners	1 Aug 06 -	31 Jul 07
(13)	The Beautiful Game, Manchester	1 Aug 06 -	31 Jul 07

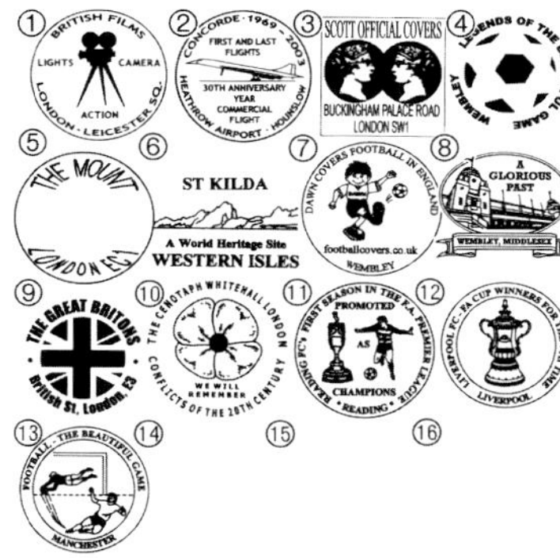

8.4 Semi-permanent handstamps in use on day of issue.

(1)	FDI - Durham (Cathedral)	22 Mar 88 -	2 Nov 98
(2)	FDI - City of London (shield)	17 Jan 89 -	2 Nov 98
(3)	FDI - GWR Swindon (train)	5 Mar 91 -	11 Jun 91
(4)	Europe '92 City of London	14 Jan 92 -	10 Nov 92
(5)	FDI - NE SHC (Tyne Bridge)	15 Sep 92 -	1 Feb 94
(6)	FDI - Scot & N.I. (Giant's Causeway)	7 Dec 93 -	11 Apr 95
(7)	FDI - Scotland (Lion) *various locations*	1 Nov 94 -	2 Nov 98
(8)	FDI - St. Albans (Abbey)	14 Mar 95 -	2 Nov 98
(9)	FDI - Glasgow (Flax & Thistle)	25 Apr 95 -	23 Apr 98
(10)	British Forces Postal Service	21 Jan 97 -	to date
(11)	William Webb Ellis, Rugby	3 Feb 98 -	2 Nov 98
(12)	Millennium Commemorative Covers	3 Oct 00 -	5 Dec 00

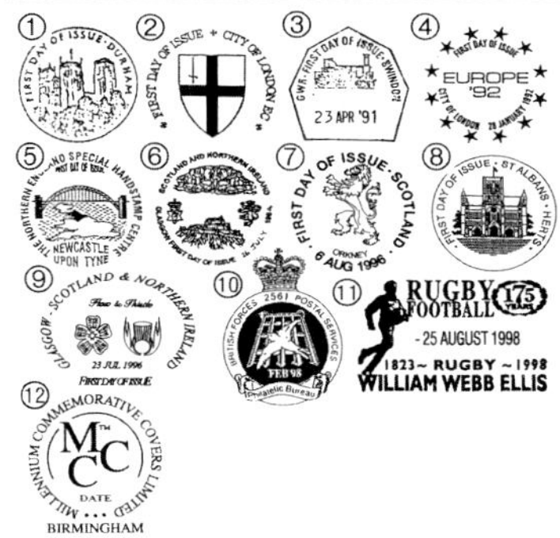

8.5 Operational style postmarks.

(1) ***Double Ring postmarks:***

Edinburgh or Glasgow	21 May 93 -	to date
Mt Pleasant, Belfast, Cardiff	28 May 99 -	to date

(2) ***Single Ring postmarks:***

Travelling Post Office, London	18 Jan 94 -	9 Jan 04

Special Handstamp (SHC) cds style postmarks:

(3)	Windsor	16 Apr 96 -	to date
(4)	London EC	30 Apr 96 -	31 Dec 02
	London SW or Heathrow Airport	30 Apr 96 -	to date
(5)	Birmingham or Stratford	30 Apr 96 -	to date
(6)	Newcastle or York	30 Apr 96 -	to date
(7)	Edinburgh or Glasgow	30 Apr 96 -	to date
(8)	Belfast, Carrickfergus or Caernarfon	30 Apr 96 -	to date
(9)	Slough-Windsor	30 Apr 96 -	to date
(10)	Cardiff *(bilingual from 16 Dec 97)*	30 Apr 96 -	to date

(11) ***Packet Style datestamps:***
Bromsgrove, Derby, Lichfield, Loughborough, Matlock, Melton Mowbray, Stoke on Trent, Walsall, Wolverhampton, West Bromwich
1 Jun 01 - to date

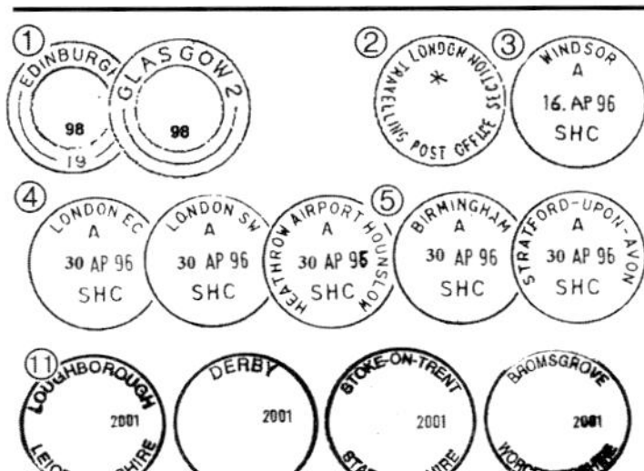

8.6 Philatelic Counter handstamps.

Armagh ....3 Jan 84 - 31 Dec 85
Ayr ....1 Feb 83 - 1 Nov 89
Ballymena ......22 Aug 83 - 1 Nov 89
Bath ....10 Jan 84 - 17 Mar 97
Belfast ....23 Sep 81 - 17 Mar 97
Birmingham .....23 Sep 81 - 17 Mar 97
Blackpool ....23 Sep 81 - 17 Nov 89
Bolton ....9 Apr 84 - 6 Jun 90
Bournemouth .23 Sep 81 - 1 Nov 89
Bradford ....15 May 84 - 6 Jun 90
Brighton ....23 Sep 81 - 17 Mar 97
Bristol ....1 Feb 83 - 17 Mar 97
Cambridge ......23 Sep 81 - 17 Mar 97
Canterbury ....1 Feb 83 - 17 Mar 97
Cardiff ....23 Sep 81 - 17 Mar 97
Carlisle ....9 Apr 84 - 1 Nov 89
Chester ....4 Jan 83 - 17 Mar 97
Chief Office ....23 Sep 81 - 16 Mar 94
Cleveland ....4 Jan 83 - 1 Nov 89
Colchester ......23 Sep 81 - 17 Mar 97
Coventry ....19 Sep 83 - 17 Mar 97
Croydon ....19 Sep 83 - 17 Mar 97
Darlington ....17 Jul 84 - 1 Nov 89
Durham ....4 Jun 85 - 17 Mar 97
Edinburgh ......23 Sep 81 - 17 Mar 97
Exeter ....21 Feb 83 - 17 Mar 97
Glasgow ....23 Sep 83 - 17 Mar 97
Gloucester ......15 Aug 83 - 17 Mar 97
Grimsby ....22 Aug 83 - 1 Nov 89
Guildford ....1 Feb 83 - 17 Mar 97
Harrogate ....19 Sep 83 - 31 May 88
Hereford ....15 Aug 83 - 6 Jun 90
Hull ....22 Aug 83 - 6 Jun 90
Inverness ....1 Feb 83 - 6 Jun 90
Leeds ....23 Sep 81 - 17 Mar 97
Leicester ....1 Feb 83 - 17 Mar 97
Lincoln ....15 May 84 - 7 Mar 90
Liverpool ....23 Sep 81 - 17 Mar 97
Londonderry ..15 May 84 - 1 Nov 89
Luton ....8 Oct 85 - 6 Jun 90
Manchester ......23 Sep 81 - 17 Mar 97
Milton Keynes ...1 Feb 83 - 1 Nov 89
Newcastle ....23 Sep 81 - 17 Mar 97
Newport ....22 Aug 83 - 6 Jun 90
Northampton ..15 Aug 83 - 29 Nov 89
Norwich ....23 Sep 83 - 6 Jun 90
Nottingham ....4 Jan 83 - 17 Mar 97
Oldham ....1 Feb 83 - 6 Jun 90
Oxford ....23 Sep 81 - 17 Mar 97
Plymouth ....15 Aug 83 - 6 Jun 90
Portadown ....21 Jul 86 - 1 Nov 89
Portsmouth ......19 Sep 83 - 17 Mar 97
Romford ....4 Jan 83 - 1 Nov 89
Sheffield ....23 Sep 81 - 6 Jun 90
Shrewsbury ......21 Feb 81 - 1 Nov 89
Southampton ..23 Sep 81 - 17 Mar 97
Southend ....21 Feb 83 - 17 Mar 97
Stoke ....23 Sep 81 - 1 Nov 89
Sunderland ....3 Jan 84 - 1 Nov 89
Swansea ....1 Feb 83 - 6 Jun 90
Swindon ....19 Sep 83 - 1 Nov 89
Torquay ....27 Sep 83 - 6 Jun 90
Trafalgar Sq ....23 Sep 81 - 17 Mar 97
Truro ....4 Jan 83 - 17 Mar 97
Windsor ....21 Feb 83 - 17 Mar 97
Worcester ....21 Feb 83 - 1 Nov 89
York ....23 Sep 83 - 17 Mar 97

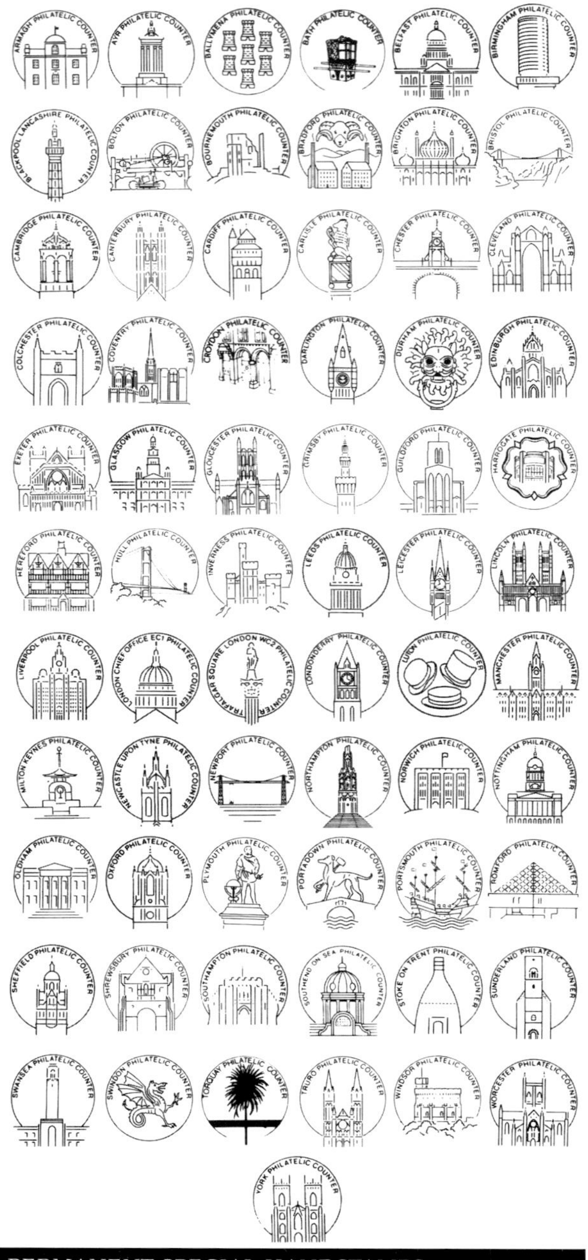

ROYAL MAIL PERMANENT SPECIAL HANDSTAMPS
for the latest information on special handstamps collectors
can subscribe to Royal Mail's ***British Postmark Bulletin*** apply to the following address:
TALLENT'S HOUSE 21 SOUTH GYLE CRESCENT EDINBURGH EH12 9PB

HOW TO USE THIS CATALOGUE

The commemorative issues follows the format below:

❶ Official date of issue of stamps

❷ Title of stamp issue

❸ Brief description of stamp designs and values. Reference to these will often explain the significance of many of the postmarks

❹ Postmark illustrations. Numbers refer to text entry.

❺

25th Jan. 1996 – ROBERT BURNS
19p To A Mouse; 25p A Red, Red Rose;
41p Scots Wha Hae; 60p Auld Lang Syne

	ordinary covers £	official/sponsored covers £	
SPECIAL HANDSTAMPS (1) Philatelic Bureau	3	–	*Royal Mail*
(2) First Day of Issue – Dumfries	3	–	*Royal Mail*
(3) First Day of Issue – Glasgow, Scotland & NI	3	–	*Royal Mail*
(4) First Day of Issue – London	8	–	*Royal Mail*
(5) Wee Sleekit Cowrin' etc, Kilmarnock	10	–	*Royal Mail*
(6) O, My Luve's Like a Red, Red Rose, Alloway	10	–	*Royal Mail*
(7) Scots Wha Hae, Dumfries	10	–	*Royal Mail*
(8) Should Auld Acquaintance etc, Ayr ❼	10	–	*Royal Mail*
(9) Spring Stampex (Red Red Rose), N1	10	–	*Royal Mail*
(10) The Burns Federation, Dumfries (mausoleum)	10	12	*LFDC 138*
(11) The Burns Federation, Alloway (portrait)	10	12	*VP 100* ❻
(12) To A Mouse, Mauchline, Ayrshire	10	15	*Bradbury*
(13) O My Luve's Like a Red, Red Rose, Dumfries	10 ❽	15	*Bradbury*
(14) Robert the Bruce, Bannockburn	10	15	*Bradbury*
(15) Auld Lang Syne, Ellisland Farm, Dumfries	10	15	*Bradbury*
(16) Robert Burns, 1759-1796 Mauchline (lion)	10	15	*Ben500(112)*
(17) Robert Burns Bicentenary, Alloway (mouse)	10	12	*BLCS 112*
(18) R.Burns, Writers' Museum, Edinburgh (rose)	10	12	*BLCS 112*
(19) Bicentenary of R. Burns, Dumfries (thistle)	10	12	*BLCS 112*
(20) Robert Burns, Radio Times, W12 0TT	10	12	*Benham*
(21) Rotary Club of Alloway, Ayr	10	15	*Rotary*
(22) Robert Burns 1759-1796, Alloway (quill)	10	12	*Gem Covers*
(23) The Immortal Memory, Edinburgh	10	10	*Keith Prowse*
(24) Should auld acquaintance GB FDC Dumfries	10	15	*FDP Co*
(25) XV Squadron Tornado Weapons BF 2498 PS	10	10	*RAF FDC 35*
C.D.S. POSTMARKS ❾			
(26) Alloway - birthplace of Robert Burns	10		
(27) Bannockburn - Scots Wha Hae	10		
(28) Burns Statue, Ayr	15		
(29) Dalswinton, Dunfermline, Kilmarnock or Tarbolton *connected with works featured on stamps*	10		
(30) Dumfries - Burns died here in 1796	10		
(31) Lincluden, Dumfries - Lincluden Abbey	10		
(32) Mauchline - where Burns lived	10		

In addition: Burnside, Burns Road, Kirkoswald, Mousehole, Nicholson Street Edinburgh, Poets Field, Rose, Sanquhar, Tam's Brig. Prices from £8.

	ordinary covers £
SLOGAN POSTMARKS	
(33) Celebrate the Legend, Robert Burns	30

Also: Luton Philatelic; Glasgow RCH; Strathclyde Univ. Prices from £8

(5) Two column price structure: *1924-1961 illustrated covers/plain covers*
1962-1967 non-phosphor covers/phosphor covers
1967- 1998 ordinary covers/official or sponsored covers
See Section 4 of General Notes (page 3)

(6) Brief description of official cover/series number **See Section 7.2 of General Notes (page 9)**

(7) Abbreviated wording of postmarks.

(8) Price guide. **See Section 5 of General Notes (page 4)**

(9) Type of postmark. **See Section 6 of General Notes (page 4)**

The purpose of this catalogue is to give the reader a guide to the variety of covers and postmarks available for each stamp issue. It is not the publisher's own price list.

Prices are a guide - see General Notes.

Whilst every care has been taken to ensure complete accuracy in the compilation of this catalogue, the publisher cannot accept responsibility for any errors or omissions.

COMMEMORATIVE ISSUES

23rd April 1924 – WEMBLEY EXHIBITION

1d, 1½d Wembley Lion

	illustrated £	plain £
SPECIAL HANDSTAMPS		
(1) Empire Exhibition, Wembley Park, 1924	–	300
(2) Palace of Engineering or Palace of Industry *each*	–	750
SLOGAN POSTMARKS		
(3) Wembley Park *(Harmer display cover £350)*	–	300
(4) British Empire	–	450
(5) British Industries Fair *1½d value only*	–	50
POSTAL STATIONERY		
(6) 1d Postcard - Wembley special h/s or slogan	–	125
(7) 1½d Postcard (foreign) - Wembley h/s or slogan	–	250
(8) 1½d Printed env. or lettercard - Wembley pmk	–	175

9th May 1925 – WEMBLEY EXHIBITION

1d, 1½d Wembley Lion

	illustrated £	plain £
SPECIAL HANDSTAMPS		
(1) British Empire Exhib., Wembley or Wembley Park	–	1,250
(2) Empire Exhibition Wembley, Palace of Industry	–	1,750
SLOGAN POSTMARKS		
(3) Wembley Park (Lion) 1925	–	1,500
POSTAL STATIONERY		
(4) 1d Postcard - Wembley special h/s or slogan	–	275
(5) 1½d Postcard (foreign) - Wembley h/s or slogan	–	220
(6) 1½d Printed env. or lettercard - Wembley pmk	–	240

10th May 1929 – POSTAL UNION CONGRESS

½d, 1d, 1½d, 2½d King George V; £1 St. George and the Dragon

	illustrated £	plain £
C.D.S. POSTMARKS		
(1) Postal Union Congress, London – £1 value	–	7,250
(2) Postal Union Congress, London – 4 low values	–	750
(3) -do- on P.U.C. stationery or env. (crest on flap)	–	900
(4) -do- on P.U.C. stationery – all 5 values	–	4,750
(5) Registered P.U.C., London (oval) – 4 low values	–	1,000
(6) Any other postmark – £1 value	–	3,650
(7) Any other postmark – 4 low values	–	350
(8) Any other postmark – all five values	–	4,000
SLOGAN POSTMARKS		
(9) Any postmark – 4 low values	–	250

7th May 1935 – KING GEORGE V SILVER JUBILEE

½d, 1d, 1½d, 2½d King George V

	illustrated £	plain £
C.D.S. POSTMARKS (1) Windsor, Berks	800	300
(2) London. SW1	525	150
(2a) -do- on Westminster Stamp Co. cover	550	–
SLOGAN POSTMARKS		
(3) London SW1 or Windsor – wavy line pmks *each*	12(s)	10
ANY OTHER POSTMARK (CDS or Slogan) *from*	400	75

13th May 1937 – KING GEORGE VI CORONATION

1½d King George VI and Queen Elizabeth

	illustrated £	plain £
C.D.S. POSTMARKS (1) Windsor, Berks.	150	25
(2) Hampton Court Camp or Kensington Gdns Camp	200	100
(3) Pirbright Camp - used for troops for Coronation	180	75
(4) Regents Park Camp - for troops for Coronation	–	35
(5) Any London SW postmark	35	8
(6) London & New York (Anglo/American Air Mail)	–	45
SLOGAN POSTMARKS		
(7) Windsor - wavy line	150	30
(8) London SW1 - wavy line	35	7
ANY OTHER POSTMARK (CDS or Slogan) *from*	20	2

6th May 1940 - POSTAGE STAMP CENTENARY

½d, 1d, 1½d, 2d, 2½d, 3d Victoria & George VI

	illustrated £	plain £
SPECIAL HANDSTAMPS		
(1) 27th Philatelic Congress, Bournemouth	125	20
(2) Adhesive Stamp Centenary Exhib., Bournemouth	50	7
(3) Stamp Centenary (Red Cross) Exhib., London	55	7
(3a) -do- on Perkins Bacon cover	95	–
(4) Pavilion, Bournemouth	35 (s)	50
C.D.S. POSTMARKS		
(5) Dundee - James Chalmers, first adhesive stamps	170	–
(6) Kidderminster - birthplace of Rowland Hill	–	20
SLOGAN POSTMARKS		
(7) Post Early in the Day	–	50
ANY OTHER POSTMARK (CDS or Slogan) *from*	25	4

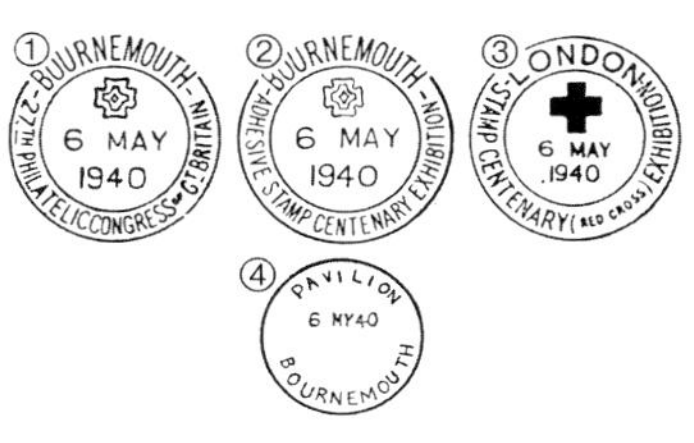

11th June 1946 - VICTORY

2½ d, 3d Peace and Reconstruction

	illustrated £	plain £
C.D.S. POSTMARKS		
(1) Any central London postmark	60	5
(2) House of Commons, London SW1	125	30
(3) Jersey or Guernsey – German occupation ....*each*	70	10
(3a) Canadian Overseas or British Fleet Mail ....*each*	n.k.	100
SLOGAN POSTMARKS		
(4) Don't Waste Bread–Others Need It	75	15
ANY OTHER POSTMARK (CDS or Slogan) ....*from*	40	3

26th April 1948 - SILVER WEDDING

2½ d, £1 Photographic portraits of the King and Queen.

	illustrated £	plain £
C.D.S. POSTMARKS		
(1) Georgetown, Jersey	500	250
(2) Any central London postmark	400	110
(3) Any other postmark	350	90
SLOGAN POSTMARKS		
(4) London SW1 or Windsor - wavy line pmks	25(s)	5(s)
(5) Any other postmark	275	60

10th May 1948 - CHANNEL ISLANDS LIBERATION

1d, 2½ d Gathering Vraic (seaweed)

	illustrated £	plain £
C.D.S. POSTMARKS		
(1) Guernsey or Jersey ....*each*	35	4
(2) Sark or Alderney ....*each*	75	10
(3) British Industries Fair, Birmingham (registered)	70	25
SLOGAN POSTMARKS		
(4) Guernsey or Jersey–wavy line pmks ....*each*	25	4
(5) A Distinguished Career–Nursing	80	20
(6) British Industries Fair, Birmingham	125	35
ANY OTHER POSTMARK (CDS or Slogan) ....*from*	30	10

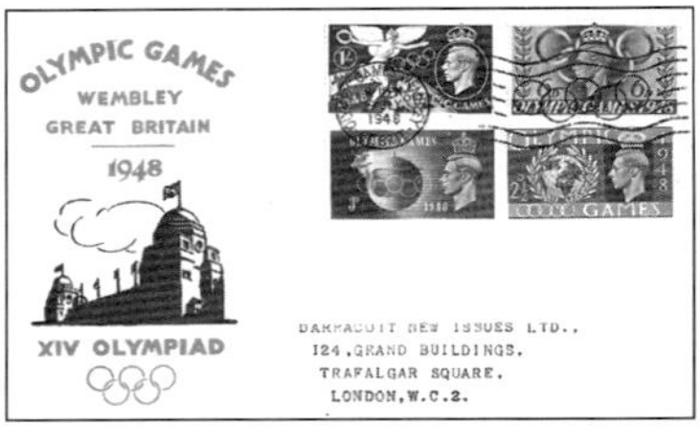

29th July 1948 - OLYMPIC GAMES, WEMBLEY

2½ d, 3d, 6d, 1s Olympic Symbols

	illustrated £	plain £
C.D.S. POSTMARKS		
(1) Wembley, Middx. (double ring metal cancel)	120	20
(1a) ditto–used at Games (nos.11 to 16 in pmk.)	100	30
SLOGAN POSTMARKS		
(2) Olympic Games, Wembley (often with cds pmk)	50	15
ANY OTHER POSTMARK (CDS or Slogan) ....*from*	40	10

10th October 1949 - UNIVERSAL POSTAL UNION

2½ d Two Hemispheres; 3d UPU Monument, Berne;
6d Goddess Concordia; 1s Posthorn and Globe

	illustrated £	plain £
C.D.S. POSTMARKS		
(1) London Chief Office–postal headquarters	100	30
ANY OTHER POSTMARK (CDS or Slogan) ....*from*	70	12

3rd May 1951 - FESTIVAL OF BRITAIN

2½ d Commerce and Prosperity; 4d Festival Symbol

	illustrated £	plain £
C.D.S. POSTMARKS		
(1) British Industries Fair, B'ham or Earl's Court	n.k.	40
(2) Registered B.I.F. Birmingham (oval)	n.k.	40
(3) Battersea SW11 – Festival Gardens	70	15
(4) Buckingham Palace, SW1 or Windsor	250	50
(5) London SE1 – Festival site was on the South Bank	75	15
SLOGAN POSTMARKS		
(6) Battersea, SW11–wavy line	50	15
(7) Festival of Britain May 3-Sept 30 (used at Cardiff)	300	175
ANY OTHER POSTMARK (CDS or Slogan) ....*from*	35	8

*A Festival handstamp and slogan were in use on the opening day of the festival, 4th May. These are commemorative covers **NOT** first day covers.*

3rd June 1953 - CORONATION

2½ d, 4d, 1s 3d, 1s 6d Portraits of Queen Elizabeth/Regalia

	illustrated £	plain £
C.D.S. POSTMARKS		
(1) Arundel–Earl Marshal/Coronation arrangements	200	–
(2) Buckingham Palace, Windsor Castle or Sandringham	1750	250
(3) House of Commons or House of Lords	250	50
(4) Windsor, Berks.	250	50
(5) Queen's Head, Queensbury (or similar) ....*each*	12(s)	
(6) London SW	75	25
(7) Any other postmark	50	10
SLOGAN POSTMARKS		
(8) Long Live the Queen, Windsor	450	40
(9) Long Live the Queen, London SW1	85	20
(10) Long Live the Queen, any other location	65	15
ANY OTHER POSTMARK (CDS or Slogan) ....*from*	30	7

1st August 1957 - SCOUT JUBILEE JAMBOREE

2½d, 4d, 1s 3d Scouting Symbols

	illustrated	plain
C.D.S. POSTMARKS	£	£
(1) Sutton Coldfield	150	20
SLOGAN POSTMARKS		
(2) World Scout Jubilee Jamboree, Sutton Coldfield	25	5
(3) -do- different design (see illustration)	35(s)	10(s)
(4) Wavy line cancellation–Sutton Coldfield	125	5
ANY OTHER POSTMARK (CDS or Slogan) *from*	15	3

12th Sept 1957 - PARLIAMENTARY CONFERENCE

4d Overprinted definitive

	illustrated	plain
SPECIAL HANDSTAMPS		
(1) 46th Parliamentary Conference, London SW1	100	20
Forged London W1 handstamps exist for this issue.		
C.D.S. POSTMARKS		
(2) House of Commons or Lords, London SW1	300	–
(3) Northern Parliament, Belfast	225	80
(4) Any London SW postmark	75	20
SLOGAN POSTMARKS		
(5) London SW1 - wavy line postmark	95	n.k.
ANY OTHER POSTMARK (CDS or Slogan) *from*	65	7

18th July 1958 - COMMONWEALTH GAMES

3d, 6d, 1s 3d Welsh Dragon & Games Emblem

	illustrated	plain
C.D.S. POSTMARKS		
(1) Empire Games Village, Barry (double ring pmk)	250	125
(2) Empire Games Village, Barry (single ring)	275	90
(3) Empire Games Village, Barry ('hooded' pmk)	300	75
(3a) -do- on R.A.F.A. Philatelic Society cover	550	–
(4) Games Mobile Post Office	–	275
(5) Mobile Post Office (sited at Games)	n.k.	525
(6) Empire Games Village, Barry Parcel Post	n.k.	25(s)
SLOGAN POSTMARKS		
(7) British Empire & Comm. Games	85	25
(8) British Empire & Comm. Games 18th-26th July	n.k.	75
ANY OTHER POSTMARK (CDS or Slogan) *from*	30	5

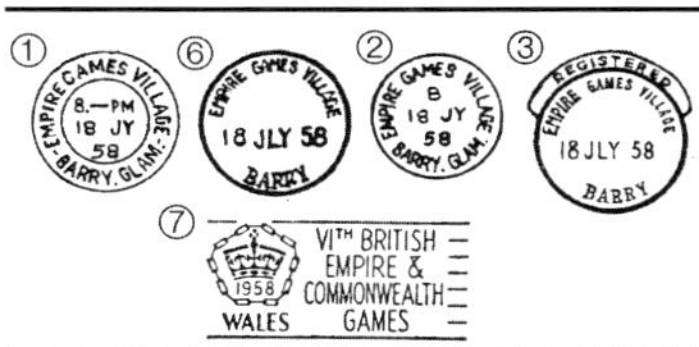

7th July 1960 - THE GENERAL LETTER OFFICE

3d, 1s 3d Post boy and Post horn of 1660

	illustrated	plain
C.D.S. POSTMARKS		
(1) Lombard Street, EC3 – General Letter Office	70	20
(2) London Chief Office, EC – postal headquarters	90	20
SLOGAN POSTMARKS		
(3) International Postal Conference, Eastbourne	150	50
ANY OTHER POSTMARK (CDS or Slogan) *from*	40	5

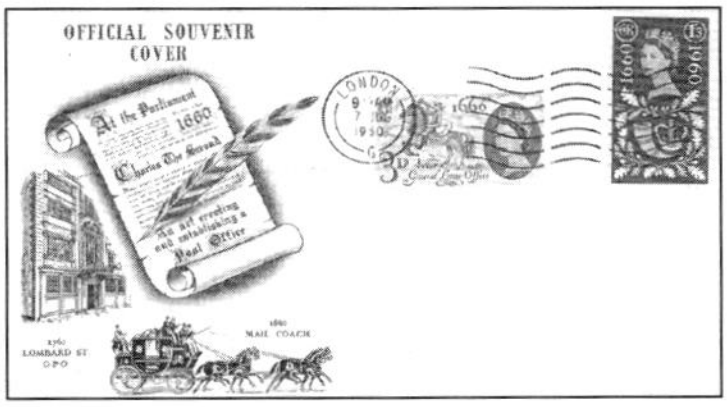

19th Sept. 1960 - 'EUROPA'

6d, 1s 6d Conference Emblem

	illustrated	plain
C.D.S. POSTMARKS		
(1) Lombard Street, EC3 – General Letter Office	100	20
(2) London Chief Office, EC – postal headquarters	100	20
(3) Norwich – first use of post codes in 1960	95	20
(4) London F.S. (Foreign Section)	95	25
SLOGAN POSTMARKS		
(5) Express Good Wishes by Greeting's Telegram	200	20
(6) London EC - wavy line	40	n.k.
ANY OTHER POSTMARK (CDS or Slogan) *from*	35	5

28th August 1961 - SAVINGS BANK CENTENARY

2½d, 3d, 1s 6d Thrift Plant and Growth of Savings

	illustrated	plain
C.D.S. POSTMARKS		
(1) Blythe Rd., W14 – HQ of the P.O.S.B.	300	75
(2) London Chief Office, EC – postal headquarters	175	25
(3) Any London postmark	100	20
SLOGAN POSTMARKS		
(4) Express Good Wishes by Greeting's Telegrams	175	20
(5) West Kensington, W14 - wavy line postmark	300	75
ANY OTHER POSTMARK (CDS or Slogan) *from*	65	6

18th September 1961 - CEPT

2d, 4d, 10d Doves and CEPT Emblem

	illustrated	plain
C.D.S. POSTMARKS		
(1) London Chief Office, EC – postal headquarters	30	n.k.
(2) Torquay – Conference venue	40	n.k.
SLOGAN POSTMARKS		
(3) CEPT European Conference, Torquay	15	5
(4) Post Office Savings Bank 1861-1961	200	25
(5) Express Good Wishes by Greeting's Telegram	n.k.	25
ANY OTHER POSTMARK (CDS or Slogan) *from*	10	2

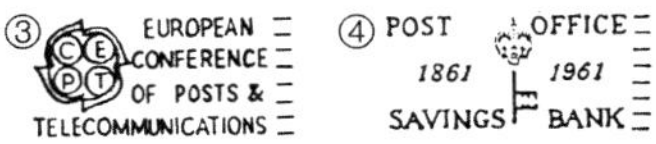

25th September 1961 - PARLIAMENT

6d Hammer Beam Roof, Westminster Hall; 1s 3d Palace of Westminster

	illustrated covers	plain covers
C.D.S. POSTMARK	£	£
(1) House of Commons, SW1	375	45
(2) House of Lords, SW1	350	60
(3) Parliament St or Westminster Bridge Rd, SW1	150	30
(4) London SW1	100	20
SLOGAN POSTMARKS		
(5) Commonwealth Parliamentary Conference	75	10
ANY OTHER POSTMARK (CDS or Slogan) *from*	45	5

With effect from the 1962 issues, all commemorative stamps were printed with & without phosphor bands. Prices are now for illustrated covers only. Plain covers are are worth considerably less.

14th Nov. 1962 - NATIONAL PRODUCTIVITY YEAR

2½d, 3d, 1s 3d Productivity Emblems

	non-phos.	phos.
SLOGAN POSTMARKS	£	£
(1) National Productivity Year, Nov 1962-63	60	130
(2) Export & Prosper, NW1	375	n.k.
(3) Southampton T – wavy line cancel	125	110
ANY OTHER POSTMARK (CDS or Slogan) *from*	50	90

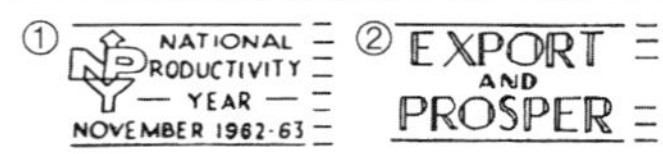

21st March 1963 - FREEDOM FROM HUNGER

2½d, 1s 3d Campaign Emblems

	non-phos.	phos.
SPECIAL HANDSTAMPS		
(1) Tenth Anniversary Stampex 1963, SW1	85	85
SLOGAN POSTMARKS		
(2) Freedom From Hunger Week 17-24 March 1963	35	40
(3) Southampton T – wavy line cancel	n.k.	35
ANY OTHER POSTMARK (CDS or Slogan) *from*	30	35

7th May 1963 - PARIS POSTAL CONFERENCE

6d 'Paris Conference'

	non-phos.	phos.
SPECIAL HANDSTAMPS		
(1) Post Office Tercentenary, Dover Packet Service	30	400
(1a) - ditto - Dover Philatelic Society official cover	45	n.k.
SLOGAN POSTMARKS		
(2) First Day of Issue–any office	20	25
(3) Norwich Addresses Need Post Codes	250	n.k.
(4) Southampton T–wavy line cancel	n.k.	30
ANY OTHER POSTMARK (CDS or Slogan) *from*	15	25

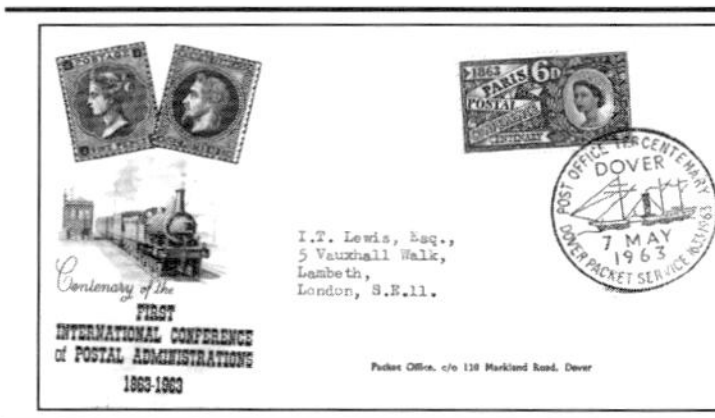

16th May 1963 - NATIONAL NATURE WEEK

3d Posy of Flowers; 4½d Woodland Life

	non-phos.	phos.
SPECIAL HANDSTAMPS		
(1) Brownsea Island Opening Week, Poole, Dorset	140	140
(2) Esperanto Kongresso, Stoke	250	n.k.
(2a) -ditto- Esperanto Kongresso official cover	350	n.k.
C.D.S. POSTMARKS		
(3) Botanic Gardens, Belfast, Forest Row etc	–	150
(4) Selborne – 'Natural History of Selborne'	95	95
SLOGAN POSTMARKS		
(5) First Day of Issue–any office	20	25
(6) Southampton T–wavy line cancel	n.k.	25
ANY OTHER POSTMARK (CDS or Slogan) *from*	20	25

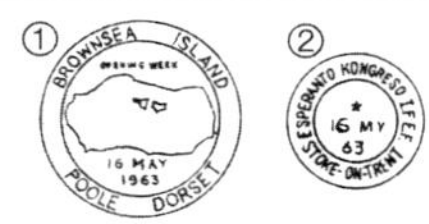

31st May 1963 - LIFEBOAT CONFERENCE

2½d Rescue at Sea; 4d Lifeboat; 1s 6d Lifeboatmen

	non-phos.	phos.
C.D.S. POSTMARKS		
(1) Edinburgh	125	n.k.
(2) Lifeboat or RN Stations, e.g. Cromer etc	125	125
SLOGAN POSTMARKS		
(3) International Lifeboat Conference, Edinburgh	60	75
(4) Southampton T–wavy line cancel	n.k.	45
(5) First Day of Issue–Edinburgh	50	55
ANY OTHER POSTMARK (CDS or Slogan) *from*	30	40

15th August 1963 - RED CROSS CENTENARY

3d, 1s 3d, 1s 6d Red Cross

	non-phos.	phos.
SPECIAL HANDSTAMPS		
(1) World Union of Catholic Teachers	400	n.k.
C.D.S. POSTMARKS		
(2) West Wellow, Romsey – Florence Nightingale	100	120
(3) Any hospital Post Office	175	175
SLOGAN POSTMARKS		
(4) Red Cross Centenary – A Century of Service	70	100
(5) Southampton T–wavy line cancel	n.k.	65
ANY OTHER POSTMARK (CDS or Slogan) *from*	40	55

3th December 1963 - COMMONWEALTH CABLE

1/6d Commonwealth Cable (COMPAC)

SLOGAN POSTMARKS	non-phos. covers £	phos. covers £
(1) First Day of Issue – Philatelic Bureau GPO, EC1 ...	50	55
(2) Southampton T – wavy line cancel	50	50
(3) First Day of Issue – any other office	30	35
(4) London WC FDI on Standard Telephones cover	100	n.k.
ANY OTHER PMK (FDI, CDS or Slogan) *from*	20	30

The 'Ordinary F.D.I. postmarks' were introduced with effect from the 1964 Shakespeare issue. In general, these were collected in preference to the F.D.I slogan (envelope design).

23rd April 1964 - SHAKESPEARE FESTIVAL

3d, 6d, 1s 3d, 1s 6d + 2s 6d (non-phos. only) scenes from plays

	non-phos.	phos.
SPECIAL HANDSTAMPS		
(1) Shakespeare 400th Anniversary, Stratford	35	35
ORDINARY F.D.I. POSTMARKS		
(2) Stratford-upon-Avon, Wks	15	20
CDS POSTMARKS		
(2a) Field Post Office 1050 (Sited in Stratford)	65	75
SLOGAN POSTMARKS		
(3) Shakespeare Anniversary Year, Stratford	975	975
(4) First Day of Issue, Stratford	15(s)	15(s)
ANY OTHER PMK (FDI, CDS or Slogan) *from*	10	15

1st July 1964 - GEOGRAPHICAL CONGRESS

2½d Flats; 4d Shipbuilding; 8d Forestry; 1s 6d Nuclear Power.

	non-phos.	phos.
SPECIAL HANDSTAMPS		
(1) Lawn Tennis Championships AELTC, Wimbledon	250	n.k.
ORDINARY F.D.I. POSTMARKS		
(2) Philatelic Bureau	25	35
(3) London	25	35
C.D.S. POSTMARKS		
(4) South Kensington – Royal Geographical Society	150	150
(5) Forest Row, Colliers Wood, Newtown or similar	60	60
SLOGAN POSTMARKS		
(6) F.D.I. - Greenwich or SE10 (with triangle) *each*	300	300
(7) Ralph Allen of Bath, Postal Pioneer	350	n.k.
(8) The Country Code–Leave no litter	275	n.k.
(9) Great Southampton Show	n.k.	75
ANY OTHER PMK (FDI, CDS or Slogan) *from*	20	30

5th August 1964 - BOTANICAL CONGRESS

3d Spring Gentian; 6d Dog Rose; 9d Honeysuckle; 1s 3d Water Lily

	non-phos.	phos.
SPECIAL HANDSTAMPS		
(1) 10th International Botanical Congress, Edinburgh	300	350
ORDINARY F.D.I. POSTMARKS		
(2) Philatelic Bureau or Edinburgh	30	50
(3) Kingston-upon-Thames (local F.D.I. for Kew)	30	50
C.D.S. POSTMARKS		
(4) Forest Row, Wood Green or similar	150	150
(5) Kew Gardens or Primrose Valley, Filey *each*	200	200
(6) Richmond & Twickenham (local CDS for Kew)	125	n.k.
SLOGAN POSTMARKS		
(7) FDI–Richmond & Twickenham (Kew)	200	200
ANY OTHER PMK (FDI, CDS or Slogan) *from*	25	35

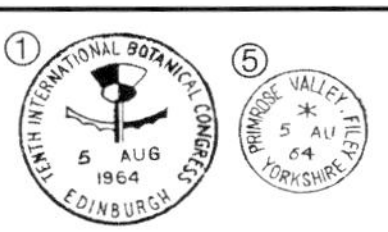

4th September 1964 -FORTH ROAD BRIDGE

3d, 6d Forth Road Bridge

	non-phos.	phos.
SPECIAL HANDSTAMPS		
(1) Forth Road Bridge, North Queensferry	45	125
(2) Forth Road Bridge, South Queensferry	35	90
(3) Apostolatus Maris - Int. Congress, Liverpool	n.k.	325
ORDINARY F.D.I. POSTMARKS		
(4) Philatelic Bureau	20	30
(5) Edinburgh (local F.D.I. for Forth Rd Bridge)	20	30
C.D.S. POSTMARKS		
(6) Balmoral Castle - The Queen proceeded to Balmoral after opening the Forth Road Bridge	225	225
(7) South Queensferry, West Lothian	90	90
(8) North Queensferry, Fife	125	125
SLOGAN POSTMARKS		
(9) F.D.I. – Edinburgh	50	50
(10) Midlothian for Industrial Sites	75	80
(11) Edinburgh – wavy line cancellation	30	n.k.
ANY OTHER PMK (FDI, CDS or Slogan) *from*	15	20

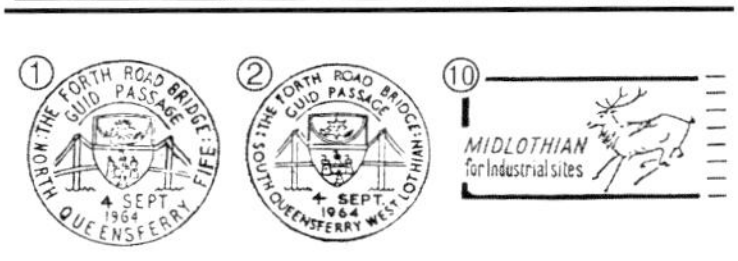

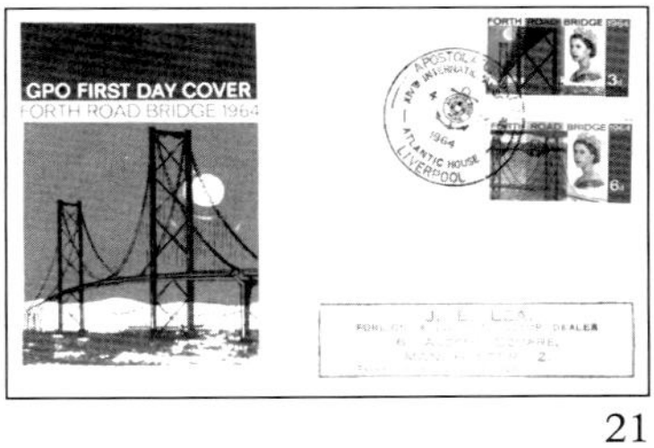

8th July 1965 - SIR WINSTON CHURCHILL

4d, 1s 3d Silhouettes of Churchill	non-phos covers	phos. covers
ORDINARY F.D.I. POSTMARKS	£	£
(1) Bladon, Oxford – Churchill buried at Bladon	25	30
(2) London SW1	10	15
(3) Philatelic Bureau	9	15
C.D.S. POSTMARKS		
(4) Churchill, Bristol or Oxford *each*	95	100
(5) Any Field or RAF Post Office	75	n.k.
(6) House of Commons, SW1	95	95
(7) House of Lords, SW1	145	145
(8) Marlborough – the Churchill ancestral home	200	n.k.
(9) Woodford Green – MP for Woodford	175	n.k.
SLOGAN POSTMARKS		
(10) First Day of Issue–Westminster, London SW1	95	95
(11) London SW1–wavy line cancellation	50	n.k.
ANY OTHER PMK (FDI, CDS or Slogan) *from*	8	9

19th July 1965 – 700th ANNIV. of PARLIAMENT

6d De Montfort's Seal; 2s 6d (non-phos. only) Parliament		
ORDINARY F.D.I. POSTMARKS		
(1) Dover or Lincoln – first to be represented at the Parliament by commoners *each*	40	40
(2) Evesham – Simon De Montfort killed here	35	35
(3) London SW	20	20
(4) Leicester – De Montfort was Earl of Leicester	35	35
(5) Oxford – Parliament sometimes met at Oxford	35	35
(6) Philatelic Bureau	15	15
(7) Any other office	12	12
C.D.S. POSTMARKS		
(8) Buckingham Palace, SW1	200	150
(9) Dover or Lincoln (see note above) *each*	60	60
(10) Evesham – Simon De Montfort killed	125	100
(11) House of Commons, SW1	100	100
(12) House of Lords, SW1	125	125
(13) North Warnborough – De Montfort's home	275	275
(14) London SW1 or Parliament Street, SW1	75	75
SLOGAN POSTMARKS		
(15) London SW1 – wavy line cancel	30	n.k.
ANY OTHER PMK (FDI, CDS or Slogan) *from*	10	10

9th August 1965 – SALVATION ARMY

3d, 1s 6d		
SPECIAL HANDSTAMPS		
(1) Portsmouth & District Philatelic Society	125	125
(1a) -ditto- on Philatelic Society official cover	100	100
ORDINARY F.D.I. POSTMARKS		
(2) London EC – HQ of Salvation Army	35	40
(3) Nottingham – Birthplace of William Booth	75	75
ANY OTHER PMK (FDI, CDS or Slogan) *from*	25	35

1st September 1965 – JOSEPH LISTER (Antiseptic Surgery)

4d Carbolic Spray; 1s Lister		
SPECIAL HANDSTAMPS		
(1) Eyam Plague Commemoration	200	n.k.
(1a) -ditto- (Eyam Plague official cover)	450	n.k.
ORDINARY F.D.I. POSTMARKS		
(2) Edinburgh – Professor of Clinical Surgery	50	50
(2a) - ditto - (Royal Infirmary special cover)	70	70
(3) Glasgow – Lister was Professor of Surgery here	60	50
(4) GPO Philatelic Bureau, London EC1	30	30
C.D.S. POSTMARKS		
(5) Royal Infirmary Edinburgh (Royal Infirmary cvr)	225	225
(6) Glasgow – Lister was Professor of Surgery here	125	150
SLOGAN POSTMARKS		
(7) First Day of Issue – Edinburgh	125	125
ANY OTHER PMK (FDI, CDS or Slogan) *from*	25	25

1st Sept. 1965 – COMMONWEALTH ARTS FESTIVAL

6d Trinidad Carnival Dancers; 1s 6d Canadian Folk Dancers		
SPECIAL HANDSTAMPS		
(1) Eyam Plague Commemoration	150	n.k.
(1a) -ditto- (Eyam Plague official cover)	650	n.k.
ORDINARY F.D.I. POSTMARKS		
(2) Cardiff, Glasgow, Liverpool or London	30	30
C.D.S. POSTMARKS		
(3) Balmoral Castle – Duke of Edinburgh travelled from Balmoral Castle to open the Festival	150	150
(4) Buckingham Palace	125	n.k.
(5) Stratford-upon-Avon (on Arts Centre cover)	125	n.k.

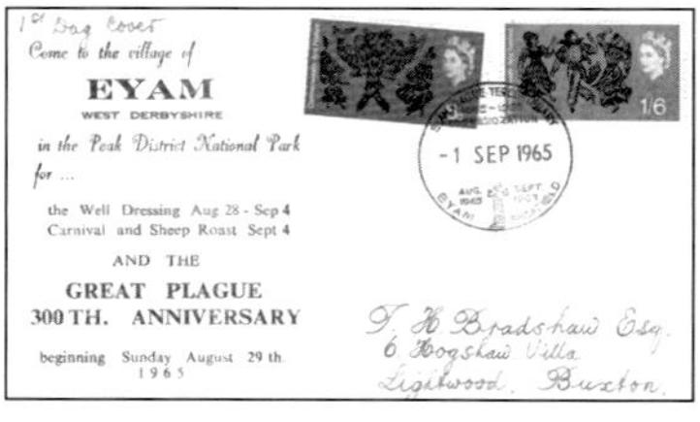

Commonwealth Arts (contd.)

	non-phos covers £	phos. covers £
SLOGAN POSTMARKS		
(6) Commonwealth Arts Festival, Glasgow	700	800
(7) Commonwealth Arts Festival, Liverpool	700	800
(8) Commonwealth Arts Festival – any other office	500	600
(9) 4th Bach Festival Bath, October 1965, Bath	500	n.k.
ANY OTHER PMK (FDI, CDS or Slogan) *from*	20	25

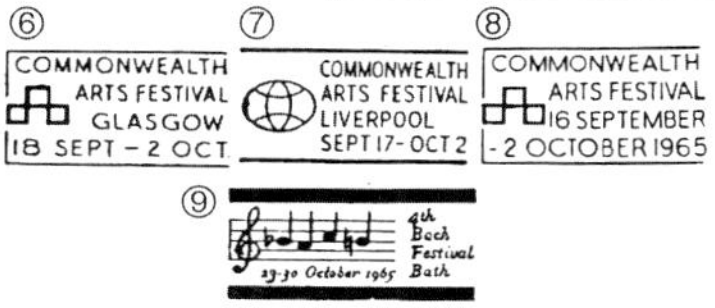

13th Sept. 1965 – THE BATTLE OF BRITAIN

6 x 4d; 9d, 1s 3d Battle scenes

ORDINARY F.D.I. POSTMARKS		
(1) Philatelic Bureau	20	25
C.D.S. POSTMARKS		
(2) Biggin Hill (packet pmk), Westerham or Cranwell..	100	100
(3) Biggin Hill (small metal cds pmk)	150	150
(4) Churchill, Bristol	75	n.k.
(5) Dover, Kent	50	75
(6) Any RAF, RN or Field Post Office (FPO) pmk	150	150
ANY OTHER PMK (FDI, CDS or Slogan) *from*	20	20

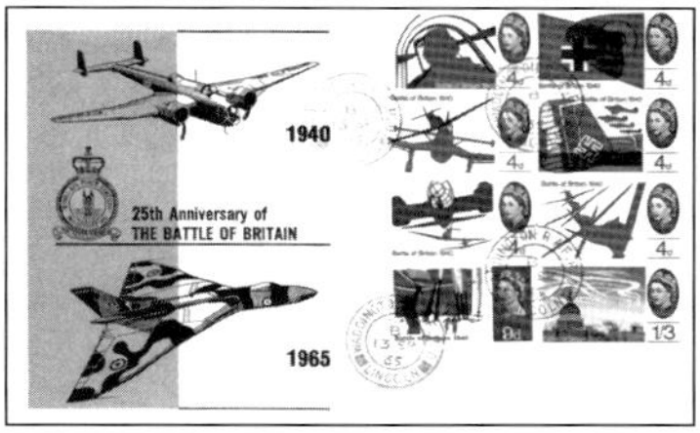

8th October 1965 – POST OFFICE TOWER

3d Georgian Bldgs & Tower; 1s 3d Nash Terrace & Tower

SPECIAL HANDSTAMPS		
(1) Leicester Philatelic Society Diamond Jubilee	75	85
(1a) ditto – on Leicester Philatelic Soc. official cover	85	95
ORDINARY F.D.I. POSTMARKS		
(2) London WC – Site of P.O. Tower	20	20
(3) Philatelic Bureau	15	15
C.D.S. POSTMARKS		
(4) Gt. Portland St. – nearest P.O. to the Tower	125	125
(5) London W1 – site of P.O. Tower	20	20
SLOGAN POSTMARKS		
(6) Have you taken out your licence for Radio-TV?	50	50
(7) London W1 (wavy line) – site of P.O. Tower	20	20
ANY OTHER PMK (FDI, CDS or Slogan) *from*	15	15

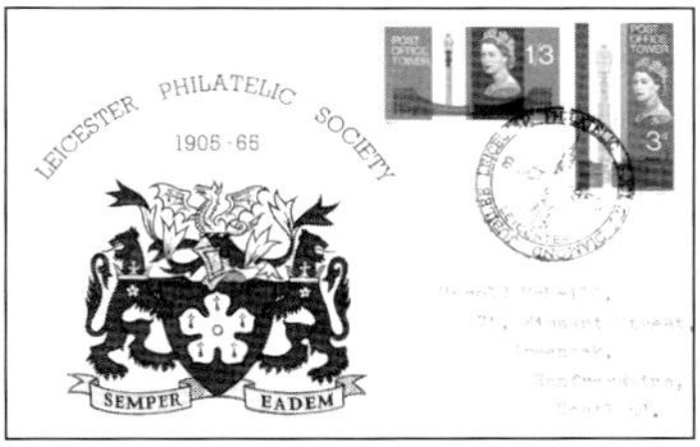

25th Oct. 1965 – U.N. & INT. CO-OPERATION YEAR

3d U.N. Emblem; 1s 6d I.C.Y. Emblem

SPECIAL HANDSTAMPS		
(1) Leicester Philatelic Society Diamond Jubilee	70	80
(1a) ditto – on Leicester Philatelic Soc. official cover	80	90
ORDINARY F.D.I. POSTMARKS		
(2) London SW – U.N. London HQ	25	35
C.D.S. POSTMARKS		
(3) House of Commons, London SW1	50	65
(4) Royal Courts of Justice, Bow WC2	200	n.k.
SLOGAN POSTMARKS		
(5) International Co-operation Year, Reading	550	550
ANY OTHER PMK (FDI, CDS or Slogan) *from*	20	25

15th Nov. 1965 – INT. TELECOMMUNICATIONS

9d Telecommunications; 1s 6d Radio Waves

C.D.S. POSTMARKS		
(1) Helston – Goonhilly Downs Ground Station	325	325
SLOGAN POSTMARKS		
(2) Have you taken out your licence for Radio-TV?	250	n.k.
ANY OTHER PMK (FDI, CDS or Slogan) *from*	20	25

25th January 1966 – ROBERT BURNS

4d, 1s 3d Portraits of Burns

SPECIAL HANDSTAMPS		
(1) The friend of man to vice alone a foe – Dumfries	20	20
(2) That man to man the warld o'er..... – Alloway	15	15
(3) That man to man the warld o'er..... – Ayr	15	15
(4) That man to man the warld o'er..... – Edinburgh	20	20
(5) That man to man the warld o'er..... – Glasgow	20	20
(6) That man to man the warld o'er..... – Greenock	35	40
(7) That man to man the warld o'er..... – Kilmarnock	20	20
(8) That man to man the warld o'er..... – Mauchline	35	40

These special handstamps were sponsored by the Post Office. Various organisations produced covers using these handstamps but they are not 'official' as described in the General Notes. However, they do command a premium.

ORDINARY F.D.I. POSTMARKS		
(9) Any Scottish postmark	8	10
C.D.S. POSTMARKS		
(10) Burns Statue, Ayr	275	275
(11) Ayr - Carlisle TPO	125	n.k.
ANY OTHER PMK (FDI, CDS or Slogan) *from*	7	8

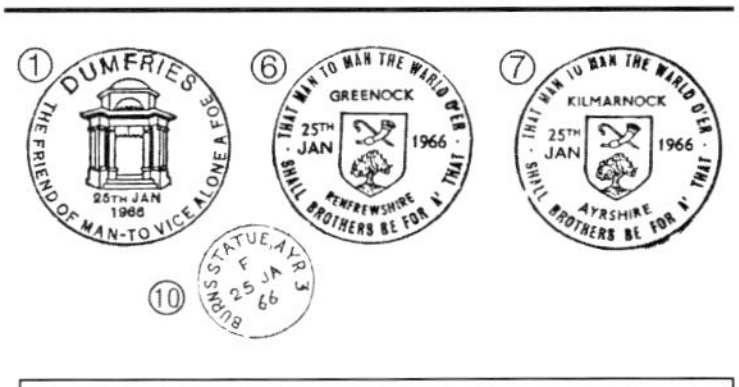

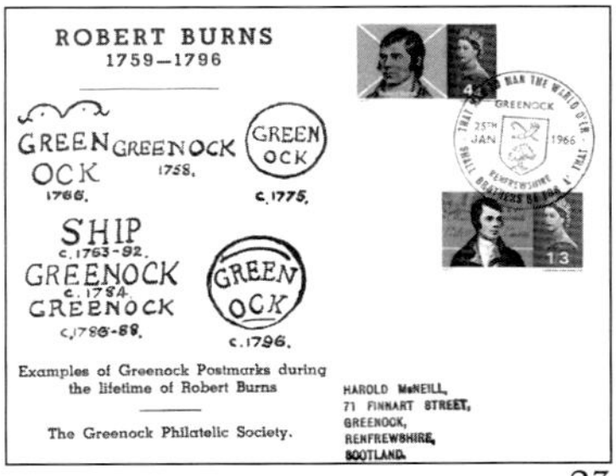

28th February 1966 - WESTMINSTER ABBEY

3d Abbey; 2s 6d (non-phos. only) Henry VII Chapel

	non-phos covers	phos. covers
ORDINARY F.D.I. POSTMARKS	£	£
(1) London SW	25	25
(2) Philatelic Bureau	15	15
C.D.S. POSTMARKS		
(3) Buckingham Palace	150	150
(4) House of Commons or Parliament St. SW1	125	100
(5) House of Lords	155	135
SLOGAN POSTMARKS		
(6) Westminster Abbey 900th Anniversary Year	150	120
(7) First Day of Issue - Westminster, London SW1	140	100
(8) London SW1 - wavy line postmark	50	15
ANY OTHER PMK (FDI, CDS or Slogan) *from*	15	15

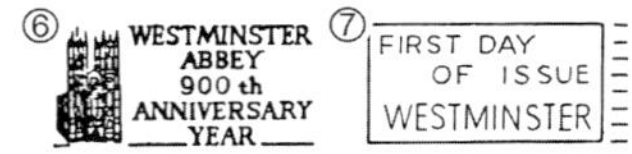

2nd May 1966 - BRITISH LANDSCAPES

4d Sussex; 6d Antrim; 1s 3d Harlech; ls 6d The Cairngorms

	non-phos covers	phos. covers
ORDINARY F.D.I. POSTMARKS		
(1) Lewes, Sussex - appropriate for 4d value	75	75
(2) Harlech, Merioneth - appropriate for 1s 3d	90	90
(3) Coleraine - appropriate for 6d value	90	90
(4) Grantown-on-Spey - appropriate for 1s 6d	125	125
(5) GPO Philatelic Bureau, London EC1	15	15
C.D.S. POSTMARKS		
(6) Antrim - appropriate for 6d value	135	135
(7) Coleraine - appropriate for 6d value	135	135
(8) Grantown-on-Spey - appropriate for 1s 6d	135	135
(9) Harlech - appropriate for 1s 3d value	135	135
(10) Forest Row, Heath Common or similar	75	75
ANY OTHER PMK (FDI, CDS or Slogan) *from*	10	10
SET 4 single stamp covers with appropriate pmks - usually (1), (2), (3) and (4)	30	40

1st June 1966 - WORLD CUP FOOTBALL

4d, 6d, 1s 3d Football scenes

	non-phos covers	phos. covers
ORDINARY F.D.I. POSTMARKS		
(1) Wembley, Middx	35	45
(2) Philatelic Bureau	20	25
(3) B'ham, Liverpool, Manchester, Middlesbrough, Sheffield, Sunderland - World Cup Games *each*	35	45
SLOGAN POSTMARKS		
(4) First Day of Issue - Harrow & Wembley	80	80
(5) World Cup City, Sheffield, City of Steel	575	n.k.
(6) The Dairy Festival, Time for Sport	300	n.k.
(7) World Cup Sunderland *plain cover*	250	n.k.
ANY OTHER PMK (FDI, CDS or Slogan) *from*	15	25

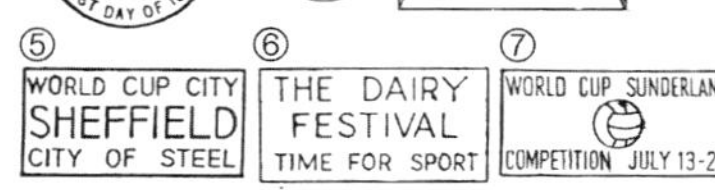

8th August 1966 - BRITISH BIRDS

4 x 4d Black-headed Gull; Blue Tit; Robin; Blackbird

	non-phos covers	phos. covers
ORDINARY F.D.I. POSTMARKS		
(1) Philatelic Bureau	30	30
C.D.S. POSTMARKS		
(2) Birdbrook (or similar)	225	–
ANY OTHER PMK (FDI, CDS or Slogan) *from*	20	20

18th August 1966 - 'ENGLAND WINNERS'

4d World Cup stamp overprinted 'England Winners' (non-phosphor only)

	non-phos covers	phos. covers
SPECIAL HANDSTAMPS		
(1) World Methodist Conference, SW1	250	–
(2) Opening of the Tay Road Bridge, Dundee	50	–
(2a) - do - on official cover	150	–
(3) Ballater Highland Games (official cover)	125	–
ORDINARY F.D.I. POSTMARKS		
(4) Harrow & Wembley	20	–
(5) B'ham, Liverpool, Manchester, Middlesbrough Sheffield, Sunderland - World Cup Games *each*	25	–
C.D.S. POSTMARKS		
(6) Harrow & Wembley, Middx	35	–
SLOGAN POSTMARKS		
(7) Harrow & Wembley - wavy line cancel	30	–
ANY OTHER PMK (FDI, CDS or Slogan) *from*	10	–

*Some **double-dated** covers exist with the set of World Cup stamps postmarked 1st June and the England Winners stamp postmarked 18th August*

	non-phos covers	phos. covers
(1) Harrow & Wembley FDI double dated	275	
(2) B'ham, Liverpool, Manchester, Middlesbrough Sheffield or Sunderland - double dated	125	
ANY OTHER PMK (FDI, CDS or Slogan) *from*	70	

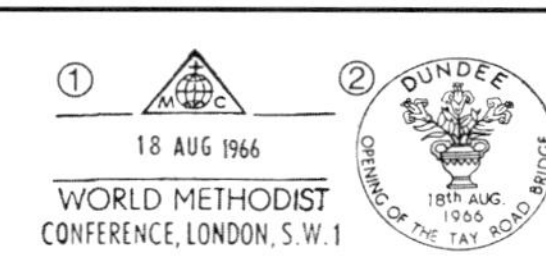

19th September 1966 - BRITISH TECHNOLOGY

4d Jodrell Bank; 6d Motor Cars; 1s 3d Hovercraft; 1s 6d Nuclear Power

	non-phos covers £	phos. covers £
ORDINARY F.D.I. POSTMARKS		
(1) Philatelic Bureau	15	15
(2) B'ham, Coventry, Oxford, Liverpool - car industry	30	35
(3) Carlisle, Cumberland - Windscale Reactor	30	35
(4) Manchester - Jodrell Bank	30	35
(5) Newport, Isle of Wight - Hovercraft	30	35
(6) Portsmouth - Hovercraft	30	35
(7) Luton, Beds - car industry	30	35
C.D.S. POSTMARKS		
(8) Macclesfield, Cheshire (with Jodrell Bank cachet)	150	175
(9) Cowes, I.O.W. (British Hovercraft Corp. cover)	175	150
(10) Calderbridge, Seascale - Windscale reactor	10(s)	–
(11) Lower Withington - Jodrell Bank	10(s)	–
SLOGAN POSTMARKS		
(12) Build Your New Factory at Grimsby	60	–
(13) Remploy (steering columns for the mini)	125	–
(14) Stop Accidents (with road sign)	175	–
ANY OTHER PMK (FDI, CDS or Slogan) *from*	10	10
SET 4 single stamp covers with appropriate pmks – usually (2), (3), (4) and (5)	30	45

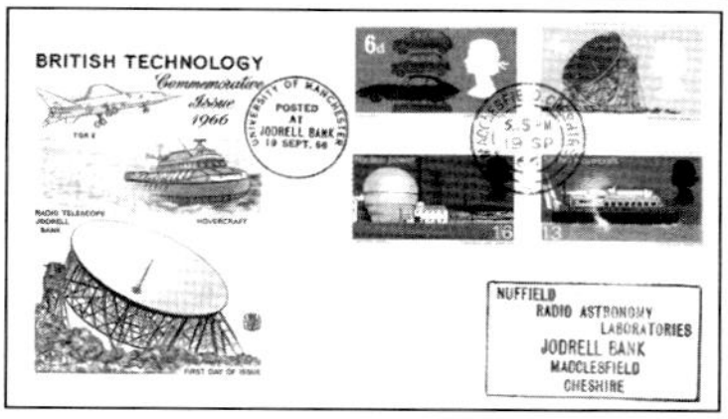

14th October 1966 - BATTLE OF HASTINGS

6 x 4d, 6d, 1s 3d Battle Scenes

	non-phos covers £	phos. covers £
SPECIAL HANDSTAMPS		
(1) Battle of Hastings 900th Anniv. Battlefield	12	15
ORDINARY F.D.I. POSTMARKS		
(2) Battle, Sussex	12	15
(3) Hastings	10	12
(4) Philatelic Bureau	10	12
(5) Guernsey or Jersey *each*	10	10
C.D.S. POSTMARKS		
(6) Battle	50	50
(7) Harold Hill, Hastings or Normandy *each*	250	250
SLOGAN POSTMARKS		
(8) Les Iles Normandes, Guernsey (on 2 covers)	400	400
(9) Les Iles Normandes, Jersey (on 2 covers)	400	400
(10) Hastings Popular with Visitors since 1066	30(s)	30(s)
ANY OTHER PMK (FDI, CDS or Slogan) *from*	10	10

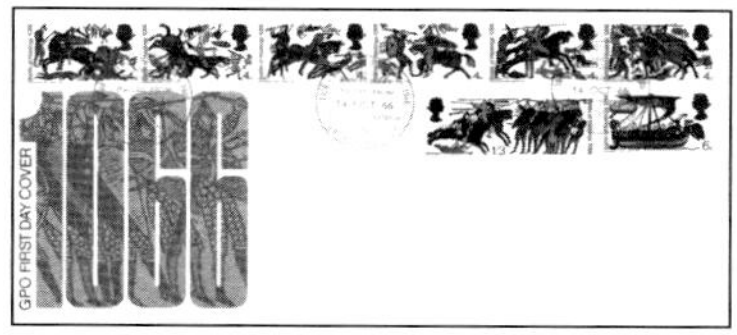

1st December 1966 - CHRISTMAS

3d, 1s 6d Children's Paintings

	non-phos covers £	phos. covers £
SPECIAL HANDSTAMPS		
(1) British Stamp Exhibition, BF 1000 PS	40	40
(1a) – ditto – on BFPS official cover	25	25
ORDINARY F.D.I. POSTMARKS		
(2) Bethlehem, Llandeilo, Carms	10	10
(3) Philatelic Bureau	10	10
C.D.S. POSTMARKS		
(4) Bethlehem or Nasareth *each*	275	275
(5) Isle of Whithorn – first seat of Christianity	150	n.k.
(6) St. Nicholas, Guildford	150	n.k.
SLOGAN POSTMARKS		
(7) Britain Leads the World in Helping Spastics	75	60
(8) Reedham School Caring for Children	90	n.k.
(9) John Groom's Cares for the Disabled	80	50
(10) Post Early for Christmas	250	n.k.
ANY OTHER PMK (FDI, CDS or Slogan) *from*	5	5

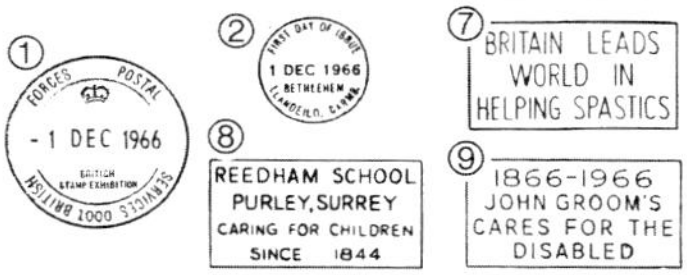

20th Feb. 1967 - EUROPEAN FREE TRADE AREA

9d Sea Freight; 1s 6d Air Freight

	non-phos covers £	phos. covers £
SPECIAL HANDSTAMPS		
(1) Radiation Biology Conference, Portmadoc	30	30
ORDINARY F.D.I. POSTMARKS		
(2) Philatelic Bureau or London SW	8	8
(3) Hounslow - Heathrow Airport	15	15
(4) Hull, Grimsby or Newcastle – EFTA Ports	25	25
C.D.S. POSTMARKS		
(5) Boston or similar – EFTA Ports	20	25
(6) House of Commons or House of Lords, SW1	60	55
SLOGAN POSTMARKS		
(7) Ship Early Through the Port of London	175	175
(8) Southend, Sunderland or Liverpool slogans	50	50
(9) Tees Side Means Business *plain covers*	15	15
(10) Are you under insured?	50	50
ANY OTHER PMK (FDI, CDS or Slogan) *from*	8	8

24th April 1967 - WILD FLOWERS

4 x 4d, 9d & 1s 9d Wild Flowers

	non-phos	phos.
SPECIAL HANDSTAMPS	£	£
(1) RSH Health Congress, Eastbourne	225	250
(1a) -ditto- on official cover	400	n.k.
ORDINARY F.D.I. POSTMARKS		
(2) Philatelic Bureau	10	10
(3) Kingston-upon-Thames (local F.D.I. for Kew)	15	15
C.D.S. POSTMARKS		
(4) Bluebell Hill, Flore, Hawthorn or Primrose St	175	175
(5) Kew Gardens or Flowery Field	150	150
(6) Hedgend, Forest Row, Welwyn Gdn City etc	50	50
ANY OTHER PMK (FDI, CDS or Slogan) *from*	12	15

OFFICIAL OR ORDINARY?

The most frequently asked question: ***'What is the difference between official covers and ordinary covers?'***

PLEASE READ GENERAL NOTES FOR MORE DETAILS

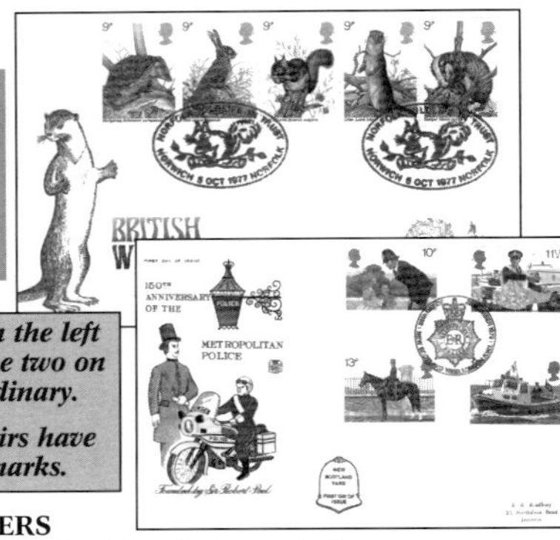

The two covers on the left are official and the two on the right are ordinary.

However both pairs have identical postmarks.

OFFICIAL COVERS

In the context of this catalogue, 'official' covers are defined as covers produced by private organisations or cover producers, who at the same time sponsor a special handstamp to accompany their cover. In the above two examples *Markton Stamps* of Norfolk produced a cover for the Norfolk Naturalists' Trust and sponsored a special postmark. The Police cover was produced for the Metropolitan Police Force by *Cotswold Covers*.

ORDINARY COVERS

These are produced primarily for the general FDC collector and are usually sold as 'blanks' (i.e with no stamps affixed). They are available from most good stamp shops before the day of issue of the postage stamps. Collectors purchase the 'blanks' then affix the stamps to the covers themselves. The Wildlife cover was produce by *Philart Covers*, and the Police cover by *Stuart Covers* - both were available as blanks. Collectors have to make their own arrangements concerning franking. They can send their covers to the Royal Mail Special Handstamp Centres and request that their covers be postmarked with any privately sponsored handstamp.

FROM THE NEXT ISSUE PRICES ARE GIVEN FOR BOTH TYPES OF COVER (WHERE AVAILABLE)

10th July 1967 - PAINTINGS

4d 'Master Lambton' (Lawrence); 9d Stubbs; 1s 6d 'Children Coming Out of School' (Lowry)

	ordinary covers	official covers	
SPECIAL HANDSTAMPS	£	£	
(1) Art on Stamps Exhibition,WC2	35	95	*P.R. O'Connell*
ORDINARY F.D.I. POSTMARKS			
(2) Philatelic Bureau	10		
(3) Bishop Auckland -'Master Lambton'	50		

24th July 1967 - SIR FRANCIS CHICHESTER

1s 9d Gipsy Moth IV

SPECIAL HANDSTAMPS			
(1) Philatelic Bureau	10	-	*Post Offfice*
(2) Greenwich, SE10	10	-	*Post Office*
(3) Plymouth	10	-	*Post Office*
(4) International Camp, E. Mersea	200	-	*n.o.c.*
ORDINARY F.D.I. POSTMARKS			
(5) Barnstaple – Birthplace of Chichester	20		
(6) Chichester, Sussex or Gosport, Hants *each*	15		
C.D.S. POSTMARKS			
(7) Barnstaple or Selsey, Chichester	25		
(8) Chichester Road, Portsmouth.	325		
(9) House of Commons (Outward Bound cover)	25		
(10) Shirwell – ancestral home of Chichester	150		
SLOGAN POSTMARKS			
(11) Ship through the Port of London	125		

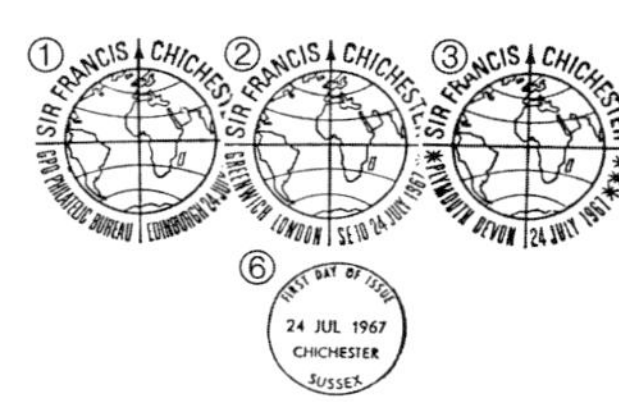

19th September 1967 - BRITISH DISCOVERY

4d Radar; 1s Penicillin; 1s 6d Jet Engine; 1s 9d Television

	ordinary covers £	official covers £	
SPECIAL HANDSTAMPS			
(1) Penicillin/Sir Alexander Fleming, W2	25	-	*n.o.c.*
(2) HMS Discovery, WC	20	-	*n.o.c.*
(3) BF 1000 PS (used at RAF Bruggen)	70	85	*Forces*
ORDINARY F.D.I. POSTMARKS			
(4) Philatelic Bureau	5		
(5) Coventry - birthplace of Whittle	15		
(6) Hounslow (jet) or Hastings (first TV images)	15		
(7) London SW (British Drug Houses cover)	25		
(8) Paddington W2 - discovery of penicillin	15		
(9) Plymouth (with Westward TV logo)	20		
(10) Any other office	5		
C.D.S. POSTMARKS			
(11) Benenden Chest Hospital, Cranbrook	375		
(12) Brechin - birthplace of Watson-Watt	25(s)		
(13) Darvel - birthplace of Fleming	25(s)		
(14) Helensburgh - birthplace Baird	150		
SLOGAN POSTMARKS			
(15) First Day of Issue - Paddington W2	100		
SET 4 single stamp covers with appropriate pmks - usually (5), (12), (13) and (14)	45		

18th October 1967 - CHRISTMAS

4d 'Madonna and Child'

	ordinary covers £
ORDINARY F.D.I. POSTMARKS	
(1) Bethlehem, Llandeilo, Carms	5
(2) Philatelic Bureau	3
C.D.S. POSTMARKS	
(3) Bethlehem, Nasareth or Jericho	150
(4) St. Nicholas	75
SLOGAN POSTMARKS	
(5) First Day of Issue - Bethlehem	10
(6) Oxfam - 25th Year	25
(7) Visit Roman Bath	100

27th November 1967 - CHRISTMAS

3d, 1s 6d 'Adoration of the Shepherds'

	ordinary covers £	official covers £
SPECIAL HANDSTAMPS		
(1) Dulwich Millennium	125	175
ORDINARY F.D.I. POSTMARKS		
(2) Philatelic Bureau	2	
(3) Bethlehem, Llandeilo, Carms	5	
C.D.S. POSTMARKS		
(4) Bethlehem or Nasareth	200	
(5) St. Nicholas, Starcross or similar	225	
SLOGAN POSTMARKS		
(6) First Day of Issue - Bethlehem	75	
(7) Christmas Illuminations, Cheltenham	325	
(8) First Ever Christmas Present, Londonderry	375	
(9) Oxfam - 25th Year	50	
(10) Visit Roman Bath (plain cover)	25	

*Some **double-dated** covers exist with the 4d stamp postmarked 18th October and the 3d & 1s 6d stamps postmarked 27th November*

(1) Bethlehem First Day of Issue	30
(2) Any other postmark	20

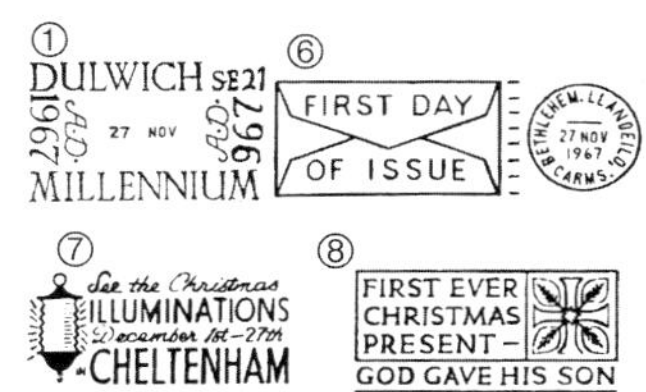

29th April 1968 - BRITISH BRIDGES

4d Tarr Steps, Dulverton; 9d Aberfeldy Bridge; 1s 6d Menai Bridge; 1s 9d M4 Viaduct, Chiswick

	ordinary covers £	official covers £	
SPECIAL HANDSTAMPS			
(1) First Day of Issue - Philatelic Bureau	10	-	*Post Office*
(2) First Day of Issue - Bridge	10	-	*Post Office*
(3) RSH Health Congress, Eastbourne	175	225	*R.S.H.*
ORDINARY F.D.I. POSTMARKS			
(4) Perth (Aberfeldy) or Exeter (Dulverton)	25		
(5) Bath (Pulteney Bridge cover)	30		
(6) Lincoln or Windsor (on special covers)	25		
C.D.S. POSTMARKS			
(7) Aberfeldy - featured on 9d value	150		
(8) Chiswick - featured on 1s 9d value	175		
(9) Dulverton - featured on 4d value	225		
(10) Menai - featured on 1s 6d value	125		
SLOGAN POSTMARKS			
(11) First Day of Issue - Bridge, Canterbury	80		
(12) First Day of Issue - Menai Bridge	80		
(13) First Day of Issue - Aberfeldy	80		
(14) Chiswick - wavy line cancellation	150		
(15) Harlow - Motorists Week (known on 2 cvrs)	350		
SET 4 single stamp covers with appropriate pmks - usually (8), (9), (12) and (13)	40		

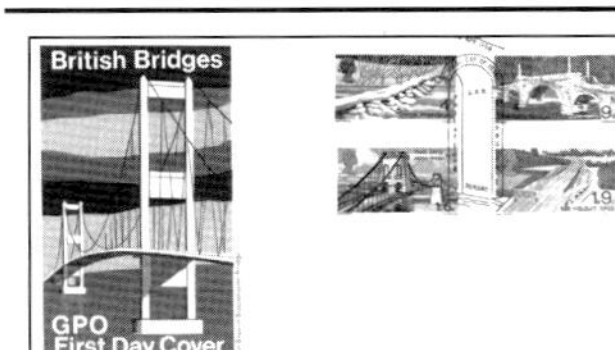

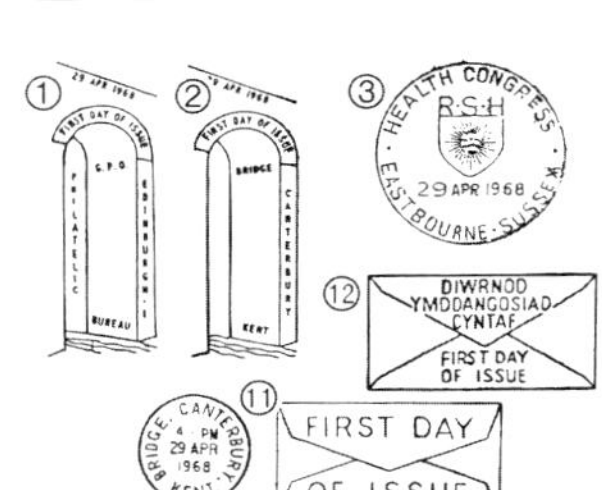

29th May 1968 - BRITISH ANNIVERSARIES

4d TUC; 9d Votes for Women; 1s RAF; 1s 9d James Cook

SPECIAL HANDSTAMPS	ordinary covers £	official covers £	
(1) First Day of Issue, Manchester TUC 100	80	-	*Post Office*
(2) First Day of Issue, Women's Suffrage	80	-	*Post Office*
(3) First Day of Issue, Hendon, NW4	80	-	*Post Office*
(4) First Day of Issue, Whitby	80	-	*Post Office*
(5) 50th Anniversary RAF Leuchars, Fife	250	20	*Forces(s)*
(6) 50th Anniv. RAF Medmenham	190	-	*n.o.c.*
(7) RAF 50th Anniv. Fylingdales	190	20	*Forces(s)*
(8) RAF 50th Anniv. RAF College Cranwell	250	20	*Forces(s)*
(9) RAF Escaping Society, BF 1067 PS	190	20	*Forces(s)*
(10) BF 1000 PS (used at RAF Laarbrucke)	190	-	*n.o.c.*
(11) P.O. Engineering Union 100000, Ealing	250	30	*P.O.E.U.(s)*
(12) RNIB Centenary , London SW1	250	-	*n.o.c.*
ORDINARY F.D.I. POSTMARKS			
(13) Philatelic Bureau	10		
(14) Any other office	8		
C.D.S. POSTMARKS			
(15) Hendon	30		
(16) House of Commons or Lords, SW1	45		
(17) Forces P.O. or any Field Post Office	50		
(18) Digby Aerodrome or Trinity (Montrose Airbase)	75		
(19) Marton-in-Cleveland - b/place Captain Cook.	10(s)		
(20) Any R.A.F. Post Office e.g. Hawkinge	100		
(21) Tolpuddle, Dorset - Tolpuddle Martyrs	15(s)		
SLOGAN POSTMARKS			
(22) Bicentenary Captain Cook ......*(on four covers)*	75		
SET 4 single stamp covers with appropriate pmks - usually (1), (2), (3) and (4)	15		

12th August 1968 - BRITISH PAINTINGS

4d Elizabeth I (artist unknown); 1s Pinkie (Lawrence); 1s 6d Ruins of St. Mary le Port (Piper); 1s 9d Hay Wain (Constable)

SPECIAL HANDSTAMPS	ordinary	official	
(1) Philatex 68 Woburn, Bletchley	35	75	*Woburn*
(2) Portsmouth & District Philatelic Society	45	60	*Phil. Soc.*
(3) Parish Church Restoration Kettering	45	60	*Parish Ch.*
(4) SAGA (Scouts & Guides), Beeley	-	30	*SAGA (s)*
ORDINARY F.D.I. POSTMARKS			
(5) Philatelic Bureau	8		
(6) Bristol - Birthplace of Lawrence	10		
(7) Ipswich - F.D.I. for 'Constable Country'	10		
(8) Any other office	8		
C.D.S. POSTMARKS			
(9) Blackheath SE3 - Queen Elizabeth	225		
(10) East Bergholt - Constable's birthplace	450		
(11) Greenwich, SE10 - Birthplace of Elizabeth I	250		
(12) Richmond - 'Pinkie'	225		
SLOGAN POSTMARKS			
(13) F.D.I. - Hatfield - Hatfield Hse	40		
(14) F.D.I. - London SE1 - B/place of Elizabeth	40		
(15) F.D.I. - London W1 - Art galleries	40		
SET 4 single stamp covers with appropriate pmks	20		

25th November 1968 - CHRISTMAS

4d, 9d, 1s 6d Childrens Toys

SPECIAL HANDSTAMPS	ordinary	official	
(1) Selfridges Toy Fair, London W1	25	35	*Selfridges(s)*
(2) HMS Hermes, BF 1074 PS	100	175	*Forces*
ORDINARY F.D.I. POSTMARKS			
(3) Philatelic Bureau	4		
(4) Bethlehem, Llandeilo, Carms	8		
(5) Any other office	3		
SLOGAN POSTMARKS			
(6) First Day of Issue - Bethlehem	40		
(7) Christmas Illuminations, Cheltenham	10(s)		

15th January 1969 - BRITISH SHIPS

5d 'Queen Elizabeth 2'; 9d 'Cutty Sark'; 9d Elizabethan Galleon; 9d East Indiaman; 1s 'SS Great Britain'; 1s RMS 'Mauretania'

SPECIAL HANDSTAMPS	ordinary	official	
(1) Lloyd's New Coffee House EC3	90	-	*n.o.c.*
(2) Cutty Sark , Greenwich SE10	35	-	*n.o.c.*
ORDINARY F.D.I. POSTMARKS			
(3) Philatelic Bureau	15		
(4) Belfast, Glasgow or Newcastle - Shipbuilding	25		
(5) Bristol, Liverpool, Plymouth or Portsmouth	25		
(6) London EC or SE1	20		
(7) Southampton (QE2) or Dover (Channel port)	20		
(8) Any other office	12		

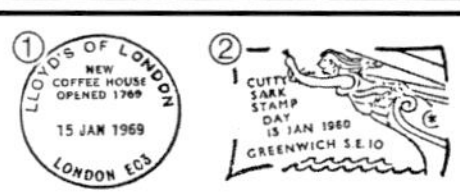

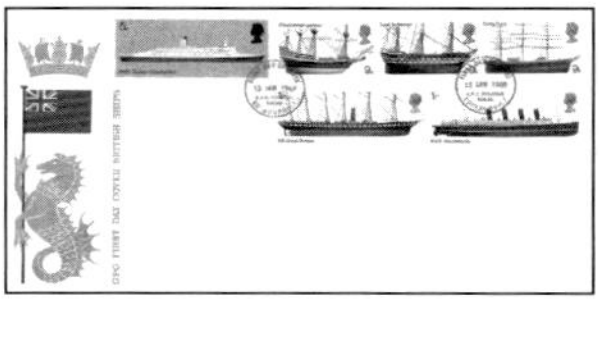

Ships (contd.)	ordinary covers	official covers	
C.D.S. POSTMARKS	£	£	
(9) Clydebank or Maritime Mail ... *each*	250		
(10) The Quarterdeck or British Fleet Mail ...	150		
(11) Southampton, Plymouth or Seaview ... *each*	50		
SLOGAN POSTMARKS			
(12) F.D.I. Greenwich or Great Britain W2 ...	20		

3rd March 1969 - CONCORDE

4d in flight, 9d plan & elevation, 1s 6d nose & tail

ORDINARY F.D.I. POSTMARKS			
(1) Filton Bristol ...	15		
(1a) -do- with 'Conseil de L'Europe' postmark ...	30		
(2) Hounslow, Middx - Heathrow ...	25		
(3) Philatelic Bureau or any other office ...	4		
C.D.S. POSTMARKS			
(4) Bristol ...	40		
(5) Farnborough ...	75		

2nd April 1969 – NOTABLE ANNIVERSARIES

5d Alcock & Brown, 9d Europa; 1s International Labour Organisation; 1s 6d NATO; 1s 9d 1st England/Australia flight

SPECIAL HANDSTAMPS			
(1) Alcock & Brown, Manchester ...	35	20	*Man.Airp.(s)*
(2) NATO HQ BF 1080 PS ...	250	250	*N.A.T.O.*
(3) NATO SHAPE BF 1081 PS ...	250	300	*N.A.T.O*
(4) Hoverlloyd, Pegwell Bay ...	425	25	*Hoverlloyd(s)*
(5) BF 1000 PS (used at Mill Hill) ...	250	150	*Forces*
(6) Grammar School Centenary, Doncaster. ...	175	200	*Grammar Sch.*
ORDINARY F.D.I. POSTMARKS			
(7) Hounslow or Manchester ...	25		
(8) London SW – Int. Labour Org. ...	15		
(9) Philatelic Bureau ...	6		
(10) Any other office ...	3		
C.D.S. POSTMARKS			
(11) Farnborough, Hants ...	125		
(12) Field Post Office postmarks ...	25		
SLOGAN POSTMARKS			
(13) Manchester Airport/Alcock & Brown ...	40(s)		
(14) Fly the Prestwick Way ...	50		
SET 5 single stamp covers with appropriate pmks ..	15		

28th May 1969 – BRITISH CATHEDRALS

4 x 5d – Durham, York, Canterbury, Edinburgh; 9d St. Paul's; 1s 6d Liverpool

SPECIAL HANDSTAMPS			
(1) Metropolitan Cathedral, Liverpool ...	30	35	*Stampex(s)*
(2) Philatex St. Pauls, London EC ...	25	–	*n.o.c.*
(3) York Minster ...	40	50	*York Mins.*
(4) Lewis's Stamp Exhibition, Manchester 1 ...	250	–	*n.oc.*
(5) Croeso 69 Tywyn Merioneth ...	40	50	*Tywyn*
(6) German British Culture Week BF 1078 PS ...	40	40	*Forces*
(7) Ulster Recruiting BF 1085 PS ...	40	40	*Forces*
ORDINARY F.D.I. POSTMARKS			
(8) GPO Philatelic Bureau, Edinburgh 1 ...	6		
(9) London EC – St. Paul's or York ...	15		
(10) Canterbury, Durham, Edinburgh or Liverpool	15		
(11) Any other office ...	5		
C.D.S. POSTMARKS			
(12) Alcester (Alcester Church Restoration cvr) ...	100		
(13) Durham or Winchester ... *each*	50		
SET single stamp covers with appropriate pmks ...	15		

1st July 1969 – PRINCE OF WALES

3 x 5d Caernarvon Castle; 9d Celtic Cross; 1s Prince Charles

SPECIAL HANDSTAMPS			
(1) Croes Geltaidd, Margam Abbey ...	120	–	*n.o.c.*
(2) Croeso 69, Investiture Day, Cardiff ...	120	–	*n.o.c.*
(3) Talyllyn Railway, Tywyn, Merioneth ...	45	50	*Tywyn*
(4) Nettleham, Lincoln ...	120	80	*Nettleham*
(5) BF 1000 PS (troop camp for Investiture) ...	175	175	*Forces*
(6) Lawn Tennis Championships ...	350	–	*n.o.c.*
ORDINARY F.D.I. POSTMARKS			
(7) GPO Philatelic Bureau, Edinburgh 1 ...	5		
(8) London SW, Windsor or Cardiff ...	15		
(9) Truro (Duchy of Cornwall) or Chester (Earl) ..	25		
(10) Day of Investiture, Caernarvon ...	5		
C.D.S. POSTMARKS			
(11) Buckingham Palace or Windsor Castle ...	275		
(12) Catterick (Royal Lancers PoWales's cover) ...	100		
(13) House of Commons or Lords ... *each*	65		
SLOGAN POSTMARKS			
(14) Dydd yr Arwisgo, Investiture Day ...	275		
(15) Wales Tomorrow Exhibition, Cardiff ...	20(s)		

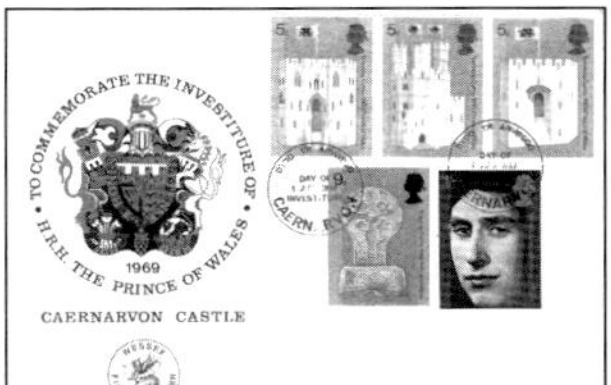

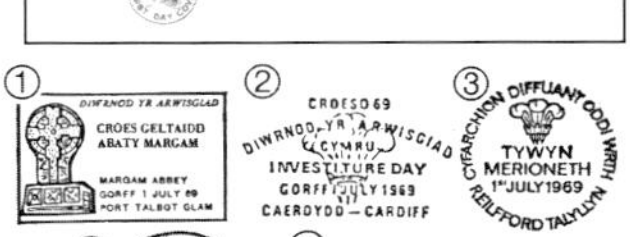

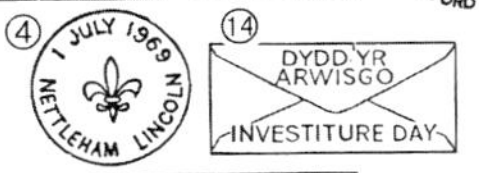

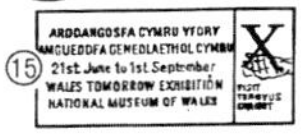

13th August 1969 - GANDHI

1s 6d Mahatma Gandhi

	ordinary covers £	official covers £	
SPECIAL HANDSTAMPS			
(1) Gandhi Centenary Year HCRC, E8	5	30	*Hackney CRC*
(2) Trade Fair & Exhibition Llanelli, Carms	175	–	*n.o.c.*
(3) International Youth Camp, Colchester	175	–	*n.o.c.*
ORDINARY F.D.I. POSTMARKS			
(4) Philatelic Bureau or any other office	2		

1st October 1969 – POST OFFICE TECHNOLOGY

5d Giro; 9d & 1s Telecommunications; 1s 6d Automatic Sorting

	ordinary	official	
SPECIAL HANDSTAMPS			
(1) Posted in the Post Office Tower, W1	7	–	*n.o.c.*
(2) P.O. Technology University College, WC1	7	–	*n.o.c.*
(3) Philatelic Stand Ideal Homes, Birmingham	250	–	*n.o.c.*
(4) Southampton Boat Show, Mayflower Park	175	35	*Boat Show(s)*
(5) National Postal Museum, EC1	80	–	*Post Office*
ORDINARY F.D.I. POSTMARKS			
(6) Philatelic Bureau or any other office	3		
(7) Norwich – first use of postal coding	10		
(8) London EC (British Week in Tokyo cover)	20		
C.D.S. POSTMARKS			
(9) Bootle – Giro HQ - featured on 5d value	20(s)		
SLOGAN POSTMARKS			
(10) Muncipal Bank Golden Jubilee Birmingham	150		
(11) Remember to use the Postcode	275		
SET 4 single stamp covers with appropriate postmarks – usually (1), (2), (7) and (9)	25		

26th November 1969 – CHRISTMAS

4d, 5d, 1s 6d The Nativity

	ordinary	official	
SPECIAL HANDSTAMPS			
(1) Jerusalem, Skellingthorpe, Lincs	40	40	*Temple of Jerusalem*
ORDINARY F.D.I. POSTMARKS			
(2) GPO Philatelic Bureau, Edinburgh 1	3		
(3) Bethlehem, Llandeilo, Carms	3		
(4) Any other office	2		
C.D.S. POSTMARKS			
(5) Bethlehem, Llandeilo, Carms	200		
(6) Nasareth, Gwynedd	150		
SLOGAN POSTMARKS			
(7) First Day of Issue – Bethlehem	60		
(8) Christmas Illuminations in Cheltenham	40(s)		
(9) Christmas Dick Whittington, Lewisham	225		
(10) National Childrens Home	50		
(11) Elgin (depicts cathedral) *plain cover*	20		

11th February 1970 – BRITISH RURAL ARCHITECTURE

5d Fife harling; 9d Cotswold limestone; 1s Welsh stucco; 1s 6d Ulster thatch

	ordinary	official	
ORDINARY F.D.I. POSTMARKS			
(1) Philatelic Bureau	4		
(2) Aberaeron – 1s Welsh stucco	12		
(3) Belfast (1s 6d) or Dunfermline (5d) *each*	12		
(4) Edinburgh (5d) or Gloucester (9d) *each*	12		
(5) Any other office	2		
C.D.S. POSTMARKS			
(6) Auchtermuchty, Fife – 5d Fife harling	125		
(7) Bibury or Chipping Campden – 9p	100		
(8) Criccieth (Criccieth Philatelic Soc cover)	40		
(9) Cirencester or Stroud – 9d Cotswold limestone	75		
(10) Culross, Fife – 5d Fife harling	80		
(11) Holywood, Co. Down – 1s 6d Ulster thatch	125		
SLOGAN POSTMARKS			
(12) Keep Britain Green – Conservation Year	175		
(13) 1970 Furniture Show *plain cover*	20		
SET 4 single stamp covers with appropriate pmks	12		

1st April 1970 – GENERAL ANNIVERSARIES

5d Declaration of Arbroath; 9d Florence Nightingale;1s Co-operative Alliance; 1s 6d Mayflower; 1s 9d Royal Astronomical Society

	ordinary	official	
SPECIAL HANDSTAMPS			
(1) Anniversary Stamps, Canterbury	20	–	*n.o.c.*
(2) Florence Nightingale Hospital NW1	60	–	*n.o.c.*
(3) Florence Nightingale Exhibition, SE1	45	50	*F.N. Cttee*
(4) The Crimean War, BF 1206 PS	350	15	*Forces(s)*
(5) Florence Nightingale, BF 1121 PS	175	15	*Forces(s)*
(6) Florence Nightingale, BF 1205 PS	300	15	*Forces(s)*
(7) London Co-op Golden Year, E15	275	20	*Co-op(s)*
(8) Int. Co-operative Alliance ICA, W1	225	–	*n.o.c.*
(9) Mayflower '70, Scrooby, Doncaster	250	30	*Scrooby(s)*
(10) Sir William Herschel, Slough	80	–	*n.o.c.*
(11) Air-sea Warfare Dev. Unit, RAF Ballykelly	225	350	RAF *Ballykelly*
(12) Air Mountains Base, Gibraltar, BF 1112 PS	225	20	*Forces(s)*

General Anniversaries (contd.)

	ordinary covers	official covers	
ORDINARAY F.D.I. POSTMARKS	£	£	
(13) Philatelic Bureau or any other office	3		
(14) Arbroath – 5d Declaration of Arbroath	45		
(15) Billericay or Boston – 'Mayflower' associations	15		
(16) London W1 – World HQ of ICA	12		
(17) Plymouth – 1s 6d Pilgrim Fathers	12		
(17a)-do- on special Plymouth cover	25		
(18) Rochdale – first Co-op	25		
(19) Slough – Sir William Herschel	20		
(20) Southampton – Pilgrim Fathers	15		
(20a)-do- on Southampton City Council cover	25		
C.D.S. POSTMARKS			
(21) Immingham or Scrooby – Pilgrim Fathers	20(s)		
(22) Southampton – Pilgrim Fathers	35		
(23) Forces P.O. (Florence Nightingale/Crimea)	35		
SLOGAN POSTMARKS			
(24) Plymouth Mayflower 70	35(s)		
(25) Boston Lincs. Mayflower 70	35(s)		
(26) Rochdale - wavy line postmark	35(s)		
(27) London W1 wavy line - HQ of ICA	25		
SET 5 single stamp covers with appropriate pmks	15		

3rd June 1970 – LITERARY ANNIVERSARIES

4 x 5d Dickens characters; 1s 6d Wordsworth

SPECIAL HANDSTAMPS			
(1) E78 Chigwell, Essex	60	95	*Chigwell*
(2) Dickens Fellowship, Broadstairs	50	90	*Broadstairs**
(3) Old Curiosity Shop, WC2	20	30	*Cameo*
(4) Dickens Centenary, Pickwick, Corsham	70	150	*Corsham*
(5) David Copperfield, Winterbourne	60	90	*Winterbourne**
(6) Living Exhibition '70, Sheffield	n.k.	150	*Sheffield Living*

** These two official covers are only known with the 4 Dickens stamps*

ORDINARY F.D.I. POSTMARKS			
(7) British Philatelic Bureau, Edinburgh 1	5		
(8) Broadstairs – 'Bleak House'	15		
(9) Cambridge – Wordsworth educated here	15		
(10) Cockermouth – b/place of Wordsworth	25		
(10a)-do- on special Wordsworth House cover	50		
(11) Portsmouth – b/place of Dickens	15		
(12) Rochester – Dickens died here in 1870	15		
(13) Any other office	5		
C.D.S. POSTMARKS			
(14) Ambleside – Wordsworth/Rydal Mount	200		
(15) Grasmere – Wordsworth/Dove Cottage	150		
(16) Portsmouth – Dickens born here in 1812	80		
SLOGAN POSTMARKS			
(17) First Day of Issue – Broadstairs	90		
(18) Int. Stamp Exhibition (4 x 5d only)	25		
PAIR of covers with appropriate pmks *from*	10		

15th July 1970 – COMMONWEALTH GAMES

5d Runners; 1s 6d Swimmers; 1s 9d Cyclists

SPECIAL HANDSTAMPS			
(1) Centenary RCT, BF 1123 PS	225	15	*Forces(s)*
(2) Enterprise Exhibition , Nottingham	165	25	*NottFest.(s)*
(3) Thos. Becket 1170-1970, Canterbury	165	25	*C.Cath.(s)*
(4) Cardigan Secondary School	165	100	*Card. Sch.*
(5) Assembly of Euro Municipalities, SE1	225	–	*n.o.c.*
(6) Great Yorkshire Show, Harrogate	165	250	*G.Y. Show*
(7) Victoria Cross, BF 1210 PS	250	15	*Forces(s)*
(8) Rorke's Drift, BF 1211 PS	250	15	*Forces(s)*
ORDINARY F.D.I. POSTMARKS			
(9) Philatelic Bureau	3		
(10) Edinburgh	10		
(11) Any other office	2		
C.D.S. POSTMARKS			
(12) Edinburgh Mobile Post Office	125		
SLOGAN POSTMARKS			
(13) The National Postal Museum	100		
(14) FDI – Edinburgh, Great Britain	55		
(15) Edinburgh – wavy line	25		

18th September 1970 – 'PHILYMPIA'

5d (Penny Black); 9d (1s Green); 1s 6d (4d Carmine)

SPECIAL HANDSTAMPS			
(1) Philatelic Bureau	2	–	*Post Office*
(2) Philympia Day, London	6	–	*Post Office*
(3) First Flight, Philympia, Calne	150	35	*B.N.I.(s)*
(4) First Flight, Philympia, Bembridge	150	35	*B.N.I.(s)*
(5) 23 Base Workshop REME, BF 1136 PS	50	50	*Forces*
(6) National Postal Museum	65	–	*n.o.c.*

Philympia (contd.)	ordinary covers	official covers	
ORDINARAY F.D.I. POSTMARKS	£	£	
(7) London W1 (local F.D.I. for Philympia)	6		
(8) Any other office	1		
C.D.S. POSTMARKS			
(9) House of Commons, SW1 (Postage Act)	40		
(10) Olympia W14	275		
SLOGAN POSTMARKS			
(11) Int Stamp Exhibition, Philympia 70	500		
(12) Any Postcode slogans	35		

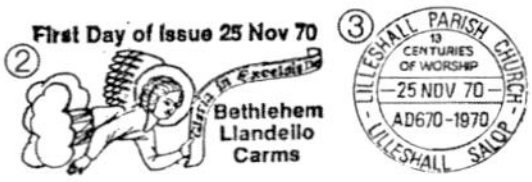

25th November 1970 - CHRISTMAS

4d, 5d, 1s 6d The Nativity

SPECIAL HANDSTAMPS			
(1) Philatelic Bureau	3	-	*Post Office*
(2) First Day of Issue - Bethlehem	6	-	*Post Office*
(3) Lilleshall Parish Church AD670-1970	175	200	*Lill. P.Ch.*
ORDINARY F.D.I. POSTMARKS			
(4) Any office	2		
SLOGAN POSTMARKS			
(5) First Day of Issue - Bethlehem	100		
(6) Fairfield Christmas Circus	150		
(7) Christmas Illuminations, Cheltenham	40(s)		

Ordinary F.D.I. pmks are now only listed if relevant to a stamp issue.

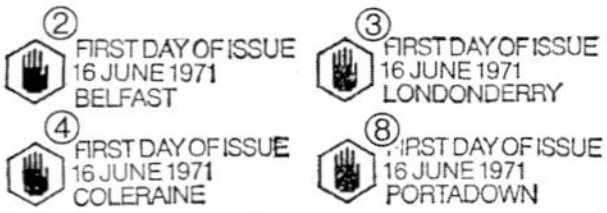

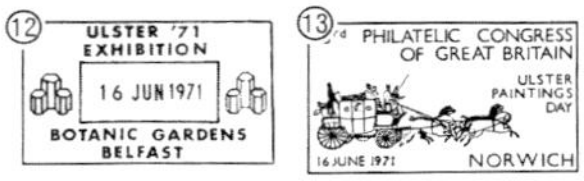

16th June 1971 - ULSTER '71 PAINTINGS

3p, 7½p, 9p Landscapes

SPECIAL HANDSTAMPS			
(1) First Day of Issue - Philatelic Bureau	3	-	*Post Office*
(2) First Day of Issue - Belfast	8	-	*Post Office*
(3) First Day of Issue - Londonderry	40	-	*Post Office*
(4) First Day of Issue - Coleraine	150	-	*Post Office*
(5) First Day of Issue - Newry	130	-	*Post Office*
(6) First Day of Issue - Ballymena	150	-	*Post Office*
(7) First Day of Issue - Armagh	145	-	*Post Office*
(8) First Day of Issue - Portadown	130	-	*Post Office*
(9) First Day of Issue - Cookstown	145	-	*Post Office*
(10) First Day of Issue - Omagh	145	-	*Post Office*
(11) First Day of Issue - Enniskillen	150	-	*Post Office*
(12) Ulster 71 Exhibition Botanic Gardens, Belfast	75	-	*n.o.c.*
(13) Ulster Paintings Day, Norwich	50	75	*Phil Congress*
C.D.S. POSTMARKS			
(14) Dungiven, Hilltown & Newcastle *situated close to the scenes on stamps*	100	*(set of three)*	
(15) Newcastle, Portadown or Northern Parliament	125		

28th July 1971 - LITERARY ANNIVERSARIES

3p Keats; 5p Gray; 7½p Scott

SPECIAL HANDSTAMPS			
(1) First Day of Issue - Philatelic Bureau	4	-	*Post Office*
(2) First Day of Issue - London EC	8	-	*Post Office*
(3) John Keats, Shanklin 1819, Isle of Wight	110	200	*Shank Library*
(4) Thomas Gray Bicentenary, Stoke Poges	35	125	*Stoke Court*
(4a) -do- with Carried by Mailcoach cachet	50	125	*Stoke Court*
(5) National Collectors Fair, Horticultural Hall	225	-	*n.o.c.*
(6) Ulster 71 Exhib, Botanic Gardens, Belfast	150	-	*n.o.c.*
ORDINARY F.D.I. POSTMARKS			
(7) Edinburgh - birthplace of Sir Walter Scott	15		
C.D.S. POSTMARKS			
(8) Melrose (7½p) - Scott/Abbotsford, Melrose	5(s)		
SET 3 single stamp covers with appropriate pmks	15		

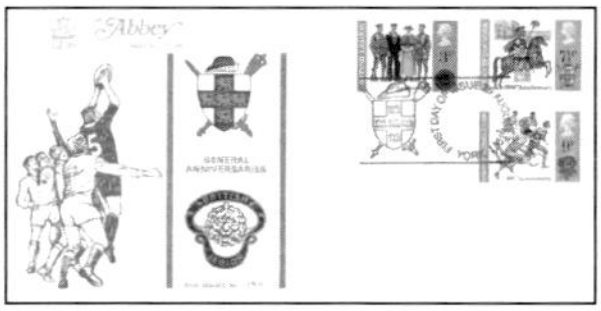

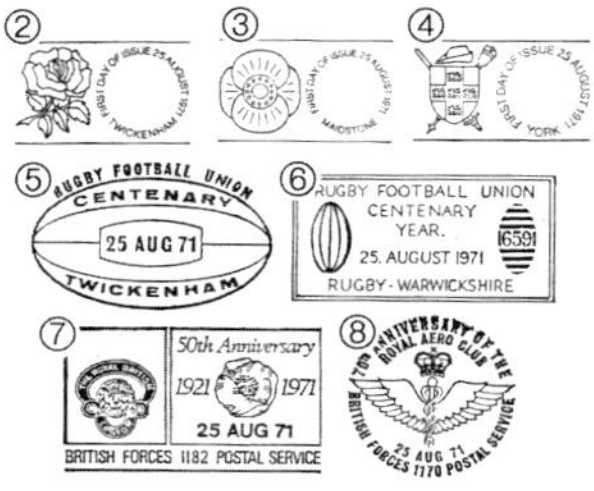

25th August 1971 - GENERAL ANNIVERSARIES

3p British Legion; 7½p City of York; 9p Rugby Football Union

SPECIAL HANDSTAMPS			
(1) First Day of Issue - Philatelic Bureau	3	-	*Post Office*
(2) First Day of Issue - Twickenham	15	-	*Post Office*
(3) First Day of Issue - Maidstone	15	-	*Post Office*
(4) First Day of Issue - York	15	-	*Post Office*
(5) Rugby Football Union, Twickenham	200	375	*R.F.U.*
(6) Rugby Football Union, Rugby	200	200	*Rugby School*
(7) Royal British Legion, BF 1182 PS	230	250	*Brit. Legion*
(8) Royal Aero Club, BF 1170 PS	300	25	*RAF Museum(s)*
(9) Ulster 71 Exhibition, Botanic Gdens, Belfast	160	-	*n.o.c.*
(10) Sir Walter Scott Bicentenary, Abbotsford	160	-	*n.o.c.*
ORDINARY F.D.I. POSTMARKS			
(11) Rugby	35		
C.D.S. POSTMARKS			
(12) Any Field Post Office	20		
(13) Richmond & Twickenham	50		
SET 3 single stamp covers with appropriate pmks - usually (2), (3) and (4)	12		

22nd September 1971 - UNIVERSITIES

3p Aberystwyth; 5p Southampton
7½p Leicester; 9p Essex

		ordinary covers £	official covers £	
SPECIAL HANDSTAMPS				
(1)	First Day of Issue - Philatelic Bureau	3	-	*Post Office*
(2)	First Day of Issue - Aberystwyth	13	-	*Post Office*
(3)	First Day of Issue - Colchester	13	-	*Post Office*
(4)	First Day of Issue - Leicester	13	-	*Post Office*
(5)	First Day of Issue - Southampton	13	-	*Post Office*
(6)	Postal Management College, Rugby	200	300	*P. Man. Coll.*
(7)	Sir Walter Scott Bicentenary, Abbotsford	150	-	*n.o.c.*
SET	4 single stamp covers with appropriate pmks - usually (2), (3), (4) and (5)	10		

13th October 1971 - CHRISTMAS

2½p, 3p, 7½p Stained Glass at Canterbury Cathedral

SPECIAL HANDSTAMPS				
(1)	First Day of Issue - Philatelic Bureau	4	-	*Post Office*
(2)	First Day of Issue - Bethlehem	10	-	*Post Office*
(3)	First Day of Issue - Canterbury	10	-	*Post Office*
(4)	Commonwealth Postal Conference, SW1	200	-	*n.o.c.*
(5)	1900th Anniv. Emperor Serverus, York	175	250	*Emp. Serv.*

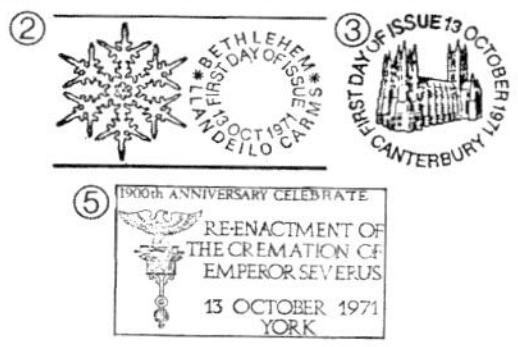

16th February 1972 - POLAR EXPLORERS

3p Ross; 5p Frobisher; 7½p Hudson; 9p Scott

SPECIAL HANDSTAMPS				
(1)	First Day of Issue - Philatelic Bureau	10	-	*Post Office*
(2)	First Day of Issue - London WC	15	-	*Post Office*
ORDINARY F.D.I. POSTMARKS				
(3)	Plymouth	20		
C.D.S. POSTMARKS				
(4)	Reykjavik BFPS (Backstamped) FPO 376	600		
(5)	FPO 129 - used in Norway	200		
(6)	Gravesend, Kent (7½p)	25(s)		
(7)	Greenwich B.O. S.E.10	25(s)		
SET	of 4 single stamp covers with appropriate pmks - usually (2), (3), (5) and (6)	35		

26th April 1972 - GENERAL ANNIVERSARIES

3p Tutankhamun; 7½p HM Coastguard; 9p Ralph Vaughan Williams

SPECIAL HANDSTAMPS				
(1)	First Day of Issue - Philatelic Bureau	3	-	*Post Office*
(2)	First Day of Issue - London EC	8	-	*Post Office*
(3)	Treasures of Tutankhamun Exhib. WC	35	75	*Tut. Exhib.*
(4)	Vaughan Williams., Down Ampney	35	50	*D. Ampney(s)*
(5)	H .M. Coastguard., Hartland Point	35	40	*Philart*
(6)	Hovercraft Trials BF 1270 PS	125	400	*Hovercraft*
SLOGAN POSTMARKS				
(7)	Treasures of Tutankhamun British Museum	250		
SET	3 single stamp covers with appropriate pmks - usually (3), (4) and (5)	15		

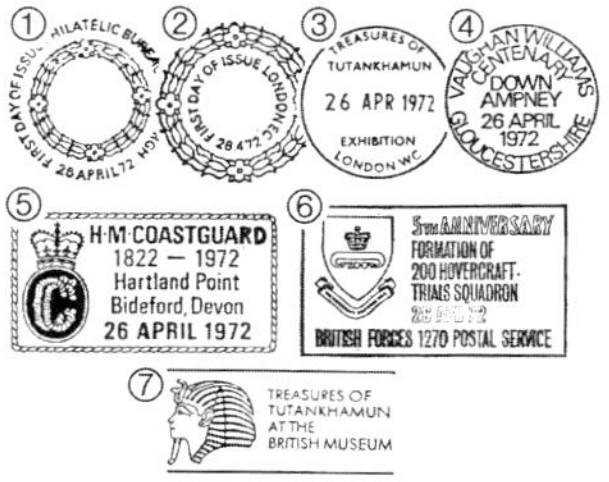

21st June 1972 - VILLAGE CHURCHES

3p Greensted; 4p Earls Barton; 5p Letheringsett;
7½p Helpringham; 9p Huish Episcopi.

SPECIAL HANDSTAMPS				
(1)	First Day of Issue - Philatelic Bureau	6	-	*Post Office*
(2)	First Day of Issue - Canterbury	8	-	*Post Office*
(3)	World's Oldest Wooden Church, Greensted	35	95	*St. Andrew's*
(4)	Village Churches, AD 970 Earls Barton	25	50	*Earls Barton*
(5)	First Day of Issue Exhib. Huish Episcopi	35	95	*St. Mary's*
(6)	Village Churches, Helpringham, Sleaford	35	90	*Helpringham*
(7)	Village Churches, Letheringsett, Holt	35	-	*n.o.c.*
(8)	Parish Church of St. Mary, Langley	150	250	*Philart*
(9)	St. Augustine's Church, Kilburn, NW6	150	250	*St.Augustine's*
(10)	Festival of Berkswell, Coventry	170	225	*Berkswell*
(11)	Treasures of Tutankhamun Exhibition, WC	100	-	*n.o.c.*
(12)	Royal Eng. Military Aeronautics, BF 1312 PS	175	175	*Royal Eng. 3*
C.D.S. POSTMARKS				
(13)	Earls Barton, Northampton	125		
(14)	Church Street, Harwich	225		
(15)	New Romney, Kent (St. Nicholas Cover)	75		
SET	5 single stamp covers with appropriate pmks - usually (3), (4), (5), (6) and (7)	25		

PLEASE READ THE GENERAL NOTES: Pages 4 - 16

These often provide the answers to enquiries received.

You will find out all about the different types of covers and postmarks.

Also lots of helpful tips on collecting British First Day Covers.

13th September 1972 - B.B.C.

3p, 5p, 7½p BBC; 9p Marconi/Kemp

		ordinary covers £	official covers £	
SPECIAL HANDSTAMPS				
(1)	First Day of Issue - Philatelic Bureau	5	-	*Post Office*
(2)	First Day of Issue - London W1	12	-	*Post Office*
(3)	Marconi-Kemp Experiments, Chelmsford	35	90	*Mar. Phil Soc*
(4)	Royal Engineers, Army Wireless, BF 1326 PS	70	80	*Royal Eng. 4*
(5)	Marconi's First Wireless, Flatholm Island	35	170	*Barry College*
(6)	BBC Radio Leicester, 5th Anniversary Year	60	100	*Radio Leics*
(7)	21st Anniv TV Network Opened Gloucester	75	250	*British Relay*
(8)	Humberside's Own Home Service, Hull	75	175	*Radio Hull*
(9)	BBC 50th Anniversary, Pebble Mill	400	*	*Pebble Mill*
(10)	John Knox - Philatelic Bureau	150	-	*n.o.c.*
(11)	Manchester City FC Kick-Off in UEFA Cup	175	475	*Dawn*
(12)	Treasures of Tutankhamun Exhibition, WC	160	-	*n.o.c.*

**Two types of Pebble Mill official covers exist:*
- covers with BBC logo only @ £170; and fully illustrated covers @ £425.

ORDINARY F.D.I. POSTMARKS			
(13)	Brighton (BBC Radio Brighton cover)	30	
(14)	Chelmsford (Marconi Philatelic Soc cover)	20	
SLOGAN POSTMARKS			
(15)	Medium Wave BBC Radio Brighton	425	
PAIR covers (3p,5p,7½p on one; 9p on the other)		12	

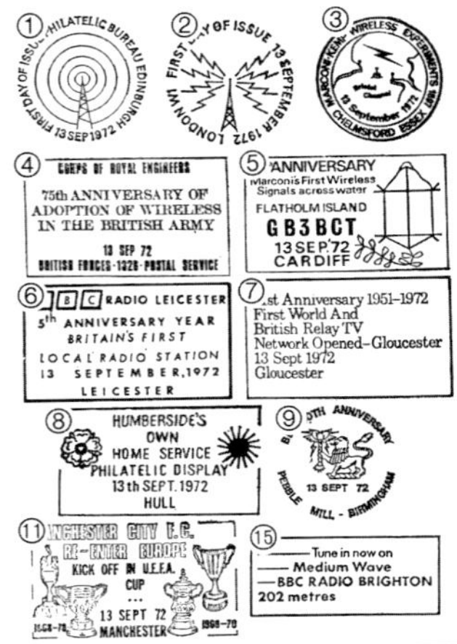

18th October 1972 - CHRISTMAS

2½p, 3p, 7½p Angels

		ordinary covers £	official covers £	
SPECIAL HANDSTAMPS				
(1)	First Day of Issue - Philatelic Bureau	5	-	*Post Office*
(2)	First Day of Issue - Bethlehem	8	-	*Post Office*
(3)	Treasures of Tutankhamun Exhibition, WC	100	-	*n.o.c.*
(4)	Rowntree's Philatelic Exhib. Scarborough	200	-	*n.o.c.*
(5)	John Knox , Philatelic Bureau	125	-	*n.o.c.*
(6)	Borough Jubilee 1922-1972, Watford	250	150	*WatfordBC (card)*

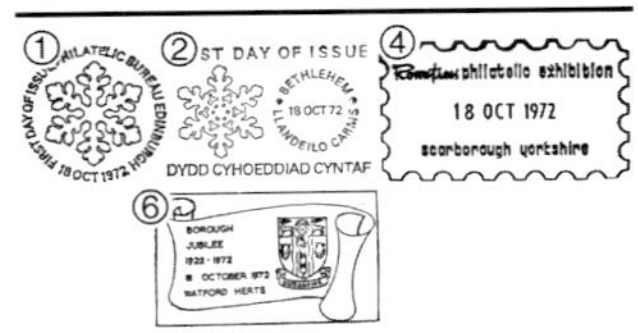

20th November 1972 - SILVER WEDDING

3p, 20p H.M. The Queen and Prince Philip

		ordinary covers £	official covers £	
SPECIAL HANDSTAMPS				
(1)	First Day of Issue - Philatelic Bureau	4	-	*Post Office*
(2)	First Day of Issue - Windsor	8	-	*Post Office*
(3)	Silver Wedding, Westminster Abbey, SW1	15	25	*Philart ACC 6*
(4)	Silver Wedding, BF 1307 PS	25	40	*RAF M/Batten*
(5)	16th/5th Queens Royal Lancers, BF 1922 PS	60	80	*R. Lancers*
(6)	Royal Regiment of Artillery, BF 1340 PS	50	140	*R.R.A.*
(7)	Royal Engineers Military Tanks, BF 1338 PS	50	175	*Royal Eng. 7*
(8)	Charlton Athletic, FA Cup Winners	110	275	*Phil. Prom.**
(9)	Fiftieth Anniv. of the BBC, W1	200	-	*n.o.c.*
(10)	Treasures of Tutankhamun Exhibition, WC	125	-	*n.o.c.*
(11)	John Knox, Philatelic Bureau	125	-	*n.o.c.*

**Beware forged official covers exist*

C.D.S. POSTMARKS			
(12)	Buckingham Palace, S.W.1	150	
(13)	House of Commons, S.W.1	40	
(14)	House of Lords,S.W.1	50	
(15)	Windsor Castle, Windsor, Berks	200	

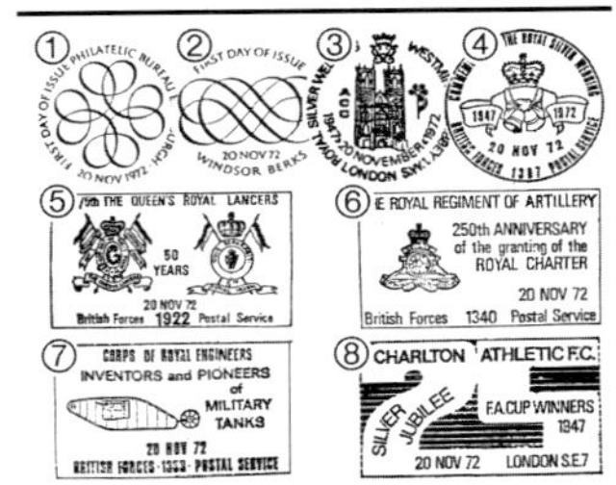

3rd January 1973 - EUROPEAN COMMUNITIES

3p, 2 x 5p Maps of Europe (jig-saw design)

		ordinary covers £	official covers £	
SPECIAL HANDSTAMPS				
(1)	First Day of Issue - Philatelic Bureau	4	-	*Post Office*
(2)	New Parcel Office, Southampton	55	125	*I.D.C.*
(3)	Royal Eng. Brennan Torpedo, BF 1343 PS	40	60	*Royal Eng. 8*
ORDINARY F.D.I. POSTMARKS				
(4)	Dover or Folkestone	10		
(4a)	-do- with PAQUEBOT markings	40		
(5)	Harrow & Wembley ('Fanfare for Europe' cvr)	65		
C.D.S. POSTMARKS				
(6)	Calais with PAQUEBOT markings	40		
(7)	Conseil de l'Europe Strasbourg	20		
(8)	Harwich (Gateway to Europe cover)	65		
(9)	House of Commons, S.W.1	50		
(10)	House of Lords, S.W.1	60		
(11)	Harrow & Wembley (Britain v. EEC cachet)	40		

28th February 1973 - BRITISH TREES - THE OAK

9p Oak Tree

		ordinary covers £	official covers £	
SPECIAL HANDSTAMPS				
(1)	First Day of Issue - Philatelic Bureau	5	-	*Post Office*
(2)	Stampex 73, Royal Horticultural Hall	10	15	*Stampex*
(3)	Hatfield Broad Oak, Plant a Tree	20	-	*n.o.c.*
(4)	Tree Planting, Westonbirt Arboretum,	20	25	*Cotswold (g)*
C.D.S. POSTMARKS				
(5)	Oakham, Four Oaks, Sevenoaks etc *each*	95		

18th April 1973 - BRITISH EXPLORERS

2 x 3p Livingstone & Stanley; 5p Drake; 7½p Raleigh; 9p Sturt

	ordinary covers £	official covers £	
SPECIAL HANDSTAMPS			
(1) First Day of Issue - Philatelic Bureau	10	-	*Post Office*
(2) Drake's Island Adventure Centre, Plymouth	35	150	*Cotswold*
(3) Sir Walter Raleigh, Budleigh Salterton	35	-	*n.o.c.*
ORDINARY F.D.I. POSTMARKS			
(4) Plymouth, Devon	25		
(5) Blantyre - birthplace of Livingstone	40		
(6) Denbigh - birthplace of Stanley	40		
(7) Gloucestershire - Sturt buried here	50		
C.D.S. POSTMARKS			
(8) Mildenhall (Scientific Explorers Soc cover)	250		
(9) Livingstone, W Lothian	90		
SET 5 single stamp covers with appropriate pmks	8		

16th May 1973 - COUNTY CRICKET CENTENARY

3p, 7½p, 9p W.G. Grace - sketches by Harry Furniss

	ordinary	official	
SPECIAL HANDSTAMPS			
(1) First Day of Issue - Philatelic Bureau	4	-	*Post Office*
(2) First Day of Issue - Lord's London NW	6	-	*Post Office*
(3) English County Cricket Exhibition, Lord's	15	20	*TCCB**
(4) County Cricket Centenary, Chelmsford	30	45	*TCCB**
(5) Surrey C.C.C., The Oval, SE11	30	45	*TCCB**
(6) Sussex C.C.C., Hove	30	45	*TCCB**
(7) Birthplace of County Cricket, Hambledon	60	325	*Porton Serv*
(8) Downend Cricket Club, W.G. Grace	25	35	*Cotswold (g)*
(9) Yorkshire v. Hamps, Headingley, Leeds	30	45	*TCCB**
(10) IBRA Exhibition Munich, BF 1400 PS	60	275	*BFPS**
ORDINARY F.D.I. POSTMARKS			
(11) Derby - Derbyshire C.C.C.*	15		
(12) Cardiff - Glamorgan C.C.C.*	15		
(13) Bristol or Gloucestershire - Glos. C.C.C.*	15		
(14) Southampton - Hampshire C.C.C.*	15		
(15) Canterbury - Kent C.C.C.*	15		
(16) Manchester - Lancashire C.C.C.*	15		
(17) Leicester - Leicestershire C.C.C.*	15		
(18) Northampton - Northamptonshire C.C.C.*	15		
(19) Nottingham - Nottinghamshire C.C.C.*	15		
(20) Taunton - Somerset C.C.C.*	15		
(21) Birmingham - Warwickshire C.C.C.*	15		
(22) Worcester - Worcestershire C.C.C.*	15		

**Note: Stamp Publicity of Worthing produced a set of 18 covers for the TCCB (Test & County Cricket Board). The set of 18 is valued at around £250.*

	ordinary		
C.D.S. POSTMARKS			
(23) Hambledon - Birthplace of County Cricket	70		

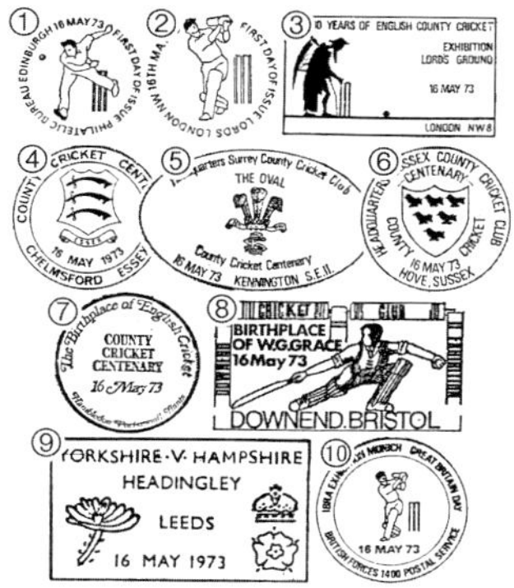

4th July 1973 - BRITISH PAINTINGS

3p, 7½p Sir Joshua Reynolds; 5p, 9p Sir Henry Raeburn

	ordinary	official	
SPECIAL HANDSTAMPS			
(1) First Day of Issue - Philatelic Bureau	5	-	*Post Office*
(2) Sir Joshua Reynolds, Royal Academy, W1	15	75	*R. Academy*
(3) Douglas, Isle of Man	40	50	*Post Office*
(4) Whitehaven, Cumberland	60	3	*Post Office(s)*
(5) 1973 AELTC, Wimbledon	200	-	*n.o.c.*
(6) Monarchy 1000, Bath	225	-	*n.o.c.*
(7) Death of General Sikorski Exhibition, SW7	225	-	*n.o.c.*
(8) Llangollen International Musical Eisteddfod	225	35	*Eisteddfod(s)*
(9) APEX 1973, Manchester	175	150	*APEX*
(10) Royal Show Stoneleigh (metal circular stamp)	250	-	*n.o.c.*
ORDINARY F.D.I. POSTMARKS			
(11) Edinburgh - birthplace of Raeburn	15		
(12) Plymouth - birthplace of Reynolds	15		
C.D.S. POSTMARKS			
(13) Raeburn Place, Edinburgh ....*(incomplete set)*	75		

15th August 1973 - INIGO JONES

3p St. Paul's, Covent Garden; 3p Court Masque Costumes; 5p Prince's Lodging, Newmarket; 5p Court Masque Stage Scene

	ordinary	official	
SPECIAL HANDSTAMPS			
(1) First Day of Issue - Philatelic Bureau	5	-	*Post Office*
(2) Inigo Jones Exhib. Wilton House, Salisbury	15	25	*Cotswold (g)*
(3) 400th Anniv. of Inigo Jones, Newmarket	15	150	*Rotary*
(4) Livestock Market Centenary, Northampton	275	-	*n.o.c.*
(5) Monarchy 1000, Bath	275	-	*n.o.c.*
(6) Third Int. Orthodontic Congress, SE	275	150	*I.O.C.*
ORDINARY F.D.I. POSTMARKS			
(7) London W.C.	5		
SLOGAN POSTMARKS			
(8) Inigo Jones Banqueting House (on 2 covers)	450		

12th Sept 1973 – PARLIAMENT

8p, 10p Palace of Westminster

	ordinary covers £	official covers £	
SPECIAL HANDSTAMPS			
(1) First Day of Issue – Philatelic Bureau	4	–	*Post Office*
(2) Houses of Parliament, London SW1	6	–	*n.o.c.*
(3) Monarchy 1000, Bath	225	–	*n.o.c.*
(4) British Pharmaceutical Conference WC	275	–	*n.o.c.*
(5) Surrey's Sixth Form College, Farnham	275	135	*Farn. Coll.*
C.D.S. POSTMARKS			
(6) Balmoral Castle	150		
(7) Buckingham Palace or Windsor Castle	100		
(8) House of Commons or Lords *each*	75		

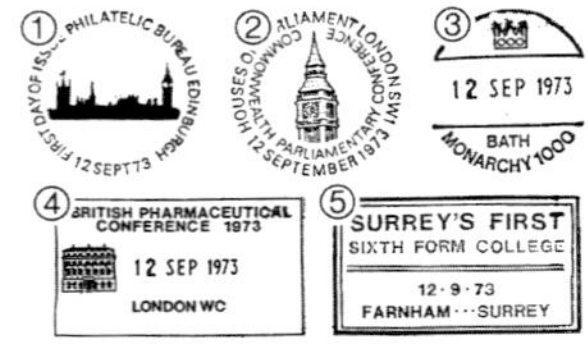

14th November 1973 – ROYAL WEDDING

3½p, 20p Princess Anne and Captain Mark Phillips

	ordinary covers £	official covers £	
SPECIAL HANDSTAMPS			
(1) First Day of Issue – Philatelic Bureau	3	–	*Post Office*
(2) First Day of Issue – Windsor	6	–	*Post Office*
(3) First Day of Issue – Westminster Abbey	6	–	*Post Office*
(4) Royal Wedding, Great Somerford	15	–	*n.o.c.*
(5) Queens Dragoon Guards BF 1434 PS	25	10	*Dragoons(s)*
(6) Royal Engineers, Gibraltar, BF 1387 PS	25	40	*Royal Eng. 17*
(7) The Chinese Exhibition, London W1	40	150	*Ch. Exhib.*
C.D.S. POSTMARKS			
(8) Buckingham Palace or Windsor Castle	175		
(9) Great Somerford or Badminton	30		
(10) House of Commons or House of Lords *each*	35		
(11) Sandhurst, Camberley	30		

28th November 1973 – CHRISTMAS

5 x 3p; 3½p 'Good King Wenceslas'

	ordinary covers £	official covers £	
SPECIAL HANDSTAMPS			
(1) First Day of Issue – Philatelic Bureau	4	–	*Post Office*
(2) First Day of Issue – Bethlehem	8	–	*Post Office*
(3) 141st Anniv. Lewis Carroll, Daresbury	225	90	*ChesHist(set of 6)*
(4) The Chinese Exhibition, London W1	75	75	*Ch. Exhib.*

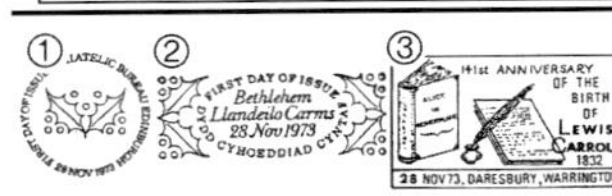

27th February 1974 – THE HORSE CHESTNUT

10p Horse Chestnut

	ordinary covers £	official covers £	
SPECIAL HANDSTAMPS			
(1) First Day of Issue – Philatelic Bureau	5	–	*Post Office*
(2) Stampex, Royal Horticultural Hall SW1	8	15	*Stampex*

24th April 1974 – FIRST FIRE SERVICE LEGISLATION

3½p, 5½p, 8p, 10p Early Fire Engines

	ordinary covers £	official covers £	
SPECIAL HANDSTAMPS			
(1) First Day of Issue – Philatelic Bureau	5	–	**Post Office*
(2) Binns Philatelic & Fire Exhib. Sunderland	40	–	*n.o.c.*
(3) Avon County Fire Brigade, Bristol	30	35	*Cotswold (g)*
(4) Cambridgeshire Fire & Rescue Service	40	200	*Cambs C.C.*
(5) Lansing Bagnall 25 Years at Basingstoke	200	525	*Lan. Bag.*
(6) MCC v Hampshire, NW8	200	200	*S.P.*

**Overprinted: 'Merryweather' £10 or 'Science Museum' £40.*

	ordinary covers £	
ORDINARY F.D.I. POSTMARKS		
(7) London S.E.1 – H.Q. London Fire Brigade	30	
(8) Bognor Regis (West Sx Fire cvr) or similar	40	
C.D.S. POSTMARKS		
(9) Burnt House Lane, Exeter	575	
(10) Hose, Melton Mowbray	250	
(11) House of Commons or House of Lords	45	
(12) Tooley St., SE 1 – Insurance Co. brigade	275	
SLOGAN POSTMARKS		
(13) The Fire Brigade Needs Men of Courage	575	

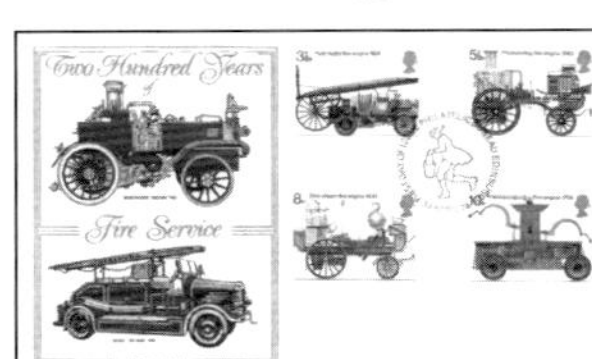

12th June 1974 – UNIVERSAL POSTAL UNION

3½p P&O Packet Steamer; 5½p First Official Airmail;
8p Air mail Blue Van and Postbox; 10p Imperial Airways Flyingboat

	ordinary covers £	official covers £	
SPECIAL HANDSTAMPS			
(1) First Day of Issue – Philatelic Bureau	5	–	*Post Office*
(1a) -do- with 'INTERNABA' cachet	10	–	*Post Office*
(2) Imp. Airways Flying Boat, Southampton	15	250	*Imp. Air.*
(3) Visit of Golden Hind ll, London E.C.	250	–	*n.o.c.*
(4) Churchill Centenary Somerset House, WC	250	–	*n.o.c.*
(5) NPM (reprinted 1890 Jubilee cover)	75	–	*n.o.c.*
ORDINARY F.D.I. POSTMARKS			
(6) Windsor – First Official Airmail	20		
(7) Southampton - Flyingboat.	20		
C.D.S. POSTMARKS			
(8) Harwich (Amsterdam Paquebot cover)	200		
(9) Southampton - Flyingboat	25		
(10) Windsor Castle – First Official Airmail	200		
SLOGAN POSTMARKS			
(11) Any Post Code slogans *from*	125		

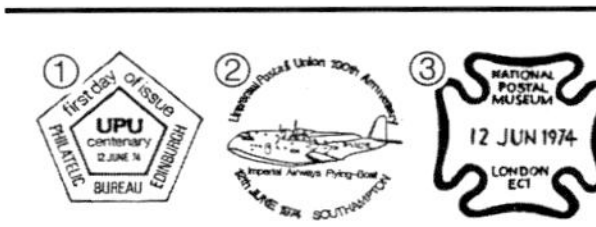

10th July 1974 - GREAT BRITONS

4½p Robert the Bruce; 5½p Owain Gyndwr; 8p Henry V; 10p Edward of Woodstock

	ordinary covers £	official covers £	
SPECIAL HANDSTAMPS			
(1) First Day of Issue - Philatelic Bureau	6	-	*Post Office*
(2) Robert the Bruce, Bannockburn	40	175	*Scot N.T.*
(3) Robert the Bruce, Dunfermline Abbey	40	150	*Dun. Abbey*
(4) Glyndwr's Parliament House, Machynlleth	40	125	*Ow. Glyn.*
(5) Royal Tournament, BF 1974 PS	70	70	*Royal T.*
(6) Visit of Golden Hind II, London EC	275	-	*n.o.c.*
(7) Churchill, Centenary Somerset House, WC	275	-	*n.o.c.*
(8) Open Golf, Lytham St. Annes	275	40	*LythamGC(s)*
(9) Trustee Savings Bank, Sunderland	275	25	*T.S.B. (s)*
ORDINARY F.D.I. POSTMARKS			
(10) Canterbury, Windsor, Dunfermline or Gwent	15		
C.D.S. POSTMARKS			
(11) Calais with PAQUEBOT markings	175		
(12) Cardross - Robert the Bruce died (4½p)	125		
(13) Glyndyfrdwy - Owain Glyndwr (5½p)	30(s)		
(14) House of Commons, S.W.1	35		
(15) House of Lords, S.W.1	45		
(16) Woodstock - Edward of Woodstock (10p)	20(s)		

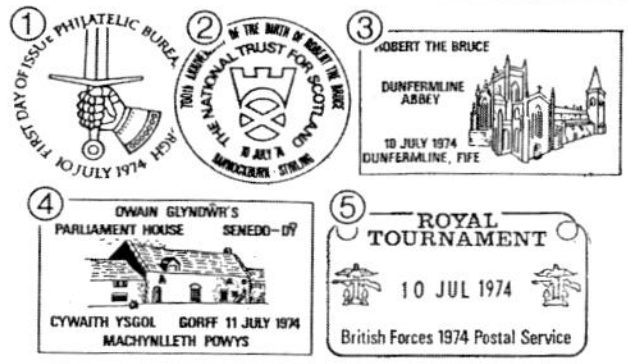

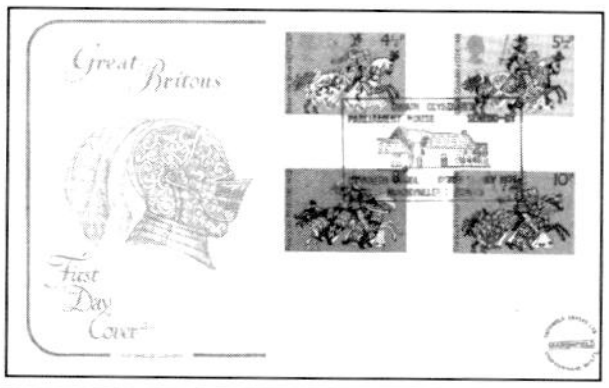

9th October 1974 - WINSTON CHURCHILL

4½p, 5½p, 8p, 10p Portraits of Churchill

	ordinary covers £	official covers £	
SPECIAL HANDSTAMPS			
(1) First Day of Issue - Philatelic Bureau	6	-	*Post Office*
(2) FDI - Blenheim, Woodstock	10	-	*Post Office*
(3) FDI - House of Commons, SW1	10	-	*Post Office*
(4) Woodford Green, Action This Day	30	45	*See Note**
(5) Churchill's First Constituency, Oldham	30	30	*Old.Conserv.*
(6) RAF Honington, BF 1874 PS	30	20	*RAF(s)*
(7) Churchill Centenary Somerset House, WC	50	125	*Som. Hse.*
(8) Universal Postal Union 1874, Clitheroe	250	-	*n.o.c.*
(9) Oldest Post Office In Britain Sanquhar	80	200	*Sanq. PO*
(10) Rotary Club of Paddington, Golden Jubilee	150	200	*Padd. R.C.*
(11) Gold Jubilee of Local Radio, Nottingham	175	250	*BBC*

Two official Wanstead & Woodford covers exist:Conservative Assoc'n & Synagogue

ORDINARY F.D.I. POSTMARKS			
(12) Tunbridge Wells (with 'Chartwell' cachet)	30		
(13) Medway (HMS Churchill Submarine cover)	50		
C.D.S. POSTMARKS			
(14) Bladon, Oxford - Churchill is buried here	150		
(15) Churchill, Bristol	150		
(16) Churchill, Oxford	150		
(17) House of Commons, S.W.1	90		
(18) House of Lords, S.W.1	125		
(19) Marlborough - Churchill's ancestral home	225		
(20) Normandy, Guildford	100		
(21) Rye - Lord Warden of the Cinque Ports	50		
(22) Sandhurst - Churchill went to Sandhurst	75		
(23) Winston, Darlington	200		

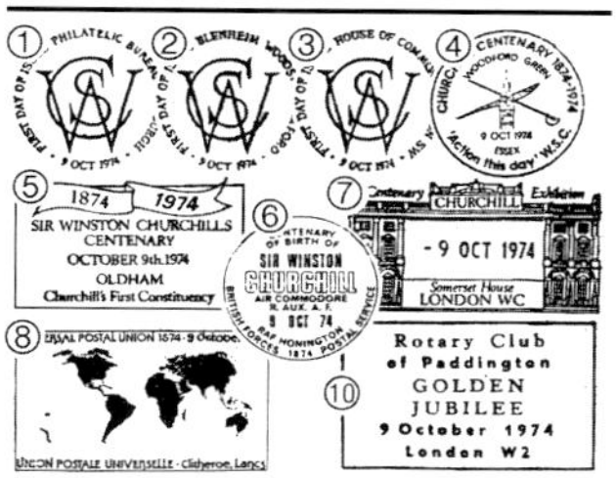

27th November 1974 - CHRISTMAS

3½p York Minster; 4½p St. Helens, Norwich; 8p Ottery St. Mary; 10p Worcester Cathedral

	ordinary covers £	official covers £	
SPECIAL HANDSTAMPS			
(1) First Day of Issue - Philatelic Bureau	4	-	*Post Office*
(2) First Day of Issue - Bethlehem	7	-	*Post Office*
(3) St. Helen's Church, Great Hospital, Norwich	25	45	*Gt. Hosp.*
(4) The Collegiate Church, Ottery St. Mary	25	45	*St. Mary*
(5) Salvation Army Christmas Supermarkets	80	20	*Sal. Army(s)*
(6) Oldest Post Office in Britain Sanquhar	60	200	*Sanq. PO*
(7) Churchill County Sec. School, Woking	120	120	*W.C. Sch.*
ORDINARY F.D.I. POSTMARKS			
(8) Norwich, Worcester or York *each*	25		

22nd January 1975 - CHARITY

4½p + 1½p donation to charities

	ordinary covers £	official covers £	
SPECIAL HANDSTAMPS			
(1) First Day of Issue - Philatelic Bureau	3	-	*Post Office*
(2) Oldest Post Office in Britain Sanquhar	25	150	*Sanq. PO*
ORDINARY F.D.I. POSTMARKS			
(3) Kettering (Winged Fellowship Trust cover)	12		
(4) Oxford - Oxfam HQ	15		
C.D.S. POSTMARKS			
(5) Stoke Charity, Winchester, Hants	275		
SLOGAN POSTMARKS			
(6) Menphys Love the Handicapped	90		
(7) Tenovus Cares, Cardiff	300		
(8) Barnardo's Cares About Children	300		

PLEASE READ THE GENERAL NOTES
These often provide the answers to enquiries received.

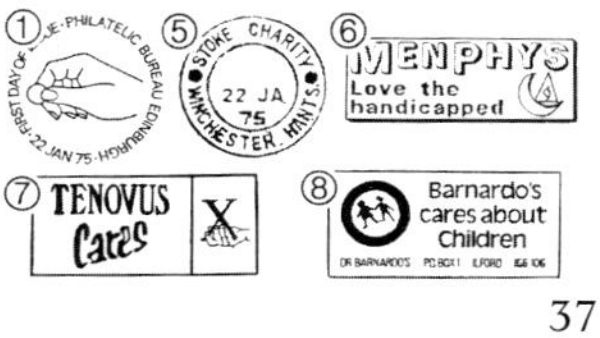

19th February 1975 - TURNER

4½p, 5½p, 8p, 10p

		ordinary covers £	official covers £	
SPECIAL HANDSTAMPS				
(1)	First Day of Issue - Philatelic Bureau	5	-	*Post Office*
(2)	First Day of Issue - London WC	7	-	*Post Office*
(3)	Oldest Post Office in Britain Sanquhar	35	200	*Sanq. PO*
(4)	Worksop & District Chamber of Trade	150	-	*n.o.c.*
(5)	Up Helly - AA Lerwick Shetland	175	-	*n.o.c.*
C.D.S. POSTMARKS				
(6)	Petworth - associated with Turner	200		
(7)	Turner's Hill, Crawley	200		
(8)	Harwich - relevant to the 5½p value	30(s)		
SLOGAN POSTMARKS				
(9)	Turner: Royal Academy (*plain cover*)	10(s)		

23rd April 1975 - ARCHITECTURE

2 x 7p Charlotte Square, Edinburgh & The Rows Chester; 8p The Royal Observatory, Greenwich; 10p St. George's Chapel, Windsor; 12p The National Theatre, London

		ordinary	official	
SPECIAL HANDSTAMPS				
(1)	First Day of Issue - Philatelic Bureau	7	-	*Post Office*
(2)	500 Years St. George's Chapel, Windsor	20	75	*St. G. Chapel*
(2a)	Ditto with 'Carried by Coach' cachet	25	75	*St. G. Chapel*
(3)	National Trust, 7 Charlotte Sq., Edinburgh	35	175	*Scot N.T.*
(4)	Corinium 1900, Heritage, Cirencester	35	100	*Corin. Mus.*
(5)	Chester Heritage City	25	100	*Chest.EAHY*
(6)	Wilton House Open Day, Wilton, Salisbury	35	50	*Cotswold*
(7)	Oldest Post Office in Britain Sanquhar	40	200	*Sanq. PO*
(8)	Meriden Junior School Pool, Watford	200	25	*MeridenSch.(s)*
ORDINARY F.D.I. POSTMARKS				
(9)	Brighton (Brighton Pier cover)	50		
(10)	Chester, Edinburgh, London SE1 or Windsor	15		
C.D.S. POSTMARKS				
(11)	Greenwich, S.E.10	275		
(12)	Dartmouth Row, Greenwich S.E.10	300		
(13)	Windsor Castle, Windsor, Berks	150		
SLOGAN POSTMARKS				
(14)	Chester Heritage City, Chester	375		
(15)	Euro Architectural Heritage Year, Leicester	375		

C.D.S = Counter Date Stamp

These are everyday operational pmks, used at Post Office counters.

Please refer to General Notes for more details

11th June 1975 - SAILING

7p Dinghies; 8p Keel Boats; 10p Yachts; 12p Multihulls

		ordinary	official	
SPECIAL HANDSTAMPS				
(1)	First Day of Issue - Philatelic Bureau	4	-	*Post Office*
(1a)	Ditto with 'Arphila 75 Paris' cachet	10	-	*Post Office*
(2)	Royal Dorset Yacht Club Weymouth	15	75	*R.D.Y. Club*
(3)	Royal Thames Yacht Club, SW	15	75	*R.T.Y. Club*
(4)	Oldest Post Office in Britain, Sanquhar	30	200	*Sanq. PO*
ORDINARY F.D.I. POSTMARKS				
(5)	Hastings - Rye Harbour Sailing Club	40		
(6)	Newport, I.O.W - famous for yachting	40		
(7)	Plymouth, Devon - sailing traditions	40		
(8)	Southampton (Boat Show cover)	40		
(9)	Weymouth, Dorset - centre for yachting	40		
(10)	Woking (Royal Yachting Assoc'n cover)	40		
C.D.S. POSTMARKS				
(11)	Cowes, I.O.W. - yachting centre	95		
(12)	Burnham-on-Crouch - yachting centre	95		
(13)	House of Commons - Yacht Club	35		
(14)	Lytham - Ribble Cruising Club	75		
(15)	Rye Harbour, West Wittering, Wells-next-the-Sea etc *locations of sailing clubs* ... *each*	75		

13th August 1975 - STOCKTON & DARLINGTON RAILWAY

7p Stephenson's Locomotion; 8p Waverley Class; 10p Caerphilly Castle; 12p High Speed Train

		ordinary	official	
SPECIAL HANDSTAMPS				
(1)	First Day of Issue - Philatelic Bureau	6	-	*Post Office*
(2)	First Day of Issue - Stockton-on-Tees	12	-	*Post Office*
(3)	First Day of Issue - Darlington	12	-	*Post Office*
(4)	First Day of Issue - Shildon	15	-	*Post Office*
(5)	Wylam, Birthplace of George Stephenson	35	100	*RoundTable*
(6)	Longmoor Military Railway, BF 1396 PS	20	40	*RoyalEng27*
(7)	Return of Steam, Buckfastleigh	25	30	*Cotswold*
(8)	Torbay Steam Railway, Paignton	20	30	*Cotswold*
(9)	Story of a Cathedral Exhibition, Canterbury	125	-	*n.o.c.*
(10)	Royal Shakespeare Theatre, Stratford	125	-	*n.o.c.*
ORDINARAY F.D.I. POSTMARKS				
(11)	Bournemouth (Big Four Rly Museum cvr)	35		
(12)	Brighton (Bluebell Railway cover)	40		
(13)	Colwyn Bay (Conwy Valley Railway cover)	40		
(14)	Crewe, Doncaster or Rugby	20		
(15)	Derby - BR Technical/Research Centre	20		

Stockton & Darlington Rly (contd.)

	ordinary covers £	official covers £	
(16) Maidstone (Kent & East Sussex Rly cover)	40		
(17) Medway (Sittingbourne & Kemsley Rly cvr)	45		
(18) Paddington or York (Rly Museum)	20		
(19) Swindon (British Rail Works cover)	45		
C.D.S. POSTMARKS (inc. T.P.O. CANCELS)			
(20) Caerphilly – Caerphilly Castle (10p)	75		
(21) Welshpool (Llanfair Light Railway cover)	50		
(22) Porthmadog (Festiniog Railway Co. cover)	50		
(23) Wylam - birthplace of George Stephenson	95		
(24) Seascale (Ravenglass & Eskdale Rly cover)	30		
(25) Any TPO (travelling post office)	40		
SLOGAN POSTMARKS			
(26) S & D Rly Jubilee Shildon Co. Durham	500		
(27) 150th S & D Rly Anniversary Darlington	500		
(28) Ravenglass & Eskdale Rly. Centenary Year	50(s)		

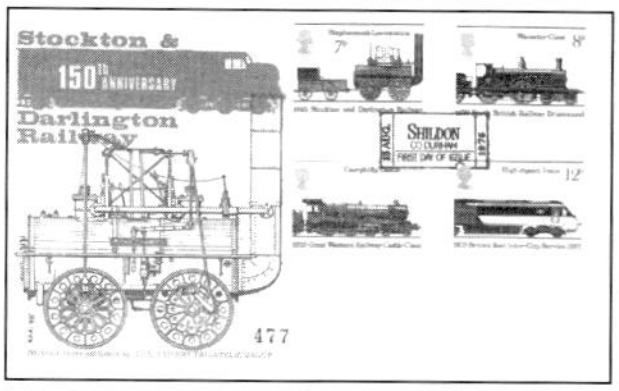

3rd September 1975 – PARLIAMENT

12p Palace of Westminster

SPECIAL HANDSTAMPS			
(1) First Day of Issue – Philatelic Bureau	3	–	*Post Office*
(2) 62nd Inter-Parliamentary Conference, SE1	8	25	*I.P. Conf.*
(3) Story of a Cathedral Exhibition, Canterbury	95	–	*n.o.c.*
(4) Stockton & Darlington Rly, 1825-1975	95	–	*n.o.c.*
C.D.S. POSTMARKS			
(5) Buckingham Palace, SW1	75		
(6) House of Commons, SW1	50		
(7) House of Lords, SW1	60		
(8) Parliament Street, SW1	50		

22nd October 1975 – JANE AUSTEN

8½p Emma and Mr. Woodhouse; 10p Catherine Moorland; 11p Mr. Darcy; 13p Mary and Henry Crawford

SPECIAL HANDSTAMPS			
(1) First Day of Issue – Philatelic Bureau	4	–	*Post Office*
(2) First Day of Issue – Steventon	6	–	*Post Office*
(2a) Ditto with 'Despatched by Mailcoach' cachet	10	–	*Post Office*
(3) Jane Austen Bi-centenary Exhibition, Bath	15	35	*City of Bath*
(4) Story of a Cathedral Exhibition, Canterbury	70	–	*n.o.c.*
C.D.S. POSTMARKS			
(5) Alton, Hants	125		
(6) Chawton, Alton – Jane Austen lived here	140		
(7) Steventon – Jane Austen's birthplace	200		
SLOGAN POSTMARKS			
(8) Jane Austen Bi-centenary 1775-1975	375		

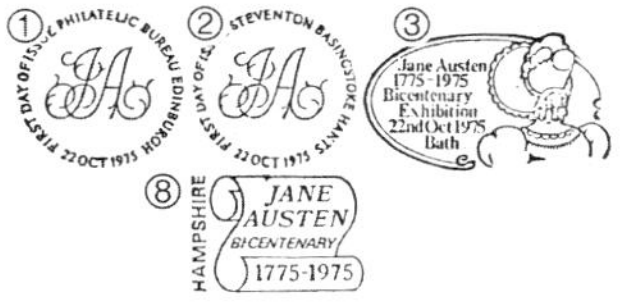

26th November 1975 – CHRISTMAS

6½p, 8½p, 11p, 13p Angels

SPECIAL HANDSTAMPS			
(1) First Day of Issue – Philatelic Bureau	2	–	*Post Office*
(2) First Day of Issue – Bethlehem	4	–	*Post Office*
C.D.S. POSTMARKS			
(3) Angel Hill, Sutton, Surrey or Nazareth	225		

10th March 1976 – TELEPHONE

8½p, 10p, 11p, 13p The Telephone in the Community

SPECIAL HANDSTAMPS			
(1) First Day of Issue – Philatelic Bureau	2	–	*Post Office*
(2) Telecommunications Museum, Taunton	6	–	*n.o.c.*
ORDINARY F.D.I. POSTMARKS			
(3) Boston – telephone invented in Boston, USA	15		
(4) Edinburgh – b/place of Alex Graham Bell	15		
(5) Hull – independent telephone service	25		
(6) Worcester (Centenary Exhibition overprint)	25		
C.D.S. POSTMARKS			
(7) Hope St., Edinburgh – near to Bell's b/place	175		
SLOGAN POSTMARKS			
(8) The Samaritans, Phone Bognor 25555	375		
(9) PO Telecommunictions Museum Taunton	325	*(set 4 single value cvrs)*	

PLEASE READ THE GENERAL NOTES
These often provide the answers to enquiries received.

28th April 1976 – SOCIAL PIONEERS & REFORMERS

8½p Thomas Hepburn; 10p Robert Owen; 11p Lord Shaftesbury; 13p Elizabeth Fry.

SPECIAL HANDSTAMPS			
(1) First Day of Issue – Philatelic Bureau	3	–	*Post Office*
(2) World of Islam Festival London SW7	35	125	*Pilgrim*
(3) 1776 Exhibition National Maritime Museum	60	100	*Pilgrim*
ORDINARAY F.D.I. POSTMARKS			
(4) Durham – National Union of Mineworkers	25		
(5) Folkestone – Lord Shaftesbury died here	25		
(6) Norwich – Birthplace of Elizabeth Fry	25		
(7) Rochdale – first Co-op	25		

Social Reformers (contd.)		ordinary covers	official covers	
C.D.S. POSTMARKS		£	£	
(8)	House of Commons, S.W. 1	30		
(9)	House of Lords, S.W. 1	40		
(10)	Magdalen St., Norwich - Fry's b/place	80		
(11)	Newton, Powys - b/place of Robert Owen	60		
(12)	Parkhurst, I.O.W. - top security prison	80		
(13)	New Lanark - Robert Owen	125		
(14)	Lanark - Robert Owen	70		
(15)	Pelton, Durham - Hepburn's birthplace	160		
(16)	Shaftesbury, Dorset	150		
(17)	Wimborne St. Giles - Earl of Shaftesbury	125		

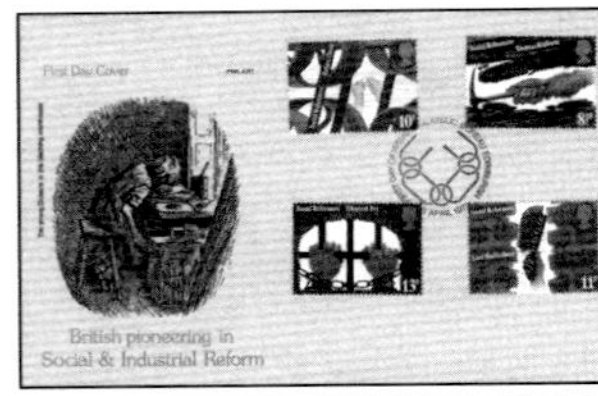

2nd June 1976 - U.S.A. BICENTENARY

11p Benjamin Franklin

SPECIAL HANDSTAMPS				
(1)	First Day of Issue - Philatelic Bureau	2	-	*Post Office*
(1a)	Ditto with 'Interphil 76 ' cachet	15	-	*Post Office*
(2)	American Independence, BF 1776 PS	12	20	*BFPS*
(3)	USA Independence, Washington	15	20	*Wash. Old Hall*
(4)	1776 Exhibition, Nati Maritime Museum	15	25	*Pilgrim*
(5)	American Museum, Bath	15	20	*Clav. Manor*
(6)	58th Philatelic Congress Plymouth	20	50	*Phil. Cong.*
(7)	World of Islam Festival, London SW7	75	150	*Pilgrim*
ORDINARY F.D.I. POSTMARKS				
(8)	Boston, Lincs	25		
(9)	Plymouth, Devon - Pilgrim Fathers	25		
C.D.S. POSTMARKS				
(10)	Bunker's Hill, Lincoln	150		
(11)	Dallas, Forres, Morayshire	150		
(12)	Denver, Downham Market	150		
(13)	House of Commons, S.W.1	30		
(14)	House of Lords, S.W.1	40		
(15)	New York, Lincoln	175		
(16)	Northborough - links with U.S.A.	50		
(17)	Sulgrave - ancestors of George Washington	60		
(18)	Washington, Pulborough, West Sussex	85		

30th June 1976 - ROSES

8½p Elizabeth of Glamis; 10p Grandpa Dickson; 11p Rosa Mundi; 13p Sweet Briar

SPECIAL HANDSTAMPS				
(1)	First Day of Issue - Philatelic Bureau	4	-	*Post Office*
(2)	Year of the Rose, Northampton	15	60	*N'ton Ph Soc*
(3)	Year of the Rose, Bath	15	40	*City of Bath*
(4)	Royal National Rose Society, Oxford	15	-	*n.o.c.*
(5)	Royal National Rose Society, St. Albans	15	-	*n.o.c.*
(6)	Royal Norfolk Show, Norwich	35	175	*Daniels*
(7)	The Mothers' Union Centenary, SW1	45	100	*Mothers Un.*
(8)	The Championships AELTC Wimbledon	200	-	*n.o.c.*
(9)	USA Independence, Washington	200	-	*n.o.c.*
(10)	Warton Bicentennial Commem., Carnforth	200	-	*n.o.c.*
(11)	1776 Exhibition, Nat Maritime Museum	200	-	*n.o.c.*
(12)	First Flight Britain/Australia, BF 1535 PS	200	-	*n.o.c.*
ORDINARY F.D.I. POSTMARKS				
(13)	Tunbridge Wells ('Sissinghurst' cachet)	25		
C.D.S. POSTMARKS				
(14)	Glamis, Forfar - 'Elizabeth of Glamis' (8½p)	100		
(15)	Kew Gardens, Richmond	175		
(16)	Rose, Truro or Rose Cottage, Hull *each*	150		
(17)	Rosebush, or Rosebank *each*	75		

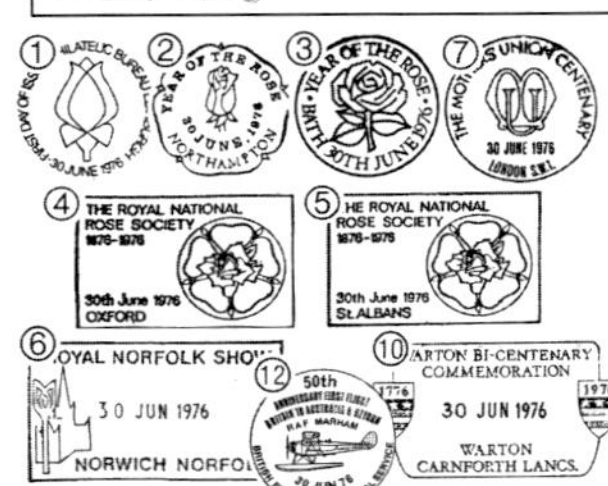

4th August 1976 - BRITISH CULTURAL TRADITIONS

8½p & 13p Eisteddfod; 10p Morris Dancing; 11p Highland Gathering

SPECIAL HANDSTAMPS				
(1)	First Day of Issue - Philatelic Bureau	3	-	*Post Office*
(2)	First Day of Issue - Cardigan	4	-	*Post Office*
(3)	Eisteddfod Genedlaethol Frenhinol Cymru	10	125	*Philart*
(4)	Bristol Morris Men, 25th Anniversary	10	150	*Bristol MM*
(5)	1776 Exhibition, Nat Maritime Museum	150	-	*n.o.c.*
(6)	USA Independence, Washington	150	-	*n.o.c.*
(7)	Story of a Cathedral Exhibition, Canterbury	100	-	*n.o.c.*
(8)	Colchester Tattoo, BF 1542 PS	150	-	*n.o.c.*
(9)	Europa 6 Cantat, Leicester	150	250	*Cantat 6*
ORDINARAY F.D.I. POSTMARKS				
(10)	Exeter ('Sidmouth Folk Festival' cachet)	30		
C.D.S, POSTMARKS				
(11)	Abbots Bromley - horn dancing	40		
(12)	Abingdon, Bampton, Britannia (Bacup), Chipping Campden or Headington Quarry - famous morris teams	40		
(13)	Padstow - famous for its 'Hobby Horse'	40		
(14)	Sidmouth ('Sidmouth Folk Festival' cachet)	50		

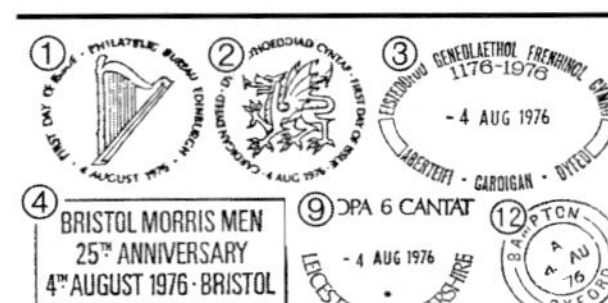

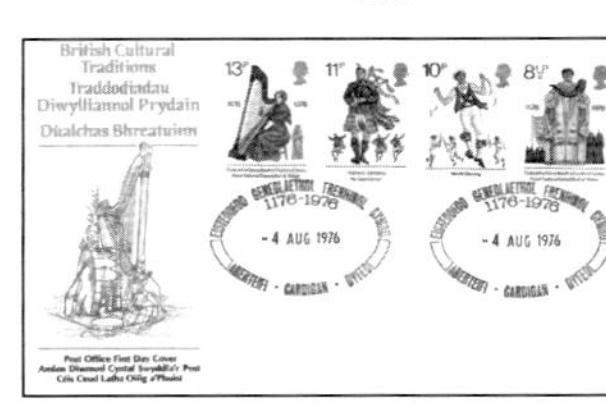

Cultural Traditions (contd.)	ordinary covers £	official covers £	
(15) Thaxted – Morris Ring meet here annually	40		
(16) Caerwys, Carmarthen or Corwen – famous eisteddfods	40		
(17) Llangollen – International Musical Eisteddfod	60		
(18) Braemar – Royal Highland Gathering	60		
(19) Dunoon – Cowal Highland Gathering	40		
SLOGAN POSTMARKS			
(20) Teeside International Eisteddfod	25 (s)		

29th September 1976 – WILLIAM CAXTON

8½p 'Canterbury Tales'; 10p Caxton's type-faces; 11p Game of Chess; 13p Printing Press

SPECIAL HANDSTAMPS			
(1) First Day of Issue – Philatelic Bureau	3	–	*Post Office*
(2) First Day of Issue – London SW1	4	–	*Post Office*
(3) 500 Years of British Printing, Westminster	20	25	*Br Pr Ind Fed*
(4) Caxton Exhibition, British Library, WC	20	50	*BL 1*
(5) William Caxton, Plymouth	20	125	*Ply. Coll.*
(6) Paper & Printing Study Group, SE1	20	100	*Philart*
(7) NATSOPA, Caxton House, SE1	20	100	*NATSOPA*
(8) De Montfort Press, Leicester	20	100	*DeM. Press*
(9) British Philatelic Exhibition, London W1	20	25	*B.P.E.*
(10) School Centenary, Stoke Poges, Bucks	30	75	*S.P. Sch.*
(11) 1776 Exhibition, Nat Maritime Museum	75	–	*n.o.c.*
(12) Royal Charter , Stow-on-the-Wold	40	125	*S-o-t-W Sch.*
(13) Manchester United v. Ajax, UEFA Cup	90	25	*Dawn (s)*
ORDINARY F.D.I. POSTMARKS			
(14) Bristol – Associated Graphics cover	50		
(15) Canterbury – 'Canterbury Tales'	10		
(16) Colwyn Bay – The Rydal Press special cover...	50		
(17) Derby – Bemrose Printing Derby spec cover ...	50		
C.D.S. POSTMARKS			
(18) Abingdon – first printing for Abbot of Abingdon	110		
(19) Caxton, Cambridge	100		
(20) Fleet St., E.C.4 – home of British printing	110		
(21) House of Commons – buried in Chapel	50		
(22) Radcliffe - East Lancs Paper Mill cover	50		
(23) Tenterden – presumed birthplace	75		

24th November 1976 – CHRISTMAS

6½p, 8½p, 11p, 13p Embroideries

SPECIAL HANDSTAMPS			
(1) First Day of Issue – Philatelic Bureau	3	–	*Post Office*
(2) First Day of Issue – Bethlehem	4	–	*Post Office*
(3) Pompeii AD79, Royal Academy of Arts	20	60	*PompExh*
(4) Tonic to the Nation, Victoria & Albert	20	60	*H.R.*
(5) 1st British Corps, Bielefeld, BF 1923 PS	30	60	*Forces*
(6) 1st British Corps, Aldershot, BF 1901 PS	30	60	*Forces*
(7) Caxton Exhibition, British Library, WC	50	–	*n.o.c.*
C.D.S. POSTMARKS			
(8) Angel Hill, Sutton	50		
(9) Pincushion, Boston – embroideries	50		

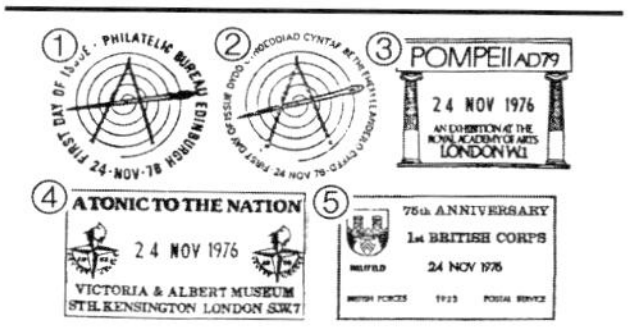

12th January 1977 – RACKET SPORTS

8½p Lawn Tennis; 10p Table Tennis; 11p Squash; 13p Badminton

SPECIAL HANDSTAMPS			
(1) First Day of Issue – Philatelic Bureau	3	–	*Post Office*
(2) The Badminton Association, Badminton	10	95	*Badm. Assoc.*
(3) Squash Rackets Association, Harrow	10	95	*Philart*
(4) Pompeii AD 79, Royal Academy of Arts	30	95	*PompExh*
(5) Caxton, Exhibition British Library, WC	50	–	*n.o.c.*
ORDINARY F.D.I. POSTMARKS			
(6) Battersea – Head PO for Wimbledon	20		
(7) Birmingham – World Table Tennis at NEC	20		
(8) Hastings – English Table Tennis Assoc'n	20		
(9) Warwick & Leamington – 1st Tennis Club	20		
C.D.S. POSTMARKS			
(10) Wimbledon SW19	250		

PLEASE READ THE GENERAL NOTES
These often provide the answers to enquiries received.

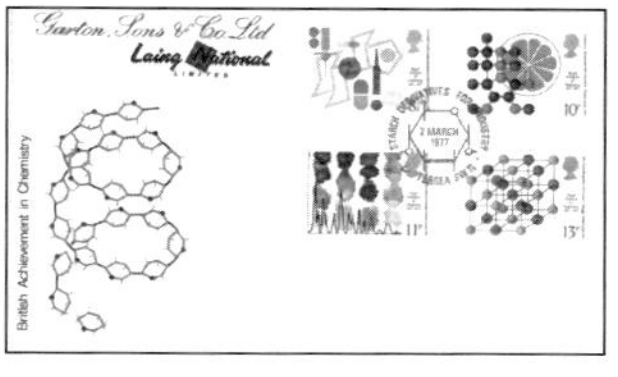

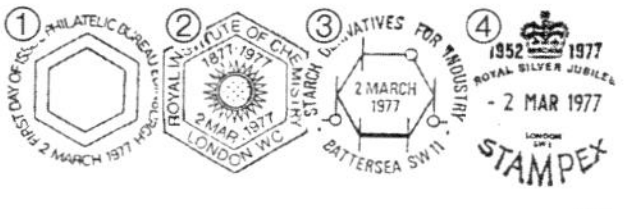

2nd March 1977 – CHEMISTRY

8½p Steroids (Barton);10p Vitamin C (Haworth); 11p Starch (Martin & Synge); 13p Salt (Bragg)

SPECIAL HANDSTAMPS			
(1) First Day of Issue – Philatelic Bureau	3	–	*Post Office*
(2) Royal Institute of Chemistry 1877-1977	8	35	*RI of Chem.*
(3) Starch Derivatives for Industry, Battersea	8	35	*Garton Ltd*
(4) Royal Silver Jubilee, Stampex, SW1	8	45	*Stampex*
(5) Pompeii AD 79, Royal Academy of Arts	30	60	*Pomp Exh.*
(6) Tonic to the Nation, Victoria & Albert	35	200	*H.R.*

Chemistry (contd.)

		ordinary covers £	official covers £	
ORDINARAY F.D.I. POSTMARKS				
(7)	Liverpool – birthplace of R.L.M. Synge	20		
C.D.S. POSTMARKS				
(8)	Barton – Barton on 8½p val	60		
(9)	Gravesend – birthplace of D H. R. Barton	60		
(10)	Haworth – Haworth on 10p value	60		
(11)	Martin – Martin on 11p value	60		
(12)	Pill, Bristol	40		
(13)	Wigton – birthplace of W. H. Bragg	60		

11th May 1977 – SILVER JUBILEE

8½p, 10p, 11p, 13p Portrait of H.M. The Queen

SPECIAL HANDSTAMPS				
(1)	First Day of Issue – Philatelic Bureau	3	–	*Post Office*
(2)	First Day of Issue – Windsor	3	–	*Post Office*
(3)	Jubilee Exhibition, Bath, England	15	30	*City of Bath*
(4)	A Royal Jubilee Exhibition, British Library	15	50	*BL 2*
(5)	Croydon Celebrates Queen's Silver Jubilee	15	150	*Croydon*
(6)	Stamp Collecting Promotion Council, SE1	15	–	*n.o.c.*
(7)	Queen Elizabeth II, RHDR, Hythe	15	30	*RHDR 1*
(8)	St. Martin-in-the-Fields, Silver Jubilee	15	150	*St. M-i-t-F*
(9)	Hayling Island Philatelic Soc.	25	175	*HI Phil Soc*
(10)	Duke of Edinburgh's Award, SW1	10	10	*DoEAScheme*
(11)	Stamp of Royalty Exhibition, Glasgow	15	30	*Pal. of Art*
(12)	Weymouth & Portland, Philatelic Exhibition	15	75	*W & P Exhib*
(13)	Tenth Conference, Dixieme Congress, W1	25	200	*ICTWO*
(14)	Exercise Makefast XXV BF 1952 PS	15	30	*Royal Eng.*
(15)	Bristol Bordeaux, 30th Anniversary	25	150	*BB Assoc*
(16)	Milton Keynes Arts Association	25	225	*MK Festival*
ORDINARY F.D.I. HANDSTAMPS				
(17)	Aberdeen ('Balmoral Castle' cachet)	20		
(18)	Croydon (Woldingham special cover)	50		
(19)	King's Lynn ('Sandringham' cachet)	35		
(20)	Leicester (Littleton special cover)	50		
(21)	Portsmouth – Review of the Fleet	20		
(22)	Warrington (Warrington Festival cover)	50		
C.D.S. POSTMARKS				
(23)	Buckingham Palace or Windsor Castle	200		
(24)	House of Commons or Lords	35		
(25)	Jubilee Cres, Jubilee Oak or Jubilee Fields	25		
(26)	Queen Elizabeth Avenue, Walsall	50		
(27)	Queen's Parade; or Queen's Head	40		
(28)	Silver Link, Tamworth	30		
SLOGAN POSTMARKS				
(29)	Silver Jubilee Appeal, Belfast	110		
(30)	Silver Jubilee Philatelic Exhib., Cardiff	125		
(31)	Silver Jubilee Philatelic Exhib., Edinburgh	125		
(32)	Silver Jubilee Philatelic Exhib., NPM, EC	125		
(33)	Review of Fleet (Jubilee logo) Portsmouth	150		
(34)	St. Neots Jubilee Riverside Festival	200		
(35)	Portsmouth & Southsea (Jubilee logo)	10(s)		

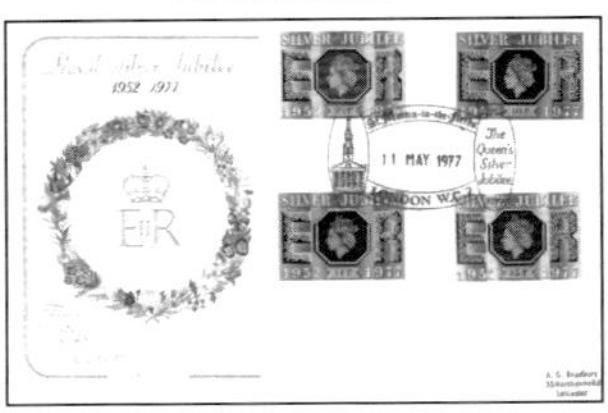

8th June 1977 – COMMONWEALTH MEETING

13p 'Gathering of Nations'

SPECIAL HANDSTAMPS				
(1)	First Day of Issue – Philatelic Bureau	2	–	*Post Office*
(2)	First Day of Issue – London SW	2	–	*Post Office*
(3)	Girl Guides Association, Open Days	20	40	*Girl Guides*
(4)	St. Martin-in-the-Field, Silver Jubilee	20	50	*St. M-i-t-F*
(5)	A Royal Jubilee Exhibition, British Library	20	–	*n.o.c.*
(6)	Croydon Celebrates Queens Silver Jubilee	20	40	*Croydon*
(7)	British Genius Exhibition, Battersea	20	–	*n.o.c.*
(8)	6000 King George V, Hereford	20	–	*n.o.c.*
(9)	City of Leicester, Silver Jubilee, EIIR	20	–	*n.o.c.*
(10)	Jubilee Exhibition, North Devon	20	–	*n.o.c.*
(11)	Royal Image Exhibition, Bristol	20	–	*n.o.c.*
(12)	The Prince of Wales Division, BF 8677 PS	20	50	*BFPS*
(13)	The Queens Silver Jubilee, Windsor	20	50	*WindsorBC*
(14)	Silver Jubilee Train, Newcastle	20	–	*n.o.c.*
(15)	Queen's Silver Jubilee, Merseyside Police	20	–	*n.o.c.*
(16)	Silver Jubilee Festival, Canon Hill Park	20	–	*n.o.c.*
C.D.S. POSTMARKS				
(17)	House of Commons, S.W.1	50		
(18)	House of Lords, S.W.1	60		
(19)	Queen Elizabeth Ave, Walsall	20		
(20)	Buckingham Palace or Windsor Castle	75		
SLOGAN POSTMARKS				
(21)	Queen's Silver Jubilee Appeal	20		
(22)	House of Commons (wavy line cancel)	15		

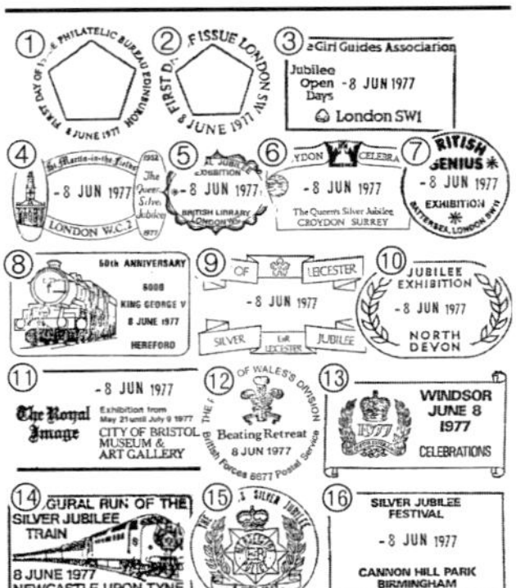

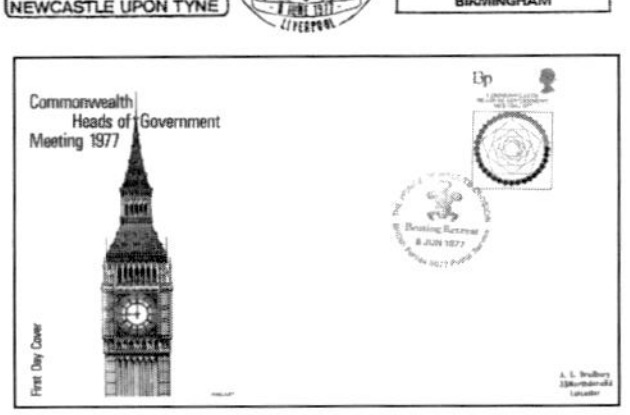

15th June 1977 - SILVER JUBILEE

9p Portrait of H.M. The Queen

		ordinary covers £	official covers £	
	SPECIAL HANDSTAMPS			
(1)	First Day of Issue - Philatelic Bureau	2	-	*Post Office*
(2)	First Day of Issue - Windsor	2	-	*Post Office*
(3)	Borough of Blackburn, Silver Jubilee	10	135	*BlackburnBC*
(4)	Jubilee Exhibition, North Devon	10	50	*N. Devon*
(5)	Silver Jubilee Exhibition, Trafalgar Square	10	-	*n.o.c.*
(6)	Royal Jubilee Exhibition, British Library	10	40	*BL 2*
(7)	City of Leicester, Silver Jubilee, EIIR	10	10	*City of Leics*
(8)	Nuneaton Council, 1952 EIIR 1977	10	50	*NuneatonBC*
(9)	Croydon Celebrates/Queen's Silver Jubilee	10	50	*Croydon*
(10)	Royal Image Exhibition, Bristol	25	60	*Royal Image*
(11)	British Genius Exhibition Battersea SW11	15	-	*n.o.c.*
	ORDINARY F.D.I. POSTMARKS			
(12)	Crewe (Sandbach special cover)	30		
(13)	Portsmouth - Review of Fleet	5		
	C.D.S. POSTMARKS			
(14)	Buckingham Palace or Windsor Castle	75		
(15)	House of Commons, S.W.1	10		
(16)	House of Lords, S.W.1	10		
(17)	Jubilee Oak; Jubilee Cresc.; Jubilee Fields	20		
(18)	Silver Link; Queens Head; Queens Parade	20		
(19)	Queen Elizabeth Avenue, Walsall	15		
	SLOGAN POSTMARKS			
(20)	The Queen's Silver Jubilee Appeal	15		
(21)	Review of the Fleet (Jubilee logo)	20		
(22)	Silver Jubilee Philatelic Exhib., Cardiff	20		
(23)	Silver Jubilee Philatelic Exhib., Edinburgh	20		
(24)	Silver Jubilee International Air Tattoo	50		
(25)	Portsmouth & Southsea (Jubilee logo)	30		

*Some **double-dated** covers exist with the set of Silver Jubilee stamps postmarked 11th May and the additional 9p value postmarked 15th June.*

(1)	special h/s (11 May) + FDI pmk (15 June)	30	30	
(2)	special h/s (11 May) + special h/s (15 June)	40	30	
(3)	appropriate CDS (both dates on one cover)	50		

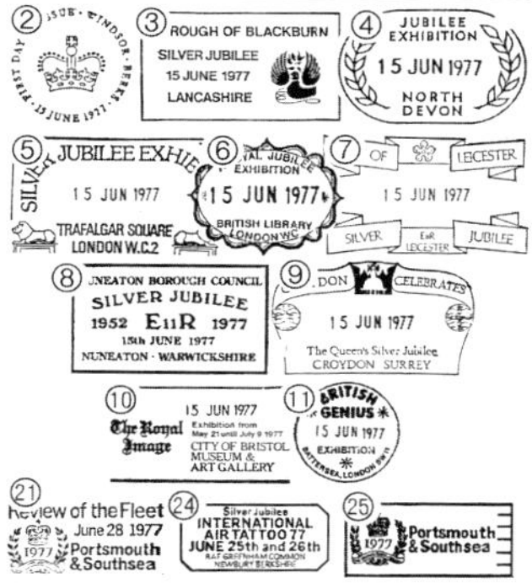

5th October 1977 - BRITISH WILDLIFE

5 x 9p: Hedgehog, Hare, Red Squirrel, Otter, Badger

		ordinary covers £	official covers £	
	SPECIAL HANDSTAMPS			
(1)	First Day of Issue - Philatelic Bureau	4	-	*Post Office*
(2)	Badger Beer, Blandford, 200th Anniversary	15	35	*Hall&Wdhse (s)*
(3)	SCT (Shropshire Conservation Trust)	15	200	*SCT*
(4)	Norfolk Wildlife in Trust, Norwich	15	15	*Markton (NNT)*
(5)	Port Lympne, Wildlife Sanctuary, Hythe	10	15	*RHDR 3*
(6)	11-13 Broad Court, Covent Garden, WC2	10	20	*Garden Studio*
(7)	Darley's, 150 Years of Print, Burton	45	600	*Darley's*
(8)	Sir Francis Drake, British Library, WC	50	-	*n.o.c.*
(9)	British Genius Exhibition, London SW11	50	-	*n.o.c.*
(10)	Army & Navy, Victoria, SW1	45	200	*A&N(set of 5)*
(11)	Manchester United, FA Cup Winners	50	45	*Dawn(set of 5)*
	C.D.S. POSTMARKS			
(12)	Badgers Mount, Sevenoaks	75		
(13)	Forest Row, East Sussex	30		
(14)	Foxton, Leics	75		
(15)	Haresfield, Harefield or Harewood ...*each*	75		
(16)	Hedge End, Southampton	15		
(17)	Nettleham - Royal Soc Nature Conservation	35		
(18)	Otterburn, Otterbourne, Ottery St Mary ...*each*	40		
(19)	Otter Ferry, Tighnabruaich	50		
(20)	Squirrels Heath, Romford	75		

23rd November 1977 - CHRISTMAS

5 x 7p; 9p 'The Twelve Days of Christmas'

		ordinary covers £	official covers £	
	SPECIAL HANDSTAMPS			
(1)	First Day of Issue - Philatelic Bureau	4	-	*Post Office*
(2)	First Day of Issue - Bethlehem	5	-	*Post Office*
(3)	Christmas Greetings, Blackpool	20	40	*Blackpool(s)*
(4)	Sir Francis Drake, British Library, WC	20	50	*Br. Lib.*
(5)	First Mail Flight, Lerwick, Shetland	30	35	*B.Airways(s)*
(6)	First Mail Flight, Dyce, Aberdeen	30	35	*B.Airways(s)*
	ORDINARY F.D.I. POSTMARKS			
(7)	Cambridge–Trinity College/original manuscript	15		
	C.D.S. POSTMARKS			
(8)	House of Lords - 'Ten Lords a-leaping'	35		
(9)	Lordship Lane, Dulwich	45		
(10)	Partridge Green or Pear Tree	45		
	SLOGAN POSTMARK			
(11)	Collect through Philatelic Bureau	50		

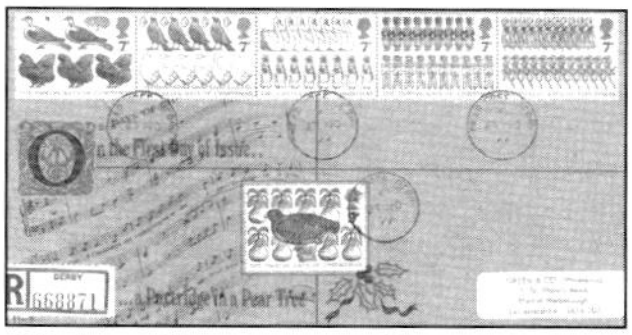

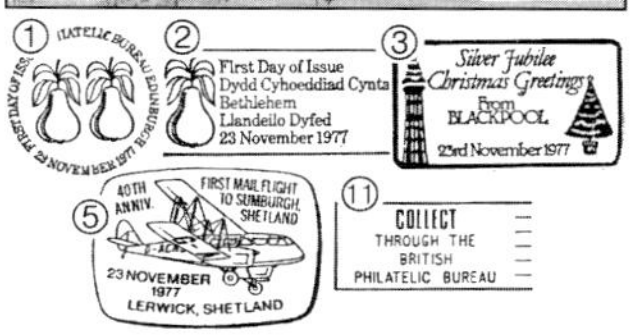

25th January 1978 - ENERGY

9p Oil; 10½p Coal; 11p Gas; 13p Electricity

		ordinary covers £	official covers £	
SPECIAL HANDSTAMPS				
(1)	First Day of Issue - Philatelic Bureau	5	-	*Post Office*
(2)	KW Claymore 'A' Project Team, Peterhead	50	200	*Claymore*
(3)	Institute of Fuel, Golden Jubilee Year, W1	10	15	*Cotswold (g)*
(4)	Coal is Precious, Ellistown	15	20	*Green(s)*
(5)	Oil is Precious, Melton Mowbray	15	20	*Green(s)*
(6)	British Speedway, Gulf Oil League, W4	15	-	*n.o.c.*
(7)	SEGAS, a part of British Gas Croydon	15	-	*n.o.c.*
(8)	Forties Field, BP, Aberdeen	10	35	*BOCS 1*
(9)	West Sole Field, BP, Hull	10	30	*BOCS 1*
(10)	21 Years Nuclear Electricity, Dungeness	10	15	*RHDR 4*
(11)	Haroldswick permanent special handstamp	50	-	*n.o.c.*
ORDINARY F.D.I. POSTMARKS				
(12)	Aberdeen (Taylor Woodrow cover)	35		
(13)	Battersea - Power Station	35		
C.D.S. POSTMARKS				
(14)	Bacton - North Sea gas pipeline	75		
(15)	Coalville, Coal Aston, Coalpit Heath or Selby	75		
(16)	Cruden Bay - Forties Field oil pipeline	75		
(17)	Seascale - first nuclear power station	100		
SLOGAN POSTMARK				
(18)	Collect through Philatelic Bureau	30		

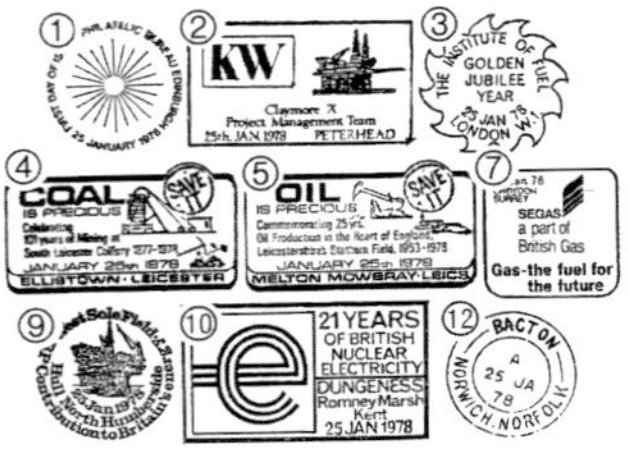

1st March 1978 - HISTORIC BUILDINGS

9p Tower of London; 10½p Holyroodhouse;
11p Caernarvon Castle; 13p Hampton Court

		ordinary covers £	official covers £	
SPECIAL HANDSTAMPS				
(1)	First Day of Issue - Philatelic Bureau	3	-	*Post Office*
(2)	First Day of Issue - London EC	3	-	*Post Office*
(3)	Tower of London, BF 9000 PS	10	25	*Tower of Lon*
(4)	British Architecture, British Library, WC	10	20	*BL 5*
(5)	Royal Heritage, Hampton Court Palace	10	25	*BOCS 2*
(6)	Hampton Court, Oldest Tennis Court	10	70	*S.P.*
(7)	Wells Cathedral, 800th Anniversary	12	15	*Cotswold (g)*
(8)	1953-1978 Stampex, Silver Jubilee, SW1	15	40	*Stampex*
(9)	Portland 900th, Dorset	20	40	*Portland*
(10)	Northwest Genius, Manchester	90	-	*n.o.c.*
ORDINARY F.D.I. POSTMARKS				
(11)	Caernarfon or Kingston-upon-Thames	25		
(12)	King's Lynn ('Sandringham' cachet)	35		
C.D.S. POSTMARKS				
(13)	Holyrood, Edinburgh 8	60		
(14)	Corfe Castle (on Saint Edward 1000 cover)	60 (s)		

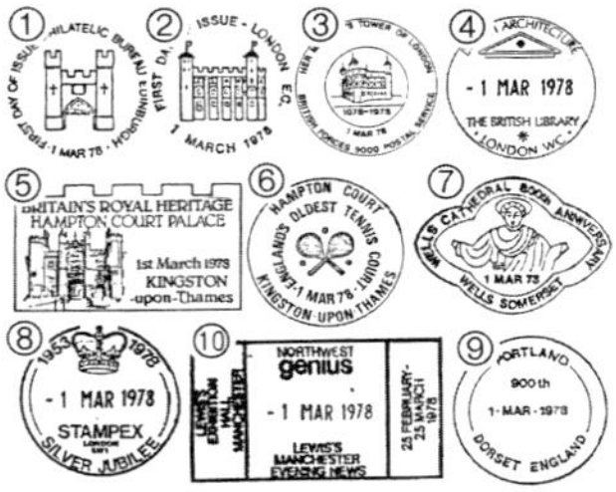

These postmarks were available for both the set of stamps and the miniature sheet issued on the same date.

1st March 1978 - HISTORIC BUILDINGS

Miniature Sheet

		ordinary covers £	official covers £	
SPECIAL HANDSTAMPS				
(1)	First Day of Issue - Philatelic Bureau	5	-	*Post Office*
(2)	First Day of Issue - London EC	5	-	*Post Office*
(3)	Tower of London, BF 9000 PS	15	20	*Tower of Lon*
(4)	British Architecture, British Library, WC	15	25	*BL 5*
(5)	Royal Heritage, Hampton Court Palace	15	100	*BOCS 2d*
(6)	Hampton Court, Oldest Tennis Court	15	-	*n.o.c.*
(7)	Wells Cathedral, 800th Anniversary	20	75	*Cotswold (g)*
(8)	1953-1978 Stampex, Silver Jubilee, SW1	15	40	*Stampex*
(9)	Portland 900th, Dorset	25	60	*Portland*
(10)	Northwest Genius, Manchester	100	-	*n.o.c.*
ORDINARY F.D.I. POSTMARKS				
(11)	Caernarfon or Kingston-upon-Thames	25		
C.D.S. POSTMARKS				
(12)	Earl's Court SW5 - venue of London 1980	40		
(13)	Holyrood, Edinburgh 8	60		

31st May 1978 - 25th ANNIVERSARY of CORONATION

9p, 10½p, 11p, 13p Coronation Regalia

		ordinary covers £	official covers £	
SPECIAL HANDSTAMPS				
(1)	First Day of Issue - Philatelic Bureau	3	-	*Post Office*
(2)	First Day of Issue - London SW	3	-	*Post Office*
(3)	1953 Coronation 1978, British Library, WC	8	25	*BL 7*
(4)	Cameo Stamp Centre, WC2	8	12	*Cameo*
(5)	RAF Wattisham, BF 1953 PS	8	45	*RAF Watt.*
(6)	Queen Elizabeth II, RHDRailway	8	10	*RHDR 6*
(7)	Caernarfon (depicting castle)	25	-	*n.o.c.*
(8)	Official Opening, Prince of Wales, Newcastle	25	50	*Freeman Hosp.*
(9)	British Philatelic Fed. Congress, Worthing	25	75	*B.P.F.*
(10)	Union of PO Workers, Blackpool	25	75	*U.P.O.W.*
(11)	RAF Hospital Wegberg, BF 1612 PS	25	50	*Forces*
(12)	Lewis's Celebrate 21 Years in Bristol	25	125	*Lewis's*
(13)	Mint, Sutton, Surrey	25	100	*Mint*
(14)	The Gatwick Park, Horley	25	125	*G. Park Hotel*

Coronation (contd.)

	ordinary covers £	official covers £	
(15) Assoc. Dairies, Royal Opening, Newcastle	25	250	*Assoc.Dairies*
(16) Visit of Prince of Wales, Newton Aycliffe	25	175	*Newton Aycl.*
(17) Temple of Jerusalem, Leicester	25	275	*Grand Priory*
ORDINARAY F.D.I. POSTMARKS			
(18) Windsor, Berks	10		
(19) Crewe (Sandbach special cover)	25		
(20) King's Lynn ('Sandringham' cachet)	35		
C.D.S. POSTMARKS			
(21) Benson RAF Station (Queen's Flight)	50		
(22) Buckingham Palace or Windsor Castle	150		
(23) Coronation Road, Parade or Square	25		
(24) House of Commons or Lords	30		
(25) Queen Elizabeth Avenue or Crown View	25		
(26) Scone – Stone of Scone/Coronation Chair	150		

5th July 1978 – SHIRE HORSE SOCIETY

9p Shire Horse; 10½p Shetland Pony; 11p Welsh Pony; 13p Thoroughbred

SPECIAL HANDSTAMPS			
(1) First Day of Issue – Philatelic Bureau	3	–	*Post Office*
(2) First Day of Issue – Peterborough	4	–	*Post Office*
(3) Havering Park Riding School	15	40	*Havering (f)*
(4) Tribute to the Horse, Market Weighton Sch.	15	30	*MW School*
(5) Horses of Britain, British Library, WC	10	40	*BL 8*
(6) Courage Shire Horse Centre, Maidenhead	10	65	*BOCS 4*
(7) The Royal Show, 1878-1978, Kenilworth	15	40	*S.P.*
(8) The Sport of Kings, Brighton	15	50	*B.Racecourse*
(9) Shetland Pony Stud Book Society	15	50	*Pilgrim*
(10) Home of the Derby, Epsom	10	–	*Post Office*
(11) World Dressage Championships Goodwood	20	75	*W Dressage*
(12) 700th Anniv. of the Cinque Ports, Hythe	10	15	*RHDR 7*
(13) RNLI Clacton 1878-1978, Clacton	25	30	*Pilgrim*
(14) Ars Gratia Artis, London W1	30	175	*MGM*
(15) Royal Scots Dragoon Guards, BF 1678 PS	20	5	*S.P.(s)*
(16) Royal Irish Rangers, BF 1621 PS	20	70	*Roy.Ir.Rang.*
(17) Lawn Tennis Championships, Wimbledon	20	–	*n.o.c.*
(18) Salvation Army, Wembley	20	15	*S. Army(s)*
(19) Sutton-on-Trent Comprehensive School	20	70	*Sutton Sch*
(20) Big Four Rly Museum, Bournemouth	20	–	*n.o.c.*
(21) Llangollen International Musical Eisteddfod	20	150	*Eisteddfod*
(22) Caernarfon (depicting castle)	15	–	*n.o.c.*
ORDINARY F.D.I. POSTMARKS			
(23) Aberystwyth ('Welsh Pony Express' cover)	35		
(24) Aylesbury (Amersham Horse Show cover)	25		
(25) Bournemouth ('Railway Horses' cover)	25		
(26) King's Lynn ('Sandringham' cachet)	25		
C.D.S. POSTMARKS			
(27) Aintree or Ascot	90		
(28) Blackhorse, Old Roan or Horsebridge	20		
(29) Darley – 'Darley Arabian'	60		
(30) Godolphin Cross – 'Goldolphin Arabian'	60		
(31) Epsom Downs – home of the Derby	100		
(32) Gt. Yarmouth (Anna Sewell cover)	45		
(33) Horsefair – Kidderminster or Rugeley *each*	25		
(34) Lerwick – Shetland pony	80		
(35) Riding Mill, Paddock or Shireoaks *each*	40		
(36) Stud Farm, Studlands or Newmarket *each*	45		

PLEASE READ THE GENERAL NOTES
These often provide the answers to enquiries received.

2nd August 1978 – CYCLING CENTENARY

9p Penny Farthing; 10½p Touring Bicycles;
11p Modern Bikes; 13p Road Racers

SPECIAL HANDSTAMPS			
(1) First Day of Issue – Philatelic Bureau	3	–	*Post Office*
(2) First Day of Issue – Harrogate	3	–	*Post Office*
(3) BCF Centenary Meeting, Leicester	10	35	*City Council*
(4) Tl Raleigh, Bicycle Manufacturer, Nott'gham	10	30	*BOCS 5*
(5) Tl Raleigh, Tour de France, Nottingham	10	25	*BOCS 5*
(6) 1953 Coronation 1978, British Library, WC	12	40	*B. Library*
(7) Colchester Searchlite Tattoo, BF 1606 PS	30	150	*C.S. Tattoo*
(8) Self-righting Lifeboat, Science Museum	40	–	*n.o.c.*
(9) Caernarfon (depicting castle)	30	–	*n.o.c.*
(10) 700th Anniv. of the Cinque Ports, Hythe	20	40	*RHDR 7*
ORDINARY F.D.I. POSTMARKS			
(11) Dumfries – invention of the bicycle	45		
(12) Guildford (Surrey Police 'Bike Safe' cover)	20		
(13) London SE1 (Holdsworthy Cycles promo cvr)	20		
C.D.S. POSTMARKS			
(14) Charlbury – Tandem Club	90		
(15) Godalming – Cylists' Touring Club	90		
(16) Meriden – Cyclists' War Memorial	90		
(17) Raleigh, Torpoint, Cornwall	250		
SLOGAN POSTMARKS			
(18) Driver – Mind that Bike	125		

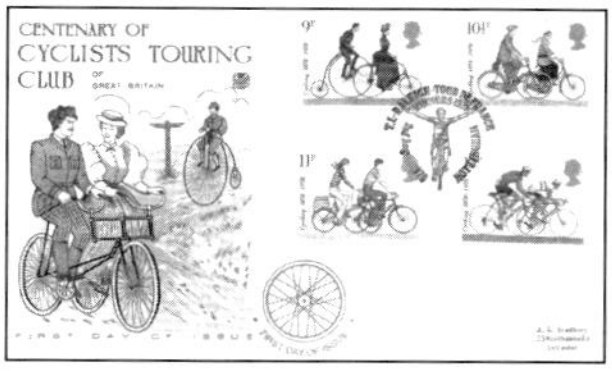

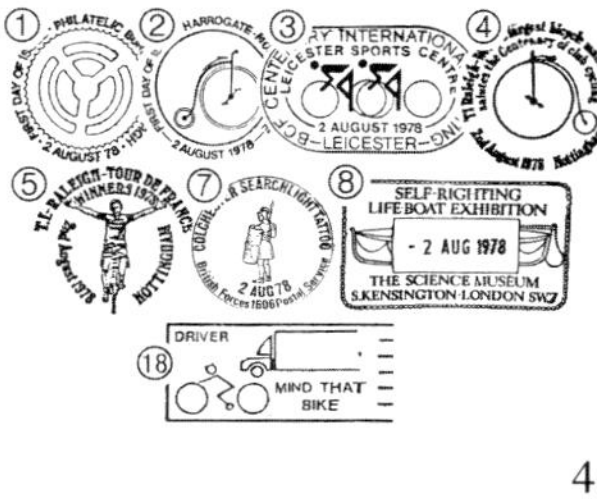

22nd Nov, 1978 - CHRISTMAS

7p, 9p, 11p, 13p Carols

	ordinary covers £	official covers £	
SPECIAL HANDSTAMPS			
(1) First Day of Issue - Philatelic Bureau	2	-	*Post Office*
(2) First Day of Issue - Bethlehem	3	-	*Post Office*
(3) Carols for Christmas, British Library, WC	10	30	*BL 9*
(4) Kings College Cambridge	10	20	*BOCS 6*
(5) Parish of Dalgety, Dunfermline	10	20	*Dal Parish*
(6) Music for All, Romford	10	15	*Havering (f)*
(7) History of Philately Exhibition, Warwick	10	30	*W & W*
(8) Meet Your Post Office, Dunfermline	25	-	*n.o.c.*
(9) Meet Your Post Office, Portsmouth	125	-	*n.o.c.*
(10) 50 Years of Rotary in Clacton	20	60	*Rotary*
(11) Gold of Eldorado, Royal Academy, W1	20	75	*Pilgrim*
(12) Croeso Cymru I'r Crysau Duon, Cardiff	20	350	*All Blacks*
ORDINARY F.D.I. POSTMARKS			
(13) Oxford - Boars Head Carol Queens College	30		
C.D.S. POSTMARKS			
(14) Boars Head, Wigan or Nasareth	125		
(15) Fairy Cross, Fir Tree or Hollybush *each*	40		

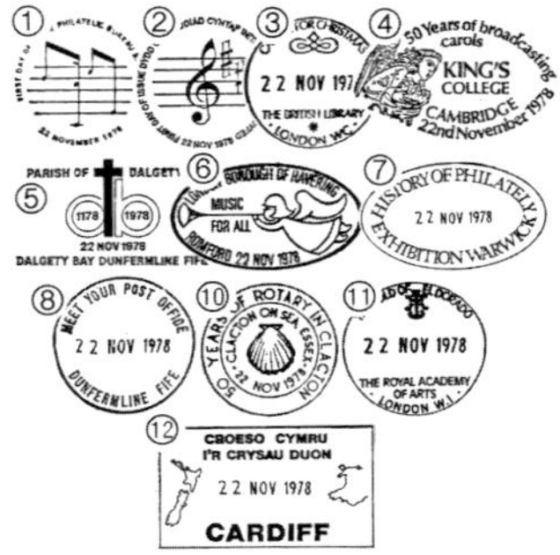

7th February 1979 - DOGS

9p Old English Sheepdog; 10½p Welsh Springer Spaniel; 11p West Highland Terrier; 13p Irish Setter

SPECIAL HANDSTAMPS			
(1) First Day of Issue - Philatelic Bureau	2	-	*Post Office*
(2) First Day of Issue - London SW	3	-	*Post Office*
(3) Spillers Congratulate Kennel Club, EC4	8	12	*BOCS 7*
(4) New Zealand Exhibition, Warwick	10	40	*W & W*
(5) Gold of Eldorado, Royal Academy, W1	10	65	*Pilgrim*
(6) England v. N. Ireland, Wembley.	15	40	*Dawn(set of 4)*
ORDINARY F.D.I. POSTMARKS			
(7) Battersea - Battersea Dogs Home	25		
(8) Brighton (Brighton & Hove Stadium cover)	50		
(9) London W1 (Dulux paints cover)	75		
(10) Paddington (CIBA-GEIGY cover)	45		
(11) Redhill (P.D.S.A. cover)	45		
C.D.S. POSTMARKS			
(12) Barking or Dogsthorpe	40		
(13) Battersea Park Road - Dogs Home	95		
(14) Black Dog or Hounds Hill	100		
(15) Dog & Gun, Dog Kennel Lane or Isle of Dogs	120		

21st March 1979 - BRITISH FLOWERS

9p Primrose; 10½p Daffodil; 11p Bluebell; 13p Snowdrop

SPECIAL HANDSTAMPS			
(1) First Day of Issue - Philatelic Bureau	2	-	*Post Office*
(2) Royal Botanic Gardens, Kew, Richmond	8	30	*Botanic Gdns*
(3) Bath Floral City Exhibition	8	10	*Cotswold (g)*
(4) Flower Arrangers Soc., St. Marys	6	9	*BOCS 8*
(5) Flower Arrangers Soc., Penzance	6	9	*BOCS 8*
(6) Founders Day, Bluebell Railway, Uckfield	10	20	*RHDR 8*
(7) Rural Blisworth Exhibition, Northampton	10	35	*Blisworth*
(8) W.I. Canterbury (Women's Institute)	15	60	*W.I.*
(9) Egypt Postage Stamp Exhibition, Warwick	15	35	*W & W*
C.D.S. POSTMARKS			
(10) Blue Bell Hill, Huddersfield	50		
(11) Botanic Gardens, Belfast or Flowery Field	50		
(12) Isles of Scilly or Snow Hill	40		
(13) Kew Gardens, Richmond	100		
(14) Primrose, Jarrow	60		
(15) Spring Gardens, Lytham St. Annes	40		
SLOGAN POSTMARKS			
(16) Bath - Europe's Floral City	85		
(17) 21st Spalding Flower Parade	85		

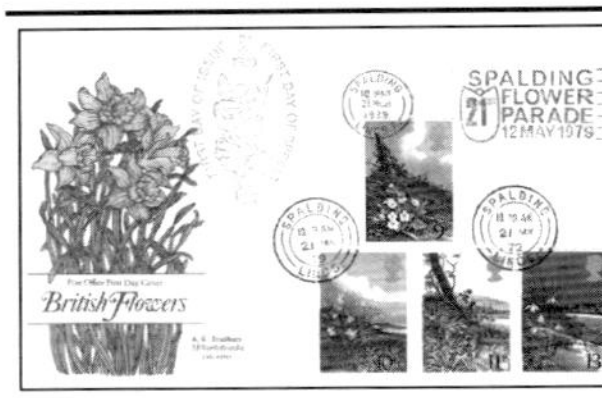

9th May 1979 - EUROPEAN ELECTIONS

9p, 10½p, 11p, 13p Flags of Member Nations

SPECIAL HANDSTAMPS			
(1) First Day of Issue - Philatelic Bureau	3	-	*Post Office*
(2) First Day of Issue - London SW	3	-	*Post Office*
(3) Strasbourg - Leicester's Twin City	6	15	*City Council*
(4) British European Elections, SW1	7	15	*BOCS 10*
(5) Entente Cordiale, Stowmarket	225	150	*Stow. Tw. Com.*
(6) Cameo Stamp Centre, WC2	6	10	*Cameo*
(7) Inst. of Gas Engineers, SW	10	40	*Gas Eng.*
(8) Worth Valley Rly Letter Service, Keighley	10	40	*W V Rly*
(9) Lions Holiday, 79 District, Hayling Island	10	100	*Lions*
(10) Barbados Postage Stamps Exhib. Warwick	10	25	*W & W*
(11) Nat. Assoc. Flower Arrangers, Blackpool	10	10	*BOCS 8*
(12) Derby 200 Exhibition, Royal Academy, W1	10	10	*BOCS 9*
(13) British Chess Federation, Norwich	10	35	*Chess Fed*
ORDINARY F.D.I. POSTMARKS			
(14) Folkestone - Gateway to Europe	10		

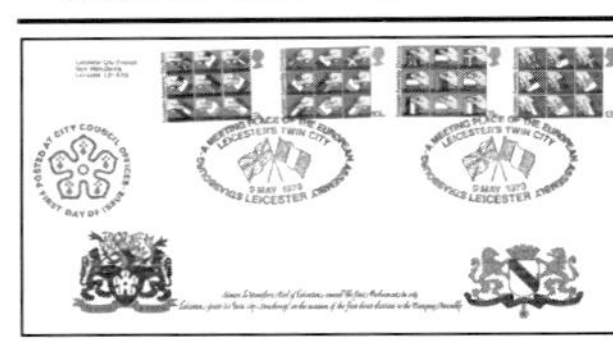

European Elections (contd.)	ordinary covers £	official covers £	
(15) Colchester (Clacton on Sea twinning cover)	20		
C.D.S. POST.MARKS			
(16) Blackrod, Bolton	35		
(17) Dover or Harwich - Gateways to Europe	15		
(18) House of Commons or Lords	25		
(19) Newhaven with PAQUEBOT markings	15		
(20) Dieppe with PAQUEBOT markings	12		
(21) Parliament St. or Northern Parliament	25		
(22) Weymouth - Gateway to Europe	15		
SLOGAN POSTMARKS			
(23) Are you on the Voters List?, Lincoln	575		
(24) Bath - Europe's Floral City	135		

6th June 1979 - HORSE RACING

9p The Derby; 10½p Aintree; 11p Newmarket; 13p Windsor

SPECIAL HANDSTAMPS			
(1) First Day of Issue - Philatelic Bureau	3	-	*Post Office*
(2) First Day of Issue - Epsom, Surrey	3	-	*Post Office*
(3) Jockey Club, Newmarket	6	30	*S.P.*
(4) Derby 200 Exhibition, Royal Academy, W1	6	9	*BOCS 9*
(5) Derby 200, Epsom, Surrey	6	10	*BOCS 11*
(6) England's Oldest Horse Race, Kiplingcotes	8	20	*MW School*
(7) Derbyshire Festival, Matlock	10	150	*Derbys Fest.*
(8) Newbury Show, Berks	8	20	*New. Ag. Soc*
(9) Chigwell School, 1629-1979	10	40	*Chigwell Sch*
(10) Nauru Postal History Exhibition, Warwick	20	30	*W & W*
(11) Norwich Union First Class Insurance	20	70	*Norwich.Un.*
(12) 35th Anniv. of D-Day, Southampton	20	-	*n.o.c.*
(13) 35th Anniv. Operation Neptune, BF 3544 PS	20	-	*n.o.c.*
(14) First Collection, Edinburgh Eurocrest Hotel	20	90	*Euro Hotel*
(15) First Collection, Glasgow Eurocrest Hotel	20	90	*Euro Hotel*
ORDINARY F.D.I. POSTMARKS			
(16) Derby, Doncaster or Liverpool	15		
(17) King's Lynn (Sandringham' cachet)	25		
(18) Windsor - Dorsett Ferry, Windsor (13p)	15		
C.D.S. POSTMARKS			
(19) Aintree, Ascot or Epsom Downs	85		
(20) Derby or Horse Fair	25		
(21) Langholm (Rotary/Red Rum cover)	75		
(22) Newmarket, Stud Farm or Studlands	50		
(23) Tattenham Corner - Epsom racecourse	250		
SLOGAN POSTMARKS			
(24) Come Racing at Great Yarmouth	75		
(25) Derby Fiesta July 3rd-7th, Derby	85		
(26) Derbyshire Festival	150		

11th July 1979 - YEAR OF THE CHILD

9p Peter Rabbit - Beatrix Potter; 10½p Wind in the Willows - Kenneth Grahame; 11p Winnie the Pooh - A. A . Milne; 13p Alice - Lewis Caroll

SPECIAL HANDSTAMPS			
(1) First Day of Issue - Philatelic Bureau	2	-	*Post Office*
(2) Yardley Primary School, Chingford	8	35	*Walth. Forest*
(3) NSPCC, Bethlehem	8	15	*BOCS Sp 1*
(4) Kent & East Sussex Rly, Tenterden	8	10	*RH 9*
(5) Winnie the Pooh, Hartfield	8	25	*BOCS 12*
(6) Beatrix Potter, Near Sawrey, Ambleside	8	-	*Post Office*
(7) Great Ormonde St., WC1	15	-	*n.o.c.*
(8) Palitoy Diamond Jubilee, Leicester	25	300	*Palitoy*
(9) New Parks Boys School Leicester	10	50	*NPB School*
(10) Lewis Carroll Society, Daresbury	10	40	*L.C. Soc*
(11) Alice in Wonderland, Llandudno	10	50	*Llan Town C*
(12) Cub Country, Birkenhead	10	20	*Dawn*
(13) Year of the Child, Wokingham	10	30	*Rotary*
(14) IYC, Westminster Cathedral, SW1	10	30	*Cotswold*
(15) Wisbech Grammar School	10	95	*Wisbech GS*
(16) Mother & Baby Life Care, Leamington	35	30	*LIFE*
(17) Royal Tournament, BF 1979 PS	10	30	*BFPS*
(18) 1979 Anniversaries, British Library	10	50	*BL 10*
(19) Home International Bowls Pontypool	15	50	*Pilgrim*
(20) Rhodesia Philatelic Exhib. Warwick	20	25	*W & W*
ORDINARY F.D.I. POSTMARKS			
(21) Birmingham (IYC Scout Conference cover)	35		
(22) Edinburgh - b/place Kenneth Grahame	15		
(23) Exeter (Exeter Childrens Orchestra cover)	25		
(24) Hartfield - home of A. A. Milne	15		
(25) London WC (F Warne cover)	55		
(26) London WC (Org. of Good Templars cover)	35		
(27) Oxford - Lewis Carroll	15		
(28) Stourbridge - designer of PO cover	15		

Year of the Child (contd.)

	ordinary covers	official covers
C.D.S. POSTMARKS	£	£
(29) Child Okeford or Child's Hill	50	
(30) Far Sawrey – home of Beatrix Potter	70	
(31) Hartfield – home of A. A. Milne	30	
(32) Playing Place, Truro	70	
SLOGAN POSTMARKS		
(33) Barnardo's Care about Children	60	
(34) Give a Child a Home Leeds	100	

22nd August 1979 – SIR ROWLAND HILL

10p Sir Rowland Hill; 11½p General Post c 1839; 13p London Post c 1839; 15p Uniform Postage 1840

SPECIAL HANDSTAMPS			
(1) First Day of Issue – Philatelic Bureau	2	–	*Post Office*
(2) First Day of Issue – London EC	2	–	*Post Office*
(3) London EC Chief Office	6	–	*n.o.c.*
(4) National Postal Museum (Maltese Cross)	6	–	*n.o.c.*
(5) Bruce Castle Museum, Tottenham N17	10	45	*Haringey*
(6) Sir Rowland Hill, Kidderminster Art Gallery	6	–	*n.o.c.*
(7) Bath Postal Museum, Centenary Exhib.	6	25	*BP Museum*
(8) Mail Coach Run, Kidderminster	6	10	*BOCS 13*
(9) Mail Coach Run, Birmingham	6	10	*BOCS 13*
(10) Commemorative Delivery, Rayleigh	10	200	*WigginsTeape*
(11) Rowland Hill 1795-1879, Coventry	6	–	n.o.c.
(12) Rowland Hill 1795-1879, Stratford	6	–	*n.o.c.*
(13) Rowland Hill 1795-1879, Warwick	6	–	*n.o.c.*
(14) First Day of Issue, Kidderminster	6	–	*n.o.c.*
(15) 1979 Anniversaries, British Library, WC	10	40	*BL 11*
(16) Military Tattoo, Edinburgh	10	75	*M Tattoo*
(17) York Races, Tote Ebor Handicap, York	10	25	*S.P.(s)*
(18) Pier Centenary, Bournemouth	10	90	*Philatex*
(19) Skirrid Energy Drive, SW1	10	70	*Skirrid*
(20) Codesort - Manchester or Liverpool	15	–	*n.o.c.*
(21) Haddo House, Aberdeen	10	20	*Scot N.T.*
ORDINARY F.D.I. POSTMARKS			
(22) Kidderminster– b/place of Rowland Hil	8		
(23) Sanquhar – Britain's oldest Post Office	8		
C.D.S. POSTMARKS			
(24) Belsize Park or Hampstead	30		
(25) Bruce Grove – Bruce Castle	25		
(26) House of Commons or Lords	20		
(27) Kidderminster – b/place of Rowland Hill	15		
(28) PAQUEBOTS – introduced by Rowland Hill	15		
(29) Rowlands Castle, Hants	25		
SLOGAN POSTMARKS			
(30) International Stamp Exhib., Earls Court, EC	80		
(31) Datapost D – a new postal service, Enfield	90		
(32) Remember to use the Postcode or similar	30		

26th Sept. 1979 – POLICE

10p Local 'bobby'; 11½p Traffic Control; 13p Mounted police; 15p Police Launch

SPECIAL HANDSTAMPS			
(1) First Day of Issue – Philatelic Bureau	2	–	*Post Office*
(2) First Day of Issue – London SW	2	–	*Post Office*
(3) New Scotland Yard, Metropolitan Police	4	10	*Cotswold*
(4) Port of London Police, E16	10	200	*Port London*
(5) Devon & Cornwall Constabulary, Exeter	10	40	*D & C Const.*
(6) West Yorks Metropolitan Police, Wakefield	10	10	*BOCS 14*
(7) Sir Robert Peel, Tamworth	10	–	*n.o.c.*
(8) RAF Police, Bruggen, BF 1665 PS	10	30	*RAF Police*
(9) 1979 Anniversaries, British Library, WC	10	40	*BL 12*
(10) Shooting First Enemy Aircraft, BF 1662 PS	10	–	*n.o.c.*
(11) Zeppelin Mail Exhibition, NPC Warwick	10	25	*W & W*
(12) Sir John Gielgud at Blackpool	10	25	*Blk Theatre*
ORDINARY F.D.I. POSTMARKS			
(13) Bedford (Bedfordshire Police cover)	25		
(14) Bolton & Bury (Manchester Police cover)	60		
(15) Bury St Edmunds (Suffolk Police cover)	60		
(16) Lincoln (Lincolnshire Police cover)	60		
(17) Norwich (Norfolk Constabulary cover)	45		
(18) Oxford (Police Training Centre cover)	60		
(19) Warrington (Cheshire Constabulary cover)	60		
C.D.S. POSTMARKS			
(20) Bow Street, Dyfed – Bow Street Runners	85		
(21) Bury, Lancs – birthplace of Sir Robert Peel	40		
(22) Constable Burton, Leyburn North Yorks	60		
(23) Constable Road, Sheffield	50		
(24) Crook, Co. Durham	35		
(25) Hendon – Police Training School	30		
(26) House of Commons, S.W.1	25		
(27) House of Lords, S.W.1	35		

Police (contd.)

	ordinary covers £	official covers £	
(28) Law, Carluke	50		
(29) Tamworth – Home of Robert Peel	20		
(30) Wapping, E.1 – River Police HQ	50		
(31) Eynsham (Police Training Centre cover)	40		
(32) Field Post Office 999 (NY Police cover)	150		
SLOGAN POSTMARKS			
(33) Durham 800 Years a City	150		

24th October 1979 – SIR ROWLAND HILL

Miniature sheet

SPECIAL HANDSTAMPS			
(1) First Day of Issue – Philatelic Bureau	2	–	*Post Office*
(2) First Day of Issue – London EC	2	–	*Post Office*
(3) London EC Chief Office	8	–	*n.o.c.*
(4) National Postal Museum	8	–	*n.o.c.*
(5) Bruce Castle Museum, Tottenham	20	50	*Haringey*
(6) London & Brighton Rly Co	8	10	*BOCS 16*
(7) Cartoonists Club Gatwick Airport	8	10	*BOCS Sp 2*
(8) 1979 Anniversaries, British Library	10	30	*BL 11a*
(9) PUC 1929 Exhibition NPC Warwick	10	–	*n.o.c.*
(10) Codesort - Manchester or Liverpool	15	–	*n.o.c.*
ORDINARY F.D.I. POSTMARKS			
(11) Kidderminster – b/place of Rowland Hill	10		
(12) Sanquhar – Britain's oldest Post Office	10		
C.D.S. POSTMARKS			
(13) Hampstead NW3 - where he died	15		
(14) House of Commons or Lords	15		
(15) Kidderminster – b/place of Rowland Hill	10		
(16) Rowlands Castle, Hants	25		
SLOGAN POSTMARKS			
(17) Int. Stamp Exhib., Earls Court	75		

*Some **double-dated** covers exist with the set of Rowland Hill stamps postmarked 22nd August and the miniature sheet postmarked 24th October. Prices from £40.*

21st November 1979 – CHRISTMAS

8p, 10p, 11½p, 13p, 15p The Nativity

SPECIAL HANDSTAMPS			
(1) First Day of Issue – Philatelic Bureau	2	–	*Post Office*
(2) First Day of Issue – Bethlehem	2	–	*Post Office*
(3) Christmas, British Library, WC	8	25	*BL 13*
(4) 25th Anniv After the Ball, Blackpool	8	25	*Blk Theatre*
(5) Cheriton & Morehall Christmas Lights	8	10	*CM Traders*
(6) Father Christmas Special, K. & E. S. Rly	8	10	*RH 10*
(7) Centenary of the War Cry, EC4	8	50	*H.R.*
(8) Rotary Club of Swansea	8	35	*Rotary*
(9) Stamp & Coin Exhib. Coventry	8	35	*D.F.*
(10) Naming Ceremony Margate Lifeboat	8	20	*Pilgrim*
(11) Air Mails, 1920-1950 NPC ,Warwick	10	25	*W & W*
(12) BIPEX, London SW	10	–	*n.o.c.*
(13) England v. Bulgaria, Wembley	10	50	*Dawn*
C.D.S. POSTMARKS			
(14) Nasareth, Caernarfon	50		

Also: Angel Hill, Holy Island, Kings Road, Star, Starcross, Shepherds Bush. Prices from £10

SLOGAN POSTMARKS

(15) Milton Keynes, Xmas Shopping 100

Also: Barnardos Cares About Children; Postcode It. Prices from £40.

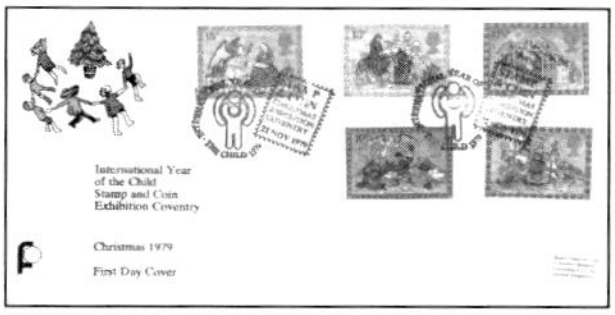

16th January 1980 – BRITISH BIRDS

10p Kingfisher; 11½p Dipper; 13p Moorhen; 15p Yellow Wagtail

SPECLAL HANDSTAMPS			
(1) First Day of Issue – Philatelic Bureau	2	–	*Post Office*
(2) First Day of Issue – Sandy, Beds	2	–	*Post Office*
(3) Essex Field Club, Centenary, Chelmsford	8	10	*Havering 5*
(4) Leicestershire & Rutland Ornithological Soc	8	20	*LFDC (f)*
(5) West Midlands Bird Club, 51st Anniversary	8	10	*P.P.S.*
(6) Wildfowl Trust, Arundel	8	10	*BOCS 17*
(7) Wildfowl Trust, Washington	8	15	*BOCS 17*
(8) Wildfowl Trust, Peakirk	8	10	*BOCS 17*
(9) Wildfowl Trust, Martin Mere	8	10	*BOCS 17*
(10) Wildfowl Trust, Slimbridge	8	10	*BOCS 17*
(11) Pioneers in Bird Protection, RSPB Sandy	8	25	*R.S.P.B.*
(12) Hull Natural History Society	8	20	*MW School*
(13) NNT Wild Birds Protection Act, Norwich	8	10	*Markton*
(14) 10th Anniv., Cotswold Wildlife Park	8	15	*Cotswold (g)*
(15) Wintertime, British Library, WC	15	80	*BL 14*
(16) The Salvation Army, 100, Harwich	15	95	*H.R.*
(17) The Royal Image Exhibition, NPC, Warwick	15	40	*W & W*
(18) Queens School Rheindahlen, BF 1671 PS	15	150	*Queens Sch*

Birds (contd.)

	C.D.S. POSTMARKS	ordinary covers £	official covers £	
(19)	Fair Isle – famous bird observatory	40		
(20)	House of Commons or Lords	30		
(21)	Sandy, Beds. – R.S.P.B. Headquarters	40		

Also: Birds Edge, Cley, Eagle, Heron Cross, Hickling, Holme, Partridge Green, Ranworth, Swallownest, Wing, Wren's Nest. Prices range from £20 each.

SLOGAN POSTMARKS

(22)	Dovecot Arts Centre (depicting doves)	475		

Also: Collect British Stamps £30.

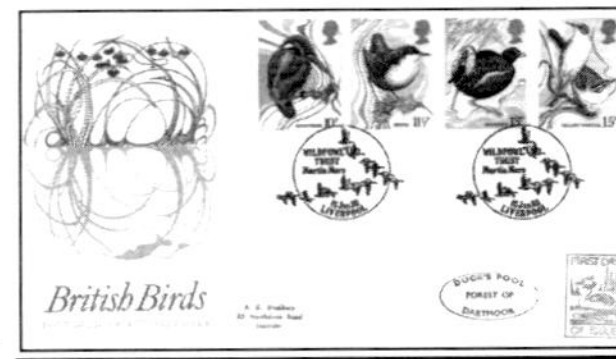

12th March 1980 – LIVERPOOL & MANCHESTER RAILWAY

5 x 12p 'The Rocket' and various railway carriages

SPECIAL HANDSTAMPS

(1)	First Day of Issue – Philatelic Bureau	2	–	*Post Office*
(2)	First Day of Issue – Manchester	2	–	*Post Office*
(3)	First Day of Issue – Liverpool	2	–	*Post Office*
(4)	Great Railway Exposition, Manchester	10	–	*n.o.c.*
(5)	Main Line Steam Trust, Loughborough	10	15	*LFDC (f)*
(6)	Newton-le-Willows, Earlstown	10	75	*Newton 150*
(7)	80th Anniversary Rother Rly, Tenterden	10	12	*RH 11*
(8)	The Railway Age, Coventry	10	40	*D.F.*
(9)	To London 1980 by Rail, BF 1682 PS	10	25	*Forces(set of 5)*
(10)	Havering's own Railway	10	10	*Havering 6*
(11)	Bressingham Steam Museum, Diss	10	10	*Markton*
(12)	T.P.O. Exhibition, Crewe	10	50	*Dawn*
(13)	Manchester (Kelloggs)	10	35	*Kelloggs*
(14)	Austro-Hungarian Postal History, Warwick	15	75	*W & W*
(15)	Volvo Diplomat Sales Consult the Experts	15	200	*Volvo*
(16)	LSP Ammeraal, Ware Herts	15	200	*LSP*
(17)	Wintertime, British Library, WC	15	60	*BL 16*
(18)	Daily Mail, Ideal Home Exhib., SW5	15	100	*Pilgrim*
(19)	Codesort Comes to Manchester, or Liverpool	20	–	*Post Office*

ORDINARY F.D.I. POSTMARKS

(20)	Aberysthwyth (Talyllyn Railway cover)	45		
(21)	Bournemouth (Big Four Railway Museum)	35		
(22)	Bradford (Worth Valley Railway cover)	45		
(23)	Caernarfon (Llanberis or Festiniog Rly cvrs)	45		
(24)	Any other FDI on private railway covers	45		

C.D.S. POSTMARKS (inc. T.P.O. CANCELS)

(25)	Crowthome Stn – station Post Office	20		
(26)	Rainhill, Prescot – 'Rainhill Trials'	35		
(27)	The Rocket, Liverpool or Wylam	75		
(28)	Sheringham (North Norfolk Railway cover)	45		
(29)	Any other CDS on private railway covers	45		
(30)	Any TPO (travelling post office) postmarks	20		

SLOGAN POSTMARKS

(31)	150 Years of Mail by Rail	50		

9th April 1980 – LONDON 1980 STAMP EXHIBITION

50p Montage of London Buildings

SPECIAL HANDSTAMPS

(1)	First Day of Issue – Philatelic Bureau	2	–	*Post Office*
(2)	First Day of Issue – London S.W.	2	–	*Post Office*
(3)	Cameo Stamp Centre	8	10	*Cameo*
(4)	London Tourist Board Victoria	8	10	*BOCS 19*
(5)	West Country-Liverpool, Inaugural Flight	8	20	*RoyalMail*
(6)	Trafalgar Square or London Chief Office	8	–	*n.o.c.*
(7)	National Postal Museum	8	–	*n.o.c.*
(8)	G.B. Major Errors Exhibition, Warwick	6	25	*W & W*
(9)	Springtime, British Library, WC	6	25	*BL 17*
(10)	C.S./R.I.C. Annual Congress, Durham	6	45	*CS/RIC*

C.D.S. POSTMARKS

(11)	Earls Court B.O.	75		
(12)	House of Commons or Lords	12		

SLOGAN POSTMARKS

(13)	Collect British Stamps	40		
(14)	Int. Stamp Exh. Earls Court – Leeds	60		

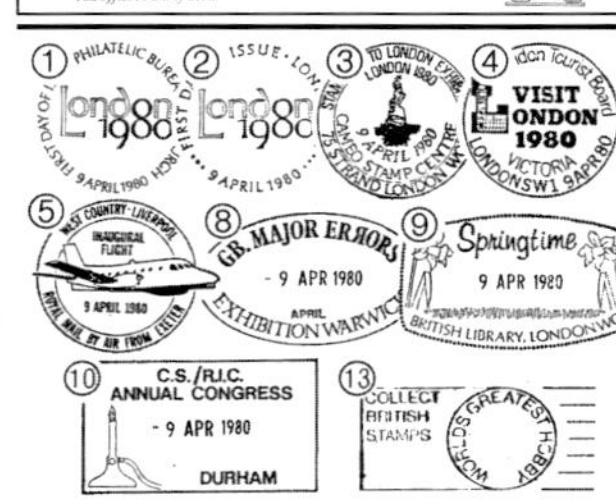

7th May 1980 – LONDON 1980

50p Miniature Sheet

SPECIAL HANDSTAMPS

(1)	First Day of Issue – Bureau (Eros)	2	–	*Post Office*
(2)	First Day of Issue – Bureau (London 1980)	2	–	*Post Office*
(3)	First Day of Issue – Kingston	2	–	*Post Office*
(4)	First Day of Issue – London SW	2	–	*Post Office*
(5)	Stamps Magazine/London 1980	8	–	*n.o.c.*
(6)	Supersonically/London 1980 BF 7580 PS	8	20	*BOCS 20*
(7)	London Union of Youth Clubs	8	–	*n.o.c.*
(8)	Leicester Philatelic Society	8	50	*LFDC Sp 1*
(9)	London Stamp Fair, London SW1	8	20	*Showpiece*
(10)	Post Office Day, London 1980, SW	8	20	*POCommCvr*
(11)	Royal Opera House, Covent Garden	8	–	*n.o.c.*
(12)	Warwick Penny Post Exhibition,	15	–	*n.o.c.*
(13)	Festival Fringe, Brighton	15	–	*n.o.c.*

London 1980 (contd.)

		ordinary covers £	official covers £	
(14)	Salvation Army, 1880-1980, Belfast	15	75	*Sal Army*
(15)	Freedom of Plymouth, BF 1694 PS	15	-	*n.o.c.*
(16)	Parish Church, Hampton-in-Arden	20	-	*n.o.c.*
(17)	Springtime, British Library, London	10	35	*BL 17a*
C.D.S. POSTMARKS				
(18)	Earl's Court, S.W.5	50		
(19)	House of Commons or Lords *each*	25		
(20)	Little London, Basingstoke	20		
SLOGAN POSTMARKS				
(21)	Collect British Stamps	30		

*Some **double-dated** covers exist with both the 50p stamp postmarked 9th April and the miniature sheet postmarked 7th May. Prices from £30.*

7th May 1980 - LONDON LANDMARKS

10½p Buckingham Palace; 12p Albert Memorial; 13½p Royal Opera House; 15p Hampton Court; 17½p Kensington Palace

SPECIAL HANDSTAMPS

		ordinary	official	
(1)	First Day of Issue - Bureau (Eros)	2	-	*Post Office*
(2)	First Day of Issue - Bureau (London 1980)	2	-	*Post Office*
(3)	First Day of Issue - Kingston-upon-Thames	2	-	*Post Office*
(4)	First Day of Issue - London SW	2	-	*Post Office*
(5)	Stamps Magazine/London 1980, Brentwood	8	-	*n.o.c.*
(6)	Supersonically to London 1980 BF 7580 PS	8	5	*RAF Mus.(s)*
(7)	London Union of Youth Clubs	8	15	*S.P. (Card)*
(8)	Leicester Philatelic Society	8	10	*LFDC 1*
(9)	London Stamp Fair, London SW1	8	15	*Showpiece*
(10)	Post Office Day London 1980, London SW	8	20	*POCommCvr*
(11)	Royal Opera House, Covent Garden, WC	8	30	*Cotswold*
(12)	Warwick Penny Post, Postal History Exhib.	8	40	*W & W*
(13)	Festival Fringe, Brighton	10	30	*BrightonFF(s)*
(14)	Salvation Army, 1880-1980, Belfast	12	75	*S. Army*
(15)	Freedom of Plymouth, BF 1694 PS	10	25	*R. Marine(s)*
(16)	Parish Church, Hampton-in-Arden	10	90	*H-i-A Church*
(17)	Springtime, British Library, London WC	10	40	*BL 18*
C.D.S. POSTMARKS				
(18)	Buckingham Palace, S.W.1	90		
(19)	Buckingham Gate, S.W.1	40		
(20)	Earl's Court - posted at the Exhibition	50		
(21)	House of Commons or Lords *each*	35		
(22)	Little London, Piccadilly or Kensington	30		

These pmks were available for both the miniature sheet & London Landmarks.

9th July 1980 - FAMOUS PEOPLE

12p Charlotte Brontë - Jane Eyre; 13½p George Eliot - Mill on the Floss; 15p Emily Brontë - Wuthering Heights; 17½p Mrs. Gaskell - North & South

SPECIAL HANDSTAMPS

		ordinary	official	
(1)	First Day of Issue - Philatelic Bureau	2	-	*Post Office*
(2)	First Day of Issue - Haworth, Keighley	2	-	*Post Office*
(3)	International Society, Mrs Gaskell	8	25	*Int. Society*
(4)	Elizabeth Gaskell Chelsea, SW3	8	30	*Hawkwood*
(5)	Leicester Writers' Club	8	10	*LFDC 2*
(6)	The Elms, Country Home of George Eliot	8	25	*The Elms*
(7)	George Eliot Centenary, Nuneaton	8	50	*D.F.*
(8)	Dent/Charlotte & Emily Brontë, Haworth	8	15	*BOCS 22*
(9)	Women Christian Temperance Union	15	-	*n.o.c.*
(10)	Rush & Tompkins, Swindon	10	200	*R & T*
(11)	Summertime, British Library, WC	10	25	*BL 19*
(12)	William Shakespeare, Stratford	10	-	*n.o.c.*
(13)	Channel Isles Occupation Exhib. Warwick	10	20	*W & W*
(14)	Llangollen International Musical Eisteddfod	10	100	*Eist 2 cvrs*
(15)	Royal Tournament Centenary, BF 1980 PS	10	30	*BFPS*
ORDINARY F.D.I. POSTMARKS				
(16)	Altrincham (with Knutsford P.O. cachet)	20		
C.D.S. POSTMARKS				
(17)	Chilvers Coton - birthplace of George Eliot	25		
(18)	Cranford - Mrs Gaskell's novel *Cranford*	25		
(19)	Haworth - home of Brontë sisters	25		
(20)	Inkpen, Newbury, Berks	20		
(21)	Knutsford - Mrs Gaskell's *Cranford*	25		
(22)	Thornton - birthplace of Brontë sisters	25		
SLOGAN POSTMARKS				
(23)	Knutsford, Mrs Gaskell's 'Cranford'	50		
(24)	Central Library & Museum, Sunderland	225		

4th August 1980 - QUEEN MOTHER'S 80th BIRTHDAY

12p Portrait of the Queen Mother

SPECIAL HANDSTAMPS

		ordinary	official	
(1)	First Day of Issue - Philatelic Bureau	2	-	*Post Office*
(2)	First Day of Issue - Glamis, Forfar	2	-	*Post Office*
(3)	Queen Mother's 80th Birthday, BF 8080 PS	8	40	*BFPS*
(4)	Clarence House	8	12	*Havering 11*
(5)	St. Paul's Walden Flower Festival, Hitchin	8	25	*Hawkwood*

Queen Mother (contd.)		ordinary covers £	official covers £	
(6)	St. Mary's Church, Ware	8	50	*St. Mary's*
(7)	Grand Theatre Blackpool	8	30	*Blk Theatre*
(8)	Queen Mother's 80th Birthday, Windsor	8	25	*Sumner*
(9)	Queen Mother's 80th Birthday, York	8	25	*Sumner*
(10)	FDCs of Royalty Exhibition, Leicester	8	10	*LFDC 3*
(11)	Hitchin Salutes the Queen Mother	8	–	*n.o.c.*
(12)	Happy Birthday, British Library, WC	8	20	*BL 20*
(13)	Lord Warden of Cinque Ports, Walmer	8	12	*BOCS 25*
(14)	St. Paul's Walden	8	25	*Sumner*
(15)	100 Years of GMT, Greenwich, SE10	8	50	*GMT*
(16)	Poppy Appeal cares all year, Richmond	8	10	*Poppy Appeal*
(17)	Forces Help Soc/Lord Roberts Workshops	8	10	*Cotswold*
(18)	Hull Kingston Rovers, Hull	8	10	*MW School*
(19)	RNLI Station Calshott	8	15	*Pilgrim*
(20)	Great Railway Exposition, Manchester	8	–	*n.o.c.*
(21)	Paramins 50 Years, Southampton	10	250	*Paramins*
(22)	Rother Railway, Tenterden	10	10	*RH 11*
(23)	1980 Promenade Concerts, SW7	10	–	*n.o.c.*
(24)	Recro '80, Kenilworth	10	40	*D.F.*
(25)	Anglo-Boer War Exhibition, Warwick	10	40	*W & W*
(26)	British Chess Congress, Brighton	10	40	*Chess Fed*
ORDINARY F.D.I. POSTMARKS				
(27)	King's Lynn ('Sandringham' cachet)	20		
(28)	Windsor, Berks	8		
C.D.S. POSTMARKS				
(29)	Bowes – Bowes-Lyon (family name)	15		
(30)	Buckingham Palace, S.W.1	120		
(31)	Glamis – Queen Mother's ancestral home	30		
(32)	House of Commons or Lords	25		
(33)	Mey (Castle of Mey) or Buckingham Gate	35		
(34)	Queen Elizabeth Avenue, Walsall	20		
(35)	Windsor Castle, Windsor, Berks	150		
SLOGAN POSTMARKS				
(36)	Isle of Man, Queen Mother Crowns	15		

Also: Elizabethan Banquets; Collect British Stamps; Post Code It. Prices from £15.

Her Majesty Queen Elizabeth, the Queen Mother 80th Birthday. Official First Day Cover 4th August 1980

PLEASE READ THE GENERAL NOTES

10th September 1980 - BRITISH CONDUCTORS

12p Sir Henry Wood; 13½p Sir Thomas Beecham; 15p Sir Malcolm Sargent; 17½p Sir John Barbirolli

SPECIAL HANDSTAMPS				
(1)	First Day of Issue – Philatelic Bureau	2	–	*Post Office*
(2)	First Day of Issue – London SW	2	–	*Post Office*
(3)	Royal Opera House, WC2	8	20	*Cotswold*
(4)	Guildhall School of Music & Drama, EC2	8	10	*Benham*
(5)	Leicester Symphony Orchestra	8	10	*LFDC 4*
(6)	Famous British Conductors, Bedford	8	50	*Bed Music Club*
(7)	Conductors of the Halle, Manchester	8	15	*P.P.S.*
(8)	1980 Promenade Concerts, SW7	8	10	*BOCS 24*
(9)	BBC Symphony Orchestra, SW7	8	10	*BOCS 24*
(10)	Royal Philharmonic Orchestra, SE1	8	20	*S.P.*
(11)	Anaesthesia 1980, Royal Festival Hall, SE1	8	10	*Hawkwood*
(12)	Sir Malcolm Sargent Cancer Fund, SW3	8	10	*Havering 12*
(13)	Birthplace Sir Thomas Beecham, St. Helens	8	55	*Th Beecham*
(14)	CBSO (City of Birmingham Symp. Orch.)	8	5	*C.B.S.O.*
(15)	TI Commemorates CBSO Birmingham	8	15	*C.B.S.O.*
(16)	Sir Thomas Beecham Rossall Sch. Fleetwood	8	3	*Benham(s)*
(17)	Fairfield, Croydon	8	35	*Fairfield*
(18)	Summertime, British Library, WC	10	45	*BL 21*
(19)	Sponne School 550th Anniv., Towcester	10	40	*Sponne Sch*
(20)	Flower Arrangements Nottingham	10	55	*NFFA*
(21)	Moorlands Festival, Leek	10	110	*Festival*
(22)	From Tom-Tom to Telex , NPC Warwick	10	80	*W & W*
(23)	Sir Geoffrey De Havilland, Hatfield	10	85	*MosquitoMus*
(24)	England v. Norway, World Cup, Wembley	10	30	*Dawn*
(25)	Great Railway Exposition, Manchester	15	–	*n.o.c.*
C.D.S. POSTMARKS				
(26)	Hitchin, Herts – Sir Henry Wood died here	15		
(27)	Marylebone, W1 – Royal Academy of Music	15		
(28)	New York – N.Y. Philharmonic (Barbirolli)	15		
(29)	Southampton Row – birthplace of Barbirolli	15		
(30)	Stamford – birthplace of Sargent	15		
(31)	St. Helens – birthplace of Beecham	15		

SLOGAN POSTMARK *B.P.E. Wembley. Prices range from £50.*

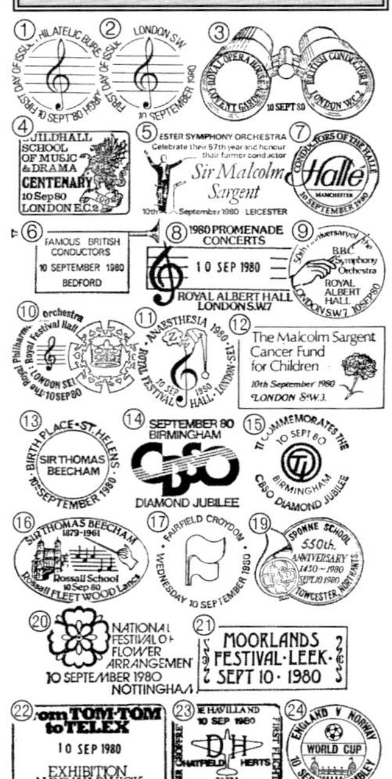

10th October 1980 - SPORTING ANNIVERSARIES

12p Athletics; 13½p Rugby; 15p Boxing; 17½p Cricket

SPECIAL HANDSTAMPS				
(1)	First Day of Issue – Philatelic Bureau	2	–	*Post Office*
(2)	First Day of Issue – Cardiff	2	–	*Post Office*
(3)	W.R.U. Centenary, Cardiff Arms Park	8	20	*W.R.U.*
(4)	The Saints 1880-1980, Northampton	8	50	*Saints RFC*
(5)	King Henry VIII, Rugby Centenary, Coventry	8	30	*D.F.*
(6)	Leicester Football Club	8	10	*LFDC 5*

Sport (contd.)

		ordinary covers £	official covers £	
(7)	Norfolk County F. A. Centenary, Norwich	8	10	*Markton*
(8)	Middlesex CCC, NW8	8	10	*Havering 13*
(9)	PO XI v Cricket Writers/Vic Lewis XI Lord's	8	10	*VicLewis(s)*
(10)	Centenary Tour, 1880-1980, Lord's, NW8	8	185	*S.P.*
(11)	Century of Tests, England v Australia, Oval	8	10	*Hawkwood*
(12)	London Union of Y.C./London Sportsmen	8	-	*n.o.c.*
(13)	Amateur Athletic Assoc., Crystal Palace	8	10	*BOCS 23*
(14)	Amateur Boxing Assoc., Wembley, M'sex	8	20	*BOCS Sp 3*
(15)	St. John Ambulance 1880-1980, Manchester	10	35	*Cotswold*
(16)	Autumntime, British Library, WC	10	45	*BL 22*
(17)	New Zealand Exhibition, Warwick	10	35	*W & W*
(18)	Post Office Philatelic Centre, Plymouth	10	-	*n.o.c.*
(19)	Nearest & Dearest, Blackpool	10	45	*Blk Theatre*

ORDINARY F.D.I. POSTMARKS

(20)	Oxford, Rugby or Twickenham	10		

C.D.S. POSTMARKS

(21)	Hambledon, Kennington, Llanelli or Neath	30		

In addition: Boycott, Bowling, Box, Brecon, Lampeter, Jump, Llandovery, Pontypool, Rugby, The Oval, Welford Road, Wells. Prices from £15.

SLOGAN POSTMARKS *Leicester Speedway. £150.*

19th November 1980 - CHRISTMAS

10p, 12p, 13½p, 15p, 17½p Christmas decorations

SPECIAL HANDSTAMPS

(1)	First Day of Issue - Philatelic Bureau	2	-	*Post Office*
(2)	First Day of Issue - Bethlehem	3	-	*Post Office*
(3)	950 Years of Worship,Waltham Abbey	8	15	*Hawkwood*
(4)	1980 Christmas, British Library, WC	8	25	*BL 23*
(5)	Regent Street Association, W1	8	10	*Havering 14*
(6)	Christmas Carols, Ivybridge	8	-	*n.o.c.*
(7)	Merry Christmas, Hollybush	8	-	*n.o.c.*
(8)	Norway's Christmas Gift, Trafalgar Square	8	10	*BOCS 26*
(9)	Commonwealth Christmas Stamps, Warwick	8	25	*W & W*
(10)	Fire Service Charity Appeal, Leicester	8	10	*LFDC 6*
(11)	Salvation Army, Mount Cross, Bramley	10	75	*H.R.*
(12)	England v Switzerland World Cup, Wembley	10	45	*Dawn*

C.D.S. POSTMARKS

(13)	Bethlehem or Nasareth	35		
(14)	Glastonbury - conversions to Christianity	35		

Also: Fairy Cross, Holly Bush, Holly Hall, Holy Island, Ivybridge, Ivychurch, Magdalen, Star. Prices from £15 each.

SLOGAN POSTMARKS *Shopping By Post. £40.*

6th February 1981 - FOLKLORE

14p St. Valentine's Day; 18p Morris Dancers; 22p Lammastide; 25p Medieval Mummers

SPECIAL HANDSTAMPS

(1)	First Day of Issue - Philatelic Bureau	2	-	*Post Office*
(2)	First Day of Issue - London WC	2	-	*Post Office*
(3)	My Valentine, Lover, Salisbury	8	10	*Cotswold (g)*
(4)	Valentines at the British Library, WC	8	75	*BL 25*
(5)	Valentines Card Exhibition, Leicester	8	20	*LFDC 7*
(6)	English Folk Song & Dance Society, SW1	8	8	*BOCS (2) 1*
(7)	Headington Morris Dancers, Oxford	8	15	*Hawkwood*
(8)	Thaxted Morris Men	8	15	*Havering 15*
(9)	Dunmow Flitch, Little Dunmow	8	15	*Havering Sp 1*
(10)	Robin Hood Society, Nottingham	8	30	*Bradbury*
(11)	Radley College, St. Helens, Abingdon	8	50	*Radley Coll*
(12)	Royal Mail Stampede, Hornsea Pottery	10	-	*n.o.c.*
(13)	Aviation History at Hendon, BF 1725 PS	10	15	*RFDC 1*
(14)	Orient F.C. Centenary, E10	10	40	*Hawkwood*
(15)	Victoria Cross Exhib., Postal Museum	15	-	*n.o.c.*
(16)	George VI, Sandringham	15	-	*n.o.c.*

C.D.S. POSTMARKS

(17)	Gretna Green or Lover	40		
(18)	Headington Quarry or Thaxted	25		

Also: Bampton, Chipping Campden, Davey Place, Honiton, Padstow, Robin Hood, St. George's, Tintagel, Widecombe-in-the-Moor. Prices from £15 each.

25th March 1981 - YEAR OF DISABLED PEOPLE

14p Guide Dog; 18p Sign Language; 22p Wheelchair; 25p Foot Artist

SPECIAL HANDSTAMPS

(1)	First Day of Issue - Philatelic Bureau	2	-	*Post Office*
(2)	First Day of Issue - Windsor	2	-	*Post Office*
(3)	Oaklands PH School, Salford	8	90	*Oaklands*
(4)	Guide Dogs Jubilee, Wallasey	8	10	*BOCS (2) 2*
(5)	Menphys Celebrate IYDP, Leicester	8	20	*LFDC 8*
(6)	MS, Exeter & District Branch	8	25	*Exeter MS*
(7)	IYDP Toynbee Hall, D.I.G., E1	8	10	*Havering 16*
(8)	Leicestershire Committee/IYDP	8	20	*P.P.S.*
(9)	Le Court: First Cheshire Home, Petersfield	8	40	*Cotswold*

Year of the Disabled (contd.)

		ordinary covers £	official covers £	
(10)	Cambridge & District Hard of Hearing	8	35	*Cam. HHA*
(11)	Arthritis Care, London SW1	8	150	*Arlington*
(12)	RAF Headley Court, BF 1726 PS	8	15	*RFDC 2*
(13)	Stoke Mandeville, Spinal Unit	8	15	*Hawkwood*
(14)	Coventry Sports Association, Charity Walk	8	25	*D.F.*
(15)	Disabled Drivers Motor Club, W3	8	35	*D.D.M.C.*
(16)	The Royal British Legion, SW1	8	175	*Brit. Leg.*
(17)	Stars for the Disabled, Peterborough	8	35	*Stars*
(18)	Carters (J & A), IYDP, Westbury	8	25	*P.P.S.*
(19)	Donington Park, 1931-1981, Derby	10	150	*Don. Park*
(20)	Daily Mail Ideal Home, Earls Court, SW5	10	40	*Pilgrim*
(21)	Swansea Philatelic Counter	10	125	*Cotswold*
(22)	March Philatelic Displays British Library	10	40	*BL 24*
(23)	Victoria Cross Exhib., Postal Museum	12	–	*n.o.c.*

ORDINARY F.D.I. POSTMARKS

(24)	Dudley (Redhill Disabled cvr) *or similar*	25	
(25)	Maidstone (Leeds Castle Disabled cover)	25	
(26)	Fylde & Blackpool (Blind Society cover)	25	

C.D.S. POSTMARKS

(27)	Any Hospital postmark	25
(28)	Leeds, Maidstone (Leeds Castle/Disabled cvr)	25
(29)	Stoke Mandeville – Spinal Injury Unit	25

Also: Bethesda, Guide,Leeds, St. Dunstans, Stoke Charity, Tredegar, Wallasey. Prices from £15 each.

SLOGAN POSTMARKS

(30)	'Can Disabled People Go Where You Go?'	35
(31)	St. Loyes College Exeter	50
(32)	The British Deaf Association, Carlisle	35

13th May 1981 - BUTTERFLIES

14p Small Tortoiseshell; 18p Large Blue; 22p Peacock; 25p Chequered Skipper

SPECIAL HANDSTAMPS

(1)	First Day of Issue – Philatelic Bureau	3	–	*Post Office*
(2)	First Day of Issue – London SW	3	–	*Post Office*
(3)	Large Blue,Quorn	10	15	*BOCS (2) 3*
(4)	Chequered Skipper, Bourton	10	15	*BOCS (2) 3*
(5)	Peacock, Sherborne	10	15	*BOCS (2) 3*
(6)	Wildfowl Trust, Slimbridge	10	15	*BOCS (2) 3*
(7)	World Wide Butterflies, Sherborne	10	15	*Havering Sp 2*
(8)	Nottingham Trust, Eakring Meadows	10	15	*Bradbury*
(9)	Margaret Fountaine Exhib., Norwich	10	15	*Markton*
(10)	Leics. Museums British Butterflies Exhib	10	15	*LFDC 9*
(11)	British Naturalist Assoc., Woodwalton	10	15	*Hawkwood*
(12)	National Butterfly Museum, Bramber	10	50	*S.P.*
(13)	Mtce Unit Conservamus, BF 1738 PS	10	15	*RFDC 3*
(14)	25 Years Freedom, RAF Locking	15	100	*RAF(set of 4)*
(15)	Sub-Postmasters Conf., Scarborough	25	–	*n.o.c.*
(16)	Victorian Postbox Postcards, Liverpool	25	–	*n.o.c.*
(17)	Victorian Postbox Postcards, Keswick	25	–	*n.o.c.*
(18)	Victorian Postbox Postcards, Buxton	25	–	*n.o.c.*
(19)	Rochdale's Unique Pillar Box	25	150	*Toad Lane Mus*
(20)	May Philatelic Displays, British Library	15	75	*BL 26*
(21)	Inauguration Wood Green Shopping	15	25	*Havering 17*
(22)	25th Christian Aid Week, Preston	15	35	*Chr. Aid*

ORDINARY F.D.I. POSTMARKS

(23)	Basildon (Marks Hill Nature Reserve cover)	40
(24)	Hemel Hempstead (Herts Nature cover)	40

C.D.S. POSTMARKS

(25)	Peacock Cross, Hamilton	35
(26)	Quorn – HQ British Butterflies Society	25

Also: Castle Acre, Dousland, Kings Norton, Nettlebed, Nettleham, Spring Gardens. Prices from £15

SLOGAN POSTMARKS

(27)	National Butterfly Museum Bramber	50

Also: Whipsnade Zoo. Prices from £40.

24th June 1981 - NATIONAL TRUSTS

14p Glenfinnan; 18p Derwentwater; 20p Stackpole Head; 22p Giant's Causeway; 25p St. Kilda

SPECIAL HANDSTAMPS

(1)	First Day of Issue – Philatelic Bureau	3	–	*Post Office*
(2)	First Day of Issue – Keswick	3	–	*Post Office*
(3)	First Day of Issue – Glenfinnan	3	–	*Post Office*
(4)	National Trust, Derwentwater	10	12	*BOCS (2) 4*
(5)	National Trust for Scotland, Glenfinnan	10	12	*BOCS Sp 4*
(6)	National Trust for Scotland, St. Kilda	10	12	*BOCS Sp 5*
(7)	National Trust, Stackpole Head	10	8	*Benham(s)*
(8)	National Trust, Giants Causeway	10	8	*Benham(s)*
(9)	N.T. Leicester, Sir Robert Shirley's Church	10	20	*LFDC 10*
(10)	Oakham Castle, 800 Years, Rutland	10	35	*Oakham Castle*
(11)	Lingholm Gardens, Open Day, Keswick	10	20	*Hawkwood*
(12)	Geology of Causeway Coast, Nottingham	10	35	*Bradbury*
(13)	Robin Hood Society, Nottingham Castle	10	30	*Bradbury*
(14)	St. Kilda, 25 Years BF 1750 PS	10	25	*BFPS*
(15)	The N.T. Scotland, Charlecote, Warwick	10	30	*Charlecote*

National Trusts (contd.)

	ordinary covers	official covers	
(16) London International Stamp Centre, WC2	10	15	*Stamp Centre*
(17) Lyke Wake Walk, BF 1739 PS	10	15	*RFDC 4*
(18) Friends of the Earth, Olympia W14	10	15	*Havering 18*
(19) Jaguar Drivers Club, 1956-1981, Luton	15	25	*Jaguar DC*
(20) Crane Schools Golden Jubilee, Nottingham	15	150	*Crane Sch.*
(21) Holkham Hall, Norfolk	15	15	*Markton*
(22) Lawn Tennis Museum, SW19	15	35	*Lawn Tennis*
(23) Christianity in Otley, Leeds	15	35	*Parish Church*
(24) June Philatelic Displays, British Library	15	45	*BL 27*
(25) Scottish Council for Spastics	15	225	*Spastics*
(26) ANTAR Service in BAOR, BF 1724 PS	15	30	*Army (s)*
(27) Humber Bridge Hull, Open to Traffic	25	270	*Scarboro'*
C.D.S. POSTMARKS			
(28) Alfriston – first building acquired by N.T.	25		
(29) Barmouth – first site acquired by N.T.	20		
(30) Buckland Monachorum – Buckland Abbey	25		
(31) Culross – first building/N.T. for Scotland	20		
(32) Glenfinnan, Stackpole, or Causeway Head	25		
(33) Tintagel – PO is National Trust property	25		
(34) Haslemere – Sir Robert Hunter (founder)	30		
(35) Lower Shiplake – Canon Rawnsley (founder)	30		
(36) Wisbech – b/place of Octavia Hill (founder)	30		
(37) Land's End & John O' Groats *pair*	95		

SLOGAN POSTMARKS *Bluebell Rly; Gawsworth Hall; Sandwich; The Pantiles; Hagley Hall. Prices from £75.*

22nd July 1981 – ROYAL WEDDING

14p, 25p Prince of Wales and Lady Diana Spencer

SPECIAL HANDSTAMPS			
(1) First Day of Issue – Philatelic Bureau	2	–	*Post Office*
(2) First Day of Issue – London EC	2	–	*Post Office*
(3) First Day of Issue – Caernarfon	2	–	*Post Office*
(4) Royal Wedding Celebrations, Leicester	8	15	*LFDC 11*
(5) Royal Wedding, Chingford Old Church	8	15	*Hawkwood*
(6) Royal Wedding, St. Paul's Cathedral	8	15	*Havering 19*
(7) Royal Wedding, Stamp Exhibition, Exeter	8	10	*Ex StampCentre*
(8) Royal Wedding, Cameo Stamp Centre	8	20	*Cameo*
(9) First Prince of Wales, Lincoln Cathedral	10	60	*Lin. Cath*
(10) Greetings from Watton-at-Stone, Hertford	10	60	*Watton Church*
(11) Prince of Wales & Lady Diana, Caernarfon	8	20	*BOCS (2) 6*
(12) Royal Wedding Greetings, Canterbury	10	–	*n.o.c.*
(13) Canoe 81/Royal Wedding, Nottingham	10	20	*Bradbury*
(14) RAF St. Clement Danes, BF 1932 PS	10	25	*RFDC 5*
(15) Royal Wedding, Althorp, Northampton	10	40	*Althorp*
(16) Loyal Greetings, Lullingstone Silk Farm	10	80	*Benham L1*
(17) St. Pauls, EC4 (changeable date)	10	40	*H.R.*
(18) East of England Show, Peterborough	10	35	*S.P.*
(19) Congratulations, Todd Scales, Cambridge	10	50	*Todd Scales*
(20) Royal Tournament, BF 1805 PS	10	25	*BFPS*
(21) Mayors Charity, City of Exeter	10	20	*ExMayor*
(22) Centenary Postcard, Cornhill P.O., Ipswich	10	25	*Corn'l p.card*
(23) Keswick/National Trust	10	–	*n.o.c.*
(24) South Lakeland/National Trust	15	–	*n.o.c.*
(25) July Philatelic Displays, British Library, WC	10	30	*BL 28*
(26) East Midlands CBI, Head P.O., Leicester	10	–	*n.o.c.*
(27) Lifeboat Week 1981, Lyme Regis	10	25	*Pilgrim*
(28) Gredington Jamboree, Whitchurch	20	175	*Jamboree*
(29) Port Sunlight, Liverpool	10	50	*Lever Bros*
(30) Windsor, Berks	10	–	*n.o.c.*
ORDINARY F.D.I. POSTMARKS			
(31) Chester – Prince Charles is Earl of Chester	15		
(32) Gloucestershire (Highgrove House cover)	25		
(33) King's Lynn (Sandringham special cover)	30		
(34) Windsor	15		
C.D.S. POSTMARKS			
(35) Buckingham Palace or Windsor Castle	175		
(36) Great Brington	100		
(37) House of Commons or Lords	25		
(38) Prince Charles Ave or Prince of Wales Ave	25		
(39) Princetown	35		
(40) Romsey, Tetbury or Buckingham Gate	35		

Also: Caernarfon, Charlestown, Dartmouth, Diss, Duffus, Highgrove, Sevenoaks, Spencers Wood, St. Paul's, Trinity St. From £20.

SLOGAN POSTMARKS	
(41) Prince Charles/Lady Diana, IoM Crowns	30
(42) Exhibition of Royal Pagentry, Hagley Hall	75
(43) Royal Westminster Exhibition	100

In addition: The Pantiles. £25.

*NOTE: **Double dated covers** exist with 22 July handstamp and 29 July (Wedding Day) handstamp. Each handstamp cancelling both stamps.* ***Prices from £20***
*In addition, **triple dated covers** were serviced with 22 July, 28 July (Wedding Fireworks) and 29 July (Wedding Day) handstamps. Each handstamp cancelling both stamps.* ***Prices from £30***

PRICES & CONDITION
Values should be taken as a guide, and are for covers in good clean condition with the full set of stamps.

12th August 1981 - DUKE OF EDINBURGH'S AWARD

14p Expeditions; 18p Skills; 22p Service; 25p Recreation

		ordinary covers £	official covers £	
SPECIAL HANDSTAMPS				
(1)	First Day of Issue - Philatelic Bureau	2	-	*Post Office*
(2)	First Day of Issue - London W2	2	-	*Post Office*
(3)	Duke of Edinburgh's Award, Belfast	8	25	*Cotswold*
(4)	Duke of Edinburgh's Award, Cardiff	8	25	*Cotswold*
(5)	Duke of Edinburgh's Award, Edinburgh	8	25	*Cotswold*
(6)	Duke of Edinburgh's Award, EC4	8	25	*Cotswold*
(7)	Duke of Edinburgh's Award, SW1	8	25	*Cotswold*
(8)	Duke of Edinburgh's Award, Devon	8	15	*Devon DoEAS*
(9)	Duke of Edinburgh's Award, Winchmore Hill	8	10	*Havering 20*
(10)	RAF Canadian Rockies, BF 1740 PS	8	15	*RFDC 6*
(11)	Duke of Edinburgh's Award, Hull	8	25	*HullDoEAS*
(12)	Leics Girl Guides Association	8	10	*LFDC 12*
(13)	August Philatelic Displays, British Library	10	40	*BL 29*
(14)	Royal Mail House, Wakefield	10	40	*Wakefield*
(15)	Cardiff Searchlight Tattoo, BF 1747 PS	10	45	*BFPS*
(16)	Stoke Mandeville Games, Aylesbury	8	15	*Hawkwood*
(17)	Military Tattoo,Edinburgh	10	40	*M Tattoo*
(18)	Keswick/National Trust	10	-	*n.o.c.*
(19)	South Lakeland/National Trust	10	-	*n.o.c.*
(20)	Royal Wedding, St. Pauls Cathedral, EC4	10	75	*H.R.*
C.D.S. POSTMARKS				
(21)	Buckingham Palace or Windsor Castle	100		
(22)	Balmoral Castle	150		
(23)	Pathfinder Village, Exeter	20		

Also: Calshot, Duffus, Dukestown, Edinburgh, Gateshead, Holyrood, Hse of Lords, Okehampton, Phillipstown. From £15

SLOGAN POSTMARKS			
(24)	Duke of Edinburgh's Award Crowns	25	

Also: Cardiff Tattoo; Highland Games; Royal Westminster Exhib. Prices from £25

23rd September 1981 - FISHING

14p Cockle dredging; 18p Hauling in a Trawl Net; 22p Lobster Potting; 25p Hoisting a Seine Net

SPECIAL HANDSTAMPS				
(1)	First Day of Issue - Philatelic Bureau	2	-	*Post Office*
(2)	First Day of Issue - Hull	2	-	*Post Office*
(3)	Catch '81, Falmouth	8	30	*Catch '81*
(4)	Manchester Weather Centre	8	15	*Dawn*
(5)	Mission Deep Sea Fishermen, Aberdeen	8	10	*BOCS (2) 5*
(6)	Heart of Scotland's Fishing Industry, Buckie	8	25	*Fish.Mut.Ass.*
(7)	Fishing Fleets of Brixham	8	200	*Pandora Press*
(8)	Leics. Amalgamated Society of Anglers	8	25	*LFDC 13*
(9)	Centuries of Trading, Billingsgate, EC3	8	25	*Hawkwood*
(10)	Ocean Tapestry, BF 1741 PS, St. Mawgan	8	25	*RFDC 7*
(11)	Fishmonger's Company, EC4	8	15	*S. Petty 1*
(12)	Sept. Philatelic Displays, British Library	10	35	*BL 30*
(13)	Transporter Bridge, Newport	10	85	*Newport BC*
(14)	Langley Grammar School, Slough	10	75	*Langley Sch*
ORDINARY F.D.I. POSTMARKS				
(15)	Grimsby or any other fishing port FDI *each*	10		
C.D.S. POSTMARKS				
(16)	Lighthouse. Fleetwood	50		
(17)	Six Bells or The Wharf *each*	35		

Also: Crab Lane, Dousland, Eyemouth, Fisherie Turriff, Fisherow, Fisher's Pond, Fishpool, Fishguard, Fleetwood, The Harbour, Hull, Milford Haven, Stafford, St. Peter's St., The Salmon Leap, Whale Hill, Whiting Bay. Prices from £15 each.

SLOGAN POSTMARKS			
(18)	Hastings/Resort for all seasons (depicts boat)	60	

In addition: Visit Sandwich. Price from £35

18th November 1981 - CHRISTMAS

11½p, 14p,18p, 22p, 25p Childrens Paintings

SPECIAL HANDSTAMPS				
(1)	First Day of Issue - Philatelic Bureau	2	-	*Post Office*
(2)	First Day of Issue - Bethlehem	2	-	*Post Office*
(3)	Children First Canterbury	8	10	*BOCS (2) 8*
(4)	Children's Christmas Book Show Blackwells	8	30	*Hawkwood*
(5)	Friends of Leicester Cathedral	8	25	*LFDC 14*
(6)	Church of St. Mary-at-Hill, EC3	8	20	*S. Petty 2*
(7)	Stamp Magazine Link House, Croydon	8	5	*Benham(s)*
(8)	Happy Xmas from Big C Appeal Norwich	8	25	*Big C Appeal*
(9)	Princess of Wales Regent St., W1	8	10	*Havering 22*
(10)	Pillar Box Postcards - Preston	20	-	*n.o.c.*
(11)	Pillar Box Postcards - Oldham	20	-	n.o.c.
(12)	Pillar Box Postcards - Manchester	20	-	*n.o.c.*
(13)	Pillar Box Postcards - Blackpool	20	-	*n.o.c.*
(14)	Nov. Philatelic, Displays British Library	10	45	*BL 31*
(15)	England v. Hungary, Wembley	10	45	*Dawn*
C.D.S. POSTMARKS				
(16)	Bethlehem or Nasareth *each*	25		

Christmas (contd.)

		ordinary covers £	official covers £	
(17)	Rhoose, Ramridge, Clutton, Horsham or Fulwood – homes of stamp designers	20		

Also: Angel Hill, Holy Island, Kings Road, Star, Starcross, St. Nicholas, Trinity. Prices from £10

10th February 1982 – CHARLES DARWIN

15½p Giant Tortoises; 19½p Iguanas; 26p Finch; 29p Skulls

SPECIAL HANDSTAMPS

(1)	First Day of Issue – Philatelic Bureau	2	–	*Royal Mail*
(2)	First Day of Issue – Shrewsbury	2	–	*Royal Mail*
(3)	Darwin Centenary, RSPB, Sandy	8	25	*R.S.P.B.*
(4)	Maer Hall Tribute to Charles Darwin	8	150	*Maer Hall*
(5)	Charles Darwin 1809-1882, Slimbridge	8	10	*BOCS(2)9*
(6)	Charles Darwin 1809-1882, Cambridge	8	10	*BOCS(2)9*
(7)	Charles Darwin 1809-1882, Shrewsbury	8	10	*BOCS(2)9*
(8)	Down House, Charles Darwin Memorial	8	15	*S. Petty 3*
(9)	Charles Darwin, Westminster Abbey, SW1	8	15	*Hawkwood*
(10)	Voyage of HMS Beagle, Plymouth	8	10	*BLS 1*
(11)	Man of Vision, London, SW7	8	10	*Havering 23*
(12)	HMS Beagle, BF 1762 PS	8	15	*RFDC 9*
(13)	1809-1882 Charles Darwin Centenary, NW1	8	35	*London Zoo*
(14)	Leicester University Jubilee Year	10	15	*LFDC 15*
(15)	February Philatelic Displays, British Library	10	40	*BL 32*
(16)	Valentines at Harrods, SW1	10	75	*Pilgrim*

C.D.S. POSTMARKS

(17)	Downe – Darwin's home or The Lizard	15		
(18)	Frankwell – near to Darwin's birthplace	30		

Also: Atcham, Falmouth, Frog Island, Oxford, Piltdown, Sandown, Shrewsbury, Slimbridge, Stonehouse, Whipsnade. From £12

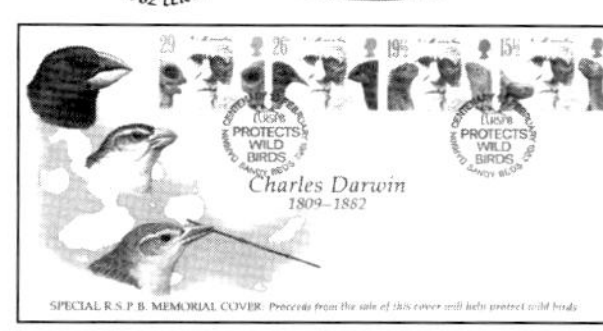

24th March 1982 – YOUTH ORGANISATIONS

15½p Boys' Brigade; 19½p Girls' Brigade; 26p Scouts; 29p Girl Guides

SPECIAL HANDSTAMPS

(1)	First Day of Issue – Philatelic Bureau	2	–	*Royal Mail*
(2)	First Day of Issue – Glasgow	2	–	*Royal Mail*
(3)	First Day of Issue – London SW	2	–	*Royal Mail*
(4)	St. Mary's 8th Hendon, NW4	8	20	*Havering 24*
(5)	Year of the Scout Celebrations, Peterborough	8	40	*Peteb. Scouts*
(6)	Lord Baden Powell, Westminster Abbey	8	15	*Hawkwood*
(7)	Loughborough, Year of Scout	8	25	*Loughb. Scouts*
(8)	Scout Movement W. Europe, BF 1742 PS	8	50	*Forces*
(9)	75th Anniversary of Scouting, Glasgow	8	40	*Glasgow Scouts*
(10)	Scouting for Boys, Baden-Powell House	8	35	*Scouts Council*
(11)	75th Anniversary of Scouting, Caterham	8	35	*Cat'm Scouts*
(12)	The Girls Brigade, SW6	8	12	*BOCS (2) 10b*
(13)	Girl Guides Association, SW1	8	20	*Cotswold*
(14)	First for Boys, SW6	8	15	*BOCS (2) 10a*
(15)	Young Enterprise, Folkestone	8	45	*S. Kent Coll.*
(16)	National Association of Youth Clubs	8	30	*Bradbury*
(17)	National Youth Bureau, Leicester	8	20	*LFDC 16*
(18)	1982 (Huyton) Sqd ATC, BF 5282 PS	8	15	*RFDC 10*
(19)	St. Donats Castle, Llantwit Major	8	20	*S. Petty 4*
(20)	Yorkshire County Bowling Assoc., York	10	20	*Yorks CBA*
(21)	Motorway Sub P.O., Rank M6 Forton	15	120	*Rank M6*
(22)	First Postbus in Yorkshire, Masham	15	–	*n.o.c.*
(23)	Four Marks Golden Jubilee, Alton	10	65	*FourMarksPO*
(24)	March Philatelic Displays, British Library	10	35	*BL 33*
(25)	Norwich Union, Mail Coach to Rayleigh	10	75	*Norwich Un.*
(26)	Daily Mail, Ideal Home, Earls Court, SW5	10	70	*Pilgrim*

ORDINARY F.D.I. POSTMARKS

(27)	Sunderland (Sunderland Scouts cover)	25		

C.D.S. POSTMARKS

(28)	Bentley, Euston, Paddington or House of Lords	20		
(29)	Fleur-de-lis – the scout's emblem	95		
(30)	Guide, Pathfinder Village or The Camp	25		
(31)	West Hampstead – girl guide on 29p value	25		

Also: Chingford, Pinkneys Road, Poole, Sandbanks, Southead, Scout Hill, Thurso. From £10.

SLOGAN POSTMARKS

(32)	Scouts help others – Chingford (Gilwell Park)	25		
(33)	Scouts help others – any other office	15		

28th April 1982 – BRITISH THEATRE

15½p Ballet; 19½p Harlequin; 26p Drama; 29p Opera

SPECIAL HANDSTAMPS

(1)	First Day of Issue – Philatelic Bureau	2	–	*Royal Mail*
(2)	First Day of Issue – Stratford-upon-Avon	2	–	*Royal Mail*
(3)	John Gay, Westminster Abbey	8	15	*Hawkwood*
(4)	Royal Shakespeare Theatre, Stratford	8	15	*BOCS (2) 11*
(5)	Royal Opera House, Covent Garden	8	7	*BLS 3*
(6)	Arts Theatre, Cambridge	10	45	*Arts Theatre*
(7)	Theatre Royal Restoration, Bath	10	30	*Cotswold*
(8)	Queens Theatre, Hornchurch	10	15	*Havering 25*
(9)	Tavistock Repertory Co., London N1	10	30	*Tav. Rep.*
(10)	Leicester Drama Society	10	50	*LFDC 17*

Theatre (contd.)

	ordinary covers £	official covers £	
(11) Theatre Royal, Norwich	10	45	*Th. Royal*
(12) Mercury Theatre, Colchester	10	45	*Mercury Th.*
(13) Shakespeare, Southwark Cathedral, SE1	10	15	*S. Petty 5*
(14) New Theatre, Hull	10	45	*New Theatre*
(15) Worthing Operatic Society	10	35	*S.P.*
(16) Barbican Centre, EC2	10	50	*Barbican*
(17) S.C.D.A., Pitlochry	10	60	*S.C.D.A.*
(18) Theatr Clwyd, Ebrill, Yr Wyddgrug, Mold	25	–	*n.o.c.*
(19) William Shakespeare, Stratford	15	–	*n.o.c.*
(20) Royal Air Force Central Band, BF 1773 PS	10	20	*RFDC 11*
(21) Rating & Valuation Association, SW1	10	60	*Bradbury*
(22) Queen Victoria's Visit of Epping Forest	15	35	*Hawkwood*
ORDINARY F.D.I. POSTMARKS			
(23) Basingstoke (Horseshoe Theatre Co. cover)	40		
(24) Bury St Edmunds (Threatre Royal cover)	40		
(25) Northampton (Royal Theatre cover)	40		
(26) Leeds (Grand Theatre cover)	60		
(27) Swindon (Wyvern Theatre card)	40		
C.D.S. POSTMARKS			
(28) Barnstaple – birthplace of John Gay	15		
(29) Ben Jonson Road or Shakespeare St	25		
(30) Great Yarmouth – first theatre	10		
(31) Stratford-upon-Avon	15		
(32) The Harlequin – harlequin (19½p)	25		

Also: Aldeburgh, Amesbury, Barbican, Bishopgate, Blackfriars, Broadway, Globe Road, Hereford, Macduff, Shoreditch, Stafford, The Circle. Prices from £10.

SLOGAN POSTMARKS		
(33) Eden Court – The Theatre of the Highlands	30	
(34) Dickens Festival – Rochester	90	

Also: Dunfermline Festival; Congleton Carnival. Aldershot Army Display. Prices from £30.

16th June 1982 – MARITIME HERITAGE

15½p Henry VIII; 19½p Blake; 24p Nelson; 26p Fisher; 29p Cunningham

	ordinary covers £	official covers £	
SPECIAL HANDSTAMPS			
(1) First Day of Issue – Philatelic Bureau	3	–	*Royal Mail*
(1a) -do- with PhilexFrance'82 Paris cachet	10	–	*Royal Mail*
(2) First Day of Issue – Portsmouth	3	–	*Royal Mail*
(3) Birthplace of Nelson, Burnham Thorpe	10	30	*Hawkwood*
(4) National Maritime Museum, Greenwich	10	12	*BLS 4*
(5) Lloyds Register of Shipping, EC3	10	45	*S. Petty 6*
(6) Maritime Heritage, Lloyds, EC3	10	45	*Cotswold*
(7) Britannia's Maritime Heritage, Dartmouth	10	90	*B.R.N.C.*
(8) Maritime Heritage Stamp Exhibition, Exeter	10	25	*Exeter Cvrs*
(9) Maritime England Year, Poole	10	60	*Poole Mar Tr*
(10) Nottinghamshire Lifeboat Appeal	10	20	*Pilgrim*
(11) Axe Valley Maritime 82, Seaton	10	75	*Fire Ser NBF*
(12) WeymouthChamber of Commerce	10	60	*Ch. of Comm.*
(13) Capt Matthew Flinders, Port Lincoln	10	90	*LincolnCath2*
(14) Cook's Endeavour Salutes Nelson's Victory	10	20	*B. Travers*
(15) Maritime Heritage Cruise, Penarth	10	20	*Post Office*
(16) Missions to Seamen, Stratford	10	50	*Eng. T. Board*
(17) Historic Ships, St. Katherines Dock, E1	10	20	*Havering 26*
(18) Missions to Seamen, Portsmouth	10	50	*S.P.*
(19) Cinque Ports Exhibition, Dover	10	65	*Cinque Ports*
(20) Mountbatten Memorial Trust, Broadlands	10	12	*S. Petty 7*
(21) Leicester Sea Cadets	10	30	*LFDC 18*
(22) RAF Marine Branch, BF 1779 PS	10	30	*RFDC 12*
(23) Peru Hovercraft Expedition, BF 1956 PS	10	45	*Forces*
(24) Worshipful Co. of Shipwrights, EC	10	10	*BOCS (2) 12*
(25) Centenary Forces Postal Service, BF 8282 PS	10	25	*Forces*
(26) Trafalgar Sq. Philatelic Counter	12	–	*n.o.c.*
(27) Philatelic Counter Opening, Coventry	12	–	*n.o.c.*
(28) Royal Shakespeare, Barbican, EC2	12	250	*Barbican*
ORDINARY F.D.I. POSTMARKS			
(29) Exeter (Exeter Maritime special cover)	40		
(30) Any other FDI on special maritime covers	40		
C.D.S. POSTMARKS			
(31) Bridgwater – birthplace of Blake	10		
(32) Buckingham Palace, S.W.1	75		
(33) Burnham Thorpe – birthplace of Nelson	20		
(34) Castle Rd. Southsea – Mary Rose	20		
(35) Devonport or Naval Barracks, Chatham	25		
(36) Falkland or Victory Street, Devonport	30		
(37) Flotta, Orkney – Scapa Flow (Home Fleet)	20		
(38) Fleet Mail Office Portsmouth or Devonport	35		
(39) Greenwich, London S.E.10	15		
(40) House of Lords, SW1	25		
(41) Marazion – b/place of Sandy Woodward	25		
(42) Nelson, Portsmouth or Trafalgar	20		
(43) The Quarterdeck or Westward Ho!	15		

Also: Blakes Corner, Blake Street, Bridgwater, Britannia, The Chart, Clyde Submarine Base, Cunningham Crescent, Dartmouth, Deptford High Street, The Docks (Bridgwater), Fisher's Pond, Fleet, Henry St., Marton-in-Cleveland, Nelson (Lancs), Portsmouth, Portsmouth Dock Yard, St. Andrew's Cross (Plymouth), Tavistock. From £10.

Maritime (contd.)

	ordinary covers	official covers
SLOGAN POSTMARKS	£	£
(44) See the Tall Ships in Southampton	45	
(45) Maritime Bristol	70	
(46) Tower Bridge Open to the Public	75	

23rd July 1982 - BRITISH TEXTILES

15½p 'Strawberry Thief' (Morris); 19½p 'Scarlet Tulips' (Steiner); 26p 'Cherry Orchard' (Nash); 29p 'Chevrons' (Foster)

SPECIAL HANDSTAMPS

(1) First Day of Issue - Philatelic Bureau	3	-	*Royal Mail*
(2) First Day of Issue - Rochdale	3	-	*Royal Mail*
(3) William Morris, Water House, E17	10	15	*Hawkwood*
(4) Sir Richard Arkwright, Preston	10	12	*BOCS (2) 13*
(5) Hockley Mill, Nottingham	10	15	*Cotswold (g)*
(6) Textile Institute, Manchester	10	15	*Pilgrim*
(7) School of Textiles, Leicester	10	50	*Bradbury*
(8) Textile Exhibition, Bradford	10	15	*Peter Scot*
(9) Leek, Centre of Textile Industry	10	80	*Staffs C.C.*
(10) Textile Design, Huddersfield Polytechnic	10	70	*Hudd.Poly*
(11) Textiles on Stamps, Liberty, W1	10	12	*BLS 5*
(12) Coldharbour Mill, Uffculme	10	70	*Coldhbr. Mill*
(13) Leicester & District Knitting Industry	10	50	*LFDC 19*
(14) Royal School of Needlework, SW7	10	15	*S. Petty 8*
(15) No.2 Squadron RAF Regiment, BF 1781 PS	10	20	*RFDC 13*
(16) Arkwright Anniv., Cromford Mills, Matlock	10	30	*Ark. Soc.*
(17) British Philatelic Federation, Southampton	10	20	*B.P.F.*
(18) European Floral City, Exeter	10	30	*Exeter C.C.*
(19) Papal Visits in Philately, SW1	10	45	*Bradbury*
(20) Royal Tournament, BF 1840 PS	10	35	*Forces*
(21) International Scout Camp, Blair Atholl	10	35	*Scot Scouts*
(22) Life Boat Week, Lyme Regis	10	25	*Pilgrim*
(23) Open Days, RNLI HQ, Poole	10	25	*Pilgrim*
(24) Caldey Island, Pope John Paul, Wales	10	35	*Caldey Isl.*

C.D.S. POSTMARKS

(25) Cherry Orchard or Silk Street	15
(26) Forest Rd., E17 - b/place of Wm. Morris	10
(27) Hall-ith-Wood - later named Spinning Mule	25
(28) Hammersmith W6 - home of Wm. Morris	10
(29) Preston - birthplace of Richard Arkwright	10
(30) Stanhill - James Hargreaves 'Spinning Jenny'	15
(31) Walthamstow, E17 - b/place of Wm. Morris	9

Also: All Saints (Derby), Arkwright Town, Axminster, Bobbers Mill, Coat, Coggeshall, Cotton Tree, Draperstown, Fair Isle, Harris, Lechlade, Merton, Milltown, New Invention, Shaftesbury,Tweed Rd, Weaver Lodge, Wilton, Wool, Worstead. Prices from £10 each.

SLOGAN POSTMARKS *Collect British Stamps, Hull. £15.*

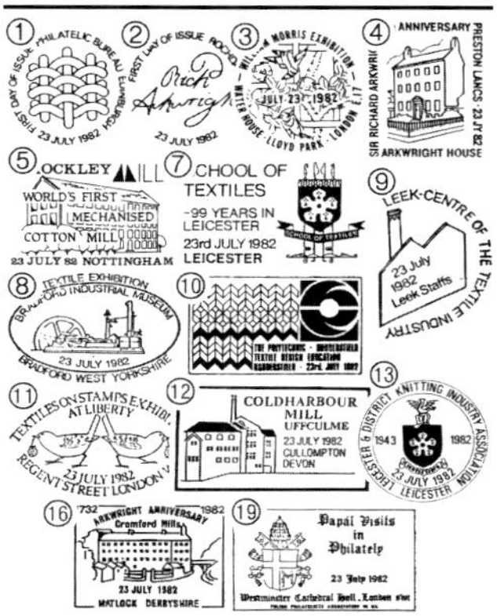

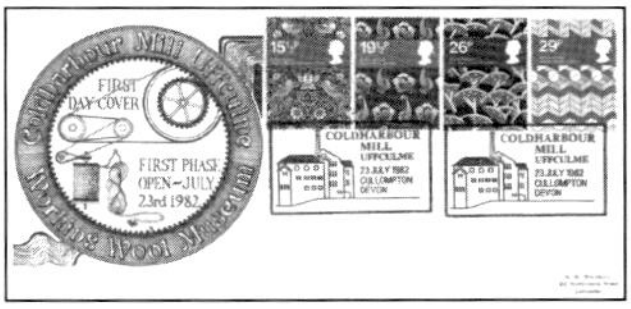

8th September 1982 - INFORMATION TECHNOLOGY

15½p History of Communications; 26p Technology Today

SPECIAL HANDSTAMPS

(1) First Day of Issue - Philatelic Bureau	2	-	*Royal Mail*
(2) First Day of Issue - London WC	2	-	*Royal Mail*
(3) Intelpost Head Post Office, E1	8	15	*Hawkwood*
(4) Computertown, Croydon	10	50	*Croy. Lib.*
(5) World Trade Centre	10	10	*Havering 28*
(6) Information Technology Year, Bedford	10	55	*Texas Instr.*
(7) RAF Supply Centre, BF 1787 PS	10	15	*RFDC 14*
(8) Best of Prestel, Martlesham	10	12	*Prestel*
(9) Artificial Earth Satellites, Jodrell Bank	10	12	*BLS 6*
(10) Information Technology UMIST, Manchester	10	12	*BOCS (2) 14*
(11) University of Leicester	10	25	*LFDC 20*
(12) Ashville College, Computer Age, Harrogate	10	-	*n.o.c.*
(13) Exercise British Prince, 82 BF 1882 PS	10	15	*Forces*
(14) Anaesthesiology, Royal Festival Hall, SE1	10	25	*Assoc Anaesth*
(15) 1982 Museum of the Year, Stoke	10	25	*Stoke Museum*
(16) Military Tattoo, Edinburgh	10	45	*Mil. Tattoo*
(17) Trishaw Marathon, Kent Fire Brigade	10	35	*Kent Fire B.*
(18) King's Cup Air Race, BF 1788 PS	10	55	*MosqMus.*

ORDINARY F.D.I. POSTMARKS

(19) London EC (Orbital Test Satellite/FT cover)	35
(20) Norwich (Hotel Norwich IT82 Exhib. cover)	35

C.D.S. POSTMARKS

(21) Helston, Mawgan, Mullion-Goonhilly Downs	10
(22) Martlesham - British Telecom Research	20
(23) New Invention, Willenhall	10

In addition: Bean, Bletchley, Bracknell, Caversham, Cheltenham, Edinburgh, Felixstowe, Helensburg, Lovelace Rd Mount Pleasant, National Insurance Blgs (Newcastle), Newton St (Manchester), Oldland Common, Oxford, The Rocket, Rosetta, South Kensington, Stock Exchange, Taunton,Telephone House, Totnes, Walworth Road. Prices from £10.

SLOGAN POSTMARKS

(24) Post Code It, Norwich	25

Also: Radio Gwent; Beat Crime Dial 999; Collect British Stamps; any Postcode slogans. From £15.

PLEASE READ THE GENERAL NOTES
These often provide the answers to enquiries received

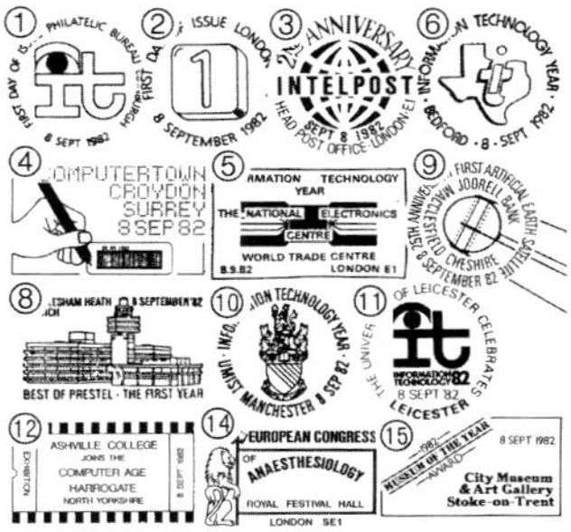

13th October 1982 - BRITISH MOTOR CARS

15½p Metro & Austin Seven;
19½p Ford Escort & Model T;
26p Jaguar XJ6 & SS1; 29p Rolls-Royce Silver Spirit & Silver Ghost

SPECIAL HANDSTAMPS

		ordinary covers £	official covers £	
(1)	First Day of Issue - Philatelic Bureau	3	-	*Royal Mail*
(2)	First Day of Issue - Birmingham	3	-	*Royal Mail*
(3)	First Day of Issue - Crewe	3	-	*Royal Mail*
(4)	National Motor Museum, Beaulieu	10	20	*Beaulieu*
(5)	Metro, World Trade Centre, E1	10	15	*Havering 29*
(6)	Year of the Car, Woodford Green	10	130	*Havering*
(7)	Millionth New Ford Escort, Halewood	10	25	*Ford*
(8)	Nuffield College, Oxford	10	25	*Univ. Covers*
(9)	Royal Flying Corps, BF 1789 PS	10	25	*RFDC 15*
(10)	Worshipful Company of Coachmakers	10	25	*S. Petty 10*
(11)	Ford Sierra, Launch Day, Chippenham	10	150	*Cotswold*
(12)	Cycle & Car Museum, Stanford Hall	10	25	*LFDC 21*
(13)	Austin 7, Brooklands, Weybridge	10	10	*BLS 7*
(14)	Transport Centenary, Chesterfield	10	20	*Dawn*
(15)	Heritage Collection, Syon Park, Brentford.	10	20	*Hawkwood*
(16)	Dagenham, Home of Ford	10	25	*Dag. Motors*
(17)	Sixty Years of Jaguar Cars, Coventry	10	15	*BOCS (2) 15*
(18)	35 Years of Silverstone Circuit	10	35	*Silverstone*
(19)	Rolls-Royce Enthusiasts', Paulerspury	10	40	*Bradbury*
(20)	Wiltshire Radio, Wootton Bassett	10	75	*Wilts Radio*
(21)	Tile Hill Wood School, Coventry	10	75	*Tile Hill*

ORDINARY F.D.I. POSTMARKS

(22)	Manchester - where Rolls met Royce	15	

C.D.S. POSTMARKS

(23)	Amersham - b/place of Sir Herbert Austin	20	
(24)	Alwalton - birthplace of Henry Royce	25	
(25)	Austin, Plymouth	20	
(26)	Brighton & Knightsbridge - car rally	20	*pair*
(27)	Dagenham - Dagenham Motors (Ford)	20	
(28)	Dover Paquebot - car ferry	20	
(29)	Foleshill - original Jaguar SS production	20	
(30)	Ford, Liverpool or Shrewsbury	25	
(31)	Halewood or Longbridge	25	
(32)	Leyland - birthplace of Leyland Motors	25	
(33)	Mount Street, W1 - b/place of Charles Rolls .	20	
(34)	N.E.C. Birmingham - Motor Show	75	
(35)	R.A.C. London SW1	525	
(36)	Rank Forton Services - first motorway PO	60	
(37)	Trafford Park - U.K. assembly for Model T	40	

Also: Allesley, Battery, Beaulieu, Bentley, Crewe, Dunlop, Fender, Hulme, Lanchester, Lewisham, Milton, Rockfield, Saltley, Silverstone, Sparkbrook (Birmingham), St. James' St., Tooting, Vauxhall, Walthamstow. From £15.

SLOGAN POSTMARKS

(41)	Hella of Banbury, Motor Show	55	

17th November 1982 - CHRISTMAS

12½p, 15½p, 19½p, 26p, 29p Christmas Carols

SPECIAL HANDSTAMPS

		ordinary covers £	official covers £	
(1)	First Day of Issue - Philatelic Bureau	3	-	*Royal Mail*
(2)	First Day of Issue - Bethlehem	3	-	*Royal Mail*
(3)	We Three Kings, Star, Glenrothes	8	10	*BLS 8*
(4)	I Saw Three Ships, Hythe	8	10	*BOCS (2) 16*
(5)	Good King Wenceslas, Salisbury	8	10	*Benham*
(6)	Seasons Greetings, Norwich Cathedral	8	25	*Nor. Cath.*
(7)	Seasons Greetings, Cutty Sark, SE10	8	10	*Havering 30*
(8)	Salvation Army, Leicester	8	25	*LFDC 22*
(9)	Christmas Carol, Dickens House, WC1	8	25	*Hawkwood*
(10)	St. John Ambulance, Leicester	8	35	*St. John Am.*
(11)	Sir Christopher Wren, East Knoyle	8	20	*S. Petty 11*
(12)	1st Highams Park Girl Guides, E4	8	30	*Girls Brig.*
(13)	North Atlantic Assembly, SW	10	-	*n.o.c.*
(14)	HMS Brilliant, Freedom of Tunbridge Wells	10	80	*H.R.*

C.D.S. POSTMARKS

(15)	Bethlehem or Nasareth	25	

In addition: Chipping Campden, East Grinstead, Fleet Street, Holly Bank, Hollybush, Holy Island, Holytown, Ivy Bush, Ivychurch, Kingsway, Kingsworthy, London SE1, Noel Road, Orient Road, St. Erth, St. Nicholas, St. Stephen, Shepherds Hill, Shepherdswell, Star, Starcross, Theobalds Road BO, Three Kingham. From £10.

26th January 1983 - BRITISH RIVER FISH

15½p Salmon; 19½p Pike; 26p Trout; 29p Perch

SPECIAL HANDSTAMPS

		ordinary covers £	official covers £	
(1)	First Day of Issue - Philatelic Bureau	2	-	*Royal Mail*
(2)	First Day of Issue - Peterborough	2	-	*Royal Mail*
(3)	Fishing the Teign, Newton Abbot	12	-	*Royal Mail*
(4)	Display of River Fish, Salisbury	12	-	*Royal Mail*
(5)	400 years of Fishing Tackle, Redditch	12	-	*Royal Mail*
(6)	British Waterways Board	12	15	*D. Taylor*
(7)	Cinque Ports Angling Society, Hythe	12	15	*BOCS (2) 17*
(8)	Pike Anglers Club, Norwich	12	40	*Pike Anglers*
(9)	London Anglers Association, E17	12	25	*Havering 1*

C.D.S. = CIRCULAR DATE STAMP
See General Notes for more details

River Fish (contd.)

		ordinary covers £	official covers £	
(10)	Izaak Walton, River Itchen, Winchester	12	20	*S. Petty 12*
(11)	RAF Stafford Angling Club, BF 1798 PS	12	30	*RFDC 17*
(12)	Tisbury Fish Farm, Romford	12	30	*Havering*
(13)	National Anglers Council, EC4	12	25	*NAC*
(14)	House of Hardy Exhibition, Pall Mall, SW1	12	25	*Hawkwood*
(15)	Return of the Salmon, Thames Water, EC	12	20	*Thames Water*
(16)	100 years of Salmon Fishing, Salmon Leap	12	10	*BLS (83) 1*
(17)	Douglas Bader Angling Club, Leicester	12	50	*Bradbury*
(18)	Birmingham Anglers Association	12	50	*Bradbury*
(19)	Izaak Walton Tercentenary, Stafford	12	60	*Staff. Museum*
(20)	Izaak Walton, 1593-1683, Stafford	12	15	*LFDC 23*
(21)	I.E.W. National Postal Museum	12	–	*n.o.c.*
C.D.S. POSTMARKS				
(22)	Fleet Street – 'The Compleat Angler'	20		
(23)	Itchen – Izaak Walton	20		
(24)	The Salmon Leap or Troutbeck	20		
(25)	Stafford – Izaak Walton's birthplace	20		
(26)	Walton, Stafford	25		
(27)	Winchester, Hants – Walton's burial place	25		

In addition: Alnwick, Angle, Bream, Coldstream, Fishbourne, Fishguard, Fishers Pond, Fishlake, Fishponds, Freshwater, Hook, Lochawe, Newton Solney, Norton Bridge, Oulton Broads, Pike Hill Pike Road, River, Potters Heigham, Romsey, Salmon Lane, Walton-on-Thames. From £15.

9th March 1983 – COMMONWEALTH

15½p Topical Island; 19½p Arid Desert; 26p Temperate Climate; 29p Mountains

SPECIAL HANDSTAMPS

(1)	First Day of Issue – Philatelic Bureau	2	–	*Royal Mail*
(2)	First Day of Issue – London SW	2	–	*Royal Mail*
(3)	Commonwealth Institute, W8	8	15	*LFDC 24*
(4)	Capt. Cook's Voyages of Discovery, Whitby	8	15	*B. Travers*
(5)	William Wilberforce, Hull	8	75	*Wilb. Council*
(6)	World Trade Centre, E1	8	15	*Havering 2*
(7)	Royal Commonwealth Society, WC2	8	15	*D. Taylor*
(8)	Romsey, Mahatma Gandhi, 1869-1948	8	15	*S. Petty 13*
(9)	No 24 Squadron, BF 1799 PS	8	25	*RFDC 18*
(10)	British Airways, London Airport W. Sussex	8	12	*BOCS (2) 18*
(11)	Geographical Magazine, London	8	20	*Hawkwood*
(12)	Association of Cricket Umpires, Leicester	10	75	*Assoc. C.U.*
(13)	Dunsmore Boy's School, Rugby	10	75	*Dunsmore Sch.*
(14)	Daily Mail Ideal Home Exhibition, SW	10	35	*Pilgrim*
(15)	Sixty years of Jaguar Cars, Coventry	8	7	*Benham*
C.D.S. POSTMARKS				
(16)	Buckingham Palace, S.W.1	80		
(17)	Gleneagles Hotel – 'Gleneagles Agreement'	50		
(18)	House of Commons or Lords	30		
(19)	Parliament Street BO. SW1	20		
(20)	Marldon – b/place of Sir Humphrey Gilbert	15		

Also: The Beach, Blantyre, Dartmouth, Falklands, Forest Town, Hull, India St., Kensington HIgh St High St, Marton-in-Cleveland, Melbourne, Mountain Ash, Queen Elizabeth Ave., Queen Victoria Rd, Romsey, Summit, Toronto,Windsor, Whitby. Prices from £10.

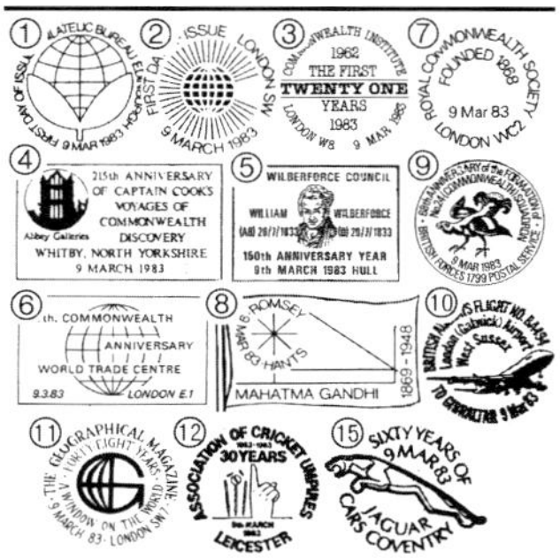

25th May 1983 – ENGINEERING

16p Humber Bridge; 20½p Thames Barrier; 28p Energy Support Vessel – Iolair

SPECIAL HANDSTAMPS

(1)	First Day of Issue – Philatelic Bureau	2	–	*Royal Mail*
(1a)	-do- with 'British Post Office Tembal' cachet	5	–	*Royal Mail*
(2)	First Day of Issue – Hull	2	–	*Royal Mail*
(3)	Institution of Civil Engineers, SW1	10	35	*LFDC 25*
(4)	Eng. Achievement, Thames Flood Barrier	10	20	*G & P*
(5)	CTH, Thames Flood Barrier, SE7	10	20	*Havering 3*
(6)	GLC Thames Barrier, Woolwich Reach	10	45	*Des. Enc.*
(7)	Engineering Achievements, AUEW, SE15	10	30	*AUEW*
(8)	British Shipbuilders lolair, SW7	10	10	*BOCS (2) 19*
(9)	BP Contribution lolair, Aberdeen	10	10	*BOCS (2) 19*
(10)	Technology to greater depths, UDI, Aberdeen.	10	20	*UDI*
(11)	Humber Bridge, Longest Single Span	10	15	*Hawkwood*
(12)	Humber Bridge, Opened 17 July 1981, Barton	10	10	*BLS (83) 3*
(13)	Institute of Mechanical Engineers, SW1	10	15	*Pilgrim*
(14)	Printing Shares the fruits of Human Genius	10	20	*Havering*
(15)	RAF Cosford, BF 1806 PS	10	25	*RFDC 19*
(16)	The Harrier, Kingston upon Thames	10	25	*S. Petty 14*
(17)	30 Years experience, Dan Air London Airport	10	15	*Benham*
(18)	Post Office Philatelic Counter, Grimsby	12	110	*Royal Mail*
(19)	Telecom Technology Showcase, EC4	12	–	*n.o.c.*
(20)	Chester-le-Street Co. Durham	12	35	*C. leS. Council*
(21)	The Wilberforce Council, Hull	12	45	*Wilb. Council*
(22)	Children's Hospital, Chippenham	12	45	*Rotary*
C.D.S. POSTMARKS				
(23)	Coalbrookdale – b/place of Ind. Revolution	15		
(24)	Eagle – 'Iolair' is gaelic for eagle	10		
(25)	Hessle & Barton – Humber Bridge *pair*	30		
(26)	Ironbridge – the world's first iron bridge	20		
(27)	New Bridge Road, Hull	20		

Engineering (contd.)

	ordinary covers £	official covers £
(28) Port Glasgow – 'Iolair' was built here	35	
(29) Silvertown & Woolwich – Barrier *pair*	20	
(30) Silvertown & Charlton – Barrier *pair*	20	

Also: Bacton, Bridge, Clydebank, Cleveland, Cruden Bay, Dundee, Hatfield, Langholm, Portsmouth, Rigside, Rotherham, Saltash, Stock Exchange, Telford. From £12.

SLOGAN POSTMARKS

(31) GLC Thames Barrier	25	
(32) Collect British Stamps Humberside	50	

In addition: Middlesbrough Philatelic Counter; Royal Mail Helping Business on Merseyside; World Communications Year. Prices from £20.

6th July 1983 - BRITISH ARMY

16p The Royal Scots; 20½ Royal Welch Fusiliers; 26p Royal Green Jackets; 28p Irish Guards; 31p Parachute Regiment

SPECIAL HANDSTAMPS

(1) First Day of Issue – Philatelic Bureau	3	–	*Royal Mail*
(2) First Day of Issue – Aldershot	3	–	*Royal Mail*
(3) Regimental Stamp Display, Glasgow	12	–	*Royal Mail*
(4) The British Army Series, BF 1983 PS	12	15	*Army*
(5) The Royal Scots, BF 0350 PS	12	35	*Army*
(6) The Royal Welch Fusiliers, BF 0294 PS	12	35	*Army*
(7) The Royal Greenjackets, BF 1800 PS	12	35	*Army*
(8) The Irish Guards, BF 1900 PS	12	35	*Army*
(9) The Parachute Regiment, BF 2000 PS	12	35	*Army*
(10) 75th Anniversary/TA in Wales, BF 1908 PS	12	50	*Forces*
(11) Rheindahlen Allied Marches, BF 1810 PS	12	60	*Forces*
(12) Royal Military Academy, Sandhurst	12	20	*G & P*
(13) Queen's Own Hussars, Warwick	12	35	*LFDC 26*
(14) Duke of York's Royal Military Sch. Dover	12	15	*BenL2*
(15) Blenheim Palace, Woodstock	12	20	*Havering 4*
(16) Soldier Print Soc., Worthing	12	45	*S.P.*
(17) National Army Museum 1971-1983, SW3	12	15	*BOCS (2) 20*
(18) Ensign Model Soldier Exhib., Boston	12	35	*Hawkwood*
(19) Duke of Edinburgh's Reg. Museum, Salisbury.	12	30	*S. Petty 15*
(20) Ancient Order of Foresters, Rugeley	15	60	*A.O.F.*
(21) Richard III 500th Anniv., Middleham	15	50	*R III Soc*
(22) Llangollen International Eisteddfod	15	150	*Eist'd*
(23) Telecom Technology Showcase, EC4	15	75	*Brit Tele*
(24) Royal Show, Kenilworth	15	–	*n.o.c.*

C.D.S. POSTMARKS

(25) Aldershot – Parachute Regiment HQ	15	
(26) Battle, or Battlefield *each*	12	
(27) Broadway, SW1 – Irish Guards Reg HQ	15	
(28) Buckingham Palace, SW1	75	
(29) Catterick Garrison, N Yorks	15	
(30) Duke of York's School, Dover – Military Sch.	20	
(31) Edinburgh – Royal Scots Regimental HQ	15	
(32) Hightown – Royal Welch Fusiliers Reg HQ	15	
(33) Marlborough, Wilts	15	
(34) Sandhurst – Royal Military Academy	15	
(35) Wilton, Salisbury – HQ UK Land Forces	15	
(36) Winchester – Royal Greenjackets Reg HQ	15	
(37) Army POs (Worthy Down, etc)	15	
(38) Any Field or Forces Post Office cancellations	20	

Also: Athelstaneford, Bannockburn, Barracks, Brunswick Road (Pirbright Camp), Bunkers Hill, Chelsea Royal Hospital, Falkland, Guard House, Gunhill, Huntingdon, Major's Green, Montgomery, Naseby, St. Andrews, Sentry Corner, Terriers, Tidworth, Waterloo, Wellington, Woodstock, Woolwich, York, Yorktown. Prices from £12.

SLOGAN POSTMARKS

(39) Join Territorial Army 75th Anniversary	525	
(40) National Army Museum – London SW	25	

ORDINARY or OFFICIAL COVERS?
See General Notes for more details

24th August 1983 - BRITISH GARDENS

16p Sissinghurst; 20½p Biddulph Grange; 28p Blenheim; 31p Pitmedden

SPECIAL HANDSTAMPS

(1) First Day of Issue – Philatelic Bureau	3	–	*Royal Mail*
(2) First Day of Issue – Oxford	3	–	*Royal Mail*
(3) Capability Brown at Bowood, Calne	12	–	*Royal Mail*
(4) Queen's Gardens, Croydon	12	75	*Croydon BC*
(5) Capability Brown, Kew Gardens	12	20	*LFDC 27*
(6) National Trust, Sissinghurst Castle	12	15	*BOCS (2) 21*
(7) League of Friends, The Grange, Biddulph	12	35	*League of F*
(8) Blenheim Palace, Woodstock	12	15	*Havering 5*
(9) National Trust for Scotland, Pitmedden	12	15	*BLS (83) 5*
(10) Capability Brown, Esher, Claremont	12	60	*Arlington*
(11) Roses in August, Syon Park, Brentford	12	15	*Hawkwood*
(12) Lancelot Capability Brown, Fenstanton	12	35	*Fenst Par Ch*
(13) National Trust for Scotland, Crathes Castle	12	12	*BenL4*
(14) National Trust, Lyme Park, Disley	12	15	*BenL3*
(15) Capability Brown, Kirkharle, Newcastle	12	35	*Landscape Ins.*
(16) Capability Brown, GRBS, Hampton Court	12	25	*S. Petty 16*
(17) Celebration of English Gardens, SW1	12	25	*DGT*
(18) RAF Gardens, Runnymede, BF 1814 PS	12	25	*RFDC 21*

Gardens (contd.)	ordinary covers £	official covers £	
(19) International camp, BB 83, Perth	12	90	*Boys Brig.*
(20) Military Tattoo Edinburgh	12	25	*Mil. Tattoo*
(21) Hornchurch Cricket Club	20	75	*H.C.C.*
C.D.S. POSTMARKS			
(22) Biddulph – featured on 20½p value	20		
(23) Botanic Gardens, Belfast	25		
(24) Fenstanton – Capability Brown buried here	20		
(25) Kew Gardens, Richmond	35		
(26) Kirkwhelpington – b/place Capability Brown	20		
(27) Mayfair, W1 – Capability Brown died here	20		
(28) Sissinghurst – featured on 16p value	20		
(29) Udny, Ellon – Pitmedden (31p)	20		
(30) Woodstock – Blenheim Palace (28p)	20		

In addition, covers are known with the following CDS pmks: Garden Suburb, Garden Village, Glamis,Harewood, Headstone Gardens, Petworth, Rake, Royal Hospital Chelsea, Sledmere, The Allotments, Trentham, Welwyn Garden City. Prices from £15.

SLOGAN POSTMARKS		
(31) Back Beautiful Britain	40	
(32) Chamber of Commerce – Devizes in Bloom	40	
(33) Your Garden Isle is Beautiful – Isle of Wight	40	
(34) Leicester City Show at Abbey Park	80	

In addition: Beautiful Bath. £30.

5th October 1983 – BRITISH FAIRS

16p Merry-go-round; 20½p Menageries and rides; 28p Side shows; 31p Early trade and produce fairs

SPECIAL HANDSTAMPS			
(1) First Day of Issue – Philatelic Bureau	3	–	*Royal Mail*
(2) First Day of Issue – Nottingham	3	–	*Royal Mail*
(3) St. Bartholomew the Great, EC	12	20	*Havering 6*
(4) Butchers Charitable Institution, EC1	12	15	*Hawkwood*
(5) Showmen's Guild, Staines	12	50	*S. Guild*
(6) Goose Fair, Tavistock	12	25	*S. Petty 17*
(7) Chipperfield's Circus, EC	12	15	*BLS (83) 6*
(8) NABMA (Markets Authority) Birmingham	12	20	*Des. Enc.*
(9) Fairfield, Croydon	12	35	*Fairfield*
(10) Turner's Northampton	12	12	*BOCS (2) 21*
(11) Goose Fair 1983, Nottingham	12	25	*LFDC 28*
(12) World's First Air Fair, BF 1815 PS	12	15	*RFDC 22*
(13) Rowell Lions, Rothwell, Kettering	12	40	*RothwellLions*
(14) British Philatelic Federation, Bath	12	20	*BPF*
(15) Samuel Pepys, Cambridge	12	20	*Univ. Covers*
(16) The Boys Brigade Centenary, Cardiff	12	60	*BB Wales*
(17) MMB (Milk Marketing Board) Newcastle	12	20	*MMB*
(17a) -do- spelling error: Newcastlf	–	125	*MMB (s)*
(18) Exhibition Garden City, Letchworth	12	–	*n.o.c.*
C.D.S. POSTMARKS			
(19) Borough High Street, S.E.1 – Southwark Fair	15		
(20) Cambridge or Chesterton – Sturbridge Fair	15		
(21) Horse Fair	15		
(22) London Chief Office – Bartholomew Fair	15		
(23) St. Giles, Oxford – largest surviving wake	20		
(24) Scarborough	15		
(25) Tavistock – Goose Fair	15		
(26) Widecombe-in-the-Moor	25		
(27) Winchester – Bishops Fair-oldest Charter Fair	15		

Also: Abingdon, Alford, Appleby-in-Westmorland, Barrus Bridge, Big Top, Brigg, Elephant & Castle, Exeter, Frome, Greenwich, Honiton, Hyson Green, King's Lynn, Marlborough, Market Sidmouth, Mayfair, North End, St. Ives, Stow-on-the-Wold, Stratford-upon-Avon, Ulverston, Warwick, Wookey Hole, Woodkirk, Yarm. Prices from £12 each.

SLOGAN POSTMARKS *Wonderland of Wales; Magnum World of Entertainment. From £85.*

16th November 1983 – CHRISTMAS

12½p, 16p, 20½p, 28p, 31p Peace and Goodwill

SPECIAL HANDSTAMPS			
(1) First Day of Issue – Philatelic Bureau	3	–	*Royal Mail*
(2) First Day of Issue – Bethlehem	3	–	*Royal Mail*
(3) Peace and Goodwill, Nasareth	10	25	*LFDC 29*
(4) Minster Gatehouse, Sheppey	10	25	*Hawkwood*
(5) Leicestershire Society for the Blind	10	5	*L. Blind Soc*
(6) Winchester Cathedral	10	15	*S. Petty 18*
(7) Peace on Earth, Peacehaven	10	10	*BLS (83) 7*
(8) St. Mary le Strand, WC2	10	15	*Havering 7*
(9) Telecom Technology Showcase, EC4	10	60	*Brit Tele*
(10) Lyminge Parish Church, Festival Year	10	10	*BOCS (2) 23*
(11) T.C. (Tandy Corporation), Walsall	15	200	*T.C.*
C.D.S. POSTMARKS			
(12) Bethlehem, Nasareth or Peacehaven	35		

Also: Birdsall, Blackbird Leys, Canterbury, Chapel, Chester-le-Street, Christchurch, Dovecot, Dove Holes, Dove House Lane, Holy Island, Kingsworthy, Minster, Quakers Rd., St. Augustine's, St. Nicholas, Star. Prices from £12.

SLOGAN POSTMARKS		
(13) Hastings, Resort for All Seasons (Xmas scene)	90	

In addition: Royal Mail Special Services, Hull. £30.

17th January 1984 - HERALDRY

16p College of Arms; 20½p Richard III; 28p The Earl Marshal; 31p City of London

	ordinary covers £	official covers £	
SPECIAL HANDSTAMPS			
(1) First Day of Issue - Philatelic Bureau	3	-	*Royal Mail*
(2) First Day of Issue - London EC	4	-	*Royal Mail*
(3) Heraldry Guildhall, City of London, EC	12	-	*Royal Mail*
(4) College of Arms, London EC4	12	35	*Cotswold*
(5) The Heraldry Society, WC	12	15	*BOCS (2) 24*
(6) Richard III Society, Leicester	12	35	*LFDC 30*
(7) Richard III, Fotheringhay Castle	12	45	*LFDC 30*
(8) Richard III Celebration, Scarborough	12	40	*Pilgrim*
(9) The City of London, The Square Mile, EC	12	25	*G&P*
(10) Deputy Norroy, King of Arms, York	12	25	*Hawkwood*
(11) Friary Meux Kings Arms, Godalming	12	25	*Hawkwood*
(12) Coat of Arms Granted in 1890, Belfast	12	30	*BLS (84) 1*
(13) Coat of Arms Granted in 1906, Cardiff	10	30	*BLS (84) 1*
(14) Coat of Arms Granted in 1975, Edinburgh	12	30	*BLS (84) 1*
(15) Spencer of Althorp	12	40	*Althorp*
(16) Heirlooms, 1 Hayhill, Berkeley Sq., W1	12	15	*Havering*
(17) Arthurian Legend, Camelot, Tintagel	12	25	*S. Petty 19*
(18) 1st RAF Badge, BF 1826 PS	12	15	*RFDC 24*
(19) NSPCC Centenary, EC4	12	60	*NSPCC*
(20) High Wycombe, Stamp Printing	12	15	*Harrisons*
(21) Lincoln Philatelic Counter Opened	25	-	*n.o.c.*
(22) Marks & Spencer, 100 Years, W1	12	15	*DGT*
(23) Berkswell Parish Church	12	35	*Parish Ch.*
(24) Good News People, Martin, Aylesbury	12	90	*Martins*
(25) Story of the Poppy, Maidstone	12	25	*Brit. Legion*
(26) London SW1 (Buckingham Palace)	12	-	*n.o.c.*
ORDINARY F.D.I. POSTMARKS			
(27) Stratford (Shakespeare Coat of Arms cover)	35		
C.D.S. POSTMARKS			
(28) Arundel - home of the Earl Marshal	20		
(29) Cannon St., EC4 - near to College of Arms	20		
(30) Fore St., EC2 - near to the Guildhall	20		
(31) Market Bosworth - Richard III	35		
(32) Middleham - Richard III's castle	35		

Also: Barony, Chester, College Town, Coneysthorpe, Fleur-de-Lis, Godalming, Gloucester, Harewood, King Arthur's Way, Leadenhall St., Lombard St., Ludgate Circus, Ludlow, Queen Elizabeth Ave., Richmond, St. Georges Cross, Sloane Square, Stock Exchange, York. From £15.

6th March 1984 - BRITISH CATTLE

16p Highland Cow; 20½p Chillingham Wild Bull; 26p Hereford Bull; 28p Welsh Black Bull; 31p Irish Moiled Cow

	ordinary covers £	official covers £	
SPECIAL HANDSTAMPS			
(1) First Day of Issue - Philatelic Bureau	4	-	*Royal Mail*
(2) First Day of Issue - Oban Argyll	4	-	*Royal Mail*
(3) Highland Cattle Society, Edinburgh	10	12	*BOCS (2) 25*
(4) Chateau Impney, Highland Cattle, Droitwich	15	-	*Royal Mail*
(5) Last Stronghold of the Chillingham Bull	10	10	*BLS (84) 2*
(6) Home of the Chillingham Wild Cattle	10	25	*CWC Assoc*
(7) Hereford Herd Book Society	10	25	*DGT*
(8) Welsh Black Cattle Society, Caernarfon	10	25	*DGT*
(9) Irish Moiled Cattle Society, Ballynahinch	10	25	*DGT*
(10) British Friesian Cattle Soc Rickmansworth	10	25	*DGT*
(11) Livestock Show, Tring	15	-	*Royal Mail*
(12) Farming the Backbone of Britain, SW1	10	25	*DGT*
(13) Rare Breeds Survival Trust, Stoneleigh	10	12	*LFDC 31*
(14) Butcher's Charitable Institution, EC1	10	10	*Hawkwood*
(15) Earl's Court - Royal Smithfield Show, SW5	10	10	*Havering*
(16) Royal Veterinary College, NW1	10	10	*S. Petty 20*
(17) Farmers Weekly Golden Jubilee, Sutton	10	60	*Des. Enc.*
(18) Dairy Crest Honours British Cattle, Crewe	10	50	*MMB*
(19) RAF Hereford, BF 1828 PS	10	15	*RFDC 25*
(20) The Martyrs, Tolpuddle	10	15	*TUC*
(21) Stampex, London, SW1	10	50	*Stampex*
(22) Daily Mail, Ideal Home Exhibition, SW	15	45	*Pilgrim*
(23) 767 Another 1st from Britannia	20	225	*Brit. Airw.*

A special handstamp 'Maiden Flight Skyship 600, Cardington' was used on 6th March, but no covers are known to exist with the British Cattle Stamps affixed.

C.D.S. POSTMARKS		
(24) Ballynahinch or Saintfield-Irish Moiled Cow	20	
(25) Black Bull St., Leeds	20	
(26) Bull Farm, Red Cow or Cattle Market	25	
(27) Caernarfon - Welsh Black Cattle	20	
(28) Chillingham - Chillingham Wild Cattle	20	
(29) Hereford	20	
(30) Kyle, Kyleakin or Oban - Highland Cattle	25	

Also: Bovey Tracey, Bull Bay, Bull Brook, Cowfold, Cowplain, Dolgellau, Heriot, Lavenham, Lincoln, Moy, Oxen Park, Royal College St., Stoneleigh, Terling, Thames Ditton, The Markets, Thirsk. From £12.

SLOGAN POSTMARKS *Collect British Stamps; Any Royal Mail slogans. From £10.*

VALUES
Values include VAT at the standard rate.
Please read the General Notes for more details about prices & condition.

10th April 1984 - URBAN RENEWAL

16p Liverpool Garden Festival; 20½ Milburngate Centre, Durham; 28p City Docks, Bristol; 31p Commercial St, Perth

		ordinary covers £	official covers £	
SPECIAL HANDSTAMPS				
(1)	First Day of Issue - Philatelic Bureau	3	-	Royal Mail
(2)	First Day of Issue - Liverpool	3	-	Royal Mail
(3)	International Garden Festival, Liverpool	10	12	BOCS (2) 26
(4)	Abbey National Building Society	10	15	G&P
(5)	Urban Renewal, City of Durham	10	25	C of Durham
(6)	Laing Development, Durham	10	50	Laing
(7)	Urban Renewal, BDP, W1	10	25	BDP
(8)	Bush House, Arnolfini Gallery, Bristol	10	25	C of Bristol
(9)	Commercial Street Redevelopment, Perth	10	25	G&P
(10)	Landscape Institute, Liverpool	10	25	Lans. Inst.
(11)	RIBA, Festival of Architecture, York	10	45	Cotswold
(12)	RIBA, Festival of Architecture, W1	10	45	Cotswold
(13)	St. John the Evangelist, (RIBA), E15	10	15	Hawkwood
(14)	Festival of Architecture, Guildhall, EC2	10	-	Royal Mail
(15)	Year of Building, CIOB, Ascot	10	25	DGT
(16)	DIADEM, Dundee Inst. of Architects	10	25	D.I.A.
(17)	Letchworth the First Garden City	10	15	LFDC 32
(18)	London Docklands, Isle of Dogs, E14	10	25	Havering
(19)	Covent Garden Market, WC	10	25	S. Petty 21
(20)	Cheshire Gibson, Surveyors, Birmingham	15	-	n.o.c.
(21)	Wigan Pier Project	15	50	Wigan Coun.
(22)	Bristol Scout, BF 1835 PS	12	15	RFDC 26
C.D.S. POSTMARKS				
(23)	Aigburth, or Cockburn St. - near to the IGF	12		
(24)	Ascot - Chartered Inst. of Building	12		
(25)	Brigend, Perth - Commercial St	12		
(26)	Letchworth - First Garden City	12		
(27)	New Buildings, Londonderry	45		
(28)	North Rd., Durham - Milburngate Centre	12		
(29)	Prince St., Bristol - near to Arnolfini Gallery	12		

Also: Fore St., Isle of Dogs, Red House, Southampton Street, Telford, Tingley, Welwyn Garden City. Prices from £10.

SLOGAN POSTMARKS			
(30)	International Garden Festival Liverpool 84	15	

In addition: Royal Mail, Hull; Beautiful Bath; Sunderland. Prices from £20.

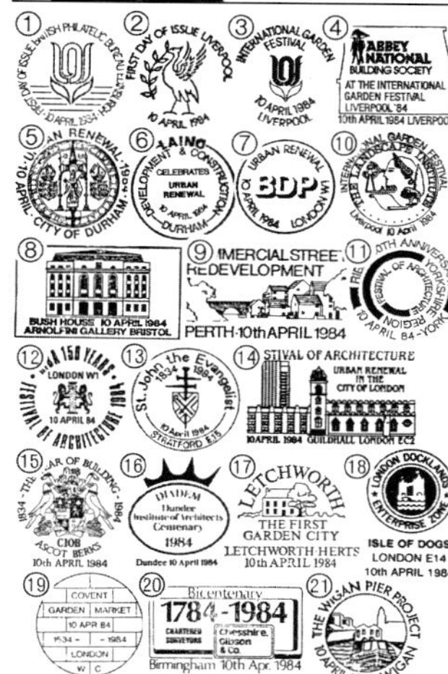

15th May 1984 - EUROPA

2 x 16p; 2 x 20½p CEPT 25th anniversary logo and the abduction of Europa

SPECIAL HANDSTAMPS				
(1)	First Day of Issue - Philatelic Bureau	3	-	Royal Mail
(2)	First Day of Issue - London SW	3	-	Royal Mail
(3)	European Elections, London, SW	10	15	Havering
(4)	Second British European Elections, SW1	10	7	BLS (84) 4
(5)	Sealink, Bridge with Europe, Folkestone	10	12	BOCS (2) 27
(6)	1606-1984 Dover Harbour Board	10	15	LFDC 33
(7)	Hawkwood Covers, Europa E1	10	15	Hawkwood
(8)	D-Day + 40 Portsmouth	10	15	S. Petty 22
(9)	35th Anniv. Formation of NATO, BF 1949 PS	12	20	RFDC 27
(10)	Mosquito Aircraft Museum, Hatfield	10	50	M.A. Mus.
C.D.S. POSTMARKS				
(11)	Bridge or Postbridge *each*	15		
(12)	Dover, Folkestone, Harwich, Weymouth	15		
(13)	House of Commons or Lords	15		
(14)	Mark Cross, Crowborough	75		
(15)	Newhaven plus PAQUEBOT	15		
(16)	Boulogne, Calais or Dieppe + PAQUEBOT	25		
(17)	Parliament Street	15		

Also: Felixstowe, Holland Fen, Montgomery, Normandy, Northern Parliament, Poling Corner, Portsmouth, Portsmouth Dockyard, York. Prices from £10.

SLOGAN POSTMARKS *Milk on your Doorstep; Historic Sandwich; Any Royal Mail slogans; Collect British Stamps. Prices from £20.*

OFFICIAL COVERS
BOCS = Benham Official Cover Series
LFDC = Leicester First Day Covers
See the General Notes for more details

5th June 1984 - LONDON ECONOMIC SUMMIT

31p Lancaster House

SPECIAL HANDSTAMPS				
(1)	First Day of Issue - Philatelic Bureau	2	-	Royal Mail
(2)	First Day of Issue - London SW	2	-	Royal Mail
(3)	Economic Summit, SW1 (50p shaped globe)	8	8	LFDC 34
(4)	London Economic Summit, SW1	8	10	Havering
(5)	London Welcomes the Economic Summit	8	7	BOCS (2) 29
(6)	Sterling Travellers Cheques, Croydon	8	-	Post Office
(7)	TSB, Chingford	8	15	Hawkwood
(8)	Brit. Philatelic Cover Producers Assoc., SW1	8	20	BPCPA
(9)	London Underwriters Centenary, EC3	8	35	Cotswold
(10)	75th Rotary Convention, Birmingham	8	25	Int. Rotary
(11)	The Queen Embarks Britannia, Portsmouth	10	50	Rembrandt
C.D.S. POSTMARKS				
(12)	Dollar	40		
(13)	Lombard St. B.O.	30		

Economic Summit (contd.)

		ordinary covers £	official covers £	
(14)	Pounds or Summit ....each	15		
(15)	St. James's St. – near to Lancaster House	8		
(16)	Stock Exchange	25		

Also: Bretton, The Forum, Lancaster, Moneyhill, Parliament Street BO. Prices from £6.

SLOGAN POSTMARKS *Sunderland Loans & Grants; Shopping by Post; Any Royal Mail slogans;Inverness Conference Capital; Sandwell Industrial. From £30.*

26th June 1984 – GREENWICH MERIDIAN

16p Astronomy; 20½p Navigation; 28p The Observatory; 31p Time

SPECIAL HANDSTAMPS

(1)	First Day of Issue – Philatelic Bureau	3	–	*Royal Mail*
(2)	First Day of Issue – Greenwich	3	–	*Royal Mail*
(3)	World's Prime Meridian, Greenwich, SE10	10	12	*BOCS (2) 28*
(4)	Greenwich Mean Time, EC4	20	–	*n.o.c.*
(5)	Geographical Magazine	10	15	*Hawkwood*
(6)	Royal Naval College	10	25	*RNC*
(7)	Meridian Road 0° 00' 00" Longitude, Boston	15	–	*Royal Mail*
(8)	Greenwich Meridian, East Lindsey, Louth	12	35	*L. Rotary*
(9)	Royal Naval Staff College, BF 1838 PS	12	35	*RFDC 28*
(10)	Longitude Zero, Somersham, Huntingdon	12	35	*PO overprint cvr*
(11)	Meridian County School, Comberton	12	45	*MCP Sch.*
(12)	Meridian Day, 0° MG GM, Swavesey	12	35	*MG Owners*
(13)	Peacehaven, Newhaven	12	100	*P'haven P.O.*
(14)	British Horological Institute, Newark	10	15	*LFDC 35*
(15)	John Longitude Harrison, Barrow	10	85	*Lincoln Cath.*
(16)	British Astronomical Association, W1	10	15	*DGT*
(17)	National Physical Laboratory, Teddington	10	100	*NPL*
(18)	Captn. Cook Study Unit, Whitby	10	35	*B. Travers*
(19)	Lloyds List, Greenwich, SE10	10	35	*Lloyds*
(20)	National Federation of Women's Institutes	10	250	*Arlington*
(21)	Steve Davis Embassy World Champion	10	35	*Havering*
(22)	Ladies Centenary Year Lawn Tennis Museum	15	35	*AELTC*

C.D.S. POSTMARKS

(23)	Alnwick – birthplace of Sir George Airy	15
(24)	Chingford – longitudinal obelisk	15
(25)	Clock Face, St. Helens	40
(26)	Hartland – Magnetic Observatory	25
(27)	Herstmonceux – new observatory	20
(28)	Greenwich or The Chart	20
(29)	Meridian Centre, Peacehaven	140
(30)	Playford, Ipswich – home of Sir George Airy	15

In addition: Cleethorpes, Comberton, East Grinstead, Globe Rd, Great Ayton, Great Portland St., Louth, Macclesfield, Station Rd (Oxted), Swavesey, Washington, World's End. Prices from £12.

SLOGAN POSTMARKS *Magyar Philatelic Society. £65.*

31st July 1984 – THE ROYAL MAIL

5 x 16p: The Bath Mail Coach; Attack on Exeter Mail Coach; Norwich Mail Coach in a thunderstorm; Holyhead & Liverpool Mail Coaches; Edinburgh Mail Coach Snowbound

SPECIAL HANDSTAMPS

(1)	First Day of Issue – Philatelic Bureau	3	–	*Royal Mail*
(1a)	-do- with Bristol-London coach run cachet	5	–	*Royal Mail*
(2)	First Day of Issue – Bristol	3	–	*Royal Mail*
(2a)	-do- with Bristol-London coach run cachet	10	–	*Royal Mail*
(3)	Bath Mail Coach Commemorative Run	10	12	*BOCS (2) 30*
(4)	Golden Age of Coaching, Bath	10	15	*LFDC 36*
(5)	Interlink Express Parcels Co, Bristol	10	15	*Hawkwood*
(6)	Royal Mail Transport, Leicester	10	50	*Mus. of Tech.*
(7)	Manchester – Altrincham Mail Coach Run	10	12	*BLS (84) 7*
(8)	Liverpool Mail Coach	10	12	*BLS (84) 7*
(9)	British Air Mail Service, BF 1845 PS	10	15	*RFDC 30*
(10)	The Islington Society, N1	10	15	*Havering*
(11)	Worshipful Company of Coachmakers, WC2	10	30	*Cotswold*
(12)	Royal Mail Commemoration, Holyhead Mail	10	–	*Royal Mail*
(13)	North Eastern Parcel Centre, Washington	15	20	*Royal Mail*
(14)	St. James's Church Piccadilly, W1	15	60	*St. J. Church*
(15)	Island of Portland Heritage Trust	15	60	*PHT*
(16)	International Essex Jamboree, Chelmsford	15	60	*Scouts*
(17)	National Postal Museum - permanent h/s	15	–	*n.o.c.*

C.D.S. POSTMARKS

(18)	Bath, Bristol, Edinburgh, Exeter, Holyhead, Liverpool or Norwich	15
(19)	Fleet Street, EC4 – 'Bolt-in-Tun' Inn	15
(20)	Holyhead or Dun Laoghaire PAQUEBOTS	20
(21)	Islington, N1 – 'The Angel Inn'	15
(22)	London Chief Office, EC1	15
(23)	Marlborough – provided Bath Mail horses	15
(24)	Moffat – snowbound Edinburgh Mail	15
(25)	Newmarket – Norwich Mail in thunderstorm	15
(26)	Thatcham – provided Bath Mail horses	15
(27)	Winterslow or Lopcombe Corner – scene of the attack on the Exeter Mail	15

In addition: Black Horse, Coach Road, Devonport. Prices from £10.

The Royal Mail (contd.)

SLOGAN POSTMARKS	ordinary covers £	official covers £	
(28) Collect British Stamps	30		
(29) Be Properly Addressed, Post Code It	40		
(30) Magyar Philatelic Society	75		
(31) Take a Break in Beautiful Bath	50		

25th September 1984 - THE BRITISH COUNCIL

17p Medicine; 22p Arts; 31p Construction; 34p Language

SPECIAL HANDSTAMPS

(1) First Day of Issue - Philatelic Bureau	3	-	*Royal Mail*
(2) First Day of Issue - London SW	3	-	*Royal Mail*
(3) The British Council, SW	8	15	*G&P*
(4) Oxford Dictionary Exhibition	8	15	*Hawkwood*
(5) Ausipex 84, Melbourne	8	10	*BOCS (2) 31*
(6) RBPD, Sutton	8	15	*Des. Enc.*
(7) Samuel Johnson, Lichfield	8	15	*LFDC 37*
(8) Battle of Britain, BF 1850 PS	8	15	*RFDC 31*
(9) St. James's Church, Piccadilly, W1	8	-	*Royal Mail*
(10) Mail Coach Service, National Postal Musuem.	10	-	*n.o.c.*
(11) Beagles Congratulate Daley Thompson, E13	10	20	*Havering*

C.D.S. POSTMARKS

(12) Southampton St. - 1st Meeting	15
(13) St. James's St. - inaugurated at Palace	15
(14) Trafalgar Sq. BO - near to British Council	15
(15) Wadhurst - 'The Midsummer Marriage'	15
(16) Walton St., Oxford - Oxford Eng Dictionary	15
(17) Westminster Bdg. Rd. - Tippett, Morley Coll	15

Also: Aberystwyth, Burgh, Dundee, King Edward VII Hospital, Lichfield, Limpsfield, Lower Broadheath, Melbourne, Oxford. From £10.

SLOGAN POSTMARKS *Doctor Johnson, Lichfield; Collect British Stamps. £25.*

20th November 1984 - CHRISTMAS

13p, 17p, 22p, 31p, 34p the Nativity

SPECIAL HANDSTAMPS

(1) First Day of Issue - Philatelic Bureau	3	-	*Royal Mail*
(2) First Day of Issue - Bethlehem	3	-	*Royal Mail*
(3) Christian Heritage Year - Durham	10	15	*BOCS (2) 32*
(4) Christian Heritage Year - Ely	10	25	*BOCS (2) 32*
(5) Christian Heritage Year - Norwich	10	12	*BLS (84) 6*
(6) Christian Heritage Year - Liverpool	10	12	*BLS (84) 6*
(7) Christmas, Isle of Iona	10	15	*Pilgrim*
(8) Glastonbury Abbey	10	35	*Fine Arts 1*
(9) Christmas Greetings, World Trade Centre	10	12	*Havering*
(10) Christmas, Weybridge	10	25	*S. Petty 25*
(11) Christmas, Theatre Royal, Stratford, E15	10	15	*Hawkwood*
(12) Telecom Technology Showcase, EC4	15	-	*n.o.c.*
(13) John Wycliffe, Lutterworth	10	15	*LFDC 38*
(14) The Lindisfarne Gospels, Holy Island	10	15	*S. Muscroft*
(15) Samuel Johnson, Lichfield	10	35	*Bradbury*
(16) Mail Coach Service, Nat Postal Museum	12	-	*n.o.c.*
(17) North Eastern Parcel Centre, Washington	12	-	*n.o.c.*

ORDINARY F.D.I. POSTMARKS

(18) Hemel Hempstead (St. Mary's cvr)	20

C.D.S. POSTMARKS

(19) Bethlehem or Nasareth	25

In addition: Canterbury, Glastonbury, Holy Island, Holytown, Horbury Bridge, Jarrow, Lutterworth, Shepherd's Bush, Shepherd's Hill, Three Kingdom. £10 each.

SLOGAN POSTMARKS

(20) Hastings - Resort for All Seasons (snowman).	40
(21) Halfpenny Green - Christmas 1984	50

In addition: Late Night Shopping, Exeter. Prices from £25.

CHRISTMAS DISCOUNT BOOKLET: Covers bearing a pair or block of 4 x 13p Christmas stamps from booklet with relevant postmark 10

22nd January 1985 - FAMOUS TRAINS

17p Flying Scotsman; 22p Golden Arrow; 29p Cheltenham Flyer; 31p Royal Scot; 34p Cornish Riviera

SPECIAL HANDSTAMPS

(1) First Day of Issue - Philatelic Bureau	5	-	*Royal Mail*
(1a) -do- carried on Orient Express cachet	7	-	*Royal Mail*
(2) First Day of Issue - Bristol	5	-	*Royal Mail*
(3) Steamtown Railway Museum, Carnforth	15	25	*LFDC 39*
(4) Flying Scotsman, Doncaster	15	25	*LFDC 39*
(5) Flying Scotsman, King's Cross, N1	15	70	*BenL6*
(6) Flying Scotsman, Scotrail, Edinburgh	25	-	*n.o.c.*
(7) Golden Arrow, Dover	15	70	*BenL8*
(8) Golden Arrow, VSOE, Victoria, SW1	15	25	*G&P*
(9) VSOE Stops at Denham Station.	25	-	*Royal Mail*
(10) GWR 150, Paddington Stn., London, W2	15	50	*CoverCraft*
(11) Great Western Hotel, Paddington, W2	15	75	*Fine Arts 2*
(12) Cheltenham Flyer, Cheltenham	15	125	*Ben500(1)*
(13) Great Western Town, Swindon	15	30	*Hawkwood*

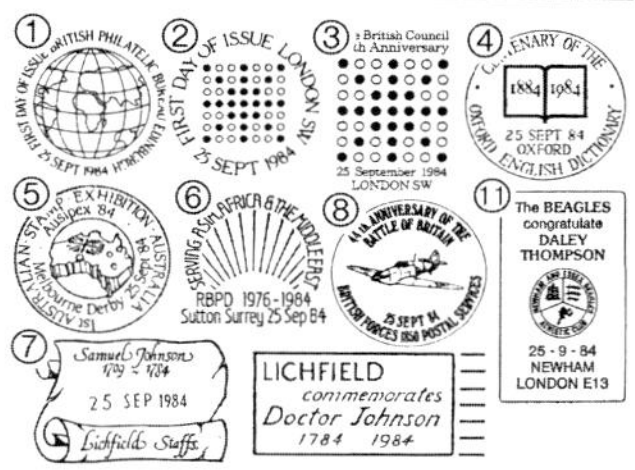

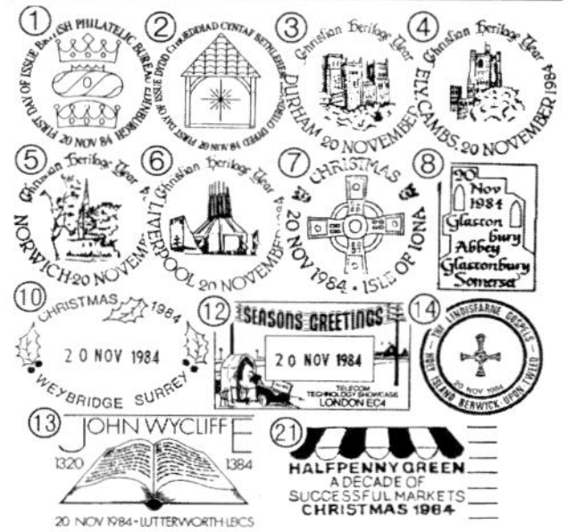

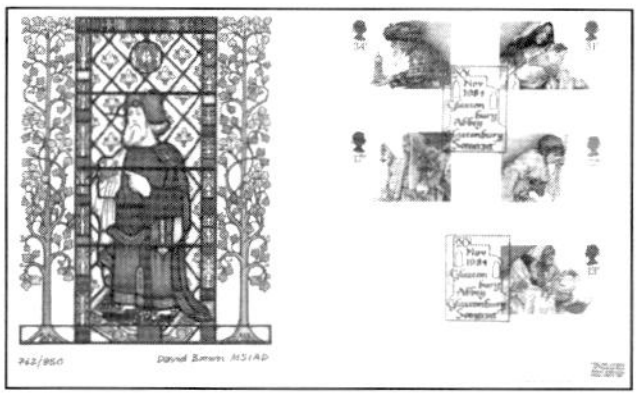

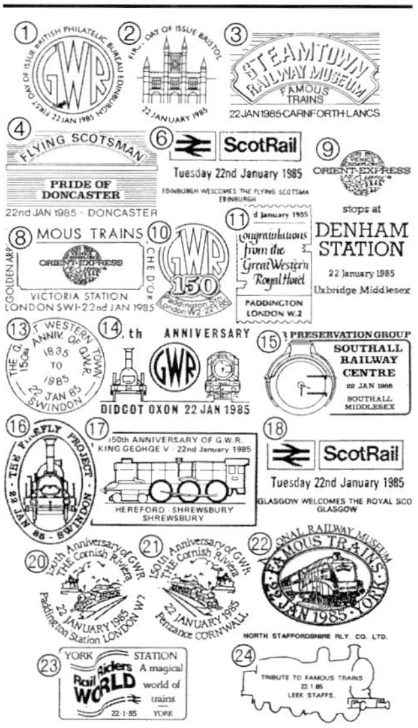

Famous Trains (contd.)

	ordinary covers £	official covers £	
(14) GWR Didcot, Oxon	15	25	*814 TPO Gp*
(15) GWR Preservation Gp, Southall Rly Centre	15	25	*DGT*
(16) Firefly Project, Swindon	15	25	*Cotswold*
(17) King George V, Hereford	25	–	*Royal Mail*
(18) ScotRail Royal Scot, Glasgow	25	–	*n.o.c.*
(19) Royal Scot, Euston, NW1	15	70	*BenL7*
(20) Cornish Riviera, Paddington	15	60	*BLCS 1*
(21) Cornish Riviera, Penzance	15	60	*BLCS 1*
(22) National Railway Museum, York	20	–	*Royal Mail*
(23) York Station, Rail Riders	15	20	*DGT*
(24) North Staffs Rly. Co. Ltd., Leek	15	85	*NSRly*
(25) Railway Loco's, British Legion, Maidstone	15	40	*Brit. Leg.*
(26) Hendon Spitfire, BF 1857 PS	15	40	*RFDC 33*
(27) Rowland Hill Loco, Crewe	30	–	*Royal Mail*
(28) National Assoc'n Boys' Clubs, Blenheim	30	60	*NABC*
ORDINARY F.D.I. POSTMARKS			
(29) Aberysthwyth (Talyllyn Railway cover)	20		
(30) Ashford (Romney Hythe Railway cover)	20		
(31) Bradford (Worth Valley Railway cover)	20		
(32) Carlisle (Ravenglass & Eskdale Rly cover)	20		
(33) Darlington (Darlington Preserv. Soc cover)	20		
(34) Any other railway society covers with FDIs	20		
C.D.S. POSTMARKS (inc. T.P.O. CANCELS)			
(35) Carnforth or Doncaster	25		
(36) Cheltenham, Penzance or Swindon *each*	25		
(37) Didcot – GWR centre	25		
(38) Euston, King's Cross or Paddington. *each*	25		
(39) Railway Place, Coleraine	25		
(40) Saltash – Brunel's famous GWR bridge	25		
(41) Any 'station' pmk e.g. Crowthorne	25		
(42) Any connected T.P.O.	25		
(43) Any other T.P.O. cancellations	20		

Also: Bristol, Corby, Edinburgh, Glasgow, Haverthwaite, Portsmouth, Silver Link, The Rocket. £15.

12th March 1985 - BRITISH INSECTS

17p Bumble Bee; 22p Ladybird; 29p Bush-Cricket; 31p Stag Beetle; 34p Dragonfly

	ordinary covers £	official covers £	
SPECIAL HANDSTAMPS			
(1) First Day of Issue – Philatelic Bureau	4	–	*Royal Mail*
(2) First Day of Issue – London SW	4	–	*Royal Mail*
(3) Royal Entomological Soc., Meadow Bank	7	50	*Ben500(2)*
(4) Royal Entomological Soc., SW7	7	20	*BLCS 2*
(5) A.E.S. Golden Jubilee, Feltham	12	30	*LFDC 40*
(6) Selborne Society Centenary, Alton	12	25	*Cotswold*
(7) Writhlington School, Radstock	15	100	*Writh. Sch.*
(8) British Museum, Natural History, SW7	10	20	*BLCS 2*
(9) Stamp Bug Club, High Wycombe	15	50	*SB Club*
(10) Bugford, I AM FIVE	20	80	*SB Club*
(11) Nature Conservation, Hummer Sherborne	15	–	*Post Office*
(12) Enfield Butterfly Centre	12	25	*Hawkwood*
(13) Robert Hooke, Freshwater	12	40	*Fine Arts 3*
(14) Scottish Wildlife Trust, Edinburgh	12	25	*Pilgrim*
(15) Mosquito Aircraft, BF 1862 PS	12	15	*RFDC 34*
(16) Pestalozzi Children's Village	35	–	*n.o.c.*
(17) National Assoc'n Boys' Clubs, Abercrave	15	40	*NABC*
C.D.S. POSTMARKS			
(18) Buckfastleigh – Abbey monks bee-keepers	25		
(19) Nettleham – Soc for Nature Conservation	25		
(20) St. Bees	25		
(21) St. James's St., or South Kensington.	25		
(22) Selborne – 'Natural History of Selborne'	25		

Also: Alexandra Park, Alexandra, Beeston, Bugbrooke, Bugthorpe, Church St., Enfield, Dunkeld, Duns, Feltham, Fleet St., Kingsstag, Lady, Meadow Bank, Northam, Sedgfield, Sheerness, Wickham, Writhlington. Prices from £15.

SLOGAN POSTMARKS *Collect British Stamps. £15.*

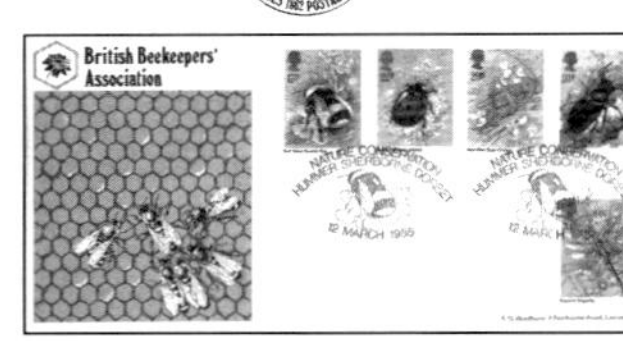

14th May 1985 - COMPOSERS

17p Handel; 22p Holst; 31p Delius; 34p Elgar

	ordinary covers £	official covers £	
SPECIAL HANDSTAMPS			
(1) First Day of Issue – Philatelic Bureau	3	–	*Royal Mail*
(2) First Day of Issue – Worcester	3	–	*Royal Mail*
(3) Handel's Birthday, Royal Opera House	6	20	*BLCS 3*
(4) Handel, Westminster Abbey, SW1	12	20	*LFDC 41*
(5) St. Paul's Cathedral, 850 Years of Music	12	40	*St. Paul's*
(6) Holst Birthplace Museum, Cheltenham	12	35	*H.B. Museum*
(7) Holst, European Music Year, Cheltenham.	12	50	*Ben500(3)*
(8) Stagenhoe Park, Mikado, Hitchin	12	15	*Hawkwood*
(9) Delius Festival, Bradford	12	25	*P. Scott*
(10) Sir Edward Elgar, Birmingham	12	–	*n.o.c.*
(11) Sir Michael Tippett, Bournemouth	12	25	*Pilgrim*
(12) British Composers, Royal Festival Hall, SE1	12	15	*G.L.C.*
(13) European Music Year, High Wycombe	12	–	*n.o.c.*
(14) Scottish National Orchestra, Aberdeen	12	30	*BenL9*
(15) Scottish National Orchestra, Dundee	12	30	*BenL10*

Composers (contd.)

		ordinary covers £	official covers £	
(16)	Royal Military School of Music, BF 2128 PS	12	20	*RFDC 35*
(17)	Music Year, National Postal Museum, EC1	12	–	*n.o.c.*
(18)	Leicester Philharmonic Society	12	25	*L.P.O.*
(19)	1st Ruislip Guides	12	40	*Ruislip GG*
(20)	St. David's Hall, Cardiff	12	30	*Pilgrim*
(21)	Haddo House, Aberdeen	12	30	*Pilgrim*
(22)	Lennon & McCartney, Composers of Today	12	60	*Fine Arts 4*
(23)	Philatelic Counter – Worcester	12	–	*n.o.c.*
(24)	Centenary of SSAFA, SW1	15	25	*Benham*
(25)	Royal Visit, The Princess of Wales, E13	15	25	*Havering*
(26)	Ultramar Fifty Years, EC	15	200	*CoverCraft*
(27)	National Assoc'n Boys' Clubs, Edinburgh	15	40	*NABC*
(28)	700th Mayoral Anniversary, High Wycombe	15	40	*High Wyc DC*

ORDINARY F.D.I. POSTMARKS

(29)	Birmingham (CBSO/M&B SimonRattle cvr)	20

C.D.S. POSTMARKS

(30)	Chichester – Holst buried in Cathedral	15
(31)	Hammersmith – Holst wrote 'Planets' here	15
(32)	Limpsfield – Delius is interred here	15
(33)	Lower Broadheath – Elgar's birthplace	15
(34)	Lowesmoor – Elgar died here	15
(35)	Pittville or Thaxted – Holst	15
(36)	South Molton St., W1 – Handel lived here	15
(37)	University, Bradford – near Delius's b/place	15
(38)	Malvern – Elgar buried nearby	15

In addition: Brigg, Chelsea, Hereford, Whitwell. Prices from £5.

SLOGAN POSTMARKS

(39)	CBSO Proms, Birmingham *(on two covers)*	50
(40)	Delius Festival, Bradford *(on two covers)*	50

In addition: Hereford Cathedral; North Wiltshire Entertains. Prices from £50.

18th June 1985 – SAFETY AT SEA

17p Lifeboat; 22p Lighthouse; 31p Satellite; 34p Buoy

SPECIAL HANDSTAMPS

(1)	First Day of Issue – Philatelic Bureau	3	–	*Royal Mail*
(2)	First Day of Issue – Eastbourne, E. Sussex	3	–	*Royal Mail*
(3)	The Plimsoll Line, Bristol	12	–	*Royal Mail*
(4)	Spurn Head Lifeboat, Hull	12	–	*Royal Mail*
(5)	Lifeboat Dedication, Cromer	12	25	*RNLI*
(6)	Lifeboat Display, Poole, Dorset	12	25	*RNLI*
(7)	Berwick-upon-Tweed Lifeboat	12	55	*B.u.T. Lifeboat*
(8)	Appledore, RNLI Lifeboat Station	12	50	*Appledore LS*
(9)	Earliest Lifeboat Design, Lowestoft	12	50	*Ben500(4)*
(10)	Grace Darling Museum, Bamburgh	12	15	*LFDC 42*
(11)	Lukin's Patent for Lifeboat Design, Hythe	12	25	*BLCS 4*
(12)	Lighthouse Club, Whitley Bay	12	40	*Light. Club*
(13)	Nore Lightship, E1	12	45	*Fine Arts 5*
(14)	Global Maritime, Safety at Sea, WC2	12	50	*Global*
(15)	Maritime Museum, SE10	12	12	*BLCS 4*
(16)	Schermuly, Greenwich, SE10	12	50	*Schermuly*
(17)	Sealion Shipping, City of London	12	125	*Sealion*
(18)	The Geographical Magazine, SW7	12	12	*Hawkwood*
(19)	No. 22 Squadrom, RAF BF 1890 PS	12	20	*RFDC 36*
(20)	British Film Year, Bristol	12	75	*CoverCraft*
(21)	The Ashes Tour, NW8	12	15	*S.P.*
(22)	London Welsh Rugby, Richmond	12	25	*LondonWelsh*
(23)	Lawn Tennis Museum, Wimbledon, SW19	12	12	*AELTA*
(24)	Nat. Assoc. of Boys' Clubs, Worcester	12	35	*NABC*
(25)	GWR 150 Exhibition Train, Shrewsbury	12	25	*BLCS 4*
(26)	Scottish National Orchestra, Glasgow	12	–	*n.o.c.*

ORDINARY F.D.I. POSTMARKS

(27)	Grimsby & Cleethorpes (Humber RNLI cvr)	35

C.D.S. POSTMARKS

(28)	Anstruther or Cromer	15
(29)	Austhorpe – b/place of Smeaton (Eddystone)	15
(30)	Bamburgh – first lifeboat station	15
(31)	Cawsand, Toward Point, Whitley Bay	15
(32)	Daventry – first successful radar experiments	15
(33)	Dover – lighthouse built by the Romans	15
(34)	E. Dean or Grand Hotel Blgs. – Beachy Head	15
(35)	Hawes – birthplace of RNLI founder	25
(36)	Hythe – Lionel Lukin is buried here	15
(37)	Lighthouse, Fleetwood	25
(38)	Little Dunmow – birthplace of Lionel Lukin	15
(39)	Poole – Headquarters of RNLI	15
(40)	Redcar – The 'Zetland' oldest lifeboat	15
(41)	Richmond – H. Greathead – 'Zetland'	15
(42)	Seething Lane, EC3 – near to Trinity House	20
(43)	Culdrose or Yeovilton RN Air Stns	25
(44)	Any RAF or RN (Air-Sea Rescue) Station	15

Also: Beacon, Marton-in-Cleveland, Sheerness, Six Bells, The Rocket, Thorpe Esplanade, Yeovil. £10

SLOGAN POSTMARKS

(45)	Relax at Sunny Weymouth	75

VALUES & CONDITION
Values should be taken as a guide, and include VAT at the standard rate. Prices are for covers in good clean condition with the full set of stamps.

30th July 1985 - THE ROYAL MAIL

17p Datapost; 22p Postbus; 31p Parcel Post; 34p Letter Post

		ordinary covers £	official covers £	
SPECIAL HANDSTAMPS				
(1)	First Day of Issue - Philatelic Bureau	3	-	*Royal Mail*
(2)	First Day of Issue - Bagshot	3	-	*Royal Mail*
(2a)	-do- carried on helicopter by Prince Charles	5	-	*Royal Mail*
(3)	P.O. Archives, 23 Glass Hill St., SE1	12	75	*Fine Arts 6*
(4)	National Postal Museum, 350 Years Service	12	-	*Royal Mail*
(5)	Thomas Witherings Postmaster, 1635	12	40	*St. Andrew's*
(6)	Royal Mail London Post, 1635-1985, EC1	12	-	*Post Office*
(7)	UCWA Public Service Union, SW4	12	15	*BLCS 5*
(8)	Royal Mail 350 Years of Service, EC	12	-	*Royal Mail*
(9)	Royal Mail SEPR Postcards, Bagshot	12	-	*Royal Mail*
(10)	Royal Mail SEPR Postcards, Windsor	12	-	*Royal Mail*
(11)	Royal Mail 350 Exhibition, Bristol	12	-	*Royal Mail*
(12)	Post Paid, Healey & Wise, EC4	12	40	*H & W*
(13)	Intelpost, Head Post Office, E1	12	15	*Hawkwood*
(14)	Postal Museum, Bath	12	50	*Ben500(5)*
(15)	National Postal Museum (Maltese Cross)	15	-	*Royal Mail*
(16)	North Eastern Parcels Centre	15	-	*Royal Mail*
(17)	10 Downing Street, SW1	12	35	*LFDC 43*
(18)	British Legion, SW1	12	35	*Brit. Leg.*
(19)	The Cardiff Tattoo, BF 1879 PS	12	45	*Forces*
(20)	Norton 100, 1885-1985, Leicester	12	150	*N. Clipper*
(21)	GWR 150 Steam Special, Gloucester	12	-	*n.o.c.*
(22)	M.C.C. Cricket Festival, Uxbridge	12	25	*MCC*
(23)	The Ashes Tour, NW8	12	25	*S.P.*
(24)	Nat. Assoc. of Boys' Clubs, Trentham Gdns	12	40	*NABC*
(25)	Ptarmigan Equipment, BF 3254 PS	12	20	*RFDC 37*
ORDINARY F.D.I. POSTMARKS				
(26)	Bromley (Bromley Post Office cover)	30		
(27)	Leeds (Yorkshire Parcel Centre cover)	30		
C.D.S. POSTMARKS				
(28)	Aberfeldy - postbus	15		
(29)	Bagshot - Charles I Proclamation	15		
(30)	Buckingham Palace, SW1	40		
(31)	Hornchurch - T. Witherings, 1st postmaster	25		
(32)	Letter, Enniskillen	30		
(33)	Llangurig or Llandloes - first ever postbus	30		
(34)	Cannon Street or Lombard Street	20		
(35)	Mount Pleasant - sorting office	20		
(36)	Sanquhar - Britain's oldest Post Office	20		
(37)	Stock Exchange - Royal Exchange (17p)	20		

Also: Brighton, Dunfermline, Edinburgh, FPO postmarks, Henfield, House of Commons, Kidderminster, Kingstanding, Postbridge. From £15.

SLOGAN POSTMARKS				
(38)	Royal Mail 350 Years Service to the Public	20		
(39)	Make any Post Office in Cleveland, etc	50		
OTHER POSTMARKS				
(40)	Parcel Post cancel - Chingford, London E4	50		
ROYAL MAIL DISOUNT BOOKLET				
	Covers bearing a pair or block of 4 x 17p 'Datapost' stamps from booklet with relevant pmk	8		
	Covers with complete pane and relevant postmark	15		

3rd September 1985 - ARTHURIAN LEGEND

17p Arthur & Merlin; 22p Lady of the Lake; 31p Guinevere & Lancelot; 34p Sir Galahad;

		ordinary covers £	official covers £	
SPECIAL HANDSTAMPS				
(1)	First Day of Issue - Philatelic Bureau	3	-	*Royal Mail*
(2)	First Day of Issue - Tintagel	3	-	*Royal Mail*
(3)	The Sword & The Stone, St. Paul's, EC4	12	40	*Fine Arts 7*
(4)	Old Post Office ,Tintagel	12	20	*BenL12*
(5)	The Legendary Camelot, Winchester.	12	15	*BLCS 6*
(6)	Morte D'Arthur, Mere, Warminster	12	50	*Ben500(6)*
(7)	The Great Hall, Winchester.	12	30	*Hants CC*
(8)	Exhibition of Celtic Legend, Glastonbury	12	35	*Arth. Exh.*
(9)	St. Margaret's Church, SW1	12	20	*Hawkwood*
(10)	King Arthur's Avalon, Glastonbury	12	15	*LFDC 44*
(11)	Royal Fleet Auxiliary, BF 1880 PS	12	15	*RFDC 38*
(12)	Leith Hall, Huntly	12	20	*Pilgrim*
(13)	Stockton on Tees, Town Hall	12	25	*Town Counc.*
(14)	Nat. Assoc. of Boys' Clubs, Guildhall, EC3	12	40	*NABC*
(15)	BI Centenary Cricket, Schaw Park	12	25	*Scot. Cricket*
(16)	23 BASE WKSP REME, BF 2340 PS	12	20	*Forces*
ORDINARY F.D.I. POSTMARKS				
(17)	Cardiff or Newport	6		
C.D.S. POSTMARKS				
(18)	Amesbury - Guinevere became a nun here	15		
(19)	Bamburgh - Lancelot's Castle	15		
(20)	Bodmin - Dozmary Pool/Excalibur	15		
(21)	Camelford - Arthur mortally wounded	15		

Arthurian Legends (contd.)

	ordinary covers £	official covers £
(22) Glastonbury – the legendary 'Isle of Avalon' ...	15	
(23) King Arthur's Way, or Lancelot Place ...	20	
(24) Merlin's Bridge ...	20	
(25) Silchester – where Arthur was crowned ...	15	
(26) South Cadbury – probable site of 'Camelot' ...	15	
(27) Stretton-under-Fosse – birthplace of Malory ...	15	
(28) Tintagel or Winchester ...	15	

In addition: Caxton, Corfe Castle, Knight's Road, Tregaron. Prices from £10.

SLOGAN POSTMARKS *Carlisle – worth a closer look. £60.*

8th October 1985 – BRITISH FILM YEAR

17p Peter Sellers; 22p David Niven; 29p Charles Chaplin; 31p Vivien Leigh; 34p Alfred Hitchcock

SPECIAL HANDSTAMPS

(1) First Day of Issue – Philatelic Bureau ...	4	–	*Royal Mail*
(2) First Day of Issue – London WC ...	4	–	*Royal Mail*
(3) British Film Year, MCMLXXXV, W1 ...	12	15	*LFDC 45*
(4) British Film Year, Bradford ...	12	50	*BLCS 7*
(5) British Film Year, Richmond ...	12	100	*Ben500(7)*
(6) British Film Year, Leicester Sq (rectangular) ...	12	20	*Arlington*
(7) British Film Year, Goldcrest London W1 ...	12	15	*G&P*
(8) British Film Year, David Niven ...	12	35	*Cotswold*
(9) British Film Year, Leicester Sq (Pink Panther) ...	12	60	*BLCS 7*
(10) Equity, Harley Street, W1 ...	12	45	*Fine Arts 8*
(11) 50 Years, National Film Archives, W1 ...	12	40	*N.F.A.*
(12) Dambusters, BF 2101 PS ...	12	50	*RFDC 39*
(13) Alfred Hitchcock, Leytonstone, E11 ...	12	20	*Hawkwood*
(14) Charrington Bass, LVNH Denham ...	12	35	*Havering*
(15) Nat. Post. Museum, Film Festival, EC1 ...	12	–	*n.o.c.*
(16) Brian Reeve New Stamp Shop, WC2 ...	12	15	*DGT*
(17) Perth Theatre ...	12	160	*Perth*
(18) Opening Arndale Centre, Luton ...	12	40	*EPR(postcard)*
(19) Nat. Assoc. of Boys' Clubs, Belfast ...	12	40	*NABC*

C.D.S. POSTMARKS

(20) Any film studio, e.g. Pinewood, Ealing ...	15
(21) Castle Road, Southsea – b/place/Peter Sellers	15
(22) Down Special T.P.O. – P.O. film 'Night Mail' ...	25
(23) East St., Walworth – b/place/Charles Chaplin ..	15
(24) Hollywood, Birmingham ...	15
(25) Kirriemuir – home of David Niven ...	15
(26) Lacock – Fox Talbot (photographic negative) .	15
(27) Leytonstone – b/place of Alfred Hitchcock ...	15
(28) Maida Vale – Friese Green (inventor of cine) .	15
(29) Victoria St., SW1 – b/place of David Niven ...	15

Also: Chancery Lane, Goonhaven, Queens Rd., Shamley Green, Sloane Square, Star. From £10.

SLOGAN POSTMARKS *Eden Court Theatre. £65.*

19th November 1985 – CHRISTMAS

12p 17p, 22p, 31p, 34p Pantomime;

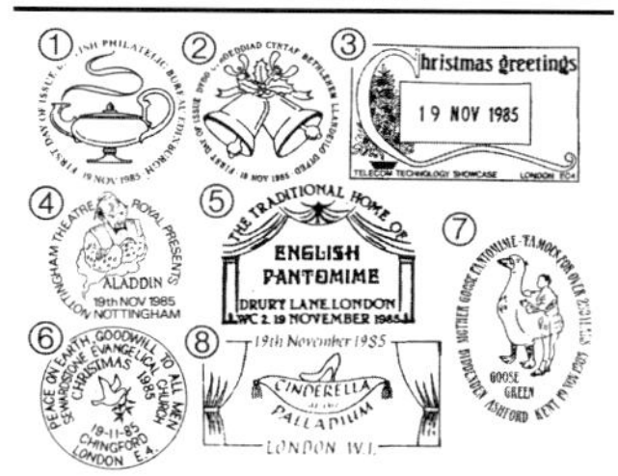

SPECIAL HANDSTAMPS

(1) First Day of Issue – Philatelic Bureau ...	3	–	*Royal Mail*
(2) First Day of Issue – Bethlehem ...	3	–	*Royal Mail*
(3) Telecom Technology Showcase, EC4 ...	12	–	*n.o.c.*
(4) Aladdin, Nottingham Theatre ...	12	15	*LFDC 46*
(5) English Pantomime, Drury Lane, WC2 ...	12	35	*Ben500(8)*
(6) Peace on Earth, Sewardstone Church, E4 ...	12	15	*Hawkwood*
(7) Mother Goose, Biddenden ...	12	15	*BLCS 8*
(8) Cinderella at the Palladium, W1 ...	12	45	*Fine Arts 9*
(9) North Eastern Parcel Centre ...	12	–	*n.o.c.*
(10) Nat. Assoc. of Boys' Clubs, Althorp ...	12	40	*NABC*

C.D.S. POSTMARKS

(11) Bethlehem, Nasareth or The Harlequin ... 30

Also: Holy Island, Lilliput, Old Whittington, Robin Hood, Star, The Circle, Whittington. From £10.

SLOGAN POSTMARKS *Eastgate or Exeter Shopping; Eden Court; Explorer Bus Tickets. £20.*

CHRISTMAS BOOKLET: Covers with pair or block of 4 x 12p stamps from bklet with special h/s ... 5

14th January 1986 – INDUSTRY YEAR

17p Energy; 22p Health; 31p Leisure; 34p Food

SPECIAL HANDSTAMPS

(1) First Day of Issue – Philatelic Bureau ...	3	–	*Royal Mail*
(2) First Day of Issue – Birmingham ...	3	–	*Royal Mail*
(3) Birthplace of Industry, Ironbridge ...	8	25	*LFDC 47*
(4) Rank Taylor Hobson, Leicester ...	8	100	*RTH*
(5) Osram, A Leading Light, Wembley ...	15	225	*G&P*
(6) British Steel, Industry Year, SE1 ...	10	75	*CoverCraft*
(7) Purveyors of Flour, Hovis, Windsor ...	15	300	*CoverCraft*
(8) The Workers Playground, Blackpool ...	10	15	*BLCS 9*
(9) Farming Feeds the Nation, Wheatacre ...	10	25	*Ben500(9)*
(10) British Steel Smelters Assoc'n, WC1 ...	10	75	*BSSA*
(11) Ulcer Therapy, Welwyn ...	15	150	*Smith Kline*
(12) All Industrious People are Happy, Blackwells ...	10	20	*Hawkwood*

Industry Year (contd.)

	ordinary covers £	official covers £	
(13) Industry Year, BP, EC	10	45	*BP*
(14) World Leading Energy Technology, Aberdeen	10	35	*Conoco(s)*
(15) British Aerospace Companies BF 2105 PS	10	25	*RFDC 41*
(16) The Salvation Army, Hoxton, N1	10	50	*H.R.*
C.D.S. POSTMARKS			
(17) Any Trading/Industrial Estate	20		
(18) Clydebank – shipbuilding	10		
(19) Cruden Bay – North Sea oil pipeline	10		
(20) Furnace, Furnace End or Ironbridge	10		
(21) Greenock – birthplace of James Watt	15		
(22) Sunderland – Joseph Swan (light bulb)	15		
(23) Steel or Steel City House	20		

Also: Bacton, Bakewell, NEC, New Invention, Pill. Prices from £7.

SLOGAN POSTMARKS *Clydebank; Sedgemoor has the Edge; Nissan. From £35.*

18th February 1986 – HALLEY'S COMET

17p Halley; 22p Giotto; 31p Twice in a Lifetime; 34p Comet

SPECIAL HANDSTAMPS

	ordinary covers £	official covers £	
(1) First Day of Issue – Philatelic Bureau	4	–	*Royal Mail*
(2) First Day of Issue – London SE10	4	–	*Royal Mail*
(3) Old Royal Observatory, SE10	10	20	*BLCS 10*
(4) A Return of Halley's Comet, Star	10	30	*Ben500(10)*
(5) Giotto, Halley's Comet Interceptor, Bristol	10	30	*CoverCraft*
(6) Halley's Comet Society, SE10	12	25	*HC Soc.*
(7) Islington Home of Halley, N1	12	20	*Hawkwood*
(8) London Planetarium, NW1	12	20	*LFDC 48*
(9) Interplanetary Society, SW	12	20	*DGT*
(10) Edmund Halley born 1656, Haggerston	12	35	*Fine Arts 11*
(11) Royal Greenwich Observatory, Herstmonceux	12	25	*K&D*
(12) Skynet 4A Satellite, BF 2109 PS	12	25	*RFDC 42*
(13) Royal Mail Fiveways, Tunbridge Wells	15	–	*Royal Mail*
(14) Royal Mail SEPR Postcards, Brighton	12	–	*Royal Mail*
(15) Ripon 1100 AD 886-1986	12	45	*Ripon Counc.*
C.D.S. POSTMARKS			
(16) Battle – Bayeux Tapestry/Halley's Comet	25		
(17) Filton – Giotto Project Team	20		
(18) Greenwich or Herstmonceux – observatories	25		
(19) Hartland – Magnetic Observatory	25		
(20) Helston – Goonhilly Downs	20		
(21) Islington – home of Edmund Halley	20		
(22) Lower Withington or Macclesfield	20		
(23) Seven Sisters or Star	20		
(24) Shoreditch – birthplace of Edmund Halley	20		

In addition: Kingsland Road. Prices from £10.

SLOGAN POSTMARKS *Shop at Post Office; Zone Tickets; Industry Year. From £18.*

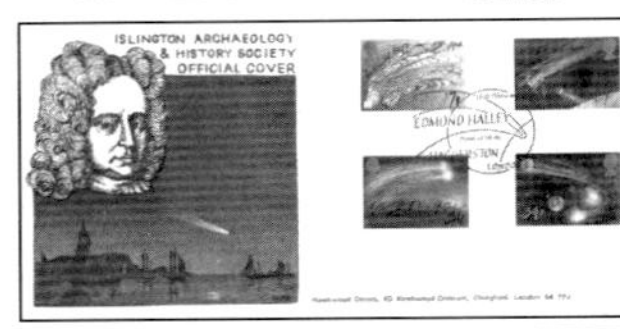

21st April 1986 – H.M. THE QUEEN'S 60th BIRTHDAY

2 x 17p; 2 x 34p Portraits of the Queen

SPECIAL HANDSTAMPS

	ordinary covers £	official covers £	
(1) First Day of Issue – Philatelic Bureau	4	–	*Royal Mail*
(2) First Day of Issue – Windsor	4	–	*Royal Mail*
(3) Birthday Greetings, London SW1 (square)	10	20	*LFDC 49*
(4) Queen's Birthday, Sandringham, Norfolk	10	15	*BLCS 11*
(5) Queen's Birthday, London SW1 (circular)	10	15	*BLCS 11*
(6) Lombard North Central, 17 Bruton St., W1	10	20	*G&P*
(7) Queen's Birthday, Windsor	10	35	*Ben500(11)*
(8) Radio Times, W1	10	25	*Arlington*
(9) Queen's 60th Birthday, SW1 (rectangular)	10	25	*Arlington*
(10) Southend Pier Train	10	15	*Hawkwood*
(11) Queen's Flight, BF 2106 PS	10	25	*RFDC 43*
(12) Queen's 60th Birthday Bruton St., W1	10	25	*K&D*
(13) Queen's Birthday, Balmoral	10	20	*BenSG1*
(14) Loyal Greetings, City of London	10	–	*n.o.c.*
(15) Many Happy Returns Nat. Postal Museum	10	15	*NPM card*
(16) Lord High Admiral, BF 2113 PS	10	75	*Royal Navy*
(17) Royal British Legion, SW1	10	35	*Brit. Leg. 26*
(18) London SW1 or Windsor permanent h/s	15	–	*n.o.c.*
(19) British Forces 1000	15	–	*n.o.c.*
(20) Tower Hill or Broadlands – permanent h/s	15	–	*n.o.c.*
(21) Royal Academy of Dancing, SW11	10	50	*CoverCraft*
(22) N. Ireland £1 Coin, Royal Mint	10	–	*n.o.c.*
(23) Women's Institutes, Denham College	10	35	*Fed. WI*
(24) Durham County Spastics Society	10	40	*DCSS*
(25) Licensed Victuallers Soc., Horsham	12	125	*RumMerc*
(26) G&J Swingler Ltd., Birmingham	10	40	*G&J Sw.*
(27) BNAI Brith District 15, London WC1	10	40	*B.B.*
(28) Austin Rover, Birmingham	10	40	*A. Rover*
(29) Open Days Broadlands	10	20	*Broadlands*
C.D.S. POSTMARKS			
(30) Aldershot – HM Queen enroled in A.T.S	20		
(31) Badminton – Horse Trials	20		
(32) Buckingham Palace or Windsor Castle	100		

Queen's 60th Birthday (contd.)

	ordinary covers £	official covers £
(33) Camberley	20	
(34) House of Commons or Lords	30	
(35) Mount Street, W1 – near Queen's birthplace	15	
(36) Romsey (honeymoon) or Crathie (Balmoral)	25	
(37) Queen Elizabeth Ave	20	
(38) Queen's Parade or Queensway	20	
(39) Windsor Great Park or Windsor	25	
(40) RAF Benson – The Queen's Flight	20	

20th May 1986 – NATURE CONSERVATION

17p Barn Owl; 22p Pine Marten; 31p Wild Cat; 34p Natterjack Toad

SPECIAL HANDSTAMPS

(1)	First Day of Issue – Philatelic Bureau	4	–	*Royal Mail*
(2)	First Day of Issue – Lincoln	4	–	*Royal Mail*
(3)	Ramblers' Association, SW8	12	20	*LFDC 50*
(4)	Barn Owl, Endangered Species, Owlsmoor	12	40	*Ben500(12)*
(5)	RSPB, Endangered Species, Sandy	12	15	*BLCS 12*
(6)	Life & Landscape, Norfolk Broads	12	45	*Bus. Inf. Ltd.*
(7)	The Wildfowl Trust, Slimbridge	12	15	*BLCS 12*
(8)	Friends of the Earth, EC1	12	15	*F.o.t.E.*
(9)	Royal Society for Nature Conservation, EC4	12	20	*Arlington*
(10)	Species at Risk, Hants & IOW	12	45	*H&IOW NT*
(11)	Herpetological Society, Studland	12	15	*Hawkwood*
(12)	Cornish Wildlife, CTNC, Truro	12	25	*CTNC*
(13)	Royal Society for Nature Conservation, W1	12	25	*Arlington*
(14)	Lady's Slipper Orchid, Grassington	12	25	*Fine Arts 13*
(15)	Friends of Arundel Castle CC	12	25	*FACCC*
(16)	Big Ack, BF 2111 PS	12	15	*RFDC 44*
(17)	British Naval Anniversary, Plymouth	12	–	*n.o.c.*
(18)	Caring & Sharing, Colchester Co-op	12	40	*Col. Co-op*
(19)	Hawk 200, First Flight, Godalming	12	85	*V.A.F.A.*

C.D.S. POSTMARKS

(20)	Aviemore, Kinloch, or Tummel Bridge – Wildcat	15
(21)	Beddgelert or Kilnlochewe – Pine Marten	15
(22)	Lincoln or Nettleham – RSNC	15
(23)	Park Road, Regents Park – London Zoo	15
(24)	Selbourne – Gilbert White/famous naturalist	15

Also: Cheltenham; Ecclestone St., SW1; Eagle; Eaglescliffe; Fair Isle;Frog Island; Isle of Rhum; Otterburn; Otterferry; Owlsmoor; Paddock Wood; Studland and Willsbridge. From £10.

SLOGAN POSTMARKS

(25)	Lincs. & Humberside Nature	70
(26)	Natureland Marine Zoo Skegness.	70

In addition: Stoke Garden Festival (2 versions). Prices from £40.

17th June 1986 - MEDIEVAL LIFE

17p Serf; 22p Freeman; 31p Knight; 34p Baron

SPECIAL HANDSTAMPS

(1)	First Day of Issue – Philatelic Bureau	4	–	*Royal Mail*
(2)	First Day of Issue – Gloucester	4	–	*Royal Mail*
(3)	Domesday Book MLXXXVI, Winchester	12	15	*LFDC 51*
(4)	Freemen of England, Oswestry	12	45	*Bradbury*
(5)	Cub Scouts Medieval Pageant, Worthing	12	45	*Worthing Cubs*
(6)	Crofters Act, Inverness	12	75	*CroftersComm*
(7)	Crofters Act, Edinburgh	12	75	*CroftersComm*
(8)	Medieval Life Stamps/Tayburn, Edinburgh	15	–	*n.o.c.*
(9)	Medieval Life Stamps/Tayburn, W14	15	–	*n.o.c.*
(10)	Domesday, 900th Anniversary, WC2	12	15	*Cotswold*
(11)	Charter Celebrations, Port of Penryn	12	50	*Penryn*
(12)	Domesday Survey 900 Years, Battle	12	25	*Ben500(13)*
(13)	Hereward Country, Isle of Ely	12	40	*E.CambsDC*
(14)	Hereward Country, Peterborough	12	40	*E.CambsDC*
(15)	The Great Hall, Domesday 900, Winchester	12	25	*Cotswold*
(16)	900th Anniversary, Domesday Survey, Exeter	12	12	*BLCS 13*
(17)	Chapter Hse, Abbey of St. Peter, Gloucester	15	50	*Fine Arts 14*
(18)	Blackwells Childrens Bookshop, Oxford	12	25	*Hawkwood*
(19)	Battle, East Sussex (permanent handstamp)	12	–	*n.o.c.*
(20)	Hastings (permanent handstamp)	12	–	*n.o.c.*
(21)	Ripon 1100, AD 886-1986	12	35	*Ripon*
(22)	Harrow Heritage Trust.	12	25	*HHT*
(23)	Tattershall Castle, BF 2116 PS	12	20	*RFDC 45*
(24)	Legal & General, London EC4	12	225	*CoverCraft*
(25)	Stamplink '86, Portsmouth	12	35	*Brit. Ferries*
(26)	Blair Castle, Pitlochry	12	35	*Pilgrim*
(27)	Friends of Arundel Castle	12	35	*S.P.*

ORDINARY F.D.I. POSTMARKS

For this issue only, many Post Offices used special F.D.I. postmarks. These were non-pictorial and incorporated both the modern and medieval spelling of the town name. Such covers (unaddressed) are valued at £10 each.

C.D.S. POSTMARKS

(28)	Battle – William's battle with Harold	25
(29)	Bosham – Manor reserved by William	20
(30)	Braunton or Laxton – ancient farming	40
(31)	Chancery Lane, WC2 – Domesday Book	25
(32)	Cherbourg PAQUEBOT – Duke of Normandy	25

PLEASE READ THE GENERAL NOTES
These often provide the answers to enquiries received

Medieval Life (contd.)	ordinary covers £	official covers £	
(33) Kingsholm – Domesday survey instigated	50		
(34) Winchester – Domesday Book compiled	15		

In addition: Castle Acre, Castle Rising, Castleton, Chertsey, Egham, Ettington, Guernsey or Jersey Paquebots, Hastings, Knight's Road, Oswestry, Saxon Ave., The Barony, Westham. From £10.

SLOGAN POSTMARKS

(35) Hereward Country – Fen Heritage	80		

In addition: Crofter's Act. Prices from £45.

15th July 1986 - SPORTS

17p Athletics; 22p Rowing; 29p Weight Lifting; 31p Shooting; 34p Hockey

SPECIAL HANDSTAMPS

(1) First Day of Issue – Philatelic Bureau	4	–	*Royal Mail*
(2) First Day of Issue – Edinburgh	4	–	*Royal Mail*
(3) Amateur Rowing Association, W6	10	15	*LFDC 53*
(4) British Rowing, Henley-on-Thames	10	25	*Ben500(14)*
(5) Cosford Arena, BF 2119 PS	15	15	*RFDC 46*
(6) 6th World Hockey Cup, NW10	10	25	*Cotswold*
(7) Scottish Brewers, Edinburgh	10	15	*DGT*
(8) The Royal British Legion, SW1	10	35	*Brit.Leg.28*
(9) Amateur Athletic Association, SW1	10	15	*DGT*
(10) Commonwealth Games, MAC, Edinburgh	10	15	*DGT*
(11) Waltham Forest, London Youth Games, E17	10	15	*Hawkwood*
(12) The Royal Tournament, BF 2118 PS	12	–	*n.o.c.*
(13) England v. N. Zealand, NW8	10	25	*S.P.*
(14) England v. India, NW8	10	25	*S.P.*
(15) Medieval Life Stamps/Tayburn, Edinburgh	10	–	*n.o.c.*
(16) Medieval Life Stamps/Tayburn, W14	10	–	*n.o.c.*
(17) Domesday 900th Anniversary, WC2	10	–	*n.o.c.*
(18) Blair Castle, Pitlochry	10	25	*Pilgrim*

C.D.S. POSTMARKS

(19) Edinburgh, Jock's Lodge, Leith Walk, Murrayfield, Musselborough, Newbridge, North Motherwell or Norton Park – venues of Games events *each*	15		
(20) Bisley or Henley	15		
(21) Gleneagles Hotel – 'Gleneagles Agreement'	20		
(22) Mobile P.O. 2 Edinburgh – Games Village	100		
(23) Willesden – World Hockey Championships	15		

Also: Badminton, Bowling Green, Clarkston, Fulham Rd, Gun Hill, Shooting Common. From £10.

22nd July 1986 - ROYAL WEDDING

12p & 17p Prince Andrew & Sarah Ferguson

SPECIAL HANDSTAMPS

(1) First Day of Issue – Philatelic Bureau	2	–	*Royal Mail*
(2) First Day of Issue – London SW1	2	–	*Royal Mail*
(3) Dummer (depicts horseshoe and church)	7	15	*G&P*
(4) Westminster Abbey (circular - front of Abbey)	7	15	*LFDC 52*
(5) Royal Wedding Greetings, Windsor	7	40	*Ben500(15)*
(6) Loyal Greetings from York	7	25	*BenSG2*
(7) The Royal Wedding, EC4	7	15	*Arlington*
(8) Westminster Abbey (circular - twin towers)	7	15	*Arlington*
(9) Loyal Greetings from Lullingstone Silk Farm	7	15	*Benham L14*
(10) Debretts Recording Royal History, SW6	20	15	*Fine Arts 16*
(11) Westminster Abbey (vertical - front of Abbey)	7	10	*Havering*
(12) The Royal Wedding, London EC	7	–	*Royal Mail*
(13) Dummer (depicts bell)	7	20	*K&D*
(14) The Lewis Carroll Society	7	20	*Hawkwood*
(15) Royal Wedding, XIII Commonwealth Games	7	15	*DGT*
(16) Westminster Abbey (rectangular - four bells)	7	15	*DGT*
(17) Woman's Weekly, SE1	7	65	*CoverCraft*
(18) Open Days Broadlands, Romsey	7	25	*Broadlands*
(19) London SW1 (Palace) – permanent h/s	7	–	*n.o.c.*
(20) Windsor (Castle) Philatelic Counter h/s	7	–	*n.o.c.*
(21) Blair Castle, Pitlochry	10	20	*Pilgrim*
(22) Wednesbury Sport Union	10	20	*Wed.SportsUnion*
(23) Lifeboat Week, Lyme Regis	10	20	*Pilgrim*
(24) Brooklands, Daily Mail Air Race	10	60	*V.A.F.A.*
(25) Head Post Office, Hemel Hempstead	10	110	*H.H.P.O.*
(26) Royal Tournament, BF 2118 PS	10	–	*n.o.c.*
(27) Amateur Athletic Association, SW1	10	20	*DGT*

C.D.S. POSTMARKS

(28) Ascot – Andrew and Sarah, schools	10		
(29) Buckingham Palace, SW1	100		
(30) Dummer – home of Sarah Ferguson	15		
(31) Great Portland St/Portman Sq – Sarah's b/place	10		
(32) House of Commons or Lords	20		
(33) Kelso – where Andrew proposed to Sarah	15		
(34) Windsor or Windsor Great Park *each*	15		
(35) Windsor Castle, Berks	130		

Also: Culdrose RNAS, Dartmouth, Duffus, Duke of York's School, Ferguson's Lane, Princetown, Romsey,St. Aldates, St. Andrews, Yeovilton RNAS. From £6.

SLOGAN POSTMARKS

St. Anne's Church, Naval Base Portsmouth; Collect British Stamps; Victorian Rose Gdn. From £15.

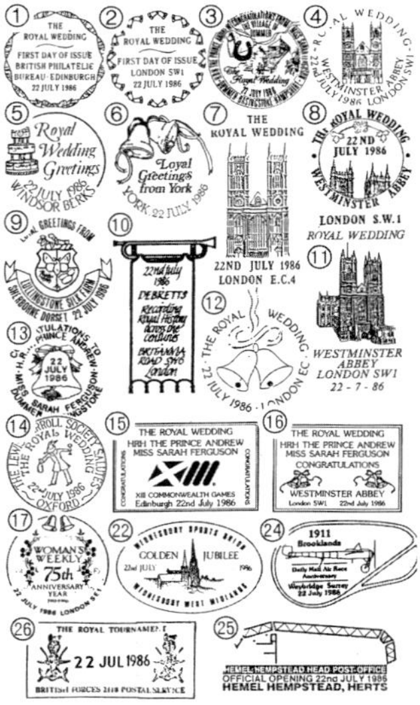

19th August 1986 - PARLIAMENTARY CONFERENCE

34p Stylised Cross and Ballot Paper

SPECIAL HANDSTAMPS	ordinary covers £	official covers £	
(1) First Day of Issue - Philatelic Bureau	2	-	*Royal Mail*
(2) First Day of Issue - London SW1	2	-	*Royal Mail*
(3) Common'lth Parl. Conf., Houses of Parliament	8	10	*LFDC 54*
(4) Common'lth Parl. Assoc., 32nd Conf., SW1	8	15	*BLCS 16*
(5) St. Margaret's Parish Church, SW1	8	20	*Hawkwood*
(6) London SW1 (Palace) permanent h/s	8	-	*n.o.c.*
(7) Dumfries Octocentenary 1186-1986	8	35	*Dumfries*
(8) World Chess Championship, W1	10	45	*H.Murray*
ORDINARY F.D.I. POSTMARKS			
(9) London N1 (Finchley Conservative cover)	10		
C.D.S. POSTMARKS			
(10) Buckingham Palace, SW1	75		
(11) Gleneagles Hotel - 'Gleneagles Agreement'	15		
(12) House of Commons, SW1	45		
(13) House of Lords, SW1	55		
(14) Huntingdon - birthplace of Oliver Cromwell	12		
(15) Kensington High St. W8 - Comm. Institute	10		
(16) Queen Elizabeth Ave., Walsall	10		
(17) Westminster Bridge Rd., SE1 - venue/Conf.	15		

SLOGAN POSTMARKS *Inverness Conference Capital; British Presidency. From £15.*

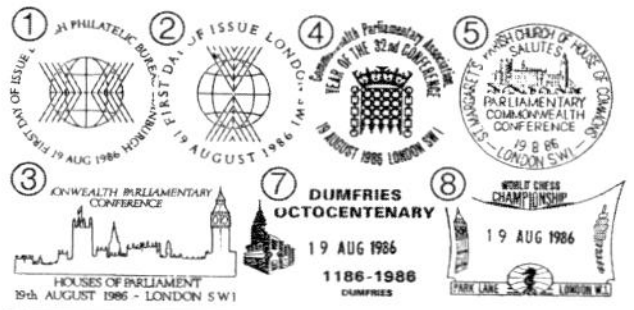

16th September 1986 - THE ROYAL AIR FORCE

17p Dowding/Hurricane; 22p Tedder/Typhoon; 29p Trenchard/DH 9A; 31p Harris/Lancaster; 34p Portal/Mosquito

SPECIAL HANDSTAMPS	ordinary covers £	official covers £	
(1) First Day of Issue - Philatelic Bureau	5	-	*Royal Mail*
(2) First Day of Issue - Farnborough	5	-	*Royal Mail*
(3) 46th Anniversary Battle of Britain, Uxbridge	7	10	*LFDC 55*
(4) Hawkinge Aerodrome, Spitfire	15	100	*Ben500(17)*
(5) RAF Scampton, Lincoln	15	30	*BLCS 17*
(6) Spitfire, 1936-1986, Eastleigh	15	20	*Bradbury*
(7) RAFA, Andover, Hants	15	15	*Cotswold*
(8) Kenley Aerodrome	15	30	*Fine Arts 18*
(9) Re-organisation of RAF, BF 2114 PS	15	20	*RFDC 49*
(10) The Battle of Britain, BF 2123 PS	15	15	*Forces*
(11) Newark on Trent, RAF	15	35	*Newark*
(12) Duxford Aviation Society	15	15	*Havering*
(13) British Philatelic Federation, Norwich	15	-	*n.o.c.*
(14) Marx Memorial Library, EC1	15	10	*Hawkwood*
(15) British Forces 1000	15	-	*n.o.c.*
C.D.S. POSTMARKS			
(16) RAF Biggin Hill *(Biggin Hill village see (22))*	100		
(17) Any other RAF station postmark *each*	25		
(18) Any Field or Forces Post Office *each*	20		
(19) House of Lords, SW1	25		
(20) Moffat, Killearn, Taunton, Cheltenham or Hungerford - birthplaces of Commanders on stamps *each*	25		
(21) Gravesend, Hawkinge, Digby Aerodrome, Manston, Kenley or Oakington - connected with aircraft featured on stamps *each*	25		
(22) Biggin Hill, Cosford Camp, Cranwell, Duxford, Honington Camp or Leuchars - RAF connections *each*	25		

Also: Churchill, Eastleigh, Gatenby, The Hyde, Hendon, Lancaster, Middle Wallop, Northolt, Pathfinder Village, Stanmore. Prices from £12.

18th November 1986 - CHRISTMAS

13p The Glastonbury Thorn; 18p The Tanad Valley Plygain; 22p The Hebrides Tribute; 31p The Dewsbury Church Knell; 34p The Hereford Boy Bishop

SPECIAL HANDSTAMPS	ordinary covers £	official covers £	
(1) First Day of Issue - Philatelic Bureau	3	-	*Royal Mail*
(2) First Day of Issue - Bethlehem, Llandeilo	3	-	*Royal Mail*
(3) The Hebrides Tribute, Stornaway	10	25	*Ben500(18)*
(4) The Devil's Knell, Dewsbury	10	45	*DewsburyPC*
(5) Christmas Greetings, Folkestone	10	15	*BenL15*
(6) St. Margaret's, Westminster, SW1	10	12	*Hawkwood*
(7) The Glastonbury Thorn	10	12	*LFDC 56*
(8) English Folk, Dance & Song Soc., Sheffield	10	10	*BLCS 18*
(9) Telecom Technology Showcase, EC1	15	-	*n.o.c.*
(10) Seasons Greetings/Railway Societies, WC1	15	-	*n.o.c.*
(11) Christmas, Hereford	10	10	*BLCS 18*
(12) NE Parcels Centre, Washington	12	-	*Royal Mail*
(13) Lloyd's of London, EC3	12	40	*CoverCraft*
(14) Battle of the Somme, BF 2124 PS	12	25	*RAF (JSF3)*
(15) Leicester Circuits	12	50	*L. Circuits*
C.D.S. POSTMARKS			
(16) Bethlehem or Nasareth *each*	15		
(17) Dewsbury, Glastonbury or Hereford *each*	15		
(18) Llanrhaeadr-ym-Mochnant (Welsh Plygain)	15		
(19) Lochboisdale or Lochmaddy (Hebrides) *each*	15		

In addition: Holy Island, St. Nicholas. Prices from £10.

SLOGAN POSTMARKS *10th Anniversary Codesort. Prices from £20*

2nd December 1986 - CHRISTMAS

12p The Glastonbury Thorn	ordinary covers		official covers
SPECIAL HANDSTAMPS	£	£	
(1) First Day of Issue - Philatelic Bureau	1	-	*Royal Mail*
(2) The Glastonbury Thorn (changeable date)	7	10	*LFDC 56*
(3) The Glastonbury Thorn, Glastonbury SC	7	10	*Cotswold*
(4) Christmas, Glastonbury, Somerset	7	15	*Ben500(19)*
(5) Telecom Technology Showcase, EC1	10	-	*n.o.c.*
(6) Biggin Hill, BF 2130 PS	10	10	*RFDC 51*
(7) Submarine 2400, Upholder, Barrow	15	50	*Vickers*
C.D.S. POSTMARKS			
(8) Bethlehem or Nasareth	25		
(9) Glastonbury or Holy Island	10		
SLOGAN POSTMARKS			
(10) Happy Christmas The Post Office	10		

Note: On the same day of issue, 2nd December, a special Christmas stamp pack was issued containing 36 x 13p Glastonbury Thorn Christmas stamps. These were identical to the 18th November 13p issue. Many of the covers produced for this issue bore both 12p and 13p values - the prices quoted above reflect this. Some covers exist with a complete pane of 18 x 13p stamps. Price from £15.

Some ***double-dated*** *covers exist with the set of Christmas stamps postmarked 18th November, and 12p value postmarked 2nd December. Prices from £30.*

20th January 1987 - FLOWERS

18p Gaillardia; 22p Echinops; 31p Echeveria; 34p Colchium

SPECIAL HANDSTAMPS			
(1) First Day of Issue - Philatelic Bureau	4	-	*Royal Mail*
(2) First Day of Issue - Richmond, Surrey	4	-	*Royal Mail*
(3) Flowers, Flore, Northampton	10	30	*Ben500(20)*
(4) Nat. Assoc. Flower Arrangement Soc., SW1	10	15	*LFDC 57*
(5) Chelsea Flower Shows, SW3	10	25	*BOCS (3) 1*
(6) Westminster Shows, SW1	10	25	*BOCS (3) 1*
(7) The Lindley Library, SW1	10	25	*BOCS (3) 1*
(8) Wisley Gardens, Royal Hort. Society,	10	25	*BOCS (3) 1*
(9) Royal Botanical Gardens, Kew	10	10	*BLCS 20*
(10) Stephen Thomas Flora & Fauna, Ovingdean	10	10	*G & P*
(11) KEB Horticultural Society, EC1A	10	35	*KEB H.S.*
(12) GQT BBC Manchester	10	60	*CoverCraft*
(13) Royal College of Art, SW1	10	60	*CoverCraft*
(14) Reformation 77 Squadron, BF 2150 PS	10	15	*RFDC 52*
(15) Bradbury Blinds, Northampton	10	150	*BradBlinds*
C.D.S. POSTMARKS			
(16) Botanic Gdns, Belfast, Kew Gardens or Kew	30		
(17) Flowery Field or Spring Gardens	15		
(18) Royal Hospital, Chelsea - Flower Show	15		
(19) Sissinghurst or Ripley - Wisley Gardens	15		

Also: Botany Bay, Ipswich, Mickleton, Ovingdean, Saffron Walden, St. Bees, Thistle Hill, Tresco. £10.

24th March 1987 - SIR ISAAC NEWTON

18p Principia; 22p Motion of Bodies; 31p Opticks; 34p The System of the World

SPECIAL HANDSTAMPS			
(1) First Day of Issue - Philatelic Bureau	3	-	*Royal Mail*
(2) First Day of Issue - Woolsthorpe, Lincs	3	-	*Royal Mail*
(3) Isaac Newton, Woolsthorpe, Grantham	10	15	*LFDC 58*
(4) Trinity College, Cambridge	10	35	*Ben500(21)*
(5) The Old Royal Observatory, SE10	10	17	*BLCS 21*
(6) Weston Favell Upper School, Northampton	10	15	*WF School*
(7) Isaac Newton, Grantham	10	40	*Maths Assoc*
(8) The George, Newton's Tercentenary, Grantham	10	50	*George Hotel*
(9) Apple's 10th Anniversary, Hemel Hempstead	10	80	*Arlington*
(10) Sir Isaac Newton, Science Museum, SW7	10	20	*Cotswold*
(11) Sir Isaac Newton, Royal Society, EC4	10	-	*n.o.c.*
(12) London College of Music, W1	10	60	*CoverCraft*
(13) Parachute Descent, BF 2151 PS	10	15	*RFDC 53*
(14) Taunton Philatelic Sales (depicts apple)	15	-	*n.o.c.*
C.D.S. POSTMARKS			
(15) Colsterworth, Lincs. - Woolsthorpe Manor	15		
(16) Grantham - Newton attended King's School	12		
(17) Greenwich - Royal Observatory	15		
(18) House of Commons-MP for Cambridge Univ.	12		
(19) Kensington - where Newton died	12		
(20) Newton - Cambridge, Swansea or Wisbech	12		
(21) Regent St., SW1 - Newton's home	12		
(22) Trinity St., Cambridge - Trinity College	12		

In addition: Globe Road and Seething Lane EC3. Prices from £10.

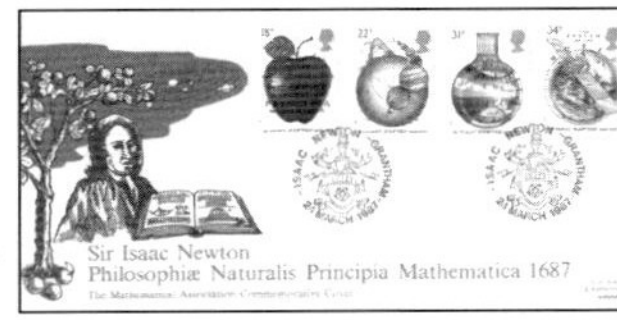

12th May 1987 - BRITISH ARCHITECTS IN EUROPE

18p Ipswich (Foster); 22p Paris (Rogers & Piano);
31p Stuttgart (Stirling & Wilford); 34p Luxembourg (Lasdun)

SPECIAL HANDSTAMPS			
(1) First Day of Issue - Philatelic Bureau	3	-	*Royal Mail*
(2) First Day of Issue - Ipswich	3	-	*Royal Mail*

Architects in Europe (contd.)

		ordinary covers £	official covers £	
(3)	British Architects in Europe, W1	10	10	*LFDC 59*
(4)	The Clore Gallery, SW1	10	20	*Ben500(22)*
(5)	R.I.B.A., Macclesfield	10	10	*BLCS 22*
(6)	R.I.B.A., Royal Charter, W1	10	15	*CoverCraft*
(7)	Willis Faber, Heritage & Progress, Ipswich	10	25	*CoverCraft*
(8)	Clinical Biochemists, Eastbourne	12	25	*A.C.B.*
(9)	Royal Engineers, BF 1987 PS	12	12	*RFDC 54*
(10)	Gallantry Awards RNLI, SE1	12	30	*Pilgrim*
(11)	London - Venice, Orient Express, Folkestone	12	60	*BenSG3*

C.D.S. POSTMARKS

(12)	Ascot – Chartered Institute of Building	10	
(13)	Euston Centre BO – James Stirling	10	
(14)	Gt. Portland St. – R.I.B.A.	10	
(15)	Hammersmith W6 – Richard Rogers	10	
(16)	Ipswich – Willis Faber Building	10	
(17)	New Buildings, Londonderry	25	
(18)	Vauxhall Bridge Rd. – Denys, Lasdun	10	

Also: Buxton Road, Macclesfield; Kirkwall; Paris Ave.; Stirling;Town Centre. From £8.

SLOGAN POSTMARKS

St. Magnus Cathedral; The Copthorne; Arndale Centre; Collect British Stamps; Nissan. From £35.

16th June 1987 – ST. JOHN AMBULANCE

18p Early Duties; 22p Wartime; 31p Pop Concert; 34p Transplant Organ Flight

SPECIAL HANDSTAMPS

(1)	First Day of Issue – Philatelic Bureau	3	–	*Royal Mail*
(2)	First Day of Issue – London EC1	3	–	*Royal Mail*
(3)	St. John's Gate, SJA Exhibition, EC1	12	15	*LFDC 60*
(4)	2nd Oldest Div. SJA Brigade, Heywood	12	15	*Cotswold*
(5)	St. John Ambulance, Hyde Park, SW1	12	30	*Ben50023*
(6)	St. John Ambulance, Stansted	12	15	*BLCS 23*
(7)	St. John Ambulance Brigade, SW1	12	15	*Arlington*
(8)	St. Margaret's Hospital, Epping	12	15	*Arlington*
(9)	London - Venice, Orient Express, Folkestone	15	125	*BenSG3*
(10)	Maiden Voyage, Waverley, Glasgow	15	50	*Benham*

ORDINARY F.D.I. POSTMARKS

(11)	Southport (Southport SJA Centre cover)	20	

C.D.S. POSTMARKS

(12)	Ashford – John Furley, Founder/Birthplace	15	
(13)	Bow or Coventry – The Blitz (22p)	15	
(14)	Epping or Stansted – The Airwing (34p)	15	
(15)	Farringdon Rd. or London EC – St. John's Gate	15	
(16)	Harrow – First road accident attended by SJA	15	
(17)	Margate (1st Corp) or Woolwich (1st Centre)	15	
(18)	Mount St., W1 – Hyde Park (31p)	15	
(19)	Papworth – Transplant surgery (34p)	15	
(20)	RAF Benson – First flight of Air Wing (34p)	20	
(21)	St. John's or St. John's Chapel	15	

Also: GWR TPO 'Up', House of Commons, House of Lords, Muswell Hill, Oldham, Orthopaedic Hospital, Royal Hospital School, and Windsor Great Park. From £10.

SLOGAN POSTMARKS *British Deaf Assoc.; Postcode your Property. From £5.*

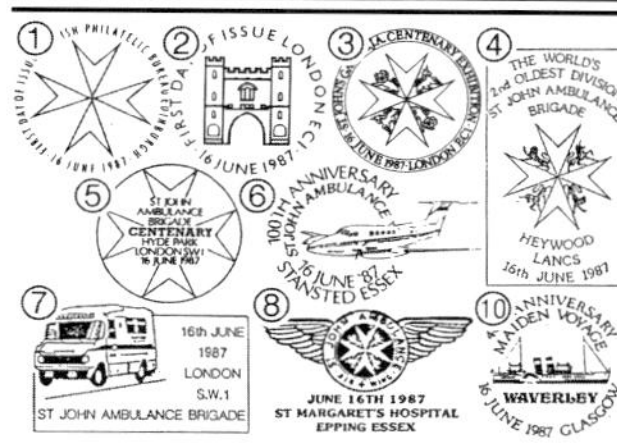

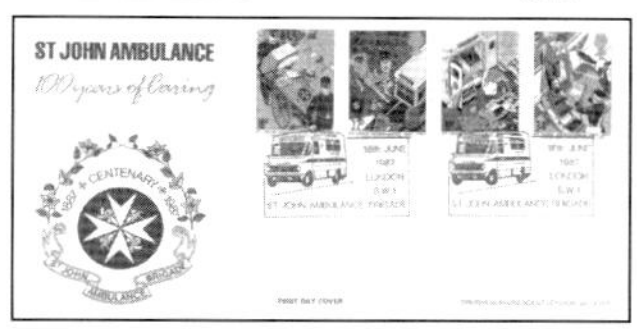

C.D.S. = CIRCULAR DATE STAMPS

These are everyday operational postmarks in use at Sub Post Offices.

Please read the General Notes for full details.

21st July 1987 – SCOTTISH HERALDRY

18p Lord Lyon King of Arms; 22p HRH The Duke of Rothesay; 31p Royal Scottish Academy; 34p Royal Society of Edinburgh

SPECIAL HANDSTAMPS

(1)	First Day of Issue – Philatelic Bureau	4	–	*Royal Mail*
(2)	First Day of Issue – Rothesay, Isle of Bute	4	–	*Royal Mail*
(3)	Order of the Thistle, Edinburgh	12	25	*Ben500(24)*
(4)	Drum Castle, Banchory	12	15	*BLCS 24*
(5)	Crathes Castle, Banchory	12	12	*BLCS 24*
(6)	Dunkeld, Perthshire	12	15	*BLCS 24*
(7)	Bannockburn, Stirling	12	12	*BLCS 24*
(8)	Mary Queen of Scots, Fotheringhay	12	15	*LFDC 61*
(9)	Royal Scottish Academy, Edinburgh	12	40	*CoverCraft*
(10)	Lord Cameron of Balhousie, BF 2144 PS	12	12	*RFDC 56*
(11)	Glasgow Herald	15	25	*Pilgrim*
(12)	Duke & Duchess of York	15	35	*Y. Minster*
(13)	Queen's School Rheindahlen, BF 21787 PS	15	35	*Queens Sch*
(14)	The Royal Tournament, BF 2142 PS	15	25	*Forces*

C.D.S. POSTMARKS

(15)	Banff – home of Lord Lyon King of Arms	15	
(16)	Bannockburn – famous battle	15	
(17)	Buckingham Palace, London SW1	50	
(18)	Edinburgh	15	
(19)	Frederick St., Edinburgh – Royal Soc. of Ed.	15	
(20)	Holyrood – Royal residence in Edinburgh	16	
(21)	House of Lords, SW1	15	
(22)	Largs or Luncarty – adoption of Thistle	15	
(23)	Rothesay – arms of Duke of Rothesay (22p)	15	
(24)	Scone – Scone Palace	35	
(25)	St. Andrews – Patron Saint of Scotland	20	
(26)	St. Mary St., Edinburgh – Royal Scot. Academy	15	

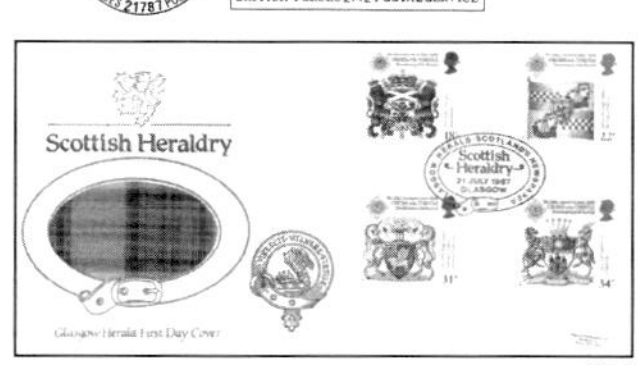

Scottish Heraldry (contd.)	ordinary covers £	official covers £	

Also: Caledonian TPO, Dingwall, Elgin, Gordon, Kintore, Linlithgow, Prince Charles Ave, Selkirk, Thistle Hill, Ullapool. Prices from £10.

SLOGAN POSTMARKS

Etterick & Lauderdale: Aberdeen Youth Fest; Inverness Conf Capital;St. Magnus Cathedral. £25.

8th September 1987 - VICTORIAN BRITAIN

18p Great Exhibition: 'Monarch of the Glen'; Grace Darling
22p 'Great Eastern'; Prince Albert; Mrs. Beeton
31p Albert Memorial; Benjamin Disraeli; Ballot Box
34p Relief of Mafeking; Marconi Wireless; Diamond Jubilee

SPECIAL HANDSTAMPS

(1) First Day of Issue - Philatelic Bureau	4	-	*Royal Mail*
(2) First Day of Issue - Newport, Isle of Wight	4	-	*Royal Mail*
(3) N.T. for Scotland, Edinburgh	12	20	*BLCS 25*
(4) Victorian Britain VA, SW7	12	15	*BLCS 25*
(5) Queen Victoria, 1837-1901, SW1	12	15	*LFDC 62*
(6) Victorian Britain, Balmoral	12	30	*Ben500(25)*
(7) Victorian Britain, Windsor.	12	50	*BenSG4*
(8) Southampton Victorian Post Office	15	-	*Royal Mail*
(9) Historic Worcester Postmarks Picture Card	15	-	*Royal Mail*
(10) Mrs. Beeton's, W1	20	75	*Arlington*
(11) Calderdale's Victorian Inheritance, Halifax	20	-	*Post Office*
(12) Marconi Philatelic Society, Gt Baddow	12	20	*G & P*
(13) Victorian Britain, Edensor, Bakewell	12	40	*CoverCraft*
(14) Henry Archer, Festiniog Rly., Porthmadog	20	50	*BenL16*
(15) National Postal Museum, 1966 -1987, EC1	12	-	*n.o.c.*
(16) Ballooning in British Army, BF 2156 PS	12	15	*RFDC 57*
(17) Ballymena Rugby Football Club	12	30	*Bally RFC*
(18) London SW (permanent handstamp)	12	-	*n.o.c.*
(19) Royal Navy Equip. Exhib., BF 2187 PS	12	25	*Forces*

C.D.S. POSTMARKS

(20) Balmoral Castle	325
(21) Bamburgh - Grace Darling	15
(22) Beaconsfield - Disraeli/Lord Beaconsfield	15
(23) Buckingham Palace, SW1	150
(24) East Cowes - near to Osborne House	15
(25) Fleet St., - 'Mafeking' on newspaper hoarding.	15
(26) Hatch End, Pinner - Mrs. Beeton	15
(27) House of Commons or Lords	15
(28) Hughenden Valley - home of Disraeli	25
(29) Kensington - V & A, Albert Memorial etc	15
(30) Maida Vale - Landseer 'Monarch of the Glen'	15
(31) Old Windsor or Windsor Great Park	15
(32) Prince Consort Rd., Queen Victoria Rd etc	15
(33) St. Margaret's Bay, Dover - wireless	30
(34) Theobald's Road - birthplace of Disraeli	15
(35) West Ferry Rd., Millwall - 'The Great Eastern'	15
(36) Westow St., Norwood - resited Crystal Palace.	15

In addition: Britannia, Paddington, Nelson, Woburn. Prices from £10.

SLOGAN POSTMARKS *Church of Latter Day Saints; The Times. From £20.*

13th OCTOBER 1987 - STUDIO POTTERY

18p Bernard Leach; 26p Elizabeth Fritsch; 31p Lucie Rie; 34p Hans Coper

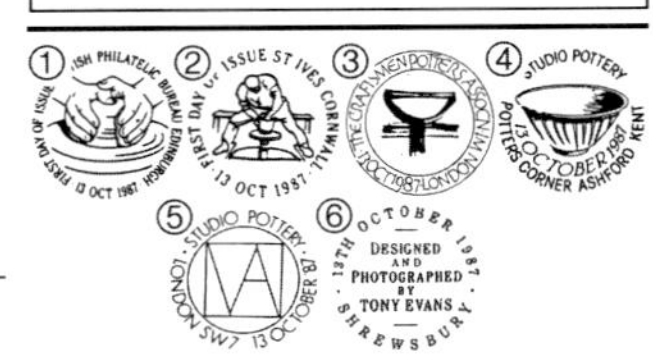

SPECIAL HANDSTAMPS

(1) First Day of Issue - Philatelic Bureau	3	-	*Royal Mail*
(2) First Day of Issue - St. Ives, Cornwall	3	-	*Royal Mail*
(3) Craftsmen Potters Assoc'n, W1	10	10	*LFDC 63*
(4) Studio Pottery, Potters Corner, Ashford	10	15	*Ben500(26)*
(5) Studio Pottery, VA, SW7	10	10	*BLCS 26*
(6) Designed by Tony Evans, Shrewsbury	10	20	*Tony Evans*
(7) Stoke-on-Trent, Philatelic Counter	10	-	*n.o.c.*
(8) Battle of Britain, BF 2154 PS	9	15	*RFDC 58*

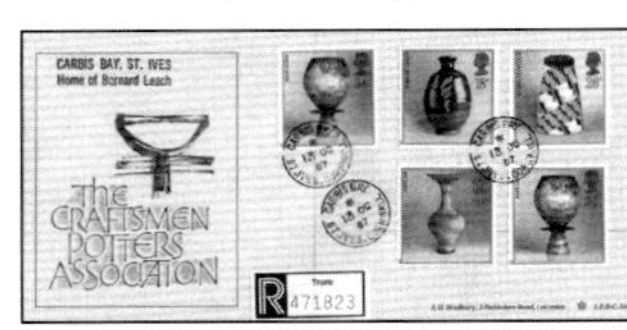

C.D.S. POSTMARKS

(9) Carbis Bay, St. Ives - home of Bernard Leach.	25
(10) Chelsea, London SW3 - annual Craft Fair	10
(11) Frome, Somerset - Hans Coper's studio	10
(12) Marble Arch, W1 - Lucie Rie's studio	10
(13) Poplar, E14 - Elizabeth Fritsch's studio	10
(14) South Kensington - V&A Museum	10
(15) St. Ives - home of studio pottery	12
(16) Stennack, St. Ives - Leach's pottery	25
(17) Welwyn Garden - Elizabeth Fritsch	10
(18) Whitchurch - birthplace of Elizabeth Fritsch	10

Also: Barlaston, Bathwick St., Dartington, Digswell, Euston Centre, Leach Ln, Potters Bar, Pottery Rd. From £8.

SLOGAN POSTMARKS *Redhill Philatelic Soc.; Royal Mail Code Show. From £15.*

17th November 1987 - CHRISTMAS

13p, 18p, 26p, 31p, 34p A child's view of Christmas

SPECIAL HANDSTAMPS

(1) First Day of Issue - Philatelic Bureau	4	-	*Royal Mail*
(2) First Day of Issue - Bethlehem, Llandeilo	4	-	*Royal Mail*
(3) Christmas, Toys Hill, Westerham	10	25	*Ben500(27)*

1987 Christmas (contd.)

	ordinary covers £	official covers £	
(4) 175th Anniv. Birth of Charles Dickens	10	15	*LFDC 64*
(5) Hamley's Toy Shop, W1	10	35	*CoverCraft*
(6) Christmas Common, Oxford	10	17	*BLCS 27*
(7) Holy Cross Church, Pattishall	10	20	*HC Church*
(8) Christmas, Christleton, Chester	10	10	*Benham*
(9) Christmas 1987, Star Underprint, Star	10	17	*B'ham500(28)*
(10) Telecom Technology Showcase, EC4	15	–	*n.o.c.*
(11) RFA Argus, BP 2157 PS	10	20	*FAAMuseum*
C.D.S. POSTMARKS			
(12) Bethlehem or Nasareth	20		
(13) Regent St – near to Hamley's Toy Shop	15		

Also: Child Okeford, Childs Hill, Fir Tree, Holy Island, Noel Road, Playing Place, St. Nicholas, Snowshill, Star, Sidmouth. From £10.

SLOGAN POSTMARKS			
(14) Gold Angels for Xmas – Pobjoy Mint	75		
(15) Church of Jesus Christ of Latter Day Saints	40		
(16) Christmas Shopping is Fun, Nottingham	140		
(17) Gold Angels available from Jewellers	10(s)		
CHRISTMAS DISCOUNT 13P MINIATURE SHEET			
Covers with gutter pair from sheet and special h/s	4		
Covers with whole miniature sheet and special h/s	20		

19th January 1988 – THE LINNEAN SOCIETY

18p Bull-rout (fish); 26p Yellow Waterlily; 31p Bewick's Swan; 34p Morel (fungus)

SPECIAL HANDSTAMPS			
(1) First Day of Issue – Philatelic Bureau	3	–	*Royal Mail*
(2) First Day of Issue – Burlington House, W1	3	–	*Royal Mail*
(3) 1788-1988 The Linnean Society, W1	12	20	*LFDC 65*
(4) British Natural History, Waterside	12	25	*Ben500(29)*
(5) The Wildfowl Trust, Welney	12	20	*BLCS 29*
(6) The Wildfowl Trust, Swan Lake	12	15	*BLCS 29*
(7) Sir Thomas Sopwith, BF 2158 PS	12	15	*RFDC 60*
(8) The Emperor's Warriors Exhibition, SW1	12	20	*Pilgrim*
C.D.S. POSTMARKS			
(9) Broadwick St., W1 – first meeting of Society	12		
(10) Norwich – B/place of founder Sir J. E. Smith	12		
(11) Fleur-de-lis – flower of the lily	15		
(12) Gotenburg, Sweden PAQUEBOT	50		
(13) POs near to Burlington House, W1	12		
(14) Holloway – Edward Lear (illustration 31p)	12		
(15) Kew Gardens or Slimbridge	35		
(16) Lambeth – James Sowerby (illustration 34p)	12		
(17) Ovingham & Mickley Sq., North'land – Bewick	12		
(18) Polperro – Dr. Jonathan Couch (manuscript 18p)	20		

Also: Abbotsbury, Badger's Mount, Bosherton, House of Commons, Lillies Leaf, Nettleham, Selbourne, Swanpool, Waterside, Welney. From £12.

1st March 1988 – THE WELSH BIBLE 1588-1988

18p William Morgan; 26p William Salesbury;
31p Richard Davies; 34p Richard Parry

SPECIAL HANDSTAMPS			
(1) First Day of Issue – Philatelic Bureau	4	–	*Royal Mail*
(2) First Day of Issue – Ty Mawr Wybrnant	4	–	*Royal Mail*
(3) Bible Society, St. David's Day, St. Asaph	10	15	*LFDC 66*
(4) Welsh Bible, Caernarfon Castle	10	30	*Ben500(30)*
(5) Y Beibl Yn Gymraeg, Llanrhaeadr	10	15	*BLCS 30*
(6) Translators of Welsh Bible, St. Asaph	10	13	*BLCS 30*
(7) Soldiers' Scripture Assoc., BF 2159 PS	10	15	*RFDC 61*
(8) 1588-1988 Ty Mawr Wybrnant, Gwynedd	10	15	*CoverCraft*
(9) Spring Stampex, SW1	10	–	*Post Office*
C.D.S. POSTMARKS			
(10) Abergwili, Bala, Conway, Cwm, Dyserth, Llandaff, Llanrhaeadr Ym, Llansanffraid, Llansannan, Penmachno, Welshpool all associated with Bible translators	15		
(11) Bethlehem, St Davids or St. Asaph	25		
(12) House of Commons or Lords	25		

In addition: Ruthin, Trinity St. Prices from £5.

SLOGAN POSTMARKS			
(13) Jesus is Alive!	75		

In addition: Oldham Education Week. £95.

22nd March 1988 – SPORT

18p Gymnastics; 26p Skiing; 31p Lawn Tennis; 34p Association Football

SPECIAL HANDSTAMPS			
(1) First Day of Issue – Philatelic Bureau	4	–	*Royal Mail*
(2) First Day of Issue – Wembley	4	–	*Royal Mail*
(3) 100 Years Ago Accrington	10	50	*Dawn*
(4) 100 Years of League Football, Aston Villa	10	50	*Dawn*

Sport (contd.)

		ordinary covers £	official covers £	
(5)	100 Years of League Football, Wolves	10	50	*Dawn*
(6)	100 Years of League Football, Everton	10	50	*Dawn*
(7)	Record Holders, Liverpool FC	10	60	*Dawn*
(8)	Manchester United	10	60	*Dawn*
(9)	Record Holders, Tottenham Hotspur	10	20	*BLCS 31*
(10)	Record Holders, Arsenal FC	10	20	*BLCS 31*
(11)	Preston North End Football Club, Preston	10	12	*LFDC 67*
(12)	Lawn Tennis at Edgbaston	10	35	*Ben500(31)*
(13)	The Lawn Tennis Association, W14	10	20	*Cotswold*
(14)	Amateur Gymnastics Assoc., Slough	10	20	*Cotswold*
(15)	'A Question of Sport', Manchester	10	15	*CoverCraft*
(16)	Physical Training Corps, BF 2161 PS	10	15	*RFDC 62*

C.D.S. POSTMARKS

(17)	Accrington, Blackburn, Bolton, Burnley, Derby, Preston, Stoke – founder members of League	15
(18)	Aviemore – ski centre	15
(19)	Deepdale Rd., Preston – Preston North End	15
(20)	Eccleston St., SW1 – HQ of Ski Association	15
(21)	Edgbaston – first lawn tennis court	15
(22)	Fleet St. – first meeting of Football League	15
(23)	Any Wimbledon pmk	20
(24)	Leamington Spa – world's first tennis club	15
(25)	Lilleshall – National Gymnastics Centre	15
(26)	Liverpool – most successful League Club	10
(27)	Lytham – HQ of the Football League	15
(28)	Meadow Lane – Notts County FC	20
(29)	Slough – HQ/Amateur Gymnastics Assoc'n	12
(30)	Villa Road – near to Aston Villa FC	50
(31)	Wembley B.O.	12
(32)	Wembley Park	20

In addition: Highbury, North End Road W14. Prices from £10.

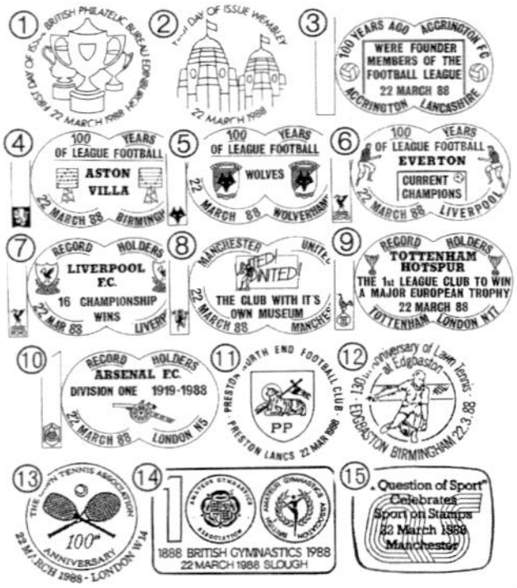

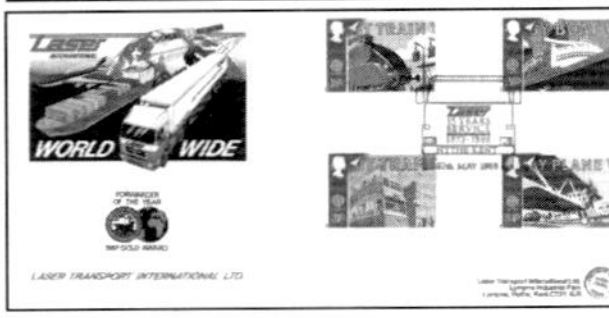

10th May 1988 – TRANSPORT & COMMUNICATIONS

18p 'Mallard'; 26p 'Queen Elizabeth'; 31p Glasgow Tram; 34p Handley Page

SPECIAL HANDSTAMPS

(1)	First Day of Issue – Philatelic Bureau	3	–	*Royal Mail*
(2)	First Day of Issue – Glasgow	3	–	*Royal Mail*
(3)	Nat Postal Museum Railways and the Post	7	–	*n.o.c.*
(4)	Mallard, National Rly. Museum, York	12	25	*BLCS 32*
(5)	Mallard, Rail Riders, York	12	75	*CoverCraft*
(6)	T.P.O. 150 Anniversary, Peterborough	12	50	*Nene V. Rly*
(7)	The Jessop Collection, Diss	12	20	*P.P.S.*
(8)	Sheffield & Rotherham Railway	12	85	*Br. Rail*
(9)	Video Cinecosse Film, Ellen	12	110	*Cinecosse*
(10)	R.M.S. Queen Elizabeth, SW1	12	20	*Arlington*
(11)	R.M.S. Queen Elizabeth, Southampton	12	15	*LFDC 68*
(12)	First Atlantic Convoy, BF 2165 PS	12	25	*FAA Museum*
(13)	The Museum of Transport, Glasgow	12	20	*BLCS 32*
(14)	Imperial Airways, Rochester	12	35	*Ben500(32)*
(15)	Croydon Airport Terminal, BF 2162 PS	12	20	*RFDC 63*
(16)	National Postal Museum (AirMail routes)	12	–	*n.o.c.*
(17)	TGWU, SW1	12	40	*CoverCraft*
(18)	Laser, 1973-1988, Hythe	12	25	*G&P*
(19)	Illustrated by Andrew Davidson, Bromley	12	–	*n.o.c.*
(20)	Designed by Carroll Dempsey & Thirkell	12	25	*CD&T(card)*
(21)	Lloyd's of London, EC3	12	30	*CoverCraft*
(22)	19th Century Post Box Discovery, Spilsby	12	30	*SpilsbyCofT*
(23)	Transams By Technology, WC1	12	125	*Transams*
(24)	Heathrow or NE Parcel Centre changeable date	12	–	*n.o.c.*

C.D.S. POSTMARKS (inc. T.P.O. CANCELS)

(25)	Berkhamsted – first use of T.P.O. apparatus	15
(26)	Central Stn., Edinburgh; or Nunthorpe Stn	15
(27)	Croydon or Purley – Croydon Airport	30
(28)	Clydebank – 'Queen Elizabeth' built here	15
(29)	Cricklewood – Handley Page HP42 built here	15
(30)	Doncaster – where 'Mallard' was built	15
(31)	Essendine – 'Mallard'/speed record	15
(32)	Garden Festival – Glasgow's trams	25
(33)	Hong Kong BFPO 1 – 'Queen Elizabeth'	100
(34)	Mosspark, Glasgow – tram destination (31p)	10
(35)	Southampton – home port/'Queen Elizabeth'	15
(36)	Springburn, Glasgow – first tram route	15
(37)	Tiverton – where HP42 ended its days	15
(38)	York – home of 'Mallard'	15
(39)	Any TPO postmark *from*	15

Also:Crich, Forton Services, Heathrow Airport, Hope St., New York, Queen Elizabeth Ave. From £10.

SLOGAN POSTMARKS

(40)	Only Fools Play on Railway Lines	25
(41)	Paisley 500 (Paisley's last tram No. 146)	20
(42)	Royal Mail/Garden Festival	25
(43)	Grampians – Going Places – Aberdeen	30
(44)	West Midlands 100 Great Days Out	35

In addition: Postcode your Property; Tobormory. Prices from £15.

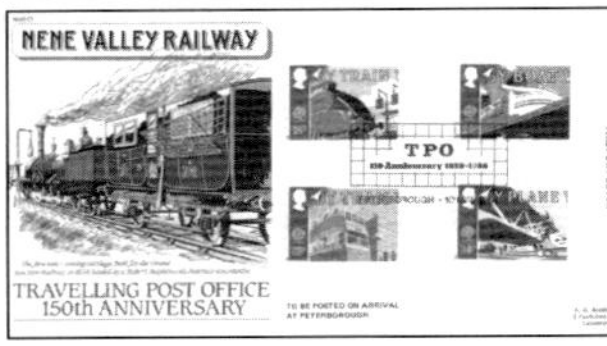

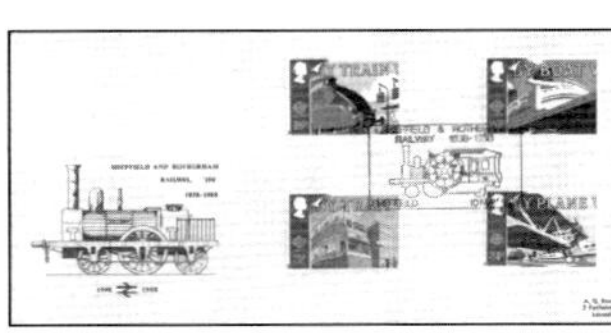

21st June 1988 - AUSTRALIAN BICENTENARY

18p Historical - Early Settler and Clipper ship;
18p Constitutional - The Queen & Parliament;
34p Sports - W.G.Grace and Tennis
34p The Arts - Lennon, Shakespeare, Sydney Opera Hse;

SPECIAL HANDSTAMPS

	ordinary covers £	official covers £	
(1) First Day of Issue - Philatelic Bureau	3	-	*Royal Mail*
(2) First Day of Issue - Portsmouth	3	-	*Royal Mail*
(3) Bicentenary of Australia, SW1	12	20	*LFDC 69*
(4) Australian Bicentenary, Portsmouth	12	40	*BenSG5*
(5) James Cook Museum, Marton-in-Cleveland	12	15	*S. Muscroft*
(6) Links with Australia, Amy Johnson, Hull	12	50	*Bradbury*
(7) GB Cricketing Links, Old Trafford	12	75	*S.P.*
(8) GB Cricketing Links, Edgbaston	12	75	*S.P.*
(9) GB Cricketing Links, Trent Bridge	12	75	*S.P.*
(10) GB Cricketing Links, The Oval, SE11	12	75	*S.P.*
(11) GB Cricketing Links, Headingley	12	75	*S.P.*
(12) GB Cricketing Links, Lords	12	15	*S.P.*
(13) Wedgwood Australian Bicentenary Barlaston	12	50	*Arlington*
(14) Botany Bay, Enfield	12	30	*Ben500(33)*
(15) Bombardment of Bardia, BF 2178 PS	12	25	*FAAMuseum*
(16) Australian Bicentennial, EC	12	35	*CoverCraft*
(17) Lawn Tennis Museum, SW19	12	25	*H.R.*
(18) R.A.F. Cottesmore, TTT3, BF 2177 PS	12	15	*RFDC 64*

C.D.S. POSTMARKS

(19) Bathampton - Capt.Phillip/first Gov. of NSW.	15
(20) Botany Bay or Penny Lane	15
(21) Downend (Grace) or Whitby (Cook) *each*	20
(22) Hambledon - birthplace of English Cricket	20
(23) House of Commons or Lords	30
(24) Portsmouth or Ryde - First Fleet	15
(25) Stratford-upon-Avon or Windsor	15

Also: Buckingham Palace, Croydon, Headingley, Kennington Park, Marton-in-Cleveland, Melbourne, Queen Elizabeth Ave., St. Bravels, Sydney, Road, Wimbledon. Prices from £12.

SLOGAN POSTMARKS

(26) 1588-1788-1988 Tobormory 200, Oban 250

In addition: Royal Mail/Glasgow G.F.; Ullapool Bicentenary. Prices from £15.

DOUBLE POSTMARKED COVERS

This issue was the first 'joint issue' involving Royal Mail. Arrangements were made for British collectors to send their British first day covers to Australia where the Australia stamps were affixed and cancelled on 21st June 1988. Prices below are for covers with the FULL SET of both British & Australian stamps.

(1) Any British handstamp + Australian h/s	35
(2) Any British C.D.S. + Australian handstamp	40

19th July 1988 - THE ARMADA 1588

5 x 18p stamps show the progress of the Armada, viz:
The Lizard; Plymouth; Isle of Wight; Calais; and North Sea.

SPECIAL HANDSTAMPS

(1) First Day of Issue - Philatelic Bureau	3	-	*Royal Mail*
(2) First Day of Issue - Plymouth	3	-	*Royal Mail*
(3) Royal Naval College, SE10	12	40	*CoverCraft*
(4) Spanish Armada Tilbury (Elizabeth on horse)	12	40	*BenSG6*
(5) Spanish Armada, Effingham	12	30	*Ben500(34)*
(6) Sighting of Armada, BF 2179 PS	12	15	*RFDC 65*
(7) Armada 400 Plymouth (circular)	12	15	*PlyPhilSoc*
(8) Armada 400 Years, Plymouth (rectangular)	12	-	*n.o.c.*
(9) Armada Anniversary, Tavistock	12	25	*TavBkShop*
(10) First Armada 400 Beacon, The Lizard	12	30	*BenL19*
(11) Armada 400, Battle of Gravelines, Dover	12	10	*BLCS 34*
(12) Spanish Armada, Tilbury (Tudor Rose)	12	20	*LFDC 70*
(13) John Hurleston, Mariner, Chester	12	10	*Havering*
(14) Royal Tournament, BF 2181 PS	12	25	*Forces*
(15) Scout Camp, Blair Atholl, Pitlochry	12	20	*Scouts*
(16) Merriott Mouldings Ltd	12	125	*Cotswold*
(17) Plymouth Philatelic Counter (Drake)	25	-	*n.o.c.*
(18) Portsmouth Philatelic Counter (Mary Rose)	15	-	*n.o.c.*

C.D.S. POSTMARKS

(19) Altofts - birthplace of Sir Martin Frobisher	20
(20) Buckland Monachorum - home of Drake	25
(21) Calais or Dover + PAQUEBOT markings *each*	35
(22) Drake, Plymouth	250
(23) Effingham - b/place of Lord Howard	20
(24) Greenwich - b/place of Queen Elizabeth I	20
(25) Maritime Mail I.S. London	100
(26) Paquebot, London or Santander	50
(27) Portland, Southwell, or Bonchurch - battles	20
(28) Plymouth or West Hoe, Plymouth	20
(29) Sandwich - prepared to meet invasion	20
(30) St. Mary's, Isle of Scilly - first sighting	20
(31) Tavistock - birthplace of Sir Francis Drake	20
(32) The Lizard & Berwick - first & last beacons	15
(33) Tilbury - where Elizabeth rallied her troops	15
(34) Tobomory, Hope and Fair Isle - wreck sites	25

Also: Beacon, Drakes Broughton, House of Commons, House of Lords. From £12.

Armada (contd.)

	ordinary covers £	official covers £	
SLOGAN POSTMARKS			
(35) 400th Anniv. of Spanish Armada	50		
(36) Tobomory 200, 1588-1788-1988	375		

In addition: Isle of Skye; Royal Mail Letters Supports G.G.F. Prices from £25.

6th September 1988 - EDWARD LEAR

19p 'The Owl and the Pussycat'; 27p Pen Sketch; 32p Alphabet 'C'; 35p Rhyme

SPECIAL HANDSTAMPS			
(1) First Day of Issue - Philatelic Bureau	4	-	*Royal Mail*
(2) First Day of Issue - London N7	4	-	*Royal Mail*
(3) Edward Lear, Foss Rampant, Learmouth	12	30	*Ben500(35)*
(4) Edward Lear Centenary, Knowsley	12	15	*LFDC 71*
(5) Hull Schools Reorganization	12	15	*HullSchools*
(6) Birthplace of Edward Lear, Holloway, N7	12	15	*BLCS 35*
(7) Designed by the Partners, Edward Lear, EC1	12	-	*n.o.c.*
(8) Knowsley, from Menagerie to Safari Park	12	25	*CoverCraft*
(9) Coeliac Symposium, St. Batholomew's, EC1	12	175	*St. Barts*
(10) Farnborough International, BF 2173 PS	10	15	*RFDC 66*
C.D.S. POSTMARKS			
(11) Camden, or Theobald's Rd. - homes of Lear	15		
(12) Chester, Gretna, Portree, Ryde - Lear's rhymes	15		
(13) Holloway - birthplace of Lear	15		
(14) Knowsley - Lear wrote his nonsense verse	15		
(15) Regents Park Rd–Lear drew birds & animals at the Zoological Gardens	15		

Also: Catsfield, Catshill, Derry Hill, East Cowes, Foss Mount, Freshwater, Luimneach, Owlsmoor, Petworth, Victoria St, Winchelsea. From £10.

SLOGAN POSTMARKS *Isle of Skye; Brighton Guide; Guide Dog Week; Tobomory. From £15.*

27th September 1988 - EDWARD LEAR

Miniature Sheet

SPECIAL HANDSTAMPS			
(1) First Day of Issue - Philatelic Bureau	5	-	*Royal Mail*
(2) First Day of Issue - London, N22	5	-	*Royal Mail*
(3) Edward Lear, Foss Rampant, Learmouth	12	20	*BLCS 36*
(4) Edward Lear Centenary, Knowsley	12	15	*LFDC 72*
(5) Edward Lear Centenary, Stampex, SW	12	12	*BLCS 36*
(6) Birthplace of Edward Lear, Holloway, N7	12	35	*Ben500(36)*
(7) Stampway to the World, Liverpool	15	-	*n.o.c.*
(8) Autumn Stampex/BPE, SW1	12	20	*Stampex*
(9) Royal Mail Exhibition Card, Stampex/BPE	12	-	*Royal Mail*
(10) Cancer & Leukaemia, BF 2182 PS	12	15	*RFDC 67*
(11) 150 Wolverton, Milton Keynes	12	-	*n.o.c.*
(12) HMS Leamington, BF 2189 PS	12	25	*FAAMuseum*
(13) RMS Queen Elizabeth, Clydebank	12	50	*Clydebank*
(14) Royal Academy of Arts, Henry Moore, W1	12	25	*Pilgrim*
C.D.S. POSTMARKS			
(15) Alexandra Park Rd - 'Stamp World 1990'	20		
(16) Chester, Gretna, Portree, Ryde–Lear's rhymes	20		
(17) Holloway, N7 - birthplace of Lear	20		
(18) Knowsley - Lear/nonsense verse	20		
(19) Park Rd., Regent's Park - Lear drew birds and animals at the Zoological Gdns	20		
(20) Portman Square - home of Lear	20		

In addition: Catsfield, Catshill, Derry Hill, East Cowes, Foss Mount, Freshwater, Luimneach, Owlsmoor, Petworth, Victoria St., Winchelsea. Prices from £10.

SLOGAN POSTMARKS			
(21) Autumn Stampex/BPE	20		
(22) Great Ormonde St. Candle	15		
(23) Philatelic Bulletin 25th Anniversary	25		

In addition: Isle of Skye; Brighton Guide; Guide Dog Week. Prices from £12.

*Some **double-dated** covers exist with the set of stamps postmarked 6th September and the miniature sheet postmarked 27th September. Prices from £35.*

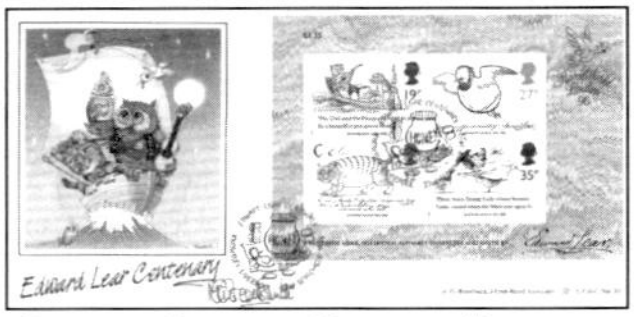

15th Nov 1988 - CHRISTMAS

14p, 19p, 27p, 32p, 35p Christmas Cards

SPECIAL HANDSTAMPS			
(1) First Day of Issue - Philatelic Bureau	4	-	*Royal Mail*
(2) First Day of Issue - Bethlehem, Llandeilo	4	-	*Royal Mail*
(3) St. Alban The Martyr, Northampton	12	35	*Ch. of St. A.*
(4) Guinea Pig Club, BF 2184 PS	12	10	*RFDC 68*
(5) York Minster Commemoration	12	25	*CoverCraft*
(6) Christmas Card Mailcoach Run, Box	12	12	*BLCS 37*
(7) Christmas Card Mailcoach Run, Luton	12	12	*BLCS 37*
(8) Christmas Card Mailcoach Run, Bath	12	15	*BLCS 37*
(9) Victorian Christmas Cards Postling, Hythe	12	25	*Ben500(37)*
(10) Saint Dunstan Millennium, Canterbury	12	15	*LFDC 73*
(11) Cartmel Priory, Grange, Cumbria	12	50	*Bradbury*
(12) Telecom Technology Showcase, EC4	12	-	*n.o.c.*
(13) Scanner, HRH Princess Margaret, Romford	12	20	*OldchHosp*
(14) Royle, Royle, Royle, N1	20	200	*Arlington*
(15) Stampway to the World, Liverpool	12	-	*n.o.c.*

Christmas (contd.)	ordinary covers £	official covers £	
(16) Royal Academy of Arts, Henry Moore, W1	12	9	*Pilgrim*
(17) The Green Howards, BF 2183 PS	12	70	*Forces*
(18) Railways and the Post, Postal Museum	12	-	*Royal Mail*
(19) Holmfirth Postcard Museum	25	-	*n.o.c.*
C.D.S. POSTMARKS			
(20) Kensington Church St. – first Xmas card	15		
(21) Nasareth, Gwynedd	25		

Also: Angel Hill, Bath, Holy Island, Lancelot Place SW7, Noel Road W3, St. Nicholas, Shepherds Bush W12, Shepherds Hill, Star. Prices from £10.

SLOGAN POSTMARKS

(22) Washington Apples/Bigger Christmas Crunch . 20

In addition: Stampway; BBC Children in Need. Prices from £15.

17th January 1989 – SEA BIRDS

19p Puffin; 27p Avocet; 32p Oyster Catcher; 35p Gannet

SPECIAL HANDSTAMPS			
(1) First Day of Issue – Philatelic Bureau	4	-	*Royal Mail*
(2) First Day of Issue – Sandy, Bedfordshire	4	-	*Royal Mail*
(3) Famous Gannet Colony, Bass Rock	12	12	*BenSG8*
(4) Leics. & Rutland Ornithological Society	12	30	*LFDC 74*
(5) Lundy Island, Bideford	12	50	*Lundy P.B.*
(6) British Sea Birds, Dungeness	12	30	*Ben500(38)*
(7) St. Kilda – Puffin Colony	12	17	*BLCS 38*
(8) RSPB, Action for Birds, Sandy	12	25	*CoverCraft*
(9) No. 201 Squadron, BF 2193 PS	12	12	*RFDC 69*
(10) HMS Quorn, BF 2194 PS	12	20	*FAA Museum*
C.D.S. POSTMARKS			
(11) Balivanich, Bempton, Papa Westray or Rathlin Is. – Puffin colonies ...*each*	15		
(12) Didsbury Village – RSPB founded here	25		
(13) Fair Isle or Ness – Gannet colonies ...*each*	25		
(14) Orford – near to Minsmere (Avocet)	15		
(15) Sandy or Slimbridge	15		
(16) Snettisham or Westleton – Oystercatcher	15		
(17) Tring – British Trust for Ornithology	35		

Also: Bideford, Birdsedge, Heron Cross, Kinlochleven, Redhill, Swallow's Nest, Wren's Nest. From £10.

SLOGAN POSTMARK *Visit the Isle of Skye. £35.*

31st January 1989 – GREETINGS STAMPS

5 x 19p: rose, cupid, sailing boat, bowl of fruit and teddy bear.

SPECIAL HANDSTAMPS			
(1) First Day of Issue – Philatelic Bureau	8	-	*Royal Mail*
(2) First Day of Issue – Lover, Salisbury	8	-	*Royal Mail*
(3) Teddy Bear Museum, Ironbridge	15	20	*BLCS 39*
(4) St. Valentine's, Lover	15	30	*Ben500(39)*
(5) Flowery Field, Hyde	15	15	*BLCS 39*
(6) Commission 'Postes' CEPT, Edinburgh	15	-	*n.o.c.*
(7) No. 6 Squadron, BF 2192 PS	15	20	*RDFC 70*
(8) Up-Helly-A, Lerwick	15	35	*UpHellyA*
(10) Holmfirth Postcard Museum	25	-	*n.o.c.*
C.D.S. POSTMARKS			
(11) Bearpark, Cowes, Flowery Field, Greet, Greetland, Gretna Green, Kew Gardens, Lover, Orchard, Pudsey, Rose, Rosehearty, Seaside, or Strawberry Hill	25		

SLOGAN POSTMARKS *Burns, Dumfries; Visit the Isle of Skye. Prices from £20.*

7th March 1989 – FOOD & FARMING YEAR

19p Fruit & vegetables; 27p Meat & Fish;32p Dairy produce; 35p Cereals

SPECIAL HANDSTAMPS			
(1) First Day of Issue – Philatelic Bureau	4	-	*Royal Mail*
(2) First Day of Issue – Kenilworth	4	-	*Royal Mail*
(3) BVA Animal Welfare Foundation, W1	10	10	*LFDC 75*
(4) British Food & Farming, Isle of Grain	10	25	*Ben500(40)*
(5) Min. of Agriculture, Fisheries and Food, SW1	10	25	*CoverCraft*
(6) Women's Land Army, BF 2195 PS	10	20	*RFDC 71*
(7) Royal Agricultural Soc., Stoneleigh	10	10	*BLCS 40*
(8) Purveyors of Flour, Hovis, Windsor	10	200	*Arlington*
(9) Taunton tourist h/s (features apple)	25	-	*n.o.c.*
ORDINARY F.D.I. POSTMARKS			
(10) Chichester (Weald & Downland Museum cvr)	25		
C.D.S. POSTMARKS			
(11) Any Farm Post Offices	20		
(12) Cheddar, Stilton or Wensley ...*each*	15		
(13) Corn Exchange or Market Place ...*each*	15		
(14) Farmers, Dyfed or Tile Farm, Orpington	15		
(15) Ham or Melton Mowbray – pork pies ...*each*	15		
(16) Isle of Grain, Rochester	15		
(17) Leek or Bramley ...*each*	15		
(18) Ivymeade, High Wycombe – shopping centre P.O.	20		
(19) Savacentre – Supermarket Post Office	40		
(20) Stoneleigh – Royal Show	15		

Also: The Allotments, Bakers Ln, Bakewell, Butterton, Evesham, The Orchard, Wheatley. From £10.

PRICES & CONDITION
Prices include VAT at the standard rate and are for clean unaddressed covers. PLEASE SEE THE GENERAL NOTES FOR MORE DETAILS

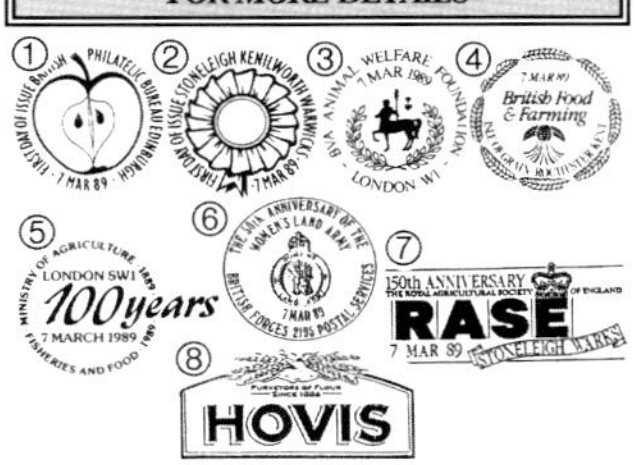

Food & Farming (contd.)

	ordinary covers £	official covers £	
SLOGAN POSTMARKS			
(21) Collect British Stamps–Bradford (sheep's head)....	25		

In addition: York Collect British Stamps; Wild about Worcestershire; Hooked on Herefordshire; County Councils; Industry Matters. Prices from £12.

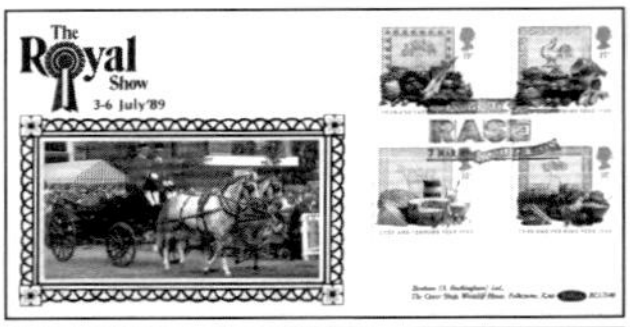

11th April 1989 - ANNIVERSARIES

19p Public Education (150th Anniversary); 19p European Parliament; 35p Postal Telegraph & Telephones Congress; 35p Inter-Parliamentary Union

SPECIAL HANDSTAMPS			
(1) First Day of Issue – Philatelic Bureau................	4	–	*Royal Mail*
(2) First Day of Issue – SW London	4	–	*Royal Mail*
(3) Strasbourg – Leicester's Twin City	10	15	*LFDC 76*
(4) 26th World Congress PTTI, W1	10	25	*Ben500(41)*
(5) Inter Parliamentary Union, SW1	10	20	*BLCS 41*
(6) Direct Elections, Downing St.	10	20	*BLCS 41*
(7) Operation Sunfish, S.E.A.C., BF 2202 PS	10	40	*FAAMuseum*
(8) RAFLET, BF 2197 PS	10	15	*RFDC 72*
(9) Centenary Derbys County Council, Matlock.....	10	35	*DerbysCC*
(10) Stampway to the World, Manchester..................	10	15	*S.P.Board*
(11) Weston Favell School, Northampton..................	10	20	*WFUS*
(12) Evesham Corps, Centenary Blood & Fire	10	15	*H.R.*
C.D.S. POSTMARKS			
(13) Brighton – PTTI Conference................................	12		
(14) Brighton Centre, Brighton – PTTI Conference.	70		
(15) Broadway, SW1 – site of IPU Congress	12		
(16) Dover or Calais + PAQUEBOT cachet......*each*	15		
(17) Hope Street, Edin. – b/place A. Graham Bell ..	15		
(18) House of Commons and Lords	25		
(19) Mark Cross or Northern Parliament	20		
(20) Duke of York's Sch. or Royal Hospital Sch.	15		
(21) Telephone House, Birmingham...........................	20		
(22) Temple Hill, Dartford – Unwin Pyrotechnics ...	12		
(23) Heathrow – main UK airport serving Europe...	30		
(24) University pmks: Bath, Bradford, Essex, Lancaster, Liverpool, Norwich & Swansea......*each*	12		

Also: Clapham Common, College Rd, Eton, Fareham, Grange Hill, Harwich, Regent St, Rochdale, Scholar Green, Sussex Coast, World's End. From £10.

SLOGAN POSTMARKS			
(25) University of Durham, Dept. of Geography	20		
(26) Mailing and Communications Show, London ..	20		
(27) Liverpool Mechanised Office – use postcodes..	20		
(28) Remember to use the Postcode – Ipswich	15		
(29) Edinburgh Festival of Science & Technology ...	20		
(30) NATO Fortieth Anniversary.................................	95		

Also: Lead Free; Derbyshire C.C.; Inverness Confe. Capital; BBC Wilts Sound; Stampway. From £14.

16th May 1989 - GAMES AND TOYS

19p train and plane; 27p building blocks; 32p board games; 35p boat, robot and doll's house

SPECIAL HANDSTAMPS			
(1) First Day of Issue – Philatelic Bureau................	4	–	*Royal Mail*
(2) First Day of Issue – Leeds	4	–	*Royal Mail*
(3) Putting Children First, NSPCC, EC.....................	10	10	*CoverCraft*
(4) Lewis Carrol, 1832-1898, Oxford	10	65	*Zanders*
(5) The Teddybears' Picnic, Ironbridge	10	20	*BLCS 42*
(6) Pollock's Toy Museum, W1..................................	10	15	*LFDC 77*
(7) Toys Hill, Westerham	10	20	*Ben500(42)*
(8) Stampway to the World, Manchester..................	10	15	*S.P.Board*
(9) Postal Museum, Uniform Exhibition, EC...........	10	–	*n.o.c.*
(10) Rotary Diamond Charter, Newcastle	10	20	*Rotary*
(11) Guisborough Priory..	10	10	*S. Muscroft*
(12) Royal Naval Air Service, BF 2200 PS	10	15	*RFDC 73*
(13) RNLI Gallantry Awards, SE1	10	15	*Pilgrim*
(14) History of the Royal Navy, Plymouth	12	–	*n.o.c.*
C.D.S. POSTMARKS			
(15) Fforestfach, Swansea – 'Corgi' toys	10		
(16) Hornby, Waddington or Playing Place	12		
(17) Mt Pleasant Liverpool–b/place Frank Hornby.....	10		
(18) Old Swan, Liverpool – 'Hornby' factory	12		
(19) Regent St., W1 – Hamley's Toy Shop	12		
(20) Any TPO postmark	10		
(21) Woodlesford or Rothwell – Waddington Games.	10		

In addition: Bathampton, Bethnal Green, Bowling, Bunny, Butlin's Holiday Camp, Child's Hill, Ironbridge, Kirton, Market, Mulberry Parade, Paddington. Prices from £8

SLOGAN POSTMARKS			
(22) 'Chess board' – Bradford	75		
(23) Save the Children Week	40		

In addition: Medway & Swale Child Safety; 40 Years Council of Europe; Lead Free; Spotless; Robin Hood; Train slogans; The Archers. Prices from £12.

4th July 1989 - INDUSTRIAL ARCHAEOLOGY

19p Ironbridge; 27p St. Agnes; 32p New Lanark; 35p Pontcysyllte Aqueduct

SPECIAL HANDSTAMPS	ordinary covers £	official covers £	
(1) First Day of Issue - Philatelic Bureau	4	-	*Royal Mail*
(2) First Day of Issue - Telford	4	-	*Royal Mail*
(3) Isambard Kingdom Brunel, Bristol	10	50	*Zanders*
(4) Water Powered Mills at New Lanark	10	20	*Ben500(43)*
(5) Pontcysyllte Aqueduct, Llangollen	10	20	*BenL21*
(6) New Lanark Conservation	10	15	*LFDC 78*
(7) Our Industrial Heritage, St. Agnes	10	17	*BLCS 43*
(8) Birthplace of British Industry, Ironbridge	10	15	*BLCS 43*
(9) Aberdulais Falls, W. Glam	10	10	*CoverCraft*
(10) Penfold Box Waterways Museum, Gloucester	10	-	*n.o.c.*
(11) Philatelic Counter, Bolton ('Spinning Mule')	20	-	*n.o.c.*
(12) Philatelic Counter, Bradford (industiral mills)	20	-	*n.o.c.*
(13) Philatelic Counter, Stoke (kiln)	20	-	*n.o.c.*
(14) Yorkshire Museum, York	10	-	*n.o.c.*
(15) Killiecrankie, National Trust Scotland	10	75	*NT for Scotland*
(16) Trenchard-Keyes Agreement, BF 2208 PS	10	25	*FAAMuseum*
(17) Lawn Tennis Museum	10	20	*H.R.*
(18) The Royal Show, Stoneleigh	10	-	*n.o.c.*
(19) No. 72 Squadron, BF 2201 PS	10	10	*RFDC 74*
C.D.S. POSTMARKS			
(20) Froncysyllte or Trevor - Pontcysyllte aqueduct	15		
(21) Ironbridge (19p)	15		
(22) Langholm - birthplace of Thomas Telford	15		
(23) New Lanark (32p)	15		
(24) St. Agnes (27p)	15		

In addition: Arkwright Town, Bolton, Camborne, Chirk, Highway, Illogen, Liverton Mines, Newtown, Preston, Saltaire, Shrewsbury, Stewarton. Prices from £10.

SLOGAN POSTMARKS£	
(25) Aveling Barford - The Earthmovers	20
(26) Collect British Stamps - Bradford (mills)	25

Also: Marine Engineers; Teesside Talent; Richmond Fest.; Post Code; Post Early; York, the Distinct Advantage. From £10.

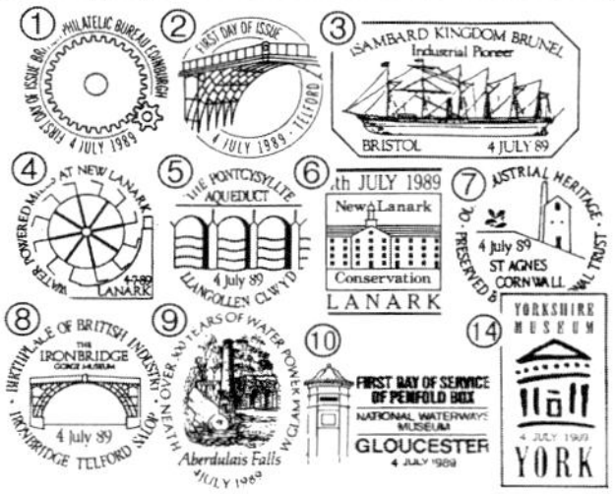

25th July 1989 - INDUSTRIAL ARCHAEOLOGY

Miniature Sheet

SPECIAL HANDSTAMPS	ordinary	official	
(1) First Day of Issue - Philatelic Bureau	4	-	*Royal Mail*
(2) First Day of Issue - New Lanark	4	-	*Royal Mail*
(3) Water Powered Mills at New Lanark	10	20	*BenL22*
(4) Pontcysyllte Aqueduct, Llangollen	10	35	*Ben500(44)*
(5) Assoc'n for Ind. Archaeology, Ironbridge	10	10	*LFDC 79*
(6) Our Industrial Heritage, Redruth	10	20	*BLCS 44*
(7) Birthplace of British Industry, Ironbridge	10	25	*BLCS 44*
(8) National Postal Museum, SWL90, EC	10	-	*n.o.c.*
(9) Killiecrankie, National Trust Scotland	10	25	*Scot.N.T.*
(10) International Scout Camp, Gosford	10	25	*Scouts*
(11) Aircraft Archaeology, BF 1968 PS	10	12	*RFDC 75*
(12) Royal Tournament, BF 2196 PS	10	12	*Forces*
(13) Philatelic Counter, Bolton ('Spinning Mule')	15	-	*n.o.c.*
(14) Philatelic Counter, Bristol (Suspension Bridge)	15	-	*n.o.c.*
(15) Philatelic Counter, Bradford (industrial mills)	15	-	*n.o.c.*
(16) Philatelic Counter, Stoke (kiln)	15	-	*n.o.c.*
C.D.S. POSTMARKS			
(17) Froncysyllte or Trevor - Pontcysyllte aqueduct	15		
(18) Ironbridge, New Lanark or St. Agnes	15		
(19) Langholm - birthplace of Thomas Telford	15		

In addition: Alexandra Park Road, Arkwright Town, Camborne, Chirk, Illogen, Liverton Mines, Muswell Hill Newtown, Preston, Saltaire, Shrewsbury, Stewarton. Prices from £10.

SLOGAN POSTMARKS	
(20) Aveling Barford - The Earthmovers	25
(21) Collect British Stamps - Bradford (mills)	20

Also: Marine Engineers; Teesside Talent Ability; Please Post Early;Post Code. From £10.

*Some **double-dated** covers exist with both the sets of stamps postmarked 4th July and the miniature sheet postmarked 25th July. Prices range from £25.*

PLEASE READ THE GENERAL NOTES AT THE BEGINNING OF THIS CATALOGUE FOR DETAILS OF THE FOLLOWING:

The scope of the catalogue - which first day covers are included and why.

Prices & condition - what to look for when buying first day covers.

Types of postmark: Special Handstamps, Ordinary FDI postmarks, CDS postmarks and Slogan postmarks.

Types of cover: Official (or sponsored) covers & Ordinary (or commercial) covers.

THE GENERAL NOTES WILL ANSWER MOST OF YOUR QUESTIONS.

5th Sept. 1989 - MICROSCOPES

19p Snowflake; 27p Fly; 32p Blood; 35p Microchip

SPECIAL HANDSTAMPS

		ordinary cvrs £	official covers £	
(1)	First Day of Issue - Philatelic Bureau	4	-	*Royal Mail*
(2)	First Day of Issue - Oxford	4	-	*Royal Mail*
(3)	Royal Microscopical Soc Oxford	10	30	*Bradbury*
(4)	Royal Microscopical Soc 1839-1989 Oxford	10	30	*Bradbury*
(5)	Cambridge Instruments	10	40	*Bradbury*
(6)	Year of the Microscope, SW7	10	30	*LFDC 80*
(7)	Year of Microscope Exh. Science Museum	10	15	*BLCS 45*
(8)	Year of the Microscope, Cambridge	10	15	*Ben500(45)*
(9)	Marconi Electronic Devices, Lincoln	10	10	*Cotswold*
(10)	Dr. Robert Hooke, Freshwater	10	75	*Zanders*
(11)	IMLS Conference, Warwick University	10	20	*H.R.*
(12)	UK North Sea Oil, Aberdeen	10	75	*Arlington*
(13)	Jeol (UK), NW9	10	75	*Arlington*
(14)	Dormeuil, The World's Best Cloths, SW1	10	30	*Dormeuil*
(15)	Battle of Britain, BF 2209 PS	10	12	*RFDC 76*
(16)	Inter-Parliamentary Union Conf., SW1	9	9	*BLCS 41*

C.D.S. POSTMARKS

(17)	Church or Freshwater - Robert Hooke	20	
(18)	Regent St., W1 - first meeting of Society	12	
(19)	St. Clements, Oxford - Society HQ	12	
(20)	South Kensington, SW7 - Science Museum	12	
(21)	Whitechapel - first meeting of Society	12	

Also: Alnwick, Holloway, Houndsditch, Lancaster, London Chief Office, Rotherhithe Lower Road, Royal Hospital School, Snowhill, Stoke Newington, Wollaston. Prices from £10.

SLOGAN POSTMARKS

(22)	Army - 50 Years of Blood Transfusion	20
(23)	CARE '89	18
(24)	Europe Against Cancer Year 1989	20

Also: Europe's Univ.; Royal Mail, Winchester; Collect British Stamps, Milton Keynes. £10.

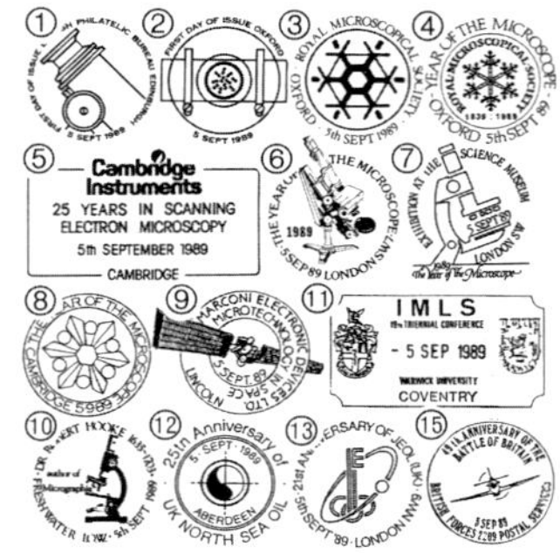

17th October 1989 - THE LORD MAYOR'S SHOW

5 x 20p Scenes from the procession

SPECIAL HANDSTAMPS

(1)	First Day of Issue - Philatelic Bureau	4	-	*Royal Mail*
(1a)	-do- carried in the Lord Mayor's Show	6	-	*Royal Mail*
(2)	First Day of Issue - London EC4	4	-	*Royal Mail*
(3)	Richard Whittington's Birthplace, Pauntley	10	110	*Bradbury*
(4)	Dick Whittington, Thrice Lord Mayor, EC	10	10	*LFDC 81*
(5)	Lord Mayor's Show, EC (trumpet)	10	15	*BenSG9*
(6)	The Lord Mayor, City of London, EC (crest)	10	15	*BLCS 46*
(7)	Exhibition at the Museum of London, EC	10	20	*Ben500(46)*
(8)	Royal Mail Open Day, WC1	10	-	*n.o.c.*
(9)	Royal Mail Exhibition Card 3, Stampex/BPE	10	-	*n.o.c.*
(10)	Autumn Stampex/BPE, 1989, SW1	10	20	*Stampex*
(11)	National Postal Museum, SWL90, EC	10	-	*n.o.c.*
(12)	Berlin Airlift, BF 2210 PS	10	12	*RFDC 77*
(13)	Sevastopol, BF 1782 PS	10	15	*FAA Museum*
(14)	Town Hall Centenary, Middlesbrough	10	9	*S.Muscroft*
(15)	Art of Photography, W1	10	12	*Pilgrim*
(16)	City of London (crest) permanent handstamp	25	-	*Royal Mail*

C.D.S. POSTMARKS

(17)	Bovingdon–Hugh Bidwell (1989 Lord Mayor)	15
(18)	Fore St.; Lombard St.; Stock Exchange; Cannon St.; London Chief Office; Fleet St. - nearest POs to scenes on the stamps	20
(19)	Ludgate Circus or Moorgate - on the route	20
(20)	Newent or Redmarley - Dick Whittington	20
(21)	Whittington, Lichfield	20

In addition: House of Lords, Richmond, Wickham, Wimbledon Park. Prices from £18.

SLOGAN POSTMARKS

Stampex; Cancer; Stampway; Gloucester Cathedral; Robin Hood; Aveling Barford; From £15.

14th November 1989 - CHRISTMAS

15p, 15p+1p, 20p+1p, 34p+1p, 37p+1p Ely Cathedral

SPECIAL HANDSTAMPS

(1)	First Day of Issue - Philatelic Bureau	4	-	*Royal Mail*
(2)	First Day of Issue - Bethlehem, Llandeilo	4	-	*Royal Mail*
(3)	First Day of Issue - Ely	4	-	*Royal Mail*
(4)	'Thomas' Invites you to Nene Valley	10	30	*N.V.Rly*
(5)	Christmas 1989, Gloucester	10	20	*Bradbury*
(6)	Telecom Technology Showcase, EC4	10	-	*n.o.c.*
(7)	Christmas 1989, Ely, Cambs	10	15	*LFDC 82*
(8)	Norman Nave, Ely Cathedral, (Mitre)	10	35	*Ben500(47)*
(9)	Norman Nave, Ely Cathedral, (3 Keys)	10	20	*BLCS 47*
(10)	Mailcoach Run, Cambridge - Ely Cathedral	10	25	*BLCS 47*
(11)	Christmas Greetings, HM Ships, BF 2214 PS	10	20	*FAA Museum*
(12)	Whitby Abbey	10	15	*S.Muscroft*
(13)	RAF Gliding Assoc'n., BF 2212 PS	10	10	*RFDC 78*
(14)	Art of Photography 1839-1989, W1	10	15	*Pilgrim*

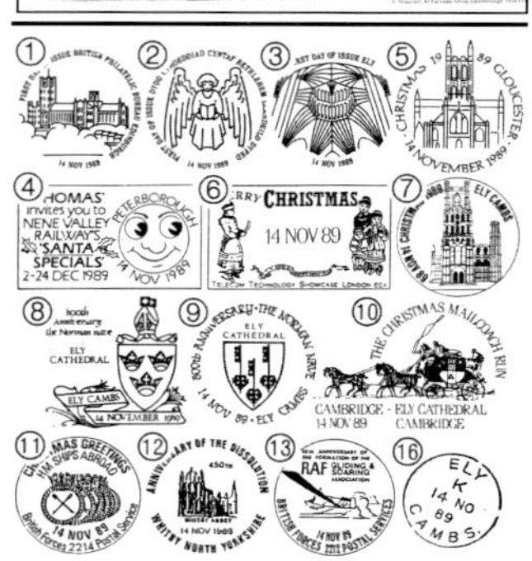

Christmas (contd.)

C.D.S. POSTMARKS

	ordinary covers £	official covers £	
(15) Barnack - Cathedral stone	15		
(16) Ely, Cambs	15		
(17) Exning – Etheldreda, Cathedral Founder	15		
(18) Primrose Hill, Tonbridge – Charities Aid HQ	12		
(19) Stoke Charity	20		
(20) Walsingham – Alan de Walsingham, architect	18		

In addition: Angel Hill, Canterbury, Holy Island, Nasareth, Northwold.Prices from £10.

SLOGAN POSTMARKS

(21) Gloucester Cathedral	20	
(22) Choose Charity Stamps or Children in Need	20	
(23) Luton Carol Aid '89	40	

Also: Unicef Cards; Beautiful Bath; Bath Royal Charter; Liverpool MLO; Collect British Stamps; Stampway. £10.

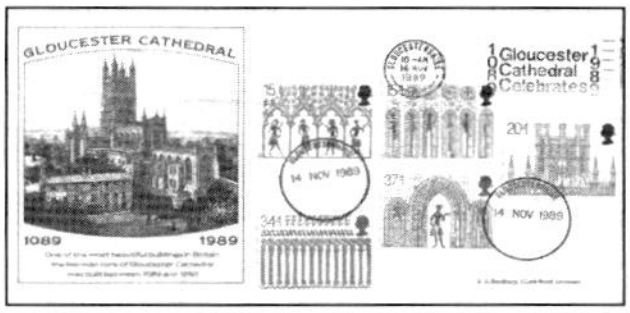

10th January 1990 – PENNY BLACK ANNIVERSARY

15p, 20p, 29p, 34p, 37p Queen Victoria & Queen Elizabeth II

SPECIAL HANDSTAMPS

(1) First Day of Issue – Philatelic Bureau	4	–	*Royal Mail*
(2) First Day of Issue – Windsor	4	–	*Royal Mail*
(3) First Roadside Pillar Box, Carlisle	12	75	*Carlisle P.O.*
(4) Postal Museum, 1840-1990, EC	12	–	*n.o.c.*
(5) Postal Museum, SWL90, Rowland Hill	12	25	*NPM postcard*
(6) Victorian Letterbox, Dean Heritage Museum	12	75	*CoverCraft*
(7) Uniform Penny Post, B.P.F., EC1	12	25	*CoverCraft*
(8) Uniform Penny Postage, Kidderminster	12	25	*CoverCraft*
(9) Sir Rowland Hill, Kidderminster	12	15	*LFDC 83*
(10) Perkins, Bacon & Co., Penny Black, Fleet St.	12	75	*Bradbury*
(11) 1840-1990 Uniform Penny Postage, SW1	12	50	*Bradbury*
(12) Etchingham Stamp Festival	12	35	*Et'ham P.C.*
(13) 150th Anniversaries, SG Plymouth	12	25	*BLCS 48*
(14) Windsor, Berks. (Maltese Cross)	12	30	*Ben500(48)*
(15) Stampway to the World, Newcastle	12	50	*S.P.Board*

C.D.S. POSTMARKS

(16) Botchergate, Carlisle – first roadside postbox	30	
(17) Buckingham Palace, SW1	75	
(18) Fleet Street – Perkins, Bacon (Penny Black)	25	
(19) House of Commons or Lords – Postage Act	35	
(20) Kidderminster – b/place of Sir Rowland Hill	15	
(21) Sanquhar – oldest Post Office	25	
(22) Windsor, Berks.	25	
(23) Windsor Castle, Berks	95	

Also: Arbroath, Bath, Birmingham, Holyrood, London Chief Office, Lordship Lane N17, Queen Elizabeth Avenue, Queensbury, Queen's Parade, Queen Victoria Rd, Scone, Seething Lane EC3, Stoke-on-Trent, Victoria Rd. From £15.

PLEASE READ THE GENERAL NOTES

SLOGAN POSTMARKS

(24) Collect British Stamps: Philatelic Counters	25	
(25) Collect British Stamps – World's Greatest Hobby	20	
(26) Be Properly Addressed, Postcode It	20	
(27) Pass on your Postcode	20	
(28) Get the Most From Your Post – Code It!	20	
(29) Remember to use the Postcode	20	
(30) Post Early in the Day	20	
(31) Liverpool is a Mechanised Letter Office	20	
(32) Senders Name & Address /back of envelopes	20	
(33) Write Now! – Say it Better in a Letter	75	
(34) Stampway to the World – Newcastle	95	

Also available: Great Expectations; Beautiful Bath. Prices from £10.

23rd January 1990 – R.S.P.C.A.

20p Kitten; 29p Rabbit; 34p Duckling; 37p Puppy

SPECIAL HANDSTAMPS

(1) First Day of Issue – Philatelic Bureau	4	–	*Royal Mail*
(2) First Day of Issue – Horsham	4	–	*Royal Mail*
(3) Bunny, Nottingham	12	60	*Bradbury*
(4) Battersea, London SW8	12	25	*LFDC 84*
(5) RSPCA, 150 Years, Horsham	12	25	*CoverCraft*
(6) RSPCA, Pett, Hastings	12	60	*Ben500(49)*
(7) Cats Protection League, Middlesbrough	12	40	*S. Muscroft*
(8) Cat World Magazine, Shoreham	12	50	*BLCS 49*
(9) Provincial Grand Masters, Hadleigh	10	25	*Masons*
(10) Ekowe, Naval Brigade, BF 2215 PS	10	35	*FAAMuseum*
(11) No. 24 Squadron, BF 2216 PS	10	20	*RFDC 79*

C.D.S. POSTMARKS

(12) Battersea, or Battersea Park Road	25	
(13) Bunny, Nottingham	25	
(14) Dog & Gun, Dog Kennel Lane or Isle of Dogs	25	
(15) Horsham – RSPCA headquarters	15	
(16) Sidmouth – birthplace of founder of RSPCA	15	
(17) Trafalgar Sq – near to RSPCA's first meeting	12	

Also: Ballynahinch, Black Dog, Catsfield, Catshill, Catsfield, Ducklington, Duckworth Ln, Middlesbrough, Regent St. From £15.

RSPCA (contd.)	ordinary covers	official covers	
SLOGAN POSTMARKS	£	£	
(18) Collect British Stamps, Bradford (ram's head)	25		
(19) Aveling Barford, the Earthmovers (horse)	80		

Also: Collect British Stamps; Liverpool MLO; Write Now etc. Prices from £7.

6th February 1990 - GREETINGS STAMPS

10 x 20p Famous 'Smiles':
Teddy Bear; Dennis the Menace, Mr. Punch, Cheshire Cat, Man in the Moon, Laughing Policeman, Clown, Mona Lisa, Queen of Hearts, Stan Laurel.

SPECIAL HANDSTAMPS			
(1) First Day of Issue - Philatelic Bureau	8	-	*Royal Mail*
(2) First Day of Issue - Giggleswick	15	-	*Royal Mail*
(3) Greetings, Clowne, Chesterfield	15	35	*BenD135*
(4) Greetings, Puncheston, Haverfordwest	15	20	*Benham*
(5) Greetings, The Teddy Bear Shop, Ironbridge	15	50	*Ben500(50)pair*
(6) Greetings, Hartford, Cheshire	15	40	*BLCS 50 pair*
(7) No.604 Squadron, BF 2217 PS	15	20	*RFDC 80*
C.D.S. POSTMARKS			
(8) Bearpark, Catsfield, or Pudsey ... *each*	25		
(9) Bow St., Constable Rd., Constable Burton, or Law	25		
(10) Fleet Street - where 'Beano' is published	25		
(11) Giggleswick	25		
(12) Greet, Birmingham	25		
(13) Oxford - Lewis Carrol/'Alice in Wonderland'	25		
(14) Ulverston - birthplace of Stan Laurel	25		

Also: Colemore Circus, Greets Green, Big Top, Merry Hill, Laurel Ln, Puncheston, London E.C. £20.

SLOGAN POSTMARKS			
(15) Take a Bite Out of Crime, Newcastle	30		
(16) Collect British Stamps, Lincoln ('Lincoln Imp')	30		

Also: Darlington Open Day; Stampex; Collect British Stamps. Prices from £15.

6th March 1990 - EUROPA

20p Alexandra Palace; 29p British Philatelic Bureau;
20p Glasgow School of Art; 37p Templeton Carpet Factory, Glasgow

SPECIAL HANDSTAMPS			
(1) First Day of Issue - Philatelic Bureau	4	-	*Royal Mail*
(2) First Day of Issue - Glasgow	4	-	*Royal Mail*
(3) Cultural Capital, Glasgow	10	25	*Arlington*
(4) Europa, Stamp World, N22	10	15	*BLCS 51*
(5) Modern Movement Blg. in Europe, Glasgow	10	35	*Ben500(51)*
(6) British Philatelic Bureau, Edinburgh	10	10	*Bureau (s)*
(7) 1st Int. Stamp Exhibition, BPF, N22	10	15	*BPF*
(8) Alexandra Palace, Victorian Heritage, N22	10	15	*CoverCraft*
(9) Europa 1990, Edinburgh	10	10	*LFDC 85*
(10) Alexandra Palace, Europa 1990, N22	10	15	*Bradbury*
(11) Oldest Post Office, Sanquhar	10	50	*Bradbury*
(12) Forth Bridge Centennial, S. Queensferry	10	45	*Bradbury*
(13) No.8 Squadron, BF 2219 PS	10	20	*RFDC 81*
C.D.S. POSTMARKS			
(14) Alexandra Park Rd - venue of Stamp World	10		
(15) Bridgeton - Templeton Carpet Factory	10		
(16) Cowcadden, City Branch, or Hope St. - near to Glasgow School of Art ... *each*	10		
(17) Warriston - near to Philatelic Bureau	10		

Also: Cove, Craigpark, Duke St., Edinburgh, Glasgow, Glasgow Airport Helensburgh, London EC1, Paisley, Sanquhar, Templeton, The Scotlands. From £8.

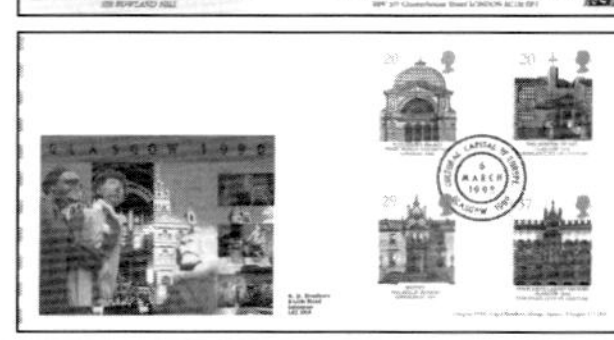

SLOGAN POSTMARKS			
(18) There's a lot of Glasgowing on	20		
(19) Collect British Stamps - World's Greatest Hobby	20		
(20) Lincoln or Bradford Philatelic Counters ... *each*	20		

Also: Burgh of Lanark; Scottish Blood Trans; Liverpool MLO. Prices from £10.

PLEASE READ THE GENERAL NOTES

10th April 1990 - QUEEN'S AWARDS TO INDUSTRY

2 x 20p, 2 x 37p Export & Technology Award emblems

SPECIAL HANDSTAMPS			
(1) First Day of Issue - Philatelic Bureau	4	-	*Royal Mail*
(2) First Day of Issue - SW London	4	-	*Royal Mail*
(3) Queen's Awards to Industry, SW1	10	30	*Ben500(52)*
(4) Queen's Award, SAGA, Folkestone	10	15	*BLCS 52*
(5) Laboratory of the Gov. Chemist	10	25	*CoverCraft*
(6) William Grant & Sons, Glenfiddich	10	85	*Arlington*
(7) CBI, Silver Jubilee, Investing in Success	10	20	*LFDC 86*
(8) Paper for the Penny Black, Northampton	10	75	*D.Rutt*
(9) No. 10 Squadron, BF 2220 PS	10	15	*RFDC 82*
(10) Konigsberg, BF 2224 PS	10	20	*FAAMuseum*
C.D.S. POSTMARKS			
(11) Buckingham Palace, SW1	75		
(12) Dover, Gatwick or Heathrow - exports ... *each*	10		
(13) Golders Green - Abram Games (stamp designer)	10		
(14) New Invention, Willenhall	15		
(15) Queen Elizabeth Avenue	15		
(16) Tufton Street, SW1 - Queen's Award Office	15		
(17) Turnpike Estate, Newbury - Quantel Ltd., (Computer Graphic artwork for stamps)	15		

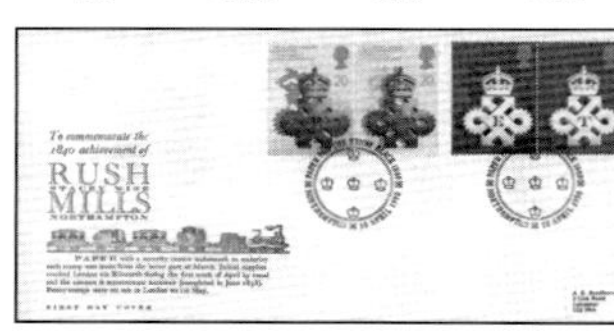

Queen's Awards (contd.)

	ordinary covers £	official covers £	
(18) Windsor Castle, Windsor, Berks	40		

Also: Aycliffe Trading Estate, Broadway SW1, Derby, Globe Road E1, House of Commons, Jubilee Crescent, Lombard St., London EC, NEC Birmingham, Newbury, Silver Link, South Lambeth SW8. Prices from £12.

SLOGAN POSTMARKS

(19) Invest in Sunderland – Enterprise Zone	20	

In addition: British Steel; Aveling Barford; Hastings Exhibition; Stamp World; Sure Plumber; Collect British Stamps; Penny Black Coin. Prices from £10.

3rd May 1990 – PENNY BLACK ANNIVERSARY

Miniature Sheet: 20p + Facsimile of Penny Black

SPECIAL HANDSTAMPS

(1) First Day of Issue – Philatelic Bureau	4	–	*Royal Mail*
(2) First Day of Issue – City of London	4	–	*Royal Mail*
(3) First Day of Issue – Alexandra Palace, N22	15	–	*Royal Mail*
(4) First Roadside Pillar Box, Carlisle	10	40	*Carlisle P.O.*
(5) Postal Museum, 1840-1990, EC	10	–	*n.o.c.*
(6) Royal Mail Exhib. Card No. 4, Edinburgh	10	–	*n.o.c.*
(7) Int. Stamp Exhibition, Stamp World, N22	10	–	*n.o.c.*
(8) Postal Museum, SWL90, EC	10	–	*n.o.c.*
(9) Penny Black, Rowland Hill, Kidderminster	10	20	*CoverCraft*
(10) Penny Black, William Wyon, Birmingham	10	20	*CoverCraft*
(11) 1d Black, Bruce Castle Museum, N17	10	20	*CoverCraft*
(12) Jacob Perkins, Printer of the Penny Black	10	20	*CoverCraft*
(13) British Philatelic Federation, N22	10	20	*CoverCraft*
(14) Sir Rowland Hill, Kidderminster	10	15	*LFDC 87*
(15) Perkins Bacon & Co., Fleet St.	10	25	*Bradbury*
(16) 'Rule Britannia', SW1	10	20	*Bradbury*
(17) Penny Black, Alexandra Palace, N22	10	20	*BenSG10*
(18) The Penny Black, Bath	10	45	*Ben500(53)*
(19) Stanley Gibbons, Stamp World, N22	10	50	*BLCS53*
(20) Perkins, Bacon, Southwark Bdge	10	20	*BLCS53*
(21) Etchingham Stamp Festival	10	25	*Etc'ham P.C.*
(22) The First Adhesive Stamp on Cover, Bath	10	25	*S. Muscroft*

C.D.S. POSTMARKS

(23) Alexandra Park Road – 'Stamp World'	10
(24) Britannia, Bacup or Porth *each*	10
(25) Buckingham Palace, SW1	40
(26) Fleet Street – Perkins, Bacon (Penny Black)	10
(27) House of Commons, SW1 – Postage Act	25
(28) House of Lords, SW1 – Postage Act	35
(29) Kidderminster – b/place of Sir Rowland Hill	10
(30) Sanquhar – oldest Post Office	10
(31) Wood Green – Mobile PO, 'Stamp World'	12
(32) Windsor, Windsor Gt Park or Old Windsor	65
(33) Windsor Castle	125

In addition: Cobham, Etchingham, Horsefair, London Chief Office, Lordship Lne N17, Queen Elizabeth Ave., South Kensington, Queen Vicoria Rd, Victoria Rd. Prices from £15.

SLOGAN POSTMARKS

(34) Visit Stamp World, Alexandra Palace	15
(35) Write Now! or Post Early in the Day	30
(36) Any Postcode slogan	30
(37) Senders name & address on back of envelopes	30
(38) New Sunday Collections, Royal Mail, B'ham	15
(39) Liverpool is a Mechanised Letter Office	20
(40) Postman of the Year	35
(41) Queen Victoria School	20

Also: Aveling Barford; Cunard; 6 May Code Change; Help Police, Postcode Valuables. From £7.

5th June 1990 – KEW GARDENS

20p Cycad + Joseph Banks Blg; 29p Stone Pine + Conservatory; 34p Willow Tree + Palm House; 37p Cedar + Pagoda

SPECIAL HANDSTAMPS

(1) First Day of Issue – Philatelic Bureau	4	–	*Royal Mail*
(2) First Day of Issue – Kew, Richmond	4	–	*Royal Mail*
(3) Arboricultural Assoc., Sevenoaks	10	12	*BLCS54*
(4) 150th Anniv. Royal Botanic Gardens, Kew	10	25	*Ben500(54)*
(5) Royal Botanic Gdns, Given to the Nation, 1840	10	15	*LFDC 88*
(6) Royal Botanic Gdns, Kew 1840-1990	10	15	*LFDC 88*
(7) Botanical Society, SW7	10	20	*CoverCraft*
(8) The Conservation Trust, Reading	10	20	*CoverCraft*
(9) Nat. Garden Festival (changeable date)	12	–	*Royal Mail*
(10) Nat. Garden Festival Tyne and Wear	12	–	*Royal Mail*
(11) Church in the Wood, St. Leonards on Sea	10	35	*Bradbury*
(12) Forth Bridge Centennial	10	25	*Bradbury*
(13) Torquay Philatelic Counter (Palm Tree)	20	–	*n.o.c.*
(14) 10th Anniversary, TTTE, BF 2247 PS	7	8	*RFDC 84*

C.D.S POSTMARKS

(15) Kew Gardens, Richmond, Surrey	25
(16) Ash, Beech, Cherry Tree, Elm, Hatfield Broad Oak, Fir Tree, Orange Tree, Pear Tree, Yew Tree	20

Also: Botanic Gdns, Broad Oak, Cedar Road, Chestnut Terrace, Forest Rd, The Firs, Glasshouses, Green Willows, Hawkhurst, Pinewoods, Sevenoaks, The Forest, The Green, The Willows, Wood End, Woodlands. Prices from £15.

1990

PLEASE READ THE GENERAL NOTES

	ordinary covers £	official covers £	
SLOGAN POSTMARKS			
(17) Royal Botanic Gardens, Kew	40		
(18) Richmond, Twin Towns, Twickenham	20		
(19) Dronfield & District Feast of Flowers	15		

Also: Steam Rally & Country Show; Royal Mail Derby/ESTF; Royal Mail Uxbridge New Sorting Office; Chester Business Park; Post Code; Collect British Stamps. Prices from £5.

10th July 1990 - THOMAS HARDY

20p Portrait of Hardy with Clyffe Clump, Dorset

SPECIAL HANDSTAMPS			
(1) First Day of Issue - Philatelic Bureau	2	-	*Royal Mail*
(2) First Day of Issue - Dorchester	2	-	*Royal Mail*
(3) Thomas Hardy Society, Higher Bockhampton	8	10	*LFDC 89*
(4) Marnhull, Tess of the D'Urbervilles	8	12	*Bradbury*
(5) Dorchester, Mayor of Casterbridge	8	12	*Bradbury*
(6) Thomas Hardy, Stinsford	8	12	*Bradbury*
(7) 150th Anniv. Thomas Hardy, Bockhampton	8	20	*Ben500(55)*
(8) Thomas Hardy, Wessex Poet & Novelist	8	10	*BLCS 55*
(9) Puddletown, Hardy's Weatherbury	8	15	*A. Pearce*
(10) Thomas Hardy, Dorchester	8	10	*Havering*
(11) Thomas Hardy, Higher Bockhampton	8	15	*CoverCraft*
(12) Nelson with Capt. Hardy, BF 2248 PS	8	15	*FAA Museum*
(13) Gibbons Stamp Monthly, Ringwood	8	10	*BenL24*
(14) Royal Navy Series, Plymouth	8	10	*Marriott*
(15) RAF Station Northolt, BF 2250 PS	8	10	*RFDC 85*
(16) Wimbledon, Lawn Tennis Museum	8	20	*H.R.*
C.D.S. POSTMARKS			
(17) Bere Regis (*Kingsbere*); Dorchester (*Casterbridge*); Maiden Newton (*Chalk Newton*); Puddletown (*Weatherbury*); Salisbury (*Melchester*); Shaftesbury (*Shaston*); Sherborne (*Sherton Abbas*); Sturminston Newton (*Stourcastle*); Weymouth (*Budmouth*); Winfrith (*Haggard Egden*) ...*each*	10		
(18) Harrow Rd or Westbourne Pk Rd - London home	10		
(19) Fordington - wrote many of his works here	10		

In addition: Amesbury, Hardy Lane, Owermoigne, Piddlehinton, Wimborne. Prices from £15.

SLOGAN POSTMARKS

Royal Mail Derby; Postcode, Dorchester; Say it Better in a Letter; Post Early; Various Post Code slogans; Uxbridge Sorting Office. Prices from £8.

2nd August 1990 - THE QUEEN MOTHER'S 90th BIRTHDAY

20p Queen Elizabeth The Queen Mother; 29p Queen Elizabeth; 34p Elizabeth Duchess of York; 37p Lady Elizabeth Bowes-Lyon

SPECIAL HANDSTAMPS			
(1) First Day of Issue - Philatelic Bureau	4	-	*Royal Mail*
(2) First Day of Issue - City of Westminster	4	-	*Royal Mail*
(3) St. Paul's, Walden, Herts - (square)	10	15	*LFDC 90*
(4) Clarence House, SW1 - (square)	10	15	*LFDC 90*
(5) Glamis, Tayside - (square)	10	15	*LFDC 90*
(6) Clarence House - (oval)	10	15	*BLCS 56*
(7) Glamis Castle - (oval)	10	25	*Ben500(56)*
(8) Windsor Castle - (oval)	10	20	*BLCS 56*
(9) St. Paul's, Hitchin - (oval)	10	15	*BenSG11*
(10) The Queen Mother, Woman & Home, SE1	10	20	*BLCS 56*
(11) Heartiest Congratulations, BF 1990 PS	10	15	*RFDC 86*
(12) Royal Mail, Birmingham	10	25	*RM B'ham*
(13) Queen Mother, Bowes Museum	10	15	*S. Muscroft*
(14) 90th Birthday HM The Queen Mother, SW1	10	30	*CoverCraft*
(15) Glamis Castle - (circle)	10	45	*CoverCraft*
(16) Clarence House - (circle)	10	45	*CoverCraft*
(17) Royal Wolverhampton School	10	35	*LFDC 90*
(18) RNLI, Thurso Lifeboat	10	25	*Pilgrim*
(19) Royal Doulton, The Potteries	10	20	*P.Withers*
C.D.S. POSTMARKS			
(20) Barnard Castle or Bowes	8		
(21) Buckingham Palace or Windsor Castle	100		
(22) Glamis - Queen Mother's ancestral home	25		
(23) House of Commons or Lords	25		
(24) Mey - Castle of Mey	25		
(25) Queen Elizabeth Ave. or Queen's Rd.	10		
(26) Whitwell, Hitchin - Bowes-Lyon family	10		
(27) Windsor, Old Windsor or Windsor Gt Park	10		

In addition: Albemarle St, Crathie, Holyrood, Rose, Scone, Walmer, York. Prices from £15.

SLOGAN POSTMARKS

Queen Victoria School; Royal Engineers Museum; Cunard; Forres Europe in Bloom; Alder Hey; Royal Mail - Car Secure; Royal Botanic Gardens. Prices from £7.

What is the difference between Ordinary & Official Covers?
The General Notes at the beginning of this catalogue will answer most of your questions.

11th Sept. 1990 - GALLANTRY

5 x 20p: Distinguished Service Cross & Medal
Distinguished Flying Cross & Medal
Military Cross & Military Medal; Victoria Cross; George Cross

1990

	ordinary cvrs £	official covers £	
SPECIAL HANDSTAMPS			
(1) First Day of Issue - Philatelic Bureau	4	-	*Royal Mail*
(2) First Day of Issue - City of Westminster	4	-	*Royal Mail*
(3) St. George, Bristol	12	30	*Bradbury*
(4) The Spirit of Britain, SW1	12	15	*LFDC 91*
(5) Battle of Britain, Hawkinge	12	25	*BLCS 57*
(6) Battle of Britain, Biggin Hill, Westerham	12	35	*BLCS 57*
(7) Victoria Cross for Valour, SW	12	60	*Ben500(57)*
(8) George Cross for Gallantry, SW	12	30	*BenSG12*
(9) Military Medal for Bravery, Chichester	12	25	*BenL26*
(10) Distinguished Service Medal, Liverpool	12	25	*BenL25*
(11) Battle of Britain, BF 2232 PS	12	15	*Forces (s)*
(12) Royal Navy Series, Plymouth	12	2	*Marriott(s)*
(13) Victoria Cross, National Postal Museum	20	-	*n.o.c.*
(14) World War II, Far East, BF 2251 PS	12	20	*FAA Museum*
(15) Defence of Rorke's Drift	12	25	*S. Muscroft*
(16) Battle of Britain, RAF Bentley Priory	12	45	*CoverCraft*
(17) Battle of Britain, BBMF, RAF Coningsby	12	25	*CoverCraft*
(18) Battle of Britain, RAF Coltishall	12	10	*Markton*
(19) George Cross, Island Siege, Bell Fund, Malta	12	75	*Cam.S.C.*
(20) Baden-Powell House	12	10	*Havering*
(21) Sunderland AFC	12	15	*Dawn*
(22) Torquay, Birthplace of Agatha Christie	12	75	*CoverCraft*
C.D.S. POSTMARKS			
(23) High Cross, Ware - b/place of first VC & Bar	20		
(24) Biggin Hill, or RAF Biggin Hill	30		
(25) Any Field Post Office or RAF Station	20		
(26) Portsmouth - Royal Navy	15		
(27) Sandhurst - Royal Military Academy	25		
(28) Royal Hospital Chelsea - Chelsea Pensioners	25		
(29) St. George, Bristol or St. Georges, Telford	25		
(30) St. George's Cross, Glasgow	20		
(31) Hawkinge or Duxford	20		
(32) Maritime Mail	40		

Also: Albemarle St. W1, Battle, Battlefield, Battlefield Rd., Battlehill, Buckingham Palace, Churchill, Cove Bay, Duke of York Sch., Dunkirk, Falklands, Gun End, House of Commons, House of Lords, Immingham Dock, King George Rd, Manor Park, Memorial Rd, Mount Ephriam, Normandy, Queen's Cross, Richmond, Sebastopol, Three Crosses, Victoria Rd, Walton-on-Thames, Wargrave, Waterloo, Windsor Castle, Wortley. From £15.

SLOGAN POSTMARKS		
(33) Royal Engineers Museum	20	
(34) RAF Finningley Air Show	20	

In addition: Nth Yorks Police; Queen Victoria Sch; Croydon. Prices from £8.

16th October 1990 - ASTRONOMY

22p Armagh Observatory; Jodrell Bank and La Palma telescopes;
26p Moon and tides; Herschel's telescope;
31p Greenwich Old Observatory and early Astronomical equipment;
37p Stonehenge: gyroscope and navigation by the stars

SPECIAL HANDSTAMPS			
(1) First Day of Issue - Philatelic Bureau	4	-	*Royal Mail*
(2) First Day of Issue - Armagh	4	-	*Royal Mail*
(3) Jodrell Bank Science Centre	10	15	*LFDC 92*
(4) Old Royal Observatory, Greenwich	10	15	*BLCS 58*
(5) Heavens Declare the Glory of God, Armagh	10	10	*BLCS 58*
(6) Sir William Herschel, Slough	10	30	*Ben500(58)*
(7) Woolsthorpe, Birthplace of Isaac Newton	10	50	*CoverCraft*
(8) Astronomical Alignments, Stonehenge	10	60	*Bradbury*
(9) Old Royal Observatory, Greenwich (globe)	10	15	*Arlington*
(10) British Astronomical Assoc., Burlington Hse	10	45	*Cam.S.C.*
(11) British Astronomical Assoc., Royal Observatory	10	65	*Cam.S.C.*
(12) Autumn Stampex/BPE, London SW1	10	-	*Royal Mail*
(13) Royal Mail Exhibition Card No. 4	10	-	*Royal Mail*
(14) No. 249 Squadron BF 2253 PS	10	15	*RFDC 88*
C.D.S. POSTMARKS			
(15) Armagh - Armagh Observatory	15		
(16) Macclesfield etc - Jodrell Bank	20		
(17) Greenwich, Herstmonceux, Castle St. Cambridge - Royal Observatory	15		
(18) Larkhill or Amesbury - Stonehenge	20		
(19) Albemarle St. - Burlington House	15		
(20) Meridian Centre, Peacehaven	20		

Also: Archer Road, Barnard Castle, Blackford Avenue Edinburgh, Ceres, Colsterworth, Comberton, The Crescent, Crown View, Denby, Five Points, Flamstead End, Globe Rd., Helston, Moore, Newton, North Pole, Oldland Common, The Rocket, Seven Sisters, Southern Cross, Starcross. From £12.

SLOGAN POSTMARKS

PO Mercurycard; Stampex; New World Dom. Appliances; Car Secure; Smugglers; Isle of Skye; Royal Soc of Chemistry; Sunderland Illuminations. Prices from £12.

13th November 1990 - CHRISTMAS

17p Children building snowman; 22p Bringing home the Christmas tree; 26p Carol singers; 31p Tobogganing; 37p Skating

SPECIAL HANDSTAMPS

	ordinary cvrs £	official covers £	
(1) First Day of Issue - Philatelic Bureau	4	-	*Royal Mail*
(2) First Day of Issue - Bethlehem, Llandeilo	4	-	*Royal Mail*
(3) Church Bell Ringers, St. Paul's, EC4	10	35	*Bradbury*
(4) Church Bell Ringers, Duffield	10	35	*Bradbury*
(5) Birmingham Cathedral	10	20	*Bradbury*
(6) 25 Years Christmas Stamps, Bethlehem	10	35	*LFDC 93*
(7) 150 Years of Stamps, Nasareth	10	35	*CoverCraft*
(8) 150 Years of Stamps, London EC1	10	35	*CoverCraft*
(9) Nat. Postal Museum, Post Early for Christmas	10	10	*Friends of NPM*
(10) Benham, First Day Covers, Folkestone	10	15	*BLCS 59*
(11) Christmas Mailcoach Run, Windsor	10	10	*BLCS 59*
(12) Christmas Tradition, Snowdown, Dover	10	20	*Ben500(59)*
(13) Stanley Gibbons Catalogue, Ringwood	10	25	*BenL27*
(14) Christmas 1990, Cambridge	10	95	*Cam.S.C.*
(15) Stampway to the World, Glasgow	10	25	*S.P. Board*
(16) Bishop Vesey, Sutton Coldfield	10	25	*BVGS*
(17) Blood & Fire in Darkest England, EC1	10	15	*S.Army*
(18) Royal Navy Series, Plymouth	10	-	*n.o.c.*

C.D.S. POSTMARKS

(19) Church, Hollybush, Fir Tree or Playing Place...	15
(20) Nasareth	25

In addition: Aviemore, Churchfield, Church Hill, Church Village, Holy Island, Jericho, Jerusalem St., Merry Hill, Noel Road, St. Nicholas, Trafalgar Square, Winter Hey. Prices from £10.

SLOGAN POSTMARKS

(21) Birmingham Cathedral	20
(22) Happy Christmas - Please Post Early	40
(23) Nadolig Llawen - Happy Christmas	40

Also: Stampway; Candlelighters; Control your Dog; Coventry/Friendship; Alder Hey. Prices from £8.

CHRISTMAS BOOKLET

Covers bearing pair or block of 4 x 17p from booklet with spec h/s (straight edges at top and bottom)	5
Full pane of ten stamps on cover	20

8th January 1991 - DOGS (George Stubbs)

22p King Charles Spaniel; 26p A Pointer; 31p Two Hounds in a Landscape; 33p A Rough Dog; 37p Fino and Tiny

SPECIAL HANDSTAMPS

	ordinary cvrs £	official covers £	
(1) First Day of Issue - Philatelic Bureau	4	-	*Royal Mail*
(2) First Day of Issue - Birmingham	4	-	*Royal Mail*
(3) PDSA, Telford	10	15	*LFDC 94*
(4) Tate Gallery, London, SW1	10	25	*Bradbury*
(5) Birmingham Dogs Home	10	30	*Bradbury*
(6) Best of British Dogs, Birmingham	10	30	*Bradbury*
(7) RVC, 200 Years, NW1	10	25	*Bradbury*
(8) Crufts Dog Show, Birmingham (badge)	10	10	*BLCS 60*
(9) Centenary Crufts Dog Show, Birmingham	10	40	*Ben500(60)*
(10) Pawprints, Stoke-on-Trent	10	20	*P. Withers*
(11) Birthplace of George Stubbs, Liverpool	10	25	*CoverCraft*
(12) National Canine Defence League, NW1	10	30	*CoverCraft*
(13) Dog World, Crufts, NEC, Birmingham	10	20	*R. Skinner*
(14) Police Guard Dog School, BF 2257 PS	10	20	*RFDC 90*
(15) Stampway to the World, Glasgow	10	20	*S.P. Board*

C.D.S. POSTMARKS

(16) Barking, Black Dog or Dogsthorpe *each*	20
(17) Battersea or NEC	20
(18) Dog & Gun, Dog Kennel Ln or Isle of Dogs	25
(19) Odiham - RVC founded by Odiham Agr Soc...	15
(20) Portman Square - Stubb's studio	15
(21) Royal College St - Royal Veterinary College	15
(22) Stubb's Cross	15

In addition: Airedale, Corn Exchange, Houndsditch, Newmarket, Pant. Prices from £12.

SLOGAN POSTMARKS

(23) Pawprints Appeal	20
(24) Take a Bite out of Crime	20

In addition: Stampway to the World. Prices from £8.

VALUES ARE FOR GOOD, CLEAN & UNADDRESSED COVERS

5th February 1991 - GREETINGS STAMPS

10 designs of '1st Class' stamps featuring good luck symbols

SPECIAL HANDSTAMPS

	ordinary cvrs £	official covers £	
(1) First Day of Issue - Philatelic Bureau	5	-	*Royal Mail*
(2) First Day of Issue - Greetwell, Lincs.	5	-	*Royal Mail*
(3) Good Luck, Rainow, Macclesfield	10	30	*BLCS 61*
(4) Good Luck, Good Easter, Chelmsford	10	25	*Ben500(61)*
(5) Good Luck, Wishford, Salisbury	10	10	*BenD158*
(6) Good Luck, Glenrothes, Fife	10	40	*BLCS 61*
(7) Good Luck, Magpie, Yelverton	10	40	*BLCS 61*
(8) Good Luck, Luckington, Chippenham	10	15	*Bradbury*
(9) Rescue Services, BF 2258 PS	10	15	*RFDC 91*

Greetings (contd.) **ordinary covers** **official covers**

C.D.S. POSTMARKS £ £

(10) Acorn St., Bell Green, Boot, Branch End, Bridge, Catsfield, Clover Rd., Cross Keys, Drakes Broughton, Ducklington, Frog Island, Frogpool, Goldenacre, Greet, Greetland, Gretna Green, Jacob's Well, Keyworth, Klondyke, Luckington, Merlin's Bridge, Primrose Hill, Silverwell, Sky Crescent, Starcross, Swallow's Nest, Well, Wing, Wren's Nest .... *each* 15

POSTMARK SLOGANS

Pawprints; Samaritans; Alder Hey; Magic of British Music; Royal Mail/Post Code. From £15.

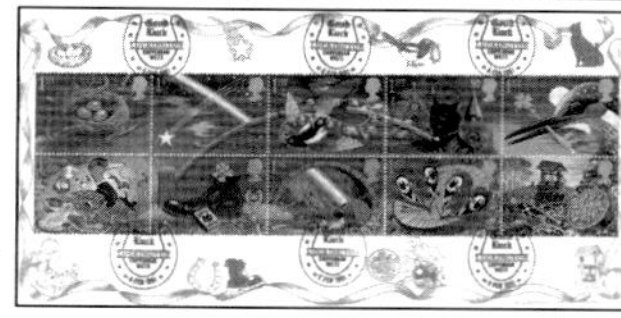

5th March 1991 - SCIENTIFIC ACHIEVEMENTS

22p Michael Faraday - electricity; 22p Charles Babbage - computers; 31p Robert Watson-Watt - radar; 37p Frank Whittle - jet engine

SPECIAL HANDSTAMPS

(1)	First Day of Issue - Philatelic Bureau	4	-	*Royal Mail*
(2)	First Day of Issue - South Kensington, SW7	4	-	*Royal Mail*
(3)	Charles Babbage, Science Museum, SW7	10	20	*Bradbury*
(4)	Royal Society of Chemistry, W1	10	20	*Bradbury*
(5)	Society British Aerospace Companies, SW1	10	20	*Bradbury*
(6)	The Royal Institution, W1	10	20	*Bradbury*
(7)	Sir Frank Whittle, Lutterworth	10	15	*LFDC 95*
(8)	Marconi Radar Systems, Chelmsford	10	20	*Bradbury*
(9)	Michael Faraday, Electrical Discovery, SW	10	17	*Ben500(62)*
(10)	A.E.U. General Office, SE15	10	20	*R. Skinner*
(11)	Loughborough University	10	20	*S. Muscroft*
(12)	Michael Faraday/Charles Babbage, IEE	10	35	*Cam.S.C.*
(13)	Industrial Soc., Peter Runge House	10	20	*P. Withers*
(14)	First Aircraft Turbo Jet Engine, BF 2260 PS	10	20	*Forces*
(15)	First Flight of Jet, Cranwell, BF 2259 PS	10	20	*RFDC 92*
(16)	Computer Innovation, Wembley	10	125	*Arlington*
(17)	Electricity, Hove	10	125	*Arlington*
(18)	Royal Signals & Radar, Malvern	10	125	*Arlington*
(19)	RMA Woolwich, Sandhurst	10	125	*Arlington*

C.D.S. POSTMARKS

(20)	Albermarle Street, W1 - Royal Institution	15
(21)	Cranwell - first official flight of the jet engine	15
(22)	Daventry - radar experiments	15
(23)	Exhibition Road, SW7 - Science Museum	15
(24)	Hucclecote - Gloster Meteor was built here	20
(25)	Lutterworth - jet engine was built here	20
(26)	New Invention	20
(27)	Weedon - first successful radar demonstrated	20

Also: Alderton, Banbury, Brechin, Brockworth, Broomfield Rd, Caversham, Earlsden, Elephant & Castle, Faraday St, Loughborough, Seascale, Southcliff, Totnes, Trinity St., Walworth Road. From £12.

SLOGAN POSTMARKS

(28)	Philips - a hundred years ahead	15
(29)	Loughborough University	15

In addition: Sunderland Enterprise Zone £8.

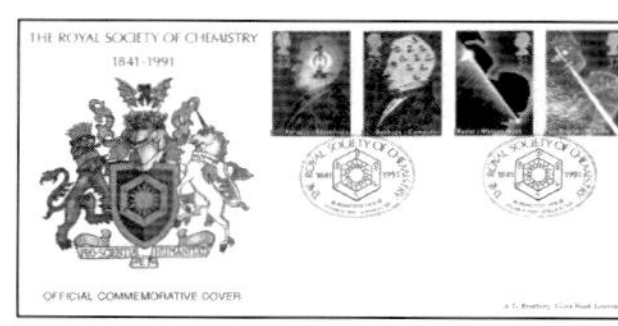

26th March 1991 - GREETINGS STAMPS

Same 'smiles' designs as 6th Feb. 1990 - values changed from 20p to '1st Class'

SPECIAL HANDSTAMPS

(1)	First Day of Issue - Philatelic Bureau	5	-	*Royal Mail*
(2)	First Day of Issue - Laughterton, Lincs.	5	-	*Royal Mail*
(3)	Puncheston, Haverfordwest, Dyfed	10	20	*BenD159*
(4)	Greetings, The Teddy Bear Shop, Ironbridge	10	25	*BLCS 63*
(5)	Greetings, Clowne, Chesterfield	10	30	*BLCS 63*
(6)	Greetings, Hartford, Cheshire	10	20	*Ben500(63)*
(7)	Birthplace of Stan Laurel, Ulverston	10	15	*Bradbury*
(8)	Battle of Cape Matapan, BF 2262 PS	10	-	*n.o.c.*

C.D.S. POSTMARKS

(9)	Bearpark, or Catsfield	12
(10)	Constable Road, or Fleet Street	12
(11)	Giggleswick, Greet or Laughterton	12
(12)	Puncheston, Clowne or Queen's Head	12
(13)	Ulverston - birthplace of Stan Laurel	12

SLOGAN POSTMARKS

(14)	Take a Bite out of Crime	12

In addition: The Samaritans; Alder Hey. Prices from £7.

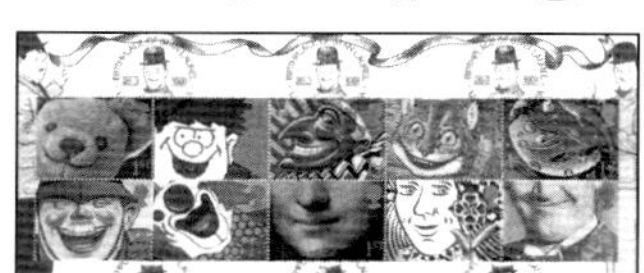

23rd April 1991 - EUROPE IN SPACE

2 x 22p Man looking into space; 2 x 37p Space looking at man

SPECIAL HANDSTAMPS

(1)	First Day of Issue - Philatelic Bureau	4	-	*Royal Mail*
(2)	First Day of Issue - Cambridge	4	-	*Royal Mail*
(3)	Soft Moon Landing, Jodrell Bank	10	20	*BLCS 64*
(4)	Vostok 1, Yuri Gargarin, The Rocket	10	20	*BLCS 64*
(5)	First Man in Space, Harwell	10	25	*Ben500(64)*
(6)	Kettering Boys School	10	20	*P. Withers*
(7)	Space: The Final Frontier, W1	10	25	*Bradbury*
(8)	Hubble Space Telescope, Cambridge	10	50	*Bradbury*

Europe in Space (contd.)	ordinary covers £	official covers £	
(9) Royal Aeronautical Society, W1	10	10	*Bradbury*
(10) British Interplanetary Society, SW8 1SZ	10	15	*Bradbury*
(11) BNSC – Britain's Space Agency, SW1	10	10	*LFDC 96*
(12) Jodrell Bank Science Centre, Macclesfield	10	45	*CoverCraft*
(13) VC10 in Military Service, BF 2272 PS	10	20	*RFDC 93*
(14) Centre for Crop Circle Studies, Guildford	10	20	*S. Muscroft*
(15) Prince & Princess of Wales, Brazil	10	75	*Forces*
(16) Salvation Army Match Factory, E3	10	30	*S.Army*

C.D.S. POSTMARKS

(17) Comberton – Mullard Radio Astron. Observatory	10		
(18) Greenwich or Cambridge – Royal Observatory	10		
(19) Helston – Goonhilly Downs Earth Station	10		
(20) The Rocket	15		
(21) Siddington, Goostrey, Macclesfield – Jodrell Bank	10		
(22) South Lambeth Rd – Interplanetary Soc	10		
(23) Surbiton–Helen Sharman/Britain's first astronaut	15		

Also: Chilton, Eye, Farnborough, Neville's Cross, Oldland Common, S. Wonston, Upton Lea. From £10.

SLOGAN POSTMARKS

(24) Squint Awareness Week	25		

Also: Loughborough Univ; BBC Radio; Samaritans; Sunday Collections; Please Control your Dog; Beat the Burglar; Postcode it. £8.

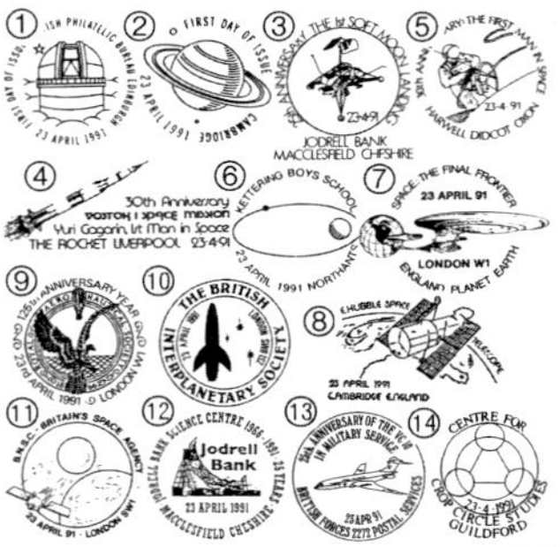

11th June 1991 – SPORTS

22p Fencing; 26p Hurdling; 31p Diving; 39p Rugby

SPECIAL HANDSTAMPS			
(1) Philatelic Bureau	4	–	*Royal Mail*
(2) First Day of Issue – Sheffield	4	–	*Royal Mail*
(3) Rugby Football, 'Grand Slam', Twickenham	10	15	*Sajal Phil*
(4) If it's on, it's in Radio Times, W1	10	20	*Radio Times*
(5) Home of Welsh Rugby, Cardiff Arms Park	10	12	*BLCS 65*
(6) Home of Scottish Rugby, Murrayfield	10	15	*BLCS 65*
(7) Home of English Rugby, Twickenham	10	12	*BLCS 65*
(8) 1991 Year of Sport, Sheffield	10	30	*Ben500(65)*
(9) Rugby School	10	10	*LFDC 97*
(10) William Webb Ellis: Game of Rugby	10	40	*VP 59*
(11) Inter. Olympic Committee, Birmingham	10	15	*Bradbury*
(12) Sport for All, Wembley	10	20	*Bradbury*
(13) World Student Games, Sheffield	10	25	*WSGames*
(14) Avon Pride, 1977-1991, Bristol	10	325	*Avon Pride*
(15) Lawn Tennis Museum	10	25	*AELT*

C.D.S. POSTMARKS

(16) The Hayes (Cardiff); Kingsholm (Gloucester); Kneller Rd. (Twickenham); Murrayfield (Edinburgh); Ravenhill Park (Belfast); Sandygate (Llanelli); Welford Rd. (Leicester); Otley; Pontypool; Pontypridd – Rugby World Cup ... *each*	20		
(17) Rugby – Rugby School	15		
(18) Sheffied – World Student Games	15		

Also: The University Bath, Fence, Jump, First Lane, Loughborough, University Bradford. From £8.

SLOGAN POSTMARKS

(19) Birmingham Welcomes IOC Committee	15		
(20) Cardiff Just Capital	20		
(21) Federation Cup, Nottingham Tennis Centre	25		

Also: Loughborough University; Convention Centre B'ham; Cub Scouting;London Docklands. £10.

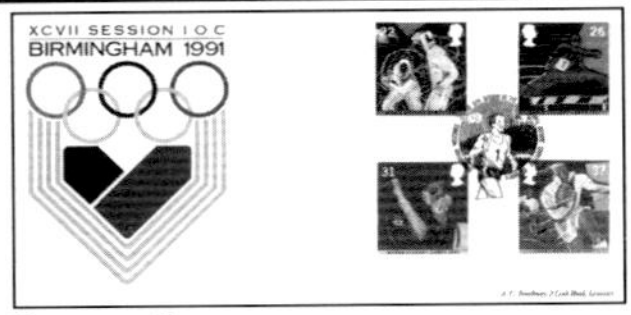

16th July 1991 – ROSES

22p Silver Jubilee; 26p Mme. Alfred Carriere; 31p Rosa Moyesii; 33p Harvest Fayre; 37p Rosa Mutabilis

SPECIAL HANDSTAMPS			
(1) Philatelic Bureau	4	–	*Royal Mail*
(2) First Day of Issue – Belfast	4	–	*Royal Mail*
(3) Royal National Rose Society, St. Albans	10	15	*LFDC 98*
(4) Royal Botanic Gardens, Kew	10	15	*Bradbury*
(5) World Rose Convention, Belfast	10	40	*VP 60*
(6) O, My Luve's Like a Red, Red Rose	10	20	*Bradbury*
(7) Roses on Stamps, Rose, Truro	10	20	*Bradbury*
(8) The Gardener, Chelsea, SW3	10	20	*BLCS 66*
(9) Rosebush, Clynderwen, Dyfed	10	25	*Ben500(66)*
(10) Rose Garden, Drum Castle, Banchory	10	22	*BLCS 66*
(11) Henry VIII, Hampton Court	10	15	*BenSG13*
(12) Hampton Court Palace, Int. Flower Show	10	50	*CoverCraft*
(13) National Gallery, WC2	10	75	*CoverCraft*
(14) Royal Tournament, Earls Court, BF 2292 PS	10	10	*Forces*
(15) London Economic Summit, SW1	10	40	*Arlington*

C.D.S. POSTMARKS

(16) Botanic Gardens, Belfast or Kew Gardens	25		
(17) Newtonards – 'Harvest Fayre' bred here	15		
(18) Rose, Truro	25		
(19) Roseacre, Rosebank, Rosebush, Rosedale Abbey, Rosehearty, Rose Green, Rose Hill, Roseland, Rosemarket, Roses Lane Ends ... *each*	25		
(20) Royal Hospital – Chelsea Flower Show	25		

In addition: Chipping Campden, Glamis, Leaves Green. Prices from £12.

PLEASE READ THE GENERAL NOTES PAGES 4 - 16

Roses (contd.)	ordinary covers	official covers	
SLOGAN POSTMARKS	£	£	
(21) Beechwood Place – Shopping in full bloom	20		

Also: Belfast 1991; Control your dog; Mansfield Show; Postcodes. Prices from £7.

20th August 1991 - DINOSAURS

22p Iguanodon; 26p Stegosaurus; 31pTyrannosaurus; 33p Protoceratops; 37p Triceratops

SPECIAL HANDSTAMPS			
(1) Philatelic Bureau	4	–	*Royal Mail*
(2) First Day of Issue – Plymouth	4	–	*Royal Mail*
(3) Dinosaur Museum, Dorchester	15	15	*BLCS 67*
(4) The Last Dinosaur? The Loch Ness Monster	15	25	*BLCS 67*
(5) Iguanodon Mantelli , Maidstone	15	15	*BenL28*
(6) 150th Anniv. of the Word Dinosaur, Oxford	15	18	*B'ham (500)67*
(7) First Discovery of Iguanodon, Cuckfield	15	45	*VP 61*
(8) Natural History Museum, Dinosaurs, SW7	15	20	*LFDC 99*
(9) First use of Word Dinosaur, Plymouth	15	35	*Bradbury*
(10) Farewell Shackletonsaurus, BF 2299 PS	15	20	*RFDC 96*
(11) Plymouth Museums & Art Gallery	15	55	*Arlington*
(12) Franklin & Andrew, London, EC4	15	125	*Arlington*
C.D.S. POSTMARKS			
(13) Plymouth – first use of Word 'Dinosaur'	20		
(14) Cuckfield, Lyme Regis, Maidstone, Stonesfield or Tilgate – dinosaur remains *each*	20		
(15) Dorchester – Dinosaur Museum	20		
(16) Exhibition Rd. – Natural History Museum	20		
(17) The Lizard	20		

Camels Head, Lancaster, Lewes, Oxford, Ness, Stonewell, Sydenham.Prices from £15.

SLOGAN POSTMARKS *Pawprints; Control Your Dog; Guide Dogs; Bite/Crime.£10.*

17th September 1991 - MAPS

24p, 28p, 33p, 39p – Hamstreet as depicted on Ordnance Survey maps.

SPECIAL HANDSTAMPS			
(1) Philatelic Bureau	4	–	*Royal Mail*
(2) First Day of Issue – Southampton	4	–	*Royal Mail*
(3) Visit the Nene Valley Railway	12	45	*N.V. Rly.*
(4) Maps and the Post Office, NPM, EC	12	85	*NPMuseum*
(5) Sir George Everest, Surveyor, Greenwich	12	45	*Bradbury*
(6) Birthplace of Tourism, Leicester	12	35	*Bradbury*
(7) RICS, London, SW1	12	12	*Bradbury*
(8) Ordnance Survey, Hamstreet	12	12	*LFDC 100*
(9) Ordnance Survey Act, Westminster, SW1	12	35	*VP 62*
(10) Ordnance Survey, Hamstreet (oast house)	12	15	*Ben500(68)*
(11) Hamstreet D490	12	15	*BLCS 68*
(12) Darling Buds of May, Hamstreet	12	12	*BLCS 68*
(13) Ordnance Survey OS, Southampton	12	60	*CoverCraft*
(14) Royal Observer Corps BF 2301 PS	12	12	*RFDC 97*
(15) Tower of London, EC3	12	10	*Sunday Mag.*
(16) Salvation Army, Hadleigh	12	15	*S. Army*
C.D.S. POSTMARKS			
(17) Ham Street, Ashford	20		
(18) House of Commons – Ordnance Survey Act	20		
(19) House of Lords – Ordnance Survey Act	30		
(20) John O'Groats/Land's End *pair*	50		
(21) Maybush – Ordnance Survey HQ	15		
(22) Newlyn – OS Tidal Observatory	15		
(23) Pathfinder Village or Ordnance Road	15		
(24) Seething Lane – original HQ of OS	15		

In addition: The Chart, Chartham, Cross Roads, Hereford, Junction, Marshfield, Meridian Centre, Richmond, Roman Way, The Triangle, Tingley, World's End. Prices from £10.

SLOGAN POSTMARKS			
(25) Royal Scottish Geographical Society	25		

Also: New Postage Rates; Yellow Brick Road; Royal Mail/Community; Control Your Dog. From £7.

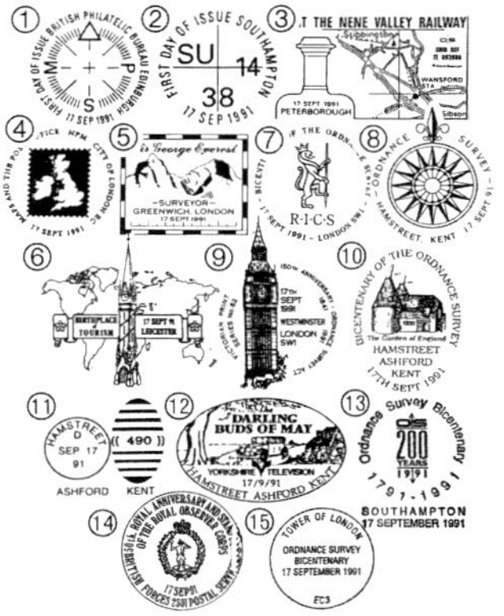

12th November 1991 - CHRISTMAS

18p, 24p, 28p, 33p, 39p Illuminated Manuscripts (Bodleian Library).

SPECIAL HANDSTAMPS			
(1) Philatelic Bureau	4	–	*Royal Mail*
(2) First Day of Issue – Bethlehem, Llandeilo	4	–	*Royal Mail*
(3) Dean & Chapter Library, Durham Cathedral	10	15	*LFDC 101*
(4) Holy Island, Berwick	10	15	*Bradbury*
(5) Illuminated Manuscripts, Bodleian Library	10	35	*Bradbury*
(6) Illuminated Manuscripts, Bethlehem	10	35	*VP 63*
(7) Cadfael Omnibus, Christmas, Shrewsbury	10	15	*BLCS 69*
(8) Christmas Manuscripts, Fountain's Abbey	10	15	*Ben500(69)*
(9) Christmas, Jerusalem, Skellingthorpe	10	20	*C. Cooke*
(10) Lindisfarne Gospels, Holy Island	10	25	*S. Muscroft*
(11) Happy Christmas Royal Mail City of London	10	–	*n.o.c.*
(12) Nat. Postal Museum Post Early for Christmas	10	10	*Friends of NPM*
(13) Christmas 1991, Cambridge	10	50	*Cam. S.C.*
(14) Joy to the World, The Salvation Army, SW1	10	15	*S. Army*
(15) Hercules, BF 2304 PS	10	20	*RFDC 98*
(16) Henry VIII, Greenwich, SE1	10	15	*BLCS 69*
(17) New Hoylake Lifeboat, Liverpool	10	12	*Pilgrim*

Christmas (contd.)	ordinary covers	official covers	
C.D.S. POSTMARKS	£	£	
(18) Exeter – birthplace of Sir Thomas Bodley	15		
(19) Holy Island or Oxford (Bodleian Library)	15		

Angel Hill, Bolton Abbey, Caldey Is., Jerusalem St., Kings Rd, Nasareth, St.Nicholas, Threekingham. £10.

SLOGAN POSTMARKS
Newcastle Brown; Clatterbridge Superscan; JVC Video Letter; Northsound Charity; Control Your Dog; Pulse Trust Appeal; Shopping in Full Bloom; Glasgow Court Hall; Alder Hey; Write Now etc. £7.

CHRISTMAS BOOKLET: Covers bearing pair or block of 4 x 18p stamps from booklet with special handstamp (these have straight edges at top and bottom) ...*each* 3
Full pane of ten stamps on cover ...*each* 15

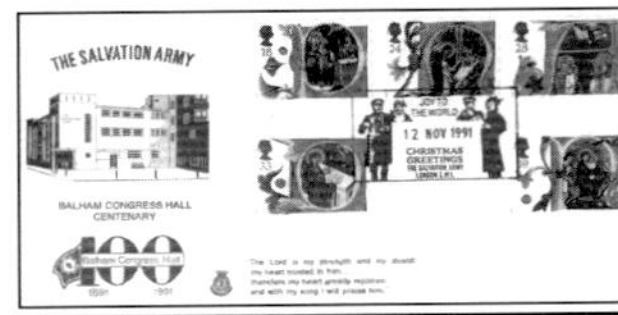

14th January 1992 – WINTERTIME

18p Deer; 24p Hare; 28p Fox; 33p Redwing; 39p Welsh Sheep.

SPECIAL HANDSTAMPS (1) Philatelic Bureau	4	–	*Royal Mail*
(2) First Day of Issue – Brecon	4	–	*Royal Mail*
(3) Emmerdale, Arncliffe, Skipton	12	–	*n.o.c.*
(4) Wintertime, Richmond Park	10	15	*B. Reeve 1*
(5) Wintertime, Owlsmoor, Camberley	10	15	*LFDC 102*
(6) Wintertime, Haresfield	10	45	*Bradbury*
(7) Wintertime, New Forest	10	25	*VP 64*
(8) The Monarch of the Glen, Glenbuck	10	25	*Ben500(70)*
(9) Wildlife in Winter, Thrushwood, Keswick	10	10	*BLCS 70*
(10) Wild About Animals, EC	10	15	*Benham*
(11) World Wide Fund for Nature, Godalming	10	20	*BLCS 70*
(12) British Wintertime, Brecon	10	20	*BLCS 70*
(13) Foxearth, Suffolk (or Sufflok)	10	20	*BenSG14*
(14) Sittingbourne's New Postbus	10	20	*RM postcard*
(15) Chester Cathedral	10	–	*n.o.c.*
(16) RAF Fylingdales, BF 2281 PS	10	20	*RFDC 99*
C.D.S. POSTMARKS			
(17) Deerpark, New Deer or Old Deer ...*each*	20		
(18) Harefield, Harehills or Harewood ...*each*	20		
(19) Foxhole or Fox Lane ...*each*	20		
(20) Sheepridge, Sheepwash or Sheepy ...*each*	20		
(21) Sheepscombe – farm Post Office	25		
(22) Brecon – sheep stamp set in Brecon area	20		

Also: Coldridge, Frosterley, Freezywater, Godalming, Lairg, Lyndhurst, Nettleham, Wing, Winterbourne, Winter Hey, Winter Rd. Winterton. Prices from £15.

SLOGAN POSTMARKS *Control your dog; Ynys Mon Isle of Anglesey; Pawprints.£12.*

28th January 1992 – GREETINGS STAMPS

10 designs of 1st Class stamps on the theme of Memories.

SPECIAL HANDSTAMPS (1) Philatelic Bureau	5	–	*Royal Mail*
(2) First Day of Issue – Whimsey	5	–	*Royal Mail*
(3) The Good Old Days, London Colney.	10	12	*BenD182*
(4) The Good Old Days, Surbiton	10	25	*Ben500(71)*
(5) The Good Old Days, Brighton	10	30	*BLCS 71*
(6) The Good Old Days, Kings Cross	10	30	*BLCS 71*
(7) The Good Old Days, Oxford	10	30	*BLCS 71*
(8) Harrogate, Yorks	10	30	*BLCS 71*
(9) Portobello Road, W11	10	15	*Bradbury*
(10) Chester Cathedral	10	–	*n.o.c.*
(11) Up Helly AA Lerwick	10	30	*A. Moncrief*
(12) Eastbourne Judgement, Salvation Army	10	25	*S. Army*
C.D.S. POSTMARKS			
(13) Bala – featured on the map	12		
(14) Greet, Lover, Letter, Rose, or Seaside	12		
(15) Portobello Road – famous antiques market	12		

Cargreen, Keyford, Kings Road, Chelsea, Market Place, Maypole, Ordnance Rd, Penny Lne. From £10.

SLOGAN POSTMARKS
(16) Southend on Sea Borough Centenary ... 20
In addition: Westmoreland; VW Audi; Please control your dog; Write Now etc. Prices from £12.

6th February 1992 – HAPPY & GLORIOUS

5 x 24p: Her Majesty as:- Head of State; Head of the Church of England; Head of the Royal Family; Head of Armed Forces; & Head of the Commonwealth.

SPECIAL HANDSTAMPS (1) Philatelic Bureau	3	–	*Royal Mail*
(2) First Day of Issue – Buckingham Palace	3	–	*Royal Mail*
(3) Happy & Glorious, National Postal Museum	10	–	*Royal Mail*
(4) Happy & Glorious, Brian Reeve, Windsor	10	12	*B. Reeve 2*
(5) Happy & Glorious, London, SW1	10	15	*VP 65*
(6) Happy & Glorious, Church Bell Ringers	10	10	*LFDC 103*
(7) Happy & Glorious, Commonwealth Institute	10	15	*Bradbury*
(8) Happy & Glorious, Windsor	10	35	*Bradbury*
(9) Happy & Glorious, TV Times, SW1	10	25	*Benham*
(10) 40th Anniv. Accession, Sandringham	10	25	*BLCS 72*
(11) 40th Anniv. Accession, Windsor Castle	10	25	*BLCS 72*
(12) 40th Anniv. Accession, Buckingham Palace	10	15	*BenSG15*
(13) 40th Anniv. Accession, Balmoral Castle	10	20	*BenSG15*
(14) 40th Anniv. Accession, Westminster Abbey	10	35	*Ben500(72)*
(15) MAJESTY, London, W1	10	35	*CoverCraft*

Happy & Glorious (contd.)	ordinary covers £	official covers £	
(16) Long Live the Queen, SW1	10	20	*CoverCraft*
(17) Sooty World Museum	10	75	*Arlington*
(18) Queen's Flight, BF 1992 PS	10	15	*RFDC 100*
(19) City of London, 40 Happy & Glorious Years	10	10	*MGN/SG/RMail*
(20) London SW1 or Windsor (permanent h/s)	10	-	*Royal Mail*
C.D.S. POSTMARKS			
(21) Buckingham Palace or Windsor Castle	120		
(22) Canterbury or York – Head of Church	20		
(23) Catterick Garrison – Head of Armed Forces	25		
(24) Duke of Yorks School	15		
(25) Any Field Post Office	15		
(26) House of Commons or Lords	20		
(27) Kensington High St. – Com'wealth Institute	15		
(28) Sandringham	300		
(29) Scone – the Coronation Chair stone	20		
(30) Terminal 2 or 4, Heathrow – H.M. first set foot on British soil as Queen	20		
(31) West Newton – near to Sandringham House	15		
(32) Windsor or Windsor Great Park	15		

Also: Coronation Parade, Crown Town, Queen Elizabeth Ave., Queens Parade, Queens Road, Queen Street, Royal Parade, Trafalgar Square. Prices from £12.

SLOGAN POSTMARKS

Control your dog; Alder Hey; Royal School for Deaf Children; Post Code Windsor. Prices from £7.

10th March 1992 – TENNYSON

24p 'Vivien'; 28p 'The Miller's Daughter'; 33p 'The Lady of Shalott'; 39p 'Mariana'.

SPECIAL HANDSTAMPS (1) Philatelic Bureau	3	–	*Royal Mail*
(2) First Day of Issue – Isle of Wight	3	–	*Royal Mail*
(3) Tennyson Centenary, Grange de Lings	10	20	*Ben500(73)*
(4) Charge of the Light Brigade, Winchester	10	10	*BLCS 73*
(5) Tennyson, The Revenge, Bude	10	12	*BLCS 73*
(6) Idylls of the King, Tintagel	10	10	*BenL29*
(7) Tennyson, Brian Reeve, Isle of Wight	10	15	*B Reeve 3*
(8) The Poetry Society, SW1	10	20	*CoverCraft*
(9) Lord Tennyson, Freshwater, Isle of Wight	10	15	*VP 66*
(10) Lord Tennyson, Haslemere	10	15	*Bradbury*
(11) Lord Tennyson, Hagworthingham	10	25	*Bradbury*
(12) The Tennyson Society, Somersby	10	12	*LFDC 104*
(13) The Salvation Army, Newport	10	15	*S. Army*
(14) Number 60 Squadron, BF 2318 PS	10	10	*RAF FDC 1*
ORDINARY F.D.I. POSTMARKS			
(15) Lincoln (Somersby/Tennyson special cover)	15		
C.D.S. POSTMARKS			
(16) Freshwater – Tennyson's home (Farringford)	15		
(17) Haselmere – Tennyson's home (Aldworth)	15		
(18) House of Lords, London SW1	35		
(19) Louth – where he attended Grammar School	15		
(20) Tetford – near to Somersby, his birthplace	15		
(21) Tintagel – inspired 'Idylls of the King'	15		
(22) Trinity St., Cambridge – Trinity College	15		

Also: King Arthurs Way, Sebastopol, Tennyson Rd., Tennyson Ave., Trumpington, Winchester. From £15.

SLOGAN POSTMARKS *Glasgow's Alive; Control your dog; Write Now!. Prices from £8.*

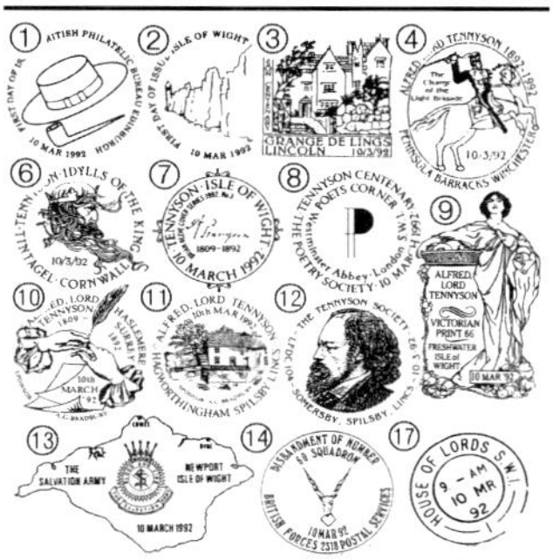

7th April 1992 – EUROPA

24p Columbus; 24p Olympics; 24p Paralympics; 39p Operation Raleigh; 39p Expo.

SPECIAL HANDSTAMPS (1) Philatelic Bureau	3	–	*Royal Mail*
(2) First Day of Issue – Liverpool	3	–	*Royal Mail*
(3) Landfall of the Americas, Columbus, Bristol	5	–	*n.o.c.*
(4) Columbus 500, Brian Reeve, Liverpool	10	15	*B Reeve 4*
(5) Columbus Quincentenary, Greenwich	10	15	*Bradbury*
(6) America, Yours to Discover, New York	10	15	*LFDC 105*
(7) America, Yours to Discover, California	10	25	*VP 67*
(8) Columbus, Discovery of America, Portsmouth	10	25	*Ben500(74)*
(9) Columbus, Discovery of America, Greenwich	10	15	*BLCS 74*
(10) Captain Cook's Endeavour, Whitby	10	20	*S. Muscroft*
(11) Peterborough, City of Europe	10	40	*N V Rly*
(12) King George's Fund for Sailors, SW1	10	85	*CoverCraft*
(13) 1992 Olympic Games, Manchester	10	15	*BLCS 74*
(14) No. 56 Squadron, BF 2319 PS	10	15	*RAF FDC 2*
(15) Royal Belfast Hospital for Sick Children	10	50	*R.B.H.S.C.*
(16) Walk Through Space, Jodrell Bank	8	40	*Bradbury*
C.D.S. POSTMARKS			
(17) Chelsea – HQ of 'Operation Raleigh'	10		
(18) Croydon – HQ of British Paralympics	10		
(19) Maritime Mail, London I.S.	15		
(20) Raleigh	10		
(21) Stoke Mandeville or Orthopaedic Hospital	10		
(22) Wandsworth – British Olympic Assoc.	10		

Also: Boston, Hagley Road, Birmingham, Lilleshall, Liverpool, Much Wenlock, New York, The Chart, The Quarterdeck, Washington, Westward Ho!, Whitechapel. Prices from £8.

SLOGAN POSTMARKS

(23) Arcadian Festival, Birmingham 25

Also: Control your dog; Post Haste; Tenovus; Hearts of Oak; Rly History; PO Charter; Impact. £7.

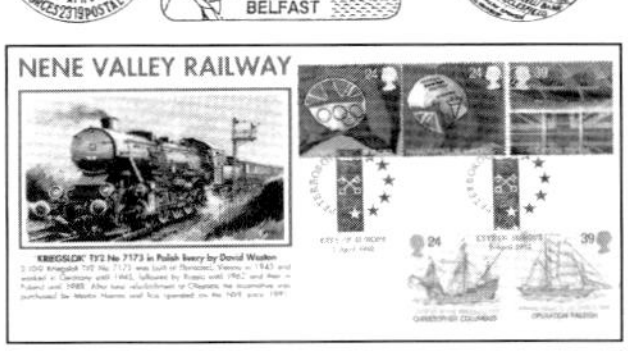

ORDINARY or OFFICIAL COVERS - Do you know the difference?

Find out more by reading the General Notes at the beginning of this catalgoue.

16th June 1992 - ENGLISH CIVIL WAR

24p Pikeman; 28p Drummer; 35p Musketeer; 39p Standard Bearer

	ordinary covers £	official covers £	
SPECIAL HANDSTAMPS (1) Philatelic Bureau	3	-	*Royal Mail*
(2) First Day of Issue - Banbury, Oxfordshire	3	-	*Royal Mail*
(3) Civil War, The Sealed Knot, Edgehill	12	15	*Bradbury*
(4) Civil War, Edgehill Battle Museum, Banbury	12	15	*Bradbury*
(5) Civil War, The Commandery, Worcester	12	15	*Bradbury*
(6) Civil War, Cromwell Museum, Huntingdon	12	15	*LFDC 106*
(7) Civil War, Naseby	12	25	*VP 68*
(8) Civil War, National Army Museum	12	12	*BLCS 75*
(9) Civil War, Robert Devereaux, Newbury	12	12	*BenL30*
(10) Civil War, Oliver Cromwell, Huntingdon	12	12	*BLCS 75*
(11) Civil War, Prince Rupert, London EC	12	25	*Ben500(75)*
(12) Civil War, Raising of the Standard, Nottingham	12	12	*BenSG17*
(13) Civil War, History Today, Kineton	12	12	*BLCS 75*
(14) Start & Finish Civil War, Bredon Covers	12	15	*Bredon Cvrs*
(15) Whitefriars, Coventry	12	40	*Coventry CC*
(16) English Civil War Society, Hull	12	30	*CoverCraft*
(17) Navy Goes Over to Parliament, Portsmouth	12	12	*BenL30*
(18) Edgehill, Brian Reeve	12	15	*B Reeve 5*
(19) Lawn Tennis Museum	12	20	*L.T.Museum*
(20) 75th Anniversary of 101 Squadron	12	15	*RAF FDC 3*
C.D.S. POSTMARKS			
(21) Castle Boulevard - Raising of the Standard	20		
(22) House of Commons or Lords	30		
(23) Huntingdon - Birthplace of Oliver Cromwell	20		
(24) Kineton, Warks - near to Edgehill	20		
(25) Marston - Battle of Marston Moor	20		
(26) Naseby - Battle of Naseby	20		
(27) Battle sites: Dunbar, Lostwithiel, Newbury, Powick, Ribbleton, Sidbury, Stow-on-the-Wold, Wash Common ... *each*	20		
(28) Oliver's Battery, Winchester	20		
(29) Southwell - where Charles I surrendered	20		

Also: Battle, Battlehill, Buckingham Palace, Castle Donington, Charles St., Cropredy, Edgehill (Scarborough), Hull, Kingsland, Lichfield, Northern Parliament, Oxford, Preston, Ratley, Windsor Castle, Worcester. Prices from £15.

SLOGAN POSTMARKS		
(30) Storming of Preston - Battle and Pageant	20	
(31) Hull Festival 1992	20	

Also: Guild Preston; Hearts of Oak; North Yorks Moors Rly. Prices from £8.

21st July 1992 - GILBERT & SULLIVAN

18p Yeoman of the Guard; 24p The Gondoliers; 28p The Mikado; 33p Pirates of Penzance; 39p Iolanthe

	ordinary covers £	official covers £	
SPECIAL HANDSTAMPS (1) Philatelic Bureau	3	-	*Royal Mail*
(2) First Day of Issue - D'Oyly Carte	3	-	*Royal Mail*
(3) D'Oyly Carte Opera Company, Birmingham	12	20	*LFDC 107*
(4) Lambeth Walk, SE11	12	20	*VP 69*
(5) Royal Academy of Music, NW1	12	20	*Bradbury*
(6) The Gilbert & Sullivan Society, WC2	12	25	*Bradbury*
(7) Birthplace of Richard D'Oyly Carte, Soho	12	35	*Bradbury*
(8) Mikado, Savoy, WC2	12	25	*Ben500(76)*
(9) Yeoman of the Guard, The Tower, EC1	12	10	*BLCS 76*
(10) Pirates of Penzance, Penzance	12	20	*BLCS 76*
(11) Iolanthe, The Sullivan Society, SW7	12	20	*BenL32*
(12) Gondoliers, The Sullivan Society, Weybridge	12	20	*BenL31*
(13) Sir Arthur Sullivan Sesquicentenary, Savoy	12	30	*CoverCraft*
(14) Ruddigore, etc., G & S Operas, Halifax	12	30	*Savoyards*
(15) Damart, Gilbert & Sullivan, Bingley	12	20	*Arlington*
(16) Gilbert & Sullivan Society, Paignton	12	35	*G&S Torbay*
(17) Symphony of Stamps, Nat Postal Museum	12	12	*N.P.M.(s)*
(18) The Salvation Army, Penzance	12	15	*H.R.*
(19) Sir Arthur Sullivan, 1842-1992, SE11	12	15	*B Reeve 6*
(20) No.47 Squadron, BF 2321 PS	12	12	*RAF FDC 4*
(21) Royal Tournament, BF 2330 PS	12	50	*Forces*
(22) Hampton Court Palace	12	65	*CoverCraft*
(23) Shoreham-by-Sea Station	12	20	*BenhamR7*
(24) Pad Cancelling Machine at SHC, Cardiff	25	-	*Royal Mail*
C.D.S. POSTMARKS			
(25) Birmingham - D'Oyly Carte Opera Co.	15		
(26) House of Commons - Iolanthe 39p value	15		
(27) House of Lords - Iolanthe 39p value	20		
(28) Kingsway (TV House) - Savoy Theatre	15		
(29) Lambeth Walk - B/place Sir Arthur Sullivan	15		
(30) Paignton or Penzance - Pirates of Penzance	15		
(31) Regent St - where G & S first met	15		
(32) Trafalgar Sq. - near to Birthplace of Gilbert	15		

Also: Broadwick Street, Castle Green, The Circle, Gilbertstone, Harrow & Wealdstone, Haymarket, London EC, Old Windsor, Pindore Street, Seething Lane, Temple, West End. Prices from £10.

SLOGAN POSTMARKS		
(33) Smugglers' Adventure, Hastings	25	

Also: Mansfield Show; Maritime Mail; Belfast Harpers; PO Charter; BBC Radio Llandudno; Edinburgh Tattoo; Royal Mail Preston; Royal Mail Cardiff; Southend Borough Centenary. From £6.

15th September 1992 - GREEN ISSUE

24p Acid Rain; 28p Ozone Layer; 33p Greenhouse Effect; 39p Bird of Hope

	ordinary covers £	official covers £	
SPECIAL HANDSTAMPS (1) Philatelic Bureau	3	-	*Royal Mail*
(2) First Day of Issue - Torridon	3	-	*Royal Mail*
(3) Without conservation..., Red Squirrel	10	15	*BLCS 77*
(4) Without conservation..., Cardigan	10	15	*BLCS 77*
(5) Without conservation..., Bristol Zoo	10	15	*BLCS 77*
(6) Without conservation..., Marsh Fritilary	10	15	*BLCS 77*
(7) Without conservation..., London Zoo	10	15	*BLCS 77*
(8) Without conservation..., The Osprey	10	18	*BLCS 77*
(9) Without conservation..., Howletts	10	15	*BLCS 77*
(10) Without conservation..., The Dormouse	10	15	*BLCS 77*
(11) Brownsea Island	10	15	*Ben500(77)*
(12) Water Wildlife, Otterhampton	10	10	*BLCS 77*
(13) Sutton Ecology Centre	10	60	*SEC & RM*
(14) The Barn Owl Trust, Ashburton	10	30	*CoverCraft*
(15) Green Charter, City of Plymouth	10	25	*LFDC 108*
(16) Greenacres, Aylesford	10	20	*VP 70*
(17) Preserve our Planet, Coventry Co-op	10	40	*Bradbury*
(18) Leicester on top of the World	10	20	*Bradbury*
(19) Carsington Water	10	40	*Bradbury*
(20) Green Issue, Fair Isle	10	15	*B Reeve 7*
(21) Manchester Metrolink	10	15	*Dawn*
(22) No.74 Squadron, BF 2322 PS	10	12	*RAF FDC 5*
(23) Shell UK, Cowdenbeath	10	125	*P.P.S.*
(24) Salvation Army, Greenford	10	15	*S. Army*
(25) National Postal Museum, London	10	-	*Royal Mail*
C.D.S. POSTMARKS			
(26) Balham, SW12 - Green Party HQ	15		
(27) Glasshouses, Greenacres, Greenhill, Greenfields, Green Island, Greenlands, Green St., Forest Green, The Green *each*	15		
(28) Islington, N1 - Green Peace Headquarters	15		
(29) Kew Gardens - conservation and seed bank	25		
(30) Leicester - first Environment City	20		
(31) Paradise	25		

Also: Boat of Garton, Globe Road, Greeness, Greenlaw, Greenside, Hope, Hopes Green, Nettleham, Park Road, Rainhill, Shepherd's Bush, Slimbridge, Sunnyside, World's End, Wren's Nest. From £10.

SLOGAN POSTMARKS

(32) Leicester - Environment City	15	
(33) Skegness is SO Bracing	15	
(34) Enrico Fermi Controlled Nuclear Fission	90	
(35) Tropical Places - exotic holiday specialists	15	
(36) Schools Poster Campaign, Glasgow	25	

Also: Wall's virtually fat free; Stamp Collecting Greatest Hobby; Please Control your Dog. From £6.

13th October 1992 - SINGLE EUROPEAN MARKET

24p Artist's interpretation of British star on European flag

	ordinary covers £	official covers £	
SPECIAL HANDSTAMPS (1) Philatelic Bureau	2	-	*Royal Mail*
(2) First Day of Issue - Westminster	2	-	*Royal Mail*
(3) First Day of Issue - Europe '92 London	8	-	*Royal Mail*
(4) Autumn Stampex, London SW1	8	-	*Royal Mail*
(5) British Presidency, Downing Street	8	15	*Ben500(78)*
(6) The Single Market, Westminster, SW1	8	10	*BLCS 78*
(7) European Arts Festival, Edinburgh	8	15	*BLCS 78*
(8) CBI Investing for the New Europe, WC1	8	10	*LFDC 109*
(9) Single European Market, Dover	8	10	*VP 71*
(10) Single European Market, Parliament Street	8	10	*B Reeve 8*
(11) European Commemorative 50 Pence	8	10	*Royal Mint*
(12) Liverpool FC - FA Cup Winners - In Europe	8	12	*Dawn*
(13) Manchester United in Europe, UEFA Cup	8	12	*Dawn*
(14) Leeds Utd - League Champions into Europe	8	12	*Dawn*
(15) Saltaire, 1853 Gallery	8	20	*1853 Gallery*
(16) No.111 Squadron, BF 2336 PS	8	10	*RAF FDC 6*
(17) HMC International	8	25	*HMC Int.*
C.D.S. POSTMARKS			
(18) Birmingham - venue for European Summit	10		
(19) House of Commons, SW1	20		
(20) House of Lords, SW1	25		
(21) Industrial and Trading Estates - various *each*	10		
(22) Lombard Street, or Stock Exchange *each*	15		
(23) Maritime Mail	10		
(24) Market, Market Place or Newmarket *each*	10		
(25) Newbridge or Aycliffe, Dover	10		
(26) Paquebot - various *each*	10		

In addition: Mastrick, Northern Parliament, Parliament Street, Pound, Runcorn (Shopping Centre), Saltaire, Starcross, Summit. Prices from £8.

SLOGAN POSTMARKS

(27) Birmingham (surrounded by circle of stars)	10	
(28) Europe for Workers Safety and Health	25	
(29) The Visaservice - Passports Renewed	10	
(30) Maritime Mail	10	

Also: WHSmiths; Royal Mail Children in Cities; Post Haste; Hearts of Oak; Times & Star. From £4.

10th November 1992 - CHRISTMAS

18p St. James's, Pangbourne
24p St. Mary's Bibury;
28p & 39p Our Lady & St. Peter's, Leatherhead; 33p All Saint's, Porthcawl

	ordinary covers £	official covers £	
SPECIAL HANDSTAMPS (1) Philatelic Bureau	3	–	*Royal Mail*
(2) First Day of Issue - Bethlehem, Llandeilo	3	–	*Royal Mail*
(3) First Day of Issue - Pangbourne	3	–	*Royal Mail*
(4) Stained Glass at Canterbury Cathedral	10	10	*BLCS 79*
(5) Stained Glass, Castle Howard, York	10	12	*BLCS 79*
(6) All Saints, Middleton Cheney	10	15	*BenL33*
(7) St. Peter & St. Paul, Cattistock	10	15	*BenL33*
(8) St. Michaels Church, Forden	10	15	*BenL34*
(9) All Hallows Church, Allerton	10	10	*BenL34*
(10) St. Martin's Church, Brampton	10	15	*BenL33*
(11) Christchurch, Cambridge	10	15	*Ben500(79)*
(12) Bethlehem, Dyfed, Victorian Print No.72	10	15	*VP 72*
(13) Church of the Lily Cross, Godshill	10	10	*LFDC 110*
(14) Our Lady & St. Peter's, Leatherhead	10	20	*Bradbury*
(15) St. Mary's Bibury, Glos	10	50	*CoverCraft*
(16) Peace on Earth, All Saint's, Porthcawl	10	20	*CoverCraft*
(17) Stained Glass Museum, Ely, Cambs	10	20	*CoverCraft*
(18) Christmas, Canterbury Cathedral	10	15	*B Reeve 9*
(19) Cambridge, Christmas 1992	10	20	*Cam. S.C.*
(20) Christmas Blessings, Salvation Army	10	15	*S. Army*
(21) National Postal Museum, EC	10	20	*FriendsNPM*
(22) Happy Christmas, Royal Mail, EC1	10	–	*n.o.c.*
(23) Seasons Greetings from Liverpool FC	10	15	*Dawn*
(24) Seasons Greetings from Newcastle United	10	15	*Dawn*
(25) CEAC 7, COSAC, London	10	–	*n.o.c.*
(26) No.84 Squadron, BF 2338 PS	10	12	*RAF FDC 7*
C.D.S. POSTMARKS			
(27) Bibury, Leatherhead, Pangbourne or Porthcawl	15		

Also: All Saints Church, Ely, Glasshouses, Holy Island, Jerusalem St., Nasareth, St. James, St. Marys, St. Nicholas, St. Peters, Threekingham. Prices from £12.

SLOGAN POSTMARKS		
(28) Leeds Light Up - Illuminations	20	
(29) Happy Christmas, Please Post Early - Inverness	25	
(30) A Happy Christmas, The Post Office - Wick	25	
(31) Jesus is Alive! - Manchester	175	

Also: Shetland for 93; Please control your Dog; Write now etc.; Senders Name and Address. From £5.

CHRISTMAS BOOKLET: Covers bearing pair or block of 4 x 18p stamps from booklet with relevant postmark (these have margin at top and bottom) *each* 3
Full pane of ten stamps on cover *each* 10

19th January 1993 - SWANS

Abbotsbury Swannery:- 18p Mute Swan Cob; 24p Cygnets;
28p Mute Swan Breeding Pair; 33p Mute Swans Eggs; 39p Winter Mute Swans

SPECIAL HANDSTAMPS (1) Philatelic Bureau	4	–	*Royal Mail*
(2) First Day of Issue - Abbotsbury	4	–	*Royal Mail*
(3) First Day of Issue - London	4	–	*Royal Mail*
(4) Wildfowl & Wetlands, Caerlaverock	12	15	*BLCS 80*
(5) Wildfowl & Wetlands, Castle Espie	12	15	*BLCS 80*
(6) Wildfowl & Wetlands, Martin Mere	12	20	*BLCS 80*
(7) Wildfowl & Wetlands, Slimbridge	12	12	*BLCS 80*
(8) Wildfowl & Wetlands, Llanelli	12	12	*BLCS 80*
(9) 600th Anniv. Abbotsbury Swannery	12	25	*BenSG18*
(10) Bird Watching Magazine, Peterborough	12	20	*Benham*
(11) Stratford upon Avon	12	20	*Ben500(80)*
(12) Dyers' Hall, London, EC4	12	35	*LFDC 111*
(13) Vintners' Company, London, EC4	12	25	*VP 73*
(14) Swan Sanctuary, Egham	12	25	*Bradbury*
(15) Independent Chapel, Swanland	12	35	*S'land Priory*
(16) Old Swan Corps, Liverpool	12	25	*S. Army*
(17) Swan Lifeline, Eton	12	35	*CoverCraft*
(18) Swan Trust, Berwick	12	25	*CoverCraft*
(19) No.115 Squadron, BF 2347 PS	12	12	*RAF FDC 8*
(20) People in the Post, National Postal Museum	12	–	*n.o.c.*
(21) William Shakespeare Stratford (swan)	12	–	*n.o.c.*
C.D.S. POSTMARKS			
(22) Abbotsbury, Egham, Sandy or Slimbridge	25		
(23) Swanland, Swanpool or Old Swan *each*	25		
(24) Thetford - British Trust for Ornithology	25		

In addition: Comber, Fleet, Hanley Swan, Henley-on-Thames, House of Lords, Ilchester, Mickley, Old Berwick, Swanmore, Swansea. Prices from £15.

SLOGAN POSTMARKS
Postcode, Doncaster; Colourful Greetings Stamps; Gloucester Citizen;Control your Dog. From £10.

All values include VAT at 17.5%
Values are a guide - please read the General Notes at the beginning of this catalogue.

2nd Feb 1993 - GREETINGS

10 x 1st Class: Long John Silver, Peter Rabbit, Tweedledee & Tweedledum, Just William, Toad and Mole, Bash Street Kids, the Snowman, Big Friendly Giant, Rupert Bear, Aladdin

	ordinary covers £	official covers £	
SPECIAL HANDSTAMPS (1) Philatelic Bureau	3	–	*Royal Mail*
(2) First Day of Issue – Greetland	5	–	*Royal Mail*
(3) First Day of Issue – London	5	–	*Royal Mail*
(4) Badger	12	6	*DailyExp(s)*
(5) Daresbury, Warrington	12	25	*Bradbury*
(6) Scottish Literary Museum	12	25	*BLCS 81*
(7) Beatrix Potter, Kensington, W8	12	25	*BLCS 81*
(8) Big Friendly Giant, Great Missenden	12	25	*BLCS 81*
(9) Aladdin, Manchester	12	20	*BenD191*
(10) Alice in Wonderland, Oxford	12	3	*Benham(s)*
(11) Rivers Corner, Sturminster Newton	12	15	*Ben500(81)*
(12) Peter Rabbit Centenary, Near Sawrey	12	8	*CoverCraft(s)*
(13) Waterstone's, London	12	15	*Waterstone's*
C.D.S. POSTMARKS			
(14) Far Sawrey – home of Beatrix Potter	15		
(15) Fleet Street – where the 'Beano' is published	15		
(16) Greet, Birmingham	15		
(17) Oxford – home of Lewis Carroll	15		

Also: Badger's Mount, Bearpark, Blackfriars Rd, Braemar, Bromley Common, Bunny, Cross Hands, Earls Court, Exchange, Fulham Palace Road, Great Missenden, Hassocks, Kensington High Street, Molehill Green, Portobello Rd, Rupert Street, Stock Exchange, Tweedle, Waterston, William Street, The Willows. Prices from £10.

SLOGAN POSTMARKS			
(18) Use Colourful Greetings Stamps	20		

In addition: Write Now, etc; Radio Nottingham. Prices from £5.

16th February 1993 – MARINE TIMEKEEPERS

24p, 28p, 33p, 39p: Four layer's of Harrison's 'H4' Clock

	ordinary covers £	official covers £	
SPECIAL HANDSTAMPS (1) Philatelic Bureau	3	–	*Royal Mail*
(2) First Day of Issue – Greenwich	3	–	*Royal Mail*
(3) First Day of Issue – John Harrison, London	3	–	*Royal Mail*
(4) Queen Elizabeth 2, Southampton	12	3	*Benham(s)*
(5) RMS Queen Mary, Southampton	12	3	*Benham(s)*
(6) The Cutty Sark, Greenwich	12	15	*BLCS 82*
(7) SS Great Britain, Bristol	12	40	*BenL35*
(8) Marine Chronometer, Portsmouth	12	3	*Benham(s)*
(9) Marine Chronometer, Plymouth	12	25	*Ben500(82)*
(10) HMS Belfast, London SE1	12	3	*Benham(s)*
(11) HMS Victory, Portsmouth	12	15	*BLCS 82*
(12) Antiquarian Horological Soc., Ticehurst	12	25	*Bradbury*
(13) British Watch & Clockmaker's Gd, Burnham	12	20	*LFDC 112*
(14) British Horological Institute, Newark	12	20	*VP 74*
(15) John Harrison Tercentenary, Greenwich	12	20	*CoverCraft*
(16) British Sailors' Society, Southampton	12	20	*SP*
(17) No.1 Squadron, BF 2346 PS	12	12	*RAF FDC 9*
(18) Salvation Army, Medical Fellowship, EC4	12	15	*S. Army*
(19) First Day of Sale, Windsor	12	–	*n.o.c.*
C.D.S. POSTMARKS			
(20) Clockface or Clock House Parade	10		
(21) Greenwich or Any Paquebot	15		
(22) Maritime Mail, London I.S.	15		
(23) Meridian Centre, Newhaven	40		
(24) New Invention, Willenhall, West Midlands	10		
(25) New Crofton – near to B/place of Harrison	10		

Also: The Chart, Cog Lane, Hampstead, Marine Parade, Marton-in-Cleveland, The Quarterdeck, Theobalds Road, Watchet, Whitby. Prices from £8.

SLOGAN POSTMARKS			
(26) Maritime Mail, London I.S.	30		
(27) SWATCH Swatch the World	250		

Also: Bedford Council/Waste Watchers; Glos. Citizen; Safeway, Plymouth; Royal Mail/Business. £6.

16th March 1993 – ORCHIDS

18p, 24p, 28p, 33p, 39p Species of Orchids

	ordinary covers £	official covers £	
SPECIAL HANDSTAMPS (1) Philatelic Bureau	3	–	*Royal Mail*
(2) First Day of Issue – Glasgow	3	–	*Royal Mail*
(3) First Day of Issue – London	3	–	*Royal Mail*
(4) Royal Botanic Gardens, Kew	12	20	*BLCS 83*
(5) Botanical Gardens, Birmingham	12	17	*BLCS 83*
(6) Botanic Gardens, Glasgow	12	17	*BLCS 83*
(7) Botanic Gardens, Belfast	12	17	*BLCS 83*
(8) Royal Botanic Garden, Edinburgh	12	17	*BLCS 83*
(9) Oldest Botanic Gardens, Oxford	12	17	*BLCS 83*
(10) Royal Orchid Service, Thai Airways	12	25	*BenSG20*
(11) World Orchid Conference, Glasgow	12	15	*Ben500(83)*
(12) Worshipful Company of Gardeners, EC	12	25	*LFDC 113*
(13) Royal Botanic Garden, Edinburgh	12	25	*VP 75*
(14) Orchid Society of Great Britain	12	55	*CoverCraft*
(15) No.30 Squadron, BF 2348 PS	12	12	*RAF FDC 10*
(16) Derwentside LDO, Consett	12	–	*n.o.c.*
(17) New Post Office, Southend-on-Sea	12	75	*Bradbury*

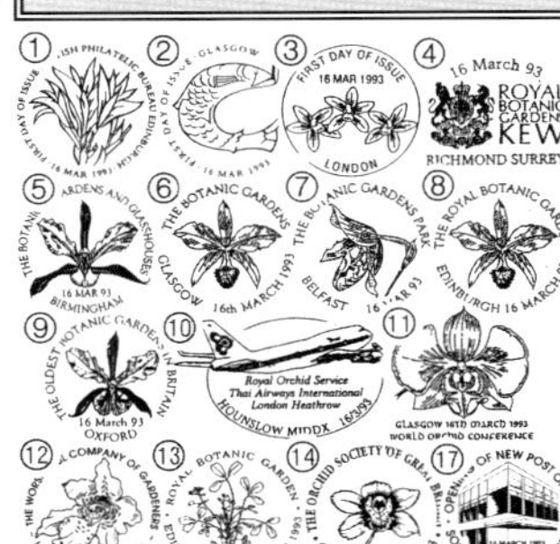

Orchids (contd.)

C.D.S. POSTMARKS	ordinary covers £	official covers £
(18) Botanic Gardens, Belfast or Kew Gardens	25	
(19) Glasgow – World Orchid Conference	20	
(20) Royal Hospital – Chelsea Flower Show	20	

In addition: Bloomfield, Flore, Flowery Field, Glasgow Airport, Glasshouses, Montague Terrace, Edinburgh, Queen Elizabeth Ave., Paradise, Ripley, Spring Gardens. From £5.

SLOGAN POSTMARKS *Daffodil Day; Royal Concert Hall; Postcodes; Royal Mail. From £5*

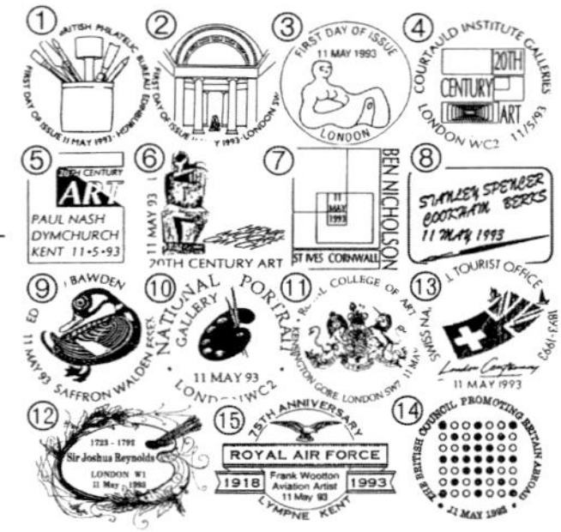

11th May 1993 – ART IN THE 20th CENTURY

24p Henry Moore – Family Group; 28p Edward Bawden – Kew Gardens; 33p Stanley Spencer – St. Francis & the Birds; 39p Ben Nicholson – Odyssey 1

SPECIAL HANDSTAMPS	ordinary	official	
(1) Philatelic Bureau	3	–	*Royal Mail*
(2) First Day of Issue – London SW	3	–	*Royal Mail*
(3) First Day of Issue – London	3	–	*Royal Mail*
(4) Courtauld Institute, WC2	8	12	*BLCS 84*
(5) Paul Nash, Dymchurch,	8	17	*Ben500(84)*
(6) Henry Moore, Leeds	8	10	*BenSG21*
(7) Ben Nicholson, St. Ives,	8	3	*Benham(s)*
(8) Stanley Spencer, Cookham,	8	3	*Benham(s)*
(9) Edward Bawden, Saffron Walden,	8	3	*Benham(s)*
(10) National Portrait Gallery, London WC2	8	15	*Westminster*
(11) Royal College of Art, SW7	8	25	*LFDC 114*
(12) Sir Joshua Reynolds, London W1	8	15	*VP 76*
(13) Swiss National Tourist Office	8	20	*CoverCraft*
(14) British Council, Promoting Britain Abroad	8	20	*CoverCraft*
(15) Frank Wootton Artist, Lympne	8	10	*BLCS 84*
(16) No.216 Squadron, BF 2349 PS	8	10	*RAF FDC 11*
(17) Cyprus, Malaya and Suez, BF 2368 PS	8	–	*n.o.c.*
(18) The Salvation Army, Sunbury,	6	20	*S. Army*
C.D.S. POSTMARKS			
(19) Albemarle Street – near to Royal Academy	8		
(20) Braintree – birthplace of Edward Bawden	8		
(21) Carbis Bay – home of Ben Nicholson	8		
(22) Castleford – birthplace of Henry Moore	8		
(23) Cookham – birthplace of Stanley Spencer	8		
(24) Denham Green – birthplace of Ben Nicholson	8		
(25) Great Bardfield – home of Edward Bawden	8		
(26) Kew Gardens or The Galleries	20		
(27) Much Hadham – Henry Moore Foundation	8		

Also: Moore, Pembroke St., Bedford; Plympton St. Maurice; Trafalgar Square, WC2; Tufton Street, SW1; Vauxhall Bridge Road, SW1. Prices from £6.

SLOGAN POSTMARKS	ordinary
(28) Barnes Cray School Arts Week	25
(29) Royal Mail Supports the Arts, Glasgow	25
(30) Milton Keynes, Festival Folk Art	75

In addition: Royal Mail Can Help Your Business; Postcodes. Prices from £5.

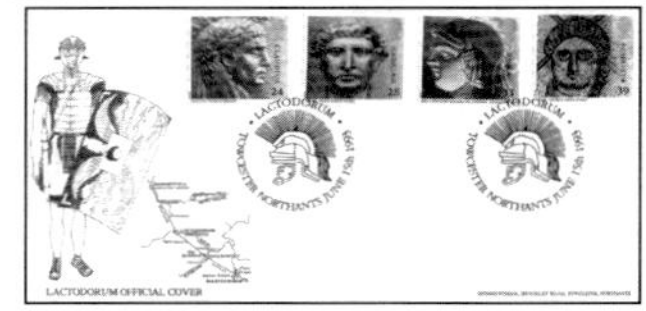

15th June 1993 – ROMAN BRITAIN

24p Claudius (Gold Coin, British Museum) found at Bredgar, Kent; 28p Hadrian (Bronze Sculpture, British Museum) found in the River Thames; 33p Roma (Gemstone, Legionary Museum, Caerleon) found at Caerleon; 39p Christ (Mosaic, British Museum) from a villa at Hinton St. Mary

SPECIAL HANDSTAMPS	ordinary	official	
(1) Philatelic Bureau	3	–	*Royal Mail*
(2) First Day of Issue – Caerllion	3	–	*Royal Mail*
(3) First Day of Issue – London	3	–	*Royal Mail*
(4) Ermine Street Guard, York	12	20	*LFDC 115*
(5) Camulodunum, Roman Britain, Colchester	12	25	*VP 77*
(6) Roman Britain, Caerleon	12	20	*BenL37*
(7) Roman Britain, Chester	12	20	*BenL37*
(8) Roman Britain, Newcastle	12	12	*BenSG21*
(9) Roman Britain, Bath	12	9	*BenSG21*
(10) Roman Britain, Colchester	12	20	*BenL37*
(11) Roman Britain, Invasion A.D. 43, Canterbury	12	20	*BenL37*
(12) White Cliffs Experience, Dover	12	10	*BenL36*
(13) Largest Roman Palace in Britain, Fishbourne	12	10	*BLCS 85*
(14) Roman Villa, Chedworth	12	10	*BLCS 85*
(15) Roman Britain, Cirencester	12	20	*BenL37*
(16) Roman Britain, Walbrook, EC4	12	20	*BenL37*
(17) Roman Britain, St. Albans	12	15	*Ben500(85)*
(18) Museum of Antiquities, Newcastle	12	35	*CoverCraft*
(19) Museum of London, London Wall	12	30	*CoverCraft*
(20) Lactodorum, Towcester,	12	40	*Sponne School*
(21) Royal Air Force Locking, Weston-super-Mare	12	200	*RAF Locking*
(22) New Relief Lifeboat, Fleetwood	12	20	*Pilgrim*
(23) Salvation Army, International Headquarters	12	20	*S. Army*
C.D.S. POSTMARKS			
(25) Bowness or Heddon – Hadrian's Wall	15		
(26) Bredgar – Claudius gold coin (24p)	15		
(27) Britannia – Roman name for Britain	15		
(28) Caerlon – Roma gemstone (33p)	15		
(29) London Bdge – Hadrian sculpture (28p)	15		
(30) Roman Way Caerlon – Roma gemstone (33p)	25		
(31) Sturminster – Mosaic of Christ (39p)	15		

PLEASE READ THE GENERAL NOTES

Roman Britain (contd.) ordinary covers £ official covers £

Also: Bacchus Road, Bath, Camp, Colchester, Eastgate, Ermine Street, Fishbourne, Fort Augustus, Garrison, High Holborn, Jerusalem, Micklegate, Occupation Rd, Prettygate, Northgate, Roman Road, Russell Square, Sandwich, Southampton Row, Southgate, Temple, The Forum, Villa Road, Wall, Wallsend, Watling Street, Westgate, York. Prices from £8.

SLOGAN POSTMARKS

(32) Christian Aid Week	35		

In addition: Stenna Sealink; Any Royal Mail slogans. Prices from £5.

20th July 1993 – INLAND WATERWAYS

24p Grand Junction Canal; 28p Stainforth & Keadby Canal; 33p Brecknock & Abergavenny Canal; 39p Crinan Canal

SPECIAL HANDSTAMPS			
(1) Philatelic Bureau	3	–	*Royal Mail*
(2) First Day of Issue – Gloucester	3	–	*Royal Mail*
(3) First Day of Issue – London	3	–	*Royal Mail*
(4) Inland Waterways Assoc'n, Mkt Harborough	15	35	*LFDC 116*
(5) Grand Union Canal, Foxton	15	35	*VP 78*
(6) Canal Museum, Stoke Bruerne	15	20	*BLCS 86*
(7) Conserving..., The Wharf, Braunston	15	3	*Benham(s)*
(8) Conserving..., Lochgilphead, Argyll	15	20	*BLCS 86*
(9) Conserving..., Sheffield, Yorks.	15	20	*BLCS 86*
(10) Conserving..., Newport, Gwent	15	20	*BLCS 86*
(11) Canals 200, Grand Junction Canal	15	20	*BLCS 86*
(12) Canals 200, Crinan Canal	15	20	*BLCS 86*
(13) Canals 200, Stainforth & Keadby Canal	15	20	*BLCS 86*
(14) Canals 200, Brecknock & Abergavenny	15	20	*BLCS 86*
(15) Grand Junction Canal, London North	15	20	*Ben500(86)*
(16) Canals Bicentenary, Regents Canal, London	15	–	*n.o.c.*
(17) Canals Bicentenary, Watford, Herts	15	–	*n.o.c.*
(18) New Lanark Visitor Centre, Lanark	15	–	*n.o.c.*
(19) The Mary-Anne Worsley Marina	15	20	*S. Army*
(20) No. 51 Squadron, BF 2383 PS	15	15	*RAF FDC 13*
(21) Royal Tournament, BF 2385 PS	15	70	*Forces*
ORDINARY F.D.I. POSTMARKS			
(22) Milton Keynes (*Leighton Lady* PO cachet)	40		
C.D.S. POSTMARKS			
(23) Abergavenny, Brecon or Pontymoile – – Brecknock & Abergavenny Canal	15		
(24) Ardrishaig or Bellanoch – Crinan Canal	15		
(25) Brentford or Braunston – Grand Junction	15		
(26) Stainforth or Keadby	15		
(27) Ellesmere Port – Inland Waterways Museum	15		
(28) House of Commons or Lords	30		

Also: Anderton, Bingley, Birchvale, Bridgwater, Burnley, Froncysllte, Lochgilphead, Locks Bottom, Locks Lane, Marsden, Patricroft, Shelton Lock, Sugar Island, Towcester, Waterside. Prices from £8.

SLOGAN POSTMARKS

Postbus; 60 Yrs Passenger Service; Royal Mail slogans; Sunbury. Prices from £4.

14th September 1993 – AUTUMN

18p Horse Chestnut; 24p Blackberry; 28p Hazel Nut; 33p Mountain Ash; 39p Pear

SPECIAL HANDSTAMPS			
(1) Philatelic Bureau	3	–	*Royal Mail*
(2) First Day of Issue – Taunton	3	–	*Royal Mail*
(3) First Day of Issue – London	3	–	*Royal Mail*
(4) Autumn – Rowanburn	10	15	*Benham L38*
(5) Autumn – Pear Tree	10	15	*Benham L38*
(6) Autumn – Berry Hill	10	15	*Benham L38*
(7) Autumn – Nutfield	10	15	*Ben500(87)*
(8) Autumn – Hazelwood	10	15	*BLCS 87*
(9) Stourhead House & Garden	10	15	*BLCS 87*
(10) Worshipful Company of Fruiterers	10	15	*LFDC 117*
(11) Worshipful Company of Gardeners, EC	10	15	*VP 79*
(12) Battle of Britain, BF 2384 PS	10	15	*RAF FDC 14*
(13) Peterborough, NVR, Wansford Stn	10	35	*NVRly*
(14) National Postal Museum, 1793-1993	10	–	*n.o.c.*
C.D.S. POSTMARKS			
(15) Chestnut Grove or Chestnut Terrace	20		
(16) Hazel Grove, Mountain Ash or Pear Tree	20		
(17) Kew Gdns or Savacentre (supermarket PO)	25		
(18) The Allotments or The Orchards	25		

Also: Berry Hill, Berrylands, Cherry Tree, Evesham, Faversham, Forest Row, Garden Fm, Hazelslade, Oundle, Peel Green, Pershore, Plantation, Rowanburn, Woodlands, Woodside, Worcester. From£15 .

SLOGAN POSTMARKS *Autumn Concerts; £££s Paid for Stamp Collections; Philatelic Cong.; Safeway; Any Royal Mail slogans. Prices from £10.*

12th October 1993 – SHERLOCK HOLMES

5 x 24p stamps: The Reigate Squire; The Hound of the Baskervilles; The Six Napoleons; The Greek Interpreter; The Final Problem

SPECIAL HANDSTAMPS			
(1) Philatelic Bureau	3	–	*Royal Mail*
(2) First Day of Issue – 221B Baker St, NW1	3	–	*Royal Mail*
(3) First Day of Issue – London	3	–	*Royal Mail*
(4) First Day of Issue – Autumn Stampex, SW1	15	–	*Royal Mail*
(5) Conan Doyle Society (silhouette)	15	30	*VP 80*
(6) Windlesham Manor, Crowborough	15	30	*Bradbury*

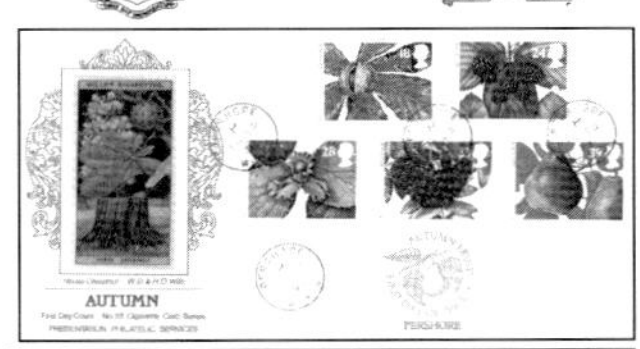

Sherlock Holmes (contd.)

		ordinary covers £	official covers £	
(7)	Sherlock Holmes Museum (silhouette)	15	35	*LFDC 118*
(8)	St. Bartholomew's Hospital	15	20	*H. Murray*
(9)	Sherlock Holmes Society, London	15	35	*CoverCraft*
(10)	Adventures of Sherlock Holmes, 221B Baker St.	15	35	*CoverCraft*
(11)	POID Bicentenary, EC	15	60	*POID*
(12)	Baker Street Post Office, W1	15	–	*n.o.c.*
(13)	Radio Times, Sherlock Holmes, Baker St.	15	30	*Benham*
(14)	Sherlock Holmes, Baker St. NW1 (silhouette)	15	20	*Benham*
(15)	Hound of the Baskervilles, Black Dog	15	50	*Ben500(88)*
(16)	Burial Place of Conan Doyle, Minstead	15	10	*Benham(s)*
(17)	The Strand, WC2	15	10	*Benham(s)*
(18)	Jeremy Brett/Sherlock Holmes, Granada TV	15	20	*BLCS 88*
(19)	Sherlock Holmes, Granada TV, Manchester	15	25	*BLCS 88*
(20)	Arthur Conan Doyle Society, ACD	15	35	*BenL39*
(21)	Conan Doyle Establishment, Crowborough	15	35	*BenL39*
(22)	Autumn Stampex, SW1 (changeable date)	15	–	*n.o.c.*
(23)	Sherlock Holmes Memorabilia Company	15	55	*SHMCo*
(24)	Province of Suffolk, Ipswich	15	35	*Arlington*
(25)	No. 100 Squadron, BF 2388 PS	8	20	*RAF FDC 15*

C.D.S. POSTMARKS

(26)	Baker Street – home of Sherlock Holmes	35
(27)	Elm Row Edinburgh – B/place Conan-Doyle	35
(28)	Beckenham, Kennington, Newhaven, Princetown, Reigate, Walkhampton, Widecombe-in-the-Moor: – locations connected with novels on stamps	35
(29)	Crowborough, Hindhead, or South Norwood: – homes of Arthur Conan-Doyle	35
(30)	Swiss Valley Park (The Final Problem)	45

Also: Crook; Constable Burton; Dog and Gun; Elm Grove, Southsea; Forest Row; Holmes Chapel; Minstead; Nicholson St., Edinburgh; Stonyhurst; North East TPO Down; The Strand. Prices from £20.

SLOGAN POSTMARKS

(31)	Post Office Investigation Dept	25
(32)	Autumn Stampex – features Sherlock Holmes	25
(33)	Please Control your Dog – features a Hound	45

In addition: £££s Paid for Stamp Collections; Postbus Silver Jubilee; Exeter Automated Processing; Collect British Stamps; Any Royal Mail slogans. Prices from £5.

9th November 1993 - CHRISTMAS

A Christmas Carol: 19p Bob Cratchit & Tiny Tim; 25p Mr & Mrs Fezziwig; 30p Scrooge; 35p Prize Turkey; 41p Mr Scrooge's Nephew

SPECIAL HANDSTAMPS

(1)	Philatelic Bureau	3	–	*Royal Mail*
(2)	First Day of Issue – Bethlehem	3	–	*Royal Mail*
(3)	First Day of Issue – City of London (top hat)	3	–	*Royal Mail*
(4)	First Day of Issue – London (cracker)	3	–	*Royal Mail*
(5)	The Dickens Fellowship, London WC1	10	15	*LFDC 119*
(6)	Birthplace of Dickens, Portsmouth	10	15	*VP 81*
(7)	Scrooge & Bob Cratchit, Rochester	10	25	*Bradbury*
(8)	Dickens House Museum	10	25	*CoverCraft*
(9)	Visit of Charles Dickens to Newcastle	12	35	*N'stle RoyalMail*
(10)	A Christmas Carol – Rochester, Kent	10	15	*BenL41*
(11)	A Christmas Carol – Portsmouth	10	20	*Ben500(89)*
(12)	A Christmas Carol – Broadstairs	10	15	*BenL41*
(13)	A Christmas Carol – Pickwick	10	15	*BenL41*
(14)	A Christmas Carol – Chatham	10	15	*BenL41*
(15)	A Christmas Carol – Old Curiosity Shop	10	10	*BLCS 89*
(16)	A Christmas Carol – Radio Times	10	15	*Benham*
(17)	A Christmas Carol – Rochester, Medway	10	12	*BLCS 89*
(18)	Scrooge's Mailcoach Run, Rochester	10	12	*BLCS 89*
(19)	Gads Hill, Higham-by-Rochester	10	8	*BenL40*
(20)	The Salvation Army	10	15	*SouthportCorps*
(21)	Happy Christmas, Royal Mail, EC1	10	–	*n.o.c.*
(22)	A Happy Christmas, News of the World	10	20	*CoverCraft*
(23)	National Postal Museum, Christmas Postcards	10	20	*Friends of NPM*
(24)	No.10 Squadron, BF 2389 PS	10	15	*RAF FDC 16*

C.D.S. POSTMARKS

(25)	Broadstairs; Marylebone; Gad's Hill or Mid-Higham, Rochester; Sultan Road, Portsmouth; Theobalds Road, London – near to the homes of Dickens	15
(26)	Camden Town – 'home' of Bob Cratchit	15

In addition: Holybush, Jerusalem Street, London Chief Office, Nasareth, St. Nicholas. Prices from £8.

SLOGAN POSTMARKS

(27)	Christmas Shopping at Rainbow Superstore	20

Also: BT; Safeway; Postbus; Collect British Stamps; Any Royal Mail slogans. Prices from £5.

£2.50 & £3.80 CHRISTMAS BOOKS OF STAMPS

With pair or block of four 19p & 25p stamps ....*pair*	7
With complete panes of 19p & 25p stamps ....*pair*	15

VALUES ARE FOR GOOD, CLEAN, UNADDRESSED COVERS WITH THE FULL SET OF STAMPS.

All values include VAT @ 17.5%

18th January 1994 - THE AGE OF STEAM

19p Bridge of Orchy; 25p "Amadis" at King's Cross;
30p Turntable at Blyth North;
35p Irlam into Wigan Central;
41p "Devizes Castle" across Worcester & B'ham Canal

	ordinary covers £	official covers £	
SPECIAL HANDSTAMPS (1) Philatelic Bureau	3	–	*Royal Mail*
(2) First Day of Issue - York	3	–	*Royal Mail*
(3) First Day of Issue - Bridge of Orchy	3	–	*Royal Mail*
(4) First Day of Issue - London	10	–	*Royal Mail*
(5) The Age of Steam, Waterloo, SE1	15	20	*VP 82*
(6) The Age of Steam, Derby	15	20	*LFDC 120*
(7) Peterborough NVR, Wansford Station	15	25	*Nene V. Rly*
(8) All Aboard Now, Collectors' Club	15	25	*C.Club (RMail)*
(9) North Yorkshire Moors Railway	15	25	*CoverCraft*
(10) Britain's Railway History, RMT, Euston	15	25	*CoverCraft*
(11) Britain's Railway Heritage, Ian Allen	15	35	*CoverCraft*
(12) Football Locomotives, Manchester United	15	20	*Dawn*
(13) Football Locomotives, Newcastle United	15	20	*Dawn*
(14) Great Central Railway, Loughborough	15	50	*Bradbury*
(15) Adventures of Sherlock Holmes, Paddington	15	40	*Bradbury*
(16) Midland Fox, Leicester	15	75	*Bradbury*
(17) Redhill, the Town and its Railway	15	40	*Redhill 150*
(18) Railway Mania, GWR Dainton Tunnel	15	30	*BenSG22*
(19) South Eastern Railway, Folkestone	15	35	*Ben500(90)*
(20) North British Rly., Edinburgh	15	20	*BLCS 90*
(21) Midland Railway, Euston	15	20	*BLCS 90*
(22) London, Brighton & South Coast Rly	15	20	*Ben500(90a)*
(23) Didcot, Great Western Railway Co.	15	25	*BenL43*
(24) Great Eastern Railway, Great Yarmouth	15	20	*BenL42*
(25) L.N.E.R., Railway Mania, Peterborough	15	20	*BenL42*
(26) LXX Sqn. Est. LXXVII, BF 2393 PS	15	20	*RAF FDC 17*
ORDINARY F.D.I. POSTMARKS			
(27) Aberystwyth (Talyllyn Railway cover)	35		
(28) Caernarfon (Festiniog Railway cover)	35		
C.D.S. POSTMARKS			
(29) Any Station postmark (e.g. Crowthorne)	20		
(30) Any TPO (Travelling Post Office) postmark	20		
(31) Blyth (or Cambois); Bridge of Orchy; King's Cross; Wigan; Worcester (or Lowesmoor) - sites on stamps	20		

Also: Branch End, Bright St. York, Carlisle, Carnforth, Darlington, Derby, Didcot, Euston, Gifford, Mallaig, Paddington, Quainton, Rainhill, The Rocket, Settle, Stephenson Square, Stockton, Swindon, Wylam. Prices from £15.

SLOGAN POSTMARKS		
(32) Sixty Years Passenger Service for the Capital	85	

In addition: British Philatelic Bulletin; Postbus. Prices from £5.

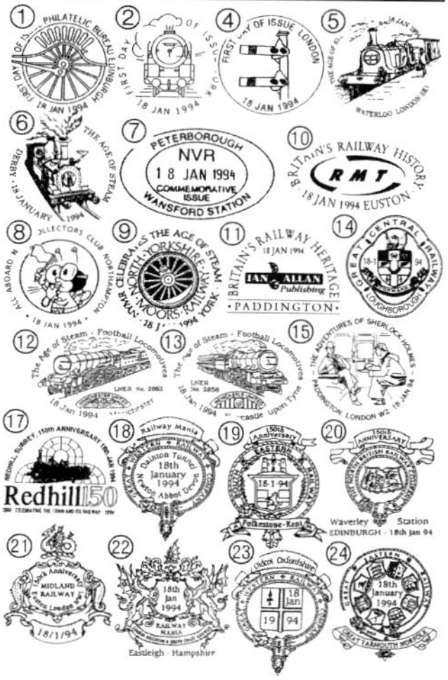

1st February 1994 - GREETINGS

10 x 1st Class – 'Messages':- Dan Dare, The Three Bears, Rupert Bear, Alice, Noggin the Nog, Peter Rabbit, Red Riding Hood, Orlando, Biggles, Paddington Bear.

SPECIAL HANDSTAMPS (1) Philatelic Bureau	3	–	*Royal Mail*
(2) First Day of Issue - Penn, Wolverhampton	4	–	*Royal Mail*
(3) First Day of Issue - London	12	–	*Royal Mail*
(4) Greetings, Daresbury	12	35	*Bradbury*
(5) Greetings from Paddington Bear, W2	12	20	*BLCS 91*
(6) Greetings from Rupert, SE1	12	20	*BLCS 91*
(7) Orlando, the Marmalade Cat, W1	12	15	*BenD223*
(8) Teddy Bear Times, Steyning	12	15	*BenD223*
(9) The Tale of Peter Rabbit, Keswick	12	15	*BenD223*
(10) Noggin the Nog, Canterbury	12	20	*Ben500(91)*
(11) Little Red Riding Hood, Wolfsdale	12	15	*BenD223*
(12) Bearsden	12	10	*ExpNews pc(s)*
(13) Evening Sentinel, Stoke on Trent	12	45	*Dawn(set of 10)*
C.D.S. POSTMARKS			
(14) Fleet St - newspapers characters	15		
(15) Greet, Letter, or Paddington	15		
(16) Oxford - home of Lewis Carroll	15		

Also: Bear Park, Bearsden, Biggleswade, Blackfriars Bridge Rd, Bunny, Catsfield, Catshill, Dunkeld, Eagle, Epsom Downs, Fulham Palace Rd,Letterston, Mount Nod, Penn, Rupert St., Wolf's Castle. £10.

SLOGAN POSTMARKS		
(17) Write Now, Say it Better in a Letter	20	

In addition: Octagon Theatre; Any Royal Mail slogans. Prices from £5.

1st March 1994 - THE PRINCE OF WALES

19p Chirk Castle; 25p Ben Arkle; 30p Mourne Mountains;
35p Dersingham; 41p Dolwyddelan Castle

SPECIAL HANDSTAMPS (1) Philatelic Bureau	3	–	*Royal Mail*
(2) First Day of Issue - Caernarfon	3	–	*Royal Mail*
(3) First Day of Issue - London	10	–	*Royal Mail*
(4) Caernarfon, St. David's Day	10	15	*Royal Mint*
(5) St. David's Day, Caernarfon Castle	10	15	*LFDC 121*
(6) St. David's Day, Caernarfon	10	15	*VP 83*
(7) St. David's, Haverfordwest (daffodils)	10	–	*Royal Mail*
(8) Investiture, Caernarfon (circle)	10	25	*CoverCraft*

Prince of Wales (contd.)	ordinary covers £	official covers £	
(9) Investiture, Caernarfon (oval)	10	15	*BLCS 92*
(10) Investiture, Highgrove	10	17	*BLCS 92*
(11) Investiture, Windsor	10	17	*BLCS 92*
(12) Radio Times, Buckingham Palace, SW1	10	12	*Benham*
(13) MAJESTY, Investiture, W1	10	20	*Benham*
(14) HRH Prince of Wales, Cardiff	10	17	*Ben500(92)*
(15) Buckingham Palace, London, SW1A 1AA	10	45	*Prince'sTrust*
(16) Prince Charles Ave. Post Office, Derby	10	–	*Royal Mail*
(17) Spring Stampex, SW1	10	–	*Royal Mail*
(18) Byddin Yr etc., Caernarfon	10	20	*S. Army*
(19) Football Locomotive Paintings, Sunderland	8	12	*Dawn*
(20) Richard I, Nottingham	8	25	*BenSG23*
(21) New £2 Coin, Bank of England, EC2	8	–	*n.o.c.*
(22) 24 Squadron, BF 2409 PS	8	12	*RAF FDC 18*
C.D.S. POSTMARKS			
(23) Achfary, Lairg – near to Ben Arkle (25p)	25		
(24) Buckingham Palace or Windsor Castle	75		
(25) Caernarfon or Windsor	15		
(26) Chirk (19p) or Dersingham (35p)	15		
(27) Dolwyddelan – (41p)	25		
(28) House of Commons or Lords	20		
(29) Nettleham – first Investiture	15		
(30) Newcastle (or Donard St., Newcastle) – (30p)	15		
(31) Prince Charles Ave., Derby	15		
(32) St. David's – issued on St. David's Day	15		
(33) St. David's Road, Caernarfon	15		

Also: Mount Charles, Prince Consort Rd, Princeville, Rhiconich, Tetbury, The Hayes, Wales. From £10.

SLOGAN POSTMARKS *Newry 850; Any Royal Mail slogans. Prices from £15.*

12th April 1994 – PICTORIAL POSTCARDS 1894–1994

19p Blackpool Tower; 25p "Where's my little lad"; 30p "Wish you were here!"; 35p Punch and Judy; 41p Tower Bridge.

SPECIAL HANDSTAMPS (1) Philatelic Bureau	3	–	*Royal Mail*
(2) First Day of Issue – Blackpool	3	–	*Royal Mail*
(3) First Day of Issue – London	12	–	*Royal Mail*
(4) Wish you were here, Blackpool	12	20	*LFDC 122*
(5) Wish you were here, Broadstairs	12	20	*VP 84*
(6) Wish you were here, Scarborough	12	20	*Bradbury*
(7) Blackpool Tower Centenary Year	12	15	*Bradbury*
(8) Picture Postcard Centenary, SW1	12	15	*BLCS 93*
(9) Tower Bridge Centenary, SE1	12	15	*BLCS 93*
(10) Picture Postcards Centenary, Brighton	12	15	*Ben500(93)*
(11) Football Locomotive Postcards, Arsenal	12	15	*Dawn*
(12) FA Cup Winners, Arsenal in Europe	12	25	*Dawn*
C.D.S. POSTMARKS			
(13) Any Seaside town, e.g. Scarborough	15		
(14) Any Butlin's Holiday Camp Post Office	50		
(15) Grand Hotel Buildings, Eastbourne	15		
(16) North Shore, or South Shore Blackpool	20		
(17) Sands, Sandy or The Strand	15		
(18) Seaside, Seaview, The Beach or The Pier	25		
(19) Whitecliff, Poole	12		

Also: Bare, Blackheath, Broadbottom, Crab Lane, Freezywater, Giggleswick, Holmfirth, Littlehampton, Pratt's Bottom, Rock, Seething Ln, Tower Hill. Prices from £10.

SLOGAN POSTMARKS	
(20) Le Shuttle, Folkestone to Calais	10
(21) Portsmouth 800	15

In addition: Collect British Stamps; Isle of Skye; Postcodes. Prices from £6.

3rd May 1994 – CHANNEL TUNNEL

25p, 41p British Lion and Le Coq; 25p, 41p Joined hands over a speeding train.

SPECIAL HANDSTAMPS (1) Philatelic Bureau	3	–	*Royal Mail*
(2) First Day of Issue – Folkestone (map)	3	–	*Royal Mail*
(3) First Day of Issue – Folkestone (Big Ben)	3	–	*Royal Mail*
(4) First Day of Issue – London	3	–	*Royal Mail*
(5) Institution of Civil Engineers, SW1	12	15	*LFDC 123*
(6) British Tunnelling Society, SW1	12	15	*VP 85*
(7) Channel Tunnel (lion and cock), Folkestone	12	15	*Bradbury*
(8) Brush Traction, Loughborough	12	15	*Bradbury*
(9) Le Shuttle, The Channel Tunnel, Folkestone	12	35	*BLCS 94 pair*
(10) Celebrating the Channel Tunnel, Folkestone	12	35	*BLCS 94 pair*
(11) Euro Tunnel Celebration '94, Folkestone	12	75	*Ben500(94)pr*
(12) Opening of the Channel Tunnel, Folkestone	12	25	*BLCS 94 pair*
(13) Radio Times, Folkestone	12	30	*Benham*
(14) First through the Tunnel, Laser, Folkestone	12	50	*Benham*
(15) Tarmac Construction Ltd, Wolverhampton	12	–	*n.o.c.*
(16) Design Consultants, Folkestone	12	175	*CoverCraft*
(17) No. 33 Squadron, BF 2421 PS	12	15	*RAF FDC 20*
(18) Woodhead Tunnel, Sheffield Wednesday	12	15	*Dawn*
(19) Busways E.S.O.P., Newcastle	12	15	*Dawn*
(20) Peterborough NVR, Wansford Station	12	25	*Nene V. Rly*

Channel Tunnel (contd.)

C.D.S. POSTMARKS	ordinary covers £	official covers £
(21) Cheriton or Folkestone – tunnel terminal	15	
(22) Ashford – international terminal	15	
(23) King's Cross – proposed new terminal	15	
(24) Waterloo Road, SE1 – existing terminal	15	
(25) Waterloo & Gare du Nord - Eurostar *pair*	35	
(26) Calais or Dover PAQUEBOTS	15	

In addition: Calais Rd., French St., Horn St., Railway Rd., Rising Bridge, Terminal Rd., Terminus Rd., The Link, Trafalgar Square, Undercliff. Prices from £10.

SLOGAN POSTMARKS

(27) Le Shuttle, Folkestone to Calais	15	

DOUBLE POSTMARKED COVERS

The Channel Tunnel stamps were a joint Royal Mail/La Poste issue. Arrangements were made for British collectors to obtain the French COQUELLES postmark at the Philatelic Bureau by authority of La Poste, the French postal administration. The Coquelles postmark was applied to the French stamps provided the covers had at least one British Channel Tunnel stamp also affixed. The French Channel Tunnel terminal is located at Coquelles.

(1) Covers with both sets (eight stamps)	30	
(2) Other combinations of English & French stamps	15	

6th June 1994 – D-DAY

25p Groundcrew reloading RAF Bostons; 25p Coastal bombardment/HMS Warspite; 25p Commandos landing on Gold Beach; 25p Infantry regrouping on Sword Beach; 25p Advancing inland from Ouistreham.

SPECIAL HANDSTAMPS			
(1) Philatelic Bureau	3	–	*Royal Mail*
(2) First Day of Issue – Portsmouth	3	–	*Royal Mail*
(3) First Day of Issue – London	3	–	*Royal Mail*
(4) Operation 'Overlord' D-Day, BF 2398 PS	12	15	*RAF FDC 21*
(5) Utah Beach, BF 2415 PS	12	100	*Forces*
(6) Sword Beach, BF 2416 PS	12	100	*Forces*
(7) Gold Beach, BF 2417 PS	12	100	*Forces*
(8) Juno Beach, BF 2418 PS	12	100	*Forces*
(9) Taking of Pegasus Bridge, BF 2419 PS	12	15	*Forces(s)*
(10) Silencing of the Merville Battery, BF 2420 PS	12	15	*Forces(s)*
(11) 50th Anniversary of 'D' Day, BF 2422 PS	12	100	*Forces*
(12) HMS Dryad, Portsmouth	12	20	*Royal Mint*
(13) D-Day, 1944-1994, Portsmouth	12	15	*Westminster*
(14) 50 Overlord, Southwick, Hampshire	12	20	*Southwick P.O.*
(15) Operation Taxable, 617 Squadron	12	50	*Cam S.C.*
(16) City of Portsmouth, D-Day, 50th Anniversary	12	60	*RM Portsmouth*
(17) D-Day Commemoration, Birmingham	12	10	*Royal Mail*
(18) D-Day + 50 (Eisenhower)	12	15	*LFDC 124*
(19) D-Day, Southampton (square map)	12	15	*VP 86*
(20) Spirit of Britain, London SW1	12	15	*Bradbury*
(21) D-Day Museum, Portsmouth	12	45	*Arlington*
(22) Imperial War Museum, SE1	12	12	*Benham*
(23) National Army Museum, Chelsea, SW3	12	25	*BenL44*
(24) Radio Times, D-Day Landings, Portsmouth	12	10	*Benham*
(25) FEARLESS, Portsmouth	12	20	*BLCS 95*
(26) D-Day Landings, Portsmouth	12	60	*BenC.I*
(27) D-Day, Tangmere	12	20	*Benham*
(28) Bletchley Park, Enigma Codebreakers	12	15	*Bletchley Trust*
(29) D-Day Preparations by Rail	12	15	*Dawn*
(30) Invasion of Europe, Portsmouth	12	50	*Cam S.C.*
(31) D-Day, News of the World, London E1	12	15	*CoverCraft*
(32) D-Day The Sun, London E1	12	15	*CoverCraft*
(33) London Taxi Benevolent Assoc'n	12	15	*CoverCraft*
(34) D-Day, 1944-1994, Portsmouth (RAF Wings)	12	15	*CoverCraft*
(35) D-Day Commemoration, Southsea	12	75	*CoverCraft*

C.D.S POSTMARKS		
(36) Calais and Dover PAQUEBOTS *pair*	20	
(37) Churchill, Bristol or Montgomery, Powys	20	
(38) House of Commons or Lords	30	
(39) Maritime Mail or Normandy (Guildford)	20	
(40) Portsmouth or Southampton	12	
(41) Southwick – SHAEF Headquarters	20	

In addition: Battle, The Beach, Boston, Bulford Barracks, Dunkirk, Pathfinder Village, RAF Scampton, Trenchard Lines, Victory Street. Prices from £10.

SLOGAN POSTMARKS		
(42) Maritime Mail	20	

In addition: Portsmouth 800; European Elections. Prices from £8.

5th July 1994 – GOLF

19p St. Andrews - The Old Course; 25p Muirfield - 18th Hole; 30p Carnoustie - Luckyslap; 35p Royal Troon - The Postage Stamp; 41p Turnberry - 9th Hole.

SPECIAL HANDSTAMPS			
(1) Philatelic Bureau	3	–	*Royal Mail*
(2) First Day of Issue – Turnberry	3	–	*Royal Mail*
(3) First Day of Issue – London	3	–	*Royal Mail*
(4) Royal and Ancient Golf Club, St. Andrews	15	30	*LFDC 125*
(5) Golfer's Alphabet, St. Andrews	15	25	*VP 87*
(6) Gleneagles Hotel, Auchterarder	15	25	*Bradbury*

Golf (contd.)

	ordinary covers £	official covers £	
(7) Tee Time, Philatelic Golf Society	15	20	*Bradbury*
(8) H-C-E-G 250 Years, Muirfield	15	30	*HCEG(s)*
(9) First Open, St. Georges, Sandwich	15	12	*BLCS 96*
(10) The British Open, Greg Norman, Turnberry	15	12	*BLCS 96*
(11) World's Oldest Golf Club, Muirfield	15	10	*Benham(s)*
(12) St. Andrew's, Home of Golf	15	25	*Ben500(96)*
(13) 250 Years of Golf, Carnoustie	15	10	*Benham(s)*
(14) Mail on Sunday, British Open, Turnberry	15	15	*Benham*
(15) 250 Years of Golf, Royal Troon	15	10	*Benham(s)*
(16) Eighth Hole, Postage Stamp, Royal Troon	15	50	*CoverCraft*
(17) No. 25 Squadron, BE 2429 PS	8	15	*RAF FDC 22*

C.D.S. POSTMARKS

(18) St. Andrews (19p); Gullane (25p); Carnoustie (30p); Troon (35p); or Turnberry (41p) *each*	35
(19) Caddy	175
(20) The Fairway, The Green or The Links	35
(21) Gleneagles Hotel, Eagle or Par *each*	50
(22) Leith Walk – 1744 home of H.C.E.G.	25

In addition: Ballybogy, Birkdale, Golf Road, Hoylake, Lytham St. Annes, Portrush, Prestwick, Sandwich, Wentworth. Prices from £15.

SLOGAN POSTMARKS

(23) New Skoda Women's Scottish Open 75

TSB Athletics; BUPA; See the Clock/Make a Wish; Any Royal Mail slogans. Prices from £7.

2nd August 1994 – SUMMERTIME

19p Llanelwedd (Royal Welsh Show); 25p Wimbledon; 30p Cowes Week; 35p Lord's; 41p Braemar Highland Gathering

SPECIAL HANDSTAMPS			
(1) Philatelic Bureau	3	–	*Royal Mail*
(2) First Day of Issue – Wimbledon	3	–	*Royal Mail*
(3) First Day of Issue – London	4	–	*Royal Mail*
(4) Birthplace of Thomas Lord, Thirsk	10	20	*S.P.*
(5) Memorial Cricket Match, NW8	10	20	*S.P.*
(6) Tribute to Lords, Derbyshire CCC	10	20	*S.P.*
(7) Tribute to Lords, Durham CCC	10	20	*S.P.*
(8) Tribute to Lords, Essex CCC	10	20	*S.P.*
(9) Tribute to Lords, Glamorgan CCC	10	20	*S.P.*
(10) Tribute to Lords, Gloucestershire CCC	10	20	*S.P.*
(11) Tribute to Lords, Hampshire CCC	10	20	*S.P.*
(12) Tribute to Lords, Kent CCC	10	20	*S.P.*
(13) Tribute to Lords, Lancashire CCC	10	20	*S.P.*
(14) Tribute to Lords, Leicestershire CCC	10	20	*S.P.*
(15) Tribute to Lords, Middlesex CCC	10	20	*S.P.*
(16) Tribute to Lords, Northamptonshire CCC	10	20	*S.P.*
(17) Tribute to Lords, Nottinghamshire CCC	10	20	*S.P.*
(18) Tribute to Lords, Somerset CCC	10	20	*S.P.*
(19) Tribute to Lords, Surrey CCC	10	20	*S.P.*
(20) Tribute to Lords, Sussex CCC	10	20	*S.P.*
(21) Tribute to Lords, Warwickshire CCC	10	20	*S.P.*
(22) Tribute to Lords, Worcestershire CCC	10	20	*S.P.*
(23) Tribute to Lords, Yorkshire CCC	10	20	*S.P.*
(24) Summertime at Lord's, NW8	10	15	*VP 88*
(25) Outside Edge, Nottingham	10	10	*Benham*
(26) Yatching at Cowes	10	15	*Ben500(98)*
(27) Braemar Gathering	10	10	*BLCS 98*
(28) Royal Welsh Show, Llanelwedd	10	10	*BenL45*
(29) Shetland Pony at Braemar	10	10	*BenL45*
(30) YMCA, 150 Years, Dulverton	10	15	*Arlington*
(31) National Association of Local Councils, WC1	10	10	*LFDC 126*
(32) Summertime Holidays by Train, Manchester	10	10	*Dawn*
(33) Summertime Holidays by Rail, Leicester	10	40	*Dawn*
(34) No.22 Squadron, BF 2431 PS	10	12	*RAF FDC 23*
(35) GSG Technology Centre, Swindon	10	150	*CSG*
(36) Postal Uniforms, National Postal Museum	10	–	*n.o.c.*

C.D.S. POSTMARKS

(37) Builth Wells (19p); Wimbledon (25p) Cowes (30p); St. John's Wood (35p); Braemar (41p) *each* 15

In addition: Bowling, Kennington, Over, Pavilion, Strawberry Hill, Summerhouse, Summerfield, Summerseat, Summertown. Prices from £8.

SLOGAN POSTMARKS

(38) Tropical Places, Exotic Holiday 12

Also: Biggleswade Festival; Inverness; Perrier; McMillans; Wilde Weekend in Worthing; Collect British Stamps; Royal Mail slogans. Prices from £7.

27th September 1994 – MEDICAL DISCOVERIES

25p Ultrasonic Imaging; 30p Scanning Electron Microscopy; 35p Magnetic Resonance Imaging; 41p Computed Tomography

SPECIAL HANDSTAMPS			
(1) Philatelic Bureau	3	–	*Royal Mail*
(2) First Day of Issue – Cambridge	3	–	*Royal Mail*
(3) First Day of Issue – London	8	–	*Royal Mail*
(4) Peak Practice, Whatstandwell	8	10	*BLCS 99*
(5) Peak Practice, Wirksworth	8	10	*BLCS 99*
(6) Peak Practice, Fritchley	8	10	*BLCS 99*
(7) Peak Practice, Crich	8	10	*BLCS 99*

Medical Discoveries (contd.)

	ordinary covers £	official covers £	
(8) The Lancet, London WC1	8	10	*BLCS 99*
(9) St. Bartholomew's, London EC1	8	15	*Ben500(99)*
(10) St. George's Hospital, London SW17	8	10	*Sajal*
(11) Cystic Fibrosis, Bromley	8	15	*Bradbury*
(12) BMA, Founded 1832, Worcester	8	35	*Bradbury*
(13) BMA, Over 100,000 Members, WC1	8	35	*Bradbury*
(14) Florence Nightingale, SE1	8	10	*VP 89*
(15) Royal College of Surgeons, WC2	8	10	*LFDC 127*
(16) Glasgow Royal Maternity Hospital	8	15	*GRMH*
(17) Blackburn Rovers UEFA Cup	8	25	*Dawn*
(18) No.360 Squadron BF 2432 PS	8	10	*RAF FDC 24*

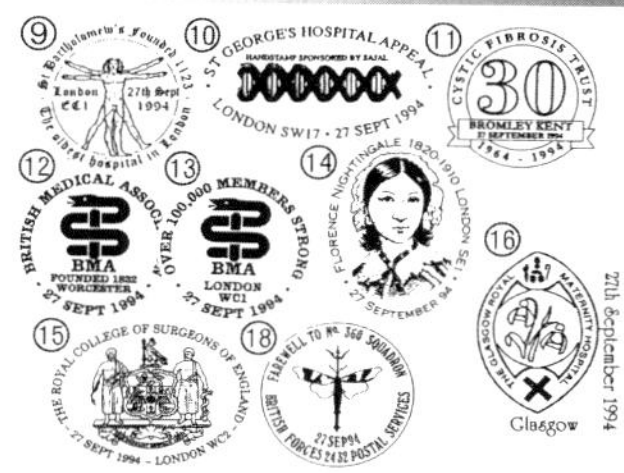

C.D.S. POSTMARKS

(19) Hospital Post Offices:- Benenden, Milford, Oswestry, Lancaster Moor or Edward VII	15		
(20) Glasgow Royal Infirmary	25		
(21) Harefield or Papworth – transplants	10		
(22) Harborne, Hammersmith or Paddington – Radiology work	15		
(23) Headington, Oxford – Electronic Microscope	15		

Also: Brentford, Cambridge, Glasgow, Healing, Lancing, Pill, New Invention, St. Clements, Oxford. £8.

SLOGAN POSTMARKS

(24) Zeneca (pharmaceuticals)	15		
(25) Health Education – Fresh Fruit & Veg	15		

In addition: Soft Rock Heart Radio; Royal Mail slogans. Prices from £7.

1st November 1994 – CHRISTMAS

19p, 25p, 30p, 35p, 41p Children's Nativity Plays

SPECIAL HANDSTAMPS (1) Philatelic Bureau	3	–	*Royal Mail*
(2) First Day of Issue – Bethlehem	3	–	*Royal Mail*
(3) First Day of Issue – London	3	–	*Royal Mail*
(4) Christmas Common	10	15	*Ben500(100)*
(5) Hollytrees Museum, Colchester	10	8	*BLCS 100*
(6) The Nativity, Bethlehem	10	8	*BLCS 100*
(7) The Nativity, Nasareth	10	8	*BLCS 100*
(8) Wiseman's Bridge	10	40	*Ben500(100a)*
(9) Christchurch Priory 1094-1994	10	25	*LFDC 128*
(10) Bethlehem (angel and trumpet)	10	15	*VP 90*
(11) Santa Claus Distrib. Fund, Stoke Newington	10	15	*G.K.Eldridge*
(12) National Postal Museum, Christmas 94	10	15	*Friends NPM*
(13) Happy Christmas, Royal Mail, EC1	10	–	*Royal Mail*
(14) Christmas Greetings, Lewes	10	15	*FDP Co*
(15) Season's Greetings, Leeds United	10	12	*Dawn*
(16) Aston Villa in Europe, Birmingham	10	12	*Dawn*
(17) Salvation Army, Hackney, E8	10	12	*S.Army*
(18) No.78 Squadron, BF 2436 PS	10	12	*RAF FDC 25*
(19) Peterborough NVR, Wansford Station	10	15	*Nene V. Rly*

C.D.S. POSTMARKS

(20) Nasareth or Holy Island	20		
(21) York – most famous Nativity play	10		

In addition: Angel Hill, Brentwood Ave., Child's Hill, Christchurch, Jerusalem Street, Narberth, Playing Place, Shepherd's Bush, Shepherd's Well, St. Nicholas, Star, Star Cross. Prices from £6.

SLOGAN POSTMARKS

(22) Walt Disney's Snow White	25		

In addition: Collect British Stamps; Control your Dog; Glasgow Concert Hall; Pass on PostCode; Mercurycard Off Peak; Any Royal Mail. Prices from £5.

£2.50 & £3.80 CHRISTMAS BOOKS OF STAMPS

With pair or block of four 19p & 25p stamps ....*pair*	7		
With complete panes of 19p & 25p stamps ....*pair*	15		

This catalogue is NOT the price list of the author or publisher. Values should be treated as a guide.

17th January 1995 – CATS

19p black cat; 25p Siamese & tabby; 30p ginger cat; 35p Abyssinian & tortoiseshell; 41p black & white cat

SPECIAL HANDSTAMPS (1) Philatelic Bureau	3	–	*Royal Mail*
(2) First Day of Issue – Kitts Green	3	–	*Royal Mail*
(3) First Day of Issue – London	3	–	*Royal Mail*
(4) Your Cat Magazine, Peterborough	15	20	*Benham*
(5) Cats, Woman & Home, SE1	15	20	*Benham*
(6) RSPCA, Horsham	15	20	*BLCS 101*
(7) Cats Protection League, Horsham	15	20	*Benham*
(8) Cats Protection League, Kirkintilloch	15	20	*Benham*
(9) Cats Protection League, Newtownards	15	20	*Benham*
(10) Cats Protection League, Bridgend	15	20	*Benham*
(11) Cats Protection League, Birmingham	15	20	*BLCS 101*
(12) Catstree, Bridgnorth	15	50	*Ben500(101)*
(13) Catfield, Great Yarmouth	15	20	*BLCS 101*
(14) Catsham, Glastonbury	15	20	*BLCS 101*
(15) Catbrook, Chepstow	15	20	*BLCS 101*
(16) Catsash, Newport	15	35	*BenSG25*
(17) Philatelic Felines, Catsfield	15	20	*VP 91*
(18) Philatelic Felines, Catshill	15	20	*LFDC 129*
(19) Celebrating Cats, Catshill	15	20	*Westminster*
(20) Wood Green Animal Shelters, Royston	15	25	*Wood Green*

Cats (contd.)

	ordinary covers £	official covers £	
(21) Cool Cats Catalogue, Catsfield	10	15	*FDP Co*
(22) Celebrating Cats, City of London	10	25	*Bradbury*
(23) Postal Cats, National Postal Museum	10	–	*n.o.c.*
(24) Tiger Squadron, Flying Pumas, BF 2439 PS	10	12	*RAF FDC 26*
C.D.S. POSTMARKS			
(25) Catfield, Catsfield, Catshill etc *each*	15		
(26) Earl's Court – Cat Show	15		
(27) Horsham – RSPCA & CPL headquarters	15		

Also: Catbrook, Catcott, Catforth, Catsworth, Lea Village, Mousehole, Whittington. From £12.

SLOGAN POSTMARKS *Please control your dog; Collect British Stamps Prices from £10.*

14th March 1995 - SPRINGTIME

19p Dandelions; 25p Sweet Chestnut Leaves; 30p Garlic Leaves; 35p Hazel Leaves; 41p Spring Grass

	ordinary covers £	official covers £	
SPECIAL HANDSTAMPS (1) Philatelic Bureau	3	–	*Royal Mail*
(2) First Day of Issue – Springfield	3	–	*Royal Mail*
(3) First Day of Issue – London	3	–	*Royal Mail*
(4) Springtime, Wingfield	10	12	*BLCS 102*
(5) Springtime, Swallownest	10	12	*BLCS 102*
(6) Springtime, Birdbrook	10	12	*BLCS 102*
(7) Springtime, Ducklington	10	15	*Ben500(102)*
(8) Springtime, Featherstone	10	12	*BLCS 102*
(9) Rupert, Bearwood	10	12	*BLCS 102*
(10) Springtime Stamps, Springvale	10	20	*LFDC 130*
(11) Springtime Stamps, Royal Botanic Gdns, Kew.	10	15	*VP 92*
(12) Springtime, North Norfolk Railway	10	12	*Dawn*
(13) Spring into the new Catalogue, Leaves Green	10	12	*FDP Co*
(14) The 'Saints', BF 2458 PS	10	12	*RAF FDC 27*
(15) Wansford Station, Peterborough	10	20	*NVRly*
C.D.S. POSTMARKS			
(16) Chestnut Grove or Hazel Grove	15		
(17) Kew Gardens	15		
(18) Springbank, Spring Grove or Springvale	15		
(19) Spring Gardens or Springfield	15		

Also: Grassmoor, Leaves Green, Long Shoot, Spring Corner, Spring Hill, Springside, Swallownest, Wrens Nest. Prices from £12.

SLOGAN POSTMARKS *Tropical Places. Postcodes Spalding. Prices from £6.*

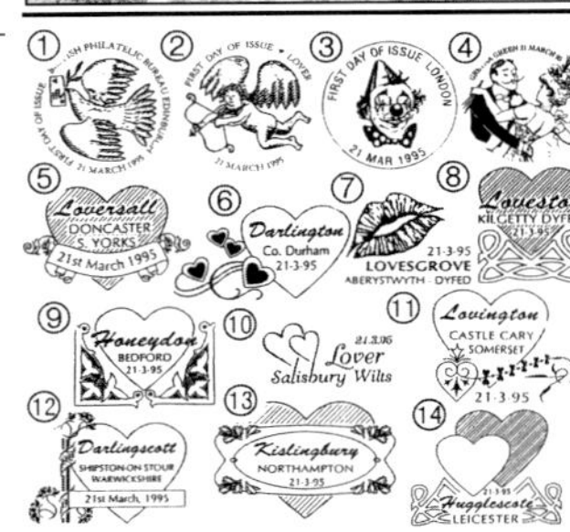

21st March 1995 - GREETINGS.

10 x 1st Class on the theme of Love & Kisses

	ordinary covers £	official covers £	
SPECIAL HANDSTAMPS (1) Philatelic Bureau	3	–	*Royal Mail*
(2) First Day of Issue – Lover	4	–	*Royal Mail*
(3) First Day of Issue – London	4	–	*Royal Mail*
(4) Gretna Green	12	25	*Bradbury*
(5) Loversall, Doncaster	12	20	*BLCS 103*
(6) Darlington, Co. Durham	12	20	*BLCS 103*
(7) Lovesgrove, Aberystwyth	12	20	*BLCS 103*
(8) Loveston, Kilgetty	12	20	*BLCS 103*
(9) Honeydon, Bedford	12	20	*BLCS 103*
(10) Lover, Salisbury	12	20	*BLCS 103*
(11) Lovington, Castle Cary	12	20	*BLCS 103*
(12) Darlingscott, Shipston on Stour	12	20	*BLCS 103*
(13) Kislingbury, Northampton	12	20	*Ben500(103)*
(14) Hugglescote, Leicester	12	20	*BenD234*
(15) Team Work, Royal Mail, Leeds	12	25	*Royal Mail NE*
(16) Discovery Day, Dundee	15	–	*n.o.c.*
C.D.S. POSTMARKS			
(17) Big Top or Playing Place	12		
(18) Greet, Gretna Green or Lover	12		

Also: Darlington, Heartsease, Kishorn, Paradise, Portobello Rd. Prices from £8.

NB These stamps were re-issued on 13th February 1996 with Blue Fluor Phosphor

11th April 1995 - NATIONAL TRUST

19p 100 Years; 25p Protecting Land; 30p Conserving Art; 35p Saving Coast; 41p Repairing Buildings.

	ordinary covers £	official covers £	
SPECIAL HANDSTAMPS (1) Philatelic Bureau	3	–	*Royal Mail*
(2) First Day of Issue – Alfriston	3	–	*Royal Mail*
(3) First Day of Issue – London	3	–	*Royal Mail*
(4) Queen Anne's Gate National Headquarters	10	–	*Royal Mail*
(5) Attingham Park, Conserving Art	10	–	*Royal Mail*
(6) St. David's, Saving Coastline	10	–	*Royal Mail*
(7) Congleton, Repairing Buildings	10	–	*Royal Mail*
(8) Crom, Enniskillen, Protecting Land	10	–	*Royal Mail*
(9) Giant's Causeway, Bushmills (oval)	10	–	*Royal Mail*
(10) Blickling Hall, Aylsham, Norfolk	10	–	*Royal Mail*
(11) This England, Oakham, Rutland	10	15	*VP 93*
(12) Country Houses Association, WC2	10	15	*LFDC 131*
(13) Steam Yacht Gondola, Coniston	10	12	*BLCS 104*
(14) Brownsea Island, Poole	10	12	*BLCS 104*
(15) Calke Abbey, Ticnall, Derby	10	12	*Benham*

National Trust (contd.)

	ordinary covers £	official covers £	
(16) Fountains, Abbey, Ripon	10	15	*Ben500(104)*
(17) Powis Castle, Welshpool	10	12	*Benham*
(18) Hidcote Manor, Chipping Camden	10	12	*Benham*
(19) Giant's Causeway, Bushmills	10	12	*Benham*
(20) The Old Post Office, Tintagel	10	12	*Benham*
(21) The Clergy House, Alfriston	10	12	*Benham*
(22) Chartwell, Westerham, Kent	10	12	*Benham*
(23) The National Trust, Radio Times, W12	10	12	*Benham*
(24) George Stephenson's Birthplace, Wylam	10	12	*Dawn*
(25) Supertrams, Sheffield	10	12	*Dawn*
(26) The catalogue you can trust, Alfriston	10	15	*FDP Co*
(27) Crathie Parish Church Centenary	10	20	*Pilgrim*
(28) Llangollen Postal Museum	10	40	*Llangollen PM*
(29) No.39 Squadron BF 2459 PS	10	12	*RAF FDC 28*
(30) Port Ellen, Isle of Islay	10	–	*Royal Mail*
C.D.S. POSTMARKS			
(31) Alfriston – first National Trust building	15		
(32) Atcham or Upton Megna – Attingham Park	15		
(33) Barmouth – first National Trust site	15		
(34) Haslemere – Robert Hunter (Founder)	15		
(35) Lower Shiplake – Canon Rawnsley (Founder)	15		
(36) St. David's (35p) or Scholar Green (41p)	15		
(37) Tintagel – National Trust Post Office	15		
(38) Wisbech – B/place Octavia Hill (Founder)	15		
(39) Land's End and John O'Groats *pair*	35		

In addition: Acorn Street, Bredon, Lacock, Montacute, Oak Tree, Oakhill, Petworth, Shipton-by-Beningbrough, Wylam. Prices from £6.

SLOGAN POSTMARKS *See the Clock etc.; Shetland Scottish Tourism. Prices from £6.*

2nd May 1995 – VE DAY

19p Liberation of Paris; 25p St. Paul's on VE night; 19p Red Cross ; 19p & 30p United Nations.

SPECIAL HANDSTAMPS (1) Philatelic Bureau	3	–	*Royal Mail*
(2) First Day of Issue – Peace & Freedom, SW	3	–	*Royal Mail*
(3) First Day of Issue – London	3	–	*Royal Mail*
(4) First Day of Issue – VE DAY London EC4	3	5	*DailyMirror(s)*
(5) United Nations Association, Whitehall	10	55	*CoverCollection*
(6) United Nations, Peacehaven	10	12	*BLCS 105*
(7) United Nations, London SW1	10	10	*BLCS 105*
(8) Victory in Europe, London	10	15	*Ben500(105)*
(9) Victory in Europe, Birmingham	10	12	*Benham*
(10) Victory in Europe, Coventry	10	12	*Benham*
(11) Victory in Europe, Edinburgh	10	12	*Benham*
(12) Victory in Europe, Cardiff	10	12	*Benham*
(13) Victory in Europe, Dover	10	12	*BLCS 105*
(14) Daily Express, Hyde Park	10	12	*Benham*
(15) The Mail on Sunday, Kensington	10	12	*Benham*
(16) Victory in Europe, Radio Times, W12	10	12	*Benham*
(17) Victory in Europe, Whitehall (cigar)	10	12	*LFDC 132*
(18) Peace & Freedom, EC4	10	15	*VP 94*
(19) British Medical Association	10	15	*Bradbury*
(20) R J Mitchell Centenary Year, Southampton	10	35	*Bradbury(set 3)*
(21) BBMF Commemoration, SW1	10	50	*CoverCraft*
(22) Enigma Codebreakers, Bletchley Park	10	20	*Arlington*
(23) St. Dunstan's, London W1	10	55	*Arlington*
(24) Birmingham Evening Mail VE DAY	10	20	*Dawn*
(25) Troops Return, Liverpool	10	20	*Dawn*
(26) British Forces Postal Service 1000	10	50	*Forces*
(27) GB FDC Catalogue, Peacehaven	10	15	*FDP Co*
(28) Llangollen Postal Museum	10	40	*Llangollen PM*
(29) No 8 Squadron, BF 2460 PS	10	12	*RAF FDC 29*
(30) Peterborough Rail 150	10	20	*NVRly*
C.D.S. POSTMARKS			
(31) Bladon, Churchill or Montgomery	15		
(32) House of Commons or Lords	50		
(33) London EC - St. Paul's Cathedral (25p)	10		
(34) Peacehaven, Cross in Hand or Hope	15		
(35) Tufton St SW1 - first meeting on UN	15		
(36) West Wellow - Florence Nightingale	15		

Also: Biggin Hill, Cranwell, Falls Rd, The Maze, New York, Normandy, Wonersh, Victory St. From £10.

6th June 1995 – SCIENCE FICTION

25p The Time Machine; 30p The First Men in the Moon; 35p War of the Worlds; 41p The Shape of Things to Come.

SPECIAL HANDSTAMPS (1) Philatelic Bureau	3	–	*Royal Mail*
(2) First Day of Issue – Wells	3	–	*Royal Mail*
(3) First Day of Issue – London H G Wells SF	3	–	*Royal Mail*
(4) Into the Future, Starboard Way, E14	12	10	*BLCS 106*
(5) Science Fiction, Star Road, W14	12	15	*Ben500(107)*
(6) War of the Worlds, Worlds End, Newbury	12	15	*BLCS 106*
(7) Time and Space, Star	12	10	*Benham(s)*
(8) Science Fiction, Radio Times, W12	12	15	*Benham*
(9) The First Men in the Moon, Bromley	12	12	*VP 95*

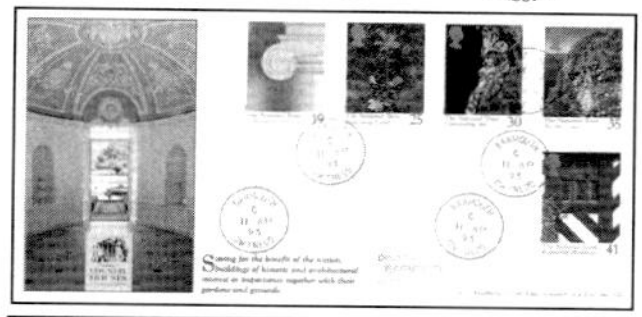

Science Fiction (contd.)	ordinary covers £	official covers £	
(10) The War of the Worlds, Bromley	12	25	*LFDC 133*
(11) H G Wells 1866-1946, Bromley	12	25	*Cam.S.C.*
(12) Blick, 70 Years Time Recording, Swindon	12	25	*Blick*
(13) Science Fiction Convention, Glasgow	12	35	*CoverCollection*
(14) Message from Mars, Bromley	12	75	*CoverCraft*
(15) Travel Back in Time, Wells	12	15	*FDP Co*
(16) No. IV (AC) Squadron BF 2469 PS	12	12	*RAF FDC 30*
C.D.S. POSTMARKS			
(17) Bromley - birthplace of H. G. Wells	15		
(18) Sandgate, Sevenoaks or Woking	15		
(19) Wells, Somerset	15		

Also: Clockface, Eagle, Globe Rd, Greenwich, Horsell, New Invention, RAF Woodbridge, Starcoast World, The Rocket, Woking, Worlds End. Prices from £12.

8th August 1995 – SHAKESPEARE'S GLOBE THEATRE

5 x 25p: The Swan Theatre 1595; The Rose Theatre 1587; The Globe Theatre 1599; The Hope Theatre 1613; The Globe Theatre 1614.

	ordinary	official	
SPECIAL HANDSTAMPS (1) Philatelic Bureau	3	–	*Royal Mail*
(2) First Day of Issue – Stratford upon Avon	3	–	*Royal Mail*
(3) First Day of Issue – Globe Theatre London	3	–	*Royal Mail*
(4) Henry V, The Barbican EC	12	15	*BenSG26*
(5) Twelfth Night, The Barbican EC	12	15	*BLCS 108*
(6) A Midsummer Night's Dream, Stratford	12	15	*BLCS 108*
(7) Love's Labours Lost, Stratford	12	15	*Ben500(108)*
(8) Romeo and Juliet, Stratford	12	15	*Benham*
(9) Stratford Upon Avon (swan)	12	15	*VP 96*
(10) Midsummer Night's Dream (portrait) Stratford	12	15	*LFDC 134*
(11) Midsummer Night's Dream (ass) Stratford	12	–	*Cam.S.C.*
(12) Celebrating Shakespeare's New Globe	12	20	*CoverCollection*
(13) Stratford upon Avon (changeable date pmk)	15	–	*Royal Mail*
(14) Shakespeare's Globe, Bankside, SE1	12	20	*Bradbury*
(15) Loughborough Grammar School	12	20	*Bradbury*
(16) Henry Purcell, City of Westminster	12	25	*MusPhilCircle*
(17) Blick Time Systems, Swindon	12	25	*Blick*
(18) The Hammers, Hamlet, Famous Locos E13	12	15	*Dawn*
(19) The new replica Globe Theatre, South Bank	12	15	*FDP Co*
(20) Covercraft Tenth Anniversary Year	12	15	*CoverCraft*
(21) Guarding the Mail, National Postal Museum	12	–	*Royal Mail*
(22) Port Ellen, Isle of Islay	12	–	*Royal Mail*
(23) No.9 First Tornado Squadron BF 2470 PS	12	12	*RAF FDC 31*
C.D.S. POSTMARKS			
(24) Blackfriars or Globe Road, London	10		
(25) London Bridge-nearest PO to the new Globe	10		
(26) Old Swan, Rose or Hope	10		
(27) Shakespeare St, Padiham Burnley	10		
(28) Stratford upon Avon	10		

In addition: Llanfair, Macduff, Talke Pits, Theatre Square, The Circle. Prices from £6.

SLOGAN POSTMARKS *PO Charter, Stratford. Prices from £7.*

5th September 1995 – COMMUNICATIONS

Rowland Hill: 19p Penny Postage; 25p Penny Black; Marconi: 41p Early wireless; 60p Marine safety & navigation.

	ordinary	official	
SPECIAL HANDSTAMPS (1) Philatelic Bureau	3	–	*Royal Mail*
(2) First Day of Issue – London EC (pillar box)	3	–	*Royal Mail*
(3) First Day of Issue – London (maltese cross)	3	–	*Royal Mail*
(4) Rowland Hill Fund - Philatelic Bureau	10	100	*Royal Mail*
(5) British Post Office Singapore '95 Edinburgh	40	–	*Royal Mail*
(6) Centenary First Wireless Message Chelmsford	10	25	*LFDC 135*
(7) Bath (Maltese Cross)	10	15	*VP 97*
(8) Radio Society of Great Britain, Herts	10	45	*LFDC 135*
(9) Alexandra Palace, London N22	10	35	*Cam.S.C.*
(10) Sir Rowland Hill, Kidderminster	10	15	*BLCS 109*
(11) Sir Rowland Hill, Bath	10	15	*Ben500(109)*
(12) First Radio Message, Chelmsford (square)	10	15	*Benham*
(13) First Radio Message, Flatholm Island	10	15	*BLCS 109*
(14) BT Portishead Radio, Highbridge	10	50	*A. Hyde/BT*
(15) ITN 40 Anniversary, WC2	10	30	*Arlington*
(16) 60th Anniv TV Trans, Alexandra Palace	10	15	*Dawn*
(17) Navy & Army Equip Exhib BF 2484 PS	10	–	*n.o.c.*
(18) Blick Time Systems Ltd, Swindon	10	25	*Blick*
(19) SRH & GM making waves, Chelmsford	10	15	*FDP Co*
(20) Mail by Rail, Sheffield	10	15	*Dawn*
(21) First Roadside Pillar Box Carlisle	10	90	*Carlisle PO*
(22) Port Ellen, Isle of Islay	10	–	*Royal Mail*
(23) National Postal Museum (maltese cross)	10	–	*n.o.c.*
(24) No.32 Commun. Squadron BF 2471 PS	10	12	*RAF FDC 32*
C.D.S. POSTMARKS			
(25) Bruce Grove - Rowland Hill/Bruce Castle	15		
(26) Great Baddow - Maroni Reseach laboratories	15		
(27) Kidderminster - Rowland Hill's birthplace	15		
(28) Mullion; Niton, IOW; or The Lizard - *trans-Atlantic experiments*	15		

Communications (contd.)	ordinary covers £	official covers £	
(29) Rathlin Island or Sandbanks - Marconi	15		
(30) Sanquhar - oldest Post Office	15		
(31) Writtle - first radio broadcast	15		

Also :Bath, Chelmsford, Hampstead Heath, Rowlands Castle, Telephone Hse, any TPOs. From £10.

SLOGAN POSTMARKS

(32) ACP Telecom, Birmingham	10		
(33) Vodaphone Centre, Wolverhampton	10		
(34) Any postcode or radio station slogan *each*	10		

In addition: Tropical Place-Teletex; Coins in cards; Please keep dogs inside. Prices from £7.

NB *Five Colchester slogans exist - these were serviced 'by favour' and are therefore outside the scope of this catalogue.*

3rd October 1995 - RUGBY LEAGUE

19p Harold Wagstaff; 25p Gus Risman; 30p Jim Sullivan; 35p Billy Batten; 41p Brian Bevan.

SPECIAL HANDSTAMPS

(1) Philatelic Bureau	3	-	*Royal Mail*
(2) First Day of Issue – Huddersfield	3	-	*Royal Mail*
(3) First Day of Issue – London	3	-	*Royal Mail*
(4) First Day of Issue – Headingley, Leeds	3	125	*RM & NZ Post*
(5) Wigan Rugby League Football Club	10	15	*LFDC 136*
(6) Halifax Rugby League Football Club	10	15	*VP 98*
(7) Salford Rugby League Club	10	15	*Dawn*
(8) Cent. of Rugby League, Bradford (rugby ball)	10	10	*Benham(s)*
(9) Cent. of Rugby League, Huddersfield (oval)	10	15	*BLCS 110*
(10) Centenary Rugby League, Leeds	10	15	*BLCS 110*
(11) Centenary Rugby League, Wigan	10	15	*BLCS 110*
(12) Cent. of Rugby League, Huddersfield (shield)	10	25	*Cam.S.C.*
(13) Association of GB FDC Collectors, Kenton	10	125	*GBFDC GB1*
(14) Radio Times, Rugby League W12	10	15	*Benham*
(15) Centenary Rugby League, Rugby	10	15	*Ben500(110)*
(16) Blick Time Systems Ltd, Swindon	10	25	*Blick*
(17) Keep in Touch with your Collection, Rugby	10	15	*FDP Co*
(18) In a League of its own, Huddersfield	10	15	*FDP Co*
(19) Get a Kick out of Collecting, Playing Place	10	15	*FDP Co*
(20) Leeds Road, shared ground, Huddersfield	10	15	*Dawn*
(21) Rugby League Centenary, Bradford (train)	10	15	*Dawn*
(22) Working with Epilepsy, Macclesfield	10	150	*G.C. Comm*
(23) No 45 Squadron Flying Camels BF 2481 PS	10	15	*RAF FDC 33*

C.D.S. POSTMARKS

(24) Fartown, Huddersfield; Hessle Road, Hull; Irwell Rd, Warrington; Salford City or Wigan - *connected with players featured on the stamps* .... *each*	15		
(25) Rugby	15		
(26) Wembley or Wembley Pk - world cup venue	15		

Also: Bradford (or Wibsey Bankfoot, Bradford); Brighouse; Castleford; Halifax (or Mount Pellon, Halifax); Hunslett; Duriding Lane, St. Helens; Englands Lane; Elland Rd, Leeds; Mount Pleasant, Batley; Rothswell; The Ball; Wakefield; Watersheddings, Oldham; Workington. £10.

SLOGAN POSTMARKS

(27) The Halifax Rugby League Centenary	40		

30th October 1995 - CHRISTMAS

19p; 25p; 30p; 41p; 60p Robins

SPECIAL HANDSTAMPS

(1) Philatelic Bureau	3	-	*Royal Mail*
(2) First Day of Issue – Bethlehem	3	-	*Royal Mail*
(3) First Day of Issue – London	3	-	*Royal Mail*
(4) Post Haste! for Christmas Nat Postal Museum.	10	20	*Friends of NPM*
(5) Christmas Greetings, York	10	15	*LFDC 137*
(6) Christmas, Canterbury	10	15	*VP 99*
(7) Happy Christmas, Royal Mail, EC1	10	-	*Royal Mail*
(8) Happy Christmas, Radio Times, W12	10	15	*Benham*
(9) Happy Christmas, Fir Tree, Crook	10	15	*BLCS 111*
(10) Yuletide Wishes, Snowdown, Dover	10	15	*Ben500(111)*
(11) Merry Christmas, Hollybush, Ayr	10	15	*BLCS 111*
(12) Christmas Greetings, Ivybridge, Devon	10	15	*Ben500(111)*
(13) Seasons Greetings, Berry Hill, Coleford	10	12	*BLCS 111*
(14) Christmas Common, Oxford (cat)	10	15	*BLCS 111*
(15) Christmas Common, Oxfordshire	10	20	*Westminster*
(16) Merry Christms, Christmas Common	10	20	*R J Smith*
(17) Blick Time Systems Ltd, Swindon	10	25	*Blick*
(18) Christmas 1995, Waddington, Lincs	10	20	*Cam.S.C.*
(19) Seasons Greetings, Middlesbrough	10	15	*Dawn*
(20) Seasons Greetings, West Ham United	10	25	*Dawn*
(21) Seasons Greetings, Nottingham Forest	10	15	*Dawn*
(22) Bletchley Park, 50 Years this Christmas	10	15	*Bletchley PO*
(23) Christmas Greetings, St. Nicholas, Norfolk	10	15	*FDP Co*
(24) Loughborough Grammar School	10	20	*Bradbury*
(25) No 28 Squadron Hong Kong BF 2482 PS	10	12	*RAF FDC 34*

C.D.S. POSTMARKS

(26) Girton, Cambridge - HQ of 'Bird Life'	10		
(27) Holy Island or Nasareth ... *each*	15		
(28) Robin's Lane, St. Helens	25		

Also: Canterbury, Fleet Street, Greet, Hollybush, Hollyhedge Road, Hopgrove, Newbottle, Prettygate, Red Lodge, Robin Hood, Wing. Prices from £8.

VALUES ARE FOR GOOD, CLEAN, UNADDRESSED COVERS WITH THE FULL SET OF STAMPS.

Christmas (contd.)	ordinary covers	official covers	
SLOGAN POSTMARKS	£	£	
(29) Happy Christmas Please Post Early	40		

In addition: Thank you for Choosing Royal Mail. Prices from £8.

£2.40, £2.50 & £3.80 CHRISTMAS BOOKS OF STAMPS

With pair or block of 19p, 25p & 60p stamps ......*set*	10		
With complete panes of 19p & 25p stamps ....*pair*	15		

25th January 1996 - ROBERT BURNS

19p To A Mouse; 25p A Red, Red Rose; 41p Scots Wha Hae; 60p Auld Lang Syne

SPECIAL HANDSTAMPS (1) Philatelic Bureau	3	–	*Royal Mail*
(2) First Day of Issue – Dumfries	3	–	*Royal Mail*
(3) First Day of Issue - Glasgow, Scotland & NI	3	–	*Royal Mail*
(4) First Day of Issue – London	8	–	*Royal Mail*
(5) Wee Sleekit Cowrin' etc, Kilmarnock	10	–	*Royal Mail*
(6) O, My Luve's Like a Red, Red Rose, Alloway	10	–	*Royal Mail*
(7) Scots Wha Hae, Dumfries	10	–	*Royal Mail*
(8) Should Auld Acquaintance etc, Ayr	10	–	*Royal Mail*
(9) Spring Stampex (Red Red Rose), N1	10	–	*Royal Mail*
(10) The Burns Federation, Dumfries (mausoleum)	10	12	*LFDC 138*
(11) The Burns Federation, Alloway (portrait)	10	12	*VP 100*
(12) To A Mouse, Mauchline, Ayrshire	10	15	*Bradbury*
(13) O My Luve's Like a Red, Red Rose, Dumfries	10	15	*Bradbury*
(14) Robert the Bruce, Bannockburn	10	15	*Bradbury*
(15) Auld Lang Syne, Ellisland Farm, Dumfries	10	15	*Bradbury*
(16) Robert Burns, 1759-1796 Mauchline (lion)	10	15	*Ben500(112)*
(17) Robert Burns Bicentenary, Alloway (mouse)	10	12	*BLCS 112*
(18) R.Burns, Writers' Museum, Edinburgh (rose)	10	12	*BLCS 112*
(19) Bicentenary of R. Burns, Dumfries (thistle)	10	12	*BLCS 112*
(20) Robert Burns, Radio Times, W12 0TT	10	12	*Benham*
(21) Rotary Club of Alloway, Ayr	10	15	*Rotary*
(22) Robert Burns 1759-1796, Alloway (quill)	10	12	*Gem Covers*
(23) The Immortal Memory, Edinburgh	10	10	*Keith Prowse*
(24) Should auld acquaintance GB FDC Dumfries	10	15	*FDP Co*
(25) XV Squadron Tornado Weapons BF 2498 PS	10	10	*RAF FDC 35*
C.D.S. POSTMARKS			
(26) Alloway - birthplace of Robert Burns	10		
(27) Bannockburn - Scots Wha Hae	10		
(28) Burns Statue, Ayr	15		
(29) Dalswinton, Dunfermline, Kilmarnock or Tarbolton *connected with works featured on stamps*	10		
(30) Dumfries - Burns died here in 1796	10		
(31) Lincluden, Dumfries - Lincluden Abbey	10		
(32) Mauchline - where Burns lived	10		

In addition: Burnside, Burns Road, Kirkoswald, Mousehole, Nicholson Street Edinburgh, Poets Field, Rose, Sanquhar, Tam's Brig. Prices from £8.

SLOGAN POSTMARKS

(33) Celebrate the Legend, Robert Burns	30		

Also: Luton Philatelic; Glasgow RCH; Strathclyde Univ. Prices from £8.

ORDINARY or OFFICIAL COVERS - Do you know the difference?
Find out more by reading the General Notes at the beginning of this catalgoue.

26th February 1996 - GREETINGS

10 x 1st Class stamps featuring cartoons.

SPECIAL HANDSTAMPS (1) Philatelic Bureau	3	–	*Royal Mail*
(2) First Day of Issue – Titterhill	3	–	*Royal Mail*
(3) First Day of Issue – London	8	–	*Royal Mail*
(4) Titterhill, Haytons Bent (laughing pillar box)	12	20	*Bradbury*
(5) Greetings - Letterfearn, Kyle	12	15	*BLCS 113*
(6) Greetings - Letterston, Haverfordwest	12	15	*BLCS 113*
(7) Greetings - Barking, Ipswich	12	15	*BLCS 113*
(8) Greetings - Yapton, Arundel	12	15	*Ben500(113)*
(9) Greetings - Purton, Swindon	12	15	*BenD245*
(10) Greetings - Braintree, Essex	12	15	*BLCS 113*
(11) Greetings - Purley, Reading	12	15	*BLCS 113*
(12) Greetings - Brington, Huntingdon	12	15	*BLCS 113*
(13) Greetings - Bonehill, Tamworth	12	15	*BLCS 113*
(14) Greetings - Nappa, Skipton	12	15	*BLCS 113*
(15) The Cartoon Art Trust, London	12	–	*n.o.c.*
(16) Greetings from Laughterton	12	15	*Gem Covers*
(17) Greetings from the 1996 Catalogue	12	20	*FDP Co*
(18) W H Smith Business Supplies, Andover	12	50	*WHS(Set3cards)*
(19) Royal Mail North East Team Work, Leeds	12	20	*Royal Mail*
C.D.S. POSTMARKS			
(20) Greet or Fleet Street ......*each*	12		

Also: Askham, Clockface, Crazies Hill, Fetcham, Idle, Laughterton, Lazy Hill,Letter, Little Snoring, Lover, Moneymore, Mumbles, New York, Penn, Point Clear, Witnesham, Yell.Prices from £8.

SLOGAN POSTMARKS

(21) Walt Disney World	15		

In addition: Collect Stamps, Luton Philatelic. Prices from £7.

All values include VAT at 17.5%
Values are a guide - please read the General Notes at the beginning of this catalogue.

12th March 1996 - THE WILDFOWL & WETLANDS TRUST

19p Muscovy Duckling; 25p Lapwing; 30p White fronted Goose; 35p Bittern; 41p Swan

	ordinary covers £	official covers £	
SPECIAL HANDSTAMPS (1) Philatelic Bureau	3	–	*Royal Mail*
(2) First Day of Issue - Slimbridge, Gloucester	3	–	*Royal Mail*
(3) First Day of Issue - London	8	–	*Royal Mail*
(4) Wildfowl & Wetlands Trust, Slimbridge (oval)	12	15	*Benham*
(5) Wildfowl & Wetlands Trust, The Mail	12	15	*Benham*
(6) Wildfowl & Wetlands Trust, Slimbridge	12	15	*BLCS 114*
(7) Wildfowl & Wetlands Trust, Washington	12	15	*BLCS 114*
(8) Wildfowl & Wetlands Trust, Arundel	12	15	*BenSG28*
(9) Wildfowl & Wetlands Trust, Caerlaverock	12	15	*Ben500(114)*
(10) Wildfowl & Wetlands Trust, Welney	12	15	*BLCS 114*
(11) Wildfowl & Wetlands Trust, Llanelli (heron)	12	12	*Gem Covers*
(12) Wildfowl & Wetlands Trust, Llanelli (duck)	12	–	*Royal Mail*
(13) Wildfowl & Wetland Birds, Sandy	12	15	*LFDC 139*
(14) Wildfowl & Wetland Birds, Malltraeth	12	15	*VP 101*
(15) Doncaster Rovers and Mallard, Doncaster	12	15	*Dawn*
(16) GB First Day Collectors, Slimbridge	12	45	*GBFDC GB2*
(17) Birds of a Feather, Arundel	12	15	*FDP Co*
(18) 202 Squadron, Search & Rescue BF 2499 PS	12	10	*RAF FDC 36*
(19) Stratford (changeable date pmk depicts swan)	12	–	*Royal Mail*
(20) Post Code Event, Team Work 96 Harrow	12	–	*Royal Mail*
(21) 45th Anniversary of Fairey FDI BF 2502 PS	12	95	*Forces*
C.D.S. POSTMARKS			
(22) Arundel - Wildfowl & Wetlands centre	20		
(23) Slimbridge - Wildfowl & Wetlands Trust HQ	15		
(24) Burscough (*Martin Mere*); Glencaple (*Caerlaverock*); Comber or Lisbane (*Castle Espie*); Llwynhendy or Llanelli; Welney; Washington	15		
(25) Malltraeth - home of Tunnicliffe	15		
(26) Sandy - RSPB headquarters	15		
(27) Tring - British Trust for Ornitholgoy HQ	15		

In addition: Drake, Goose Green, The Pond, Waterside. Prices from £10.

SLOGAN POSTMARKS

Oilbank; Visit the Isle of Skye. Recycle Used Oil. Prices from £10.

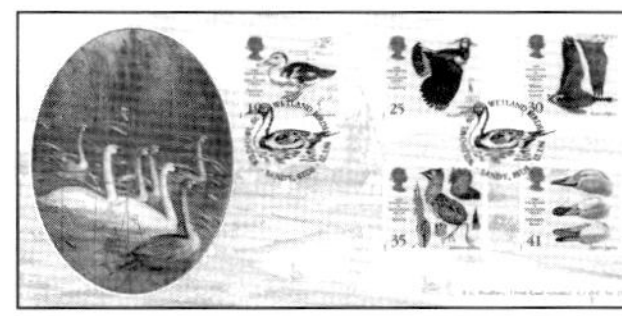

16th April 1996 - 100 YEARS OF THE CINEMA

19p Harrogate Odeon; 25p The Screen Kiss; 30p Cinema Ticket; 35p Pathe News; 41p 'Big Screen Showing', Manchester Odeon.

	ordinary covers £	official covers £	
SPECIAL HANDSTAMPS (1) Philatelic Bureau	3	–	*Royal Mail*
(2) First Day of Issue - London WC2	3	–	*Royal Mail*
(3) First Day of Issue - London (Cinema 100)	8	–	*Royal Mail*
(4) Leicester Square, WC2 (Superman)	10	15	*LFDC 140*
(5) Leicester Square, WC2 (Chaplin)	10	15	*VP 102*
(6) Leicester Square, WC2 (Cinema 100 logo)	10	25	*Cam.S.C.*
(7) The Harrogate Odeon	10	15	*Bradbury*
(8) The Projected Picture Trust, Bletchley	10	15	*Bletchley PO*
(9) Sense and Sensibility, Steventon	10	20	*BenSG30*
(10) Centenary of the Cinema, Pinewood Studios	10	15	*Ben500(115)*
(11) 100 Years of Cinema, Elstree	10	15	*BLCS 115*
(12) 100 Years of Cinema, Shepperton	10	15	*BLCS 115*
(13) 100 Years of Going to Pictures, Ealing	10	15	*BLCS 115*
(14) 100 British Cinema MOMI Museum, SE1	10	15	*BenL46*
(15) Star Road, London W14	10	15	*Benham*
(16) Starboard Way, E14	10	15	*Benham*
(17) Star Place, SE1	10	15	*Benham*
(18) Star, Clydey	10	15	*Benham*
(19) Starcross, Exter	10	15	*Benham*
(20) Shepperton Studios	10	15	*Gem Covers*
(21) Great Scott! 100 Years of Cinema, Windsor	10	15	*Steven Scott*
(22) A Star Performer!, Star	10	15	*FDP Co*
(23) RNLI Cinema Centenary, Star	10	15	*StampSearchers*
(24) Bradford City on Film	10	15	*Dawn*
(25) Warwickshire County Cricket, Edgbaston	10	65	*S.P.*
(26) No 617 Dam Busters Squadron	10	10	*RAF FDC 37*
(27) SG (Stanley Gibbons) Strand WC2	10	10	*Benham*
(28) Post Haste! National Postal Musuem, EC	10	–	*Royal Mail*
(29) 1746 Battle of Culloden 1996, Inverness	10	25	*Bradbury*
(30) 70th Birthday Celebrations, London SW1*	10	25	*Bradbury*
(31) 70th Birthday Celebrations, Windsor*	10	25	*Bradbury*
(32) 70th Birthday Celebrations, Balmoral*	10	25	*Bradbury*
(33) 70th Birthday Celebrations, Bruton St, SW1*	10	–	*Benham*
(34) 70th Birthday, Queen St, W1*	10	–	*Benham*
(35) 70th Birthday, Windsor*	10	–	*Benham*
(36) 70th Birthday, Westminster Abbey, SW1*	10	–	*Benham*

** Sponsored primarily to coincide with the issue of the Royal Mail commemorative label to celebrate the Queen's 70th birthday.*

C.D.S. POSTMARKS		
(37) Bray, Denham Green, Ealing, Elstree, Iver Heath (Pinewood), Shepperton	15	
(38) Barnet - first showing of a moving film	15	
(39) Harrogate; Oxford Street, Oldham or Manchester (featured on 19p, 30p and 41p values)	15	

Going to the Pictures (contd.)	ordinary covers £	official covers £	
(40) Hollywood or The Circle	15		
(41) Perry Bar, Birmingham - first Odeon	15		
(42) Regent St - 1st commercial screening of film	15		
(43) Victoria St. SW1 - 1st Picture House	15		

Also: Attenborough, Borehamwood, Dorking, Hamilton, Leigh, Long Shoot, Lover, South Bank Street, Waterloo Rd. Prices from £8.

SLOGAN POSTMARKS

(44) Walt Disney World, Instant Win	15		

In addition: Blackpool Pleasure Beach; Trafford Park. Prices from £7.

14th May 1996 - FOOTBALL LEGENDS

19p 'Dixie' Dean; 25p Bobby Moore; 35p Duncan Edwards; 41p Billy Wright; 60p Danny Blanchflower.

SPECIAL HANDSTAMPS			
(1) Philatelic Bureau	3	–	*Royal Mail*
(2) First Day of Issue – Wembley	3	–	*Royal Mail*
(3) First Day of Issue – Philatelic Bureau	3	–	*Royal Mail*
(4) First Day of Issue – Manchester	3	–	*Royal Mail*
(5) First Day of Issue – London	12	–	*Royal Mail*
(6) Bobby Moore, West Ham United	12	25	*Dawn*
(7) Billy Wright, Wolves & England	12	20	*Dawn*
(8) Dixie Dean, Everton FC	12	25	*Dawn*
(9) 60th Anniv 1st FA Semi-Final, Grimsby	12	15	*Dawn*
(10) Manchester United FC Museum	12	25	*Dawn*
(11) Hull City 50 Years at Boothferry Park	12	15	*Dawn*
(12) 25 Yrs Official Football Covers - 8 locations	12	35	*Dawn*
(13) A Celebration of Football, Wembley	12	20	*Westminster*
(14) Autographed Editions, Wembley	12	20	*Westminster*
(15) Wembley, Middlesex (trophy)	12	15	*Gem Covers*
(16) Jackie Milburn, St. James' Park, Newcastle	12	15	*FourPennyPost*
(17) Danny Blanchflower, Tottenham N17	12	50	*G.Blanchflower*
(18) 1966 England Winners, Wembley (player)	12	15	*LFDC 141*
(19) Football Legends, Bolton, Lancs	12	15	*VP 103*
(20) Football Legends, Stoke on Trent (player)	12	50	*Bradbury*
(21) Preston North End FC	12	50	*Bradbury*
(22) Wolverhampton Wanderers (player)	12	30	*Bradbury*
(23) Football Heroes Wolverhampton (trophy & ball)	12	30	*Ben500(117)*
(24) Football Heroes, Wolverhampton (ball)	12	10	*Benham(s)*
(25) Football Heroes, The Mail on Sunday, Stoke	12	15	*Benham*
(26) Football Heroes, Stoke on Trent (ball)	12	15	*BLCS 117*
(27) Football Heroes, Manchester (ball & flag)	12	–	*n.o.c.*
(28) Football Heroes, Manchester (ball & net)	12	10	*Benham(s)*
(29) Football Heroes, Everton Liverpool (ball)	12	10	*Benham(s)*
(30) Football Heroes, Wembley (ball & flag)	12	20	*B'hamCoinCvr*
(31) Football Heroes, Tottenham (ball on banner)	12	10	*Benham(s)*
(32) England World Cup Winners, Sunday, E1	12	10	*Benham*
(33) Arsenal, FA Cup Winners, Highbury, N5	12	10	*BLCS 117*
(34) Evening Standard, Wembley	12	12	*RM/EveningStd*
(35) Brewers Fayre, Wembley	12	12	*RM/BrewFayre*
(36) Wembley (lettering in half circle plus ball)	12	10	*RM/MasterCard*
(37) Winning New Readers, Wembley	12	12	*FDP Co*
(38) RNLI Football Legends, Wembley	12	12	*StampSearchers*
(39) Matthew Sea Trials, Bristol	12	35	*R Higgs*
(40) 80th Anniv No 54 Squadron BF 2581 PS	12	12	*RAF FDC 38*

C.D.S. POSTMARKS

(41) County Rd, Liverpool - Everton (Dixie Dean)	15		
(42) Barking Rd, E13 - West Ham (Bobby Moore)	15		
(43) Trafford Pk - Man United (Duncan Edwards)	15		
(44) Staveley Rd. Wolverhampton - (Billy Wright)	15		
(45) Park Lne, Tottenham - (Danny Blanchflower)	20		
(46) Benwell Grove (Newcastle), Elland Road (Leeds) Hillsborough (Sheffield), Priory Road (Liverpool) Radcliffe Rd (Nottingham), Villa Rd (Birmingham) *all venues for Euro '96*	15		
(47) Wembley or Wembley Park	15		

Also: Birkenhead, Bolton, Moore, Preston, Stoke on Trent.The Ball. Prices from £10.

SLOGAN POSTMARKS

(48) Snickers - Proud to Sponsor Euro '96	15		

Also: Racial Equality, Europe Day, BBC Midlands Today, Trafford Park Centenary. Prices from £7

NB Royal Mail also issued a Prestige Book for the 1996 European Football Championships on this date - these books also contained the new stamps in various se-tenant and miniature sheet formats - please refer to definitive section for prices.

PLEASE READ THE GENERAL NOTES

9th July 1996 - OLYMPIC GAMES

5 x 26p: Olympic and Paralympic Teams 1996

SPECIAL HANDSTAMPS			
(1) Philatelic Bureau	3	–	*Royal Mail*
(2) First Day of Issue – Much Wenlock	3	–	*Royal Mail*
(3) First Day of Issue – London	8	–	*Royal Mail*
(4) Meadowbank, Edinburgh	8	10	*Benham*
(5) Pond's Forge, Sheffield	8	10	*Benham*
(6) Gateshead, Tyne & Wear	8	25	*Ben500(118)*
(7) Crystal Palace, London (running)	8	15	*Ben500(118)*
(8) Crystal Palace, London (hurdles)	8	10	*Benham*

Olympic Games (contd.)	ordinary covers £	official covers £	
(9) Alexander Stadium, Perrybarr Birmingham	8	8	*Benham*
(10) 100th Olympic Games, Wembley (torch)	8	17	*B'hamCoinCvr*
(11) Olympic Champion, Badminton	8	10	*BLCS 118*
(12) Henley on Thames	8	10	*BLCS 118*
(13) The Mail on Sunday	8	10	*Benham*
(14) Wembley (laurels)	8	10	*VP 104*
(15) Amateur Athletic Association, Birmingham	8	10	*LFDC 142*
(16) Kodak, Hemel Hempstead	8	10	*Gem Covers*
(17) Crystal Palace Gold Medal Winners, SE19	8	10	*Westminster*
(18) Autographed Editions Crystal Palace, SE19	8	18	*Westminster*
(19) Olympic Centenary 1896-1996 Crystal Palace	8	15	*Keith Prowse*
(20) Olympic Centenary 1896-1996 Wembley	8	160	*Keith Prowse*
(21) Olympic Centenary 1896-1996 Hickstead	8	160	*Keith Prowse*
(22) Olympic Centenary 1896-1996 Henley	8	160	*Keith Prowse*
(23) Olympic Centenary 1896-1996 Bisley	8	160	*Keith Prowse*
(24) Duke of Edinburgh's Award, Bewdley	8	15	*Bredon Cvrs*
(25) Olympics and Paralympics, Runwell Essex	8	15	*Steven Scott 1*
(26) To the Games by Train Barnsley	8	10	*Dawn*
(27) Running rings around competition, Runwell	8	15	*FDP Co*
(28) Royal Tournament BF 1996 PS	8	25	*Forces*
(29) RNLI Speedwell	8	12	*StampSearchers*
(30) XI Squadron Swifter & Keener BF 2525 PS	8	12	*RAF FDC 39*
C.D.S. POSTMARKS			
(31) Croydon – Headquarters of Paralympics	15		
(32) London SE19 – Crystal Palace	15		
(33) Much Wenlock – early olympic style games	15		
(34) Wandsworth – British Olympic Assoc'n	15		
(35) Wembley or Wembley Park – 1948 Olympics	15		

Also: Anerley Rd., Badminton, Beetham, Boston, Birmingham, Chipping, Campden, Cosford Camp, Jump, Klondyke, Melbourne, New York, Paris Ave., Perry Bar, Sheriffhales, Silver End, Stoke Mandeville. Prices from £10.

SLOGAN POSTMARKS *Trafford Park Centenary; New Postage Rates. Prices from £7.*

6th August 1996 - WOMEN OF ACHIEVEMENT

20p Dorothy Hodgkin; 26p Margot Fonteyn; 31p Elisabeth Frink; 37p Daphne du Maurier; 43p Marea Hartman.

	ordinary covers £	official covers £	
SPECIAL HANDSTAMPS (1) Philatelic Bureau	3	–	*Royal Mail*
(2) First Day of Issue – Fowey	3	–	*Royal Mail*
(3) First Day of Issue – London	8	–	*Royal Mail*
(4) Royal Academy of Dancing SW11	8	15	*LFDC 143*
(5) Jane Eyre, Haworth Keighley	8	10	*VP 105*
(6) Marea Hartman, AAA Birmingham	8	25	*LFDC 142 Spec*
(7) Margot Fonteyn (portrait), London EC1	8	15	*Ben500(119)*
(8) Marea Hartman (portrait), Edgbaston B'ham	8	15	*BenhamPilgrim*
(9) Daphne du Maurier (portrait), Par Cornwall	8	12	*BLCS 119*
(10) Dorothy Hodgkin (portrait), Oxford	8	15	*BenhamPilgrim*
(11) Elisabeth Frink (portrait), Thurlow Suffolk	8	15	*BenhamPilgrim*
(12) Ruth Rendell, Colchester	8	10	*BLCS 119*
(13) Votes for Women, Parliament Square SW1	8	10	*BLCS 119*
(14) Parliament Street, London SW1	8	15	*Steven Scott 2*
(15) GBFDC Margot Fonteyn, Covent Garden	8	25	*GBFDC GB3*
(16) Women's Royal Voluntary Service, SW19	8	12	*Bredon Cvrs*
(17) St Thomas' Hospital, London SE1	8	15	*Westminster*
(18) Autographed Editions, House of Lords SW1	8	50	*Westminster*
(19) Autographed Editions, BBC TV, London W12	8	20	*Westminster*
(20) Women's World Bowls, Leamington Spa	8	25	*Bradbury*
(21) Nurse Edith Cavell, Peterborough	8	12	*NVRly*
(22) Lisa Clayton's Voyage Around World, B'ham	8	12	*JRiceStampCo*
(23) We Value Women of Achievement	8	12	*FDP Co*
(24) RNLI, Ladybank, Cupar	8	15	*StampSearchers*
(25) 42 (Torpedo Bomber) Squadron BF 2528 PS	8	12	*RAF FDC 40*
C.D.S. POSTMARKS			
(26) Fowey or Par - Daphne du Maurier	10		
(27) Lady or Lady Margaret Rd	10		
(28) Reigate - birthplace of Margot Fonteyn	10		
(29) Shipston on Stour - Dorothy Hodgkin	10		

Also: Amwell St., Bodmin, Bristol, Cambridge, Canterbury, Coventry, Durham, Haworth, Manchester Airport, Oxford, Pill, Roman Rd., The Galleries, Tiptoe. Prices from £7

SLOGAN POSTMARKS *Various Royal Mail slogans; Voters List. From £7.*

3rd September 1996 - CHILDREN'S TV

20p Muffin the Mule: 26p Sooty; 31p Stingray; 37p The Clangers; 43p Dangermouse.

	ordinary covers £	official covers £	
SPECIAL HANDSTAMPS (1) Philatelic Bureau	3	–	*Royal Mail*
(2) First Day of Issue – Alexandra Palace	3	–	*Royal Mail*
(3) First Day of Issue – London	8	–	*Royal Mail*
(4) Blue Peter, Shepherds Bush W12	10	50	*Royal Mail*
(5) Sooty, Blackpool	10	15	*LFDC 144*
(6) Treasure Island, Edinburgh	10	15	*VP 106*
(7) Just William, Bury Lancs	10	15	*BLCS 120*
(8) The Railway Children, Halstead, Kent	10	15	*BLCS 120*
(9) Bagpuss, The Mail, London W8	10	35	*Benham*

Children's Television (contd.)	ordinary covers £	official covers £	
(10) Children's TV (Mermaid) W1P 7LB	10	25	*BenhamPilgrim*
(11) Children's TV (Mule) Wood Lane W12	10	25	*BenhamPilgrim*
(12) Children's TV (Mouse) Cosgrove Hall	10	25	*BenhamPilgrim*
(13) Children's TV (Sooty) Guiseley, Leeds	10	25	*BenhamPilgrim*
(14) Children's TV (Sooty) Child Okeford	10	25	*BenhamPilgrim*
(15) Children's TV (Clangers) Blean, Kent	10	15	*Ben500(120)*
(16) Children's TV (TV set) London WC2	10	15	*Steven Scott 3*
(17) Big Stars/Small Screen, Autographed, Shipley	10	18	*Westminster*
(18) Paddington Stn (Paddington Bear) W2	10	15	*Westminster*
(19) Booth Catalogue, Corsham Wilts	10	20	*FDP Co*
(20) RNLI, Jubilee	10	20	*StampSearchers*
(21) Robin Hood, Nottingham (changeable date)	12	–	*Royal Mail*
(22) 29 Squadron (Energetic & Keen) BF 2540 PS	4	12	*RAF FDC 41*

C.D.S. POSTMARKS

(23) Alexandra Pk Rd - 1st Children's TV broadcast	12	
(24) Blackpool - where Harry Corbett purchased Sooty	12	
(25) Grange Hill - famous children's TV series	12	
(26) Playing Place	12	
(27) London W12 or Teddington - TV studios	12	

In addition: Baird Ave., Baker St., Blackwater, Blyton, Eccles, Edinburgh, Foxhole, Gotham, Mousehole, Mutley, Paddington, Pandy, Ramsbottom, Recreation Road, School Lane, Slough, Tobermory, Weedswood, Welbourne, Wellington, Wimbledon, Woodtop. Prices from £10.

SLOGAN POSTMARKS *BBC; Kit Kat; Royal Mail; Severn Valley Rly; Wigan 750. From £8.*

1st October 1996 – CLASSIC CARS

20p Austin Healey 100; 26p MG TD; 37p Triumph TR3; 43p Jaguar XK 120; 63p Morgan Plus 4.

SPECIAL HANDSTAMPS (1) Philatelic Bureau	3	–	*Royal Mail*
(2) First Day of Issue – Beaulieu	3	–	*Royal Mail*
(3) First Day of Issue – London (vintage car)	3	–	*Royal Mail*
(4) First Day of Issue – London (steering wheel)	8	8	*RM/Times*
(5) Cent Emancipation Rally (map) – London	8	–	*Royal Mail*
(6) Cent Emancipation Rally (map) – Brighton	8	–	*Royal Mail*
(7) British Motoring GB London	8	12	*Royal Mint*
(8) National Postal Museum	10	–	*Royal Mail*
(9) Heritage Motor Centre, Gaydon	10	15	*LFDC 145*
(10) London to Brighton Car Rally, Brighton	10	15	*VP 107*
(11) London to Brighton Car Rally, London	10	15	*VP 107*
(12) MG Owners' Club, Swavesey	10	20	*Bradbury*
(13) National Motor Museum, Beaulieu	10	15	*BLCS 121*
(14) Nigel Mansell, Silverstone	10	15	*BLCS 121*
(15) Genevieve, Hyde Park, London W2	10	20	*B'hamCoinCvr*
(16) Genevieve, Brighton	10	20	*B'hamCoinCvr*
(17) John Surtees, Goodwood, Sussex	10	15	*BenSG31*
(18) RAC, Pall Mall	10	15	*Benham*
(19) A Tribute from Toyota, Redhill Surrey	10	15	*Benham*
(20) A Tribute from Aston Martin, Newport Pagnell	10	15	*Benham*
(21) A Tribute from Landrover, Solihull	10	15	*Benham*
(22) A Tribute from Lotus, Norwich	10	15	*Benham*
(23) A Tribute from Vauxhall, Luton	10	15	*Benham*
(24) A Tribute from Daimler, Coventry	10	15	*Benham*
(25) A Tribute from Rover Group, Birmingham	10	15	*Benham*
(26) A Tribute from Morgan, Malvern	10	20	*Ben500(121)*
(27) A Tribute from Jaguar, Coventry	10	15	*Benham*
(28) A Tribute from Ford Motor Co, Dagenham	10	15	*Benham*
(29) Practical Classics, Peterborough	10	15	*Benham*
(30) Autographed - Motor Sport Legends, Aintree	10	20	*Westminster*
(31) Autographed - Classic Cars, Carr, Rotherham	10	20	*Westminster*
(32) Classic British Cars, Beaulieu	10	20	*West Set of 5*
(33) 100th Anniv London-Brighton Rally Hyde Park	10	15	*Westminster*
(34) MG Car Club, Abingdon	10	15	*FourPennyPost*
(35) Aston Martin, Newport Pagnell	10	30	*Bletchley PO*
(36) 60th Anniv Morgan Four Wheeler, Malvern	10	25	*GBFDC GB4*
(37) Great Scott - It's A Classic Hyde Park W2	10	15	*Steven Scott 4*
(38) Silverstone, Northants	10	15	*G Lovell*
(39) British International Motor Show, NEC	10	20	*Arl'ton/T'graph*
(40) National Exhibition Centre (changeable date)	10	–	*Royal Mail*
(41) Driving Force, Booth Catalogue, Redcar	10	15	*FDP Co*
(42) RNLI Cargo, Carlisle	10	15	*StampSearchers*
(43) Trafford Park Centenary, Manchester	10	15	*Dawn*
(44) Derby County Locomotive, Derby	10	15	*Dawn*
(45) In Celebration of Lux, Malmesbury	10	95	*D Pratten*
(46) 80th Anniv. No. Squadron BF 2541 PS 41	10	12	*RAF FDC 42*
(47) The Queen's Stamps, Mauritius, NPM	10	–	*Royal Mail*

C.D.S. POSTMARKS

(48) Abingdon - where MG TD was built	10
(49) Allesley - where Jaguar XK 120 was built	10
(50) Beaulieu - National Motor Museum	10
(51) Canley - home of Standard Triumph (TR3)	10
(52) London & Brighton - car rally *pair*	20
(53) Longbridge - where Austin Healey 100 was built	10

Classic Cars (contd.)

	ordinary covers £	official covers £	
(54) Malvern Link - Morgan Plus Four was built	10		
(55) NEC - Motor Show or Silverstone	20		
(56) Royal Automobile Club, SW1	50		

Also: Austin, Bentley, Cowley Centre, Dunlop, The Fender, Ford, Healey, Humber Rd,Leyland, Morganstown, Morris Green, Swavesey, Tickford St, Newport Pagnell, Trafford Park. Prices from £10.

SLOGAN POSTMARKS

(57) Trafford Park 15

Also: Better Music Mix. PO Charter, Coventry. Prices from £7.

28th October 1996 - CHRISTMAS

2nd The Three Kings; 1st The Annunciation; 37p Journey to Nazareth; 43p The Nativity; 63p The Shepherds.

SPECIAL HANDSTAMPS (1) Philatelic Bureau	3	-	*Royal Mail*
(2) First Day of Issue - Bethlehem	3	-	*Royal Mail*
(3) First Day of Issue - London	8	-	*Royal Mail*
(4) Happy Christmas, Royal Mail, London EC1	8	-	*Royal Mail*
(5) Westminster Abbey, SW1	8	15	*BLCS 122*
(6) 900th Anniversary Norwich Cathedral	8	15	*BLCS 122*
(7) Season's Greetings, Jerusalem, Lincoln	8	15	*Ben500(122)*
(8) Tidings of Great Joy, Nasareth	8	15	*BLCS 122*
(9) Unto us a King is born, Bethlehem	8	15	*Benham*
(10) Jesus College Cambridge	8	25	*LFDC 146*
(11) The Christmas Story, Bethlehem	8	15	*VP 108*
(12) Christmas Stamps, Bethlehem	8	20	*CoverCraft*
(13) Seasons Greetings, Angel Islington	8	15	*Steven Scott 5*
(14) Autographed, Cathedral, Canterbury	8	35	*Westminster*
(15) Christmas 1996 Bethlehem (star)	8	15	*Westminster*
(16) Booth Catalogue, St. Nicholas	8	15	*FDP Co.*
(17) RNLI Christmas Common, Watlington	8	15	*StampSearchers*
(18) No.18 Squadron Courage & Faith	8	15	*RAF FDC 43*
(19) Heathrow Airport, 50th Anniversary	8	30	*Cam.S.C.*
(20) Christmas 1996, Woodhall Spa, Lincs	8	30	*Cam.S.C.*
(21) The Queen's Stamps, Mauritius, NPM	8	25	*FriendsNPM*

C.D.S. POSTMARKS

(22) Holy Island or Nasareth, Caernarfon ..... *each* 15

Also: Angel Hill, Apple Cross, Cambridge, Capel St. Mary, Holytown, Lord Lane, Mary Pk, Noel Rd, Oaktree, Orangefield, Orange Tree, St. Nicholas, Shepherd's Bush, Shepherdswell, Threekingham. £7.

SLOGAN POSTMARKS *Breast Cancer, Childline, Youth Service Week; Heart Check Week; Shopping by Post; The Beautiful South, Various Royal Mail slogans. Prices from £7.*

£2.60 & £4 CHRISTMAS BOOKLETS

With pair or block of 4 20p & 26p stamps ..... *pair* 10

With complete panes of 20p & 26p stamps ..... *pair* 25

SLOGAN POSTMARKS

With effect from November 1996 Royal Mail withdrew the re-posting facility for slogan postmarks. It is now therefore very difficult to obtain first day covers with all the stamps cancelled as described in the General Notes. Covers are known to exist, but not in sufficient quantity to warrant listing.

6th January 1997 - GREETINGS

10 x 1st Class stamps featuring flowers.

SPECIAL HANDSTAMPS (1) Philatelic Bureau	3	-	*Royal Mail*
(2) First Day of Issue - Kew (Butterfly)	3	-	*Royal Mail*
(3) First Day of Issue - London	10	-	*Royal Mail*
(4) Greetings Stamps, Kew Gardens (rose)	12	15	*Bradbury*
(5) Greetings Flying Flowers, Staines	12	15	*BLCS 123*
(6) Blooms of Bressingham, Norfolk	12	15	*BLCS 123*
(7) Blooms of Bressingham, Dorney Windsor	12	15	*BenD290*
(8) Blooms of Bressingham, Elton Peterborough	12	15	*BLCS 123*
(9) Wisley Gardens, Surrey	12	20	*BenhamPilgrim*
(10) Greetings Gardening Direct, Chelmsford	12	15	*BLCS 123*
(11) Royal Botanic Gardens, Edinburgh	12	15	*Ben500(123)*
(12) Greetings Flower Girl, Romford	12	25	*T Hurlstone*
(13) Red, Red Rose - Robert Burns Alloway	12	-	*n.o.c.*
(14) Autographed - Flowers, Kew Gardens	12	27	*Westminster:*
(15) Autographed - RHS Gardens, Wisley	12		*pair of covers*
(16) Floral Greetings, Kew Gardens (rose)	12	20	*Westminster:*
(17) Floral Greetings, Kew Gardens (daffodil)	12		*pair of covers*
(18) Floral Greetings, Kew Gardens (fuchsia)	12	20	*Westminster*

C.D.S. POSTMARKS

(19) Botanic Gardens Belfast or Kew Gardens	20		
(20) Bloomfield or Flore or Flowery Field	15		
(21) Royal Hospital, Chelsea or Greet	15		

Also: Garden Village, Moffat, Pleasure Gardens, Spalding Prices from £10.

This catalogue is NOT the price list of the author or publisher.
Values should be treated as a guide.
PLEASE READ THE GENRAL NOTES AT THE BEGINNING OF THIS CATALOGUE.

21st January 1997 - THE GREAT TUDOR

7 x 26p featuring portraits of Henry and his six wives.

SPECIAL HANDSTAMPS (1) Philatelic Bureau	3	-	*Royal Mail*
(2) First Day of Issue - Hampton Court	3	-	*Royal Mail*
(3) First Day of Issue - London	10	-	*Royal Mail*
(4) Henry VIII & Six Wives, Peterboro' Cathedral	12	25	*BenhamPilgrim*

Henry VIII (contd.)

		ordinary covers £	sponsored covers £	
(5)	Henry VIII & Six Wives, Sudeley Castle	12	20	*BenhamPilgrim*
(6)	Henry VIII & Six Wives, Windsor	12	35	*Ben500(124)*
(7)	Henry VIII & Six Wives, Tower of London	12	20	*BenSG32*
(8)	Henry VIII & Six Wives, Hampton Ct Palace	12	15	*BLCS 124*
(9)	Henry VIII & Six Wives, Hever Castle	12	15	*BLCS 124*
(10)	Henry VIII & Six Wives, Dover Castle	12	20	*BenhamPilgrim*
(11)	Great Tudor (silhouette of Henry & wives)	12	60	*Westminster*
(12)	Hampton Court (silhouette Henry full length)	12	15	*Westminster*
(13)	450th Anniv of Death (silhouette of Hampton Ct)	12	7	*Westminster(s)*
(14)	Hampton Ct (silhouette Henry head/shoulders)	12	15	*Westminster:*
(15)	6 Wives of Henry Tudor (silhouette six wives)	12	25	*Set of 7 covers*
(16)	Birthplace of Henry VIII Greenwich	12	15	*LFDC 147*
(17)	Henry VIII Hampton Wick	12	15	*VP 109*
(18)	Autographed - Hampton Court Palace	12	30	*Westminster:*
(19)	Autographed - Tower of London EC3	12	–	*pair of covers*
(20)	The Mary Rose Portsmouth	12	6	*Westminster(s)*
(21)	Henry VIII & Wives (Hampton Ct Palace)	12	15	*Cover Collection*
(22)	Henry VIII & Wives (Crown & Rose) The Mail	12	15	*Benham*
(23)	Henry VIII & Wives (Tudor Rose) Hampton Ct	12	20	*Steven Scott 6*
(24)	Henry VIII & Wives Kimbolton, Huntingdon	12	25	*Cam.S.C.*
(25)	Henry VIII School Coventry	12	30	*H.VIII School*
(26)	The Great Tudor, Tower Hill (rectangular)	12	25	*GBFDC GB5*
(27)	Greetings Flower Girl, Romford	12	20	*T Hurlstone*
(28)	Tower Hill, London EC3	15	–	*Royal Mail*
(29)	Portsmouth Philatelic Counter (Mary Rose)	15	–	*Royal Mail*
(30)	GWR Loco King Henry VIII Leamington Spa	12	20	*Dawn*
(31)	The Booth Catalogue, Henryd Gwynedd	12	15	*FDP Co*
(32)	RNLI Official Postmark, Six Bells	12	15	*StampSearchers*
(33)	No.7 Squadron, Farnborough	12	12	*RAF FDC 44*
C.D.S. POSTMARKS				
(34)	Dunstable, Kimbolton, or Peterborough - connections with Catherine of Aragon	15		
(35)	Greenwich - birthplace of Henry VIII	15		
(36)	Hampton, Hampton Wick or East Molesey	15		
(37)	Seething Lane - near to Tower of London	15		
(38)	Windsor - burial place of Henry VIII	15		

Also: Bolton Abbey, Broadway, Calais, Chelsea, Henry St., Howard Place, King's Est., King's Head, Maidenhead, Marlborough, Queen's Parade, Royal Parade, Seymour Hill, St. Georges, Tower Hill, Tudor Drive, Winchcombe. From £10.

11th March 1997 – MISSIONS OF FAITH

26p & 37p Saint Columba; 43p & 63p Saint Augustine.

SPECIAL HANDSTAMPS (1)	Philatelic Bureau	3	–	*Royal Mail*
(2)	First Day of Issue – Isle of Iona	4	–	*Royal Mail*
(3)	First Day of Issue – London	10	–	*Royal Mail*
(4)	First Day of Issue – Durham	10	–	*Royal Mail*
(5)	First Day of Issue – St. Albans	10	–	*Royal Mail*
(6)	St. Columba 521-597, Iona	10	–	*n.s.c.*
(7)	Missions of Faith, Canterbury	10	15	*VP 110*
(8)	Missions of Faith, Isle of Iona	10	15	*LFDC 148*
(9)	Uckfield Philatelic Soc, Missions of Faith	10	20	*Uckfield PS*
(10)	Autographed Editions, Isle of Iona	10	20	*Westminster*
(11)	Missions of Faith, Canterbury Cathedral	10	20	*Westminster*
(12)	World's Oldest Wooden Church, Ongar	10	20	*T. Hurlstone*
(13)	St. Andrew's Church, Hornchurch, Essex	10	20	*T. Hurlstone*
(14)	St. Augustine's Church, Queensgate, SW7	10	15	*Steven Scott 7*
(15)	St. Columba, Iona Abbey, Isle of Iona	10	15	*BLCS 125*
(16)	597-1997 Canterbury	10	15	*BLCS 125*
(17)	Lindisfarne, Holy Island	10	15	*Ben500(125)*
(18)	St.Augustine/English Heritage Canterbury	10	15	*BLCS 125*
(19)	Downside, Bath	10	35	*St.Gregory's*
(20)	Any Royal Mail cathedral permanent h/s	10	–	*Royal Mail*
(21)	RNLI Missions of Faith, St. Columb, Cornwall	10	15	*StampSearchers*
(22)	St. Columba, Res Class 47, Newcastle	10	20	*Dawn*
(23)	No.14 Squadron, RAF's Crusades, Shoreham	10	12	*RAF FDC 45*
C.D.S. POSTMARKS				
(24)	All Saints or Holy Island	10		
(25)	Canterbury - St. Augustine first Archbishop	10		
(26)	Dunkeld - Home of St. Columba's relics	10		
(27)	Isle of Iona - St. Columba's monastery	10		
(28)	St. Augustine or St. Columb	10		

Also: Bede, Cliffs End, Coleraine, Edinburgh, Glasgow, Inverness, Jarrow, Londonderry, Morvern, Pagan Hill, The Priory, Rannoch, St. Cross, Saintfield, St. Peter's St (St. Albans), Urquhart,Whitby. £7.

21st April 1997 – GOLDEN WEDDING

1st Class & 26p Golden Definitives

SPECIAL HANDSTAMPS (1)	Philatelic Bureau	3	–	*Royal Mail*
(2)	First Day of Issue – Windsor	3	–	*Royal Mail*
(3)	First Day of Issue – London	10	–	*Royal Mail*
(4)	Westminster Abbey London SW1	10	15	*Westminster*
(5)	Autographed Editions Westminster Abbey	10	20	*Westminster*
(6)	50th Anniv Golden Wedding West. Abbey	10	12	*BLCS 128*

Golden Wedding (contd.)	ordinary covers £	sponsored covers £	
(7) Queen Street, London W1	10	15	*Ben500(128)*
(8) Golden Wedding Anniv Year Windsor	10	15	*BenSG33*
(9) 50th Anniv Golden Wedding Windsor	10	15	*BLCS 128*
(10) The Mail on Sunday	10	15	*Benham*
(11) Golden Wedding Year Westminster Abbey	10	10	*Bradbury*
(12) Golden Wedding Sandringham Norfolk	10	-	*Royal Mail*
(13) Westminster Abbey London SW1	10	10	*Steven Scott 8*
(14) Golden & Glorious National Postal Museum	10	-	*NPM*
(15) Prototype Letterboxes Nat Postal Museum	10	-	*NPM*
(16) Kendal & Windermere Railway, Kendal	10	15	*Benham*
(17) Royal Mail London SW (permanent h/s)	10	-	*Royal Mail*
(18) Royal Mail Windsor (permanent handstamp)	10	-	*Royal Mail*
C.D.S. POSTMARKS			
(19) Buckingham Palace, London SW1	150		
(20) House of Commons or Lords	15		
(21) Queen Elizabeth Avenue	15		
(22) Windsor Castle, Windsor Berks	100		
(23) Windsor, Berks	15		

In addition: Edinburgh. Prices from £6.

13th May 1997 - TALES OF HORROR

26p Dracula; 31p Frankenstein; 37p Dr Jekyll & Mr. Hyde; 43p The Hound of the Baskervilles.

SPECIAL HANDSTAMPS (1) Philatelic Bureau	3	-	*Royal Mail*
(2) First Day of Issue - Whitby	3	-	*Royal Mail*
(3) First Day of Issue - London	10	-	*Royal Mail*
(4) Bram Stoker Society Whitby North Yorks	10	15	*LFDC 149*
(5) The Whitby Dracula Xociety	10	15	*VP 111*
(6) Carfax Estate, Purfleet Essex	10	20	*Bradbury*
(7) Hound of the Baskervilles Princetown	10	15	*Bradbury*
(8) Batman Close London W12	10	15	*GBFDC GB6*
(9) Mary Shelley Frankenstein London SW17	10	15	*Ben500(126)*
(10) The Sherlock Holmes Museum London NW1	10	15	*BLCS 126*
(11) Centenary of Dracula Bradford	10	15	*BLCS 126*
(12) Dr Jeykll & Mr Hyde Edinburgh	10	20	*BenhamPilgrim*
(13) Tales of Terror Whitby	10	15	*Westminster*
(14) Autographed Editions Mary Shelley	10	25	*Westminster*
(15) Havering's Witch Queen Romford	10	35	*T Hurlstone*
(16) Tales of Horror, Elstree	10	50	*Cam.S.C.*
(17) Hound of the Baskervilles, Dartmoor	10	50	*Cam.S.C.*
(18) Swains Lane Highgate N6	10	15	*CoverCollection*
(19) Birmingham Ghost Trails	10	75	*GhostTrail*
(20) Sherlock Holmes Society of London	10	15	*Steven Scott*
(21) Hound of the Baskervilles Baker Street	10	12	*Steven Scott 9*
(22) Visit of Endeavour Replica Whitby	10	25	*B.Downham*
(23) RNLI Tales of Horror, Horrabridge, Devon	10	12	*StampSearchers*
(24) Sunderland Champions FA Carling	10	40	*Dawn*
(25) No.13 Squadron, We Assist by Watching	10	12	*RAF FDC 46*
C.D.S. POSTMARKS			
(26) Hindhead - Conan Doyle wrote H of the B	10		
(27) Marlow - where Shelley wrote Frankenstein	10		
(28) Princetown - Hound of the Baskervilles	10		
(29) Purfleet or Whitby - Dracula settings	10		
(30) Westbourne - Stevenson wrote Dr J & Mr H	10		

Also: Beast Banks, Bitteswell, Bournemouth,Cemetery, Cruden Bay, Devil's Bdge, Edinburgh, Elstree, Golders Green, Hammerwich, Headless Cross, Horrabridge, Houndsditch, Hyde, Shelley, Stoneyhurst, Whitstable, Widecombe, Wolf's Castle. Prices from £7.

10th June 1997 - ARCHITECTS OF THE AIR

20p R J Mitchell (Spitfire); 26p R Chadwick (Lancaster); 37p R E Bishop (Mosquito); 43p G Carter (Meteor); 63p S Camm (Hunter)

SPECIAL HANDSTAMPS (1) Philatelic Bureau	3	-	*Royal Mail*
(2) First Day of Issue - Duxford Cambridge	3	-	*Royal Mail*
(3) First Day of Issue - London	10	-	*Royal Mail*
(4) British Aerospace Farnborough	10	15	*BAe/Royal Mail*
(5) Supermarine Spitfire R J Mitchell Duxford	12	20	*BenhamPilgrim*
(6) Avro Lancaster Roy Chadwick Waddington	12	15	*BLCS 129*
(7) DeHaviland Mosquito R E Bishop Marham	12	15	*BLCS 129*
(8) Gloster Meteor W G Carter Manston	12	20	*BenhamPilgrim*
(9) Hawker Hunter Sir Sidney Camm Leuchars	12	15	*Ben500(129)*
(10) Supermarine Spitfire Southampton Int Airport	12	15	*BenSG34*
(11) Shuttleworth Collection Biggleswade	12	15	*BLCS 129*
(12) Supermarine Spitfire The Mail on Sunday	12	15	*Benham*
(13) Royal Naval Air Station Culdrose	12	15	*BenL47*
(14) Architects of the Air Scampton Lincs	12	20	*Westminster(set 5)*
(15) Architects of the Air Autographed Editions	12	25	*Westminster*
(16) Home of the 617 Squadron Lossiemouth	12	15	*LFDC 150*
(17) The Dambusters 617 Squadron Scampton	12	25	*LFDC 150*
(18) Tribute to Aircraft Designers Farnborough	12	15	*VP 112*
(19) Bletchley Park	12	15	*Bletchley PO*
(20) Lancaster Lancashire	12	35	*RAF (P&P1)*
(21) Architects of the Air Biggin Hill	12	15	*Steven Scott 10*

Architects of the Air (contd.)	ordinary covers £	sponsored covers £	
(22) Battle of Britain Flight RAF Coningsby	12	15	*Steven Scott*
(23) Spitfire Way, Hounslow	12	15	*GBFDC GB7*
(24) National Postal Museum City of London	12	–	*n.s.c*
(25) Roy Chadwick Designer Scampton	12	25	*Cam.S.C.*
(26) RJMitchell & Spitfire Duxford Cambridge	12	25	*Cam.S.C.*
(27) Architects of the Air Heathrow Airport	12	25	*Cam.S.C.*
(28) RAF Hornchurch Remembering the Few	12	25	*T Hurlstone*
(29) Duxford Aviation Society Cambs	12	25	*T Hurlstone*
(30) Eurofighter 2000 GEC Marconi Stanmore	12	45	*GEC-Marconi*
(31) City of Lancaster LMS loco6243 Lancaster	12	25	*Dawn*
(32) Nene Valley Rly Return to Steam	12	20	*NVRly*
(33) Heathrow Airport London, Houslow	12	–	*n.s.c*
(34) Royal Mail Gatwick	12	–	*n.s.c.*
(35) Booth Catalogue, Lancaster	12	15	*FDP Co*
(36) RNLI Lancaster	12	20	*StampSearchers*
(37) No.19 Squadron Castle Bromwich	12	15	*RAF FDC 47*
C.D.S. POSTMARKS			
(38) Cranwell - First flight of Meteor	12		
(39) Duxford - RAF Spitfire base	12		
(40) Eastleigh & Woolston - Spitfires built here	12		
(41) Edgware & Hatfield - Mosquitos built here	12		
(42) Farnborough - British Aerospace & Air Show	12		
(43) Hucclecote - Meteors built here	12		
(44) Kingston - Hawker Hunters built here	12		
(45) Lancaster	12		
(46) Leuchars - associated with Hawker Hunters	12		
(47) Lossiemouth & Scampton - Dambusters	12		
(48) Manston - associated with Meteor	12		
(49) Marham RAF Stn - associated with Mosquito	12		
(50) Newton Heath - Lancasters built here	12		

In addition: Biggin Hill, Bletchley, Butt Lane, Churchill, Coningsby, Cranfield, Hawkinge, Herne Bay, North Berwick, Southampton, Victory St., Woodhall Spa. Prices from £10.

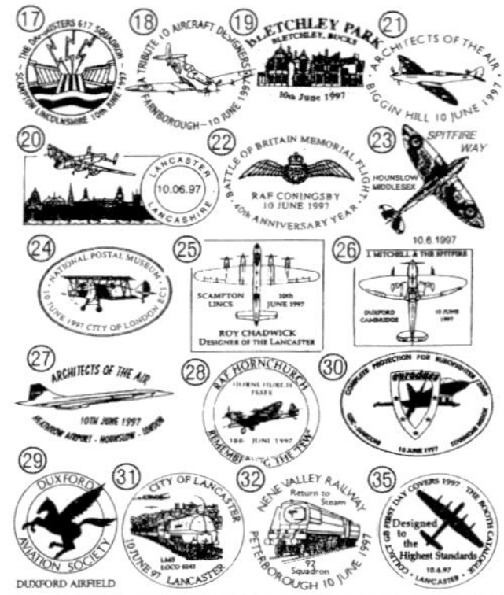

8th July 1997 – ALL THE QUEEN'S HORSES

20p Royal Mews (St Patrick); 26p Lifeguards (Thompson); 43p Blues & Royals (Janus); 63p Royal Mews (River Star).

SPECIAL HANDSTAMPS (1) Philatelic Bureau	3	–	*Royal Mail*
(2) First Day of Issue – Windsor	3	–	*Royal Mail*
(3) First Day of Issue – London	10	–	*Royal Mail*
(4) British Horse Society Stoneleigh	10	15	*LFDC 151*
(5) British Horse Society Windsor Great Park	10	15	*VP 113*
(6) Household Cavalry London	10	20	*Bradbury*
(7) Horse Guards Avenue SW1 (Banner at base)	10	15	*Ben500(130)*
(8) Horse Guards Avenue SW1 (circle)	10	15	*Westminster*
(9) Hyde Park Gardens W2	10	15	*BLCS 130*
(10) Golden Wedding Horse Guards Ave	10	15	*BenSG35*
(11) Pony Club Kenilworth	10	15	*BenL50*
(12) Badminton Gloucester (showjumper)	10	15	*BLCS 130*
(13) Windsor Great Park (jockey on horseback)	10	15	*BLCS 130*
(14) The Guards Toy Soldier Centre	10	15	*Steven Scott 11*
(15) King's Troop Royal Horse Artillery Whitehall	10	15	*FourPennyPost*
(16) The Coronation Coach Westminster Abbey	10	15	*T Hurlstone*
(17) Autographed Editions Badminton	10	20	*Westminster*
(18) RNLI Horsehay Telford	10	15	*StampSearchers*
(19) No.203 Squadron Newquay Cornwall	10	12	*RAF FDC 48*
(20) Vasco da Gama Sea Route to India, London	10	–	*n.s.c*
C.D.S. POSTMARKS			
(21) Broadway - Wellington Barracks	12		
(22) Lancelot Pl. - Knightsbridge Barracks	12		
(23) Victoria St. - Royal Mews	12		
(24) Windsor - where Queen's horses are trained	12		

Also: Badminton, Black Horse, Constantine, Duke Street, Guardhouse, Horsebridge, Horsehay, Horsefair, Horseman's Green, Kenilworth, King's Lynn, Queen's Dr., Queen's Parade, Stud Farm, Thompson, Whitehorse Hill. From £10

12th August 1997 – POST OFFICES

20p Haroldswick; 26p Painswick; 43p Beddgelert; 63p Ballyroney.

SPECIAL HANDSTAMPS (1) Philatelic Bureau	3	–	*Royal Mail*
(2) First Day of Issue – Wakefield	3	–	*Royal Mail*
(3) First Day of Issue – London	10	–	*Royal Mail*
(4) National Fed of SubPostmasters Wakefield	10	20	*LFDC 152*
(5) National Fed of SubPostmasters Shoreham	10	15	*VP 114*
(6) National Postal Museum Sub Post Offices	10	–	*n.s.c*
(7) Britain's Post Office Heritage the NPM,	10	15	*Westminster*
(8) Autographed Editions Painswick Glos	10	25	*Westminster*
(9) The Old Post Office Castle Combe	10	15	*BLCS 131*
(10) Blisland Post Office Bodmin	10	15	*BLCS 131*
(11) The Old Post Office Tintagel Cornwall	10	15	*Ben500(131)*
(12) Sanquhar Post Office Dumfriesshire	10	12	*BLCS 131*
(13) Earliest known posting of the 1d Black Bath	10	15	*Steven Scott 12*
(14) Hedge End Southampton	10	20	*HedgeEnd PO*
(15) Haroldswick Post Office	10	–	*n.o.c.*
(16) Painswick Post Office	10	–	*n.o.c.*

Post Offices (contd.)

	ordinary covers £	sponsored covers £	
(17) Beddgelert Gwynedd	10	15	*GBFDC GB8*
(18) The Oldest Working Post Office Sanquhar	10	15	*FourPennyPost*
(19) Haroldswick Post Office - permanent h/s	10	–	*n.s.c*
(20) TPO Restoration Scheme Peterborough	10	15	*NVRly*
(21) Bicentenary of the Copper Penny Liverpool	10	20	*B'hamCoinCvr*
(22) Operation Pedestal Malta Gourock	10	15	*RN CvrsGp 1-10*
(23) 750 Years Romford Market	10	15	*T Hurlstone*
(24) No.20 Squadron Netheravon Salisbury	10	12	*RAF FDC 49*
(25) Post Office at Bletchley Park	10	15	*Bletchley PO*
(26) RNLI Sub Post Office Letters Ross-shire	10	15	*StampSearchers*
C.D.S. POSTMARKS			
(27) Ballyroney, Beddgelert, Haroldswick or Painswick Post Offices featured on the stamps	12		
(28) Sanquhar - Oldest working Post Office	10		
(29) Shoreham by Sea - Federation's HQ	12		
(30) Wakefield or Kirkgate - Fed founded here	15		

Also: Belstone, Carlisle (Mobile PO), Glenelg, Hargrave, Hilborough, Lanelli Hill, The Lizard, Maidford, RAC, Rowelton,Witcham, Spooner Row, Starcoast World, Thurcaston, Trafford Park, TPOs. Prices from £7.

9th September 1997 – ENID BLYTON'S FAMOUS FIVE

20p Noddy; 26p Famous Five; 37p Secret Seven; 43p Faraway Tree; 63p Malory Towers.

SPECIAL HANDSTAMPS (1) Philatelic Bureau	3	–	*Royal Mail*
(2) First Day of Issue – Beaconsfield	3	–	*Royal Mail*
(3) First Day of Issue – London	10	–	*Royal Mail*
(4) First Day of Issue – Birmingham	10	–	*Royal Mail*
(5) Children's Stories for Sunny Days, Blyton	12	15	*LFDC 153*
(6) World's Favourite Aunt, Blyton	12	15	*VP 115*
(7) Centenary of Birth of Enid Blyton, Blyton	12	15	*Westminster*
(8) Autographed Editions Blyton	12	20	*Westminster*
(9) Enid Blyton Beaconsfield (teddy & doll)	12	20	*Cam.S.C.*
(10) Enid Blyton Corfe Castle	12	15	*BLCS 132*
(11) Enid Blyton London W1 (Noddy)	12	15	*BLCS 132*
(12) Enid Blyton Beaconsfield (open book)	12	15	*BLCS 132*
(13) Enid Blyton Bickley, Bromley (Noddy)	12	15	*Ben500(132)*
(14) Enid Blyton Surbiton, Surrey	12	15	*BenhamPilgrim*
(15) Enid Blyton East Dulwich (pile of books)	12	15	*BLCS 132*
(16) Enid Blyton The Mail on Sunday	12	15	*Benham*
(17) Variety Club London W1	12	15	*Benham*
(18) Childhood Adventures, Childs Way NW11	12	15	*Steven Scott 13*
(19) Swan Libraries, Booksellers, Upminster	12	20	*T Hurlstone*
(20) Southampton, Hampshire	12	15	*RAF (P&P2)*
(21) RNLI Enid Blyton, Blyton Gainsborough	12	15	*StampSearchers*
(22) Operation Avalanche, Eastney, Southsea	12	15	*RN CvrsGp 1-11*
(23) No.5 Squadron Famous Five Farnborough	12	12	*RAF FDC 50*
C.D.S. POSTMARKS			
(24) Beaconsfield – home of Enid Blyton	12		
(25) Blyton, Gainsborough or Playing Place	15		
(26) East Dulwich – birthplace of Enid Blyton	12		

Also: Beckenham, Bourne End, Child's Hill, Corfe Castle, Fiveways. From £10

27th October 1997 – CHRISTMAS

2nd, 1st, 31p, 43p, 63p - Tom Smith's Christmas Crackers 1847-1997

SPECIAL HANDSTAMPS (1) Philatelic Bureau	3	–	*Royal Mail*
(2) First Day of Issue – Bethlehem	3	–	*Royal Mail*
(3) First Day of Issue – London	10	–	*Royal Mail*
(4) First Day of Issue – Birmingham	10	–	*Royal Mail*
(5) Happy Christmas Royal Mail London EC1	10	–	*Royal Mail*
(6) Drury Lane WC2 (bells and holly)	10	15	*BLCS 135*
(7) Norwich (crackers)	10	15	*BLCS 135*
(8) Regent Street (boxed presents)	10	15	*BLCS 135*
(9) Trafalgar Square (Christmas tree)	10	15	*BLCS 135*
(10) Bethlehem (candle)	10	15	*Ben500(135)*
(11) Christmas Crackers Bethlehem	10	15	*LFDC 155*
(12) Christmas Crackers 150 Years Nasareth	10	15	*VP 117*
(13) Charles Dickens Rochester	10	15	*Bradbury*
(14) Christmas Crackers, Bangor	10	12	*Blechley PO*
(15) Happy Christmas, Rainham Royals	10	20	*T Hurlstone*
(16) Christmas Crackers, West Langdon, Dover	10	15	*SouthernCvr.1*
(17) Great Scott, Crackers	10	15	*Steven Scott 15*
(18) Christmas Cracker, Finsbury Square	10	15	*Westminster*
(19) Autographed Editions, Christmas Common	10	25	*Westminster*
(20) Snowdrop Close Hampton Middx	10	15	*GBFDC GB10*
(21) Christmas Greetings HM Ships Abroad	10	12	*RN CvrsGp 1-14*
(22) Santa Specials Nene Valley Railway	10	15	*NVRly*
(23) RNLI Christmas, St. Nicholas	10	15	*StampSearchers*
(24) Battle of Britain Flight, RAF Coningsby	10	20	*Cam.S.C.*
(25) No.72 Squadron, Upavon, Pewsey	10	12	*RAF FDC 51*
(26) Queen's Stamps National Postal Museum	10	–	*NPM*
(27) Halifax, West Yorkshire	10	15	*RAF (P&P4)*

Values are a guide - please read the General Notes at the beginning of this catalogue.

Christmas (contd.)	**ordinary covers**	**sponsored covers**	
C.D.S. POSTMARKS	**£**	**£**	
(28) Heartease or Norwich - Tom Smith factory	12		
(29) Bishop's Stortford, Colman Street EC2, Stockport all connected with Tom Smith's Crackers	10		
(30) St Nicholas - Santa	12		

Also: Holy Island, Nasareth. Prices from £7.

£2.60 & £4 CHRISTMAS BOOKLETS		
With pair or block of 4 20p & 26p stamps	5	
With complete panes of 20p & 26p stamps	10	

13th November 1997 - QUEEN'S GOLDEN WEDDING

20p & 43p Wedding day portrait; 26p & 63p Present day portrait

SPECIAL HANDSTAMPS			
(1) Philatelic Bureau	3	-	*Royal Mail*
(2) First Day of Issue - London SW Fifty Years	3	-	*Royal Mail*
(3) First Day of Issue - London (bells & doves)	10	-	*Royal Mail*
(4) First Day of Issue - Birmingham	10	-	*Royal Mail*
(5) Queen & Duke of Ed 1947-1997 (W.Abbey)	12	15	*LFDC 154*
(6) Golden Wedding West. Abbey (three bells)	12	15	*VP 116*
(7) Buckingham Palace Rd SW1 (showing Palace)	12	20	*BenhamPilgrim*
(8) Westminster SW1 (showing Abbey)	12	15	*BLCS 134*
(9) Crathie (showingBalmoral)	12	15	*BLCS 134*
(10) Windsor (showing Castle)	12	15	*Ben500(134)*
(11) 50th Wedd Anniv Congratulations, Romsey	12	20	*BenhamPilgrim*
(12) Golden Wedd Anniv Congrat., Romsey	12	150	*BenhamCoinCvr*
(13) The Queen & the Duke of Ed, Windsor	12	20	*BenhamCoinCvr*
(14) Golden Wedding Year, Windsor	12	20	*BenhamCoinCvr*
(15) Royal Golden Wedd Year Congrat. Windsor	12	15	*BenSG36*
(16) Royal Golden Wedding Anniv Ballater	12	15	*BLCS 134*
(17) HM QEII HRH Prince Philip Westminster	12	15	*BLCS 134*
(18) Royal Golden Wedding Mail on Sunday	12	15	*Benham*
(19) Westminster Abbey (wreath)	12	12	*Steven Scott 15*
(20) Westminster Abbey (text within bell)	12	20	*Cam.S.C.*
(21) Royal Mews, Buckingham Palace Road (rose)	12	15	*FourPennyPost*
(22) 50th The Mall London SW1	12	15	*Cover Collection*
(23) Best Wishes/GBFDC Queen Elizabeth St	12	15	*GBFDC GB9*
(24) Royal Naval Covers Group	12	10	*RN CvrsGp 1-12*
(25) Autographed Editions, Westminster Abbey	12	20	*Westminster*
(26) Britannia Royal Naval College	12	15	*Westminster*
(27) Buckingham Palace Rd (hands)	12	12	*Bletchley PO*
(28) Royal Mail Windsor - permanent handstamp	12	-	*Royal Mail*
(29) Royal Mail London SW - permanent h/s	12	-	*Royal Mail*
(30) Redhill Philatelic Society	12	15	*Redhill PS*
(31) Nat West Philatelic Society	12	30	*NatWest PS*
(32) Uckfield Philatelic Society	12	15	*Uckfield PS*
(33) The Queen's Stamps National Postal Museum	12	20	*NPM*
(34) Int Brotherhood Golden Fleece, Romford	12	20	*T Hurlstone*
(35) Ardleigh House Comm. Assocn, Hornchurch	12	20	*T Hurlstone*
(36) Havering Covers 150 Club	12	15	*T Hurlstone*
(37) Sunderland Tyne & Wear	12	15	*RAF (P&P3)*
(38) Manchester City Royal Sovereign	12	15	*Dawn*
(39) RNLI Golden Wedding, Wedmore Somerset	12	15	*Stamp Searchers*
(40) Happy Christmas Royal Mail London EC1	12	-	*Royal Mail*
(41) No.11 Squadron, Farnborough Hants	12	15	*RAF FDC 52*
(42) 50th Anniv. Armstrong Whitworth, Baginton	12	20	*RAF JSPCC*
C.D.S. POSTMARKS			
(43) Buckingham Palace	150		
(44) Dartmouth - couple first met at RNCollege	10		
(45) House of Commons or House of Lords	20		
(46) Romsey - Honeymoon at Broadlands	10		
(47) Queen Elizabeth Ave or Windsor	10		
(48) Windsor Castle	250		

Also: Broadway, Dolgellau,Duke St, Edinburgh, Gretna Grn, Prince Consort Rd, Royal Pde. From £8.

20th January 1998 - ENDANGERED SPECIES

20p Dormouse; 26p Lady's slipper orchid; 31p Song thrush;
37p Shining ram's-horn snail; 43p Mole cricket; 63p Devil's bolete

SPECIAL HANDSTAMPS			
(1) Philatelic Bureau	3	-	*Royal Mail*
(2) First Day of Issue - Selborne, Alton	3	-	*Royal Mail*
(3) First Day of Issue - London	10	-	*Royal Mail*
(4) First Day of Issue - Birmingham	10	-	*Royal Mail*
(5) Common dormouse, London Zoo	12	15	*BLCS 137*
(6) Song Thrush, Sandy	12	15	*BLCS 137*
(7) Mole Cricket, London Zoo	12	15	*BLCS 137*
(8) Devil's Bolete, Kew, Richmond	12	15	*BLCS 137*
(9) Lady's Slipper Orchid, Kew, Richmond	12	15	*Ben500(137)*
(10) Shining Ram's-Horn Snail, Norwich	12	20	*BenhamPilgrim*
(11) RSPB Saving the future, Sandy	12	15	*Benham*
(12) Thames Salmon Trust Campaign	12	15	*BenL53*
(13) Endangered Species, Selborne, Alton	12	15	*LFDC 156*
(14) Endangered Species, Sandy, Beds	12	15	*VP 118*
(15) Endangered Species, Grassington, Skipton	12	15	*Bradbury*
(16) Charles Lutwidge Do-do-Dodgson, Guildford	12	15	*Bradbury*
(17) Birthplace of Lewis Carroll, Daresbury	12	15	*Bradbury*
(18) Endangered Species, London Zoo (elephant)	12	15	*Steven Scott*

Endangered Species (contd.)	ordinary covers £	sponsored covers £	
(19) Endangered Species, Birdcage Walk, SW1	12	15	*Steven Scott 16*
(20) Endangered Species, Mousehole	12	20	*Westminster*
(21) Autographed Editions Regents Park	12	25	*Westminster*
(22) Autographed Editions Attenborough	12	25	*Westminster*
(23) Ashford Stamp Shop	12	20	*SouthernCvr.2*
(24) Grassington Habitat of Lady's Slipper Orchid	12	20	*T Hurlstone*
(25) Ardleigh Green Habitat/Great Crested Newt	12	20	*T Hurlstone*
(26) Tusk Force Birmingham	12	–	*Royal Mail*
(27) Sinking of the Santorre Santarosa	12	15	*RN CvrsGp 2-1*
(28) No.43 Squadron, Fighting Cocks, Stirling	12	12	*RAF FDC 53*
(29) RNLI Mousehole	12	15	*Stamp Searchers*
C.D.S. POSTMARKS			
(30) Botanic Gdns, Belfast, Kew Gardens or Mold	15		
(31) Grassington - Lady's Slipper Orchid	15		
(32) Lincoln or Selborne	12		

Also: Attenborough, Mousehole, Otterburn, Snailbeach, Throstle Ln. From £10.

3rd February 1998 – DIANA - PRINCESS OF WALES

5 x 26p - Portraits of Diana

SPECIAL HANDSTAMPS (1) Philatelic Bureau	3	–	*Royal Mail*
(2) First Day of Issue – Kensington	3	–	*Royal Mail*
(3) Diana, Kens. Palace Gdns (roses & candle)	10	30	*BLCS 138*
(4) Diana, Kens. Palace Gdns (roses in bud)	10	15	*BenSG39*
(5) Diana, St. Paul's Cathedral (roses)	10	15	*BenhamPilgrim*
(6) Diana, Althorp (roses)	10	15	*Benham*
(7) Diana, Sandringham (roses)	10	25	*BenhamPilgrim*
(8) Diana, Cardiff (roses)	10	30	*BLCS 138*
(9) Diana, Kensington Palace Gdns	10	15	*Benham*
(10) Diana, St. Paul's Cathedral	10	50	*Ben(500)138*
(11) Diana, Althorp	10	35	*BenCoin*
(12) Diana, Sandringham	10	30	*BLCS 138*
(13) Diana, Cardiff	10	30	*BLCS 138*
(14) Diana, The Mail on Sunday	10	15	*Benham*
(15) Diana, KM Canterbury Kent	10	15	*Benham*
(16) Diana, St. Paul's Cathedral	10	175	*Benham*
(17) Diana, The People's Princess, Great Brington	10	15	*LFDC 160*
(18) Diana, Kensington (single rose in circle)	10	15	*VP 122*
(19) Queen of Hearts, Lewis Carroll Centenary	10	25	*Bradbury*
(20) Diana, Althorp (Althorp House)	10	25	*GtBringtonPO*
(21) Kensington, London W8 (Kensington Palace)	10	20	*Westminster*
(22) Autographed Editions, Kens. Palace Gdns	10	35	*Westminster*
(23) A Tribute to Diana, London E1	10	15	*NewsOfWorld*
(24) A Tribute to Diana, Kensington	10	15	*CoverCraft*
(25) A Tribute to the People's Princess Kensington	10	15	*CoverCollection*
(26) Diana Commemoration London WC2	10	15	*Steven Scott 17*
(27) England's Rose, Kensington	10	15	*CoverCraft*
(28) Diana Princess of Wales BFPS 3298	10	15	*Forces*
(29) Althorp Northamptonshire	10	15	*T Hurlstone*
(30) Kensington Palace Gardens	10	15	*T Hurlstone*
(31) London SW1 Diana, Princess of Wales	10	15	*T Hurlstone*
(32) Kensington London W8, Princess of Wales	10	15	*T Hurlstone*
(33) The City of London, EC4	10	15	*T Hurlstone*
(34) Limited Editions, Arundel	10	15	*T Hurlstone*
(35) England's Rose, Postcombe, Oxford	10	15	*FourPennyPost*
(36) Diana, Bletchley Park	10	12	*Bletchley PO*
(37) Capital of Wales, Cardiff	10	–	*Royal Mail*
(38) The Helping Hand, Diana Place, NW1	10	15	*GBFDC GB*
(39) The Booth Catalogue	10	12	*FDP Co*
(40) Madame Tussaud's Baker Street	10	–	*n.s.c*
(41) London EC (St.Paul's) or London SW (Palace)	10	–	*n.s.c*
(42) North York Moors Railway, Pickering	10	15	*NYMoorsRly*
(43) Nene Valley Railway, Peterborough	10	15	*NVRly*
(44) HMShips Cornwall & Vanguard, Devonport	10	15	*RN CvrsGp 2-2*
(45) RNLI Althorp	10	15	*StampSearchers*
(46) Stirling	10	30	*RAF (P&P6)*
(47) NO.3 Squadron, Larkhill Salisbury	10	20	*RAF FDC 56*
C.D.S. POSTMARKS			
(48) Buckingham Palace or Windsor Castle	40		
(49) Great Brington - Althorp	60		
(50) Kensington High Street - Kensington Palace	35		
(51) Sandringham	275		

Also: Broadway, Earls Court, Elton, Forest Hall, Ludgate Circus, The Jewel, Memorial Rd Paris Ave., Princess Street, Sevenoaks, Spencers Wood, Spencer Road, Wales From £10.

24th February 1998 - THE QUEEN'S BEASTS

5x26p: Lion of England/Griffin of Edward III; Falcon of Plantagenet/Bull of Clarence; Lion of Mortimer/Yale of Beaufort; Greyhound of Richmond/Dragon of Wales; Unicorn of Scotland/Horse of Hanover

SPECIAL HANDSTAMPS (1) Philatelic Bureau	3	–	*Royal Mail*
(2) First Day of Issue – London SW1 (3 lions)	3	–	*Royal Mail*
(3) First Day of Issue – London (single lion)	10	–	*Royal Mail*
(4) First Day of Issue – Birmingham (Richard I)	10	–	*Royal Mail*
(5) Greyhound of Richmond	10	15	*BLCS 139*

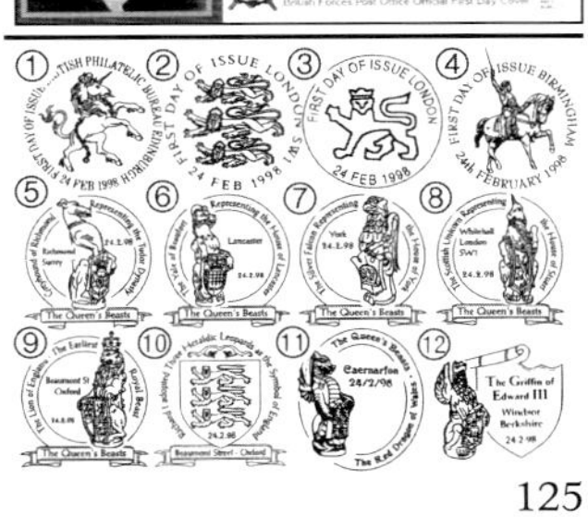

Queen's Beasts (contd.)	ordinary covers £	sponsored covers £	
(6) The Yale of Beaufort, Lancaster	10	20	*BenhamPilgrim*
(7) The Silver Falcon, York	10	20	*BenhamPilgrim*
(8) The Scottish Unicorn, London SW1	10	15	*BLCS 139*
(9) The Lion of England, Oxford	10	15	*BLCS 139*
(10) Richard I, Three Heraldic Leopards, Oxford	10	15	*Ben(500)139*
(11) The Red Dragon of Wales, Caernarfon	10	15	*BenhamCoinCvr*
(12) The Griffin of Edward III, Windsor	10	15	*BenSG40*
(13) Royal Armouries, Leeds	10	15	*BLCS 139*
(14) The Heraldry Society, WC1	10	15	*LFDC 157*
(15) The Age of Chivalry, Windsor	10	15	*VP 119*
(16) 650th Anniv Order of the Garter, Windsor	10	20	*Bradbury*
(17) Debrett's London SW6	10	25	*Bradbury*
(18) The Queen's Beasts, Westminster Abbey	10	15	*Westminster*
(19) Autographed Editions, Westminster Abbey	10	20	*Westminster*
(20) City of Westminster, SW1	10	15	*RoyalMail/Mint*
(21) The Heraldic City, London (changeable date)	10	20	*T Hurlstone*
(22) Noak Hill Romford (changeable date)	10	20	*T Hurlstone*
(23) Herald's Place London SE11	10	15	*GBFDC GB11*
(24) Forgotten Beasts	10	30	*PMPayne*
(25) Order of the Garter, Buckingham Old Gaol	10	15	*Bletchley PO*
(26) Queens Road Post Office, Bristol	10	–	*n.s.c*
(27) NatWest Philatelic Society	10	30	*NWPhilSoc*
(28) Queen's Beasts Historic Windsor	10	20	*CoverCraft*
(29) Henry V Lancaster	10	15	*Steven Scott 18*
(30) Lincoln	10	15	*RAF (P&P7)*
(31) Dortmund-Ems Canal, Woodhall Spa	10	20	*Cam S.C.*
(32) The Flying Scotsman, Doncaster	10	15	*Benham(s)*
(33) Oldest Working Steam Loco, Liverpool	10	15	*Dawn*
(34) Mine Warfare Force in Gulf War	10	15	*RN CvrsGp 2-3*
(35) RNLI Shieldfield	10	15	*StampSearchers*
(36) Lewis Carroll, Darlington	10	25	*Bradbury*
(37) No.23 Squadron, Gosport Hants	10	15	*RAF FDC 54*
C.D.S. POSTMARKS			
(38) Arundel - home of the Earl Marshal	10		
(39) Beaufort or Richmond	10		
(40) Broadway, SW1 - Westminster Abbey	10		
(41) Buckingham Palace or Windsor Castle	125		
(42) House of Common or House of Lords	25		
(43) Oxford - birthplace of Richard I	10		
(44) Windsor or Windsor Great Park	25		

Beast Bank, Clarence St. York, Falcon Lodge, Kew Gdns, Lion Green, Royal Pde, Shield Row. £7.

PLEASE READ THE GENERAL NOTES

24th March 1998 – LIGHTHOUSES

20p St. John's Point; 26p the Smalls; 37p the Needles; 43p Bell Rock; 63p Eddystone

SPECIAL HANDSTAMPS (1) Philatelic Bureau	3	–	*Royal Mail*
(2) First Day of Issue – Plymouth	3	–	*Royal Mail*
(3) First Day of Issue – London	10	–	*Royal Mail*
(4) First Day of Issue – Birmingham	10	–	*Royal Mail*
(5) Flannan Lighthouse, Lewis	12	–	*Royal Mail*
(6) Grace Darling, Bamburgh	12	15	*BLCS 141*
(7) The Original Eddystone, Plymouth	12	15	*BLCS 141*
(8) The Smalls, St. Davids	12	25	*BenhamPilgrim*
(9) The Needles, Freshwater	12	25	*BenhamPilgrim*
(10) St. John's Point, Killough	12	25	*BenhamPilgrim*
(11) The Bell Rock, Arbroath	12	15	*BLCS 141*
(12) 300th Anniv Eddystone Lighthouse	12	15	*Ben(500)141*
(13) The Roman Pharos at Dover	12	15	*BenL54*
(14) Belle Tout Lighthouse, Beachy Head	12	15	*BenL55*
(15) 300 Years of the Eddystone Lighthouse	12	15	*Westminster*
(16) Autographed Editions, Eddystone	12	20	*Westminster*
(17) Corp. of Trinity House EC3	12	15	*LFDC 158*
(18) Corp. of Trinity House, Eddystone EC3	12	15	*VP 120*
(19) Seamark: Magazine about Lighthouses	12	45	*Bradbury*
(20) Skerries Court, Langley	12	15	*GBFDC GB12*
(21) Belle Tout Eastbourne	12	45	*HDMcIntyre*
(22) A Guiding Light, Alum Bay	12	15	*Steven Scott 19*
(23) Lighthouse, Reigate	12	65	*Steven Scott*
(24) Beacons Close E6	12	40	*PMPayne*
(25) The Pharos Dover	12	20	*PBarrett*
(26) Beachy Head Eastbourne	12	20	*UckPhilSoc*
(27) Eddystone Lighthouse, Plymouth	12	12	*JC Stamps*
(28) Royal Mail Plymouth (changeable date)	12	–	*Royal Mail*
(29) RNLI Eddystone	12	20	*StampSearchers*
(30) Preserved Loco Eddystone	12	20	*Dawn*
(31) Lewis Carroll Beachy Head	12	20	*Bradbury*
(32) No201 Squadron, Gosport	12	15	*RAF FDC 55*
(33) Hastings, East Sussex	12	15	*RAF (P&P8)*
(34) Royal Marines Act, Whitehall	12	15	*RN CvrsGp 2-4*
(35) Leicester Synagogue	12	35	*SKacher*
C.D.S. POSTMARKS			
(36) Cawsand, Plymouth; Cliffburn, Arbroath; Dale; Killough; Totland Bay - nearest POs to lighthouses	15		
(37) Lightouse or Seething Lane	15		

Also: Fair Isles, Lightcliffe, Lightwater, Sandbanks, Seahouses. Prices from £8.

23rd April 1998 – COMEDIANS

20p Tommy Cooper; 26p Eric Morecambe
37p Joyce Grenfell; 43p Les Dawson; 63p Peter Cook

	ordinary cvrs £	sponsored covers £	
SPECIAL HANDSTAMPS (1) Philatelic Bureau	3	–	*Royal Mail*
(2) First Day of Issue – Morecambe	3	–	*Royal Mail*
(3) First Day of Issue – London	10	–	*Royal Mail*
(4) First Day of Issue – Birmingham	10	–	*Royal Mail*
(5) Int. Stamp Exhibition, Stamp 98 Wembley	10	–	*Royal Mail*
(6) Stamp 98 Wembley	10	20	*WalsallSecPrint*
(7) Tommy Cooper, Caerphilly	10	15	*BenhamPilgrim*
(8) Eric Morecambe, Morecambe	10	15	*Ben500(142)*
(9) Joyce Grenfell, London	10	15	*BLCS 142*
(10) Les Dawson, Manchester	10	20	*BenhamPilgrim*
(11) Peter Cook, Torquay	10	20	*BenhamPilgrim*
(12) Heroes of British Comedy The Mail, W8	10	15	*Benham*
(13) Comedy, London W1	10	15	*BLCS 142*
(14) Great British Comedy, Knightsbridge	10	35	*Benham(Print)*
(15) Great British Comedy, Cambridge	10	15	*BenSG41*
(16) Great British Comedy, Slade	10	15	*BLCS 142*
(17) Variety Club, London W1P	10	15	*BenhamPilgrim*
(18) Hell's Bells, Shepperton	10	15	*BLCS 142*
(19) Best of British Comedy, Morecambe	10	15	*LFDC 159*
(20) Oscar Wilde, Windermere	10	15	*VP 121*
(21) Tony Hancock, Birmingham	10	20	*Bradbury*
(22) British Comedy Greats, Blackpool	10	20	*SculptureWks*
(23) Britain's Comedy Legends	10	15	*Westminster*
(24) Autographed Editions, London Palladium	10	25	*Westminster*
(25) Autographed Editions, Morecambe	10	25	*Westminster*
(26) Clowne, Chesterfield	10	10	*GBFDC GB13*
(27) Comedians, Bletchley Park	10	8	*Bletchley PO*
(28) Peter Cook, Satirist, London W1	10	15	*T.Hurlstone*
(29) Charlie Chaplin, Walworth, SE17	10	15	*T.Hurlstone*
(30) Frankie Howerd, Eltham, SE	10	15	*T.Hurlstone*
(31) Laughter, the best Medicine	10	15	*Steven Scott 20*
(32) Carry on Sergeant, Cambridge	10	25	*Cam.S.C.*
(33) Passport to Pimlico, Ealing W5	10	25	*Cam.S.C.*
(34) Caerffill, Caerfphilly	10	–	*Royal Mail*
(35) Lewis Carroll, Rugby School	10	25	*Bradbury*
(36) No208 Squadron, Valley Holyhead	10	15	*RAF FDC 57*
(37) RNLI Laughton	10	15	*StampSearchers*
(38) HMS Hesperus, Bootle	10	15	*RN CvrsGp 2-6*
(39) Manchester	10	15	*RAF (P&P9)*
C.D.S. POSTMARKS			
(40) Any Butlin's Holiday Camp	25		
(41) Caerphilly; Collyhurst; Fulham Rd; Morecambe or Torquay – birthplace or homes of comedians featured on stamps	15		
(42) Giggleswick	15		

Also: Coopers Rd., The Circle, Grenfell Rd., Knotty Ash, Pratts Bottom, Reading, Shepherd's Bush. £10.

23rd June 1998 – NATIONAL HEALTH SERVICE

20p Blood Donors; 26p Vaccinations; 43p Babies; 63p Outpatients.

	ordinary cvrs £	sponsored covers £	
SPECIAL HANDSTAMPS (1) Philatelic Bureau	3	–	*Royal Mail*
(2) First Day of Issue – Tredegar	3	–	*Royal Mail*
(3) First Day of Issue – London	10	–	*Royal Mail*
(4) First Day of Issue – Birmingham	10	–	*Royal Mail*
(5) National Blood Service, Watford	10	15	*Benham*
(6) The Royal Hospitals NHS Trust, Whitechapel	10	15	*BLCS 143*
(7) Guy's & St.Thomas', London SE1	10	15	*BLCS 143*
(8) Ebbw Vale, South Wales (portrait of Bevan)	10	15	*BenL57*
(9) Trafford General Hospital, Manchester	10	15	*Ben500(143)*
(10) NHS Edlington, Doncaster	10	15	*LFDC 161*
(11) Florence Nightingale, East Wellow	10	15	*VP 123*
(12) Heart of the Nations Healthcare, WC1	10	20	*Bradbury*
(13) NHS Sydney Street, London SW3	10	15	*Steven Scott 21*
(14) 50th Anniv NHS, Tredegar	10	15	*Westminster*
(15) Health Autographed, Tredegar	10	20	*Westminster*
(16) William Beveridge, Westminster SW1	10	20	*T Hurlstone*
(17) William Gladstone, Westminster SW1	10	20	*T Hurlstone*
(18) Gladstone Centenary, Hawarden Deeside	10	20	*T Hurlstone*
(19) 50 years of getting better, Hale Gardens W3	10	15	*PMPayne*
(20) The heart of the matter, Vale of Health NW3	10	10	*GBFDC GB14*
(21) NatWest Philatelic Soc, St. Thomas' SE1	10	15	*NWPhilSoc*
(22) Health in the Community, Uckfield	10	15	*PBarrett*
(23) National Health Service, Canterbury	10	20	*HDMcIntyre*
(24) Ambrex Harrogate ASA	10	25	*WMAmbulance*
(25) Scottish National Blood Transfusion	10	20	*GlasgowBlood*
(26) Carry On Nurse, Iver Bucks	10	25	*Cam.S.C.*
(27) MKCCG Milton Keynes	10	20	*Bletchley PO*
(28) 100 Years Manufacturing, Enfield	10	20	*Arlington*
(29) Royal Army Medical Corps	10	20	*Arlington*
(30) The Most Famous Blood Donor, Birmingham	10	15	*Bradbury*
(31) Lewis Carroll Centenary, Oxford	10	25	*Bradbury*
(32) Leonard Cheshire, Westminster	10	15	*WSORandle (s)*
(33) Beverley	10	15	*RAF (P&P10)*

CATALOGUE VALUES ARE A GUIDE

Health Service (contd.)	ordinary covers £	sponsored covers £	
(34) HMS Scylla, Portsmouth	6	10	*RN CvrsGp 2-7*
(35) Wimbledon Tennis, London SW19	6	15	*Arlington*
(36) RNLI Healing	6	10	*StampSearchers*
(37) No55 Squadron, Castle Bromwich	6	8	*RAF FDC 58*
(38) Nene Valley Railway	6	8	*NVRly*
C.D.S. POSTMARKS			
(39) Any hospital/infirmary postmark ... *each*	10		
(40) Tredegar - birthplace of Aneurin Bevan	10		

Also: Healing, Pill. from £8.

21st July 1998 – MAGICAL WORLDS

20p The Hobbit (J.R.R.Tolkien); 26p The Lion, the Witch & Wardrobe (C.S.Lewis); 37p The Phoenix and the Carpet (E.Nesbit); 43p The Borrowers (Mary Norton); 63p Through the Looking Glass (Lewis Carroll)

SPECIAL HANDSTAMPS (1) Philatelic Bureau	3	–	*Royal Mail*
(2) First Day of Issue – Oxford	3	–	*Royal Mail*
(3) First Day of Issue – London	10	–	*Royal Mail*
(4) First Day of Issue – Birmingham	10	–	*Royal Mail*
(5) Aberdeen (cat: The Boggart)	10	20	*RM Airletter*
(6) Variety Club, London W1	10	15	*Benham*
(7) Magical Worlds C.S.Lewis, Belfast	10	15	*BLCS 144*
(8) Magical Worlds Lewis Carroll, Daresbury	10	15	*BLCS 144*
(9) Magical Worlds E.Nesbit, Halstead, Kent	10	15	*BLCS 144*
(10) Magical Worlds Mary Norton, Leighton Buzzard	10	15	*BLCS 144*
(11) Magical Worlds J.R.R.Tolkien, Birmingham	10	15	*Ben500(144)*
(12) Centenary of the Birth of CS Lewis, Oxford	10	15	*BenL58*
(13) Lewis Carroll, Oxford (Mad Hatter)	10	20	*LFDC 162*
(14) 'Twas Brillig, and the Slithy Toves, Oxford	10	15	*VP 124*
(15) Birthplace of Lewis Carroll, Daresbury	10	20	*Bradbury*
(16) Alice Liddell, Lyndhurst Hants	10	25	*Bradbury*
(17) Lewis Carroll, Tom Quad, Oxford	10	25	*Bradbury*
(18) Sarehole Mill Inspired Tolkien, Birmingham	10	25	*RMail B'ham*
(19) Magical Worlds, Daresbury (open book)	10	15	*Westminster*
(20) Autographed Editions, Daresbury	10	20	*Westminster*
(21) Magical Authors, Guildford Surrey	10	15	*Steven Scott*
(22) St. Aldates, Oxford	10	15	*Steven Scott 22*
(23) Yellow Brick Road Appeal, Newcastle	10	20	*FourPennyPost*
(24) Dillons Bookstore, Newcastle	10	15	*FourPennyPost*
(25) The Barley Field, Upminster Essex	10	20	*T Hurlstone*
(26) Dick Whittington, London	10	20	*T Hurlstone*
(27) Child's Way, London NW11	10	12	*GBFDC GB15*
(28) Paradise Place, London SE18	10	15	*PMPayne*
(29) The Railway Children, Keighley	10	35	*Cam S.C.*
(30) HMS Quilliam, Belfast	10	15	*RN CvrsGp 2-8*
(31) Belfast	10	15	*RAF(P&P11)*
(32) No27 Squadron, Hounslow	10	10	*RAF FDC 59*
(33) Royal Tournament	10	35	*Forces*
(34) Blair Atholl Jamborette	10	70	*Scouts*
(35) Electrical Tramroad, Blackpool	10	35	*Dawn*
C.D.S. POSTMARKS			
(36) Guildford, Headington, Leighton Buzzard, Oxford - all associated with authors ... *each*	12		
(37) Llandudno or Lyndhurst - Alice Liddell ... *each*	12		

Also: Castle St., Belfast, Chessington, Child's Hill, Lewis Road, Lewisham, Lilliput, Old Penshaw, Paradise, St. Mary's Bay, Underhill Circus. Prices from £10

25th August 1998 - CARNIVALS

20p,26p,43p & 63p Scenes from the Notting Hill Carnival.

SPECIAL HANDSTAMPS (1) Philatelic Bureau	3	–	*Royal Mail*
(2) First Day of Issue – London W11 (drum)	3	–	*Royal Mail*
(3) First Day of Issue – London (sax & bongo)	10	–	*Royal Mail*
(4) First Day of Issue – Birmingham	10	–	*Royal Mail*
(5) Notting Hill, W11 (face in sun)	10	15	*RoyalMail/Mint*
(6) London Celebrates Notting Hill (dancer)	10	15	*Ben500(145)*
(7) London Celebrations Notting Hill (dancer)	10	15	*BLCS 145*
(8) London Celebrations Chinatown, W1	10	15	*BLCS 145*
(9) London Celebrations City Pageantry	10	15	*BLCS 145*
(10) London Celebrations Pearly Kings & Queens	10	15	*BLCS 145*
(11) Leicester Caribbean Carnival	10	15	*LFDC 163*
(12) Notting Hill, London W11 (dancer)	10	15	*VP 125*
(13) Carnival, Notting Hill (maracas)	10	15	*Westminster*
(14) Autographed Editions, Notting Hill	10	20	*Westminster*
(15) Largest Carnival in Europe, Notting Hill	10	15	*Steven Scott 23*
(16) Europe's Largest Street Carnival	10	15	*Cover Collection*
(17) Carnival Notting Hill Gate	10	20	*T Hurlstone*
(18) Torchlight Carnival, Hornchurch	10	20	*T Hurlstone*
(19) The Spirit of Carnival, Notting Hill Gate	10	10	*GBFDC GB16*
(20) Carnival, Notting Hill Gate (mask)	10	15	*PMPayne*
(21) Brazil Close, Beddington Croydon	10	15	*PMPayne*
(22) Come & Join the Dance, Daresbury	10	25	*Bradbury*
(23) No17 Squadron, Gosport	10	15	*RAF FDC 60*
(24) RNLI postmark Merrymeet	10	15	*Stamp Searchers*
(25) Holiday on the Buses	10	15	*Cam.SC*
(26) HMS Wanderer, Devonport	10	15	*RN CvrsGp 2-9*

PLEASE READ THE GENERAL NOTES

Carnivals (contd.)	ordinary covers £	sponsored covers £	
(27) Lerwick	5	13	*RAF(P&P12)*
C.D.S. POSTMARKS			
(28) Notting Hill or Leicester - Caribbean Carnivals	10		
(29) Ladbroke Grove or Portobello Rd - on route	10		

Also: Bridgewater, Durham, Jamaica Street, Jamaica Road, Lerwick, Lewes, Lichfield, The Parade, Sloane Square, West India Dock. Prices from £7.

29th September 1998 - SPEED

20p Bluebird (Sir Malcolm Campbell); 26p Sunbeam (Sir Henry Seagrave); 30p Babs (John G Parry Thomas); 43p Railton Mobil Special (John R Cobb); 63p Bluebird (Donald Campbell)

SPECIAL HANDSTAMPS (1) Philatelic Bureau	3	-	*Royal Mail*
(2) First Day of Issue - Pendine	3	-	*Royal Mail*
(3) First Day of Issue - London	10	-	*Royal Mail*
(4) First Day of Issue - Birmingham	10	-	*Royal Mail*
(5) Sir Malcolm Campbell Castle Silverstone	12	15	*BLCS 146*
(6) Donald Cambell Horley	12	15	*BLCS 146*
(7) Sir Malcolm Campbell Castle Combe	12	15	*BLCS 146*
(8) Sir Malcolm Campbell Thruxton	12	20	*BenhamPilgrim*
(9) Sir Malcolm Campbell Snetterton	12	20	*BenhamPilgrim*
(10) Sir Malcolm Campbell Castle Donington	12	15	*BLCS 146*
(11) Sir Malcolm Campbell Pendine	12	15	*Ben500(146)*
(12) Sir Malcolm Campbell Mail on Sunday	12	15	*Benham*
(13) National Motor Museum Beaulieu	12	15	*BenSG42*
(14) Donald Campbell Bluebird Coniston	12	15	*LFDC 164*
(15) Land Speed Records Pendine	12	15	*VP 126*
(16) Legends of Speed Pendine	12	15	*Westminster*
(17) Autographed Editions Silverstone	12	25	*Westminster*
(18) Speedy Place London WC2	12	15	*Steven Scott 24*
(19) Lakeland Motor Museum Holker Hall	12	15	*Steven Scott*
(20) Graham Hill Hendon	12	20	*T Hurlstone*
(21) Jim Clark Duns Berwickshire	12	20	*T Hurlstone*
(22) Silverstone Golden Jubilee	12	25	*G Lovell*
(23) Speed 98 Silverstone	12	15	*Bletchley PO*
(24) Bluebird Don Wales Speed Record Attempt	12	15	*FourPennyPost*
(25) Bentley Farnham	12	25	*HDMcIntyre*
(26) Genevieve Brighton	12	25	*Cam S.C.*
(27) Eric Morecambe	12	25	*Cam S.C.*
(28) The Sound Barrier Heathrow Airport	12	25	*Cam S.C.*
(29) Speed Heathrow Airport	12	25	*Cam S.C.*
(30) Speedwell Street London	12	15	*PMPayne*
(31) Hermes Way Wallington	12	15	*PMPayne*
(32) Speed House Barbican	12	12	*GBFDC GB17*
(33) Concorde Filton Bristol	12	-	*R Pratten*
(34) Lewis Carroll Coniston	12	20	*Bradbury*
(35) Harrow	12	15	*RAF(P&P13)*
(36) No12 Squadron, Salisbury	12	15	*RAF FDC 61*
(37) RNLI Postmark Speedwell	12	15	*StampSearchers*
(38) RAFLET Stamp Club	12	15	*RAFLET*
(39) Liverpool FC Return to Europe	12	15	*Dawn*
(40) The Fast Ball Instow Bideford	12	20	*Instow PO*
(41) A Tribute to the Brave Men....Scapa Flow	12	15	*RN CvrsGp 2-10*
C.D.S. POSTMARKS			
(42) Beaulieu - National Motor Museum	15		
(43) Chislehurst - Birthplace of Malcolm Campbell	15		
(44) Silverstone , Weybridge or RAC	15		
(45) Pendine, Coniston or Windermere	15		

Also: The Drive, Elvington, Fort Augustus, Mansell Rd, The Rocket. Prices from £10.

2nd November 1998 - CHRISTMAS

20p, 26p, 30p, 43p, 63p Angels

SPECIAL HANDSTAMPS (1) Philatelic Bureau	3	-	*Royal Mail*
(2) First Day of Issue - Bethlehem	3	-	*Royal Mail*
(3) First Day of Issue - London	10	-	*Royal Mail*
(4) First Day of Issue - Birmingham	10	-	*Royal Mail*
(5) Happy Christmas Royal Mail London EC1	10	-	*Royal Mail*
(6) Hear the Christmas Angels Nasareth	10	15	*BLCS 148*
(7) Silent Night Holy Night Bethlehem	10	15	*BLCS 148*
(8) Sing Choirs of Angels Chrismas Common	10	15	*BLCS 148*
(9) Born a King Wiseman's Bridge	10	15	*BLCS 148*
(10) Gloria in Excelcis Angel Bank	10	15	*Ben500(148)*
(11) Bethlehem	10	15	*LFDC 165*
(12) Nasareth	10	15	*VP 127*
(13) Godshill Isle of Wight	10	15	*Bradbury*
(14) Christmas Greetings Lewis Carroll	10	15	*Bradbury*
(15) Autographed Editions Bethlehem	10	20	*Westminster*
(16) Merry Christmas Bethlehem	10	15	*Westminster*
(17) Canterbury Cathedral	10	15	*Steven Scott*
(18) Angel Court London EC2	10	15	*Steven Scott 25*
(19) The Angel Islington	10	15	*T Hurlstone*
(20) Chronic Pain South Ockendon	10	15	*T Hurlstone*
(21) Bletchley Milton Keynes	10	15	*Bletchley PO*
(22) The Alhambra Theatre Bradford	10	15	*J Cook*
(23) North Pole Road London W10	10	15	*PMPayne*
(24) St Nicholas Road London SE18	10	15	*PMPayne*

Christmas (contd.)

	ordinary covers £	sponsored covers £	
(25) Angel Lane London E15	10	12	*GBFDC GB18*
(26) The Salvation Army Kettering	10	15	*DCopper*
(27) Murder on the Orient Express	10	15	*Cam S.C.*
(28) Imperial War Museum Duxford	10	15	*Cam S.C.*
(29) Are You Being Served? Oxford Street	10	15	*Cam S.C.*
(30) Oxford	10	15	*RAF(P&P14)*
(31) No 31 Squadron, Farnborough	10	10	*RAF FDC 62*
(32) RNLI Postmark Bethlehem	10	15	*StampSearchers*
(33) Christmas Angels Whitfield	10	15	*PBarrett*
(34) 25th Anniversary Tandy Walsall	10	20	*Tandy*
(35) The Midweek Club Farnborough	10	25	*ROsborne*
(36) Christmas Greetings HM Ships Plymouth	10	15	*RN CvrsGp 2-11*
(37) Royal Mail New HQ Birmingham	10	75	*Royal Mail*
C.D.S. POSTMARKS			
(38) Angel Hill, Holy Island or Nasareth *each*	10		

Also: Godshill, Chapel House, Jerusalem Street, Kew, Noel Road. Prices from £7

MILLENNIUM STAMPS

To celebrate the new millennium Royal Mail has devoted the whole of its special stamps programme for 1999 to British history and achievement over the past 1,000 years. Each stamp is numbered, the first issue being numbered 48, 47, 46 and 45 - the final set of the year being 4, 3, 2 and 1 - Royal Mail's countdown to the new millennium.

12th January 1999 – INVENTORS' TALE

20p Time, 26p Steam Power, 43p Photography, 63p Computers

SPECIAL HANDSTAMPS	Price Guide Ordinary Covers £4-£9 /	SPONSOR Sponsored Covers:
(1) FDI - Bureau		*Royal Mail (n.s.c.)*
(2) FDI - Greenwich		*Royal Mail (n.s.c.)*
(3) -do- non pictorial version		*Royal Mail (n.s.c.)*
(4) Inventors' Tale Glasgow		*Royal Mail (n.s.c.)*
(5) Steam Power Birmingham		*Royal Mail (n.s.c.)*
(6) Photography Lacock	£15	*Benham BLCS150*
(7) Steam Power Newcastle	£20	*Benham Pilgrim*
(8) Technology London SW7	£15	*Benham BLCS150*
(9) Timekeeping Greenwich	£15	*Benham BLCS150*
(10) John Harrison Greenwich	£25	*Benham Coin Mil.1*
(11) John Harrison Foulby	£25	*Benham 500(150)*
(12) Stonehenge	£20	*Benham Eng.Heritage*
(13) Steam Power Glasgow	£20	*Bradbury LFDC 166*
(14) Steam Power Paddington	£20	*Bradbury VP 128*
(15) Robert Stephenson Newc'tle	£20	*Bradbury*
(16) Autographed Editions	£25	*Westminster*
(17) Greenwich Millennium	£15	*Westminster*
(18) Lacock Chippenham	£30	*Steven Scott Plat.1*
(19) Euston London	£20	*Steven Scott 26*
(20) John Harrison Foulby	£25	*FourpennyPost*
(21) Millennium Dome	£25	*T Hurlstone*
(22) Collosus	£35	*Bletchley PO*
(23) Trevithick Trust	£30	*J Henty*
(24) Bell Drive	£30	*P M Payne*
(25) The Locomotive	£30	*M Brazier (Pubs.1)*
(26) Engineers Way	£20	*GB19*
(27) Homer Drive	£30	*M J Kingsland*
(28) Power Road	£30	*P Sheridan*
(29) Timeball Tower	£30	*H D MacIntyre*
(30) Shuttleworth Collection	£20	*BritHerCollect*
(31) Charles Babbage	£20	*RN CvrsGpTDFC1-01*
(32) Operation Pungent	£20	*RN CvrsGpNFDC3-01*
(33) East Grinstead Stamp Club	£25	*E GrinStampClub*
(34) Adhesive Postage Stamp	£25	*P Barrett*
(35) Sion Cop Whitehall	£20	*Benham/JS Medal 1*
(36) The Wooden Horse	£35	*Cam S.C.*
(37) Man in White Suit	£35	*Cam S.C.*
(38) Whisky Galore	£35	*Cam S.C.*
(39) Flying Scotsman	£35	*Cam S.C.*
(40) She Elstree Studios	£35	*Cam S.C.*
(41) Satanic Rites Elstree	£35	*Cam S.C.*
(42) Total Eclipse Penzance	£35	*Bradbury*

C.D.S. POSTMARKS Price Guide £10-£15

(43) James Watt Dock, New Invention or The Rocket
(44) Clockface, Greenwich, Meridian Centre or Salisbury
(45) Any colliery pmk, Lacock, New Crofton or Smethwick
(46) Bletchley or Whitworth (Manchester)
(47) Science Museum

2nd February 1999 - TRAVELLERS' TALE

20p Global travel, 26p Bicycle, 43p Linking the Nation, 63p Captain Cook - Exploration.

SPECIAL HANDSTAMPS — SPONSOR

Price Guide Ordinary Covers £4-£9 / Sponsored Covers:

(1) FDI - Bureau .... *Royal Mail (n.s.c.)*
(2) FDI - Coventry .... *Royal Mail (n.s.c.)*
(3) -do- non pictorial version .... *Royal Mail (n.s.c.)*
(4) Travellers' Tale Glasgow .... *Royal Mail (n.s.c.)*
(5) Longbridge Birmingham .... *Royal Mail (n.s.c.)*
(6) Air Travel Concorde .... £20 *Benham BLCS 151*
(7) Linking the Nation Ports'th ... £15 *Benham BLCS 151*
(8) Marton in Cleveland .... £15 *Benham BLCS 151*
(9) Brunel, Paddington Station .... £25 *Benham 500(151)*
(10) The Rocket Rainhill Prescot .. £25 *Benham Coin Mil.2*
(11) Courthill Dumfries .... £20 *Benham Pilgrim*
(12) English Heritage Tintagel .... £20 *Benham Eng.Heritage*
(13) Global Travel Heathrow .... £20 *Bradbury LFDC 167*
(14) Meriden Coventry .... £20 *Bradbury VP 129*
(15) Sir Frank Whittle .... £35 *Bradbury*
(16) Flying Scotsman .... £35 *Bradbury*
(17) Global Travel The Comet .... £30 *Bradbury*
(18) The Millennium Pall Mall ...... £15 *Westminster*
(19) Autographed Editions .... £25 *Westminster*
(20) Sir Francis Drake Tavistock .. £30 *Steven Scott Plat.2*
(21) Whittle Cranford Sleaford ...... £20 *Steven Scott 27*
(22) James Cook Marton .... £25 *FourpennyPost*
(23) Luton Airport .... £30 *T Hurlstone*
(24) James Cook Barking Essex ..... £30 *T Hurlstone*
(25) The Bike Man, Upminster ...... £30 *T Hurlstone*
(26) Mail Travels the World .... £25 *Bletchley PO*
(27) The Travellers Rest .... £25 *M Brazier (Pubs.2)*
(28) Ulysses Road .... £30 *P M Payne*
(29) Great Malvern .... £35 *A Wright*
(30) Captain Cook £15 *GB20*
(31) Chichester Sussex .... £30 *M J Kingsland*
(32) Transporter Bridge .... £30 *P Sheridan*
(33) NYMR Millennium Stamps ... £25 *NYMRly*
(34) St Andrew the Great .... £30 *B A Downham*
(35) Supermarine S6 .... £25 *BritHerCollect*
(36) Linking Nations Saltash .... £25 *RN CvrsGpTDFC1-02*
(37) HMS Westcott .... £25 *RN CvrsGpNFDC3-02*
(38) King George V loco .... £25 *Dawn*
(39) Raflet Stamp Club .... £25 *RAFLET*
(40) Anglo-Boer War Whitehall .... £25 *Benham/JS Medal 2*
(41) Royal Mail Norwich .... £30 *Royal Mail*
(42) Princess Diana Tribute .... £30 *Steven Scott*
(43) The Belles of St.Trinians .... £40 *Cam S.C.*
(44) Private's Progress .... £40 *Cam S.C.*
(45) On The Buses .... £40 *Cam S.C.*
(46) The Blue Lamp .... £40 *Cam S.C.*
(47) Death of Howard Carter .... £40 *Cam S.C.*
(48) Scott of the Antarctic .... £40 *Cam S.C.*
(49) Dutch U-Boat Pens .... £40 *Cam S.C.*
(50) Total Eclipse Torquay .... £30 *Bradbury*

C.D.S. POSTMARKS Price Guide £10-£15

(51) Heathrow Airport, Luton, Filton or Glasgow Airport
(52) Dumfries, Thornhill, Raleigh or Marton in Cleveland
(53) Any TPO, station or junction postmark, Whitby

2nd March 1999 - PATIENTS' TALE

20p Vaccination, 26p Nursing, 43p Penicillin, 63p Test-tube bady.

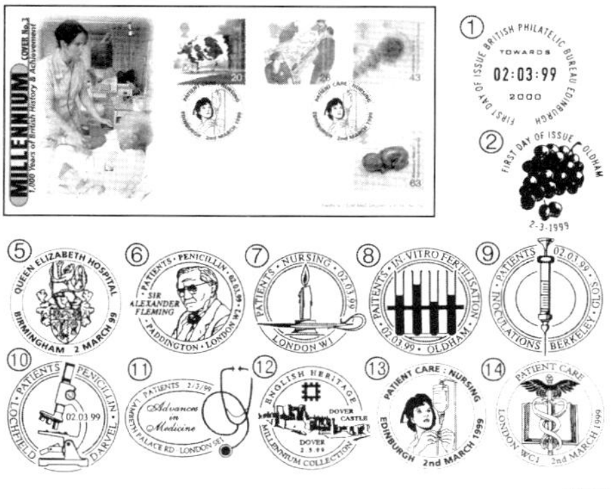

SPECIAL HANDSTAMPS — SPONSOR

Price Guide Ordinary Covers £4-£9 / Sponsored Covers:

(1) FDI - Bureau .... *Royal Mail (n.s.c.)*
(2) FDI - Oldham .... *Royal Mail (n.s.c.)*
(3) -do- non pictorial version .... *Royal Mail (n.s.c.)*
(4) Patients' Tale Glasgow .... *Royal Mail (n.s.c.)*
(5) QE Hospital Birmingham .... *Royal Mail (n.s.c.)*
(6) Sir Alexander Fleming W2 ..... £25 *Benham 500(153)*
(7) Patients, Nursing W1 .... £15 *Benham BLCS 153*
(8) In-vitro Fertilisation .... £15 *Benham BLCS 153*
(9) Inoculations Berkeley .... £25 *Benham Pilgrim*
(10) Penicillin Lochfield .... £15 *Benham BLCS 153*
(11) Lambeth Palace Road .... £20 *Benham Coin Mil.3*
(12) English Heritage Dover .... £20 *Benham Eng.Heritage*
(13) Nursing Edinburgh .... £20 *Bradbury LFDC 168*
(14) Patient Care WC1 .... £20 *Bradbury VP 130*
(15) Aneurin Bevan Tredegar .... £40 *Bradbury*
(16) Jenner Museum Berkeley .... £50 *Bradbury*
(17) Festival of Medicine .... £35 *Bradbury (for BMA)*
(18) The Millennium .... £15 *Westminster*
(19) Autographed Editions .... £25 *Westminster*
(20) 1st Test Tube Baby Oldham ... £20 *Steven Scott 28*

(21) Penicillin Norfolk Place W2..£30 *Steven Scott Plat.3*
(22) Nightingale School ....£20 *FourpennyPost*
(23) Florence Nightingale ....£30 *T Hurlstone*
(24) Fleming Laboratory ....£30 *T Hurlstone*
(25) Brains Surgery..........................£25 *M Brazier (Pubs.3)*
(26) Biggin Hill.................................£30 *PMPayne*
(27) Victoria Hospital, Deal ....£35 *G Cordwell*
(28) Mental Health Farnborough..£35 *R Osborne*
(29) Nightingale Way......................£15 *GB21*
(30) Accident Hospital Widnes .....£25 *P Sheridan*
(31) D.H.98 Mosquito Hatfield......£20 *BritHerCollect*
(32) The Heart of Nursing.............£20 *RN CvrsGpTDFC1-03*
(33) HMS Ariadne...........................£20 *RN CvrsGpNFDC3-03*
(34) Campaign in Tibet...................£25 *Benham/JS Medal 3*
(35) Perth...£25 *RAF(P&P15)*
(36) Filton Bristol ....£30 *Cam S.C.*
(37) Nurse on Wheels.....................£30 *Cam S.C.*
(38) Dr. Jekyll & Sister Hyde............... *Cam S.C. (n.s.c.)*
(38) The Cruel Sea...........................£30 *Cam S.C.*
(40) Doctor Crippen........................£30 *Cam S.C.*
(41) Total Eclipse Falmouth...........£30 *Bradbury*
(42) Macclesfield Football Club.....£20 *Dawn*

C.D.S. POSTMARKS Price Guide £10-£15

(43) Any Hospital or Infirmary pmks; Harrow (Patients Assoc'n)
(44) Berkeley (Jenner); Coldhurst or Oldham (Test-tube baby)
(45) Brown Ave; Fleming Way; Healing; Pill or Ward End
(46) West Wellow or Nightingale Lane
(47) Barnard Castle; Darvel or Paddington (Fleming/Penicillin)

6th April 1999 - SETTLERS' TALE

20p Migration to Scotland, 26p Pilgrim Fathers, 43p Colonisation of Australia, 63p Migration to UK.

SPECIAL HANDSTAMPS SPONSOR
Price Guide Ordinary Covers £4-£9 / Sponsored Covers:

(1) FDI - Bureau.................................. *Royal Mail (n.s.c.)*
(2) FDI - Plymouth .... *Royal Mail (n.s.c.)*
(3) -do- non pictorial version .... *Royal Mail (n.s.c.)*
(4) Settlers' Tale Glasgow................... *Royal Mail (n.s.c.)*
(5) Destination Australia, S'ton...£20 *Benham*
(6) Migration to the UK, B'ham..£20 *Benham Pilgrim*
(7) Migration to the Scotland......£15 *Benham BLCS 154*
(8) Pilgrim Fathers (circle)...........£15 *Benham BLCS 154*
(9) Pilgrim Fathers (oval).............£25 *Benham 500(154)*
(10) Spirit of Expansion.................£20 *Benham Coin Mil.4*
(11) The Mail on Sunday ....£20 *Benham*
(12) Osborne House.........................£20 *Benham Eng.Heritage*
(13) Pilgrim Fathers, Plymouth......£20 *Bradbury LFDC 169*
(14) Pilgrim Fathers, Boston..........£20 *Bradbury VP 131*
(15) William Wilberforce, Hull......£35 *Bradbury*
(16) The Millennium Plymouth.....£15 *Westminster*
(17) Autographed Editions ....£25 *Westminster*
(18) Captain Cook...........................£30 *Steven Scott Plat.4*
(19) The Barbican, Plymouth.........£20 *Steven Scott 29*
(20) Mayflower Plymouth Mass.....£25 *FourpennyPost*
(21) The Mayflower, Rotherhithe..£25 *T Hurlstone*
(22) The Mayflower Inn ....£25 *M Brazier (Pubs.4)*
(23) Settlers, Bletchley Park...........£20 *Bletchley PO*
(24) Nile Road..................................£30 *P M Payne*
(25) Mayflower Road, SW9...........£20 *GB22*
(26) Leaving Liverp'l (ship)...........£25 *P Sheridan*
(27) Leaving Liverp'l (Liver Blg)...£20 *Dawn*
(28) British Bulldog, Filton............£20 *BritHerCollect*
(29) Pilgrim Fathers New World...£20 *RN CvrsGpTDFC1-04*
(30) HMS Fearless...........................£20 *RN CvrsGpNFDC3-04*
(31) Mons 85th Anniversary ....£25 *Benham/JS Medal 4*
(32) Bristol ....£25 *RAF(P&P16)*
(33) The Servant, Shepperton........£35 *Cam S.C.*
(34) A Kind of Loving......................£35 *Cam S.C.*
(35) Odette, War Office..................£35 *Cam S.C.*
(36) Total Eclipse Plymouth...........£35 *Bradbury*

C.D.S. POSTMARKS Price Guide £10-£15

(37) Boston, Any Plymouth pmk or New England
(38) Melbourne, Jamaica Rd, or West India Dock
(39) Settle, Paradise or Seaforth, Liverpool

4th May 1999 - WORKERS' TALE

19p Weaver's Craft, 26p Mill Towns, 44p Shipbuilding, 64p City Finance.

SPECIAL HANDSTAMPS SPONSOR
Price Guide Ordinary Covers £4-£9 / Sponsored Covers:

(1) FDI - Bureau.................................. *Royal Mail (n.s.c.)*
(2) FDI - Belfast.................................. *Royal Mail (n.s.c.)*
(3) -do- non pictorial version .... *Royal Mail (n.s.c.)*
(4) The Jewellery Qtr, Birmingham... *Royal Mail (n.s.c.)*
(5) Workers' Tale Glasgow .... *Royal Mail (n.s.c.)*
(6) Salts Mill Saltaire Shipley............ *Royal Mail (n.s.c.)*

(7) Shipbuilding Belfast..................£15 *Benham*
(8) Mill Towns Blackburn.............£15 *Benham BLCS 155*
(9) City Finance, EC.......................£15 *Benham BLCS 155*
(10) Weaver's Craft..........................£20 *Benham Pilgrim*
(11) Barrow-in-Furness ....£25 *Ben500(155)*
(12) Shipbuilding & Tunnels..........£20 *Benham Coin Mil.5*
(13) Lindisfarne.................................£20 *Benham Eng.Heritage*
(14) Financial Trading, EC ....£20 *Bradbury LFDC 170*
(15) Lavenham, Suffolk....................£20 *Bradbury VP 132*
(16) Richard Arkwright ....£40 *Bradbury*
(17) City of London...........................£15 *Westminster*
(18) Autographed Editions ....£25 *Westminster*
(19) Armoury Way, SW18 ....£20 *Steven Scott Plat.5*
(20) Great Western Dock ....£30 *Steven Scott 30*
(21) Wallsend, Shipbuilding...........£25 *FourpennyPost*
(22) Financial Capital ....£25 *T Hurlstone*
(23) The Dry Dock Londonderry..£30 *M Brazier (Pubs.5)*
(24) Beehive Place ....£30 *PMPayne*
(25) Post Office Way, SW8.............£15 *GB23*
(26) Quarry Bank Mill Wilmslow .£25 *P Sheridan*
(27) The Dambusters........................£20 *BritHerCollect*
(28) Worker's Tales, London ....£20 *RN CvrsGpTDFC1-05*
(29) HMS Sheffield ....£20 *RN CvrsGpNFDC3-05*
(30) New Romney.............................£35 *H D MacIntyre*
(31) NatWest Philatelic Soc ....£25 *NWPhilSoc*
(32) Operation Kindertransports...£40 *S Kacher*
(33) Salvation Army Sunbury.........£20 *J A Deakins*
(34) National Postal Museum ....£25 *NPM (AGM 98 cvr)*
(35) Gallipoli 84th Anniversary.....£20 *Benham/JS Medal 5*
(36) Andover.......................................£20 *RAF(P&P17)*
(37) Total Eclipse Camborne ....£35 *Bradbury*

C.D.S. POSTMARKS Price Guide £10-£15

(38) Arkwright Town, Cranbrook, Saltaire, Lavenham,
(39) Cotton Tree, Lombard Street, Wool, Pounds, Jarrow
(40) Any Colliery pmk., Barrow, Belfast, Clydebank, Govan

1st June 1999 – ENTERTAINERS' TALE

19p Freddie Mercury, 26p 1966 World Cup, 44p Doctor Who, 64p Charlie Chaplin.

SPECIAL HANDSTAMPS SPONSOR
Price Guide Ordinary Covers £4-£9 / Sponsored Covers:

(1) FDI - Bureau.................................. *Royal Mail (n.s.c.)*
(2) FDI - Wembley.............................. *Royal Mail (n.s.c.)*
(3) -do- non pictorial version .... *Royal Mail (n.s.c.)*
(4) Hollywood, Birmingham............... *Royal Mail (n.s.c.)*
(5) Entertainers' Tale Glasgow........... *Royal Mail (n.s.c.)*
(6) Birmingham Repertory .... *Royal Mail (n.s.c.)*
(7) Cinema Classics, Walworth ...£15 *BLCS 158*
(8) Football's Glory, Wembley......£15 *BLCS 158*
(9) Cult Television, London W1..£20 *Benham Pilgrim*
(10) Charity Concerts, Wembley ...£40 *Benham 500(158)*
(11) That's Entertainment, Ealing.£25 *Benham Coin Mil.6*
(12) Kenwood House.......................£20 *Benham Eng.Heritage*
(13) Cult Television, W12..............£20 *Bradbury LFDC 171*
(14) Music Festival, Aldeburgh......£20 *Bradbury VP 133*
(15) Lillie Langtry, Drury Lane .....£45 *Bradbury*
(16) 1966 World Cup, Wembley ...£20 *Bradbury (s)*
(17) Pop Culture, Wembley............£35 *Bradbury(LiveAid cvr)*
(18) The Millennium Wembley......£15 *Westminster*
(19) Autographed The Palladium..£25 *Westminster*
(20) Autographed Wembley ....£25 *Westminster*
(21) Autographed Wood Lane.......£25 *Westminster*
(22) East Street London SE17 ....£30 *Steven Scott Plat.6*
(23) Olympic Way, Wembley.........£20 *Steven Scott 31*
(24) Baker Street, London NW1...£20 *Steven Scott*
(25) John Logie Baird, ...£25 *FourpennyPost*
(26) Charlie Chaplin, ...£30 *T Hurlstone*
(27) The King of Comedy................£25 *M Brazier (Pubs.6)*
(28) World Cup Rugby, ...£30 *P M Payne*
(29) Wimbledon ....£30 *P M Payne*
(30) Football Lane Harrow.............£20 *GB24*
(31) Auto Quest Stadium Widnes.£25 *P Sheridan*
(32) D-Day 1944-1999 Ramsgate..£25 *BritHerCollect*
(33) Freddie Mercury........................£50 *Richard Gray*
(34) Entertaining at Wembley........£20 *RN CvrsGpTDFC1-07*
(35) HMS Renown Devonport ......£20 *RN CvrsGpNFDC3-07*
(36) Augusta Rd Twickenham........£25 *M J Kingsland*
(37) Home of Legends.....................£20 *P Barrett*
(38) American Express Brighton ...£20 *Woodford Sports Cvrs*
(39) Bobby Moore/West Ham ....£20 *Dawn*
(40) Toy & Model Shop, Margate.£20 *Ashford Stamp Shop*
(41) Dr Who & Daleks,....................£35 *Cam S.C.*
(42) Leicester Square ....£20 *A. Wright*
(43) The Somme, Whitehall ....£20 *Benham/JS Medal 6*
(44) Aldershot...................................£20 *RAF(P&P18)*
(45) Total Eclipse, Helston ....£35 *Bradbury*

C.D.S. POSTMARKS Price Guide £10-£15
(46) Aldeburgh, Cults, Hollywood, West End
(47) Moore, Wembley, Wembley Park,
(48) Rock, Shepherd's Bush, World's End, Walworth

15th June 1999 - ROYAL WEDDING

26p & 64p HRH Prince Edward & Miss Sophie Rhys-Jones.

SPECIAL HANDSTAMPS **SPONSOR**
Price Guide Ordinary Covers £4-£9 / Sponsored Covers:
(1) FDI - Bureau .... *Royal Mail (n.s.c.)*
(2) FDI - Windsor .... *Royal Mail (n.s.c.)*
(3) -do- non pictorial version .... *Royal Mail (n.s.c.)*
(4) Sandringham, Norfolk .... *Royal Mail (n.s.c.)*
(5) Buckingham Palace Rd ....£20 *Benham Coin Cover*
(6) Windsor (rose) ....£25 *Benham 500(161)*
(7) Royal Wedding, Windsor ....£15 *Benham BLCS 161*
(8) The Mail on Sunday ....£15 *Benham*
(9) Windsor (Cypher) ....£15 *Bradbury LFDC 178*
(10) Windsor (Chapel) ....£15 *Bradbury VP 140*
(11) Autographed Windsor ....£25 *Westminster*
(12) Royal Wedding Windsor ....£15 *Westminster*
(13) Castle Hill Windsor (Chapel) £15 *Steven Scott*
(14) Castle Hill Windsor (Heart) ..£15 *Steven Scott*
(15) St Georges Chapel (circle) ....£20 *T Hurlstone*
(16) St Georges Chapel (oval) ....£20 *T Hurlstone*
(17) St Georges Chapel (rectangle) ....£20 *T Hurlstone*
(18) Windsor (bells) ....£20 *T Hurlstone*
(19) Prince Edward Road (roses) ..£20 *P M Payne*
(20) Prince Edward Road (cupid) .£15 *GB25*
(21) Windsor (rings) ....£20 *BritHerCollect*
(22) Windsor (bells, horseshoes) ...£20 *RN CvrsGpTDFC1-08*
(23) Dracula Prince of Darkness ...£35 *Cam S.C.*
(24) Victory in the Falklands ....£20 *RN CvrsGpNFDC3-08*
(25) Tavistock Cricket Club ....£20 *Stuart Mundy*

C.D.S. POSTMARKS Price Guide £10-£15
(26) Any Windsor pmk, Bagshot, Brenchley or Oxford
(27) Buckingham Palace or Windsor Castle £75 each

6th July 1999 - CITIZENS' TALE

19p Votes for Women, 26p Right to Health,
44p Right to Learn, 64p Magna Carta.

SPECIAL HANDSTAMPS **SPONSOR**
Price Guide Ordinary Covers £4-£9 / Sponsored Covers:
(1) FDI - Bureau .... *Royal Mail (n.s.c.)*
(2) FDI - Powys Newtown .... *Royal Mail (n.s.c.)*
(3) -do- non pictorial version .... *Royal Mail (n.s.c.)*
(4) Education for All, Birmingham.... *Royal Mail (n.s.c.)*
(5) Citizens' Tale Glasgow .... *Royal Mail (n.s.c.)*
(6) Votes for Women ....£15 *Benham BLCS 162*
(7) Right to Health, Enfield ....£20 *Benham Pilgrim*
(8) Right to Learn, Lanark ....£15 *Benham BLCS 162*
(9) First Rights, Runnymede ....£20 *Benham*
(10) Signing of the Magna Carta ...£25 *Benham 500(162)*
(11) People's Rights Parl. Sq ....£20 *Benham Coin Mil.7*
(12) Audley End ....£20 *Benham Eng.Heritage*
(13) Magna Carta 1215, Egham ....£20 *Bradbury LFDC 172*
(14) Parliament Square ....£20 *Bradbury VP 134*
(15) Emmeline Pankhurst ....£35 *Bradbury*
(16) The Millennium Runnymede .£15 *Westminster*
(17) Autographed New Lanark ......£25 *Westminster*
(18) Davidson Terrace, E7 ....£20 *Steven Scott 32*
(19) Parliament Square, SW1 ....£30 *Steven Scott Plat.7*
(20) New Lanark ....£25 *FourpennyPost*
(21) John Stuart Mill ....£25 *T Hurlstone*
(22) Environmental Health ....£25 *T Hurlstone*
(23) Runnymede Hotel, Egham .....£25 *M Brazier (Pubs.7)*
(24) Milton Keynes Citizen ....£20 *Bletchley PO*
(25) French Place, London E1 ....£30 *P M Payne*
(26) Pankhurst Close, SE14 ....£20 *GB26*
(27) Right to Vote, Widnes ....£20 *P Sheridan*
(28) Avro Lancaster Whitehall ......£20 *BritHerCollect*
(29) Citizens' Rights London ....£20 *RN CvrsGpTDFC1-09*
(30) HMS Shark Harwich ....£20 *RN CvrsGpNFDC3-09*
(31) East Borough School ....£20 *EBorough Sch & PTA*
(32) South Cerney 999-1999 ....£40 *South Cerney PO*
(33) 617 Sqn Woodhall Spa ....£35 *Cam S.C.*
(34) Top Secret, Borehamwood .....£35 *Cam S.C.*
(35) Carry on Teacher, Ealing ....£35 *Cam S.C.*
(36) Compiegne, Whitehall ....£20 *Benham/JS Medal 7*
(37) York ....£20 *RAF(P&P19)*
(38) Total Eclipse, St. Just ....£35 *Bradbury*

C.D.S. POSTMARKS Price Guide £10-£15
(39) Egham, Salisbury, New Lanark or Newtown
(40) Manchester, Parliament Street, House of Commons
(41) Waterloo, Kielder

3rd August 1999 - SCIENTISTS' TALE

19p Decoding DNA, 26p Darwin's Theory, 44p Faraday's Electricity, 64p Newton.

SPECIAL HANDSTAMPS **SPONSOR**

Price Guide Ordinary Covers £4-£9 / Sponsored Covers:

(1) FDI - Bureau .... *Royal Mail (n.s.c.)*
(2) FDI - Cambridge .... *Royal Mail (n.s.c.)*
(3) -do- non pictorial version .... *Royal Mail (n.s.c.)*
(4) Scientists' Tale, Birmingham .... *Royal Mail (n.s.c.)*
(5) Scientists' Tale Glasgow .... *Royal Mail (n.s.c.)*
(6) Electricity, London SE1 .... £15 *Benham*
(7) Evoulution, Shrewsbury .... £20 *Benham Pilgrim*
(8) Space Observation .... £15 *Benham BLCS 163*
(9) Decoding DNA, Cambridge ... £15 *Benham BLCS 163*
(10) The Royal Society .... £20 *Benham 500(163)*
(11) Down House, Downe .... £20 *Benham Coin Mil.8*
(12) Battle Abbey .... £20 *Benham Eng.Heritage*
(13) Theory of Evolution, SW7 ...... £20 *Bradbury LFDC 173*
(14) Sir Isaac Newton .... £20 *Bradbury VP 135*
(15) Charles Darwin, SW7 .... £35 *Bradbury*
(16) The Hubble Telescope, SW7 . £45 *Bradbury*
(17) Festival of Medicine .... £35 *Bradbury for BMA*
(18) Royal Institution, London ...... £15 *Westminster*
(19) Autographed Newington .... £25 *Westminster*
(20) Jupiter Way, London N7 .... £30 *Steven Scott Plat.8*
(21) Moon Street, London N1 .... £20 *Steven Scott 33*
(22) Michael Faraday, Southwark . £25 *FourpennyPost*
(23) Charles Darwin, SW7 .... £25 *T Hurlstone*
(24) Sir Isaac Newton, Grantham . £25 *M Brazier (Pubs.8)*
(25) Turing Bombe, Bletchley .... £20 *Bletchley PO*
(26) Twining Ave, Middx .... £25 *P M Payne*
(27) Pierre & Marie Curie .... £25 *P M Payne*
(28) Faraday Way, London SE18 .. £20 *GB27*
(29) Jodrell Bank Macclesfield .... £20 *P Sheridan*
(30) Jodrell Bank Macclesfield .... £20 *P Barrett*
(31) Birmingham (microscope) ...... £20 *RN CvrsGpTDFC1-10*
(32) HMS Dauntless .... £20 *RN CvrsGpNFDC3-10*
(33) Lord of the Flies, Newquay .... £35 *Cam S.C.*
(34) The Mindbenders, Chelsea ..... £35 *Cam S.C.*
(35) Dr Jekyll & Sister Hyde .... £35 *Cam S.C.*
(36) Miramshah, Whitehall .... £20 *Benham/JS Medal 8*
(37) Total Eclipse, Falmouth .... £35 *Bradbury*
(38) Red Dwarf, London .... £25 *Steven Scott*

C.D.S. POSTMARKS Price Guide £10-£15

(39) Science Museum, Cambridge, Albermarle St., Teddington
(40) Faraday Avenue, Newton
(41) Colsterworth, Downe, Frankwell

11th August 1999 - TOTAL SOLAR ECLIPSE

£2.56 Miniature Sheet comprising 4 x 64p Scientists' Tale.

SPECIAL HANDSTAMPS **SPONSOR**

Price Guide Ordinary Covers £4-£9 / Sponsored Covers:

(1) FDI - Bureau .... *Royal Mail (n.s.c.)*
(2) FDI - Falmouth .... *Royal Mail (n.s.c.)*
(3) -do- non pictorial version .... *Royal Mail (n.s.c.)*
(4) Falmouth (oval) .... £15 *Benham BLCS 164*
(5) Falmouth (circle) .... £15 *Benham BLCS 164*
(6) Falmouth (circle) .... £30 *Ben500(164)*
(7) Falmouth (film strip) .... £30 *Benham Coin C46*
(8) Line of Totality, Falmouth ...... £25 *Bradbury*
(9) Line of Totality, Kingston .... £50 *Bradbury*
(10) Total Solar Eclipse .... £15 *Westminster*
(11) Autographed, Isles of Scilly ... £25 *Westminster*
(12) Falmouth (sun) .... £20 *P Barrett*
(13) Land's End, Penzance .... £20 *S Wales Collectables*
(14) Eclipse Road .... £20 *P M Payne*
(15) Walking on the Moon .... £20 *BritHerCollect*
(16) BAA Total Eclipse Truro .... *Cam S.C. (n.s.c.)*
(17) Jodrell Bank Macclesfield .... £25 *P Sheridan*
(18) Folland Midge, Hamble .... £25 *C Greaves*

C.D.S. POSTMARKS Price Guide £15-£20

(19) Falmouth, St. Ives, Greenwich, The Science Museum
(20) Shade, Blackshade

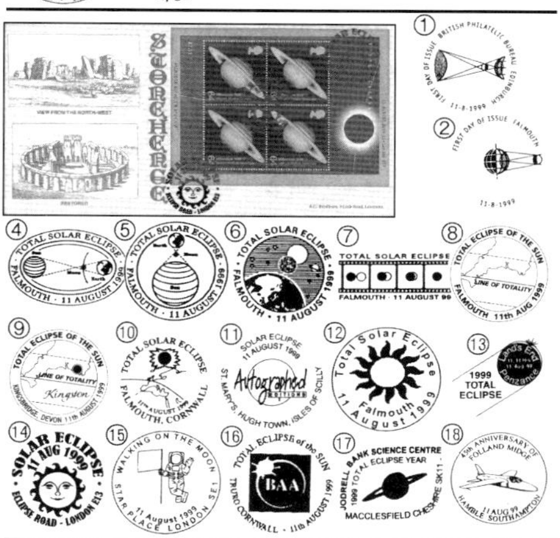

7th September 1999 - FARMERS' TALE

19p Strip Farming, 26p Mechanical Farming, 44p Food from afar, 64p Satellite Agriculture.

SPECIAL HANDSTAMPS **SPONSOR**

Price Guide Ordinary Covers £4-£9 / Sponsored Covers:

(1) FDI - Bureau .... *Royal Mail (n.s.c.)*
(2) FDI - Laxton, Newark .... *Royal Mail (n.s.c.)*
(3) -do- non pictorial version .... *Royal Mail (n.s.c.)*
(4) Bull Ring Centre, Birmingham ..... *Royal Mail (n.s.c.)*
(5) Farmers' Tale Glasgow .... *Royal Mail (n.s.c.)*
(6) Strip Farming, Laxton .... £15 *Benham BLCS 165*

(7) Mechanical Farming................£15 *Benham BLCS 165*
(8) Food from afar..........................£20 *Benham*
(9) Satellite Agriculture..................£20 *Benham Pilgrim*
(10) Sir Walter Raleigh/Potato......£20 *Benham 500(165)*
(11) The Changing Land, Laxton..£20 *Benham Coin Mil.9*
(12) English Heritage Kenilworth.£20 *Benham Eng.Heritage*
(13) Farmers, Stoneleigh.................£20 *Bradbury LFDC 174*
(14) Farmers, Sheepscombe............£20 *Bradbury VP 136*
(15) Robert Bakewell, Leicester.....£45 *Bradbury*
(16) NFU Shaftesbury Ave.............£15 *Westminster*
(17) Autographed Whitehall...........£25 *Westminster*
(18) Farm Lane London SW6........£20 *Steven Scott 34*
(19) King William Street, EC4.......£30 *Steven Scott Plat.9*
(20) Emmerdale, Esholt Shipley....£15 *Steven Scott*
(21) Jethro Tull, Reading.................£25 *FourpennyPost*
(22) Old Macdonalds Farm............£25 *T Hurlstone*
(23) The Farmers, Charlbury..........£25 *M Brazier (Pubs.9)*
(24) Farmers Road, London SE5..£25 *P M Payne*
(25) Farmer's Road London SE5..£20 *GB28*
(26) Congleton, Cheshire................£20 *P Sheridan*
(27) Farmer's Training.....................£20 *RN CvrsGpTDFC1-11*
(28) HMS Swiftsure..........................£20 *RN CvrsGpNFDC3-11*
(29) Spitfire, Biggin Hill..................£20 *BritHerCollect*
(30) Young Farmers.........................£25 *Ashford Stamp Shop*
(31) Eastry Sandwich.......................£25 *H D MacIntyre*
(32) Cowland Avenue, Enfield.......£25 *D Legg*
(33) Left, Right & Centre................£35 *Cam S.C.*
(34) The Elephant Man...................£35 *Cam S.C.*
(35) Arawazi, Whitehall..................£20 *Benham/JS Medal 9*
(36) Sikorski Museum.....................£40 *Gen Sikorski Museum*
(37) Total Eclipse, Falmouth..........£35 *Bradbury*

C.D.S. POSTMARKS Price Guide £10-£15

(38) Farmers, Bull Farm, Cattle Market, Wheatfield
(39) Isle of Grain, Savacentre, Laxton

5th October 1999 - SOLDIERS' TALE

19p Bannockburn, 26p Civil War,
44p World Wars, 64p Peace keeping.

SPECIAL HANDSTAMPS **SPONSOR**
Price Guide Ordinary Covers £4-£9 / Sponsored Covers:

(1) FDI - Bureau.................................. *Royal Mail (n.s.c.)*
(2) FDI - London SW.......................... *Royal Mail (n.s.c.)*
(3) -do- non pictorial version .... *Royal Mail (n.s.c.)*
(4) Soldiers' Tale, Birmingham........... *Royal Mail (n.s.c.)*
(5) Soldiers' Tales, Glasgow................ *Royal Mail (n.s.c.)*
(6) Scottish Independence............£20 *Benham Pilgrim*
(7) Civil War, Marston...................£15 *Benham BLCS 169*
(8) World Wars, Biggin Hill.........£20 *Benham*
(9) Peace Keeping, Whitehall........£15 *Benham BLCS 169*
(10) Battle of Bannockburn............£20 *Ben500(169)*
(11) Britain at War, Whitehall.......£25 *Benham Coin Mil.10*
(12) Carisbrooke..............................£20 *Benham Eng.Heritage*
(13) Soldiers, Sandhurst.................£20 *Bradbury LFDC 175*
(14) Soldiers, Whitehall..................£20 *Bradbury VP 137*
(15) Oliver Cromwell.......................£35 *Bradbury*
(16) Hastings Kent...........................£15 *Westminster*
(17) Autographed The Cenotaph...£25 *Westminster*
(18) Victory Way SE16....................£20 *Steven Scott 35*
(19) Battle Close SW19...................£30 *Steven Scott Plat.10*
(20) National Army Museum.........£15 *Steven Scott*
(21) Public Record Office, Kew.....£15 *Steven Scott*
(22) Lest We Forget, Whitehall.....£25 *FourpennyPost*
(23) Sir William Brereton, WC1....£25 *T Hurlstone*
(24) Oliver Cromwell.......................£35 *Cam S.C.*
(25) The Cenotaph...........................£35 *Cam S.C.*
(26) The Bold Dragoon...................£25 *M Brazier (Pubs.10)*
(27) Oxf. & Bucks Bletchley..........£15 *Bletchley PO*
(28) Russia Row, EC2......................£25 *P M Payne*
(29) Richard the Lionheart SW3...£25 *P M Payne*
(30) Cavalry Crescent, Hounslow.£15 *GB30*
(31) To Our Glorious Dead............£20 *P Sheridan*
(32) Robert the Bruce.....................£20 *RN CvrsGpTDFC1-13*
(33) HMS Aurora & Catterick.......£20 *RN CvrsGpNFDC3-13*
(34) Handley Page Halifax..............£20 *BritHerCollect*
(35) Achilles Close SE1...................£30 *M J Kingsland*
(36) Start of World War II...............£20 *Benham/JS Medal 10*
(37) Total Eclipse, Falmouth..........£40 *Bradbury*
(38) Clarity of Vision.......................£40 *Helio*
(39) Ice Cold In Alex, Elstree........£35 *Cam S.C.*

C.D.S. POSTMARKS Price Guide £10-£15

(40) Battle, The Barracks, Guardhouse, Wargrave
(41) Bannockburn, Aldershot, Naseby, Edgehill, Sandhurst
(42) Chelsea Royal Hospital, Sandhurst, Catterick Garrison

2nd November 1999 - CHRISTIANS' TALE

19p Wesley, 26p King James Bible,
44p St. Andrews Pilgrimage, 64p First Christmas.

SPECIAL HANDSTAMPS SPONSOR
Price Guide Ordinary Covers £4-£9 / Sponsored Covers:

(1) FDI - Bureau.................................... *Royal Mail (n.s.c.)*
(2) FDI - St. Andrews, Fife.................. *Royal Mail (n.s.c.)*
(3) -do- non pictorial version .... *Royal Mail (n.s.c.)*
(4) Christians' Tale, Birmingham....... *Royal Mail (n.s.c.)*
(5) Christians' Tales, Glasgow .... *Royal Mail (n.s.c.)*
(6) Methodism, Epworth...............£15 *Benham BLCS 170*
(7) Pilgrimage, St. Andrews...........£15 *Benham BLCS 170*
(8) First Christmas, Bethlehem....£20 *Benham Pilgrim*
(9) The Bible, Hampton Court .....£20 *Benham*
(10) King James Bible, Edinburgh.£20 *Benham 500(170)*
(11) Trafalgar Square ....£25 *Benham Coin Mil.11*
(12) Rievaulx Abbey ....£20 *Benham Eng.Heritage*
(13) 1999 Christmas, Bethlehem...£20 *Bradbury LFDC 176*
(14) 1999 Christmas, Nasareth ......£20 *Bradbury VP 138*
(15) John Wesley, Epworth.............£35 *Bradbury*
(16) Christians' Tale, Bethlehem ...£25 *Bradbury*
(17) Canterbury, Kent ....£15 *Westminster*
(18) Autographed, Canterbury ....£25 *Westminster*
(19) Jerusalem Passage, EC1 ....£20 *Steven Scott 36*
(20) Reform Street, SW11...............£30 *Steven Scott Plat.11*
(21) St. Andrew's Cathedral ....£25 *FourpennyPost*
(22) St. Andrew's Kaleidoscope.....£25 *T Hurlstone*
(23) St. Andrew's Fife ....£25 *T Hurlstone*
(24) Merchant's Assoc'n...................£25 *T Hurlstone*
(25) The Pilgrim's Progress.............£25 *M Brazier (Pubs.11)*
(26) Christians Code Bletchley......£20 *Bletchley PO*
(27) Christian St, London E1.........£25 *P M Payne*
(28) Christian St, London E1.........£15 *GB31*
(29) Cathedrals Liverpool ....£20 *P Sheridan*
(30) Christians' Tale, Bethlehem ...£20 *RN CvrsGpTDFC1-14*
(31) HMS Gloucester.........................£20 *RN CvrsGpNFDC3-15*
(32) Vickers Wellington ....£20 *BritHerCollect*
(33) John Wesley, Oxford ....£20 *P Barrett*
(34) Thomas Beckett.........................£30 *H D MacIntyre*
(35) Zionist Federation....................£40 *Zionist Federation*
(36) Happy Christmas, London............ *Royal Mail (n.s.c.)*
(37) Total Eclipse, Falmouth...........£35 *Bradbury*
(38) Laughter in Paradise, Elstree.£35 *Cam S.C.*
(39) Last Holiday, Elstree ....£35 *Cam S.C.*
(40) Guy Gibson, Woodhall Spa...£35 *Cam S.C.*
(41) Sinking of the Tirpitz ....£35 *Cam S.C.*
(42) Biggin Hill, Whitehall..............£20 *Benham/JS Medal 11*
(43) The Gunners Shot at Europe £20 *Dawn*
(44) Manchester Untd in Europe .£20 *Dawn*

C.D.S. POSTMARKS Price Guide £10-£15

(45) Holy Island, Nasareth, Angel Hill, St. Andrews
(46) Canterbury, Christchurch, Church, Epworth
(47) All Saints, All Hallows, Chapel Lane, Chapel Hill

7th December 1999 - ARTISTS' TALE

19p World of Stage, 26p World of Music,
44p World of Literature, 64p New Worlds.

SPECIAL HANDSTAMPS SPONSOR
Price Guide Ordinary Covers £4-£9 / Sponsored Covers:

(1) FDI - Bureau.................................... *Royal Mail (n.s.c.)*
(2) FDI - Stratford upon Avon........... *Royal Mail (n.s.c.)*
(3) -do- non pictorial version .... *Royal Mail (n.s.c.)*
(4) Artists' Tale, Birmingham............. *Royal Mail (n.s.c.)*
(5) Artists' Tales, Glasgow.................. *Royal Mail (n.s.c.)*
(6) The Stage, Stratford.................£15 *Benham BLCS 171*
(7) Music, Brook St, London W1 £20 *Benham*
(8) Literature, Portsmouth............£15 *Benham BLCS 171*
(9) New Worlds, Chelsea SW3.....£20 *Benham*
(10) Royal Academy of Music........£20 *Benham Coin Mil.12*
(11) George Frideric Handel...........£20 *Benham 500(171)*
(12) Eng. Heritage Stonehenge......£20 *Benham Eng.Heritage*
(13) William Shakespeare...............£20 *Bradbury LFDC 177*
(14) Glyndebourne, Lewes..............£20 *Bradbury VP 139*
(15) Charles Dickens, Rochester...£35 *Bradbury*
(16) Autographed, Gadshill ....£25 *Westminster*
(17) -do-, Royal Opera House........£25 *Westminster*
(18) Stratford-upon-Avon ....£15 *Westminster*
(19) Covent Garden, WC2..............£20 *Steven Scott 38*
(20) Handel Street, WC1.................£30 *Steven Scott Plat.12*
(21) Gary Hume at Whitechapel...£25 *T Hurlstone*
(22) Leicester Sq, Theatre Land ....£25 *T Hurlstone*
(23) DanceStorm North East.........£25 *FourpennyPost*
(24) The Charles Dickens................£25 *M Brazier (Pubs.12)*
(25) Bletchley Park Post Office .....£20 *Bletchley PO*
(26) 400th Anniv Van Dyck...........£25 *P M Payne*

(27) Guerin Square, London E3....£25 *P M Payne*
(28) Last Xmas of 20th Century....£25 *P M Payne*
(29) Painters Road, Ilford £20 *GB32*
(30) Philharmonic Hall....................£20 *P Sheridan*
(31) Artists' Tale London ....£20 *RN CvrsGpTDFC1-15*
(32) Cockleshell Raid, Helensb'h..£20 *RN CvrsGpNFDC3-14*
(33) Philatelic Music Circle ....£30 *Phil. Music Circle*
(34) Glyndebourne Opera...............£20 *P Barrett*
(35) Star Place, London SE1 ....£20 *D Legg*
(36) Total Eclipse, Falmouth..........£35 *Bradbury*
(37) 6.5 Special Shepherds Bush...£35 *Cam S.C.*
(38) Tobruk, Whitehall....................£20 *Benham/JS Medal 12*
(39) Merry Christmas, B'ham............... *Royal Mail (n.s.c.)*
(40) German U-Boats, Whitehall ..£20 *BritHerCollect*
(41) National Postal Museum ....£25 *Friends of NPM*
(42) Happy Christmas, London........... *Royal Mail (n.s.c.)*

C.D.S. POSTMARKS Price Guide £10-£15
(43) Ben Jonson Rd., Stratford-upon-Avon, Macduff
(44) Rochester, Theatre Square, The Galleries, Theatre
(45) Saltaire, Poets Field, Globe Road

14th Dec 1999 - MILLENNIUM TIMEKEEPER

4 x 64p Globes/Time ~ Miniature Sheet

SPECIAL HANDSTAMPS **SPONSOR**
Price Guide Ordinary Covers £4-£9 / Sponsored Covers:
(1) FDI - Bureau.................................... *Royal Mail (n.s.c.)*
(2) FDI - Greenwich............................ *Royal Mail (n.s.c.)*
(3) -do- non pictorial version .... *Royal Mail (n.s.c.)*
(4) London SW1 ....£15 *Benham BLCS 172*
(5) Edinburgh...................................£15 *Benham BLCS 172*
(6) Belfast..£20 *Benham*
(7) Cardiff ....£20 *Benham*
(8) Parliament Square. ....£20 *Benham*
(9) Greenwich ....£20 *Benham Coin 54*
(10) Greenwich ....£25 *Bradbury*
(11) Greenwich ....£25 *Bradbury*
(12) Stonehenge ....£25 *Bradbury*
(13) The Millennium Greenwich...£15 *Westminster*
(14) Autographed Greenwich ....£25 *Westminster*
(15) Millennium Dome...................£25 *T Hurlstone*
(16) Holy Cross Church ....£25 *M Brazier*
(17) Houses of Parliament ....£20 *P M Payne*
(18) Century Road, London E17...£20 *P M Payne*
(19) The Clock Tower, Chester......£20 *P Sheridan*
(20) East Grinstead Stamp Club....£20 *East Grinstead SC*
(21) 20th to 21st Century................£20 *RN CvrsGpTDFC1-16*
(22) Graf Spee Exeter ....£20 *RN CvrsGpNFDC3-16*
(23) Parliament Square....................£25 *Steven Scott*
(24) Last Stamp of Millennium .....£25 *J L Englert*
(25) Merry Christmas Birmingham...... *Royal Mail (n.s.c.)*
(26) Happy Christmas London............ *Royal Mail (n.s.c.)*

C.D.S. POSTMARKS Price Guide £15-£25
(27) Greenwich, Clockface or Clockhouse Parade

NB This Miniature Sheet was re-issued with a 'Stamp Show 2000' overprint on 1st March. Price with Stampex pmk £100

6th JAN 2000 - NEW MILLENNIUM

1st Class: Millennium Definitive

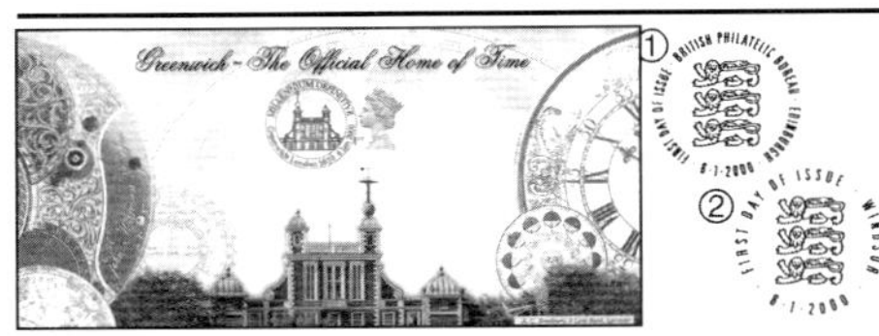

SPECIAL HANDSTAMPS **SPONSOR**
Price Guide Ordinary Covers £4-£9 / Sponsored Covers:
(1) FDI - Bureau.................................... *Royal Mail (n.s.c.)*
(2) FDI - Windsor .... *Royal Mail (n.s.c.)*
(3) -do- non pictorial version .... *Royal Mail (n.s.c.)*
(4) Royal Residences, Windsor.....£15 *Benham BLCS Sp7*
(5) Royal Residences, SW1...........£15 *Benham BLCS Sp7*
(6) -do- Sandringham.....................£20 *Benham D341*
(7) -do- Edinburgh..........................£20 *Benham*
(8) Greenwich (observatory).........£20 *Bradbury*
(9) Greenwich (sundial).................£15 *Bradbury*
(10) Stonehenge, Salisbury..............£15 *Bradbury*
(11) H M The Queen Mother ....£15 *Westminster*
(12) The Millennium, Greenwich...£15 *Westminster*
(13) Guns of Wembury, Plymouth.£15 *RN CvrsGp 4-01*
(14) French Stamp Anniversary .....£15 *P M Payne*
(15) Ladysmith, Whitehall...............£20 *Benham*

NB These stamps were also issued in stamp books - please see Definitive Section.

ORDINARY or SPONSORED COVERS - Do you know the difference?
Find out more by reading the General Notes at the beginning of this catalgoue.

PRICES & CONDITION
Values include VAT at the standard rate and are for clean unaddressed covers. PLEASE SEE THE GENERAL NOTES FOR MORE DETAILS

18th January 2000 - ABOVE & BEYOND

19p Owl Centre Muncaster, 26p Space Science Centre Leicester, 44p Torrs Walkway/New Mills, 64p Seabird Centre, North Berwick.

SPECIAL HANDSTAMPS **SPONSOR**

Price Guide Ordinary Covers £4-£9 / Sponsored Covers:

(1) FDI - Bureau .... *Royal Mail (n.s.c.)*
(2) FDI - Muncaster, Ravenglass .... *Royal Mail (n.s.c.)*
(3) -do- non pictorial version .... *Royal Mail (n.s.c.)*
(4) Above & Beyond, Birmingham.... *Royal Mail (n.s.c.)*
(5) Muncaster ....£15 *Benham BLCS 173*
(6) Leicester ....£15 *Benham BLCS 173*
(7) Matlock ....£20 *Benham Pilgrim*
(8) North Berwick ....£20 *Benham*
(9) Matlock ....£20 *Benham 500(173)*
(10) World of Birds, Sandy.............£20 *Benham Coin Mill.1*
(11) Muncaster Castle.....................£20 *CoverCraft*
(12) Bolsover Castle........................£20 *Benham Eng.Heritage*
(13) Muncaster ....£20 *Bradbury LFDC 179*
(14) North Berwick ....£20 *Bradbury VP 134*
(15) The Future is Now....................£20 *Bradbury*
(16) National Space Centre.............£25 *Bradbury*
(17) Scottish Seabird Centre ....£25 *Bradbury*
(18) The Millennium, Leicester .....£15 *Westminster*
(19) Autographed, RAF Cranwell..£25 *Westminster*
(20) Air Street, London W1 ....£30 *Steven Scott Plat.12*
(21) Bird Street, London W1 ....£20 *Steven Scott 38*
(22) Hawk & Owl Trust..................£25 *FourpennyPost*
(23) The Oadby Owl ....£25 *M Brazier (Pubs.13)*
(24) Flamingo Gardens, Northolt..£25 *P M Payne*
(25) Jupiter Way, London N7 ....£20 *GB33*
(26) Ullswater, Penrith....................£25 *P Sheridan*
(27) Walkway New Mills ....£25 *Derbyshire Council*
(28) North Berwick ....£20 *RN CvrsGpTDFC2-01*
(29) HMS Wilton..............................£20 *RN CvrsGpNFDC4-02*
(30) Death of Dickens, Rochester.£35 *Cam S.C.*
(31) Holly & Ivy, Shepperton........£35 *Cam S.C.*
(32) Zulu War, Whitehall................£20 *Benham/JS Medal 13*
(33) Operation Millennium ....£20 *Benham*
(34) Daleks Invasion Earth.............£35 *Cam S.C.*

C.D.S. POSTMARKS Price Guide £10-£15

(35) Owlsmoor, Ravenglass, Leicester, Macclesfield, Starcross
(36) New Mills, Greenwich, North Berwick

NB The 26p value was issued as a 1st Class NVI on 26th May ~ Please see page 142.

1st February 2000 - FIRE & LIGHT

19p Beacon Millennium, 26p Ffestiniog Railway, 44p Dynamic Earth, Edinburgh, 64p Croydon Skyline.

SPECIAL HANDSTAMPS **SPONSOR**

Price Guide Ordinary Covers £4-£9 / Sponsored Covers:

(1) FDI - Bureau .... *Royal Mail (n.s.c.)*
(2) FDI - Edinburgh.......................... *Royal Mail (n.s.c.)*
(3) -do- non pictorial version .... *Royal Mail (n.s.c.)*
(4) Birmingham.................................. *Royal Mail (n.s.c.)*
(5) Great Yarmouth ....£15 *Benham BLCS 174*
(6) Ffestiniog...................................£20 *Benham Pilgrim*
(7) Edinburgh ....£15 *Benham BLCS 174*
(8) Croydon.....................................£20 *Benham*
(9) Edinburgh ....£20 *Benham 500(174)*
(10) Welsh Mountain Rail ....£20 *Benham Coin Mill.2*
(11) Chiswick House........................£20 *Benham Eng.Heritage*
(12) King's Cross, London ....£20 *Bradbury LFDC 180*
(13) Victoria Station, London.........£20 *Bradbury VP 135*
(14) Porthmadog, Gwynedd ....£20 *Bradbury*
(15) The Millennium, Met Office ..£15 *Westminster*
(16) Autographed, Met Office........£25 *Westminster*
(17) Phoenix Place, WC1 ....£30 *Steven Scott Plat.13*
(18) Sunray Ave, London SE24.....£20 *Steven Scott 39*
(19) Our Dynamic Earth.................£20 *Steven Scott*
(20) Beacons, Great Yarmouth......£25 *FourpennyPost*
(21) Railwaymen's Armsh ....£20 *M Brazier (Pubs.14)*
(22) Jupiter Way, London N7 ....£20 *P M Payne*
(23) Railway Rise, London SE22 ..£15 *GB34*
(24) Bridge at Night, Widnes ....£20 *P Sheridan*
(25) Illuminations, Blackpool ....£20 *P Sheridan*
(26) Holyrood Park ....£20 *RN CvrsGpTDFC2-02*
(27) HMS Welshman ....£20 *RN CvrsGpNFDC4-03*
(28) Beacon Tower Bridge..............£20 *CoverCraft*
(29) Stealth Fighter..........................£20 *BritHerCollect*
(30) Limoges Aero-Engine..............£35 *Cam S.C.*
(31) Snowdon Mountain Railway .£20 *Dawn*
(32) Arakan Campaign, Whitehall £20 *Benham/JS Medal 14*

C.D.S. POSTMARKS Price Guide £10-£15

(33) Ffestiniog, Porthmadog, Croydon, Beacon, Thunder Lane
(34) Edinburgh, King's Cross, Caernarfon, Burnt Ash Lane

7th March 2000 - WATER & COAST

19p Durham Coast, 26p National Pondlife Liverpool, 44p Llanelli Coast, 64p Portsmouth Harbour.

SPECIAL HANDSTAMPS SPONSOR

Price Guide Ordinary Covers £4-£9 / Sponsored Covers:

(1) FDI - Bureau .... *Royal Mail (n.s.c.)*
(2) FDI - Llanelli .... *Royal Mail (n.s.c.)*
(3) -do- non pictorial version .... *Royal Mail (n.s.c.)*
(4) Birmingham .... *Royal Mail (n.s.c.)*
(5) Durham ....£15 *Benham BLCS 176*
(6) Liverpool ....£20 *Benham Pilgrim*
(7) Llanelli ....£15 *Benham BLCS 176*
(8) Portsmouth ....£20 *Benham*
(9) Liverpool ....£20 *Benham 500(176)*
(10) Maritime Portsmouth ....£20 *Benham Coin Mill.3*
(11) Eng. Heritage Stonehenge......£20 *Benham Eng.Heritage*
(12) Land's End, Penzance............£20 *Bradbury LFDC 181*
(13) Pondlife, Liverpool (frog).......£20 *Bradbury VP 136*
(14) Pondlife, Liverpool (lily).........£20 *Bradbury*
(15) Porstmouth Harbour 2000.....£25 *Bradbury*
(16) The Millennium, Portsmouth.£15 *Westminster*
(17) Autographed, Pembroke.........£25 *Westminster*
(18) Tideway Walk, SW8...............£30 *Steven Scott Plat.14*
(19) Pond Place, SW3....................£20 *Steven Scott 40*
(20) NEPA Durham ....£20 *FourpennyPost*
(21) The Mary Rose, Portsmouth..£20 *M Brazier (Pubs.15)*
(22) Ocean Street, London E1.......£25 *P M Payne*
(23) Puffin Close, Beckenham £20 *GB35*
(24) National Pondlife, Prescot.....£20 *P Sheridan*
(25) Turning the Tide, Durham.....£15 *CoverCraft*
(26) Water & Coast, Prescot..........£20 *RN CvrsGpTDFC2-03*
(27) HMS Wolverine.....................£20 *RN CvrsGpNFDC4-04*
(28) Bletchley Park Post Office.....£15 *Bletchley PO*
(29) Dover ....£30 *H D MacIntyre*
(30) Tidal Basin Road....................£30 *M J Kingsland*
(31) Doodle Bugs, Whitehall..........£20 *BritHerCollect*
(32) I Was Monty's Double...........£30 *Cam S.C.*
(33) Long, Short and the Tall........£30 *Cam S.C.*
(34) Hendon....................£20 *RAF(P&P19)*
(35) S.E.Asia Command ....£20 *Benham/JS Medal 15*

C.D.S. POSTMARKS Price Guide £10-£15

(36) Durham, Easington Colliery, Prescott, Llanelli, Portsmouth
(37) The Pond, Pathfinder Village, Waterbeach, Frogpool

4th April 2000 - LIFE & EARTH

2nd ECOS, Ballymena; 1st Web of Life, London Zoo, 44p Earth Centre, Doncaster; 64p Project SUZY Middlesbrough.

SPECIAL HANDSTAMPS SPONSOR

Price Guide Ordinary Covers £4-£9 / Sponsored Covers:

(1) FDI - Bureau .... *Royal Mail (n.s.c.)*
(2) FDI - Doncaster .... *Royal Mail (n.s.c.)*
(3) -do- non pictorial version .... *Royal Mail (n.s.c.)*
(4) Birmingham .... *Royal Mail (n.s.c.)*
(5) Ballymena ....£20 *Benham Pilgrim*
(6) London NW1 ....£15 *Benham BLCS 178*
(7) Doncaster ....£20 *Benham*
(8) Middlesbrough ....£15 *Benham BLCS 178*
(9) Regents Park....................£20 *Benham Coin Mill.4*
(10) Biodiversity, London NW1....£20 *Benham 500(178)*
(11) Brodsworth Hall....................£20 *Benham Eng.Heritage*
(12) Kew Gardens, Richmond ....£20 *Bradbury LFDC 182*
(13) Life & Earth, Ballymena.........£20 *Bradbury VP 137*
(14) Kew Gardens (rose)................£20 *Bradbury*
(15) ECOS, Ballymena....................£30 *Bradbury*
(16) 'SUZY' Middlesbrough ....£25 *Bradbury*
(17) The Millennium, Kew.............£15 *Westminster*
(18) Autographed, Earth Centre....£25 *Westminster*
(19) World's End Place, SW10......£20 *Steven Scott 41*
(20) Discovery Walk ....£30 *Steven Scott Plat.16*
(21) The Reptile Trust, Newcastle.£20 *FourpennyPost*
(22) The Spider's Web, Aberdeen .£20 *M Brazier (Pubs.16)*
(23) Regent's Park, London NW1.£20 *P M Payne*
(24) Frog Lane, West Malling........£15 *GB36*
(25) The Earth Centre, Doncaster.£15 *CoverCraft*
(26) Life & Earth, London ....£20 *RN CvrsGpTDFC2-04*
(27) NATO ....£20 *RN CvrsGpNFDC4-05*
(28) Ness Botanic Gdns, Neston...£20 *P Sheridan*
(29) Nightingale, London SW12...£20 *J & M Arlington*
(30) E. London's Natural Habitat.£25 *T Hurlstone*
(31) Supermarine Walrus...............£20 *BritHerCollect*
(32) Met. Police Philatelic Soc.......£20 *Bradbury*
(33) Blackburn....................£20 *RAF(P&P20)*
(34) Operation Shingle ....£20 *Benham/JS Medal 16*

A further seven handstamps were sponsored on this date to coincide with the issue of the commemorative label featuring

the Botanic Gardens of Wales ~ Please see definitive section.

C.D.S. POSTMARKS Price Guide £10-£15

(35) Acklam, Ballymena, Middlesbrough, Regents Park Road

(36) Doncaster, Primrose, Webheath

2nd May 2000 - ART & CRAFT

2nd Ceramica, Stoke; 1st Tate Modern;
45p Cycle Network Artworks; 65p The Lowry, Salford.

SPECIAL HANDSTAMPS		SPONSOR
Price Guide Ordinary Covers £4-£9 /		**Sponsored Covers:**
(1) FDI - Bureau		*Royal Mail (n.s.c.)*
(2) FDI - Salford		*Royal Mail (n.s.c.)*
(3) -do- non pictorial version		*Royal Mail (n.s.c.)*
(4) Birmingham		*Royal Mail (n.s.c.)*
(5) Stoke on Trent	£15	*Benham BLCS 180*
(6) London SE1	£20	*Benham Pilgrim*
(7) Bristol	£20	*Benham*
(8) Salford	£15	*Benham BLCS 180*
(9) Fine Art Painting	£20	*Benham Coin Mill.5*
(10) Mother town of Potteries	£20	*Benham 500(180)*
(11) Stokesay Castle	£20	*Benham Eng.Heritage*
(12) Art & Craft, Burslem	£20	*Bradbury LFDC 183*
(13) Art & Craft, St. Ives	£20	*Bradbury VP 138*
(14) Tower Bridge, London	£25	*Bradbury*
(15) Ceramica, Burslem	£25	*Bradbury*
(16) Tate Modern	£15	*Westminster*
(17) Autographed, Tate Modern	£25	*Westminster*
(18) Bankside, London SE1	£30	*Steven Scott Plat.17*
(19) Tranquil Passage, SE3	£20	*Steven Scott 42*
(20) Coronation Street	£15	*Steven Scott*
(21) L S Lowry in the N. East	£20	*FourpennyPost*
(22) The Wobbly Wheel	£20	*M Brazier (Pubs.17)*
(23) Turner, Temeraire St, SE16	£20	*P M Payne*
(24) Lowry Crescent, Mitcham	£15	*GB37*
(25) The Lowry, Salford	£15	*CoverCraft*
(26) Life & Earth, Salford	£20	*RN CvrsGpTDFC2-05*
(27) HMS Conqueror	£20	*RN CvrsGpNFDC4-06*
(28) The Lowry, Salford	£20	*P Sheridan*
(29) Art Centre of World	£25	*T Hurlstone*
(30) Gallery Road, SE21	£25	*M J Kingsland*
(31) British Midland/Lufthansa	£30	*Karl-Jurgen Schepers*
(32) B17 Football Loco	£25	*Dawn*
(33) Bunbury Cricket Club	£25	*Woodford Sports*
(34) Arundel Castle Cricket Club	£25	*Woodford Sports*
(35) Ripon	£20	*RAF(P&P21)*
(36) Operation Overlord	£20	*Benham/JS Medal 17*
(37) World WIZO Russell Sq	£40	*S Kacher*

C.D.S. POSTMARKS Price Guide £10-£15

(38) Salford, The Galleries, Raleigh, Dresden, Hanley, Barlaston

(39) Pottery Road, Stoke-on-Trent, Exchange Key (Salford).

22nd May 2000 - 'SMILERS' STAMPS

Miniature Sheet issued for the 'Stamp Show 2000' containing a reprinted version of the 1991 'Smiles' stamps and labels.

SPECIAL HANDSTAMPS		SPONSOR
Price Guide Ordinary Covers £4-£9 /		**Sponsored Covers:**
(1) The Stamp Show 2000, SW5		*Royal Mail (n.s.c.)*
(2) Art & Entertainment		*Royal Mail (n.s.c.)*
(3) Smilers, Stamp Show 2000	£20	*Benham (11 versions)*

Other handstamps were sponsored on this date to for the 'Artist's Palette' Souvenir Sheet. Please see Definitive Section.

23rd May 2000 - THE QUEEN'S STAMPS

Miniature Sheet issued for the 'Stamp Show 2000' containing a reprinted version of the 1/3d 1953 Coronation stamp with a £1 denomination plus 4 Millennium Definitive stamps.

SPECIAL HANDSTAMPS		SPONSOR
Price Guide Ordinary Covers £4-£9 /		**Sponsored Covers:**
(1) FDI - Bureau		*Royal Mail (n.s.c.)*
(2) FDI - Westminster		*Royal Mail (n.s.c.)*
(3) -do- non pictorial version		*Royal Mail (n.s.c.)*
(4) The Stamp Show 2000, SW5		*Royal Mail (n.s.c.)*
(5) Stamp Show - Royalty		*Royal Mail (n.s.c.)*
(6) New £1 Coronation Stamp	£25	*Bradbury*
(7) Stamp Show, Earl's Court	£20	*Benham BLCS 183*
(8) Stamp Show, Westminster	£20	*Benham BLCS 183*
(9) Stamp Show, Westminster	£20	*Benham*
(10) Coronation of Q. Elizabeth	£20	*Westminster*
(11) Lyceum Post Office	£25	*P Sheridan*
(12) Stamp Show Earl's Court	£25	*T Hurlstone*
(13) 160 Years Since First Stamp	£20	*P M Payne*
(14) The Penny Black, Bicester	£25	*M Brazier (Pubs.19)*
(15) Royal Horticultural Society	£35	*RHS*

C.D.S. POSTMARKS Price Guide £10-£15

(16) Balmoral, Buckingham Palace, Windsor Castle *(£150 each)*

(17) Windsor, Earls Court, Broadway

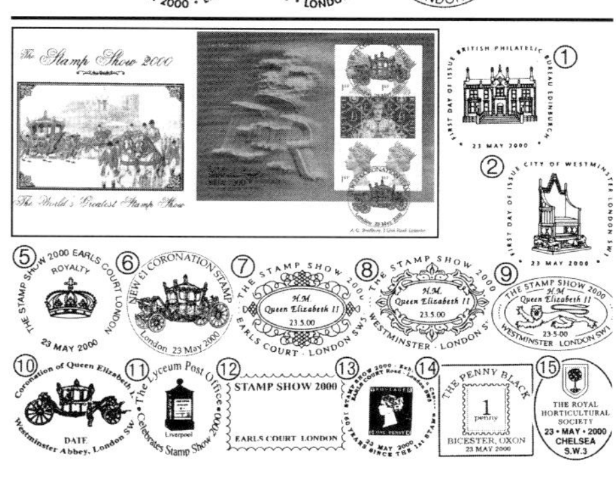

26th May 2000 - SPECIAL RETAIL BOOK

Se-tenant pair of 1st Class stamps: Space Science Centre (Above & Beyond); Web of Life, London Zoo (Life & Earth). The Space Centre stamp was previously issued as a 26p, making this 1st Class value a new stamp.

SPECIAL HANDSTAMPS SPONSOR
Price Guide Ordinary Covers £4-£9 / Sponsored Covers:

(1) FDI - Bureau .... *Royal Mail (n.s.c.)*
(2) FDI - Leicester.................................. *Royal Mail (n.s.c.)*
(3) -do- non pictorial version .... *Royal Mail (n.s.c.)*
(4) The Stamp Show 2000, SW5 .... *Royal Mail (n.s.c.)*
(5) Stamp Show - Technology........... *Royal Mail (n.s.c.)*
(6) Space Centre/London Zoo ....£15 *Bradbury*
(7) National SpaceCentre ....£20 *Bradbury*
(8) Space Leicester........................£20 *Benham*
(9) Above & Beyond, Space.........£15 *Benham BLCS 184*
(10) Life & Earth, NW1 ....£15 *Benham BLCS 184*
(11) Lyceum Post Office..................£20 *P Sheridan*
(12) Stamp Show Earl's Court.......£25 *T Hurlstone*
(13) deHaviland, Hatfield ....£25 *Cam S.C.*

6th June 2000 - PEOPLE & PLACE

2nd Millennium Greens; 1st Gateshead Millennium Bridge; 45p Mile End Park, London; 65p On the Line (Greenwich)

SPECIAL HANDSTAMPS SPONSOR
Price Guide Ordinary Covers £4-£9 / Sponsored Covers:

(1) FDI - Bureau.................................. *Royal Mail (n.s.c.)*
(2) FDI - Gateshead............................ *Royal Mail (n.s.c.)*
(3) -do- non pictorial version .... *Royal Mail (n.s.c.)*
(4) People & Place, Birmingham....... *Royal Mail (n.s.c.)*
(5) Birmingham...............................£15 *Benham BLCS 185*
(6) Gateshead ....£15 *Benham BLCS 185*
(7) London E14...............................£20 *Benham Pilgrim*
(8) Oxford.......................................£20 *Benham*
(9) Greenwich ....£20 *Benham 500(185)*
(10) Oxford.......................................£20 *Benham Coin Mill.6*
(11) Mt Grace Priory........................£20 *Benham Eng.Heritage*
(12) People & Place, London ....£20 *Bradbury LFDC 184*
(13) People & Place, Brighton.......£20 *Bradbury VP 139*
(14) Gateshead Millennium Bdge .£25 *Bradbury*
(15) Sponsored Scooter Trek ....£40 *Bradbury*
(16) Trafalgar Square ....£15 *Westminster*
(17) Autographed, Hyde Park........£25 *Westminster*
(18) Mile End Road, E1 ....£15 *Steven Scott 43*
(19) Meridian Road, SE7 ....£30 *Steven Scott Plat.18*
(20) We Shall Remember................£15 *Steven Scott*
(21) Gateshead Millennium Bdge .£20 *FourpennyPost*
(22) The Morris Man ....£20 *M Brazier (Pubs.18)*
(23) David Livingstone, E1.............£20 *P M Payne*
(24) All Souls Place, W1 ....£15 *GB38*
(25) Baltic Centre, Gateshead........£15 *CoverCraft*
(26) People & Place, Gateshead....£20 *RN CvrsGpTDFC2-06*
(27) Operation Neptune..................£20 *RN CvrsGpNFDC4-07*
(28) Community Centre Widnes....£20 *P Sheridan*
(29) Normandy Invasion.................£20 *BritHerCollect*
(30) Rowland Hill, Kidderminster.£15 *Assoc. of GBFDC*
(31) Bletchley Park..........................£15 *Bletchley PO*
(32) The Gilbert Collection ....£20 *T Hurlstone*
(33) Ramsgate ....£35 *H D MacIntyre*
(34) Old England XI, Hove ....£30 *Woodford Sports*
(35) Wistaston Jnr School...............£25 *M Wilson*
(36) Felixstowe ....£20 *RAF(P&P22)*
(37) V1 & V2 Assaults.....................£20 *Benham/JS Medal 18*

C.D.S. POSTMARKS Price Guide £10-£15

(38) Gateshead, Greenwich, Mile End, Meridian Centre
(39) Playing Place, Daisy Hill, The Green or similar

4th July 2000 - STONE & SOIL

2nd Strangford Stone, Killyleagh; 1st Trans-Pennine Trail; 45p Kingdom of Fife Cycleways; 65p Changing Places

SPECIAL HANDSTAMPS SPONSOR
Price Guide Ordinary Covers £4-£9 / Sponsored Covers:

(1) FDI - Bureau.................................. *Royal Mail (n.s.c.)*
(2) FDI - Killyleagh............................ *Royal Mail (n.s.c.)*
(3) -do- non pictorial version .... *Royal Mail (n.s.c.)*
(4) Birmingham.................................... *Royal Mail (n.s.c.)*
(5) Killyleagh ....£15 *Benham BLCS 186*
(6) Barnsley....................................£20 *Benham*
(7) Glenrothes ....£15 *Benham BLCS 186*
(8) Birmingham..............................£20 *Benham Pilgrim*
(9) Salisbury...................................£20 *Benham Coin Cover*
(10) Barnsley....................................£20 *Benham 500(186)*
(11) Pendennis Castle ....£20 *Benham Eng.Heritage*
(12) Stone & Soil, Barnsley............£20 *Bradbury LFDC 185*
(13) Stone & Soil, Stonehenge......£20 *Bradbury VP 140*

(14) Trans Pennine Trail .... £25 *Bradbury*
(15) Stonehenge .... £15 *Westminster*
(16) Autographed, Garden City ..... £25 *Westminster*
(17) The Plantation, SE1 .... £20 *Steven Scott 44*
(18) English Grounds, SE1 .... £30 *Steven Scott Plat.19*
(19) Long Distance Walkers .... £20 *FourpennyPost*
(20) The Rambler, Edale .... £20 *M Brazier (Pubs.20)*
(21) Rushmore Close, Bromley ...... £20 *P M Payne*
(22) Summer Olympics .... £20 *P M Payne*
(23) Stone £15 *GB39*
(24) Changing Places .... £15 *CoverCraft*
(25) Stone & Soil, Glenrothes .... £20 *RN CvrsGpTDFC2-07*
(26) HMS Foylebank, Portland ..... £20 *RN CvrsGpNFDC4-08*
(27) Ditton Brook, Widnes .... £25 *P Sheridan*
(28) Wimbledon Championships... £25 *Post Office Network*
(29) Wellington .... £20 *RAF(P&P23)*
(30) End of WWII, Whitehall .... £20 *Benham/JS Medal 19*

C.D.S. POSTMARKS Price Guide £10-£15
(31) Killyleagh, Strangford, Glenrothes, Kingdom Ctre, Southport
(32) Bluebell Hill, Stone, Stonesfield, Limestone Walk or similar

1st August 2000 – TREE & LEAF

2nd Yews for the Millennium; Eden Project, St. Austell; 45p Millennium Seed Bank, Kew; 65p Forest for Scotland

SPECIAL HANDSTAMPS — SPONSOR
Price Guide Ordinary Covers £4-£9 / Sponsored Covers:

(1) FDI - Bureau .... *Royal Mail (n.s.c.)*
(2) FDI - St. Austell .... *Royal Mail (n.s.c.)*
(3) -do- non pictorial version .... *Royal Mail (n.s.c.)*
(4) Birmingham .... *Royal Mail (n.s.c.)*
(5) London SW7 .... £20 *Benham Pilgrim*
(6) St. Austell .... £15 *Benham BLCS 187*
(7) Ardingley .... £20 *Benham*
(8) Glasgow .... £15 *Benham BLCS 187*
(9) Sherwood .... £20 *Benham Coin Cover*
(10) Glasgow .... £20 *Benham*
(11) Walmer Castle .... £20 *Benham Eng.Heritage*
(12) Kew (oak leaf) .... £20 *Bradbury LFDC 186*
(13) Kew (fern) .... £20 *Bradbury VP 141*
(14) Wistow, Leics .... £30 *Bradbury*
(15) Millennium Forest, Glasgow.. £25 *Bradbury*
(16) Caverswall Garden .... £20 *Bradbury*
(17) The Millennium, New Forest. £15 *Westminster*
(18) Autographed, New Forest ...... £25 *Westminster*
(19) Leafy Oak Road, SE12 .... £30 *Steven Scott Plat.20*
(20) Sycamore Gdns, W6 .... £20 *Steven Scott 45*
(21) Great North Forest .... £20 *FourpennyPost*
(22) Brave Old Oak, Towcester ..... £20 *M Brazier (Pubs.21)*
(23) Rhodes Avenue, N22 .... £20 *P M Payne*
(24) Isle of Pabay £15 *GB40*
(25) Yews for the Millennium .... £15 *CoverCraft*
(26) Tree & Leaf, St. Austell .... £20 *RN CvrsGpTDFC2-08*
(27) HMS Euryalus, Plymouth .... £20 *RN CvrsGpNFDC4-09*
(28) Mersey Forest, Widnes .... £20 *P Sheridan*
(29) Molash, Canterbury .... £25 *H D MacIntyre*
(30) Milton Keynes Philatelic Soc. £25 *M Brazier*
(31) Eden Project, St. Austell .... £15 *Mill.Com.Covers (s)*
(32) Stranraer .... £20 *RAF(P&P24)*
(33) HMS Amethyst, Whitehall ..... £20 *Benham/JS Medal 20*

C.D.S. POSTMARKS Price Guide £10-£15
(34) Ardingly, Kew, Kew Gardens, Eden, St. Austell, Yew Tree
(35) Woodlands Park, The Forest, Pinewoods - or similar

4th August 2000 – QUEEN MOTHER

Miniature Sheet celebrating the 100th Birthday of The Queen Mother, containing 4 x 27p stamps depicting HM The Queen, The Queen Mother, Prince Charles & Prince William

SPECIAL HANDSTAMPS — SPONSOR
Price Guide Ordinary Covers £4-£9 / Sponsored Covers:

(1) FDI - Bureau .... *Royal Mail (n.s.c.)*
(2) FDI - London SW1 .... *Royal Mail (n.s.c.)*
(3) -do- non pictorial version .... *Royal Mail (n.s.c.)*
(4) Clarence House .... *Royal Mail*
(5) The Queen Mother, SW1 .... £20 *Royal Mail/Royal Mint*
(6) Life of the Century, Glamis ... £20 *Royal Mail*
(7) Sandringham, Norfolk .... *Royal Mail (n.s.c.)*
(8) St. James's .... £15 *Benham BLCS 188*
(9) Westminster .... £15 *Benham BLCS 188*
(10) Castle of Mey .... £15 *Benham BLCS 188*
(11) Buckingham Pal Rd .... £15 *Benham BLCS 188*
(12) Hundreth Birthday, Hitchin .. £20 *Benham*
(13) The Mail on Sunday .... £20 *Benham*
(14) Grosvenor Gardens .... £20 *Benham*
(15) Glamis (lion) .... £25 *Benham Coin Cover*

(16) Cinque Ports, Dover ....£20 *Benham (Prestige Bk)*
(17) Cinque Ports, Hythe ....£20 *Benham (Prestige Bk)*
(18) Cinque Ports, Rye.....................£20 *Benham (Prestige Bk)*
(19) Cinque Ports, Walmer.............£20 *Benham (Prestige Bk)*
(20) Cinque Ports, Hastings............£20 *Benham*
(21) Ancestral Home, Glamis ....£15 *Bradbury LFDC 191*
(22) Clarence House ....£15 *Bradbury VP 146*
(23) St Paul's Walden ....£15 *Bradbury*
(24) Clarence House ....£15 *Bradbury*
(25) Windsor Berkshire ....£15 *Bradbury*
(26) 100 Years, Clarence House....£15 *Westminster*
(27) 100th Birthday, Glamis...........£15 *Westminster*
(28) Majesty, Buck Palace Rd........£15 *Steven Scott*
(29) Savoy Ct, Gilbert & Sullivan.£20 *Steven Scott*
(30) Queen of Hearts, Daventry....£20 *M Brazier (Pubs.22)*
(31) Clarence House, SW1 ....£20 *T Hurlstone*
(32) Windsor Castle ....£20 *T Hurlstone*
(33) Elizabeth Way...........................£20 *P M Payne*
(34) Queen Elizabeth's Drive.........£20 *P M Payne*
(35) Regal Way, Kenton £15 *GB41*
(36) Royal Naval Cvrs Plymouth...£20 *RN CvrsGpTDFC2-09*
(37) HMS Ark Royal, Rosyth.........£20 *RN CvrsGpNFDC4-10*
(38) Halton Celebrates, Widnes ....£20 *P Sheridan*
(39) Prince William of Wales.........£20 *BritHeritCollections*
(40) Moor House School Oxted....£20 *BritHeritCollections*
(41) Windsor.....................................£20 *BritHeritCollections*
(42) Wedgwood, Barlaston ....£20 *Mill.Commem.Covers*
(43) Raflet Stamp Club'...................£15 *Raflet Stamp Club*
(44) Colonel in Chief BF2611PS...£25 *Group Capt Randle*
(45) Colonel in Chief BF2612PS...£25 *Group Capt Randle*
(46) Colonel in Chief BF2613PS...£25 *Group Capt Randle*
(47) Colonel in Chief BF2614PS...£25 *Group Capt Randle*
(48) Colonel in Chief BF2615PS...£25 *Group Capt Randle*
(49) Colonel in Chief BF2616PS...£25 *Group Capt Randle*
(50) Colonel in Chief BF2617PS...£25 *Group Capt Randle*
(51) Colonel in Chief BF2618PS...£25 *Group Capt Randle*
(52) Internat'l Prisoners of War ....£15 *Steven Scott*
(53) Leonard Cheshire, Oxford ......£20 *Cam S.C.*
(54) Eden Project, St. Austell.........£20 *Mill.Commem.Covers*

C.D.S. POSTMARKS Price Guide £10-£15

(55) Buckingham Palace, Windsor Castle *(each £200)*
(56) Glamis, Mey, Bowes, Windsor, Clarence Road Windsor
(57) Whitwell, Windsor Great Park, Hundred House,

5th September 2000 - MIND & MATTER

2nd Wildscreen at - Bristol; 1st Norfolk & Norwich Project; 45p Millennium Point, Birmingham; 65p SCRAN Edinburgh.

SPECIAL HANDSTAMPS SPONSOR
Price Guide Ordinary Covers £4-£9 / Sponsored Covers:

(1) FDI - Bureau.................................. *Royal Mail (n.s.c.)*
(2) FDI - Norwich............................... *Royal Mail (n.s.c.)*
(3) -do- non pictorial version .... *Royal Mail (n.s.c.)*
(4) Mind & Matter, Birmingham....... *Royal Mail (n.s.c.)*
(5) millenniumpoint ....20 *Royal Mail/MCC*
(6) Bristol...15 *Benham BLCS 190*
(7) Norwich..15 *Benham BLCS 190*
(8) Birmingham ....20 *Benham*
(9) Edinburgh.....................................20 *Benham Pilgrim*
(10) Bristol..20 *Benham Coin Cover*
(11) Bristol..20 *Benham*
(12) Eng. Heritage, Kirby Hall ....20 *Benham Eng.Heritage*
(13) Edinburgh...................................20 *Bradbury LFDC 187*
(14) Birmingham ....15 *Bradbury VP 142*
(15) www.britishfirstdaycovers.........35 *Bradbury*
(16) www.millenniumpoint.org.uk ..25 *Bradbury*
(17) Birmingham ....15 *Westminster*
(18) Autographed ....25 *Westminster*
(19) Braintree Street, E2...................20 *Steven Scott 46*
(20) Ram Place, E9 ....30 *Steven Scott Plat.21*
(21) Norwich, Norfolk ....20 *FourpennyPost*
(22) The Boat Inn ....20 *M Brazier (Pubs.23)*
(23) Botticelli, Venus Rd SE18 ....20 *P M Payne*
(24) Bristol Rd, London E7 ....15 *GB41*
(25) Special Stamp @ Bristol............15 *CoverCraft*
(26) Mind & Matter, Bristol ....20 *RN CvrsGpTDFC2-09*
(27) HMS Endymion, Portsmouth ..20 *RN CvrsGpNFDC4-10*
(28) Halton Electronic, Widnes.......20 *P Sheridan*
(29) Friends of NPM EC1 ....15 *R. Pottle (postcards)*
(30) Imjin River, Whitehall...............20 *Benham/JS Medal 21*
(31) Leonard Cheshire, Oxford........30 *Cam S.C.*
(32) Pembroke BF 2609 PS ....20 *RAF(P&P25)*

A further seven handstamps were sponsored on this date to coincide with the issue of the fourth Retail Pane featuring a setenant pair of Trans-Pennine Trail & Eden Project stamps ~ Please see definitive section for details

C.D.S. POSTMARKS Price Guide £7-£10

(33) Birmingham, Bristol, Edinburgh, Norwich

3rd October 2000 - BODY & BONE

2nd Body/The Dome, Greenwich; 1st Hampden Pk, Glasgow; 45p Bath Spa; 65p Centre for Life, Newcastle.

SPECIAL HANDSTAMPS SPONSOR

Price Guide Ordinary Covers £4-£9 / Sponsored Covers:

(1)	FDI - Bureau		*Royal Mail (n.s.c.)*
(2)	FDI - Glasgow		*Royal Mail (n.s.c.)*
(3)	-do- non pictorial version		*Royal Mail (n.s.c.)*
(4)	Birmingham		*Royal Mail (n.s.c.)*
(5)	Greenwich	£15	*Benham BLCS 193*
(6)	Glasgow	£15	*Benham BLCS 193*
(7)	Bath	£20	*Benham*
(8)	Newcastle	£20	*Benham Pilgrim*
(9)	Bath	£20	*Benham Coin Cover*
(10)	Bath	£20	*Benham Coin Cover*
(11)	Cleeve Abbey	£20	*Benham Eng.Heritage*
(12)	Greenwich	£20	*Bradbury LFDC 188*
(13)	Greenwich	£15	*Bradbury VP 143*
(14)	Crystal Palace	£25	*Bradbury*
(15)	Bath's Spa Revival	£20	*Bradbury*
(16)	Hampden Stadium	£25	*Bradbury*
(17)	Sci & Nat History	£15	*Westminster*
(18)	Autographed, The Dome	£25	*Westminster*
(19)	Sportsbank St, SE6	£20	*Steven Scott 47*
(20)	Hands Walk, E16	£30	*Steven Scott Plat.22*
(21)	Life, Newcastle upon Tyne	£20	*FourpennyPost*
(22)	The Bath Tap, Bath	£20	*M Brazier (Pubs.24)*
(23)	Sir Francis Drake, E1	£20	*P M Payne*
(24)	Bath	£15	*GB42*
(25)	Prime Meridian Greenwich	£15	*CoverCraft*
(26)	Hampden Park	£20	*RN CvrsGpTDFC2-10*
(27)	HMS Kenya	£20	*RN CvrsGpNFDC4-11*
(28)	Total Body Fitness, Widnes	£20	*P Sheridan*
(29)	Oldest Body & Bone	£15	*Assoc. of GBFDC*
(30)	Football at Wembley	£20	*Dawn*
(31)	Kidderminster Harriers	£20	*Dawn*
(32)	City are Back! Manchester	£20	*Dawn*
(33)	Burnley are Back in Div.One	£20	*Dawn*
(34)	Charlton are Back, SE7	£20	*Dawn*
(35)	Any football permanent h/s	£20	*Dawn*
(36)	Kenya, 26th Anniversary	£20	*Benham/JS Medal 22*
(37)	Warwick	£20	*RAF(P&P26)*
(38)	Millennium Fair, Redhill	£25	*Redhill Philatelic Soc*
(39)	Polish Roman Catholic	£30	*J L Englert*
(40)	General Sikorski	£30	*J L Englert*
(41)	The Dome (changeable date)		*Royal Mail*

C.D.S. POSTMARKS Price Guide £10-£15

(42) Millennium Dome, Mount Florida Glasgow, Hampden Park

(43) Glasgow, Bath, Newcastle, Orthopeadic Hospital

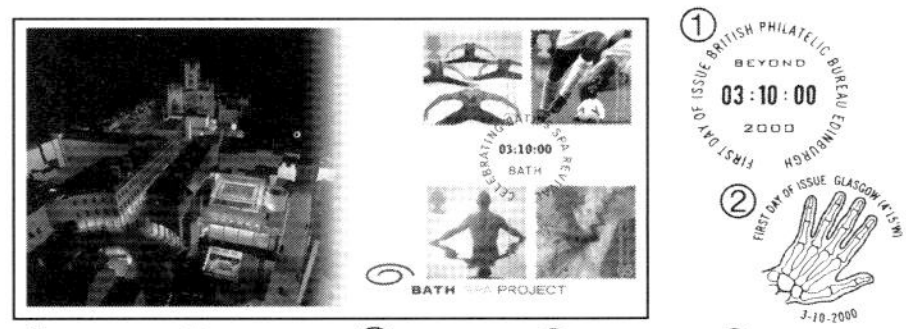

3rd October 2000 - CHRISTMAS Generic

The first Generic Customised Christmas stamps

A re-issue of the 1995 19p Robins Christmas stamp in sheets of 20 with labels & 1997 1st Class Crackers Christmas stamp in sheets of 10 with labels.

SPECIAL HANDSTAMPS SPONSOR

Price Guide Ordinary Covers £4-£9 / Sponsored Covers:

(1)	Bethlehem	£25	*Bradbury*
(2)	Hollybush	£15	*Benham BLCS 195*
(3)	Christmas Common	£15	*Benham BLCS 195*

These stamps were issued on the same day as the Body & Bone set. Therefore all of the Body & Bone handstamps (with the exception of the Bureau and Glasgow FDIs) were available for this issue. Conversely, the above three handstamps were also available for the Body & Bone issue.

7th November 2000 - SPIRIT & FAITH

2nd St. Edmundsbury Cathedral; 1st Church Floodlighting; 45p St. Patrick Ctre, Downpatrick; 65p Mystery Plays, York Minster

SPECIAL HANDSTAMPS SPONSOR

Price Guide Ordinary Covers £4-£9 / Sponsored Covers:

(1)	FDI - Bureau		*Royal Mail (n.s.c.)*
(2)	FDI - Downpatrick		*Royal Mail (n.s.c.)*
(3)	-do- non pictorial version		*Royal Mail (n.s.c.)*
(4)	Spirit & Faith, Birmingham		*Royal Mail (n.s.c.)*
(5)	Seasons Greetings Bethlehem		*Royal Mail (n.s.c.)*
(6)	Bury St Edmunds	£15	*Benham BLCS 194*
(7)	Walton-on-Thames	£20	*Benham Pilgrim*
(8)	Downpatrick	£15	*Benham BLCS 194*
(9)	York	£20	*Benham*

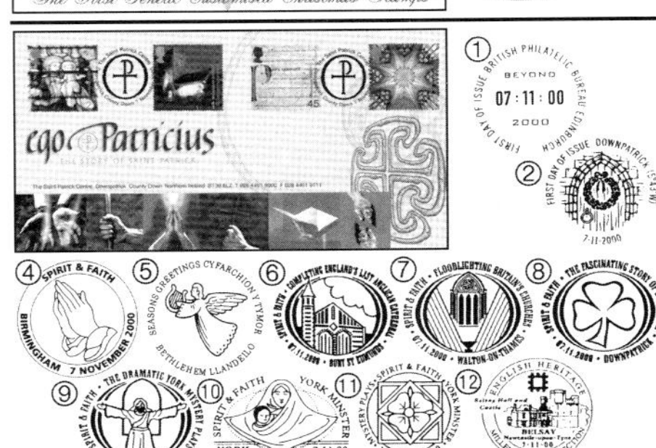

(10) York Minster ....£20 *Benham Coin Cover*
(11) Mystery Plays, York ....£20 *Benham*
(12) Belsay Hall................................£20 *Benham Eng.Heritage*
(13) Bethlehem.................................£20 *Bradbury LFDC 189*
(14) Nasareth ....£20 *Bradbury VP 144*
(15) The Saint Patrick Centre ....£30 *Bradbury*
(16) York Minster ....£15 *Westminster*
(17) Autographed, York Minster ...£25 *Westminster*
(18) Christian St, E1........................£20 *Steven Scott 48*
(19) Cathedral Place, EC4 ....£30 *Steven Scott Plat.23*
(20) Church Floodlighting ....£20 *FourpennyPost*
(21) The Minster Inn, York ....£20 *M Brazier (Pubs.25)*
(22) 1st Xmas/3rd Millennium .....£20 *P M Payne*
(23) Faith Street, Bolton.................£15 *GB43*
(24) St Edmunsbury Cathedral ......£15 *CoverCraft*
(25) Bletchley Park..........................£15 *Bletchley PO*
(26) Spirit & Faith, York ....£20 *RN CvrsGpTDFC2-11*
(27) HMS Fearless...........................£20 *RN CvrsGpNFDC4-12*
(28) Church Floodlighting ....£20 *P Sheridan*
(29) St Edmund, Greensted ....£25 *T Hurlstone*
(30) St Martins Hill, Canterbury ...£30 *H D MacIntyre*
(31) HMS Petard..............................£35 *Cam S.C.*
(32) Sinking of the Tirpitz ....£35 *Cam S.C.*
(33) Concorde, Test & Delivery ....£35 *Cam S.C.*
(34) 60th Anniv Battle of Britain ..£35 *Cam S.C.*
(35) Suez, 44th Anniversary ....£20 *Benham/JS Medal 23*
(36) London with SARO ....£20 *RAF(P&P27)*
(37) Friends of NPMuseum ....£25 *R G Pottle*

C.D.S. POSTMARKS Price Guide £10-£15
(38) Bury St. Edmunds, Nether Stowey, Downpatrick, York
(39) Holy Island, Angel Hill, St. Faith, Christchurch, Norwich

5th December 2000 - SOUND & VISION

2nd Ringing in the Millennium; 1st Year of the Artist; 45p Canolfan Mileniwm,Cardiff; 65p Talent & Skills 2000.

SPECIAL HANDSTAMPS SPONSOR
Price Guide Ordinary Covers £4-£9 / Sponsored Covers:
(1) FDI - Bureau .... *Royal Mail (n.s.c.)*
(2) FDI - Cardiff .... *Royal Mail (n.s.c.)*
(3) -do- non pictorial version .... *Royal Mail (n.s.c.)*
(4) Sound & Vision, Birmingham...... *Royal Mail (n.s.c.)*
(5) Seasons Greetings Bethlehem...... *Royal Mail (n.s.c.)*
(6) Merry Christmas, Birmingham..... *Royal Mail (n.s.c.)*
(7) Happy Christmas, London EC1 .. *Royal Mail (n.s.c.)*
(8) Loughborough..........................£20 *Benham*
(9) Sheffield.....................................£20 *Benham Pilgrim*
(10) Cardiff.......................................£15 *Benham BLCS 196*
(11) London NW5..........................£15 *Benham BLCS 196*
(12) London E1...............................£20 *Benham Coin Cover*
(13) Bridgwater ....£20 *Benham*
(14) Castle Acre...............................£20 *Benham Eng.Heritage*
(15) Shepherd's Bush.......................£20 *Bradbury LFDC 190*
(16) Shepherd's Bush.......................£15 *Bradbury VP 145*
(17) Taylor Bellfounders.................£25 *Bradbury*
(18) Royal Albert Hall ....£15 *Westminster*
(19) Autographed, Abbey Road .....£25 *Westminster*
(20) Ringmore Rise, SE23..............£20 *Steven Scott 49*
(21) Theatre Street, SW11 ....£30 *Steven Scott Plat.24*
(22) Music/Arts Gateshead ....£20 *FourpennyPost*
(23) The Five Bells, Bugbrooke .....£20 *M Brazier (Pubs.26)*
(24) Oxford Bell Ringers ....£25 *M Brazier*
(25) Telephone Place, SW6 ....£20 *P M Payne*
(26) Bell Street, NW1 ....£15 *GB44*
(27) Year of the Artist, Sheffield ...£15 *CoverCraft*
(28) Four Lads who..........................£15 *Assoc. of GBFDC*
(29) Sound & Vision, Cardiff.........£20 *RN CvrsGpTDFC2-12*
(30) Bickleigh Plymouth.................£20 *RN CvrsGpNFDC4-13*
(31) Chester Cathedral ....£20 *P Sheridan*
(32) Whitechapel Bell Foundry .....£30 *T Hurlstone*
(33) SunsetSunrise School.............£35 *J L Englert*
(34) Concorde, Test & Delivery ....£35 *Cam S.C.*
(35) 60th Anniv Battle of Britain ..£35 *Cam S.C.*
(36) Borneo 38th Anniversary.......£20 *Benham/JS Medal 23*

C.D.S. POSTMARKS Price Guide £10-£15
(37) Eye, The Galleries, Six Bells
(38) Loughborough, Sheffield, Cardiff, London

16th January 2001 - THE FUTURE

2nd Nuture Children (flower); 1st Listen to Children (tiger); 45p Teach Children (owl); 65p Children's Freedom (butterfly).

SPECIAL HANDSTAMPS SPONSOR
Price Guide Ordinary Covers £4-£9 / Sponsored Covers:
(1) FDI - Bureau .... *Royal Mail (n.s.c.)*
(2) FDI - Hope Valley .... *Royal Mail (n.s.c.)*
(3) -do- non pictorial version .... *Royal Mail (n.s.c.)*
(4) The Future, Birmingham .... *Royal Mail (n.s.c.)*

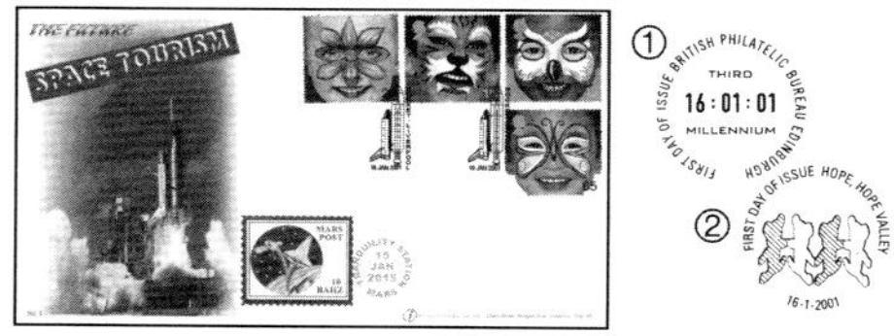

(5) Nuture Children ....£15 *Benham BLCS 197*
(6) Listen to Children ....£15 *Benham BLCS 197*
(7) Teach Children ....£20 *Benham*
(8) Children's Freedom ....£20 *Benham Pilgrim*
(9) A Child for the Future, N1.....£20 *Benham Coin Cover*
(10) The Earth's Children, N1 ....£20 *Benham*
(11) Savile Row, W1 ....£20 *Benham Eng.Heritage*
(12) Greenwich ....£15 *Bradbury Sovereign 1*
(13) Greenwich ....£20 *Bradbury Britannia 1*
(14) Millennium, Hope Park ....£15 *Westminster*
(15) Autographed, Hope Close ......£25 *Westminster*
(16) Hope Park, Bromley Kent ......£15 *Westminster*
(17) Child's Place, SW5..................£30 *Steven Scott Plat.25*
(18) Freedom Street, SW11 ....£20 *Steven Scott 50*
(19) Hope Primary School.............£20 *FourpennyPost*
(20) Pattishall Primary School.......£20 *M Brazier (Pubs.27)*
(21) Child's Place SW5 ....£20 *P M Payne*
(22) Butterfly Lane, Elstree............£15 *GB45*
(23) CHF, Gateshead ....£15 *CoverCraft*
(24) Hope for the Future, Hope ....£15 *RN CvrsGpTDFC2-13*
(25) HMS Porpoise, Gosport ....£15 *RN CvrsGpNFDC4-14*
(26) Rocket, Liverpool.....................£20 *Buckingham Cvrs 1*
(27) The Future, Salisbury ....£20 *P Sheridan*
(28) Greenwich ....£25 *T Hurlstone*
(29) Iona Post Office 150 Anniv ...£20 *Royal Mail*
(30) South Georgia, Falkland Is ....£20 *Benham/JS Medal 24*
(31) Duxford, Cambridge ....£20 *BritHerCollections*

C.D.S. POSTMARKS Price Guide £10-£15

(32) Hope, Playing Place, Child's Hill, Child Okeford
(33) High Holborn (UNICEF)

The Future finishes the Millennium Issues

6th February 2001 - OCCASIONS

5 x 1st Class: New Baby, Love, Cheers, Thanks & Welcome.

SPECIAL HANDSTAMPS SPONSOR
Price Guide Ordinary Covers £4-£9 / Sponsored Covers:

(1) FDI - Bureau .... *Royal Mail (n.s.c.)*
(2) FDI - Merry Hill............................ *Royal Mail (n.s.c.)*
(3) -do- non pictorial version .... *Royal Mail (n.s.c.)*
(4) Occasions, Birmingham................ *Royal Mail (n.s.c.)*
(5) Childrey Wantage.....................£15 *Benham BLCS 199*
(6) Greet Birmingham ....£15 *Benham BLCS 199*
(7) Lover Salisbury.........................£20 *Benham*
(8) Thankerton Biggar ....£20 *Benham Pilgrim*
(9) Welcombe Bideford ....£20 *Benham*
(10) Greet Cheltenham....................£20 *Benham Coin Cover*
(11) Occasions..................................£20 *Benham 500(199)*
(12) Gretna Green ....£20 *Bradbury Windsor 3*
(13) Autographed, Merryfield.........£25 *Westminster*
(14) Smiles Place, SE13..................£15 *Westminster*
(15) The Silver Jubilee ....£15 *M Brazier (Pubs.28)*
(16) Silver Street, London £15 *GB47*
(17) Lover Salisbury Wilts ....£15 *Buckingham Cvrs 2*
(18) N.I. Tourist Board ....£20 *P Sheridan*
(19) Hatton Garden ....£20 *T Hurlstone*
(20) Friends of NPMuseum ....£15 *NPM(postcard issue)*
(21) Boscombe Down ....£20 *BritHerCollections*

C.D.S. POSTMARKS Price Guide £10-£15

(22) Lover, Silver Link

13th February 2001 - CATS & DOGS

10 x 1st Class: Black & white photographic images.

SPECIAL HANDSTAMPS SPONSOR
Price Guide Ordinary Covers £4-£9 / Sponsored Covers:

(1) FDI - Bureau .... *Royal Mail (n.s.c.)*
(2) FDI - Petts Wood........................... *Royal Mail (n.s.c.)*
(3) -do- non pictorial version .... *Royal Mail (n.s.c.)*
(4) Cats & Dogs, Birmingham............ *Royal Mail (n.s.c.)*
(5) Catshill, Bromsgrove ....£15 *Benham BLCS 200*
(6) Kittywell Braunton...................£20 *Benham Pilgrim*
(7) Catsfield, Battle........................£20 *Benham*
(8) Catstree Bridgnorth ....£20 *Benham D372*
(9) Pant, Oswestry ....£15 *Benham BLCS 200*
(10) Dog Little, Enniskillen............£20 *Benham Pilgrim*
(11) Dog Big, Enniskillen................£20 *Benham*
(12) Bonehill, Tamworth.................£20 *Benham*
(13) Barking, Ipswich......................£20 *Benham Pilgrim*
(14) Pawlett, Bridgwater..................£20 *Benham Coin Cover*
(15) Cats Protection, Horsham ......£20 *Benham Pilgrim*
(16) Pett, Hastings ....£20 *Benham (500)200*
(17) Isle of Dogs..............................£15 *Bradbury Sovereign 2*
(18) Catshill......................................£15 *Bradbury Britannia 2*
(19) Battersea, London SW8..........£15 *Westminster*
(20) Autographed, Battersea..........£20 *Westminster*
(21) Battersea Sq, SW11 ....£15 *Steven Scott 51*
(22) The Greyhound........................£20 *M Brazier (Pubs.29)*

(23) Cat Hill, Barnet Herts £15 *GB48*
(24) Our Dogs Manchester ....£15 *CoverCraft*
(25) Cats Ash, Newport ....£15 *Buckingham Cvrs 4*
(26) Black Dog, Crediton ....£15 *Buckingham Cvrs 4*
(27) PDSA Huyton, Liverpool ....£20 *P Sheridan*
(28) Your dog, Isle of Dogs ....£25 *T Hurlstone*
(29) Your cat, Catford.....................£25 *T Hurlstone*
(30) Celia Hammond Trust.............£25 *T Hurlstone*
(31) Lawton & Stokes ....£25 *T Hurlstone*
(32) The Shackleton........................£20 *BritHerCollections*
(33) Biggin Hill, Westerham...........£20 *BritHerCollections*

C.D.S. POSTMARKS Price Guide £10-£15

(34) Battersea, Dog & Gun, Isle of Dogs, Dog Kennel Lane
(35) Catsfield, Catshill, Barking, Terriers, Pett, Horsham

These self-adhesive stamps were issued in books of 10 1st Class stamps. Additionally they were also issued in a booklet of 12 1st class stamps: the 10 Cats & Dogs stamps plus 2 Definitives - price range £7 - £10.

13th March 2001 - THE WEATHER

19p Rain; 27p Fair; 45p Stormy; 65p Very Dry/Set Fair.
Set of Stamps & Miniature Sheet issued on same date.

SPECIAL HANDSTAMPS SPONSOR
Price Guide Ordinary Covers £4-£9 / Sponsored Covers:

(1) FDI - Bureau .... *Royal Mail (n.s.c.)*
(2) FDI - Fraserburgh .... *Royal Mail (n.s.c.)*
(3) -do- non pictorial version .... *Royal Mail (n.s.c.)*
(4) The Weather, Birmingham............ *Royal Mail (n.s.c.)*
(5) Rainy Weather, Bracknell ......£20 *Benham Coin Cover*
(6) Fair Weather, Fair Isle ....£20 *Benham Pilgrim*
(7) Stormy Weather, Oxford ....£20 *Benham 500(202)*
(8) Dry Weather, Reading.............£20 *Benham 500(202)*
(9) First Weather Map ....£20 *Benham Coin Cover*
(10) The Weather, Bracknell..........£20 *Benham 500(203)*
(11) First Weather Map...................£20 *Benham 500(203)*
(12) Wild Weather, Exton S'ton....£15 *Benham BLCS 203*
(13) Wild Weather, Eastbourne.....£15 *Benham BLCS 203*
(14) RSPB Hope Farm.....................£20 *Benham*
(15) Windygages...............................£15 *Bradbury Sovereign 3*
(16) 150 Years Progress Reading...£20 *Bradbury Sovereign 3*
(17) Snowshill...................................£15 *Bradbury Britannia 3*
(18) Sunnyside..................................£15 *Bradbury Windsor 2*
(19) Autographed, Sunny Cresc.....£15 *Westminster*
(20) Weatherley Close, E3 ....£15 *Steven Scott 52*
(21) Weather Cock ....£20 *M Brazier (Pubs.30)*
(22) Sunbeam Rd, NW10................£15 *GB48*
(23) Planting for Future, Uckfield .£15 *Buckingham Cvrs 5*
(24) Scottish Wildlife Trust.............£15 *CoverCraft*
(25) Windyridge Close, SW19........£20 *P M Payne*
(26) 150 Years Weather Charts .....£15 *Dawn*
(27) British Weather London.........£10 *Assoc. of GBFDC*
(28) London's Maritime Borough .£20 *T Hurlstone*
(29) The Weather, Bracknell..........£15 *RN CvrsGp*
(30) Capt Walker Liverpool ....£15 *RN CvrsGp*
(31) Manchester Weather Centre..£15 *P Sheridan*
(32) Exmouth Stamp Club.............£20 *Exmouth Stamp Club*
(33) Old England XI St Albans .....£20 *Woodford Sports*
(34) Grosvenor Square, W1...........£15 *BritHerCollections*
(35) Jade Crossing Fund..................£35 *Jade Crossing Fund*
(36) Gulf War, Kuwait Whitehall..£15 *Benham/JS Medal 25*
(33) Biggin Hill, Westerham..........£15 *BritHerCollections*

C.D.S. POSTMARKS Price Guide £10-£15

(34) Bracknell, Fair Isle, Sunnybrow, Windygates, Sunnyhill
(35) Puddletown, Windwhistle, Thunder Lane, Freezy Water
(36) Frazerburgh, Fog Lane, Gale Street, Rainhill - or similar

10th April 2001 - SUBMARINES

2nd Vanguard Class; 1st Swiftsure Class;
45p Unity Class; 65p Holland Class

SPECIAL HANDSTAMPS SPONSOR
Price Guide Ordinary Covers £4-£9 / Sponsored Covers:

(1) FDI - Bureau .... *Royal Mail (n.s.c.)*
(2) FDI - Portsmouth.......................... *Royal Mail (n.s.c.)*
(3) -do- non pictorial version .... *Royal Mail (n.s.c.)*
(4) Submarines, Birmingham.............. *Royal Mail (n.s.c.)*
(5) Vanguard, Plymouth................£15 *Benham BLCS 204*
(6) Swiftsure, Faslane....................£15 *Benham BLCS 204*
(7) Barrow-in-Furness (circle) .....£20 *Benham Coin Cover*
(8) Barrow-in-Furness (oval)........£25 *Benham 500(204)*
(9) Centenary, Portsmouth ....£20 *Benham Coin Cover*
(10) Centenary, Barrow...................£20 *Benham*
(11) HMS Conquerors.....................£20 *Bradbury Sovereign 4*
(12) Nemo & the Nautilus.............£15 *Bradbury Britannia 4*
(13) Submarines, Portsmouth.........£15 *Westminster*
(14) Submarines, Portsmouth.........£15 *Westminster*
(15) Autographed, Portsmouth ......£25 *Westminster*

(16) Ocean Street, E1 ....£15 *Steven Scott 53*
(17) The Nautilus, North Shields ..£20 *M Brazier (Pubs.31)*
(18) Target Close, Feltham..............£15 *GB50*
(19) RN Submarine Museum ....£15 *Buckingham Cvrs 6*
(20) Inst. of Marine Engineers.......£15 *CoverCraft*
(21) 20,000 Leagues Under Sea.....£20 *P M Payne*
(22) RN Submarine Service............£15 *RN CvrsGp*
(23) HM Sub Spearfish....................£15 *RN CvrsGp*
(24) Dock Road Birkenhead ....£15 *P Sheridan*
(25) Enigma Code Breakers ....£10 *Bletchley PO*
(26) Centenary Dover ....£25 *H D McIntyre*
(27) Dive! Dive! Dive! Devonport.£25 *R G Howe*
(28) Cody War Kite BF2624PS......£15 *Group Capt Randle*
(29) Capture of Badajoz ....£20 *Benham/JS Medal 26*
(30) Mountbatten Plymouth ....£20 *BritHerCollections*
(31) Gosport (changeable date).....£15 *RN CvrsGp*
(32) Faslane (changeable date)......£15 *RN CvrsGp*
(33) Vickerstown Barrow................£30 *Cam S.C.*
(34) BF 2628 PS RN Sub Service .... *British Forces (n.s.c.)*
(35) BF 2630 PS Bureau .... *British Forces (n.s.c.)*
C.D.S. POSTMARKS Price Guide £10-£15
(36) Clyde Submarine Base, Barrow in Furness, Clydebank,
(37) Drake Barracks, Gosport, Devonport, Holland on Sea

PLEASE READ THE GENERAL NOTES

17th April 2001 - SUBMARINES Self Adhesive

1st Swiftsure Class (x2) issued in self-adhesive stamp book with four 1st Class definitives

SPECIAL HANDSTAMPS SPONSOR
Price Guide Ordinary Covers £4-£9 / Sponsored Covers:
(1) Barrow-in-Furness ....£40 *Bradbury Sovereign 4*
(2) Barrow-in-Furness ....£30 *Benham BLCS 205*
(3) Gosport.......................................£35 *Benham*
(4) Chatham Kent...........................£30 *Benham BLCS 205*
(5) H M Submarine Affray ....£30 *RN CvrsGp*
(6) Gosport (changeable date)........... *RN CvrsGp* (n.s.c.)*
(7) Faslane (changeable date)............ *RN CvrsGp* (n.s.c.)*
(8) Vickerstown Barrow..................£30 *Cam S.C.**
** Postmark same design as for the 10th April issue.*
C.D.S. POSTMARKS Price Guide £10-£15
(9) Barrow in Furness

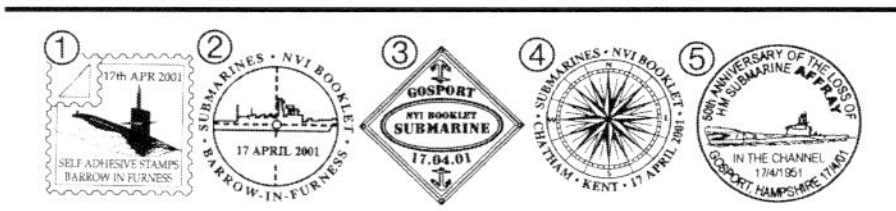

15th May 2001 - BUSES

5 x 1st Class featuring Classic Double-Decker Buses
Set of Stamps & Miniature Sheet issued on same date.

SPECIAL HANDSTAMPS SPONSOR
Price Guide Ordinary Covers £4-£9 / Sponsored Covers:
(1) FDI - Bureau.................................... *Royal Mail (n.s.c.)*
(2) FDI - London WC2........................ *Royal Mail (n.s.c.)*
(3) -do- non pictorial version .... *Royal Mail (n.s.c.)*
(4) Double-Deckers, Birmingham...... *Royal Mail (n.s.c.)*
(5) Double-Deckers, Southall ......£15 *Benham BLCS 207*
(6) Double-Deckers, Guildford....£20 *Benham Pilgrim*
(7) Double-Deckers, Bristol ....£15 *Benham BLCS 208*
(8) Double-Deckers, W4 ....£15 *Benham BLCS 207*
(9) Double-Deckers, E4.................£15 *Benham BLCS 208*
(10) Double-Deckers, WC2 ....£20 *Benham 500(208)*
(11) Stop Here, London SW1........£20 *Benham 500(207)*
(12) Transportation ....£20 *Benham Coin Cover*
(13) Leyland, Lancashire.................£20 *Bradbury Britannia 5*
(14) Leyland, Lancs..........................£20 *Bradbury Sovereign 5*
(15) Westminster, London..............£20 *Bradbury Windsor 5*
(16) Victoria, London ....£15 *Westminster*
(17) Autographed, Victoria.............£25 *Westminster*
(18) Oxford Street, W1....................£15 *Steven Scott 54*
(19) London's Transport Museum £15 *Steven Scott*
(20) Stagecoach, Perth.....................£15 *M Brazier (Pubs.32)*
(21) Piccadilly Circus, W1 ....£15 *GB51*
(22) Buses, Bus Magazine...............£15 *Buckingham Cvrs 7*
(23) Classic Bus, Edinburgh ....£20 *CoverCraft*
(24) British Buses, London.............£15 *Assoc. of GBFDC*
(25) British Buses, Tuckingmill......£15 *RN CvrsGp*
(26) HMS/m Sickle ....£15 *RN CvrsGp*
(27) British Bus Archives, Bury.....£20 *P Sheridan*
(28) Electric Trams, Croydon.........£15 *Dawn*
(29) Electric Trams, Manchester ...£15 *Dawn*
(30) Manchester & Salford.............£15 *Dawn*
(31) Covent Garden ....£25 *T Hurlstone*
(32) TransBus International ....£10 *Bletchley PO*
(33) Code Breakers...........................£10 *Bletchley PO*
(34) Double Deckers, Victoria ....£30 *M J Kingsland*
(35) Buses of East Kent...................£20 *P J Barrett*
(36) Last Stand at Gandamak........£20 *Group Capt Randle*
(37) Red Arrows, Cranwell.............£20 *BritHerCollections*
C.D.S. POSTMARKS Price Guide £10-£15
(38) Leyland, Paddington, Victoria St, Tuckingmill, Coach Rd
(39) Terminus Rd, Trafford Park, Herne Bay *etc*

5th June 2001 - OCCASIONS Generic Issue

A re-issue of the February 2001 Occasions stamps issued in sheets of 20 1st Class stamps with labels attached: New Baby, Love, Cheers, Thanks & Welcome. These were also issued on 1st May with Customised Labels - Prices £10 - £15.

SPECIAL HANDSTAMPS SPONSOR
Price Guide Ordinary Covers £4-£9 / Sponsored Covers:
(1) Letters Lochbroom ....£20 *Benham*
(2) Lover Salisbury.........................£30 *Bradbury*
C.D.S. POSTMARKS Price Guide £10-£15
(3) Silverstone, Silverdale, Silver Street

19th June 2001 - FABULOUS HATS

Hats by the following designers: 1st Pip Hackett; 'E' Dai Rees; 45p Stephen Jones; 65p Philip Treacy.

SPECIAL HANDSTAMPS SPONSOR
Price Guide Ordinary Covers £4-£9 / Sponsored Covers:
(1) FDI - Tallents House...................... *Royal Mail (n.s.c.)*
(2) FDI - Ascot....................................... *Royal Mail (n.s.c.)*
(3) -do- non pictorial version .... *Royal Mail (n.s.c.)*
(4) Fabulous Hats, Birmingham......... *Royal Mail (n.s.c.)*
(5) Blackstock Road, N5...............£20 *Benham*
(6) Belgravia, SW1 ....£15 *Benham BLCS 209*
(7) Gt. Western Road, W9............£20 *Benham Pilgrim*
(8) Great Queen Street, WC2......£15 *Benham BLCS 209*
(9) Hat & Mitre Court, EC1 ....£20 *Benham 500(209)*
(10) Ascot ....£20 *Benham Coin Cover*
(11) Ascot Berks................................£15 *Bradbury Sovereign 6*
(12) Ascot Berkshire ....£15 *Bradbury Britannia 6*
(13) Ascot Berkshire ....£15 *Westminster*
(14) Autographed, Ascot ....£25 *Westminster*
(15) Hat & Mitre Court, EC1 ....£15 *Steven Scott 55*
(16) The Boater, Luton Beds..........£20 *M Brazier (Pubs.33)*
(17) Hatters Lane.............................£15 *GB52*
(18) Royal Ascot Ladies Day...........£15 *Buckingham Cvrs 9*
(19) British Hat Guild, Luton ....£25 *CoverCraft*
(20) Fabulous Hats, Stockport.......£15 *RN CvrsGp*
(21) Falkland Islands ....£15 *RN CvrsGp*
(22) Hat Works, Stockport.............£20 *P Sheridan*
(23) Fabulous Hats Carnaby St .....£25 *T Hurlstone*
(24) Wimbledon, London SW1 .....£20 *P M Payne*
(25) Derby Street, London W1......£30 *M J Kingsland*
(26) Civil Defence Memorial...........£30 *C J Young*
(27) Bunbury Cricket Club ....£25 *Woodford Sports*
(28) Capture of Chuenpee ....£20 *Benham*
(29) Debden, Cambridgeshire ....£20 *BritHerCollections*
(30) Carrickfergus ....£50 *Consignia*
C.D.S. POSTMARKS Price Guide £10-£15
(31) Ascot, Luton, Carnaby Street, Silk Street, Busby
(32) Hatt, Hatfield, Hatton, Top o' the Brow

3rd July 2001 - 'SMILERS' Generic Issue

Reprinted version of the Miniature Sheet issued for the Stamp Show 2000 'Smilers' stamps plus revised label designs.

SPECIAL HANDSTAMPS SPONSOR
Price Guide Ordinary Covers £4-£9 / Sponsored Covers:
(1) Smile with Mr Punch ....£30 *Bradbury*
(2) Smilers Greetwell Lincoln......£20 *Benham*
(3) Wimbledon Championships...£25 *Paul Inwood (pair)*

10th July 2001 - PONDLIFE

1st Common Frong; 'E' Great Diving Beetle; 45p Stickleback; 65p Dragonfly.

SPECIAL HANDSTAMPS SPONSOR
Price Guide Ordinary Covers £4-£9 / Sponsored Covers:
(1) FDI - Tallents House...................... *Royal Mail (n.s.c.)*
(2) FDI - Oundle, Peterborough .... *Royal Mail (n.s.c.)*
(3) -do- non pictorial version .... *Royal Mail (n.s.c.)*
(4) Pondlife, Birmingham .... *Royal Mail (n.s.c.)*
(5) Pondlife, Liverpool ....£15 *Benham BLCS 210*
(6) Pondlife, Sutton Park ....£20 *Benham Pilgrim*
(7) Pondlife, Barnes SW13 ....£15 *Benham BLCS 210*
(8) Pondlife, Alverley ....£20 *Benham 500(210)*
(9) Pondlife, Liverpool ....£20 *Benham Coin Cover*
(10) Pondersbridge, Huntingdon...£15 *Bradbury Sovereign 7*
(11) Fishers Pond, Eastleigh...........£25 *Bradbury Britannia 7*
(12) Freshwater Rd, London SW7 £15 *Westminster*
(13) Autographed, Pond Place.......£25 *Westminster*
(14) Pond Place, London SW3.......£15 *Steven Scott 56*
(15) The Pike & Eel, Daventry......£20 *M Brazier (Pubs.34)*
(16) Pond Street, London NW3 ....£15 *GB53*
(17) Scotney Castle Garden............£15 *Buckingham Cvrs 10*
(18) Scottish Wildlife Trust.............£15 *CoverCraft*
(19) Pondlife, Poole Dorset ....£15 *RN CvrsGp*
(20) Operation Husky......................£15 *RN CvrsGp*
(21) Town Pond Runcorn ....£20 *P Sheridan*

(22) Hampstead Heath, NW3........£20 *T Hurlstone*
(23) Vocal Pondlife..........................£25 *M J Kingsland*
(24) Frog Lane, Bristol ....£20 *D Legg*
(25) Eden Project, St. Austell.........£30 *Mill.Commem.Covers*
(26) Rotary Club of London...........£20 *Benham*
(27) Battle of Meeanee ....£20 *Benham*
(28) Biggin Hill, Westerham...........£15 *BritHerCollections*
(29) Battle of Britain Mem Day.....£20 *Squadron Leader Hill*

C.D.S. POSTMARKS Price Guide £10-£15

(30) Watermeadow, Fishlake, The Pond, Fishponds, Frogmore
(31) Oundle, Fishers Pond, Waterside, Riverbank, Fishpool

4th September 2001 - PUNCH & JUDY

6 x 1st: Policeman, Clown, Punch, Judy, Beadle & Crocodile. Also issued on same day a Self Adhesive Stamp Book containing 6 x 1st: Mr Punch, Judy & 4 Definitives.

SPECIAL HANDSTAMPS SPONSOR
Price Guide Ordinary Covers £4-£9 / Sponsored Covers:

(1) FDI - Tallents House..................... *Royal Mail (n.s.c.)*
(2) FDI - Blackpool .... *Royal Mail (n.s.c.)*
(3) -do- non pictorial version .... *Royal Mail (n.s.c.)*
(4) Punch & Judy, Birmingham .... *Royal Mail (n.s.c.)*
(5) Punch & Judy, Blackpool.......£15 *Benham BLCS 211*
(6) Punch & Judy, Margate ....£15 *Benham BLCS 212*
(7) Punch & Judy, Brighton ....£20 *Benham Pilgrim*
(8) Punch & Judy, Scarborough..£20 *Benham 500*
(9) Punch & Judy, Eastbourne.....£20 *Benham BLCS 211*
(10) Punch & Judy, Weston ....£20 *Benham 500*
(11) Punch & Judy, Blackpool.......£20 *Benham Coin Cover*
(12) Birthplace of Mr Punch..........£15 *Bradbury Sovereign 8*
(13) Covent Garden ....£15 *Bradbury Britannia 8*
(14) Self Adhesives.........................£30 *Bradbury Britannia 8*
(15) Blackpool, Lancashire.............£15 *Westminster*
(16) Autographed, Blackpool.........£25 *Westminster*
(17) Theatre Street, SW11 ....£15 *Steven Scott 57*
(18) Northampton............................£20 *M Brazier (Pubs.35)*
(19) Croft New Ash Green £15 *GB54*
(20) Punch & Judy Inn...................£15 *Buckingham Cvrs 11*
(21) Puppeteers UK, Bicester ....£15 *CoverCraft*
(22) Punch & Judy Fellowship ....£15 *Bletchley PO*
(23) Harlequin Puppet Theatre......£20 *P Sheridan*
(24) Punch & Judy, Covent Gdn...£25 *T Hurlstone*
(25) Nat West Philatelic Society ...£15 *Nat West Phil Society*
(26) Punch & Judy, Margate ....£25 *H D MacIntyre*
(27) East Grinstead Rotary Club...£20 *E Grins'd Stamp Club*
(28) Debden, Saffron Walden ....£15 *BritHerCollections*
(29) Battle of Moodkee ....£15 *Group Capt Randle*

C.D.S. POSTMARKS Price Guide £10-£15

(25) The Beach, South Shore, Seaside, The Pier, Loggerheads
(26) East Beach, Butlin's Camp, Funcoast World Skegness

2nd October 2001 - NOBEL PRIZES

2nd Chemistry; 1st Economic Sciences; E Peace; 40p Medicine; 45p Literature; 65p Physics.

SPECIAL HANDSTAMPS SPONSOR
Price Guide Ordinary Covers £4-£9 / Sponsored Covers:

(1) FDI - Tallents House..................... *Royal Mail (n.s.c.)*
(2) FDI - Cambridge .... *Royal Mail (n.s.c.)*
(3) -do- non pictorial version .... *Royal Mail (n.s.c.)*
(4) Nobel Prizes Birmingham............ *Royal Mail (n.s.c.)*
(5) FDI - Oxford .... *Royal Mail (n.s.c.)*
(6) Brighton - Chemistry...............£20 *Benham Pilgrim*
(7) London WC2 - Econ Sciences....£20 *Benham*
(8) London EC1 - Peace ....£20 *Benham Coin Cover*
(9) London NW1 -Medicine ....£20 *Benham (500)213*
(10) Literature - Oxford..................£15 *Benham BLCS 213*
(11) London SW7 - Physics............£15 *Benham BLCS 213*
(12) Alfred Nobel, Ardeer...............£20 *Bradbury Sovereign 9*
(13) Sir Winston Churchill ....£20 *Bradbury Britannia 9*
(14) Nobel Road, N18 ....£15 *Westminster*
(15) Autographed, N18....................£25 *Westminster*
(16) Alfred Place, WC1...................£15 *Steven Scott 58*
(17) The Swedish Flag, E1 ....£20 *M Brazier (Pubs.36)*
(18) Nobel House, SE5....................£15 *GB55*
(19) Cambridge.................................£15 *Buckingham Cvrs 12*
(20) Rudyard Kipling, Burwash .....£15 *Buckingham Cvrs*
(21) Inst of Internat'l Affairs ....£15 *CoverCraft*
(22) Marconi Way, Southall ....£20 *JFE Payne*
(23) The Washing Machine ....£20 *JFE Payne*
(24) Nobel Rd (changeable date) ..£20 *JFE Payne*
(25) Rudyard Kipling, Burwash .....£20 *P Sheridan*
(26) 5th Generation of Churchills.£15 *Bletchley PO*
(27) Nobel Rd, N18.........................£15 *Assoc. of GBFDC*
(28) Jean Henri Dunant...................£20 *Britcross Ltd*
(29) Lech Walesa ....£30 *J L Englert*
(30) Forever Heroes, Duxford........£15 *BritHerCollections*

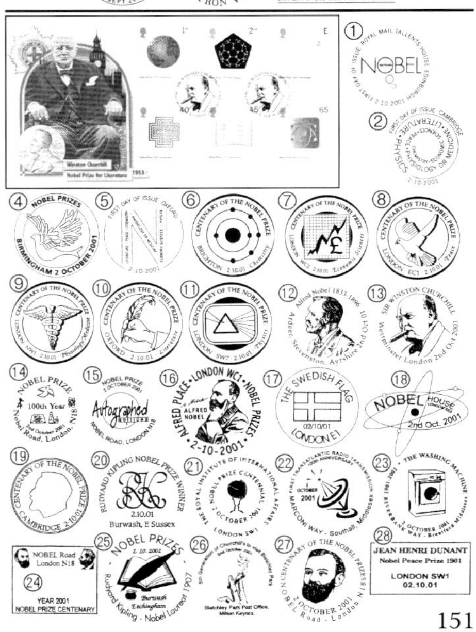

(31) The Siege of Mooltan..............£15 *Group Capt Randle*
(32) Northern Ireland, Armagh........... *Royal Mail (n.s.c.)*
C.D.S. POSTMARKS Price Guide £10-£15
(33) Churchill, Peacehaven, Science Museum,
(34) Cambridge, Oxford

22nd October 2001 - FLAGS & ENSIGNS

(1) Miniature Sheet 4x1st: White Ensign; Union Flag; Jolly Roger; Chief of Defence Staff.
(2) Self Adhesive Stamp Book containing 6 x 1st Class Stamps: White Ensign, Jolly Roger & 4 Definitives.
(3) Prestige Stamp Book (see definitives section), which also contained the Flags & Ensigns miniature sheet.

SPECIAL HANDSTAMPS SPONSOR
Price Guide Ordinary Covers £4-£9 / Sponsored Covers:
(1) FDI - Tallents House..................... *Royal Mail (n.s.c.)*
(2) FDI - Rosyth, Dunfermline........... *Royal Mail (n.s.c.)*
(3) -do- non pictorial version .... *Royal Mail (n.s.c.)*
(4) Flags & Ensigns Birmingham....... *Royal Mail (n.s.c.)*
(5) Unseen & Unheard Birmingham.. *Royal Mail (n.s.c.)*
(6) Faslane...£20 *Benham (500)215*
(7) Portsmouth ....£15 *Benham BLCS 215*
(8) Whitehall....................................£15 *Benham BLCS 216*
(9) Dartmouth ....£20 *Benham (500)214*
(10) Flags & ..., SW1........................£15 *Benham BLCS 214*
(11) Flags & ..., Greenwich.............£15 *Benham BLCS 216*
(12) Flags & ..., Penzance ....£20 *Benham D378*
(13) Flags & ..., Plymouth ....£20 *Benham*
(14) Flags & ..., Admiralty Arch......£20 *Benham Coin Cover*
(15) Elgar, Lower Broadheath ....£20 *Bradbury (s)*
(16) Rule Britannia, Edinburgh .....£15 *Bradbury Windsor 11*
(17) Flags & Ensigns, Romsey ....£25 *Bradbury*
(18) Self Adhesive Stamps ....£25 *Bradbury*
(19) Unseen & Unheard, Barrow..£15 *Bradbury*
(20) Flags & Ensigns, Gosport.......£15 *Westminster*
(21) Submarines, Gosport...............£15 *Westminster*
(22) Autographed, Gosport.............£25 *Westminster*
(23) Royal Standard Way.................£15 *Steven Scott 59*
(24) The Union Jack, Rugby...........£20 *M Brazier (Pubs.37)*
(25) Victory Way London SE16....£15 *GB56*
(26) RN Sub Museum, Gosport.....£15 *Buckingham Cvrs 13*
(27) Admirals Flag Loft ....£20 *T Hurlstone*
(28) Historic Dockyard....................£20 *T Hurlstone*
(29) The Flag Insitute, York ....£20 *T Hurlstone*
(30) Battle of the Atlantic ....£20 *P Sheridan*
(31) Chatham 1901-2001 ....£30 *H D MacIntyre*
(32) The Boat Brewery ....£30 *A Sheriff*
(33) Peace in Kaffraria....................£15 *Group Capt Randle*
(34) Coningsby, Lincoln..................£15 *BritHerCollections*
(35) Corfu Channel Incident..........£15 *RN CvrsGp*
(36) Gosport (changeable date).....£20 *RN CvrsGp*
(37) Faslane (changeable date)......£20 *RN CvrsGp*
(38) HMS Petard...............................£25 *Cam S.C.*
(39) Royal Yacht Britannia (-do-)..... *Royal Mail (n.s.c.)*
(40) Royal Mail Portsmouth (-do-)... *Royal Mail (n.s.c.)*
(41) BF 2644 PS Forces Bureau........... *British Forces (n.s.c.)*
(42) Norfolk Philatelic Society ......£20 *Philatelic Society*
C.D.S. POSTMARKS Price Guide £10-£15
(43) St Andrews, St Georges Cross, Clyde Submarine Base
(43) Chatham, Union Street

6th November 2001 - CHRISTMAS

2nd, 1st, E, 45p, & 65p Robins

SPECIAL HANDSTAMPS SPONSOR
Price Guide Ordinary Covers £4-£9 / Sponsored Covers:
(1) FDI - Tallents House..................... *Royal Mail (n.s.c.)*
(2) FDI - Bethlehem .... *Royal Mail (n.s.c.)*
(3) -do- non pictorial version .... *Royal Mail (n.s.c.)*
(4) Christmas, Birmingham................. *Royal Mail (n.s.c.)*
(5) Snowhill, Walcot, Bath...........£15 *Benham BLCS 217*
(6) Merry Hill, Wolverhampton ..£20 *Benham Pilgrim*
(7) Christmas Common....................£20 *Benham (500)217*
(8) Frostrow, Sedbergh..................£20 *Benham Coin Cover*
(9) Bird in Hand, Whiteshill........£15 *Benham BLCS 217*
(10) Hadrian's Wall..........................£20 *Benham Eng.Heritage*
(11) Nasareth.....................................£15 *Bradbury Sovereign 10*
(12) Bethlehem..................................£15 *Bradbury Britannia 10*
(13) Robins Lane, Norwich............£15 *Westminster*
(14) Autographed..............................£25 *Westminster*
(15) Holly Tree Close SW19 ....£15 *Steven Scott 60*
(16) The Robins, Bristol ....£20 *M Brazier (Pubs.38)*
(17) Robin Close, NW7 ....£15 *GB57*
(18) Robins, Midhurst......................£15 *Buckingham Cvrs 14*
(19) Pudding Lane, EC3..................£20 *CoverCraft*
(20) North Pole Road, W10 ....£30 *M J Kingsland*
(21) Robins Lane, St. Helens ....£25 *P Sheridan*

(22) Bletchley Park ....£10 *Bletchley PO*
(23) Kings Cliffe, Peterborough .....£15 *BritHerCollections*
(24) Battle of Khoosh-Ab ....£15 *Group Capt Randle*
(25) Target Tirpitz Lossiemouth ....£25 *Cam S.C.*
C.D.S. POSTMARKS Price Guide £10-£15
(26) Robins Lane, Winter Gardens, Hollybush, Jerusalem St
(27) Holy Island, St. Nicholas-at-Wade, Nasareth

18th Dec 2001 - CARTOONS Generic Issue

Reprinted version of the 1996 Cartoons Greetings stamps in sheet format plus revised label designs.

SPECIAL HANDSTAMPS SPONSOR
Price Guide Ordinary Covers £4-£9 / Sponsored Covers:
(1) Laughterton ....£25 *Bradbury*
(2) Lover, Salisbury ....£20 *Benham BLCS 221*
(3) Clock Face, St. Helens ....£10 *Benham(s)*
(4) World's End, Waterlooville....£10 *Benham(s)*
(5) Fetcham, Leatherhead ....£10 *Benham(s)*
(6) Falstone, Hexham ....£10 *Benham(s)*
(7) Nutts Corner, Crumlin ....£20 *Benham BLCS 221*
(8) Braintree, Essex ....£10 *Benham(s)*
(9) Letters, Lochbroom ....£10 *Benham(s)*
(10) Ringmore, Kingsbridge ....£10 *Benham(s)*
(11) Money More, Magherafelt......£10 *Benham(s)*

15th Jan 2002 - THE JUST SO STORIES

10 x 1st Class:Whale, Camel, Rhinoceros, Leopard, Elephant, Kangaroo, Armadillo, Crab, Cat and Butterfly.

SPECIAL HANDSTAMPS SPONSOR
Price Guide Ordinary Covers £4-£9 / Sponsored Covers:
(1) FDI - Tallents House..................... *Royal Mail (n.s.c.)*
(2) FDI - Burwash, Etchingham......... *Royal Mail (n.s.c.)*
(3) -do- non pictorial version .... *Royal Mail (n.s.c.)*
(4) Rudyard Kipling Birmingham ...... *Royal Mail (n.s.c.)*
(5) Cat...Wetwood, Stafford...........£15 *Benham BLCS 218*
(6) Elephant...Ledbury ....£20 *Benham Coin Cover*
(7) Rhinoceros..Church Stretton .£15 *Benham BLCS 218*
(8) Butterfly...Palacefields ....£20 *Benham Pilgrim*
(9) Camel...Pity Me, Durham ....£10 *Benham (s)*
(10) Whale...Whale, Penrith ....£20 *Benham Pilgrim*
(11) Kangaroo...Hopperton.............£10 *Benham (s)*
(12) Armadillo...New Invention.....£15 *Benham 500(218)*
(13) Crab...Chacewater, Truro........£20 *Benham Pilgrim*
(14) Leopard...Spott, Dunbar...........£20 *Benham Coin Cover*
(15) Rudyard, Leek, Staffs...............£20 *Bradbury Sovereign 11*
(16) Burwash (palette) ....£15 *Westminster*
(17) Burwash (whale) ....£15 *Westminster*
(18) Autographed, Burwash ....£25 *Westminster*
(19) The Rudyard Kipling ....£20 *M Brazier (Rly.1)*
(20) Towcester Book Shop ....£20 *M Brazier (Pubs.39)*
(21) Cat Hill, Barnet £15 *GB58*
(22) Bateman's, Home of Kipling..£15 *Buckingham Cvrs 15*
(23) Knowsley Safari Park ....£20 *P Sheridan*
(24) Kipling Society, Rottingdean .£15 *CoverCraft*
(25) Kipling Drive, SW19................£30 *M J Kingsland*
(26) Zoological Gardens, Chester .£30 *A Sheriff*
(27) Kipling's Just So Stories..........£15 *Bletchley PO*
(28) Just So Stories, Humpage.......£20 *Phil Stamp Covers 18*
(29) HMS Kipling, Glasgow ....£15 *RN CvrsGp*
(30) Linton-on-Ouse ....£15 *BritHerCollections*
(31) 2002 Anniversaries ....£20 *J F E Payne*
(32) Tales of Horror ....£30 *Cam S.C.*
(33) London Aquarium....................£30 *T Hurlstone*
C.D.S. POSTMARKS Price Guide £7-£10
(34) Burwash, Rottingdean, Westward Ho!
(35) Crab Lane, Whale Hill, Camel's Head

6th Feb 2002 - QUEEN'S GOLDEN JUBILEE

(1) 2nd, 1st, E, 45p & 65p Portraits of the Queen.
(2) ***Gracious Accession*** *Prestige Stamp Book containing reprinted versions of the $1^1/_2$d and $2^1/_2$d 1952 definitives*
- see also Definitive Section.

SPECIAL HANDSTAMPS SPONSOR
Price Guide Ordinary Covers £4-£9 / Sponsored Covers:
(1) FDI - Tallents House...................... *Royal Mail (n.s.c.)*
(2) FDI - Windsor .... *Royal Mail (n.s.c.)*
(3) -do- non pictorial version .... *Royal Mail (n.s.c.)*
(4) Golden Wedding, Birmingham .... *Royal Mail (n.s.c.)*
(5) Golden Jubilee, London (circle) ... *Royal Mail (n.s.c.)*
(6) Golden Jubilee, London (oval) ..... *Royal Mail (n.s.c.)*
(7) Windsor, Berks ....£15 *Benham BLCS 219*
(8) Buckingham Palace Rd...........£15 *Benham BLCS 219*
(9) Sandringham, Norfolk ....£20 *Benham Pilgrim*
(10) Royal Mile, Edinburgh ....£30 *Benham 500(219)*
(11) Balmoral, Ballater ....£20 *Benham*
(12) Windsor (coat of arms) ....£20 *Benham*
(13) King George VI.........................£20 *Benham*

(14) London (square)........................£20 *Benham*
(15) Edinburgh (square)...................£20 *Benham*
(16) Buckingham Palace Rd............£20 *Benham Coin Cover*
(17) Westminster (Cathedral).........£15 *Bradbury Sovereign 12*
(18) A Gracious Accession, SW1..£20 *Bradbury Windsor 15*
(19) London SW1 (crown).............£15 *Westminster*
(20) Windsor (palette)....................£15 *Westminster*
(21) Autographed, Windsor............£20 *Westminster*
(22) Buckingham Palace Road........£15 *Steven Scott 61*
(23) Canterbury.................................£15 *Steven Scott*
(24) Blandford Camp.......................£15 *Steven Scott*
(25) Princess Elizabeth...................£20 *M Brazier (Rly.2)*
(26) Q. Elizabeth Elmley Castle....£20 *M Brazier (Pubs.40)*
(27) Jubilee Way, London SW19...£15 *GB59*
(28) London SW1 (Palace)............£15 *Buckingham Cvrs 16*
(29) Sandringham............................£15 *Buckingham Cvrs 16*
(30) Windsor.....................................£15 *Buckingham Cvrs 16*
(31) Windsor (Castle).....................£15 *CoverCraft*
(32) Westminster (flowers).............£15 *P Sheridan*
(33) Queen Street, Harwood..........£20 *P M Payne*
(34) Jubilee Place, London SW3...£20 *P M Payne*
(35) Windsor.....................................£15 *Assoc. of GBFDC*
(36) Cranwell, Sleaford...................£15 *BritHerCollections*
(37) RN Covers, Plymouth..............£15 *RN CvrsGp*
(38) Q. Elizabeth II Square............£20 *Phil Stamp Covers 19*
(39) Jubilee Close, Castle Cary.......£20 *Phil Stamp Covers 20*
(40) Mazel Tov.................................£35 *S Kacher*
(41) Havengore Trust.......................£25 *T Hurlstone*
(42) Tony Penberthy Benefit..........£20 *Woodford Sports*
(43) Storming of Bomarsund..........£15 *Group Capt Randle*
(44) Windsor or SW1 (changeable date).. *Royal Mail*
(45) 2002 Anniversaries..................£15 *P M Payne*
C.D.S. POSTMARKS Price Guide £7-£10
(46) Jubilee Oak, Jubilee Fields, Jubilee Cresc, Queen's Parade
(47) Heathrow, Windsor, Windsor Great Park, Crathie
(48) Windsor Castle, Sandringham (each £100)

5th March 2002 - OCCASIONS

5 x 1st: Moving House, Best Wishes, Hello, Love, New Baby

SPECIAL HANDSTAMPS SPONSOR
Price Guide Ordinary Covers £4-£9 / Sponsored Covers:
(1) FDI - Tallents House..................... *Royal Mail (n.s.c.)*
(2) FDI - Merry Hill............................. *Royal Mail (n.s.c.)*
(3) -do- non pictorial version .... *Royal Mail (n.s.c.)*
(4) Occasions Birmingham................. *Royal Mail (n.s.c.)*
(5) Greetwell, Gainsborough ....£25 *Benham 500(222)*
(6) Birthorpe, Sleaford...................£15 *Benham BLCS 222*
(7) Bloomfield, Tipton...................£20 *Benham Coin Cover*
(8) Home Meadow, Worcester....£20 *Benham*
(9) Love Lane, London N17........£15 *Benham BLCS 222*
(10) Gretna Green...........................£15 *Bradbury Windsor 12*
(11) Merry Hill Rd (cake)...............£15 *Westminster*
(12) Merry Hill Rd (palette)..........£15 *Westminster*
(13) Autographed, Merry Hill Rd £25 *Westminster*
(14) Best Wishes Great Occasion .£20 *M Brazier*
(15) Titanic Ship Yard, SW14........£15 *GB60*
(16) Motherwell................................£15 *Buckingham Cvrs 17*
(17) Hugo Bicentenary, N19..........£20 *P M Payne*
(18) Flowergirl, Romford................£20 *T Hurlstone*
(19) Heart in Hand Rd....................£20 *Phil Stamp Covers 21*
(20) Duxford, Cambridge................£15 *BritHerCollections*
C.D.S. POSTMARKS Price Guide £7-£10
(21) Lover, Greet, Weddington, Daisy Hill

19th March 2002 - BRITAIN'S COASTLINES

10 x 27p Studland; Luskentyre; Dover; Padstow; Broadstairs; St.Abb's Head; Dunster; Newquay; Portrush; Conwy.

SPECIAL HANDSTAMPS SPONSOR
Price Guide Ordinary Covers £4-£9 / Sponsored Covers:
(1) FDI - Tallents House..................... *Royal Mail (n.s.c.)*
(2) FDI - Poolewe................................ *Royal Mail (n.s.c.)*
(3) -do- non pictorial version .... *Royal Mail (n.s.c.)*
(4) Coastlines, Birmingham................ *Royal Mail (n.s.c.)*
(5) Dover, Kent..............................£15 *Benham BLCS 223*
(6) Padstow, Cornwall...................£15 *Benham BLCS 223*
(7) Conwy.......................................£20 *Benham 500(223)*
(8) Dunster, Minehead..................£20 *Benham Coin Cover*
(9) Broadstairs, Kent......................£20 *Benham Coin Cover*
(10) Luskentyre, Harris...................£20 *Benham Pilgrim*
(11) Newquay, Cornwall.................£10 *Benham (s)*
(12) Studland, Swanage..................£10 *Benham (s)*
(13) St. Abb's, Eyemouth................£20 *Benham Pilgrim*
(14) Portrush, Co. Antrim...............£20 *Benham Pilgrim*
(15) Pembrokeshire Coast...............£15 *Bradbury Sovereign 13*
(16) Studland (sun and waves)......£15 *Westminster*
(17) Studland (palette)....................£15 *Westminster*

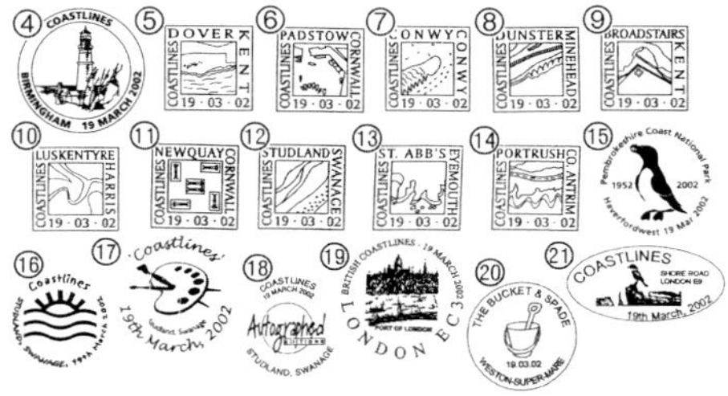

(18) Autographed, Studland ....£25 *Westminster*
(19) Port of London ....£15 *Steven Scott 62*
(20) Bucket & Spade, Weston ....£20 *M Brazier (Pubs.41)*
(21) Shore Road, London E9 ....£15 *GB61*
(22) White Cliffs, Dover ....£15 *Buckingham Cvrs 18*
(23) St Michael's Mount..................£15 *Buckingham Cvrs 18*
(24) Giant's Causeway.....................£20 *P Sheridan*
(25) White Cliffs of Dover ....£30 *M J Kingsland*
(26) St Margaret's Bay ....£30 *H D MacIntyre*
(27) Coastline Signals, Bletchley ...£15 *Bletchley PO*
(28) Adnams, Southwold ....£20 *Fourpenny Post*
(29) North Coates, Grimsby ....£15 *BritHerCollections*
(30) Operation Paraquat ....£15 *RN CvrsGp*
(31) Coast View, Bude ....£20 *Phil Stamp Covers 22*
(32) Baltasound, Unst (changeable date).. *Royal Mail*
(33) Giant's Causeway (changeable date). *Royal Mail*
(34) Battle of Balaklava...................£15 *Group Capt Randle*
(35) Relief of Lucknow ....£15 *Group Capt Randle*
(36) Ladies Curling Team ....£25 *T Hurlstone*

C.D.S. POSTMARKS Price Guide £7-£10

(37) Dunster, Portrush, Studland, Dover, Sandbanks, Padstow
(38) Broadstairs, Newquay, Harris, The Rock, The Harbour
(39) St Davids, Haverfordwest: Pemb. Coast Path 50th Anniversary

9th April 2002 - CIRCUS

2nd Slack Wire Act; 1st Lion Tamer; E Trick Tri Cyclyists; 40p Krazy Kar; 45p The Equestrienne.

SPECIAL HANDSTAMPS SPONSOR
Price Guide Ordinary Covers £4-£9 / Sponsored Covers:

(1) FDI - Tallents House...................... *Royal Mail (n.s.c.)*
(2) FDI - Clowne Chesterfield............ *Royal Mail (n.s.c.)*
(3) -do- non pictorial version .... *Royal Mail (n.s.c.)*
(4) Circus, Big Top Birmingham........ *Royal Mail (n.s.c.)*
(5) Westminster Bridge Rd, SE1 .£15 *Benham BLCS 224*
(6) Blackfriar's Road, SE1 ....£10 *Benham (s)*
(7) London Bridge, SE1 ....£20 *Benham Coin Cover*
(8) Bank Hey Street, Blackpool ..£20 *Benham (500)224*
(9) Belle Vue, Manchester ....£15 *Benham BLCS 224*
(10) Gerry Cottle's Circus ....£20 *Bradbury Sovereign 14*
(11) Circus Rd, NW8 (clown) ....£15 *Westminster*
(12) Circus Rd, NW8 (palette)......£15 *Westminster*
(13) Autographed, Circus Rd ....£25 *Westminster*
(14) Circus Place, London EC2.....£15 *Steven Scott 63*
(15) Conjuror's Half Crown ....£20 *M Brazier (Pubs.42)*
(16) Circus Road, NW8...................£15 *GB62*
(17) Great Circus Parade, SW1 .....£15 *Buckingham Cvrs 19*
(18) Circus Unlimited, Hemel........£15 *P Sheridan*
(19) Circus Friends Association.....£15 *CoverCraft*
(20) F14 Tomcat, Grosvenor Sq....£15 *BritHerCollections*
(21) HMS Hermes, Plymouth ....£15 *RN CvrsGp*
(22) Circus, Kings Langley..............£20 *Phil Stamp Covers 23*
(23) Circus of Horrors....................£25 *Cam S.C.*
(24) Concorde 33rd Anniversary........£25 *Cam S.C.*
(25) W Reid VC Memorial..............£25 *Cam S.C.*
(26) Capture of the Taku Forts......£25 *Group Capt Randle*
(27) Sir Walter Raleigh, Feltham...£20 *P M Payne*
(28) Old England XI, Hove ....£15 *Woodford Sports*

C.D.S. POSTMARKS Price Guide £7-£10

(29) Big Top, Clowne, Chipperfield, Castle Circus or similar

23rd April 2002 - OCCASIONS Generic Issue

Reprinted version of the 2002 Occasions stamps with labels.

SPECIAL HANDSTAMPS SPONSOR
Price Guide Ordinary Covers £4-£9 / Sponsored Covers:

(1) Greetwell, Gainsborough ....£15 *Benham*
(2) Gretna Green, Carlisle............£15 *Bradbury Windsor 12*
(3) Alexander Dumas, SE5 ....£15 *P M Payne*

VALUES SHOULD BE TREATED AS A GUIDE.
Please read the General Notes.

25th April 2002 - THE QUEEN MOTHER

1st The Queen Mother; E Queen Elizabeth; 45p Elizabeth, Duchess of York; 65p Lady Elizabeth Bowes-Lyon

SPECIAL HANDSTAMPS SPONSOR
Price Guide Ordinary Covers £4-£9 / Sponsored Covers:

(1) FDI - Tallents House...................... *Royal Mail (n.s.c.)*
(2) FDI - London SW1 .... *Royal Mail (n.s.c.)*
(3) -do- non pictorial version .... *Royal Mail (n.s.c.)*
(4) Queen Mother, Sandringham....... *Royal Mail (n.s.c.)*
(5) Castle of Mey ....£20 *Benham Pilgrim*
(6) Glamis, Forfar ....£35 *Benham (500)228*
(7) St James's, London SW1 ....£15 *Benham BLCS 228*
(8) Buckingham Palace Rd...........£15 *Benham BLCS 228*
(9) Windsor Berks ....£20 *Benham Coin Cover*
(10) In Memoriam, Glamis.............£15 *Bradbury*
(11) In Memoriam, The Mall ....£15 *Bradbury*
(12) In Memoriam, Windsor ....£15 *Bradbury Sovereign 21*
(13) In Memorian QM, Windsor...£15 *Westminster*
(14) Windsor (palette) ....£15 *Westminster*

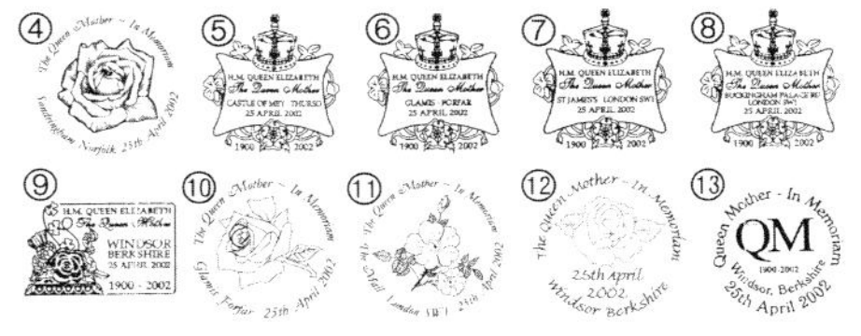

(15) Autographed, Windsor............£25 *Westminster*
(16) A Lifetime Remembered.........£15 *Steven Scott 64*
(17) Queen of Hearts, Daventry....£20 *M Brazier (Pubs.43)*
(18) Regal Way, Harrow ....£15 *GB 64*
(19) Windsor......................................£15 *Buckingham Cvrs 26*
(20) Memorial Tribute, Glamis......£15 *P Sheridan*
(21) Tribute to Queen Mother.......£15 *CoverCraft*
(22) Payne FDC Sympathy.............£20 *P M Payne*
(23) London SW1.............................£20 *H Athanassiades*
(24) Windsor (Lillies)......................£15 *Phil Stamp Covers*
(25) Windsor.....................................£20 *Cam S.C.*
(26) Life of Devotion and Joy........£20 *Bletchley PO*
(27) HMS Ark Royal........................£15 *RN CvrsGp*
(28) Yacht Britannia (changeable date)... *Royal Mail*
(29) Windsor (changeable date) .... *Royal Mail*
(30) Buck Palace (changeable date) ...... *Royal Mail*
C.D.S. POSTMARKS Price Guide £7-£10
(31) Bowes, West Newton, Windsor, Mey, Glamis
(32) Windsor Great Park, Clarence Rd, Windsor, Walmer
(33) Windsor Castle, Buckingham Palace (£100 each)

2nd May 2002 - AIRLINERS

(1) 2nd Airbus; 1st Concorde; E Trident; 45p VC10; 65p Comet.
(2) Miniature Sheet with above stamps;
(3) Self Adhesive Stamp Book containing 6 x 1st Class Stamps: 2 Concorde & 4 Definitives.

SPECIAL HANDSTAMPS SPONSOR
Price Guide Ordinary Covers £4-£9 / Sponsored Covers:
(1) FDI - Tallents House...................... *Royal Mail (n.s.c.)*
(2) FDI - Heathrow Airport................ *Royal Mail (n.s.c.)*
(3) -do- non pictorial version............. *Royal Mail (n.s.c.)*
(4) Aircraft, Birmingham..................... *Royal Mail (n.s.c.)*
(5) Concorde, Filton Bristol.........£20 *Benham BLCS 227*
(6) Airbus, Broughton Chester.....£20 *Benham BLCS 226*
(7) Comet, Hatfield Herts.............£20 *Benham BLCS 225/6*
(8) Trident, St. James's London...£20 *Benham*
(9) VC10, Brooklands....................£20 *Benham Pilgrim*
(10) Concorde, Heathrow...............£30 *Benham (500) 225*
(11) Commercial Jet Travel............£25 *Bradbury Windsor 13*
(12) Fifty Years Jet Travel...............£20 *Bradbury Sovereign 15*
(13) Self Adhesives, Hounslow......£35 *Bradbury Windsor 18*
(14) Airliners, Heathrow (plane)...£15 *Westminster*
(15) Airliners, Heathrow (palette).£15 *Westminster*
(16) Autographed, Heathrow ....£25 *Westminster*
(17) Evolution of Aircraft, W1.......£20 *Steven Scott 65*
(18) The Spitfire, Stockton ....£25 *M Brazier (Pubs.44)*
(19) Henri Coanda, Jetstar Way....£20 *GB63*
(20) The Comet, Croydon...............£20 *Buckingham Cvrs 20*
(21) Concorde, Heathrow...............£20 *Buckingham Cvrs 20*
(22) Liverpool Airport.....................£20 *P Sheridan*
(23) Airliners Commemoration......£25 *CoverCraft*
(24) Vulcan, Waddington................£25 *BritHerCollections*
(25) Stansted, Essex.........................£25 *T Hurlstone*
(26) Charles Lindberg......................£25 *P M Payne*
(27) Leonardo da Vinci....................£25 *P M Payne*
(28) Heathrow Airport.....................£30 *Cam S.C.*
(29) Manston Airport.......................£30 *H D MacIntyre*
(30) Gatwick Top Flight..................£15 *Assoc. of GBFDC*
(31) RAFLET Stamp Club................£20 *P Barrett*
(32) Exter International Airport....£20 *R Howe*
(33) Airliners, Concorde..................£20 *Phil Stamp Covers 25*
(34) Airliners, Comet Way..............£20 *Phil Stamp Covers 24*
(35) 26th Anniv Year Concorde....£40 *Cam S.C.*
(36) Royal Mail, Gatwick...................... *Royal Mail (n.s.c.)*
(37) Bletchley Park Post Office......£20 *Bletchley PO*
(38) Nimrod, BF2676PS..................£20 *Sqn Ldr Hill*
(39) VC10, BF2674PS......................£20 *Sqn Ldr Hill*
(40) Sinking of the Belgrano..........£20 *RN CvrsGp*
(41) Mildenhall.................................£20 *A Sherriff*
(42) Bunbury Cricket Club.............£25 *Woodford Sports*
(43) Attack on the Gate Pa............£20 *Group Capt Randle*
C.D.S. POSTMARKS Price Guide £7-£10
(44) Heathrow Terminal 2 or 4, Gatwick, Filton, Duxford,
(45) Manchester or Glasgow Airport, Hatfield, Biggin Hill

21st May 2002 - WORLD CUP FOOTBALL

(1) Miniature Sheet 4 x 1st St. George Flag & Footballs plus 1 x 1st Crowned Lion of England.
(2) 1st Crowned Lion of England - in sheet format.
(3) Self Adhesive Stamp Book containing 6 x 1st Class Stamps: 2 St George Flag/Footballs & 4 Definitives.
(4) Generic Sheet of 20 x 1st (St George Flag) & 16 labels.

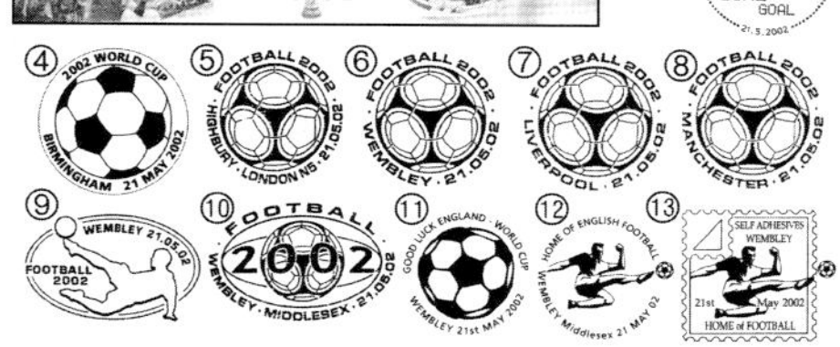

SPECIAL HANDSTAMPS SPONSOR
Price Guide Ordinary Covers £4-£9 / Sponsored Covers:
(1) FDI - Tallents House...................... *Royal Mail (n.s.c.)*
(2) FDI - Wembley............................... *Royal Mail (n.s.c.)*
(3) -do- non pictorial version............. *Royal Mail (n.s.c.)*

(4) World Cup, Birmingham .... *Royal Mail (n.s.c.)*
(5) Football 2002, Highbury.........£15 *Benham BLCS 229*
(6) Football 2002, Wembley.........£15 *Benham BLCS 230*
(7) Football 2002, Liverpool ....£15 *Benham BLCS 230*
(8) Football 2002, Manchester.....£15 *Benham BLCS 229*
(9) Football 2002, Wembley.........£20 *Benham Coin Cover*
(10) Football 2002, Wembley.........£20 *Benham Coin Cover*
(11) Good Luck, Wembley ....£15 *Bradbury Sovereign 17*
(12) Home of English Football ......£15 *Bradbury Windsor 16*
(13) Self Adhesives, Wembley........£25 *Bradbury Sovereign 17*
(14) Wembley (football) ....£15 *Westminster*
(15) Wembley (palette) ....£15 *Westminster*
(16) Autographed, Wembley ....£25 *Westminster*
(17) Tom Finney Way, Preston......£15 *Steven Scott*
(18) Good Luck to England ....£15 *Steven Scott 66*
(19) The Goal Post ....£20 *M Brazier (Pubs.45)*
(20) Wembley Stadium ....£15 *GB 65*
(21) World Cup 2002, Wembley ...£15 *Buckingham Cvrs 19*
(22) Becks - Good Luck.................£20 *P Sheridan*
(23) Historic Wembley ....£20 *CoverCraft*
(24) World Cup 2002, Wembley ...£20 *T Hurlstone*
(25) World Cup Qualifiers ....£20 *P M Payne*
(26) World Cup, Korea - Japan.......£25 *Cam S.C.*
(27) Winners World Cup 1966 ......£25 *D Harper*
(28) Englands Way ....£15 *Phil Stamp Covers 26*
(29) Korea Road, Preston................£15 *Phil Stamp Covers 27*
(30) Football Legends ....£20 *M Jennings*
(31) Best Wishes, Manchester........£15 *Dawn*
(32) M United (changeable date) ..£15 *Dawn*
(33) Liverpool (changeable date) ..£15 *Dawn*
(34) Norwich (changeable date)....£15 *Dawn*
(35) Typhoon, Duxford...................£15 *BritHerCollections*
(36) First Solo Crossing Atlantic ...£15 *Group Capt Randle*
(37) Reduction of Magdala ....£15 *Group Capt Randle*
(38) Royal Horticultural Society ...£25 *A W Mailing Services*
(39) HMS Ardent.............................£15 *RN CvrsGp*

C.D.S. POSTMARKS Price Guide £7-£10
(40) Wembley or Wembley Park, Trafford Park
(41) The Ball, Ball Green, St George's Cross

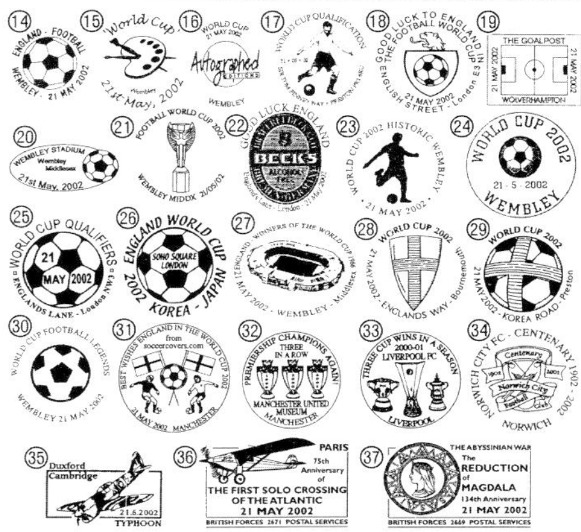

5th June 2002 - GOLDEN JUBILEE

1st Class Gold Self Adhesive Definitive.

SPECIAL HANDSTAMPS SPONSOR
Price Guide Ordinary Covers £4-£9 / Sponsored Covers:
(1) Parliament Square....................£15 *Benham BLCS 231*
(2) Canterbury ....£15 *Benham BLCS 231*
(3) Buckingham Palace Road.......£20 *Benham Coin Cover*
(4) Westminster Abbey ....£25 *Benham (500)231*
(5) Self Adhesives SW1 ....£15 *Bradbury Windsor 19*
(6) The Mall, London ....£15 *Westminster*
(7) Pall Mall, London SW1 ....£15 *Buckingham Cvrs*
(8) Championships, Wimbledon....£15 *New Malden PO*

16th July 2002 - COMMONWEALTH GAMES

2nd Swimming; 1st Running; E Cycling; 47p Long-jumping; 68p Wheelchair athletics.

SPECIAL HANDSTAMPS SPONSOR
Price Guide Ordinary Covers £4-£9 / Sponsored Covers:
(1) FDI - Tallents House..................... *Royal Mail (n.s.c.)*
(2) FDI - Manchester........................... *Royal Mail (n.s.c.)*
(3) -do- non pictorial version .... *Royal Mail (n.s.c.)*
(4) Manchester 2002........................... *Royal Mail (n.s.c.)*
(5) Friendly Games, Birmingham ...... *Royal Mail (n.s.c.)*
(6) Games 2002, Manchester.......£15 *Benham BLCS 232*
(7) Games 2002, Manchester.......£20 *Benham Coin Cover*
(8) Games 2002, Belfast................£20 *Benham*
(9) Games 2002, Edinburgh ....£20 *Benham*
(10) Games 2002, London.............£15 *Benham BLCS 232*
(11) Games 2002, Cardiff...............£20 *Benham*
(12) Commonwealth Games ....£25 *Benham Gold(232)*
(13) The 2002 Games ....£15 *Bradbury Sovereign 16*
(14) The Games, Manchester.........£15 *Westminster*
(15) Manchester (palette)...............£15 *Westminster*
(16) Autographed, Manchester .....£25 *Westminster*
(17) Friendly Games........................£15 *Steven Scott 67*
(18) The Torch, Wembley ....£20 *M Brazier (Pubs 46)*
(19) Olympic Way, Wembley.........£15 *GB 66*
(20) Sporting Heroes, Henley ....£15 *Buckingham Cvrs 21*
(21) Sporting Heroes, Henley ....£15 *Buckingham Cvrs 21*
(22) Manchester, The Games.........£15 *P Sheridan*
(23) Wimbledon, London SW19...£15 *P M Payne*
(24) The Friendly Games, Manch .£20 *Cam S.C.*
(25) Commonwealth Way..............£20 *M J Kingsland*
(26) The Friendly Games ....£15 *Phil Stamp Covers 28*
(27) Royal Navy Athletics...............£15 *RN CvrsGp*
(28) Spitfire, West Malling.............£15 *BritHerCollections*
(29) The Fenian Raid ....£15 *Group Capt Randle*
(30) Anniversaries, Games Rd ....£20 *P M Payne*

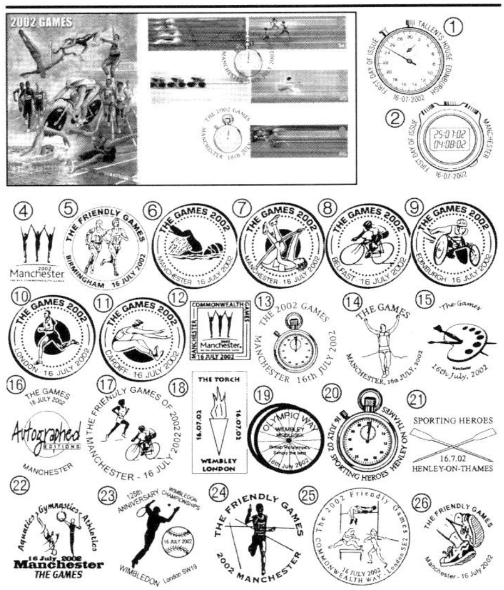

C.D.S. POSTMARKS Price Guide £7-£10
(31) M2002 Games Village (£50), Jump, Stoke Mandeville,
(32) any Manchester postmarks near to venues for the Games

20th August 2002 - PETER PAN

2nd Tinkerbell; 1st Wendy, John & Michael; E Crocodile; 47p Hook; 68p Peter Pan.

SPECIAL HANDSTAMPS **SPONSOR**
Price Guide Ordinary Covers £4-£9 / Sponsored Covers:

(1) FDI - Tallents House .... *Royal Mail (n.s.c.)*
(2) FDI - Hook .... *Royal Mail (n.s.c.)*
(3) -do- non pictorial version .... *Royal Mail (n.s.c.)*
(4) Peter Pan, Birmingham................. *Royal Mail (n.s.c.)*
(5) Great Ormond Street ....£15 *Benham BLCS 233*
(6) London ....£20 *Benham Coin Cover*
(7) Kirriemuir ....£15 *Benham BLCS 233*
(8) Edinburgh ....£25 *Benham (500)233*
(9) Hook, Hampshire.....................£20 *Benham Pilgrim*
(10) Peter Pan, Kensington Gdns..£15 *Bradbury Sovereign 22*
(11) Peter Pan, Hook ....£15 *Westminster*
(12) Hook (palette) ....£15 *Westminster*
(13) Autographed, Hook ....£25 *Westminster*
(14) Peter Street, London W1........£15 *Steven Scott 68*
(15) The Peter Pan ....£15 *M Brazier (Pubs 47)*
(16) Barrie House, Addlestone ......£15 *GB 67*
(17) Great Ormond Street ....£15 *Buckingham Cvrs 27*
(18) Kensington Gardens ....£15 *Buckingham Cvrs 27*
(19) Birthplace, Kirriemuir ....£20 *CoverCraft*
(20) Chicken Shed Theatre Co ......£15 *P Sheridan*
(21) Hooks Close, SE15 ....£20 *P M Payne*
(22) James Barrie, Kirriemuir ....£15 *Assoc. of GBFDC*
(23) Peter Pan, Bletchley Park.......£15 *Bletchley PO*
(24) Peter Pan, Kirriemuir...............£15 *Phil Stamp Covers 29*
(25) Duke of York's Theatre ....£20 *T Hurlstone*
(26) Lambert School, Hull..............£25 *John Bryan*
(27) Concorde, Duxford ....£25 *Cam S.C.*
(28) Phantom, Manston...................£15 *BritHerCollections*
(29) The Capture of Coomassie.....£15 *Group Capt Randle*
(30) U-43 Sinking off Brighton......£15 *RN CvrsGp*

C.D.S. POSTMARKS Price Guide £7-£10
(31) Kensington Church Street, Kirriemuir, Farnham
(32) Hook, Pan, Clockface

10th Sept 2002 - BRIDGES OF LONDON

(1) 2nd Millennium Bridge; 1st Tower Bridge; E Westminster Bridge; 47p Blackfriars Bridge; 68p London Bridge.
(2) Self Adhesive Stamp Book containing 6 x 1st Class Stamps: 2 Tower Bridge & 4 Definitives.

SPECIAL HANDSTAMPS **SPONSOR**
Price Guide Ordinary Covers £4-£9 / Sponsored Covers:

(1) FDI - Tallents House .... *Royal Mail (n.s.c.)*
(2) FDI - London SE1 .... *Royal Mail (n.s.c.)*
(3) -do- non pictorial version .... *Royal Mail (n.s.c.)*
(4) Bridges of London, Birmingham . *Royal Mail (n.s.c.)*
(5) Westminster Bridge..................£15 *Benham BLCS 234*
(6) Tower Hill...................................£20 *Benham Coin Cover*
(7) Bankside......................................£15 *Benham BLCS 234*
(8) London Bridge ....£30 *Benham (500)234*
(9) Blackfriars Road ....£20 *Benham Pilgrim*
(10) Tower Hill NVI Booklet.........£20 *Benham*
(11) Guildhall NVI Booklet ....£20 *Benham*
(12) Bridges of London (crest) ......£20 *Bradbury Sovereign 18*
(13) Self Adhesives ....£25 *Bradbury Britannia 12*
(14) Riverview Road........................£15 *Westminster*
(15) Riverview Road (palette) ....£15 *Westminster*
(16) Autographed, Riverview Rd ...£25 *Westminster*
(17) London Bridges (Big Ben) .....£15 *Steven Scott 69*
(18) The Giddy Bridge ....£15 *M Brazier (Pubs 48)*
(19) The Square Arch ....£15 *GB 68*
(20) London Bridge ....£15 *Buckingham Cvrs 22*
(21) Tower Bridge ....£15 *Buckingham Cvrs 22*
(22) Westminster Bridge..................£15 *P Sheridan*
(23) Structural Engineers ....£20 *CoverCraft*
(24) Tower Bridge ....£20 *T Hurlstone*
(25) Thomas Gainsborough............£20 *P M Payne*
(26) London Bridges ....£25 *Cam S.C.*
(27) London SE1 ....£20 *H D MacIntyre*
(28) London's Bridges......................£15 *Assoc. of GBFDC*
(29) London Bridges ....£20 *N McInnes*
(30) Westminster Bridge..................£15 *Phil Stamp Covers 30*
(31) Tower Bridge ....£15 *Phil Stamp Covers 31*
(32) London Bridge Mustang.........£15 *BritHerCollections*
(33) London's Fire Brigade............£15 *Bletchley PO*
(34) Jade's Crossing, Detling ....£25 *Jade Crossing Fund*
(35) Battle of Isandhlwana ....£15 *Group Capt Randle*
(36) HMS Warspite ....£15 *RN CvrsGp*

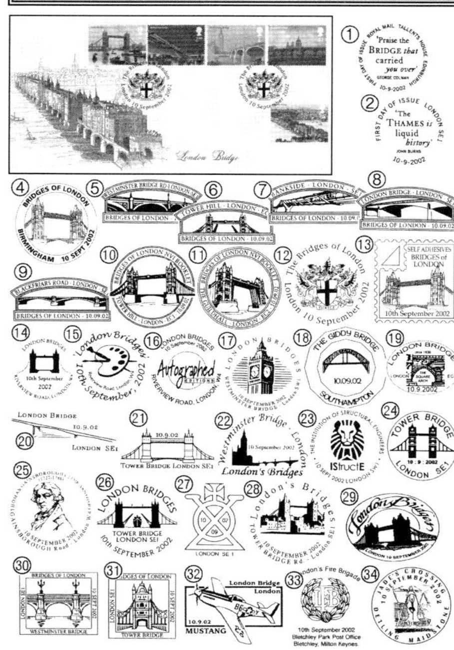

C.D.S. POSTMARKS Price Guide £7-£10
(37) London Bridge, Blackfriars Road, Westminster Bridge Road
(38) Rising Bridge, Ironbridge, Thames View, New Bridge

24th September 2002 - ASTRONOMY

(1) 4 x 1st: Planetary Nebula in Aquila & Norma; Seyfert 2 Galaxy in Pegasus & Circinus.
*(2) **Across the Universe** Prestige Stamp Book.*

SPECIAL HANDSTAMPS **SPONSOR**
Price Guide Ordinary Covers £4-£9 / Sponsored Covers:

(1) FDI - Tallents House .... *Royal Mail (n.s.c.)*
(2) FDI - Star, Glenrothes .... *Royal Mail (n.s.c.)*
(3) -do- non pictorial version .... *Royal Mail (n.s.c.)*
(4) Across the Universe, B'ham......... *Royal Mail (n.s.c.)*
(5) Piccadilly ....£20 *Benham*
(6) Greenwich ....£15 *Benham BLCS 236*
(7) Leicester ....£20 *Benham Coin Cover*
(8) Armagh ....£20 *Benham*
(9) Windsor......................................£15 *Benham BLCS 236*
(10) London W1 ....£20 *Benham (500)236*
(11) Macclesfield..............................£15 *Benham*
(12) Edinburgh ....£15 *Benham*
(13) Macclesfield...............................£25 *Bradbury Sovereign 19*
(14) Space Shuttle, Cambridge ......£30 *Bradbury Windsor 17*
(15) Apollo Way, Birmingham.......£15 *Westminster*
(16) Apollo Way (palette) ....£15 *Westminster*
(17) Autographed, Apollo Way......£25 *Westminster*
(18) Greenwich Observatory..........£15 *Steven Scott 70*
(19) The North Star..........................£15 *M Brazier (Pubs 49)*
(20) Starcross Street........................£15 *GB 69*
(21) Jodrell Bank (oval)...................£15 *Buckingham Cvrs 23*
(22) Jodrell Bank (circle) ....£15 *Buckingham Cvrs 23*
(23) The Blue Planet ....£20 *P Sheridan*
(24) British Astronomical Ass'n ......£20 *CoverCraft*
(25) Sir William Ramsey ....£20 *P M Payne*
(26) Starfield Road ....£20 *M J Kingsland*
(27) Greenwich Park, SE10..............£25 *Cam S.C.*
(28) Constellation St, Cardiff ....£15 *Phil Stamp Covers 32*
(29) HMS Echo ....£15 *RN Philatelic Society*
(30) Attack on the Tirpitz ....£15 *RN CvrsGp*
(31) The George Cross, SW1 ....£15 *Westminster*
(32) Tempest, Manston ....£15 *BritHerCollections*
(33) Capture of Ali Musjid...............£15 *Group Capt Randle*

C.D.S. POSTMARKS Price Guide £7-£10
(34) Kennedy Centre, Greenwich, The Science Museum
(35) World's End, Meridian Centre, Star Cross, Seven Sisters

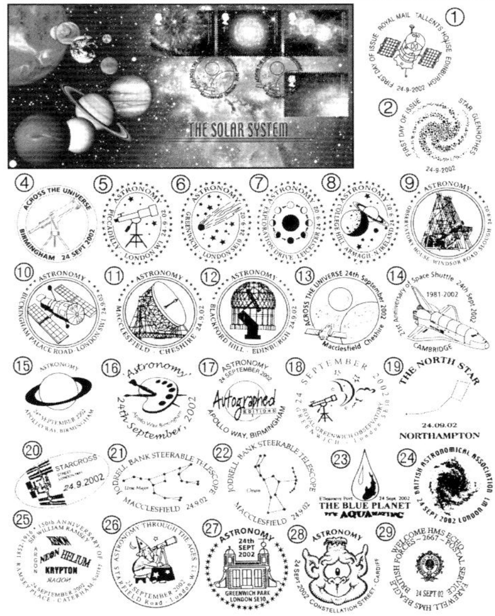

1st October 2002 - SMILERS GENERIC

3 x 1st: Father Christmas; Teddy Bear; Dennis the Menace.

SPECIAL HANDSTAMPS **SPONSOR**
Price Guide Ordinary Covers £4-£9 / Sponsored Covers:

(1) Smilers Issue, Bethlehem........£20 *Bradbury Windsor 22*
(2) Bear Park, Durham..................£20 *Benham (500)239*
(3) Bearstead, Maidstone ....£15 *Benham BLCS 239*
(4) Bean, Dartford ....£15 *Benham BLCS 239*

8th October 2002 - PILLAR TO POST

2nd 1857 Decorative box; 1st 1874 Mainland box; E 1933 Airmail box; 47p 1939 Dual-aperture box; 68p 1980 New-style

SPECIAL HANDSTAMPS **SPONSOR**
Price Guide Ordinary Covers £4-£9 / Sponsored Covers:

(1) FDI - Tallents House..................... *Royal Mail (n.s.c.)*
(2) FDI - Bishops Caundle .... *Royal Mail (n.s.c.)*
(3) -do- non pictorial version .... *Royal Mail (n.s.c.)*
(4) Pillar to Post, Birmingham............ *Royal Mail (n.s.c.)*
(5) Pillar to Post, Solihull ....£20 *Benham Pilgrim*
(6) Pillar to Post, Windsor............£15 *Benham BLCS 238*
(7) Pillar to Post, Edinburgh ....£20 *Benham Coin Cover*
(8) Pillar to Post, Salford ....£30 *Benham (500)238*
(9) Pillar to Post, London ....£15 *Benham BLCS 238*
(10) Letter Box Study Group ....£20 *Bradbury Sovereign 20*
(11) Post Box Lane Abingdon........£15 *Westminster*
(12) Post Box Lane (palette) ....£15 *Westminster*
(13) Autographed, Post Box Ln.....£25 *Westminster*
(14) Mount Pleasant........................£15 *Steven Scott 71*
(15) The Pillar Box, EC1 ....£15 *M Brazier (Pubs 50)*
(16) Ye Olde Post Box Horsham ..£15 *R Park*
(17) Post Office Way, SW8.............£15 *GB 70*
(18) Bath Postal Museum................£15 *Buckingham Cvrs 24*
(19) Local Post, Runcorn ....£20 *P Sheridan*
(20) First Pillar Box, EC1 ....£20 *CoverCraft*
(21) Post Office Way, SW8.............£20 *P M Payne*
(22) Royal Hospital, Chelsea..........£20 *FourpennyPost*
(23) Folkestone.................................£20 *H D MacIntyre*
(24) Secret Postbox 111 ....£15 *Bletchley PO*
(25) Botchergate, Carlisle................£15 *Phil Stamp Covers 33*
(26) Exmouth Stamp Club..............£25 *Exmouth Stamp Club*

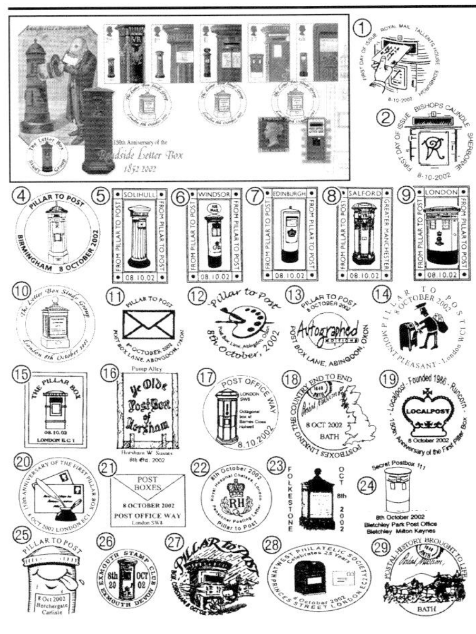

(27) Box, Corsham ....£15 *Stick with Stamps*
(28) NatWest Philatelic Soc.............£15 *NW Phil Soc*
(29) Bath (changeable date)...........£15 *Buckingham Cvrs 24*
(30) "Dolphin", Portsmouth ....£15 *RN CvrsGp*
(31) Lossiemouth, 617 Squadron ..£15 *BritHerCollections*
(32) Capture of Kabul ....£15 *Group Capt Randle*
(33) Baltasound, Unst, Shetland .... *Royal Mail (n.s.c.)*
C.D.S. POSTMARKS Price Guide £7-£10
(34) Box, Send, Bishops Caundle, Sanquhar, Botchergate
(35) Mount Pleasant, Postbridge, Baltasound

5th November 2002 - CHRISTMAS

2nd Spruce; 1st Holly; E Ivy; 47p Mistletoe; 68p Pine Cone
SPECIAL HANDSTAMPS SPONSOR
Price Guide Ordinary Covers £4-£9 / Sponsored Covers:
(1) FDI - Tallents House..................... *Royal Mail (n.s.c.)*
(2) FDI - Bethlehem .... *Royal Mail (n.s.c.)*
(3) -do- non pictorial version .... *Royal Mail (n.s.c.)*
(4) Seasons Greetings, Bethlehem..... *Royal Mail (n.s.c.)*
(5) Christmas, Birmingham .... *Royal Mail (n.s.c.)*
(6) Christmas, Bethlehem ....£15 *Benham BLCS 240*
(7) Christmas, Nasareth ....£20 *Benham Coin Cover*
(8) Christmas, Shepherds Green .£15 *Benham BLCS 240*
(9) Christmas, Star..........................£20 *Benham*
(10) Christmas, Wisemans Bridge .£20 *Benham (500)240*
(11) Christmas Kiss, Bethlehem.....£15 *Bradbury Sovereign 23*
(12) Holly Gardens, Margate ....£15 *Westminster*
(13) Holly Gardens (palette) ....£15 *Westminster*
(14) Autographed, Holly Gdns ......£25 *Westminster*
(15) Holly Way, Mitcham ....£15 *Steven Scott 72*
(16) The Ivy Bush Inn, Llandybie .£15 *M Brazier (Pubs 51)*
(17) Robin Close, NW7 ....£15 *GB 71*
(18) Coventry Cathedral..................£15 *Buckingham Cvrs 25*
(19) Trafalgar Square ....£15 *P Sheridan*
(20) Peace & Goodwill, Bletchley £10 *Bletchley PO*
(21) Merry Christmas, Dartford.....£15 *Phil Stamp Covers*
(22) Mistletoe Green, Oxford.........£15 *Phil Stamp Covers 34*
(23) Hollybush, Blackwood ....£15 *Stick with Stamps*
(24) Classic British Films, Ealing ..£25 *Cam S.C.*
(25) 617 Squadron, Lincoln ....£25 *Cam S.C.*
(26) Minewatchers, London ....£15 *RN CvrsGp*
(27) Mildenhall, 15 Squadron........£15 *BritHerCollections*
(28) Battle of Tel-el-Kebir...............£15 *Group Capt Randle*
C.D.S. POSTMARKS Price Guide £7-£10
(29) Holy Island, Ivy Bush, Ivy Mount, Winter Gardens
(30) Hollybush, Holly Hall, Botanic Gardens, Woodberry Grove
(31) Holly Lane, Pinewoods, Berryhill, Holly Hedge

Values include VAT @ 17.5%

5th December 2002 - WILDINGS

1p, 2p, 5p, 2nd, 1st, 30p, 37p, 47p, 50p Reprint of Wilding Definitives
SPECIAL HANDSTAMPS SPONSOR
Price Guide Ordinary Covers £4-£9 / Sponsored Covers:
(1) FDI - Tallents House..................... *Royal Mail (n.s.c.)*
(2) FDI - Windsor .... *Royal Mail (n.s.c.)*
(3) -do- non pictorial version .... *Royal Mail (n.s.c.)*
(4) Buckingham Palace Rd............£15 *Benham BLCS 241*
(5) Portman Square.......................£20 *Benham*
(6) Regent Street ....£20 *Benham*
(7) Old Bond Street........................£15 *Benham BLCS 241*
(8) King Edward Street..................£20 *Benham Coin Cover*
(9) Longford...................................£20 *Benham Pilgrim*
(10) High Wycombe.........................£20 *Benham Pilgrim*
(11) Basingstoke...............................£20 *Benham Pilgrim*
(12) The Octagon, Bath...................£20 *Benham*
(13) Wild about Wildings................£25 *Bradbury Windsor 21*
(14) 1952 to 2002, George St.........£15 *Westminster*
(15) George Street, (palette)...........£15 *Westminster*
(16) Autographed, George St ....£25 *Westminster*
(17) Westminster Abbey, SW1........£15 *Westminster*
(18) Elizabethan Definitives...........£15 *Buckingham Cvrs 28*
(19) George St, Portman Square ...£15 *P Sheridan*
(20) Bond Street, London W5 ....£15 *Phil Stamp Covers 35*
(21) Battles of El-Teb & Tamaai ...£15 *Group Capt Randle*
(22) Charlton Athletic......................£15 *Dawn*
C.D.S. POSTMARKS Price Guide £7-£10
(23) Portman Sq., Queen's Parade, Crown House, Throne

14th January 2003 - BIRDS of PREY

5 x 1st Barn Owl; 5 x 1st Kestrel
SPECIAL HANDSTAMPS SPONSOR
Price Guide Ordinary Covers £4-£9 / Sponsored Covers:
(1) FDI - Tallents House..................... *Royal Mail (n.s.c.)*
(2) FDI - Hawkshead .... *Royal Mail (n.s.c.)*
(3) -do- non pictorial version .... *Royal Mail (n.s.c.)*
(4) Birds of Prey, Birmingham............ *Royal Mail (n.s.c.)*
(5) Birds of Prey, Newent ....£20 *Benham Pilgrim*

(6) Birds of Prey, Oakham............£20 *Benham Pilgrim*
(7) Birds of Prey, Ravenglass ....£20 *Benham (500)242*
(8) Birds of Prey, Bangor..............£20 *Benham Coin Cover*
(9) Birds of Prey, Carradale..........£20 *Benham*
(10) Birds of Prey, Edinburgh ....£20 *Benham*
(11) Birds of Prey, Thetford............£15 *Benham BLCS 242*
(12) Birds of Prey, Sandy ....£15 *Benham BLCS 242*
(13) Birds of Prey, Andover............£20 *Benham*
(14) Birds of Prey, Ringwood.........£20 *Benham Pilgrim*
(15) Birds of Prey, Sandy ....£15 *Bradbury Sovereign 24*
(16) Barn Owl Close, Torquay.......£15 *Westminster*
(17) Barn Owl Close (palette)........£15 *Westminster*
(18) Autographed, Barn Owl Cl ....£25 *Westminster*
(19) Bird in Bush Road ....£15 *Steven Scott 75*
(20) The Kestrel & the Falcon.......£20 *M Brazier (Rly.3)*
(21) The Barn Owl ....£15 *M Brazier (Pubs 52)*
(22) Eagle Street, London WC1 ....£15 *GB 72*
(23) Barn Owl Ctre, Brockworth ..£15 *Buckingham Cvrs 29*
(24) Eagle Heights, Eynesford........£15 *Buckingham Cvrs 29*
(25) The Hawk & Owl Trust..........£15 *CoverCraft*
(26) Hoo Farm..................................£15 *P Sheridan*
(27) Barn Owl, Owlswick ....£15 *Phil Stamp Covers 36*
(28) Wing, Leighton Buzzard.........£15 *Phil Stamp Covers 37*
(29) Eagle, Lincoln ....£15 *Stick with Stamps*
(30) Many Hoots Owl Centre ....£20 *H D MacIntrye*
(31) Papagallos Restaurant ....£15 *P M Payne*
(32) HMS/M Triumph, Gosport....£20 *RN CvrsGp*
(33) Expedition Against Mlanje.....£15 *Group Capt Randle*
(34) Expedition Benin Territory ....£15 *Group Capt Randle*

C.D.S. POSTMARKS Price Guide £7-£10
(35) Owlsmoor, Wing, Falconwood, Eagle, Sandy
(36) Hawkshead, Hawkswood, Hawkhurst, Falcon Lodge

VALUES SHOULD BE TREATED AS A GUIDE
Please read the General Notes at the front of catalogue where you will find the answers to most of your questions.

21st January 2003 - FLOWERS Generic Issue

Reprinted version of the 1997 Flowers Greetings stamps in sheet format plus revised label designs.

SPECIAL HANDSTAMPS SPONSOR
Price Guide Ordinary Covers £4-£9 / Sponsored Covers:
(1) Botanical Fine Arts, Kew........£20 *Bradbury Windsor 23*
(2) Smilers, Rettendon Common.£20 *Benham*
(3) Smilers, Ardingly......................£15 *Benham BLCS 243*
(4) Smilers, St. Austell...................£20 *Benham Pilgrim*
(5) Smilers, Torrington..................£20 *Benham*
(6) Smilers, Llanarthney................£20 *Benham*
(7) Smilers, Mevagissey.................£20 *Benham Pilgrim*
(8) Smilers, Woking.......................£20 *Benham*
(9) Smilers, Kew..............................£15 *Benham BLCS 243*
(10) Smilers, Chelsea.......................£20 *Benham (500)243*
(11) Smilers, Harrogate...................£20 *Benham Pilgrim*

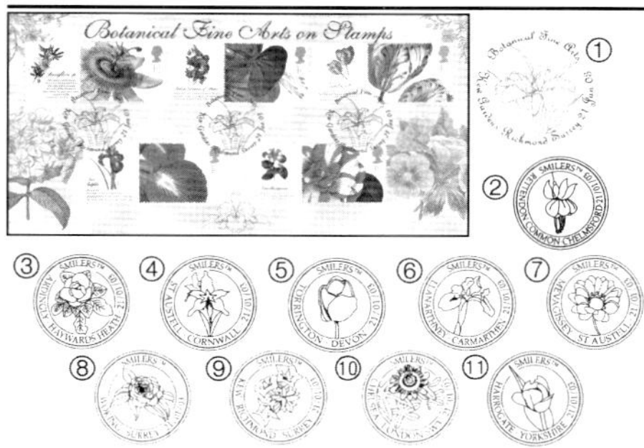

4th February 2003 - OCCASIONS

(1) 6 x 1st: Gold Star; I Love You; Angel; Yes; Oops!; I did it!
(2) 6 x 1st Stamps as above with generic labels.

SPECIAL HANDSTAMPS SPONSOR
Price Guide Ordinary Covers £4-£9 / Sponsored Covers:
(1) FDI - Tallents House..................... *Royal Mail (n.s.c.)*
(2) FDI - Merry Hill............................ *Royal Mail (n.s.c.)*
(3) -do- non pictorial version .... *Royal Mail (n.s.c.)*
(4) Occasions, Birmingham................ *Royal Mail (n.s.c.)*
(5) Flowerdown, Winchester........£15 *Benham BLCS 244*
(6) Angel Bank, Ludlow................£20 *Benham (500)244*
(7) May Street, London.................£20 *Benham Pilgrim*
(8) Jump, Barnsley..........................£20 *Benham Coin Cover*
(9) Star, Glenrothes........................£20 *Benham*
(10) Loversall, Doncaster................£15 *Benham BLCS 244*
(11) Gretna Green, Carlisle............£15 *Bradbury Sovereign 25*
(12) Angel Street, Worcester...........£15 *Westminster*
(13) Angel Street (palette)...............£15 *Westminster*
(14) Autographed, Angel Street.....£25 *Westminster*
(15) The True Lovers Knot.............£15 *M Brazier (Pubs 53)*
(16) Donkey Lane, Enfield ....£15 *GB 73*
(17) Just Married, Sandwich Kent.£15 *Buckingham Cvrs 30*
(18) Tickenham, Clevedon..............£15 *Phil Stamp Covers 38*
(19) Lover, Salisbury........................£20 *Stick with Stamps*
(20) Nostradamus ....£15 *P M Payne*

C.D.S. POSTMARKS Price Guide £7-£10
(21) Angel Hill, Playing Place, Lover, Gretna Green, Send, Mark

25th Feb 2003 - DNA: The SECRET of LIFE

2nd The End of the Beginning; 1st Comparative Genetics; E Cracking the Code; 47p Genetic Engineering; 68p Medical Futures. Also issued on the same day the ***Microcosmos*** *Prestige Stamp Book.*

SPECIAL HANDSTAMPS SPONSOR

Price Guide Ordinary Covers £4-£9 / Sponsored Covers:

(1) FDI - Tallents House.................... *Royal Mail (n.s.c.)*
(2) FDI - Cambridge .... *Royal Mail (n.s.c.)*
(3) -do- non pictorial version .... *Royal Mail (n.s.c.)*
(4) Secret of Life, Birmingham.......... *Royal Mail (n.s.c.)*
(5) Cambridge (fingerprint) ....£20 *Royal Mail/Royal Mint*
(6) London W1 ....£15 *Benham BLCS 245*
(7) London W12 ....£20 *Benham (500)245*
(8) Harley Street, London W1.....£20 *Benham*
(9) Belfast ....£20 *Benham*
(10) Edinburgh ....£20 *Benham Coin Cover*
(11) Cambridge..................................£15 *Benham BLCS 245*
(12) Harwell, Didcot ....£20 *Benham Pilgrim*
(13) Discovery of DNA....................£15 *Bradbury Sovereign 26*
(14) Secret of Life, Cambridge.......£15 *Westminster*
(15) Cambridge (palette) ....£15 *Westminster*
(16) Autographed, Cambridge........£25 *Westminster*
(17) Discovery Walk, London E1 .£15 *Steven Scott 76*
(18) The Eagle, Cambridge ....£15 *M Brazier (Pubs 54)*
(19) Discovery Walk,SE1 ....£15 *GB 74*
(20) Cambridge..................................£15 *Buckingham Cvrs 31*
(21) Genetic Interest Group............£15 *P Sheridan*
(22) Chemistry, Whitchurch...........£15 *Phil Stamp Covers 39*
(23) Crick, Northampton ....£20 *Stick with Stamps*
(24) Code, Bletchley Park ....£15 *Bletchley PO*
(25) Secret of Life, Cambridge.......£10 *Assoc. of GBFDC*
(26) Cavendish Laboratory.............£25 *Cam S.C.*
(27) William Harvery, E11 ....£15 *P M Payne*
(28) HMS Ark Royal........................£15 *RN CvrsGp*
(29) The Relief of Chitral ....£15 *Group Capt Randle*

C.D.S. POSTMARKS Price Guide £7-£10

(30) Crick, Cambridge, Watson Way, Weston Favell

4th March 2003 - 'HELLO' Self Adhesive

1st Occasions Hello (x2) issued in self-adhesive stamp book with four 1st Class definitives

SPECIAL HANDSTAMPS SPONSOR

Price Guide Ordinary Covers £4-£9 / Sponsored Covers:

(1) Hounslow, Middlesex.............£15 *Bradbury Windsor 26*
(2) Greetwell, Lincoln ....£15 *Benham BLCS 247*
(3) Waverton, Chester ....£15 *Benham BLCS 247*
(4) Flyford Flavell, Worcester......£20 *Benham*
(5) HMS Vanguard.........................£15 *RN CvrsGp*

25th March 2003 - FUN FRUIT & VEG

10 x 1st Strawberry, Potato, Apple, Pepper, Pear, Orange, Tomato, Lemon, Sprout, Aubergine.

SPECIAL HANDSTAMPS SPONSOR

Price Guide Ordinary Covers £4-£9 / Sponsored Covers:

(1) FDI - Tallents House.................... *Royal Mail (n.s.c.)*
(2) FDI - Pear Tree, Derby................. *Royal Mail (n.s.c.)*
(3) -do- non pictorial version .... *Royal Mail (n.s.c.)*
(4) Fun Fruit & Veg, Birmingham..... *Royal Mail (n.s.c.)*
(5) Pear Tree, Derby.......................£15 *Benham BLCS 248*
(6) Pepper Arden, Northallerton ..£15 *Benham BLCS 248*
(7) Brusselton, Shildon.................£20 *Benham*
(8) Garden Village, Hull ....£20 *Benham*
(9) Chipping, Preston....................£20 *Benham Coin Cover*
(10) Appleby, Scunthorpe...............£20 *Benham Pilgrim*
(11) Ripe, Lewes ....£20 *Benham*
(12) Bittering, Dereham..................£20 *Benham (500)248*
(13) Grove, Canterbury ....£20 *Benham*
(14) Strawberry Valley....................£20 *Benham*
(15) Covent Garden ....£15 *Bradbury Sovereign 27*
(16) Appletree, Daventry.................£15 *Westminster*
(17) Appletree (palette) ....£15 *Westminster*
(18) Autographed, Appletree..........£25 *Westminster*
(19) Sainsburys...............................£15 *M Brazier (Pubs 55)*
(20) Great Ormond Street ....£15 *Buckingham Cvrs 32*
(21) Eat for Health, Covent Gdn ..£15 *P Sheridan*
(22) Appledore, Ashford..................£15 *Phil Stamp Covers 40*
(23) Covent Garden ....£25 *Cam S.C.*
(24) Sainsbury Drury Lane ....£20 *A Bard*
(25) Sticker St. Austell....................£20 *A Bard*
(26) Child's Place, London ....£20 *H Athanassiades*
(27) Greens Turriff...........................£15 *Stick with Stamps*
(28) Operation Iceberg ....£15 *RN CvrsGp*

C.D.S. POSTMARKS Price Guide £7-£10

(29) Strawberry Hill, Orange Tree, Pear Tree, Apple Cross, Ripe
(30) The Allotments, The Orchards, Orchard Way, Jersey Farm

29th April 2003 - EXTREME ENDEAVOURS

(1) 2nd Amy Johnson; 1st Everest Team; E Freya Stark; 42p Ernest Shackleton; 47p Francis Chichester; 68p Robert Falcon Scott.

(2) Self Adhesive Stamp Book containing 6 x 1st Class Stamps: 2 Everest & 4 Definitives.

SPECIAL HANDSTAMPS — **SPONSOR**

Price Guide Ordinary Covers £4-£9 / Sponsored Covers:

(1) FDI - Tallents House .... *Royal Mail (n.s.c.)*
(2) FDI - Plymouth .... *Royal Mail (n.s.c.)*
(3) -do- non pictorial version .... *Royal Mail (n.s.c.)*
(4) Ext. Endeavours, Birmingham ..... *Royal Mail (n.s.c.)*
(5) Amy Johnson, Hull ....£15 *Benham BLCS 250*
(6) Edmund Hillary, SW1 ....£20 *Benham*
(7) Freya Strark, WC1 ....£20 *Benham (500)250*
(8) Francis Chichester ....£20 *Benham Coin Cover*
(9) Robert Falcon Scott ....£20 *Benham*
(10) Ernest Shackleton ....£15 *Benham BLCS 250*
(11) Ascent of Everest, SW1 ....£20 *Benham Pilgrim*
(12) Ascent of Everest, SW1 ....£15 *Benham BLCS 251*
(13) Amy Johnson, Derby ....£20 *Benham*
(14) Conquest of Everest, SW1 ......£20 *Bradbury Sovereign 28*
(15) Amy Johnson Memorabilia ....£15 *Anniv & Events 9*
(16) Self Adhesives, London ....£20 *Bradbury Windsor 29*
(17) Everest Place ....£15 *Westminster*
(18) Everest Place (palette) ....£15 *Westminster*
(19) Autographed, Everest Place ...£25 *Westminster*
(20) The Three Compasses ....£20 *M Brazier (Pubs 56)*
(21) Shackleton House, SE1 ....£20 *GB 75*
(22) Conquest of Mount Everest ...£20 *Buckingham Cvrs 33*
(23) Price's Candles, Bedford ....£20 *P Sheridan*
(24) Mountain Ash ....£15 *Phil Stamp Covers 42*
(25) Endeavour Way, SW19 ....£15 *Assoc. of GBFDC*
(26) Polemarch St, Seaham ....£15 *Stick with Stamps*
(27) RRS Discovery, Dundee ....£15 *Stick with Stamps*
(28) Dulwich College, SE21 ....£20 *CoverCraft*
(29) High Peak, Derby ....£25 *Cam S.C.*
(30) Self Adhesive Booklet ....£15 *A Bard*
(31) Summit, Littleborough ....£15 *A Bard*
(32) Greenwich, London SE1 ....£20 *H D MacIntyre*
(33) Endeavour Way, Barking ....£15 *Steven Scott*
(34) Endeavour High School ....£20 *J Bryan*
(35) Endeavour Way, SW19 ....£15 *P M Payne*
(36) HMS Scott, Devonport ....£15 *RN CvrsGp*
(37) Capture of Coomassie ....£15 *Group Capt Randle*

C.D.S. POSTMARKS Price Guide £7-£10

(38) Summit, Chichester, The Heights, North Pole Rd, The Camp
(39) any Hull pmk, Croydon, Buckingham Palace (£75)

20th May 2003 - WILDINGS

4p, 8p, 10p, 20p, 28p, 34p, E, 42p, 68 Reprint of Wilding Definitives

SPECIAL HANDSTAMPS — **SPONSOR**

Price Guide Ordinary Covers £4-£9 / Sponsored Covers:

(1) FDI - Tallents House .... *Royal Mail (n.s.c.)*
(2) FDI - Windsor .... *Royal Mail (n.s.c.)*
(3) -do- non pictorial version .... *Royal Mail (n.s.c.)*
(4) Wildings, Old Bond Street ....£25 *Benham (500)252*
(5) Wildings, Regent Street ....£20 *Benham Pilgrim*
(6) Wildings, Portman Square ......£20 *Benham*
(7) Wildings, King Edward St ......£20 *Benham Pilgrim*
(8) Wildings, London SW1 ....£20 *Benham*
(9) Wildings, Longford ....£20 *Benham Coin Cover*
(10) Wildings, High Wycombe ....£15 *Benham BLCS 252*
(11) Wildings, Basingstoke ....£15 *Benham BLCS 252*
(12) Wildings, The Octagon, Bath £20 *Benham*
(13) Wilding Revivals, Windsor .....£25 *Bradbury Windsor 24*
(14) Autographed, George Street ..£25 *Westminster*
(15) George Street (palette) ....£15 *Westminster*
(16) Wilding Defins, George St .....£15 *Westminster*
(17) Elizabethan Definitives ....£15 *Buckingham Cvrs*
(18) Wilding Defins Portman Sq ...£15 *P Sheridan*
(19) Old Bond Street, W5 ....£15 *Phil Stamp Covers 43*
(20) Chelsea, SW3 ....£25 *Royal Hort. Society*

C.D.S. POSTMARKS Price Guide £7-£10

(21) Portman Sq., Throne, Windsor, Innsworth

The General Notes at the beginning of this catalogue gives details of the following topics:

The scope of the catalogue - which first day covers are included and why.

Prices & condition - what to look for when buying first day covers.

Types of pmk: Special Handstamps, CDS, FDI, Slogans. **Types of cover: Sponsored or Ordinary.**

2nd June 2003 - CORONATION

*10 x 1st Scenes from the 1953 Coronation. Also issued on the same day the **A Perfect Coronation** Prestige Stamp Book.*

SPECIAL HANDSTAMPS SPONSOR
Price Guide Ordinary Covers £4-£9 / Sponsored Covers:

(1) FDI - Tallents House........................ *Royal Mail (n.s.c.)*
(2) FDI - London SW1 .... *Royal Mail (n.s.c.)*
(3) -do- non pictorial version .... *Royal Mail (n.s.c.)*
(4) Long Live the Queen, EC1.......... *Royal Mail (n.s.c.)*
(5) Coronation Anniversary, SW1..... *Royal Mail (n.s.c.)*
(6) Coronation, Birmingham .... *Royal Mail (n.s.c.)*
(7) Westminster - horses...............£15 *Benham BLCS 253*
(8) Westminster - coach................£30 *Benham (500)253*
(9) Westminster - crown & lion..£20 *Benham*
(10) Westminster - rose & thistle..£20 *Benham*
(11) Westminster - 50th Anniv......£20 *Benham Pilgrim*
(12) Westminster - Abbey...............£20 *Benham*
(13) London SW1 - crown ....£20 *Benham Coin Cover*
(14) Buck Palace Rd - lion ....£15 *Benham BLCS 253*
(15) God Save the Queen ....£20 *Benham*
(16) Buck Palace Rd - emblems ....£20 *Benham Pilgrim*
(17) 50th Anniv of Coronation......£15 *Bradbury Sovereign 29*
(18) Westminster Abbey.................£15 *Westminster*
(19) Abbey (palette).........................£15 *Westminster*
(20) Autographed, Abbey.................£25 *Westminster*
(21) Coronation Road, E13............£15 *Steven Scott*
(22) The Crown & Sceptre.............£15 *M Brazier (Pubs 57)*
(23) Coronation, Euston..................£15 *M Brazier (Rly.4)*
(24) Coronation Road, E13............£15 *GB 76*
(25) Westminster Abbey, SW1.......£15 *Buckingham Cvrs 34*
(26) Buckingham Palace, SW1......£15 *Buckingham Cvrs 34*
(27) Express Newspapers, SW1.....£15 *Buckingham Cvrs*
(28) Heraldry Society, SW1............£20 *CoverCraft*
(29) Queen Elizabeth St, SE1........£15 *P Sheridan*
(30) £1 The Coronation, SW1........£15 *Phil Stamp Covers 45*
(31) Windsor....................................£15 *Phil Stamp Covers 44*
(32) Coronation Court.....................£10 *Assoc. of GBFDC*
(33) Coronation Chair, SW1..........£10 *Stick with Stamps*
(34) Coronation Crown, SW1.........£10 *Stick with Stamps*
(35) Westminster Abbey, SW1.......£15 *Cam S.C.*
(36) Happy Birthday, Wawne........£20 *J Bryan*
(37) Three Crowns..........................£15 *P M Payne*
(38) Coronation Tram, Blackpool.£20 *Dawn*
(39) HMS Invincible, London......£15 *RN CvrsGp*
(40) Morris Light Commercial.......£20 *DTL Enterprises*
(41) Battle of Omdurman................£15 *Group Capt Randle*
(42) Battle of Battle of Atbara ....£15 *Group Capt Randle*
(43) Royal Hospital Haslar.............£20 *R F John*

C.D.S. POSTMARKS Price Guide £7-£10

(44) Scone, Windsor
(45) Throne, Coronation Parade, Queen's Parade or similar
(46) Buckingham Palace, Windsor Castle (£75 each)

17th June 2003 - PRINCE WILLIAM

28p, E, 47p, 68p Photographic portraits of the Prince

SPECIAL HANDSTAMPS SPONSOR
Price Guide Ordinary Covers £4-£9 / Sponsored Covers:

(1) FDI - Tallents House........................ *Royal Mail (n.s.c.)*
(2) FDI - Cardiff .... *Royal Mail (n.s.c.)*
(3) -do- non pictorial version .... *Royal Mail (n.s.c.)*
(4) 21st Birthday, Birmingham.......... *Royal Mail (n.s.c.)*
(5) Prince William, St. Andrews..£15 *Benham BLCS 255*
(6) Prince William, Windsor........£15 *Benham BLCS 255*
(7) Prince William, W2 ....£20 *Benham (500)255*
(8) Prince William, SW1 ....£20 *Benham Coin Cover*
(9) Windsor......................................£15 *Bradbury Sovereign 31*
(10) Highgrove House, Tetbury.....£15 *Westminster*
(11) St Andrews, Fife......................£15 *Westminster*
(12) St Andrews (palette)...............£15 *Westminster*
(13) Autographed, St Andrews......£25 *Westminster*
(14) Prince of Wales Road.............£15 *Steven Scott*
(15) Windsor Castle........................£15 *M Brazier (Pubs 58)*
(16) William Road, NW1................£15 *GB 77*
(17) Caernarfon...............................£15 *Buckingham Cvrs 35*
(18) Caernarfon...............................£15 *P Sheridan*
(19) Fort William ....£15 *Phil Stamp Covers 46*
(20) Prince of Wales, Windsor.......£15 *Stick with Stamps*
(21) Prince of Wales Road.............£15 *P M Payne*
(22) Sailing Ship Prince William...£15 *RN CvrsGp*
(23) National Ecumenical...............£20 *Methodist Philat. Soc*
(24) John Wesley, Epworth............£20 *Methodist Philat. Soc*
(25) The Attack on Fort Lubwas...£15 *Group Capt Randle*

C.D.S. POSTMARKS Price Guide £7-£10

(26) Eton, St. Andrews, Cardiff, Windsor, Great Brington
(27) Caernarfon, Tetbury, Paddington (Born St. Mary's Hosp),
(28) Princes Avenue, William Street, or similar

15th July 2003 - SCOTLAND

(1) 2nd Loch Assynt, Sutherland; 1st Ben More, Isle of Mull; E Rothiemurchus, Cairngorms; 42p Dalveen Pass, Lowther Hills; 47p Glenfinnan Viaduct, Lochaber; 68p Papa Little, Shetlands
(2) Self Adhesive Stamp Book containing 6 x 1st Class Stamps: 2 Ben More & 4 Definitives.

SPECIAL HANDSTAMPS SPONSOR
Price Guide Ordinary Covers £4-£9/Sponsored Covers:

(1) FDI - Tallents House .... *Royal Mail (n.s.c.)*
(2) FDI - London SW1 .... *Royal Mail (n.s.c.)*
(3) -do- non pictorial version .... *Royal Mail (n.s.c.)*
(4) Scotland, Birmingham .... *Royal Mail (n.s.c.)*
(5) Papa Little, Baltasound...........£15 *Benham BLCS 256*
(6) Aviemore...................................£20 *Benham Coin Cover*
(7) Glenfinnan.................................£15 *Benham BLCS 256*
(8) Crianlarich................................£20 *Benham*
(9) Ullapool......................................£20 *Benham (500)256*
(10) Wanlockhead, Biggar..............£20 *Benham Pilgrim*
(11) Ben More, Isle of Mull...........£15 *Benham BLCS 257*
(12) Crianlarich................................£20 *Benham*
(13) Ben More, Isle of Mull...........£20 *Benham (500)257*
(14) Beautiful Britain, Edinburgh..£15 *Bradbury Sovereign 30*
(15) Self Adhesives, Alloway..........£15 *Bradbury Windsor 32*
(16) Fort William ....£15 *Westminster*
(17) Fort William (palette)..............£15 *Westminster*
(18) Autographed, Fort William ....£25 *Westminster*
(19) Aberdeen Place, NW8.............£15 *Steven Scott*
(20) Scotland Place, EC1 ....£15 *GB 78*
(21) Loch Ness, Inverness ....£15 *Buckingham Cvrs 36*
(22) Glenfinnan Viaduct ....£15 *P Sheridan*
(23) Drumnadrochit, Inverness .....£15 *Phil Stamp Covers 47*
(24) Thistle St., Edinburgh.............£15 *Stick with Stamps*
(25) Beauties of Scotland................£20 *Cam S.C.*
(26) Dalmally.....................................£20 *H D MacIntyre*
(27) Naval Base, Faslane.................£15 *RN CvrsGp*
(28) Scott's View, Melrose..............£15 *A Bard*
(29) Letters, Lochbroom Garve.....£15 *A Bard*
(30) Steyn's War Cabinet ....£15 *Group Capt Randle*

C.D.S. POSTMARKS Price Guide £7-£10

(31) The Scotlands, Glenfinnan, Aviemore, Lochside
(32) Leadhills, Lochinver, Highland Dykes, Aith, Thistle Hill

29 July 2003 - CROSSWORDS Generic Issue

Reprinted version of the 1996 Cartoons Greetings stamps in sheet format plus labels featuring Crosswords in miniature.

SPECIAL HANDSTAMPS SPONSOR
Price Guide Ordinary Covers £4-£9/Sponsored Covers:

(1) Crosswords on Stamps .... *Bradbury Windsor 35*

12th August 2003 - PUB SIGNS

1st The Station; 'E' Black Swan; 42p The Cross Keys; 47p The Mayflower; 68p The Barley Sheaf

SPECIAL HANDSTAMPS SPONSOR
Price Guide Ordinary Covers £4-£9 / Sponsored Covers:

(1) FDI - Tallents House..................... *Royal Mail (n.s.c.)*
(2) FDI - Cross Keys, Hereford.......... *Royal Mail (n.s.c.)*
(3) -do- non pictorial version .... *Royal Mail (n.s.c.)*
(4) Pub Signs, Birmingham .... *Royal Mail (n.s.c.)*
(5) Rotherham.................................£15 *Benham BLCS 258*
(6) Leicester ....£30 *Benham (500)258*
(7) Southsea....................................£20 *Benham Coin Cover*
(8) Lincoln ....£15 *Benham BLCS 258*
(9) Bodmin.......................................£20 *Benham Pilgrim*
(10) The Inn Sign Society...............£20 *Bradbury Sovereign 32*
(11) Cross Keys, Hereford...............£15 *Westminster*
(12) Cross Keys, (palette)................£15 *Westminster*
(13) Autographed, Q.Victoria St ...£25 *Westminster*
(14) Autographed, Cross Keys ....£25 *Westminster*
(15) Lords Cricket Ground.............£15 *Steven Scott*
(16) Original Pub Cover Series......£15 *M Brazier (Pubs 60)*
(17) Taverners Way, E4..................£15 *GB 79*
(18) Shepherd Neame.....................£15 *Buckingham Cvrs 37*
(19) Beer & Pub Assoc, SW8.........£20 *CoverCraft*
(20) The Crown, Widnes.................£15 *P Sheridan*
(21) Beer, Seaton ....£15 *Phil Stamp Covers 48*
(22) Drinker's End Gloucester.......£15 *Stick with Stamps*
(23) Captain Ridley's Billets...........£15 *Bletchley PO*
(24) The Big Match, Manchester...£15 *Dawn*
(25) The Scapehouse Inn ....£20 *R C Productions*
(26) Life of 'HMS Black Swan' .....£15 *RN CvrsGp*
(27) Real Ale Tasting Soc, WC1....£20 *P M Payne*
(28) Pubs & Stars of Jazz................£15 *P M Payne*
(29) Relief of Peking........................£15 *Group Capt Randle*

C.D.S. POSTMARKS Price Guide £7-£10

(30) Beer, Barley Mow, Brewery Road, Cross Keys
(31) Old Swan, Royal Oak, Black Bull

18th Sept 2003 - TRANSPORTS of DELIGHT

(1) 1st Meccano Constructor Biplane; E Wells-Brimtoy Clockwork Omnibus; 42p Hornby Clockwork Locomotive; 47p Dinky Ford Zephyr; 68p Mettoy Space Ship Eagle
(2) Miniature Sheet.
(3) Self Adhesive Stamp Book containing 6 x 1st Class Stamps: 2 Meccano Biplane & 4 Definitives.

SPECIAL HANDSTAMPS **SPONSOR**
Price Guide Ordinary Covers £4-£9 / Sponsored Covers:

(1) FDI - Tallents House .... *Royal Mail (n.s.c.)*
(2) FDI - Toye, Downpatrick .... *Royal Mail (n.s.c.)*
(3) -do- non pictorial version .... *Royal Mail (n.s.c.)*
(4) Transports of Delight, Stampex ... *Royal Mail (n.s.c.)*
(5) Stampex 50th Anniversary .... *Royal Mail (n.s.c.)*
(6) Birmingham .... *Royal Mail (n.s.c.)*
(7) Epping .... £15 *Benham BLCS 260*
(8) Margate .... £15 *Benham BLCS 260*
(9) Northampton .... £15 *Benham BLCS 261*
(10) Liverpool .... £20 *Benham Coin Cover*
(11) TLiverpool .... £15 *Benham BLCS 259*
(12) York .... £20 *Benham (500)259*
(13) Duxford .... £20 *Benham Coin Cover*
(14) Beaulieu .... £20 *Benham (500)260*
(15) Corgi Leicester .... £15 *Benham BLCS 259*
(16) Hornby Lancaster .... £15 *Bradbury Sovereign 33*
(17) Hornby Lancaster .... £15 *Bradbury Windsor 30*
(18) Self Adhesives, Hornby .... £15 *Bradbury Windsor 31*
(19) Hornby Close, London .... £15 *Westminster*
(20) Hornby Close (palette) .... £15 *Westminster*
(21) Autographed, Hornby Cl .... £25 *Westminster*
(22) www.scificollector.co.uk .... £15 *Steven Scott*
(23) Orient Way, London E5 .... £15 *GB 80*
(24) Hornby, Margate .... £20 *Buckingham Cvrs 38*
(25) Hornby, Stampex .... £20 *Buckingham Cvrs 38*
(26) Pollock's Toy Museum .... £20 *P Sheridan*
(27) Toy & Hobby Association .... £20 *CoverCraft*
(28) Bletchley Park Post Office .... £15 *Bletchley PO*
(29) Hornby, Lancaster .... £15 *Phil Stamp Covers 50*
(30) Eagle, Lincoln .... £15 *Phil Stamp Covers 49*
(31) Dinky Trams & Buses .... £20 *Dawn*
(32) Memory Lane, Leicester .... £20 *Stick with Stamps*
(33) Transport Revisited .... £20 *P M Payne*
(34) Barry Potter Toy Collectors ... £20 *M Brazier (Pubs.61)*
(35) Duke Ellington .... £20 *P M Payne*
(36) Ford Centenary, Dagenham ... £20 *D T L Enterprises*
(37) Recapture of Kumassi .... £15 *Group Capt Randle*
(38) Off Tripoli, Faslane .... £15 *RN CvrsGp*

C.D.S. POSTMARKS Price Guide £7-£10
(39) The Rocket, Playing Place, Hornby, Eagle, Model Village

30 Sept 2003 - ROBINS Generic Issue

Reprinted version of the 2001 1st Class Christmas Robins stamps in sheet format plus labels.

SPECIAL HANDSTAMPS **SPONSOR**
Price Guide Ordinary Covers £4-£9 / Sponsored Covers:

(1) Christmas Common .... £20 *Benham*
(2) Christmas, Bethlehem .... £10 *Bradbury Windsor 37*
(3) RAF Coltishall .... £10 *British Forces*

7th October 2003 - BRITISH MUSEUM

2nd Coffin of Denytenamun; 1st Alexander the Great; 'E' Sutton Hoo Helmet; 42p Sculpture of Parvati; 47p Mask of Xiuhtecuhtli; 68p Hoa Hakananai'a

SPECIAL HANDSTAMPS **SPONSOR**
Price Guide Ordinary Covers £4-£9 / Sponsored Covers:

(1) FDI - Tallents House .... *Royal Mail (n.s.c.)*
(2) FDI - London WC1 .... *Royal Mail (n.s.c.)*
(3) -do- non pictorial version .... *Royal Mail (n.s.c.)*
(4) London WC1 .... *Royal Mail*
(5) Birmingham .... *Royal Mail (n.s.c.)*
(6) Great Russell St (Egyptian) ... £20 *Benham Coin Cover*
(7) British Museum .... £20 *Benham (500)262*
(8) British Museum (coin) .... £20 *Benham*
(9) Great Russell St (snake) .... £20 *Benham Pilgrim*
(10) British Museum (circle) .... £10 *Benham BLCS 262*
(11) British Museum (oval) .... £10 *Benham BLCS 262*
(12) 250 Years British Museums ... £10 *Bradbury Sovereign 34*
(13) British Museums (helmet) .... £10 *Westminster*
(14) British Museums (palette) .... £10 *Westminster*
(15) Autographed, Museums .... £20 *Westminster*
(16) 250 Years of Excellence .... £10 *Steven Scott*
(17) Museum Tavern, WC1 .... £15 *M Brazier (Pubs.62)*
(18) Headstone Road, Harrow .... £10 *GB 81*
(19) Egyptian Art .... £15 *P Sheridan*
(20) The British Museum .... £10 *Phil Stamp Covers 51*
(21) Museum Street .... £10 *Assoc. of GBFDC*
(22) Sutton Hoo, Woodbridge .... £10 *Stick with Stamps*

(23) Sloane Square, SW1 ....£10 *A Bard*
(24) Woodnesborough ....£20 *H D McIntyre*
(25) Canford School, Wimborne ...£20 *T Hurlstone*
(26) Morris Traveller, Cowley ....£20 *D T L Enterprises*
(27) HMS Unruly ....£10 *RN CvrsGp*
(28) Concorde Farewell Flight ....£20 *Buckingham Cvrs*
C.D.S. POSTMARKS Price Guide £7-£10
(29) Russell Square, Elgin, Sutton, The Galleries, Sloane Sq.

4th November 2003 - CHRISTMAS

2nd Ice Spiral; 1st Icicle Star; 'E' Wall of Frozen Snow; 53p Ice Ball; 68p Ice Hole; £1.12 Snow Pyramids
Also issued on same date 2nd & 1st Generic Sheets

SPECIAL HANDSTAMPS SPONSOR
Price Guide Ordinary Covers £4-£9 / Sponsored Covers:
(1) FDI - Tallents House...................... *Royal Mail (n.s.c.)*
(2) FDI - Bethlehem .... *Royal Mail (n.s.c.)*
(3) -do- non pictorial version .... *Royal Mail (n.s.c.)*
(4) Seasons Greetings, Bethlehem..... *Royal Mail (n.s.c.)*
(5) Christmas, Snow Hill, B'ham....... *Royal Mail (n.s.c.)*
(6) Chilwell, Nottingham ....£20 *Benham Coin Cover*
(7) Frostrow, Sedbergh ....£15 *Benham*
(8) Crystal Peaks, Sheffield...........£15 *Benham*
(9) Winterburn, Skipton................£30 *Benham (500)267*
(10) Snowhill, Enniskillen ....£10 *Benham BLCS 267*
(11) Cold Blow, Narberth ....£10 *Benham BLCS 267*
(12) Bethlehem.................................£15 *Bradbury Sovereign 35*
(13) Snowball Hill, Maidenhead ...£10 *Westminster*
(14) Snowball Hill (palette)............£10 *Westminster*
(15) Autographed, Snowball Hill ..£20 *Westminster*
(16) St Nicholas Rd, SE18..............£10 *Steven Scott*
(17) Wise Man, Dorchester ....£15 *M Brazier (Pubs.63)*
(18) Snowy Fielder Waye................£10 *GB 82*
(19) Freezywater, Enfield ....£10 *P Sheridan*
(20) Merry Christmas, Dartford.....£10 *Phil Stamp Covers*
(21) Cold Christmas, Ware ....£10 *Phil Stamp Covers 52*
(22) Freezywater, Enfield ....£10 *ABC-FDC*
(23) Bletchley Park ....£10 *Bletchley PO*
(24) Hector Berlioz ....£10 *P M Payne*
(25) Loch Striven, Dunoon ....£10 *RN CvrsGp*
C.D.S. POSTMARKS Price Guide £7-£10
(26) Freezywater, Winter Gdns, North Pole Rd, Frosterley

19 Dec 2003 - RUGBY WORLD CHAMPIONS

1st Flags; 1st Team Circle; 68p World Cup; 68p Rear of Team

SPECIAL HANDSTAMPS SPONSOR
Price Guide Ordinary Covers £4-£9 / Sponsored Covers:
(1) FDI - Tallents House...................... *Royal Mail (n.s.c.)*
(2) FDI - Twickenham .... *Royal Mail (n.s.c.)*
(3) -do- non pictorial version .... *Royal Mail (n.s.c.)*
(4) Congratulations, Birmingham ...... *Royal Mail (n.s.c.)*
(5) England Rugby, WC2 ....£20 *Benham*
(6) England Rugby, SW1 ....£15 *Benham BLCS 270*
(7) England Rugby, Twick'ham ...£20 *Benham*
(8) England Rugby, Rugby............£20 *Benham*
(9) World Champions.....................£20 *Benham*
(10) World Champions, Leics ....£15 *Bradbury Sovereign 44*
(11) Birthplace of Rugby ....£15 *Anniv & Events 21*
(12) Leicester Tigers.........................£20 *Bradbury*
(13) Rugby ....£15 *Westminster*
(14) Rugby (palette)..........................£15 *Westminster*
(15) Autographed, Rugby ....£25 *Westminster*
(16) Twickenham ....£15 *Steven Scott*
(17) William Webb Ellis, Rugby ....£15 *M Brazier (Pubs.65)*
(18) Northampton Saints ....£15 *M Brazier (Sports.1)*
(19) GB Covers, Kenton...................£15 *GB 84*
(20) England Rugby World Cup ....£15 *Buckingham Cvrs 41*
(21) Rugby School ....£15 *CoverCraft*
(22) World Champions, Rugby ......£15 *Phil Stamp Cvrs 52a*
C.D.S. POSTMARKS Price Guide £7-£10
(23) Twickenham, Rugby

13th Jan 2004 - CLASSIC LOCOMOTIVES

(1) 20p Talyllyn Railway; 28p Bo'ness & Kinneil Railway; E Great Central Railway; 42p Severn Valley Railway; 47p Bluebell Railway; 68p Keighley & Worth Valley Rly
(2) Miniature Sheet.

SPECIAL HANDSTAMPS SPONSOR
Price Guide Ordinary Covers £4-£9 / Sponsored Covers:
(1) FDI - Tallents House...................... *Royal Mail (n.s.c.)*
(2) FDI - York .... *Royal Mail (n.s.c.)*
(3) -do- non pictorial version .... *Royal Mail (n.s.c.)*
(4) 2004 Penydarren Merthyr Tydfil . *Royal Mail (n.s.c.)*
(5) New Street Birmingham .... *Royal Mail (n.s.c.)*
(6) Tywyn, Gwynedd......................£20 *Benham BLCS 269*
(7) Bo'ness, West Lothian.............£25 *Benham Pilgrim*
(8) Loughborough...........................£20 *Benham BLCS 269*

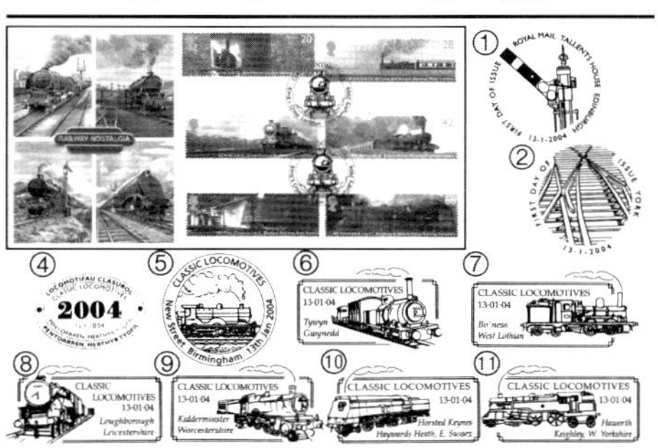

(9) Kidderminster ....£15 *Benham(s)*
(10) Horsted Keynesx ....£20 *Benham BLCS 268*
(11) Haworth, Keighley ....£15 *Benham(s)*
(12) Euston Station, NW1 ....£20 *Benham BLCS 268*
(13) King's Cross, N1 ....£25 *Benham Coin Cover*
(14) Penydarren, Merthyr Tydfil....£30 *Benham (500)268*
(15) King's Cross, London ....£20 *Bradbury Sovereign 36*
(16) King's Cross, London ....£20 *Westminster*
(17) Penydarren, Merthyr Tydfil....£20 *Westminster*
(18) Penydarren, Merthyr Tydfil....£20 *Westminster*
(19) Penydarren (palette) ....£20 *Westminster*
(20) Autographed, Penydarren.......£30 *Westminster*
(21) Charing Cross...........................£15 *Steven Scott*
(22) The North Western ....£20 *M Brazier (Pubs.64)*
(23) King Arthur Close, SE15........£20 *GB 83*
(24) Railway Magazine, SE1 ....£20 *Buckingham Cvrs 201*
(25) Great Central Railway.............£20 *Buckingham Cvrs 201*
(26) National Railway Museum.....£20 *Buckingham Cvrs 201*
(27) Bo'ness & Kinneil Railway ....£20 *CoverCraft*
(28) Keighley & Worth Valley ....£20 *P Sheridan*
(29) Classic Locos, Bridgnorth ......£15 *Phil Stamp Covers 53*
(30) Classic Locos, York ....£15 *Phil Stamp Covers 54*
(31) Railtrail Tours, Leek, Staffs....£15 *Dawn*
(32) Canterbury ....£20 *H D MacIntyre*
(33) Flying Scotsman, Euston ....£15 *Assoc. of GBFDC*
(34) London Victoria ....£25 *Cam S.C.*
(35) Bletchley Park Post Office .....£15 *Bletchley PO*
(36) Rheilffordd Talyllyn Rly..........£25 *Talyllyn Rly Company*
(37) Wrenn Railways Collectors....£20 *B Fentiman*
(38) NATO Atlantic Squadron ......£15 *RN CvrsGp*
(39) Royal Navy Football Assoc'n.£15 *R F John*
(40) Chattanooga Choo Choo........£15 *P M Payne*
C.D.S. POSTMARKS Price Guide £7-£10
(41) Keighley, Bewdley, Loughborough, Bo'ness
(42) Uckfield, Ffestiniog, Tywyn, Railway Road

30th January 2004 - 'HELLO' Generic Issue

1st Occasions Hello stamp + labels to mark the Hong Kong Stamp Expo and Year of the Monkey

SPECIAL HANDSTAMPS SPONSOR
Price Guide Ordinary Covers £4-£9 / Sponsored Covers:
(1) Year of the Monkey.................£10 *Bradbury Windsor 42*

3rd February 2004 - OCCASIONS

(1) 5 x 1st Entertaining Envelopes; (2) Generic Sheet

SPECIAL HANDSTAMPS SPONSOR
Price Guide Ordinary Covers £4-£9 / Sponsored Covers:
(1) FDI - Tallents House..................... *Royal Mail (n.s.c.)*
(2) FDI - Merry Hill............................ *Royal Mail (n.s.c.)*
(3) -do- non pictorial version .... *Royal Mail (n.s.c.)*
(4) Valentine Road, Birmingham....... *Royal Mail (n.s.c.)*
(5) Happisburgh, Norwich............£15 *Benham Pilgrim*
(6) Penn, High Wycombe ....£10 *Benham BLCS 271*
(7) Lovington, Castle Cary............£10 *Benham BLCS 271*
(8) Newsome, Huddersfield..........£15 *Benham (500)271*
(9) Babel, Landovery ....£15 *Benham Coin Cover*
(10) Gretna Green ....£10 *Bradbury Sovereign 37*
(11) Letter Box Lane, Sevenoaks..£10 *Westminster*
(12) -do- Autographed Editions.....£15 *Westminster*
(13) -do- (palette design)................£10 *Westminster*
(14) Postling, Hythe ....£10 *Buckingham Cvrs 202*
(15) Laughterton, Lincoln..............£10 *Phil Stamp Covers 55*
C.D.S. POSTMARKS Price Guide £7-£10
(16) Greet, Manchester Airport, Send, Duckworth Lane

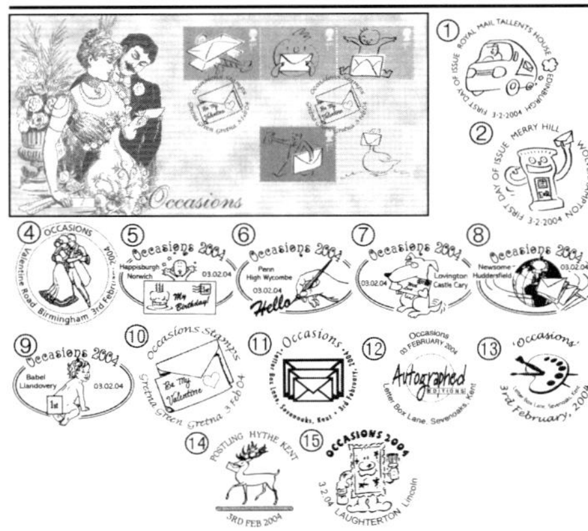

26th February 2004 - LORD of the RINGS

10 x 1st Map of Middle Earth; Lothlorien Forest; Fellowship of the Ring; Rivendell; Bag End; Orthanc; Doors of Durin; Barad-dur; Minas Tirith; Fanghorn Forest.

SPECIAL HANDSTAMPS SPONSOR
Price Guide Ordinary Covers £4-£9 / Sponsored Covers:
(1) FDI - Tallents House..................... *Royal Mail (n.s.c.)*
(2) FDI - Oxford .... *Royal Mail (n.s.c.)*
(3) -do- non pictorial version .... *Royal Mail (n.s.c.)*
(4) Stampex - Lord of the Rings .... *Royal Mail (n.s.c.)*
(5) Ryde, Isle of Wight ....£20 *Benham BLCS 272*
(6) Arrow, Alcester.........................£20 *Benham*
(7) Elphin, Lairg..............................£25 *Benham Coin Cover*
(8) Forest Green, Dorking ....£20 *Benham*
(9) Spellbrook.................................£20 *Benham Pilgrim*
(10) Battlefield, Shrewsbury ....£20 *Benham BLCS 272*
(11) Treeton, Rotherham.................£20 *Benham*
(12) Crow Bank, Wallsend ....£20 *Benham Pilgrim*
(13) Mountain, Holyhead ....£30 *Benham (500)272*
(14) Shirehampton, Bristol ....£20 *Benham Pilgrim*
(15) Tolkien Society, Sarehole.......£20 *Anniv & Events 14*

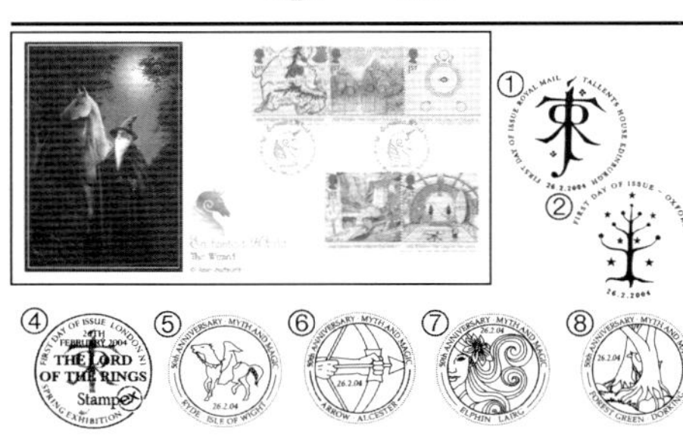

(16) Enchanted World....................£20 *Bradbury Sovereign 38*
(17) Sarehole Mill............................£15 *Westminster*
(18) -do- (palette design)................£15 *Westminster*
(19) -do- Autographed Editions.....£25 *Westminster*
(20) Middle Way, London SW1 ....£15 *Steven Scott*
(21) Eagle and Child, Oxford.........£20 *M Brazier (Pubs.66)*
(22) Ring Road, London W12........£15 *GB 85*
(23) King Arthur, Machynlleth ......£20 *P Sheridan*
(24) Ringwould, Deal.......................£15 *Buckingham Cvrs 203*
(25) Rings End, Wisbech................£15 *Buckingham Cvrs 203*
(26) Sarehole Mill............................£15 *Phil Stamp Covers 56*
(27) Oxford...£15 *Phil Stamp Covers 57*
(28) Spring Stampex, MCC.............£10 *MachinCollectorsClub*
(29) Spring Stampex, N1 ....£15 *Royal Mail*
(30) Lords of the Strings.................£15 *P M Payne*
(31) George Cross 56th Anniv.......£15 *RN CvrsGp*
C.D.S. POSTMARKS Price Guide £7-£10
(32) The Shires, Wolvercote, Ringmer, Underhill Circus
(33) Oxford, High Holborn, Hurst Green, Edgbaston

16th March 2004 - NORTHERN IRELAND

(1) 2nd Ely Island, Lough Erne; 1st Giant's Causeway; E Slemish, Antrim Mountains; 42p Banns Road, Mourne Mountains; 47p Glenelly Valley, Sperring; 68p Islandmore, Strangford Lough.
(2) Self Adhesive Stamp Book containing 6 x 1st Class Stamps: 2 Giant's Causeway & 4 Definitives.

SPECIAL HANDSTAMPS SPONSOR
Price Guide Ordinary Covers £4-£9 / Sponsored Covers:
(1) FDI - Tallents House..................... *Royal Mail (n.s.c.)*
(2) FDI - Garrison, Enniskillen.......... *Royal Mail (n.s.c.)*
(3) -do- non pictorial version .... *Royal Mail (n.s.c.)*
(4) Northern Ireland, Birmingham.... *Royal Mail (n.s.c.)*
(5) Ballymena, County Antrim ....£10 *Benham BLCS 273*
(6) Bushmills, County Antrim......£15 *Benham Coin Cover*
(7) Newcastle, County Down.......£20 *Benham (500)273*
(8) Enniskillen.................................£10 *Benham BLCS 273*
(9) Downpatrick.............................£15 *Benham*
(10) Omagh, County Tyrone ....£15 *Benham Pilgrim*
(11) Belfast...£15 *Bradbury Sovereign 39*
(12) Self Adhesives..........................£10 *Bradbury Windsor 40*
(13) A British Journey, Bushmills..£10 *Westminster*
(14) -do- (palette design)................£10 *Westminster*
(15) -do- Autographed Editions.....£20 *Westminster*
(16) Ireland Place, N22...................£10 *Steven Scott*
(17) Saint Molaise Tower................£10 *GB 86*
(18) Glens of Antrim, Glenariff.....£10 *P Sheridan*
(19) White Park Bay, Bushmills ....£10 *Buckingham Cvrs 204*
(20) Northern Ireland, Belfast ....£15 *Phil Stamp Covers 58*
(21) Hunt Class, Belfast..................£10 *RN CvrsGp*
(22) Giants Causeway - permanent..... *Royal Mail (n.s.c.)*
(23) Battle of Maldon ....£15 *Heritage of Britain 1*

*NB The **Letters by Night** Prestige Stamp Book was also issued on 16th March. Therefore Northern Ireland covers may also exist with postmarks listed below.*

C.D.S. POSTMARKS Price Guide £7-£10
(24) Bushmills, Antrim, Warrenpoint, Strangford
(25) Strabane, Draperstown, Monea, Ballykeel

16th March 2004 - LETTERS BY NIGHT

*Prestige Stamp Book with four stamp panes including Classic Locomotives stamps (Jan 2004) and Pub Signs - The Station (Aug 2003). **Values for set of 4 covers.***

SPECIAL HANDSTAMPS SPONSOR
Price Guide Ordinary Covers £20 / Sponsored Covers:
(1) FDI - Tallents House..................... *Royal Mail (n.s.c.)*
(2) FDI - London NW10..................... *Royal Mail (n.s.c.)*
(3) -do- non pictorial version .... *Royal Mail (n.s.c.)*
(4) New Street, Birmingham.............. *Royal Mail (n.s.c.)*
(5) Letters by Night, Crewe..........£40 *Benham*
(6) Letters by Night, Newcastle...£40 *Benham*
(7) Letters by Night, Calisle ....£40 *Benham*
(8) Letters by Night, Edinburgh ..£40 *Benham*
(9) Letters by Night, Euston.........£40 *Benham*
(10) The Night Mail, York.............£40 *Buckingham Cvrs*
(11) Final Journey of TPO Bristol.£40 *P Sheridan*
(12) Royal Scot Class, Glasgow.....£40 *M Brazier*
(13) Letters by Night, Bristol ....£40 *Phil Stamp Covers 59*

*NB **Northern Ireland** stamps were also issued on 16th March. Therefore Letters by Night covers may also exist with postmarks listed above.*

C.D.S. POSTMARKS Price Guide £10 (each cover)
(14) The Station, Railway Road, Penzance, Kidderminster

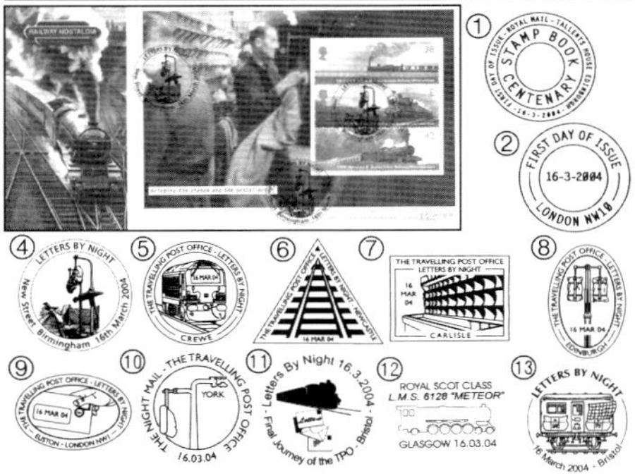

WHAT ARE CDS POSTMARKS?
Counter Date Stamps or Circular Date Stamps are the everyday cancellations used at Post Offices.
Please see General Notes for more information.

6th April 2004 - ENTENTE CORDIALE

28p Lace 1; 57p Coccinelle.

SPECIAL HANDSTAMPS **SPONSOR**

Price Guide Ordinary Covers £4-£9 / Sponsored Covers:

(1) FDI - Tallents House .... *Royal Mail (n.s.c.)*
(2) FDI - London SW1 .... *Royal Mail (n.s.c.)*
(3) -do- non pictorial version .... *Royal Mail (n.s.c.)*
(4) Entente Cordiale 1904-2004......... *Royal Mail/Royal Mint*
(5) Premier Jour, Paris......................... *See note below*
(6) Twinned Lyon - Birmingham....... *Royal Mail (n.s.c.)*
(7) King Charles St, SW1.............£10 *Benham BLCS 277*
(8) Parliament Sqe, SW1..............£20 *Benham (500)277*
(9) Knightsbridge, SW1 ....£10 *Benham BLCS 277*
(10) London-Paris Rail Link ....£15 *Bradbury Sovereign 42*
(11) London SW1............................£10 *Westminster*
(12) -do- (palette design)................£10 *Westminster*
(13) -do- Autographed Editions.....£20 *Westminster*
(14) Allied Way, London W3.........£10 *Steven Scott*
(15) Concorde, Filton, Bristol ....£15 *M Brazier (Pubs)*
(16) Bleriot Road, Hounslow ....£10 *GB 87*
(17) L'Entente Cordiale, SW1........£15 *Buckingham Cvrs 205*
(18) Entente Cordiale, SW1 ....£15 *Phil Stamp Covers 60*
(19) Grecian Cresc, SE19...............£10 *P M Payne*
(20) Hunt Class, Belfast..................£10 *RN CvrsGp*
(21) Battle of Stamford Bridge.......£15 *Heritage of Britain 2*

C.D.S. POSTMARKS Price Guide £7-£10

(22) Paris Avenue, Dunkirk, Calais Road, Britannia

DOUBLE POSTMARKED COVERS

The Entente Cordiale stamps were a joint Royal Mail/LaPoste issue. Arrangements were made for British collectors to obtain the Paris posmark (see item 5 above) at Tallents House by authority of LaPoste, the French postal administration. The Paris postmark was applied to the French stamps provided the covers had the Royal Mail's Entente Cordiale stamps also affixed

Please see the General Notes for lots of useful tips about Collecting British First Day Covers

13th April 2004 - OCEAN LINERS

(1) 1st RMS Queen Mary 2 (2004); E SS Canberra; 42p RMS Queen Mary (1936); 47p RMS Mauretania; 57p SS City of New York; 68p PS Great Western.
(2) Miniature Sheet
(3) Self Adhesive Stamp Book containing 6 x 1st Class Stamps: 2 Queen Mary 2 & 4 Definitives.

SPECIAL HANDSTAMPS **SPONSOR**

Price Guide Ordinary Covers £4-£9 / Sponsored Covers:

(1) FDI - Tallents House .... *Royal Mail (n.s.c.)*
(2) FDI - Southampton .... *Royal Mail (n.s.c.)*
(3) -do- non pictorial version .... *Royal Mail (n.s.c.)*
(4) Spanning the Oceans.................. *Royal Mail/Mint*
(5) Canberra Way, Birmingham......... *Royal Mail (n.s.c.)*
(6) RMS Queen Mary 2, S'ton.....£20 *Benham BLCS 279*
(7) SS Canberra, Belfast...............£20 *Benham BLCS 278*
(8) RMS Queen Mary ....£20 *Benham BLCS 278*
(9) RMS Mauretania, Wallsend...£25 *Benham Coin Cover*
(10) SS City of New York..............£25 *Benham (500)278*
(11) PS Great Western, Bristol......£20 *Benham Pilgrim*
(12) Ocean Liners, Liverpool.........£20 *Bradbury Sovereign 40*
(13) Ocean Liners, Glasgow..........£15 *Bradbury Windsor 36*
(14) Self Adhesives, Ocean Liners £15 *Bradbury Windsor 41*
(15) Ocean Liners, Southampton..£15 *Westminster*
(16) -do- (palette design)...............£15 *Westminster*
(17) -do- Autographed Editions.....£25 *Westminster*
(18) Tilbury Road, E10 ....£15 *Steven Scott*
(19) Southampton...........................£20 *Buckingham Cvrs 206*
(20) QM2, Southampton................£20 *Buckingham Cvrs 206*
(21) Crown & Anchor ....£15 *M Brazier (Pubs.67)*
(22) Merchant Navy Class ....£15 *M Brazier (Rly.9A)*
(23) Great Western Rd, W9...........£15 *GB 88*
(24) Cunard, Southampton............£15 *P Sheridan*
(25) Belfast.....................................£15 *Phil Stamp Covers 61*
(26) Southampton...........................£15 *Phil Stamp Covers 62*
(27) Southampton...........................£15 *Assoc. of GBFDC*
(28) Bristol ....£20 *H D Macintyre*
(29) Queen Mary 2 Southampton.£15 *RN CvrsGp*
(30) Cruise Control, Bletchley ....£15 *Bletchley PO*
(31) Flight Approach......................£10 *P M Payne*
(32) Battle of Hastings...................£15 *Heritage of Britain 3*

C.D.S. POSTMARKS Price Guide £7-£10

(33) Southampton, Bristol, Belfast, Glasgow, Sea Lane
(34) Sea Street, Quarterdeck, Seaview, The Harbour

SPONSORED COVERS or ORDINARY COVERS?
Sponsored covers, also referred to as 'official covers', are those covers which have been produced by the sponsor of the postmark. Ordinary covers are those which are available as 'blanks'. *Please see General Notes for more information.*

25 May 2004 - ROYAL HORTICULTURAL SOC.

(1) 2nd Dianthus; 1st Dahlia; E Clematis; 42p Miltonia; 47p Lilium; 68p Delphinium
(2) Miniature Sheet (3) Prestige Stamp Book Stamps
(4) Generic Sheet of 20 x 1st Class + labels.

SPECIAL HANDSTAMPS — SPONSOR
Price Guide Ordinary Covers £4-£9 / Sponsored Covers:

(1) FDI - Tallents House .... *Royal Mail (n.s.c.)*
(2) FDI - Wisley, Woking .... *Royal Mail (n.s.c.)*
(3) -do- non pictorial version .... *Royal Mail (n.s.c.)*
(4) RHS 1804-2004 .... *Royal Mail/Mint*
(5) Chelsea Flower Show FDI .... *Royal Mail*
(6) Chelsea Flower Show RHS .... *Royal Mail*
(7) Canberra Way, Birmingham .... *Royal Mail (n.s.c.)*
(8) Chelsea, London .... £20 *Benham (500)281*
(9) Knutsford, Cheshire .... £20 *Benham Coin Cover*
(10) Great Torrington, Devon .... £15 *Benham*
(11) Wisley, Woking .... £10 *Benham BLCS 281*
(12) Rettendon, Chelmsford .... £10 *Benham BLCS 281*
(13) Harrogate, N. Yorkshire .... £15 *Benham*
(14) Kew Gardens, Richmond .... £15 *Bradbury Sovereign 41*
(15) Chelsea, London .... £15 *Bradbury Windsor 43*
(16) Flower Girl, Chelsea .... £15 *Bradbury Windsor 44*
(17) Royal Horticultural Society ... £15 *Westminster*
(18) -do- (palette design) .... £15 *Westminster*
(19) -do- Autographed Editions ..... £25 *Westminster*
(20) Chelsea Embankment .... £15 *Steven Scott*
(21) RHS Chelsea .... £15 *Buckingham Cvrs 207*
(22) RHS Wisley .... £15 *Buckingham Cvrs 207*
(23) The Tulip .... £15 *M Brazier (Pubs.69)*
(24) Wisley Road, SW11 .... £10 *GB 89*
(25) Flowers & Plants Ass'n .... £10 *P Sheridan*
(26) Chelsea .... £15 *Phil Stamp Covers 63*
(27) The Glory of the Garden .... £15 *Phil Stamp Covers 65*
(28) Wisley, Woking .... £15 *Phil Stamp Covers 64*
(29) Battle of the Standard .... £15 *Heritage of Britain 4*
(30) Mount Everest Expedition ..... £20 *ABC-FDC*
(31) Poland - United Europe .... £25 *J L Englert*
(32) HMS Coventry .... £15 *RN CvrsGp*

C.D.S. POSTMARKS Price Guide £7-£10
(33) Chelsea Royal Hospital, Botanical Gardens, Primrose
(34) New Covent Gdn, Ripley, Garden Village, Rose Lane

15th June 2004 - WALES

(1) 2nd Barmouth Bridge; 1st Hyddgen, Plynlimon; 40p Brecon Beacons; 43p Pen-pych, Rhondda Valley; 47p Rhewl, Dee Valley; 68p Marloes Sands.
(2) Self Adhesive Stamp Book containing 6 x 1st Class Stamps: 2 Hyddgen, Plynlimon & 4 Definitives.

SPECIAL HANDSTAMPS — SPONSOR
Price Guide Ordinary Covers £4-£9 / Sponsored Covers:

(1) FDI - Tallents House .... *Royal Mail (n.s.c.)*
(2) FDI - Llanfair .... *Royal Mail (n.s.c.)*
(3) -do- non pictorial version .... *Royal Mail (n.s.c.)*
(4) Prince of Wales Lane, B'ham .... *Royal Mail (n.s.c.)*
(5) Machynlleth, Powys .... £10 *Benham BLCS 285*
(6) Llangollen, Clwyd .... £20 *Benham (500)284*
(7) Snowdonia, Barmouth .... £20 *Benham Coin Cover*
(8) Marloes, Pembrokeshire .... £15 *Benham*
(9) Brecon, Powys .... £10 *Benham BLCS 284*
(10) Blaenrhonnda, Glamorgan ..... £20 *Benham*
(11) Machynlleth, Powys .... £10 *Benham BLCS 284*
(12) Tenby, Dyfed .... £10 *Bradbury Sovereign 43*
(13) Merthyr Tydfil .... £10 *Bradbury Windsor 45*
(14) Brecon, Powys .... £10 *Westminster*
(15) -do- (palette design) .... £10 *Westminster*
(16) -do- Autographed Editions ..... £20 *Westminster*
(17) Prince of Wales Road, NW5 .. £10 *Steven Scott*
(18) The National Trust .... £10 *Buckingham Cvrs 208*
(19) The Welsh Harp .... £10 *M Brazier (Pubs.70)*
(20) Owens Way, London SE23 .... £10 *GB 90*
(21) Portmeirion .... £10 *P Sheridan*
(22) Cymru - Wales, Cardiff .... £10 *Phil Stamp Covers 66*
(23) Battle of Lewes .... £15 *Heritage of Britain 5*
(24) HMS Cardiff .... £10 *RN CvrsGp*

C.D.S. POSTMARKS Price Guide £7-£10
(25) Barmouth, Brecon, Marloes, Wales, Blaenrrhondda
(26) Llangollen, Rhewl, Machynlleth

NB Values should be treated as a guide. Find out more from the General Notes at the beginning of this catalogue.

27 July 04 - RULE BRITANNIA Generic Issue

1st Union Jack stamp + labels featuring all things British

SPECIAL HANDSTAMPS SPONSOR

Price Guide Ordinary Covers £4-£9 / Sponsored Covers:

(1) Rule Britannia, W1 ....£20 *Benham BLCS 287*
(2) Rule Britannia, SW1 ....£20 *Benham (500)287*
(3) Union Jack Generic Issue.......£25 *Bradbury Britannia 17*
(4) Smilers, Union Jack, Flagg .....£15 *Phil Stamp Covers*
(5) 55th Anniversary The Comet £20 *Group Capt Randle*

10th August 2004 - ROYAL SOCIETY of ARTS

1st Sir Rowland Hill; 40p William Shipley; 43p RSA Examinations; 47p Appartus for sweeping chimnies; 57p Eric Gill's typeface; 68p Zero Waste.

SPECIAL HANDSTAMPS SPONSOR

Price Guide Ordinary Covers £4-£9 / Sponsored Covers:

(1) FDI - Tallents House..................... *Royal Mail (n.s.c.)*
(2) FDI - London WC2......................... *Royal Mail (n.s.c.)*
(3) -do- non pictorial version .... *Royal Mail (n.s.c.)*
(4) Rowland Hill, Birmingham........... *Royal Mail (n.s.c.)*
(5) John Adam Street, WC2 ....£10 *Benham BLCS 286*
(6) Henrietta Street, WC2.............£15 *Benham (500)286*
(7) Millbank, SW1 ....£10 *Benham*
(8) Kensington Gore, SW1 ....£15 *Benham Coin Cover*
(9) Regent Street, Cambridge.......£10 *Benham*
(10) Kidderminster ....£10 *Benham BLCS 286*
(11) The 1851 Great Exhibition ....£10 *Bradbury Sovereign 45*
(12) RSA John Adam Street ....£10 *Westminster*
(13) -do- (palette design).................£10 *Westminster*
(14) -do- Autographed Editions.....£20 *Westminster*
(15) RSA John Adam Street ....£10 *Steven Scott*
(16) Anniversary, London WC2 ....£10 *Buckingham Cvrs 209*
(17) The Printers Devil, Fleet St....£15 *M Brazier (Pubs.71)*
(18) Milton Keynes Philatelic Soc.£10 *M Brazier*
(19) Smart Street..............................£10 *GB 91*
(20) Assoc. Chimney Sweeps ....£15 *P Sheridan*
(21) 250 Anniversary, WC2............£10 *Phil Stamp Covers 67*
(22) RSA Stoke on Trent ....£15 *T Hurlstone*
(23) Battle of Evesham ....£15 *Heritage of Britain 6*
(24) New Orleans Walk ....£10 *P M Payne*
(25) Alexandra Athanassiades........£10 *P M Payne*
(26) Op. Pedestal Gourock ....£10 *RN CvrsGp*

C.D.S. POSTMARKS Price Guide £7-£10

(27) Kidderminster, Shipley, Trafalgar Square

16th Sept 2004 - WOODLAND ANIMALS

10 x 1st: Pine marten, Roe deer, Badger, Yellow-necked mouse, Wild cat, Red squirrel, Stoat, Natterer's bat, Mole, Fox

SPECIAL HANDSTAMPS SPONSOR

Price Guide Ordinary Covers £4-£9 / Sponsored Covers:

(1) FDI - Tallents House..................... *Royal Mail (n.s.c.)*
(2) FDI - Woodland, Bhp Auckland. *Royal Mail (n.s.c.)*
(3) -do- non pictorial version .... *Royal Mail (n.s.c.)*
(4) Stampex Woodland Animals........ *Royal Mail (n.s.c.)*
(5) Autumn Stampex .... *Royal Mail (n.s.c.)*
(6) Fox Green, Birmingham............... *Royal Mail (n.s.c.)*
(7) Great Molewood, Hertford ....£15 *Benham*
(8) Badger, Burnhill Green...........£15 *Benham*
(9) Mousehole, Penzance..............£20 *Benham (500)288*
(10) Bats Corner, Farnham.............£15 *Benham*
(11) Catshill, Bromsgrove ....£20 *Benham Coin Cover*
(12) Foxholes, Driffield...................£15 *Benham BLCS 288*
(13) Nutgrove, Blandford Forum ..£15 *Benham BLCS 288*
(14) Stotfield, Lossiemouth............£15 *Benham*
(15) Deerhurst, Gloucester ....£20 *Benham Coin Cover*
(16) Marten, Marlborough..............£15 *Benham*
(17) Badger's Mount, Sevenoaks...£15 *Bradbury Sovereign 46*
(18) Woodland Walk ....£15 *Westminster*
(19) -do- (palette design).................£15 *Westminster*
(20) -do- Autographed Editions.....£25 *Westminster*
(21) Highwood Gardens, Ilford.....£15 *Steven Scott*
(22) Brownsea Island, Poole ....£10 *Buckingham Cvrs 210*
(23) Dinefwr Deer Park..................£10 *Buckingham Cvrs 210*
(24) The Squirrel, Cannock ....£15 *M Brazier (Pubs.72)*
(25) British Deer Society.................£15 *P Sheridan*
(26) Woodlands, Harrow Middx ...£15 *GB 92*
(27) Stoat's Nest Village..................£15 *Phil Stamp Covers 69*
(28) Badger, Wolverhampton.........£15 *Phil Stamp Covers 68*
(29) Naturewatch HQ......................£20 *Naturewatch*
(30) Wildlife across the Park..........£15 *Bletchley PO*
(31) Scouting, Harwick ....£20 *I Tack*
(32) Woodland Animals, Extinct...£15 *P M Payne*
(33) Battle of Stirling Bridge ....£15 *Heritage of Britain 7*

C.D.S. POSTMARKS Price Guide £7-£10

(34) Mole Hill Green, Mousehole, Foxhole, Woodland
(35) Beddgelert, Kinloch Rannoch, New Deer, Deerpark

5th Oct 2004 - SCOTTISH PARLIAMENT

Miniature Sheet containing 1 x 2nd, 2 x 1st, 2 x 40p, Scottish Country Pictorial stamps

SPECIAL HANDSTAMPS SPONSOR

Price Guide Ordinary Covers £4-£9 / Sponsored Covers:

(1) Tallents House................................ *Royal Mail (n.s.c.)*
(2) Edinburgh EH99............................ *Royal Mail (n.s.c.)*
(3) -do- non pictorial version .... *Royal Mail (n.s.c.)*
(4) Scotland Street, Birmingham....... *Royal Mail (n.s.c.)*
(5) Holyrood (lion).........................£10 *Benham BLCS 289*
(6) Holyrood (thistle)......................£15 *Benham (500)289*
(7) Holyrood...................................£10 *Benham BLCS 289*
(8) Scottish Parliament...................£10 *Bradbury Sovereign 49*
(9) New Scottish Parliament.........£10 *Buckingham Cvrs 213*
(10) The Scottish Parliament..........£10 *Phil Stamp Covers 70*
(11) City of Edinburgh.....................£10 *M Brazier*
(12) HMS's Catterick & Aurora....£10 *RN CvrsGp*

C.D.S. POSTMARKS Price Guide £75

(13) The Scottish Parliament, Edinburgh

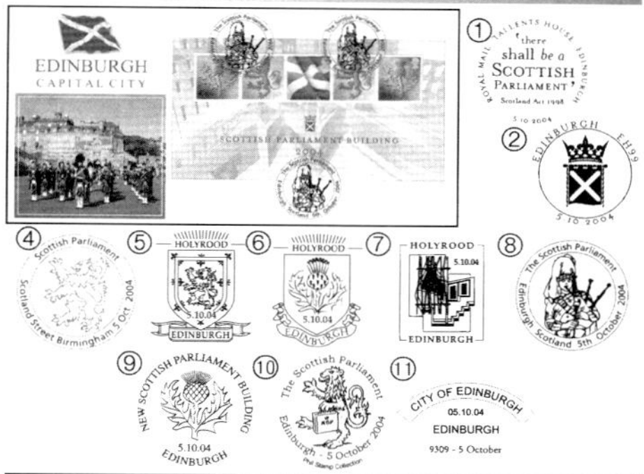

12th Oct 2004 - CRIMEAN WAR

2nd Private McNamara,(Charge at Battle of Balaclava)
1st Piper Muir, (Amphibious raid on Kerch & Yenikale)
40p Sgt Major Edwards, (Gallant action at Inkerman)
57p Sgt Powell, (Battles of Alma and Inkerman)
68p Sgt Major Poole,(Front Line at Battle of Inkerman)
£1.12 Sgt Glasgow,(Gun Battery, Sebastopol)

SPECIAL HANDSTAMPS SPONSOR

Price Guide Ordinary Covers £4-£9 / Sponsored Covers:

(1) FDI - Tallents House..................... *Royal Mail (n.s.c.)*
(2) FDI - London SW3... .... *Royal Mail (n.s.c.)*
(3) -do- non pictorial version .... *Royal Mail (n.s.c.)*
(4) Balaclava Road, Birmingham....... *Royal Mail (n.s.c.)*
(5) Crimean War Research Soc...£15 *Bradbury Sovereign 47*
(6) Royal Leicestershire Reg.........£20 *Bradbury*
(7) Alma Road, London E4.........£15 *Westminster*
(8) -do- (palette design)...............£15 *Westminster*
(9) -do- Autographed Editions.....£20 *Westminster*
(10) Victoria Cross Road................£15 *Westminster*
(11) Inkerman Road, NW5............£10 *Steven Scott*
(12) National Army Museum ....£10 *Buckingham Cvrs 211*
(13) Hyde Park, London W1 ....£10 *Buckingham Cvrs 211*
(14) The Victoria Cross..................£15 *M Brazier (Pubs.73)*
(15) Bomb, Lucas Avenue...............£10 *GB 93*
(16) CWRS, London SW1 ....£15 *P Sheridan*
(17) Alma Cut, St. Albans...............£15 *Phil Stamp Covers 71*
(18) Inkerman Road, NW5............£10 *Assoc. of GBFDC*
(19) HMS's Catterick & Aurora....£10 *RN CvrsGp*
(20) Crimean War Victoria Cross .£10 *RN CvrsGp*
(21) CWRS, Sowerby Bridge..........£10 *P M Payne*
(22) Battle of Falkirk.......................£15 *Heritage of Britain 8*
(23) The Buffs, Canterbury ....£20 *H D Macintyre*
(24) The Fall of Sevastopol............£15 *Benham*
(25) The Treaty of Paris..................£15 *Benham*
(26) Expedition to Kerch ....£15 *Benham*
(27) The Battle of Inkerman...........£15 *Benham*
(28) The Battle of Balaklava...........£15 *Benham*
(29) The Battle of Alma..................£15 *Benham*
(30) K2 1954-2004 Cho Oyu..........£10 *ABC-FDC*

C.D.S. POSTMARKS Price Guide £7-£10

(31) Battle, Raglan, Chelsea Royal Hospital, West Wellow
(32) Aldershot, Gun Hill, Alma Vale

2nd November 2004 - CHRISTMAS

(1) 2nd, 1st, 40p, 57p, 68p, £1.12 'Father Christmas'
(2) Miniature Sheet
(3) Generic Sheet containing 2nd and 1st Class stamps.

SPECIAL HANDSTAMPS SPONSOR

Price Guide Ordinary Covers £4-£9 / Sponsored Covers:

(1) FDI - Tallents House..................... *Royal Mail (n.s.c.)*
(2) FDI - Bethlehem... .... *Royal Mail (n.s.c.)*
(3) -do- non pictorial version .... *Royal Mail (n.s.c.)*
(4) Father Christmas, Tallents Hse.... *Royal Mail (n.s.c.)*
(5) Snow Hill, Birmingham................ *Royal Mail (n.s.c.)*
(6) Seasons Greetings, Bethlehem..... *Royal Mail (n.s.c.)*
(7) Toys Hill, Edenbridge..............£10 *Benham BLCS 291*
(8) Christmas Street, SE1..............£15 *Benham 500(292)*
(9) Yule Tide Close, NW10..........£10 *Benham BLCS 292*
(10) Rudolf Road, London E13.....£10 *Benham BLCS 291*
(11) Winerley, Sandbach.................£15 *Benham 500(291)*
(12) St Nicholas, Goodwick...........£15 *Benham Coin Cover*
(13) St Nicholas, Cardiff ....£10 *Bradbury Sovereign 48*
(14) Yuletide Close (palette) ....£10 *Westminster*
(15) -do- Autographed Editions.....£10 *Westminster*
(16) Angel Street, EC1.....................£10 *Steven Scott*
(17) Bloomsbury, WC1....................£10 *Buckingham Cvrs 212*
(18) Christmas Common.................£10 *Buckingham Cvrs 212*

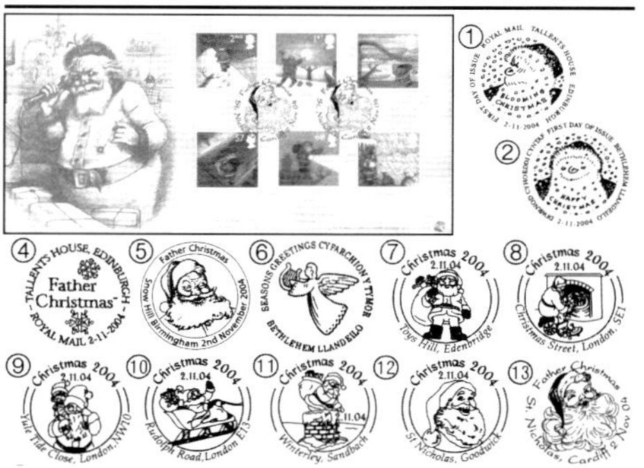

(19) The Plum Pudding....................£15 *M Brazier (Pubs.74)*
(20) Noel Road, London N1..........£10 *GB 94*
(21) Charity Christmas Cards.........£15 *P Sheridan*
(22) Reindeer Close, Horncastle....£15 *Phil Stamp Covers 72*
(23) Cold Christmas, Ware.............£15 *Phil Stamp Covers 73*
(24) St Nicholas Rd, SE18..............£10 *P M Payne*
(25) Battle of Bannockburn............£15 *Heritage of Britain 9*
(26) Christmas - HMS Richmond .£10 *RN CvrsGp*
(27) Marylebone Cricket Club ....£10 *Bletchley PO*

C.D.S. POSTMARKS Price Guide £7-£10

(28) Frosterley, Freezywater, Winter Gardens
(29) North Pole Road, St. Nicholas at Wade

11th January 2005 - FARM ANIMALS

(1) 10 x 1st British Saddleback Pig; Khaki Campbell Duck; Suffolk Punch; Shorthorns; Border Collie; Chicks; Suffolk Sheep; Bagot Goat; Norfolk Black Turkeys; Emden Geese.
(2) Generic Sheet of 20 x 1st Class stamps (2 of each design).

SPECIAL HANDSTAMPS SPONSOR
Price Guide Ordinary Covers £4-£9 / Sponsored Covers:

(1) FDI - Tallents House..................... *Royal Mail (n.s.c.)*
(2) FDI - Paddock, Huddersfield......... *Royal Mail (n.s.c.)*
(3) -do- non pictorial version .... *Royal Mail (n.s.c.)*
(4) Farmers Walk, Birmingham .... *Royal Mail (n.s.c.)*
(5) Trumpington, Cambridge........£15 *Benham BLCS 293*
(6) Bentley Heath, Solihull...........£15 *Benham*
(7) Market Hill, Woodbridge ....£20 *Benham Coin Cover*
(8) Stoneleigh Park, Kenilworth..£15 *Benham*
(9) Llangwm, Corwen....................£20 *Benham 500(293)*
(10) Frampton, Boston ....£15 *Benham BLCS 293*
(11) Llanelwedd, Builth Wells ....£15 *Benham*
(12) Bovey Tracey............................£15 *Benham*
(13) Great Eversden, Cambridge...£15 *Benham*
(14) Gelly, Clynderwen....................£15 *Benham*
(15) Farmers, Llanwrda...................£15 *Bradbury Sovereign 50*
(16) Farm Lane (palette design) ....£15 *Westminster*
(17) -do- Autographed Editions.....£20 *Westminster*
(18) Horseshoe Lane........................£15 *GB 95*
(19) Kentish Town City Farm ....£15 *P Sheridan*
(20) Sowerby Bridge, N. Yorks......£10 *Buckingham Cvrs 214*
(21) Thirsk, N. Yorks ....£10 *Buckingham Cvrs 214*
(22) Farm Animals on Pub Signs ..£15 *M Brazier (Pubs.75)*
(23) Farm Animals, Hereford ....£10 *Phil Stamp Covers 74*
(24) Farm Animals, Woolley ....£10 *Phil Stamp Covers 75*
(25) HMS/m Tallyho ....£10 *RN CvrsGp*
(26) Battle of Boroughbridge..........£15 *Heritage of Britain 10*

C.D.S. POSTMARKS Price Guide £7-£10

(27) Goose Green, Bull Farm, Sheepwash, Fieldgate etc

8th February 2005 - SOUTH WEST ENGLAND

2nd Old Harry Rocks, Studland; 1st Wheal Coates, St. Agnes; 40p Start Point, Start Bay; 43p Horton Down, Wilts; 57p Chiselcombe, Exmoor; 68p St. James's Stone, Lundy.

SPECIAL HANDSTAMPS SPONSOR
Price Guide Ordinary Covers £4-£9 / Sponsored Covers:

(1) FDI - Tallents House..................... *Royal Mail (n.s.c.)*
(2) FDI - The Lizard, Helston... .... *Royal Mail (n.s.c.)*
(3) -do- non pictorial version .... *Royal Mail (n.s.c.)*
(4) Cornwall Rd, Birmingham........... *Royal Mail (n.s.c.)*
(5) Studland, Swanage, Dorset ....£10 *Benham*
(6) St. Agnes, Cornwall ....£10 *Benham BLCS 294*
(7) Hallsands, Kingsbridge............£15 *Benham 500(294)*
(8) Avebury, Marlborough ....£10 *Benham BLCS 294*
(9) Lynmouth, Devon ....£10 *Benham*
(10) Bideford to Lundy Island ....£15 *Benham Coin Cover*
(11) Penzance, Cornwall ....£10 *Bradbury Sovereign 51*
(12) The Lizard (palette design) ....£10 *Westminster*
(13) -do- Autographed Editions.....£15 *Westminster*
(14) Stourhead, Warminster...........£10 *Buckingham Cvrs 215*
(15) Cornwall Road, SE1 ....£10 *Steven Scott*
(16) Lynmouth Road, N2................£10 *GB 96*
(17) SW England, Penzance...........£15 *Phil Stamp Covers 76*
(18) The White Horse, Uffington ..£10 *P Sheridan*
(19) Air, Rail, Sea, Bristol ....£15 *Cam S.C.*
(20) South West Naval Base ....£10 *RN CvrsGp*
(21) Battle of Neville's Cross..........£15 *Heritage of Britain 11*

C.D.S. POSTMARKS Price Guide £7-£10

(22) St. Agnes, Studland, Torcross, Bideford, Penzance etc

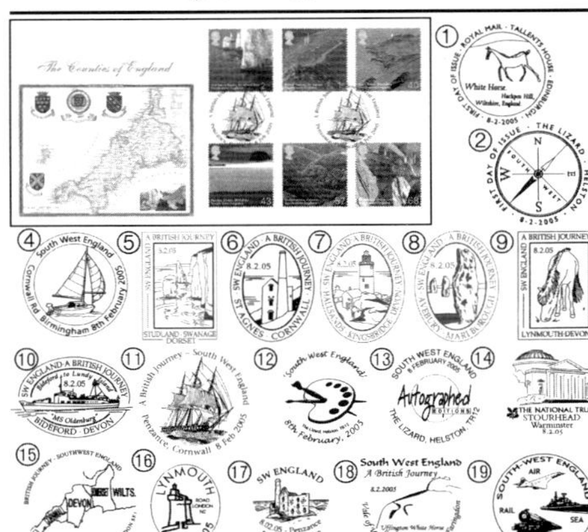

24th February 2005 - JANE EYRE

(1) 2nd Mr Rochester; 1st Jane; 40p Jane at George Inn; 57p Adele and Jane; 68p & £1.12 Jane at Lowton School.
(2) Miniature Sheet & (3) Prestige Stamp Book.

SPECIAL HANDSTAMPS SPONSOR
Price Guide Ordinary Covers £4-£9 / Sponsored Covers:

(1) FDI - Tallents House..................... *Royal Mail (n.s.c.)*

(2) FDI - Haworth Parsonage............ *Royal Mail (n.s.c.)*
(3) -do- non pictorial version .... *Royal Mail (n.s.c.)*
(4) Hay-on-Wye.................................... *Royal Mail/Royal Mint*
(5) Spring Stampex .... *Royal Mail (n.s.c.)*
(6) Stampex, Jane Eyre......................... *Royal Mail (n.s.c.)*
(7) Eyre Rd., Birmingham..................... *Royal Mail (n.s.c.)*
(8) Norton Conyers, Ripon...........£10 *Benham BLCS 296*
(9) The Parsonage, Haworth........£15 *Benham Coin Cover*
(10) Cowan Bridge School.................£10 *Benham BLCS 296*
(11) Thornton, Bradford..................£10 *Benham BLCS 295*
(12) Tunstall, Carnforth....................£10 *Benham BLCS 295*
(13) Wycoller, Colne, Lancs............£15 *Benham 500(295)*
(14) Jane Eyre - Charlotte Bronte .£15 *Bradbury Sovereign 53*
(15) Bronte Grove (palette)............£10 *Westminster*
(16) -do- Autographed Editions.....£20 *Westminster*
(17) BS, Haworth, Keighley............£10 *Buckingham Cvrs 216*
(18) Bronte Parsonage Museum....£10 *Buckingham Cvrs 216*
(19) Wuthering Heights Inn...........£10 *M Brazier (Pubs.76)*
(20) Society of Authors, SW10......£10 *P Sheridan*
(21) Chestnut Lane, N20.................£10 *GB 97*
(22) Eyre Street Hill, EC1...............£10 *Steven Scott*
(23) Safety Matches, Rochester .....£15 *Phil Stamp Covers 77*
(24) Aspirin, Gateshead...................£15 *Phil Stamp Covers 78*
(25) Charlotte Bronte, York ....£10 *Cotswold*
(26) Literature & Fables, SE5........£10 *P M Payne*
(27) Loss of HMS Dainty................£10 *RN CvrsGp*
(28) Battle of Otterburn ....£15 *Heritage of Britain 12*

C.D.S. POSTMARKS Price Guide £7-£10

(29) Thornton, Rochester, Haworth, Rawdon, Gateshead

15th March 2005 - MAGIC

(1) 1st Heads or Tails; 40p Rabbit and Top Hat; 47p Scarves; 68p Ace of Hearts; £1.12 Fezzes.
(2) Generic Sheet of 20 x 1st Class stamps (and labels).

SPECIAL HANDSTAMPS SPONSOR
Price Guide Ordinary Covers £4-£9 / Sponsored Covers:

(1) FDI - Tallents House..................... *Royal Mail (n.s.c.)*
(2) FDI - London NW1... .... *Royal Mail (n.s.c.)*
(3) -do- non pictorial version .... *Royal Mail (n.s.c.)*
(4) Daniels Road, Birmingham........... *Royal Mail (n.s.c.)*
(5) Stephenson Way, NW1...........£10 *Benham BLCS 299*
(6) Southport.....................................£10 *Benham BLCS 299*
(7) Selly Oak, Birmingham ....£15 *Benham 500(299)*
(8) St. Austell, Cornwall................£15 *Benham Coin Cover*
(9) Glasgow.......................................£15 *Benham Coin Cover*
(10) A Century of Magic ....£15 *Bradbury Sovereign 54*
(11) The Magic Circle Centenary ..£25 *Bradbury*
(12) Stephenson Way (palette) ......£10 *Westminster*
(13) -do- Autographed Editions.....£15 *Westminster*
(14) Prestolee, Bolton ....£10 *Buckingham Cvrs 217*
(15) Conjurors 1/2 Crown, Poole..£10 *M Brazier (Pubs.77)*
(16) Hand Court, WC1.....................£10 *GB 98*
(17) Stephenson Way, NW1...........£10 *Steven Scott*
(18) Wandsworth.............................£15 *Phil Stamp Covers 79*
(19) Bletchely Park Post Office .....£10 *Bletchley PO*
(20) Magic through the Ages..........£10 *P M Payne*
(21) Merlin Close, Croydon............£10 *Assoc. of GBFDC*
(22) Operation Marstrike................£10 *RN CvrsGp*
(23) Battle of Shrewsbury ....£10 *Heritage of Britain 13*

C.D.S. POSTMARKS Price Guide £7-£10

(24) Bunny, Hatt, King's Cross

22nd March 2005 - CASTLES

50p Carrickfergus & Windsor; £1 Caernarfon & Edinburgh

SPECIAL HANDSTAMPS SPONSOR
Price Guide Ordinary Covers £4-£9 / Sponsored Covers:

(1) FDI - Tallents House..................... *Royal Mail (n.s.c.)*
(2) FDI - Windsor... .... *Royal Mail (n.s.c.)*
(3) -do- non pictorial version .... *Royal Mail (n.s.c.)*
(4) Castle Road, Birmingham .... *Royal Mail (n.s.c.)*
(5) Carrickfergus..............................£15 *Benham BLCS 300*
(6) Edinburgh ....£15 *Benham BLCS 300*
(7) Windsor...£20 *Benham Coin Cover*
(8) Caernarfon...................................£20 *Benham(500)300*
(9) 50th Anniversary of Castles...£15 *Bradbury Sovereign 52*
(10) Windsor (palette design)........£15 *Westminster*
(11) -do- Autographed Editions........£25 *Westminster*
(12) QEII High Values ....£15 *Buckingham Cvrs 218*
(13) British Castles Windsor ....£15 *M Brazier (Pubs.78)*
(14) Windsor Way, London W14..£15 *GB DWX*
(15) The Windsor Castle ....£15 *Steven Scott*
(16) The 1955 Castle Definitives...£15 *P Sheridan*
(17) The Castle Definitives ....£15 *Phil Stamp Covers 80*
(18) Second Battle of Sirte ....£10 *RN CvrsGp*
(19) Battle of St. Albans..................£15 *Heritage of Britain 14*

C.D.S. POSTMARKS Price Guide £7-£10

(20) Windsor, Caernarfon, Edinburgh, Carrickfergus

8th April 2005 - ROYAL WEDDING

2 x 30p; 2 x 68p Prince Charles & Mrs Camilla Parker Bowles in Miniature Sheet format.

SPECIAL HANDSTAMPS SPONSOR

Price Guide Ordinary Covers £4-£9 / Sponsored Covers:

(1) FDI - Tallents House .... *Royal Mail (n.s.c.)*
(2) FDI - Windsor... .... *Royal Mail (n.s.c.)*
(3) -do- non pictorial version .... *Royal Mail (n.s.c.)*
(4) Prince of Wales, Birmingham ...... *Royal Mail (n.s.c.)*
(5) Royal Wedding, Windsor........£15 *Benham BLCS 301*
(6) Charles & Camilla ....£15 *Benham BLCS 301*
(7) Tudor Rose, Windsor................£20 *Benham(500)301*
(8) Royal Wedding Celebrations .£15 *Bradbury Sovereign 62*
(9) Windsor (palette design).........£15 *Westminster*
(10) -do- Autographed Editions.....£20 *Westminster*
(11) Majesty Magazine, Windsor...£10 *Buckingham Cvrs 227*
(12) The Guildhall, Windsor ....£15 *M Brazier*
(13) Royal Wedding ....£15 *Phil Stamp Covers 84*
(14) Rotary, Romford ....£10 *T Hurlstone*
(15) Rotary, Brentford ....£10 *T Hurlstone*
(16) Battle of Towton.......................£15 *Heritage of Britain 16*
(17) No.32 (The Royal) Squadron £10 *S Hill*
(18) HMS Glowworm ....£10 *RN CvrsGp*

C.D.S. POSTMARKS Price Guide £7-£10

(19) Windsor, Windsor Great Park, Wales, Caernarfon

The Royal Wedding was postponed from 8th April to 9th April as a mark of respect for Pope John Paul II's funeral. Royal Mail therefore agreed that all sponsors of postmarks could obtain a free postmark for 9th April provided it was of an identical design (except of course for the date). Double dated covers also exist - these will fetch a premium over the prices listed above.

21st April 2005 - WORLD HERITAGE SITES

2nd, Hadrian's Wall; 2nd Uluru-Kata Tjuta; 1st Stonehenge; 1st Wet Tropics Queensland; 47p Blenheim Palace; 47p Greater Blue Mountains; 68p Heart of Neolithic, Orkney; 68p Purnululu National Park

Also issued on same day: Pacific Explorer Generic Sheet with 20 x Hello Stamps and labels.

SPECIAL HANDSTAMPS SPONSOR

Price Guide Ordinary Covers £4-£9 / Sponsored Covers:

(1) FDI - Tallents House .... *Royal Mail (n.s.c.)*
(2) FDI - Blenheim Palace... .... *Royal Mail (n.s.c.)*
(3) -do- non pictorial version .... *Royal Mail (n.s.c.)*
(4) Stonehenge, Amesbury .... *Royal Mail (n.s.c.)*
(5) Stonehenge Croft, Birmingham ... *Royal Mail (n.s.c.)*
(6) Hounslow, West London ....£15 *Benham Coin Cover*
(7) Invergowrie, Dundee ....£10 *Benham*
(8) The Strand, London WC2......£10 *Benham BLCS 302*
(9) Great Russell Street, WC1 .....£10 *Benham*
(10) Prehistoric Britain, Salisbury.£10 *Benham*
(11) Roman Britain, Carlisle...........£10 *Benham*
(12) Year of the Sea, Greenwich...£10 *Benham BLCS 302*
(13) Year of the Sea, South'ton .....£10 *Benham BLCS 302*
(14) Stonehenge ....£10 *Bradbury Sovereign 55*
(15) Blenheim (palette design).......£10 *Westminster*
(16) -do- Autographed Editions.....£15 *Westminster*
(17) Blenheim Palace ....£10 *Buckingham Cvrs 219*
(18) Captain Cook ....£10 *Buckingham Cvrs 219*
(19) Bark Endeavour........................£10 *Buckingham Cvrs 219*
(20) The Hadrian, Wall ....£10 *M Brazier (Pubs.79)*
(21) Stonehenge, Salisbury ....£10 *P Sheridan*
(22) Barrier Approach, SE7............£10 *GB 99*
(23) Dean's Yard, London SW1....£10 *Steven Scott*
(24) World Heritage Sites, Perth ...£15 *Phil Stamp Covers 81*
(25) Battle of Blore Heath ....£15 *Heritage of Britain 15*
(26) Bombardment of Tripoli ....£10 *RN CvrsGp*

C.D.S. POSTMARKS Price Guide £7-£10

(27) Heddon on the Wall, Stromness, Woodstock, Amesbury

This was a joint issue with Australia Post. Pairs of covers exist with both sets of stamps. Priced approx double the above.

7th June 2005 - TROOPING THE COLOUR

2nd Ensign of Scots Guard; 1st H M the Queen; 42p Trumpeter, Household Cavalry; 60p Welsh Guards Sgt; 68p H M the Queen as Colonel of the Coldstream Guards; £1.12 H M the Queen with the Duke of Edinburgh. Stamps and Miniature Sheet.

SPECIAL HANDSTAMPS SPONSOR

Price Guide Ordinary Covers £4-£9 / Sponsored Covers:

(1) FDI - Tallents House...................... *Royal Mail (n.s.c.)*
(2) FDI - London SW1... .... *Royal Mail (n.s.c.)*
(3) -do- non pictorial version .... *Royal Mail (n.s.c.)*
(4) Queen's Road, Birmingham.......... *Royal Mail (n.s.c.)*
(5) Horse Guards Avenue, SW1..£10 *Benham BLCS 304*

(6) Whitehall, SW1........................£10 *Benham BLCS 303*
(7) St. James's St., SW1...................£10 *Benham BLCS 303*
(8) Buckingham Palace Rd............£15 *Benham(500)303*
(9) Tower Hill, EC3.........................£15 *Benham(500)304*
(10) Birdcage Walk, SW1.................£10 *Benham BLCS 304*
(11) Horse Guards Ave....................£15 *Bradbury Sovereign 56*
(12) 1805-2005, London........................ *Bradbury (n.s.c.)*
(13) London SW1 (palette)............£15 *Westminster*
(14) -do- Autographed Editions.....£20 *Westminster*
(15) Buckingham Palace Road.......£10 *Steven Scott*
(16) The Mall, SW1..........................£10 *Buckingham Cvrs 220*
(17) Horse Guards Parade, SW1...£10 *Buckingham Cvrs 220*
(18) The Royal & The Parade........£10 *M Brazier (Pubs.80)*
(19) Coldstream (Gdns) Guards....£10 *GB 100*
(20) Trooping the Colour................£10 *P Sheridan*
(21) The Parade, SW1......................£10 *Assoc. of GBFDC*
(22) Trooping the Colour................£15 *Phil Stamp Covers 82*
(23) Trooping the Colour................£15 *Phil Stamp Covers 83*
(24) Rotary Club of London...........£20 *Bradbury*
(25) Battle of Northampton............£15 *Heritage of Britain 16*
(26) Trooping the BP Colour.........£10 *Bletchley PO*
(27) 61st Anniversary D-Day +1...£10 *RN CvrsGp*
(28) Kangchenjunga, Watford........£15 *ABC-FDC*
(29) Makalu 1955, Mt Pleasant.....£15 *ABC-FDC*
(30) Annapurna South Face...........£15 *ABC-FDC*

C.D.S. POSTMARKS Price Guide £7-£10

(31) Coldstream, Windsor, Trafalgar Square
(32) Queensway, Queens Parade, Queen's Drive, March

21st June 05 - WHITE ENSIGN Generic Issue

1st White Ensign stamp + labels featuring signal flags

SPECIAL HANDSTAMPS SPONSOR

Price Guide Ordinary Cvrs £3-£5 / Sponsored Covers:

(1) Horatio Nelson........................£15 *Bradbury Windsor 55*
(2) The White Ensign, Flagg.........£15 *Phil Stamp Covers*
(3) Wimbledon...................................... *Royal Mail (n.s.c.)*

5th July 2005 - END OF THE WAR

Miniature Sheet comprising of:
1st Floodlit St. Paul's; 5 x 1st Gold Definitives

SPECIAL HANDSTAMPS SPONSOR

Price Guide Ordinary Covers £3-£5 / Sponsored Covers:

(1) FDI - Tallents House..................... *Royal Mail (n.s.c.)*
(2) FDI - Peacehaven.......................... *Royal Mail (n.s.c.)*
(3) -do- non pictorial version............ *Royal Mail (n.s.c.)*
(4) St Pauls London EC4.................... *Royal Mail (n.s.c.)*
(5) Winston Drive, Birmingham........ *Royal Mail*
(6) Whitehall, London SW1.........£10 *Benham BLCS 305*
(7) St Pauls, London SW1............£10 *Benham BLCS 305*
(8) Peacehaven, East Sussex..........£15 *Benham(500)305*
(9) Peace, London SW1.................£15 *Bradbury Sovereign 57*
(10) St. Paul's (palette design).......£10 *Westminster*
(11) -do- Autographed Editions.....£15 *Westminster*
(12) Victory Road, SW19................£10 *Steven Scott*
(13) Peace on Earth, EC4...............£10 *Buckingham Cvrs 221*
(14) The Soldiers Return.................£10 *M Brazier (Pubs.81)*
(15) Wall End Road, E6..................£10 *GB 101*
(16) End of War, London...............£10 *P Sheridan*
(17) Victory Walk............................£15 *Phil Stamp Covers 84*
(18) End of War BF 2865 PS.........£10 *Forces BFPS*
(19) 60th Anniv End of War..........£10 *Bletchley PO*
(20) End of War BF 2867 PS.........£10 *RN CvrsGp*
(21) Battle of Barnet.......................£15 *Heritage of Britain 18*

C.D.S. POSTMARKS Price Guide £7-£10

(22) Montgomery, Peacehaven, Wargrave, Bletchley,
(23) Churchill, Woodstock, King George Road

VALUES SHOULD BE TREATED AS A GUIDE
Please read the General Notes where you will find the answers to most of your questions.

19th July 2005 - BRITISH MOTORCYCLES

1st Norton F1; 40p BSA Rocket; 42p Vincent Black Shadow; 47p Triumph Twin Speed; 60p Brough Superior; 68p Royal Enfield

SPECIAL HANDSTAMPS SPONSOR

Price Guide Ordinary Covers £3-£5 / Sponsored Covers:

(1) FDI - Tallents House..................... *Royal Mail (n.s.c.)*
(2) FDI - Solihull................................. *Royal Mail (n.s.c.)*
(3) -do- non pictorial version............ *Royal Mail (n.s.c.)*
(4) Sheen Road, Birmingham............ *Royal Mail*
(5) Wolverhampton........................£15 *Benham*
(6) Birmingham..............................£20 *Benham Coin Cover*
(7) Stevenage.................................£15 *Benham*

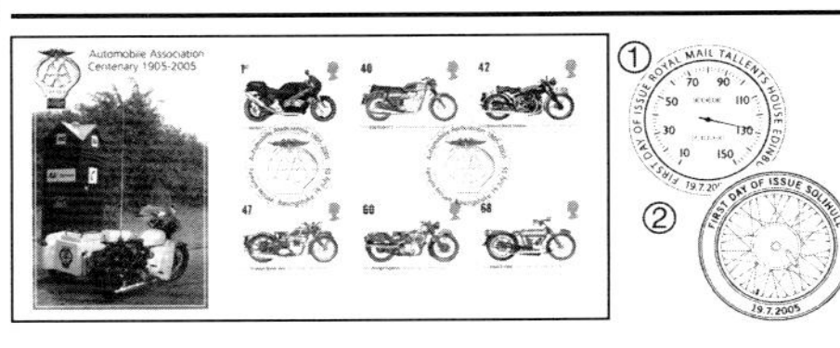

(8)	Coventry	£20	*Benham(500) 306*
(9)	Nottingham	£15	*Benham BLCS 306*
(10)	Redditch	£15	*Benham BLCS 306*
(11)	Automobile Association	£15	*Bradbury Sovereign 58*
(12)	Brands Hatch (palette)	£15	*Westminster*
(13)	-do- Autographed Editions	£25	*Westminster*
(14)	Motorcycles, Norwich	£15	*Steven Scott*
(15)	Beaulieu	£10	*Buckingham Cvrs 222*
(16)	Classic Bike, Silverstone	£10	*Buckingham Cvrs 222*
(17)	Stirling Moss, Aintree	£15	*Buckingham Cvrs 222*
(18)	The Norton & the Sun Inn	£15	*M Brazier (Pubs.82)*
(19)	Harley Davidson, Towcester	£15	*M Brazier*
(20)	Biko Close, Uxbridge	£10	*GB 102*
(21)	Sammy Miller Motorcycles	£10	*P Sheridan*
(22)	TMC Southfield Rd, W4	£15	*H D MacIntyre*
(23)	Silverstone, Towcester	£20	*G Lovell*
(24)	Motorcycles, Birmingham	£20	*Phil Stamp Covers 86*
(25)	Ace Corner, NW10	£15	*Farrukh Jamil Covers*
(26)	Ace Corner, NW10	£15	*Farrukh Jamil Covers*
(27)	Brough Superior, Tonbridge	£25	*W H Pugh*
(28)	AJS, Andover	£25	*W H Pugh*
(29)	BSA, Southampton	£25	*W H Pugh*
(30)	Verralls, Haywards Heath	£25	*W H Pugh*
(31)	Royal Enfield, Moreton	£25	*W H Pugh*
(32)	Post Office Urgent Despatch	£10	*Bletchley PO*

C.D.S. POSTMARKS Price Guide £7-£10

(33) Brereton, Small Heath, Allesley, Sherwood, The Rocket

(34) Redditch, Brough, Silverstone, Norton, Enfield, Dunlop

5th August 2005 - LONDON 2012

Miniature Sheet comprising of: 1st Athlete; 1st Javelin; 1st Basketball; 1st Swimming; 2 x 1st Triumphant Athlete

SPECIAL HANDSTAMPS SPONSOR

Price Guide Ordinary Covers £3-£5 / Sponsored Covers:

(1)	FDI - Tallents House		*Royal Mail (n.s.c.)*
(2)	FDI - London E15		*Royal Mail (n.s.c.)*
(3)	-do- non pictorial version		*Royal Mail (n.s.c.)*
(4)	London Road, Birmingham		*Royal Mail*
(5)	2012 (Finishing Line)	£10	*Benham BLCS 310*
(6)	2012 (Javelin)	£15	*Benham(500) 310*
(7)	2012 (Swimming)	£10	*Benham*
(8)	2012 (Runner)	£15	*Benham BLCS 310*
(9)	2012 (Basketball)	£10	*Benham*
(10)	Hat Trick for London	£15	*Bradbury Sovereign 64*
(11)	Host City, E15 (palette)	£10	*Westminster*
(12)	-do- Autographed Editions	£15	*Westminster*
(13)	London Wins Stratford	£10	*Steven Scott*
(14)	London (torch)	£10	*Buckingham Cvrs 228*
(15)	Raffles, Romford	£10	*M Brazier (Pubs.84)*
(16)	Olympic Way, Wembley	£10	*GB 104*
(17)	It's London Host City 2012	£10	*P Sheridan*
(18)	London Host City	£15	*Phil Stamp Covers*
(19)	Soc of Olympic Collectors	£10	*Soc of Olympic Coll.*
(20)	Congratultions, York	£10	*Cotswold*
(21)	Havering Sports Council	£15	*T Hurlstone*
(22)	HMS Belfast	£10	*RN CvrsGp*

C.D.S. POSTMARKS Price Guide £7-£10

(23) Stratford, City (London)

23rd August 2005 - CHANGING TASTES

2nd Rice; 1st Tea; 42p Sushi; 47p Pasta; 60p Chips; 68p Apples

SPECIAL HANDSTAMPS SPONSOR

Price Guide Ordinary Covers £3-£5 / Sponsored Covers:

(1)	FDI - Tallents House		*Royal Mail (n.s.c.)*
(2)	FDI - Cookstown		*Royal Mail (n.s.c.)*
(3)	-do- non pictorial version		*Royal Mail (n.s.c.)*
(4)	Oliver Street, Birmingham		*Royal Mail*
(5)	Ashdown Forest, E. Sussex	£10	*Benham BLCS 309*
(6)	Guiseley, Leeds	£15	*Benham(500) 309*
(7)	Hillingdon, Uxbridge	£10	*Benham*
(8)	St. Austell, Cornwall	£10	*Benham BLCS 309*
(9)	Victoria, London SW1	£15	*Benham Coin Cover*
(10)	Chagford, Devon	£10	*Benham*
(11)	Covent Garden	£10	*Bradbury Sovereign 59*
(12)	Curry Rise (palette)	£10	*Westminster*
(13)	-do- Autographed Editions	£15	*Westminster*
(14)	Curry Rise, NW7	£10	*Steven Scott*
(15)	Great British Food, W1	£10	*Buckingham Cvrs 223*
(16)	The Bramley Apple	£15	*M Brazier (Pubs.83)*
(17)	Cooksway, Hatfield	£10	*GB 103*
(18)	Vegetarian Society	£15	*P Sheridan*
(19)	Cookham, Maidenhead	£15	*Phil Stamp Covers 87*
(20)	Nando's, South Bank SE1	£15	*ABC FDC*
(21)	Food you can trust, Iceland	£15	*W H Pugh*
(22)	Changing Rations	£10	*Bletchley PO*
(23)	Battle of Bosworth	£15	*Heritage of Britain 20*

(24) HMS Hero..............................£10 *RN CvrsGp*

C.D.S. POSTMARKS Price Guide £7-£10

(25) Bramley, Strawberry Hill, Curry Rivel, Isle of Grain

(26) Wheatley, Rowelton, New Covent Garden, Sugar Island

15th September 2005 - CLASSIC ITV

(1) 2nd Inspector Morse; 1st Emmerdale; 42p Rising Damp; 47p Avengers; 60p South Bank Show; 68p Who wants to be a Millionaire

(2) Generic Sheet of 20 x 1st Class stamps.

SPECIAL HANDSTAMPS SPONSOR

Price Guide Ordinary Covers £3-£5 / Sponsored Covers:

(1) FDI - Tallents House.................... *Royal Mail (n.s.c.)*
(2) FDI - London SE19...................... *Royal Mail (n.s.c.)*
(3) -do- non pictorial version .... *Royal Mail (n.s.c.)*
(4) Stampex, London N1.................... *Royal Mail*
(5) Stampex ITV, London N1 .... *Royal Mail*
(6) Broad Street, Birmingham .... *Royal Mail*
(7) Oxford......................................£10 *Benham BLCS 311*
(8) The Woolpack, Harewood.....£15 *Benham Coin Cover*
(9) Burley Road, Leeds..................£10 *Benham*
(10) Elstree, Borehamwood ....£15 *Benham(500) 311*
(11) Upper Ground, SE1..................£10 *Benham BLCS 311*
(12) Grays Inn Road, WC..................£10 *Benham*
(13) Commercial TV, Manchester.£10 *Bradbury Sovereign 60*
(14) South Bank (palette) ....£10 *Westminster*
(15) -do- Autographed.....................£15 *Westminster*
(16) Gray's Inn Road, WC2...........£10 *Steven Scott*
(17) TV Times, SE1 ....£10 *Buckingham Cvrs 224*
(18) 50 Years of Classic ITV ....£10 *Buckingham Cvrs 224*
(19) The Sweeney, Charlton...........£15 *M Brazier (Pubs.85)*
(20) Cooper Road, London ....£10 *GB 105*
(21) Police Station Lane, Herts .....£10 *GB 105*
(22) National Museum, Bradford..£15 *P Sheridan*
(23) Classic ITV, Watchet..............£15 *Phil Stamp Covers 85*
(24) Scott's View, Melrose ....£10 *ABC-FDC*
(25) Riot of Steam 150 Years.........£10 *Dawn*
(26) HMS Valient ....£10 *RN CvrsGp*
(27) Battle of East Stoke ....£15 *Heritage of Britain 21*

C.D.S. POSTMARKS Price Guide £7-£10

(28) Harewood, South Bank, Esholt, Oxford, Woodsley

(29) Teddington, Blackfriars Road, Elstree

4th October 2005 - SMILERS

6 x 1st featuring small versions of the previously issued 'Smilers' stamps: Hello, Love, Union Jack, Teddy Bear, Flowers and Robin. (Self Adhesives issued in Stamp Book)

SPECIAL HANDSTAMPS SPONSOR

Price Guide Ordinary Covers £3-£5 / Sponsored Covers:

(1) FDI - Tallents House.................... *Royal Mail (n.s.c.)*
(2) FDI - Windsor .... *Royal Mail (n.s.c.)*
(3) -do- non pictorial version .... *Royal Mail (n.s.c.)*
(4) Garden Village, Hull ....£10 *Benham*
(5) Greet, Cheltenham..................£10 *Benham BLCS 312*
(6) Lovington, Castle Cary...........£10 *Benham BLCS 312*
(7) Flagg, Buxton ....£10 *Benham D461*
(8) Bearwood, Leominster...........£15 *Benham Coin Cover*
(9) Birdwood, Gloucester ....£15 *Benham(500) 312*
(10) Teddy Bears Picnic ....£15 *Bradbury Windsor 57*
(11) Bearwood, Birmingham..........£10 *Buckingham Cvrs 229*
(12) Stamp Bk, Greetham...............£10 *Phil Stamp Covers 9*
(13) 1st Pictorial Defins, York.......£10 *Cotswold*

6th October 2005 - CRICKET (The Ashes)

2 x 1st; 2 x 68p Scenes from the 2005 Ashes

SPECIAL HANDSTAMPS SPONSOR

Price Guide Ordinary Covers £3-£5 / Sponsored Covers:

(1) FDI - Tallents House.................... *Royal Mail (n.s.c.)*
(2) FDI - London SE11...................... *Royal Mail (n.s.c.)*
(3) -do- non pictorial version .... *Royal Mail (n.s.c.)*
(4) Edgbaston, Birmingham .... *Royal Mail*
(5) Birmingham..............................£10 *Benham BLCS 316*
(6) Manchester..............................£15 *Benham(500) 316*
(7) Nottingham..............................£15 *Benham Coin Cover*
(8) London SE11 ....£10 *Benham BLCS 316*
(9) Hambledon ....£15 *Bradbury Sovereign 70*
(10) London SE11 (palette)............£10 *Westminster*
(11) -do- Autographed....................£15 *Westminster*
(12) Ashes Come Home, Oval ....£10 *Buckingham Cvrs*
(13) Test Match, W Bridgford........£10 *M Brazier (Pubs.87)*
(14) Cricketers Arms Rd, Enfield ..£10 *GB 107*
(15) Victory, The Oval ....£10 *Cotswold*
(16) Bletchley Park ....£10 *Bletchley PO*
(17) Winning the Ashes..................£10 *Phil Stamp Covers*
(18) Mine Counter Measures ....£10 *RN CvrsGp*

C.D.S. POSTMARKS Price Guide £7-£10

(19) St. John's Wood, Edgbaston, Old Trafford, Trent Bridge

(20) Kennington

18th October 2005 - TRAFALGAR

(1) 2 x 1st, 2 x 42p, 2 x 68p Battle of Trafalgar
(2) Miniature Sheet
(3) Prestige Stamp Book

SPECIAL HANDSTAMPS		SPONSOR
Price Guide Ordinary Covers £3-£5 / Sponsored Covers:		
(1) FDI - Tallents House		*Royal Mail (n.s.c.)*
(2) FDI - Portsmouth		*Royal Mail (n.s.c.)*
(3) -do- non pictorial version		*Royal Mail (n.s.c.)*
(4) Burnham Thorpe		*Royal Mail*
(5) Nelson Road, Birmingham		*Royal Mail*
(6) Trafalgar Square, WC2	£15	*Benham BLCS 313*
(7) Burnham Thorpe	£15	*Benham BLCS 313*
(8) Merton, London SW19	£15	*Benham BLCS 314*
(9) St. Paul's Churchyard, EC4	£25	*Benham Coin Cover*
(10) Portsmouth	£30	*Benham(500) 314*
(11) Whitehall, London SW1	£15	*Benham BLCS 314*
(12) Trafalgar Square, London	£15	*Bradbury Sovereign 61*
(13) H M Naval Base	£15	*Westminster*
(14) -do- Palette Design	£15	*Westminster*
(15) -do- Autographed	£25	*Westminster*
(16) Trafalgar Square, London	£15	*Steven Scott*
(17) The Victory, Portsmouth	£15	*Buckingham Cvrs 225*
(18) HMS Victory, Chatham	£15	*Buckingham Cvrs 225*
(19) The Trafalgar, Hythe	£15	*M Brazier (Pubs.86)*
(20) Victory Way, London	£15	*GB 106*
(21) Royal Naval Museum	£15	*P Sheridan*
(22) Portsmouth	£15	*Phil Stamp Covers 89*
(23) Nelson	£15	*Phil Stamp Covers 90*
(24) Victory Place, E14	£15	*Assoc. of GBFDC*
(25) Southsea, Hants	£20	*H D Macintyre*
(26) Trafalgar BF 2878 PS	£15	*Forces*
(27) Eng Expects BF 2885 PS	£15	*Forces*
(28) Trafalgar 1805 Matapan	£15	*Bletchley PO*
(29) Battle of Flodden	£20	*Heritage of Britain 22*

C.D.S. POSTMARKS Price Guide £7-£10
(30) Trafalgar Sq, Nelson, Trafalgar Rd, Portsmouth, Merton
(31) Burnham Market, The Quarterdeck, Deal, HMS Nelson

1st November 2005 - CHRISTMAS

(1) Madonna & Child through the eyes of different cultures: 2nd Haiti; 1st & 42p Europe; 60p North American Indian; 68p India; £1.12 Australian Aborigine.
(2) Miniature Sheet
(3) Generic Sheet with 2nd and 1st Class Robin stamps.

SPECIAL HANDSTAMPS		SPONSOR
Price Guide Ordinary Covers £3-£5 / Sponsored Covers:		
(1) FDI - Tallents House		*Royal Mail (n.s.c.)*
(2) FDI - Bethlehem		*Royal Mail (n.s.c.)*
(3) -do- non pictorial version		*Royal Mail (n.s.c.)*
(4) Mary Street, Birmingham		*Royal Mail (n.s.c.)*
(5) Wiseman's Bridge, Narberth	£10	*Benham BLCS 319*
(6) Christchurch, Newport	£15	*Benham(500) 318*
(7) Bethlehem, Llandeilo	£10	*Benham BLCS 318*
(8) Maryhill, Isle of Lewis	£10	*Benham BLCS 318*
(9) Stableford, Newcastle	£15	*Benham Coin Cover*
(10) Shepherdswell, Dover	£15	*Benham(500) 319*
(11) Madonna and Child	£15	*Bradbury Sovereign 63*
(12) Noel Street, W1 Palette	£15	*Westminster*
(13) -do- Autographed	£25	*Westminster*
(14) North Pole Road, W10	£10	*Steven Scott*
(15) 1300 Years, Wells	£10	*Buckingham Cvrs 226*
(16) Christmas, Canterbury	£10	*Buckingham Cvrs 226*
(17) Season's Greetings		*Royal Mail (n.s.c.)*
(18) St Katherine's Way, E1	£10	*GB 108*
(19) Holytown	£10	*P Sheridan*
(20) Christmas Robins, Ware	£10	*Phil Stamp Covers 10*
(21) Bethlehem (angel)	£15	*Phil Stamp Covers 92*
(22) Bethlehem (crown)	£15	*Phil Stamp Covers 91*
(23) Madonna and Child, York	£10	*Cotswold*
(24) York Minster	£10	*Cotswold*
(25) Allendale, Hexham	£15	*T Beaumont*
(26) Philatelic Music Circle	£15	*G Datson*
(27) Bletchley Park Post Office	£10	*Bletchley PO*
(28) Wolver'ton Art Gallery	£10	*Royal Mail (n.s.c.)*
(29) H M Ships at Christmas	£10	*RN CvrsGp*
(30) Battle of Solway Moss	£15	*Heritage of Britain 23*

C.D.S. POSTMARKS Price Guide £7-£10
(31) Holy Island, Canterbury, Bethlehem, Jerusalem Street

The General Notes at the beginning of this catalogue gives details of the following topics:

The scope of the catalogue - which first day covers are included and why.

Prices & condition - what to look for when buying first day covers.

Types of pmk: Special Handstamps, CDS, FDI, Slogans. **Types of cover: Sponsored or Ordinary.**

10th January 2006 - ANIMAL TALES

(1) 2nd Jeremy Fisher; 2nd Kipper; 1st Enormous Crocodile; 1st Paddington Bear; 42p Boots; 42p White Rabbit; 68p The Very Hungry Caterpillar; 68p Maisy.
(2) Generic Sheet with 20 x Paddington Bear stamps.

SPECIAL HANDSTAMPS SPONSOR
Price Guide Ordinary Covers £3-£5 / Sponsored Covers:

(1) FDI - Tallents House...................... *Royal Mail (n.s.c.)*
(2) FDI - Mousehole........................... *Royal Mail (n.s.c.)*
(3) -do- non pictorial version .... *Royal Mail (n.s.c.)*
(4) Dogpool Lane, Birmingham......... *Royal Mail (n.s.c.)*
(5) Inkpen, Hungerford..................£10 *Benham BLCS 319*
(6) Paddington, Warrington ....£10 *Benham*
(7) Near Sawrey, Ambleside..........£15 *Benham Coin Cover*
(8) Llandaff, Cardiff.......................£15 *Benham (500) 319*
(9) Stratford-upon-Avon ....£15 *Benham (500) 319*
(10) Daresbury, Warrington ....£10 *Benham BLCS 319*
(11) Catshill, Bromsgrove ....£10 *Benham BLCS 319*
(12) Mousehole, Penzance..............£10 *Benham BLCS 319*
(13) Animal Tales, London.............£15 *Bradbury Sovereign 65*
(14) Paddington St, W1 (Palette) ..£10 *Westminster*
(15) -do- Autographed.....................£20 *Westminster*
(16) Paddington, London W2 ....£10 *Steven Scott*
(17) A Bear Called Paddington.......£10 *Buckingham Cvrs 231*
(18) Paddington, London W2 ....£10 *Buckingham Cvrs 231*
(19) The White Rabbit, Maidstone£15 *M Brazier (Pubs.89)*
(20) Animal Tales, Waverton ....£10 *P Sheridan*
(21) Snapper ....£15 *Phil Stamp Covers 93*
(22) Windsor Gardens.....................£15 *Phil Stamp Covers 91*
(23) 1st Stamp Issue 2006, York...£10 *Cotswold*
(24) Bletchley Park Post Office .....£10 *Bletchley PO*
(25) Battle of Pinkie.........................£15 *Heritage of Britain 24*
(26) HMS Gallant.............................£10 *RN CvrsGp*

C.D.S. POSTMARKS Price Guide £7-£10
(27) Bunny, Catfield, Mousehole, Frogmore
(28) Paddington, Hawkshead

7th February 2006 - ENGLAND

12 x 1st: Cardigan Mill Valley; Beachy Head; St. Paul's Cathedral; Brancaster; Derwent Edge; Robin Hood's Bay; Buttermere; Chipping Campden; St. Boniface Down; Chamberlain Square Birmingham

SPECIAL HANDSTAMPS SPONSOR
Price Guide Ordinary Covers £3-£5 / Sponsored Covers:

(1) FDI - Tallents House...................... *Royal Mail (n.s.c.)*
(2) FDI - Tea Green, Luton .... *Royal Mail (n.s.c.)*
(3) -do- non pictorial version .... *Royal Mail (n.s.c.)*
(4) Chamberlain Sq, Birmingham...... *Royal Mail (n.s.c.)*
(5) St Paul's Churchyard...............£10 *Benham BLCS 320*
(6) Brancaster Staithe....................£15 *Benham (500) 320*
(7) Bamford, Hope Valley.............£10 *Benham*
(8) Birmingham...............................£10 *Benham*
(9) Robin Hood's Bay, Whitby ....£10 *Benham*
(10) Church Stretton, Shropshire..£10 *Benham*
(11) Buttermere, Cockermouth.......£10 *Benham BLCS 320*
(12) Chipping Campden, Glos.......£10 *Benham*
(13) Eastbourne, East Sussex ....£10 *Benham*
(14) Cowes, Isle of Wight................£15 *Benham Coin Cover*
(15) Animal Tales, London.............£15 *Bradbury Sovereign 66*
(16) St Paul's Courtyard..................£10 *Westminster*
(17) -do- Autographed.....................£20 *Westminster*
(18) London - New York ....£15 *Westminster*
(19) Ramblers, Eastbourne ....£10 *Buckingham Cvrs 232*
(20) Ramblers, Buttermere..............£10 *Buckingham Cvrs 232*
(21) Birmingham - Beachy Head ..£10 *M Brazier (Rly.14)*
(22) Buttermere Lake.......................£10 *P Sheridan*
(23) Journeys End (ointment) ....£15 *Phil Stamp Covers 95*
(24) Journeys End (boots)...............£15 *Phil Stamp Covers 94*
(25) HMS Orwell..............................£10 *RN CvrsGp*
(26) Defeat of Spanish Armada.....£15 *Heritage of Britain*

C.D.S. POSTMARKS Price Guide £7-£10
(27) Church Stretton, Chipping Campden, Brancaster,
(28) Robin Hoods Bay, Bamford, Birmingham, East Dean

23rd February 2006 - BRUNEL

(1) 1st Royal Albert Bridge, Saltash; 40p Box Tunnel; 42p Paddington Station; 47p PSS Great Eastern; 60p Clifton Suspension Bridge; 68p Maidenhead Bridge
(2) Miniature Sheet
(3) Prestige Stamp Book

SPECIAL HANDSTAMPS SPONSOR
Price Guide Ordinary Covers £3-£5 / Sponsored Covers:

(1) FDI - Tallents House...................... *Royal Mail (n.s.c.)*
(2) FDI - Bristol.................................... *Royal Mail (n.s.c.)*
(3) -do- non pictorial version .... *Royal Mail (n.s.c.)*
(4) Brunel Close, Birmingham............ *Royal Mail (n.s.c.)*

(5) Brunel - Stampex......................£15 *Royal Mail*
(6) Spring Stampex.........................£15 *Royal Mail*
(7) Engineer - Paddington ....£20 *Royal Mail*
(8) Clifton Suspension Bridge......£15 *Benham BLCS 321*
(9) Maidenhead Bridge..................£20 *Benham(500) 322*
(10) Box Tunnel, Corsham ....£15 *Benham BLCS 321*
(11) Royal Albert Bridge, Saltash..£15 *Benham BLCS 322*
(12) Paddington Station ....£20 *Benham Coin Cover*
(13) Great Eastern, Millwall...........£15 *Benham BLCS 322*
(14) Saltash, Cornwall ....£15 *Bradbury Sovereign 67*
(15) Brunel Road, W3 (Palette).....£15 *Westminster*
(16) -do- Autographed ....£20 *Westminster*
(17) Great Western Railway...........£15 *Westminster*
(18) Paddington................................£15 *Buckingham Cvrs 233*
(19) Saltash ....£15 *Buckingham Cvrs 233*
(20) The Enterprise - Bristol ....£15 *M Brazier (Pubs.90)*
(21) Brunel University ....£15 *P Sheridan*
(22) Brunel Road, London W3......£10 *Steven Scott*
(23) Portsea, Portsmouth ....£15 *Phil Stamp Covers 97*
(24) Millwall, London E14 ....£15 *Phil Stamp Covers 96*
(25) Saltash Cornwall ....£10 *Cotswold*
(26) Brunel Road, London W3......£10 *GB 109*
(27) Britain Street, Portsea ....£10 *ABC FDC*
(28 Battle of Newburn Ford..........£15 *Heritage of Britain 25*
(29) 2006 Anniversaries ....£10 *P M Payne*
(30) HMS Bicester ....£10 *RN CvrsGp*
C.D.S. POSTMARKS Price Guide £7-£10
(31) Saltash, Box, Paddington, Clifton Village, Maidenhead
(32) ....

1st March 2006 - WELSH ASSEMBLY

Miniature Sheet containing 1 x 2nd, 2 x 1st, 2 x 68p, Welsh Country Pictorial stamps

SPECIAL HANDSTAMPS SPONSOR
Price Guide Ordinary Covers £3-£5 / Sponsored Covers:
(1) Tallents House................................ *Royal Mail (n.s.c.)*
(2) Cardiff... *Royal Mail (n.s.c.)*
(3) -do- non pictorial version .... *Royal Mail (n.s.c.)*
(4) Daffodil Way, Birmingham........... *Royal Mail (n.s.c.)*
(5) Llanberis, Caernarfon..............£10 *Benham BLCS 325*
(6) Caernarfon ....£15 *Benham Coin Cover*
(7) Builth Wells..............................£15 *Benham (500)325*
(8) Cardiff.......................................£10 *Benham BLCS 325*
(9) Cardiff Bay, Cardiff (Palette) .£10 *Westminster*
(10) -do- Autographed....................£15 *Westminster*
(11) Cardiff.......................................£10 *Buckingham Cvrs 234*
(12) Cardiff/Caerdydd.....................£10 *Phil Stamp Covers 98*
(13) Cymru, Cardiff ....£10 *Cotswold*
(14) Battle of Powick Bridge..........£10 *Heritage of Britain*
(15) RFA Fort George......................£10 *RN CvrsGp*
C.D.S. POSTMARKS Price Guide £7-£10
(16) National Assembly for Wales (English or Welsh version)
(17) Cardiff, St. Davids

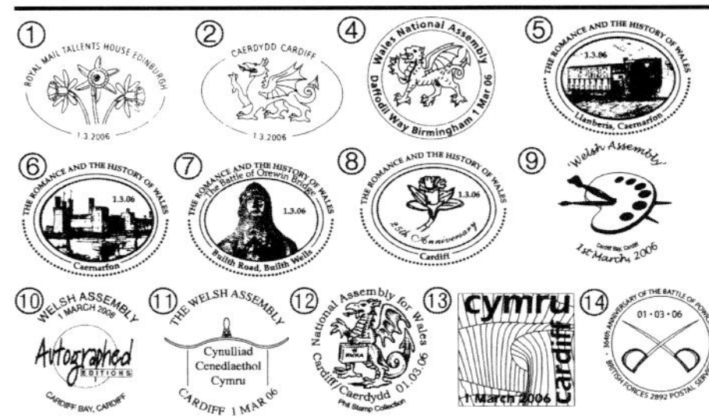

7th Mar 2006 - FRUIT & VEG Generic Issue

20 x 1st Strawberry, Potato, Apple, Pepper, Pear, Orange, Tomato, Lemon, Sprout, Aubergine + labels

SPECIAL HANDSTAMPS SPONSOR
Price Guide Ordinary Covers £3-£5 / Sponsored Covers:
(1) Saffron Walden, Essex ....£15 *Benham 500(326)*
(2) Winchester, Hampshire ....£10 *Benham BLCS 326*
(3) Wells, Somerset ....£10 *Benham BLCS 326*
(4) Covent Garden ....£10 *Buckingham Cvrs 32*
(5) Potato Town ....£10 *Phil Stamp Covers 12*

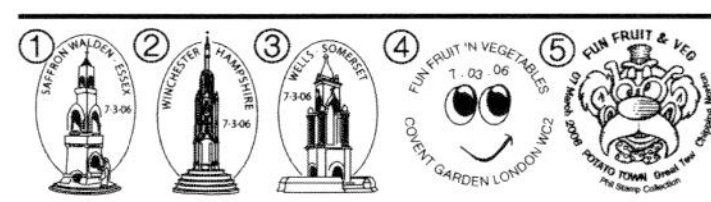

Fruit & Veg Generic Issue

21st March 2006 - ICE AGE MAMMALS

1st Sabre-Tooth Cat; 42p Giant Deer; 47p Woolly Rhino; 68p Woolly Mammoth; £1.12 Cave Bear

SPECIAL HANDSTAMPS SPONSOR
Price Guide Ordinary Covers £3-£5 / Sponsored Covers:
(1) FDI - Tallents House .... *Royal Mail (n.s.c.)*
(2) FDI - Tea Green, Luton .... *Royal Mail (n.s.c.)*
(3) -do- non pictorial version .... *Royal Mail (n.s.c.)*
(4) Coldbath Road, Birmingham........ *Royal Mail (n.s.c.)*
(5) Ilford ....£15 *Benham Coin Cover*
(6) Lowestoft ....£15 *Benham BLCS 327*
(7) Lancaster...................................£15 *Benham 500(327)*
(8) Burton-on-Trent ....£10 *Benham BLCS 327*
(9) Torquay ....£10 *Benham*
(10) London ....£15 *Bradbury Sovereign 69*
(11) Cromwell Road (Palette) ....£10 *Westminster*
(12) -do- Autographed ....£15 *Westminster*
(13) Bearsted, Maidstone ....£10 *Buckingham Cvrs 235*
(14) Iceland & The Great Stone ...£10 *M Brazier (Pubs.91)*
(15) Save the Rhino.........................£10 *P Sheridan*
(16) Piltdown ....£15 *Phil Stamp Covers 99*

(17) Cromwell Road, SW7 .... *GB 110*
(18) Bletchley Park Post Office .... *Bletchley PO*
(19) Battle of Edgehill .... *Heritage of Britain*
(20) HMS Bulldog .... *RN CvrsGp*
C.D.S. POSTMARKS Price Guide £7-£10
(21) Freezywater, Frosterley, Coldstream, or similar
(22) Ilford, Deerpark, Bearsden, New Deer, Bear Flat etc

18th April 2006 – QUEEN'S 80th BIRTHDAY
2 x 2nd; 2 x 1st; 2 x 44p; 2 x 72p Portraits of the Queen

SPECIAL HANDSTAMPS SPONSOR
Price Guide Ordinary Covers £3-£5 / Sponsored Covers:
(1) FDI - Tallents House .... *Royal Mail (n.s.c.)*
(2) FDI - Windsor .... *Royal Mail (n.s.c.)*
(3) -do- non pictorial version .... *Royal Mail (n.s.c.)*
(4) Queens Drive, Birmingham .... *Royal Mail (n.s.c.)*
(5) Sandringham, Norfolk ....£15 *Benham 500(328)*
(6) London SW1 ....£10 *Benham BLCS 328*
(7) Windsor Berkshire ....£10 *Benham BLCS 328*
(8) Crathie, Ballater.......................£15 *Benham Coin Cover*
(9) Edinburgh ....£10 *Benham*
(10) Buckingham Palace Rd ....£15 *Bradbury Sovereign 71*
(11) Bruton Street (Palette) ....£10 *Westminster*
(12) -do- Autographed ....£15 *Westminster*
(13) Buckingham Palace ....£10 *Westminster*
(14) Windsor, Berkshire ....£10 *Buckingham Cvrs 236*
(15) The Crown and Sceptre ....£10 *M Brazier (Pubs.92)*
(16) Buckingham Palace Road.......£10 *P Sheridan*
(17) Windsor ....£15 *Phil Stamp Cvrs 100*
(18) London 80 ....£10 *Cotswold*
(19) Grenadier Street, E16..............£10 *GB 111*
(20) Bletchley Park Post Office .....£10 *Bletchley PO*
(21) Jewish Community ....£10 *ABC-FDC*
(22) Stanley Gibbons 150 ....£15 *Stanley Gibbons*
(23) Battle of Braddock Down ......£15 *Heritage of Britain 26*
(24) HMS Sandown ....£10 *RN CvrsGp*
C.D.S. POSTMARKS Price Guide £7-£10
(25) Throne, Britannia, Windsor, Queen's Rd or similar
(26) Windsor Castle, Buckingham Palace (£50)

6th June 2006 – WORLD CUP WINNERS
(1) 1st England; 42p Italy; 44p Argentina; 50p Germany; 64p France; 72p Brazil
(2) Generic Sheet with 20 x England World Cup Winners.

SPECIAL HANDSTAMPS SPONSOR
Price Guide Ordinary Covers £3-£5 / Sponsored Covers:
(1) FDI - Tallents House .... *Royal Mail (n.s.c.)*
(2) FDI - Balls Park, Hertford .... *Royal Mail (n.s.c.)*
(3) -do- non pictorial version .... *Royal Mail (n.s.c.)*
(4) Bobby Moore, OBE ....£15 *Royal Mail*
(5) Hurst Street, Birmingham .... *Royal Mail (n.s.c.)*
(6) Wembley (Ball) ....£10 *Benham BLCS 329*
(7) Wembley (Boots) ....£15 *Benham Coin Cover*
(8) A Glorious Past, Wembley .....£10 *Benham BLCS 329*
(9) England 4 - W Germany 2 .....£15 *Bradbury Sovereign 73*
(10) Wembley (silhouette) ....£10 *Westminster*
(11) Champion Rd, SE26 ....£10 *Westminster*
(12) -do- Autographed ....£15 *Westminster*
(13) Wembley ....£10 *Buckingham Cvrs 238*
(14) World Cup Willie ....£10 *Buckingham Cvrs 238*
(15) Football Lane, Harrow.............£10 *GB 112*
(16) The Ball, Widnes ....£10 *P Sheridan*
(17) Referees' Association ....£10 *P Sheridan*
(18) World Cup Winners ....£10 *Phil Stamp Cvrs 101*
(19) Football Tavern, Derby ....£10 *M Brazier (Pubs.93)*
(20) World Cup Winners ....£10 *GBFDC*
(21) footballcovers.co.uk ....£10 *Dawn*
(22) Bletchley Park ....£10 *Bletchley PO*
(23) Numerical Symmetry ....£10 *Royal Mail (n.s.c.)*
(24) Battle of Hopton Heath ....£10 *Heritage of Britain 27*
C.D.S. POSTMARKS Price Guide £7-£10
(25) Wembley, The Ball, New England, Gerrards Cross
(26) Moore, Ramsey, Charlton or similar

20th June 2006 – MODERN ARCHITECTURE
1st 30 St. Mary Axe, London; 42p Maggies Centre, Dundee; 44p Selfridges, Birmingham; 50p Downland Gridshell, Chichester; 64p An Turas, Isle of Tiree; 72p The Deep, Hull

SPECIAL HANDSTAMPS SPONSOR
Price Guide Ordinary Covers £3-£5 / Sponsored Covers:
(1) FDI - Tallents House .... *Royal Mail (n.s.c.)*
(2) FDI - Balls Park, Hertford .... *Royal Mail (n.s.c.)*
(3) -do- non pictorial version .... *Royal Mail (n.s.c.)*
(4) The Bull Ring, Birmingham .... *Royal Mail (n.s.c.)*
(5) Birmingham .... *Benham BLCS 330*
(6) Oban, Argyll .... *Benham 500(330)*
(7) Portland Place, London W1 .... *Benham Coin Cover*

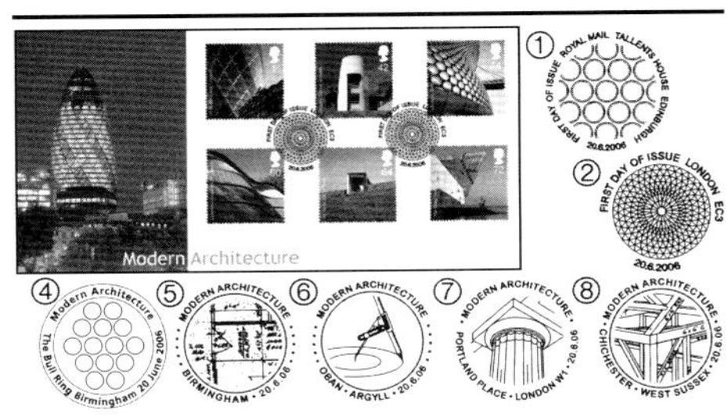

(8) Chichester, West Sussex ....£10 *Benham BLCS 330*
(9) St Mary Axe (palette) ....£10 *Westminster*
(10) -do- Autographed ....£15 *Westminster*
(11) Architectural Review ....£10 *Buckingham Cvrs 239*
(12) The Gherkin ....£10 *GB 113*
(13) Glasgow Science Centre ....£10 *P Sheridan*
(14) St. Mary Axe ....£10 *Phil Stamp Cvrs 102*
(15) Maggie's, Dundee ....£10 *Maggie's Cancer Care*
(16) 1st Ascent of Manaslu ....£10 *ABC FDC*
(17) 1st Ascent of LHOTSE ....£10 *ABC FDC*
(18) Indian Ocean Deployment.....£10 *RN CvrsGp*

C.D.S. POSTMARKS Price Guide £7-£10

(19) Downlands, Scarinish (Isle of Tiree), Lowgate (Hull),
(20) Singleton (Chichester), City of London, New Buildings

4th July 2006 - SMILERS Generic Issue

6 x 1st small 'Smilers' stamps with labels: Hello, Love, Union Jack, Teddy Bear, Flowers and Robin. (Self Adhesives)

SPECIAL HANDSTAMPS SPONSOR

Price Guide Ordinary Covers £3-£5 / Sponsored Covers:

(1) Buckingham Palace Rd...........£10 *Benham BLCS 331*
(2) Giggleswick ....£10 *Phil Stamp Covers 14*

18th July 2006 - National Portrait Gallery

10 x 1st: Sir Winston Churchill; Joshua Reynolds; T S Elliot; Mrs Pankhurst; Virginia Woolf; Sir Walter Scott; Mary Seacole; William Shakespeare; Dame Cicely Saunders; Charles Darwin

SPECIAL HANDSTAMPS SPONSOR

Price Guide Ordinary Covers £3-£5 / Sponsored Covers:

(1) FDI - Tallents House...................... *Royal Mail (n.s.c.)*
(2) FDI - London WC2....................... *Royal Mail (n.s.c.)*
(3) -do- non pictorial version .... *Royal Mail (n.s.c.)*
(4) London WC2 ....£15 *Royal Mail*
(5) Rowlands Rd, Birmingham........... *Royal Mail (n.s.c.)*
(6) Plympton, Plymouth ....£10 *Benham*
(7) Trafalgar Square ....£15 *Benham*
(8) Southwark, SE1 ....£10 *Benham*
(9) Walmer, Deal ....£10 *Benham*
(10) Great Britons on Canvas........£10 *Westminster*
(11) St Martin's Place (palette)......£10 *Westminster*
(12) -do- Autographed ....£15 *Westminster*
(13) International Churchill Soc ...£10 *Buckingham Cvrs 240*
(14) National Portrait Gallery........£10 *Buckingham Cvrs 240*
(15) Royal Soc Portrait Painters....£10 *P Sheridan*
(16) St Martin's Place ....£10 *Phil Stamp Cvrs 103*
(17) Portraits of Pub Signs.............£10 *M Brazier (Pubs.95)*
(18) From Paint to Pixel..................£10 *Bletchley PO*
(19) HMS Enterprise - Caen ....£10 *RN CvrsGp*
(20) Battle of Chalgrove ....£10 *Heritage of Britain*

C.D.S. POSTMARKS Price Guide £7-£10

(21) Trafalgar Square, Plympton, East Coker, Sydenham
(22) Shrewsbury, Melrose, Manchester, Churchill.

31st Aug 2006 - YEAR of the THREE KINGS

£3 Definitive plus reproductions of 1d definitives for each of the Three Kings.

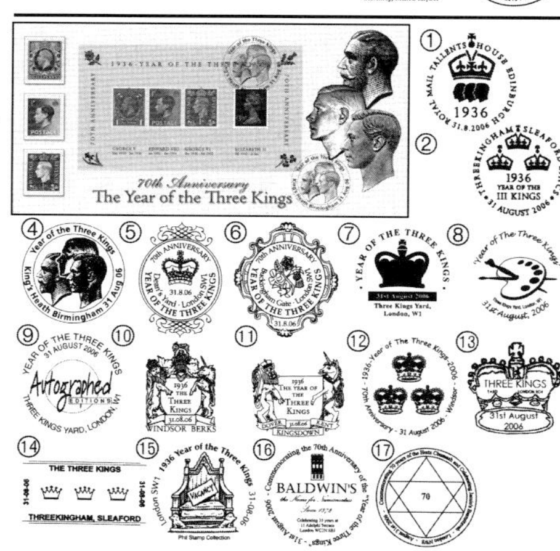

SPECIAL HANDSTAMPS SPONSOR

Price Guide Ordinary Covers £3-£5 / Sponsored Covers:

(1) FDI - Tallents House...................... *Royal Mail (n.s.c.)*
(2) FDI - Threekingham, Sleaford ..... *Royal Mail (n.s.c.)*
(3) -do- non pictorial version .... *Royal Mail (n.s.c.)*
(4) King's Heath, Birmingham........... *Royal Mail (n.s.c.)*
(5) Dean's Yard, SW1 ....£10 *Benham*
(6) Buckingham Gate, SW1 ....£15 *Benham*
(7) Three King's Yard, W1...........£10 *Westminster*
(8) Three King's Yard (palette)....£10 *Westminster*
(9) -do- Autographed ....£15 *Westminster*
(10) Windsor.....................................£10 *Buckingham Cvrs 241*
(11) Kingsdown ....£10 *Buckingham Cvrs 241*
(12) Windsor.....................................£10 *P Sheridan*
(13) Three Kings Yard, EC4...........£10 *Assoc. of GBFDC*
(14) The Three Kings ....£10 *M Brazier (Pubs.96)*
(15) London SW1 (Vacancy).........£10 *Phil Stamp Cvrs 104*
(16) Baldwins....................................£10 *ABC-FDC*
(17) 70 Years Hertz Chumash ....£10 *I Balcombe*

C.D.S. POSTMARKS Price Guide £7-£10

(18) *details to follow in next edition*

21st Sept 2006 - VICTORIA CROSS

1st Brave Gurkha; 1st Boy VC; 64p Midshipman; 64p Army Doctor; 72p Feared Lost; 72p Colditz Hero

SPECIAL HANDSTAMPS SPONSOR

Price Guide Ordinary Covers £3-£5 / Sponsored Covers:

(1) FDI - Tallents House...................... *Royal Mail (n.s.c.)*
(2) FDI - Potters Bar .... *Royal Mail (n.s.c.)*
(3) -do- non pictorial version .... *Royal Mail (n.s.c.)*
(4) Stampex, London N1.................... *Royal Mail (n.s.c.)*

(5) Stampex, Victoria Cross .... *Royal Mail (n.s.c.)*
(6) Hyde Park .... *Royal Mail (n.s.c.)*
(7) Victoria Road, Birmingham .... *Royal Mail (n.s.c.)*
(8) Whitehall, SW1 ....£10 *Benham*
(9) Chelsea, SW3 ....£10 *Benham*
(10) Lambeth Road, SE1 ....£10 *Benham*
(11) For Valour, Duxford ....£10 *Benham*
(12) Portsmouth ....£10 *Benham*
(13) Hyde Park ....£10 *Benham*
(14) Hyde Park ....£10 *Westminster*
(15) Hyde Park (palette) ....£10 *Westminster*
(16) -do- Autographed ....£15 *Westminster*
(17) Hyde Park (canon) ....£10 *Buckingham Cvrs 242*
(18) Hyde Park (VC) ....£10 *Buckingham Cvrs 242*
(19) Warrior, London E12 ....£12 *GB 115*
(20) Victoria Square ....£12 *Assoc. of GBFDC*
(21) Victoria Cross Society ....£12 *P Sheridan*
(22) Malet Lambert School ....£12 *Malet Lambert School*
(23) Mereworth, Maidstone ....£10 *Phil Stamp Crs 105/6*
(24) Thornton Heath, Surrey ....£10 *M Brazier (Pubs.97)*
(25) For Valour ....£10 *H D MacIntyre*
(26) Captain Fenton John Aylmer.£10 *ABC FDC*
(27) BF 2916 PS ....£10 *RNPS*
(28) Bletchley Park ....£10 *Bletchley PO*
(29) Zeebrugge Raid ....£10 *P Barrett*
(30) RAFLET Stamp Club ....£10 *RAFLET*
(31) St. Sepulchre ....£10 *T Wyard*
(32) Albert Ball ....£10 *Trent College, Notts*
(33) Battle of Lansdowne Hill ....£10 *Heritage of Britain*

C.D.S. POSTMARKS Price Guide £7-£10
(34) *details to follow in next edition*

3rd Oct 2006 - SOUNDS of BRITAIN

1st Bollywood and Bhangra; 42p Africa and the Caribbean; 50p Celtic; 72p Jazz and Blues; £1.19 Latin American

SPECIAL HANDSTAMPS SPONSOR
Price Guide Ordinary Covers £3-£5 / Sponsored Covers:

(1) FDI - Tallents House .... *Royal Mail (n.s.c.)*
(2) FDI - Rock, Kidderminster .... *Royal Mail (n.s.c.)*
(3) -do- non pictorial version .... *Royal Mail (n.s.c.)*
(4) Osbourne Rd, Birmingham .... *Royal Mail (n.s.c.)*
(5) Harpswell, Gainsborough ....£10 *Benham*
(6) Fiddlers Hamlet, Epping ....£10 *Benham*
(7) Rock, Kidderminster ....£10 *Benham*
(8) Rock Street (palette) ....£10 *Westminster*
(9) -do- Autographed ....£15 *Westminster*
(10) The Stables, Milton Keynes ...£10 *Buckingham Cvrs 243*
(11) The Louis Armstrong ....£10 *M Brazier (Pubs.98)*
(12) India Way, London W12 ....£12 *GB 116*
(13) Dublin Street, Liverpool ....£12 *P Sheridan*
(14) the brindley, Runcorn ....£12 *P Sheridan*
(15) Sound, Nantwich ....£10 *Phil Stamp Crs 107*
(16) CDT Design, London WC1 ....£12 *CDT Design Ltd*
(17) Children in Need, Pudsey ....£12 *Gerald Lovell*
(18) Battle of Roundhay Down .....£10 *Heritage of Britain*

C.D.S. POSTMARKS Price Guide £7-£10
(19) *details to follow in next edition*

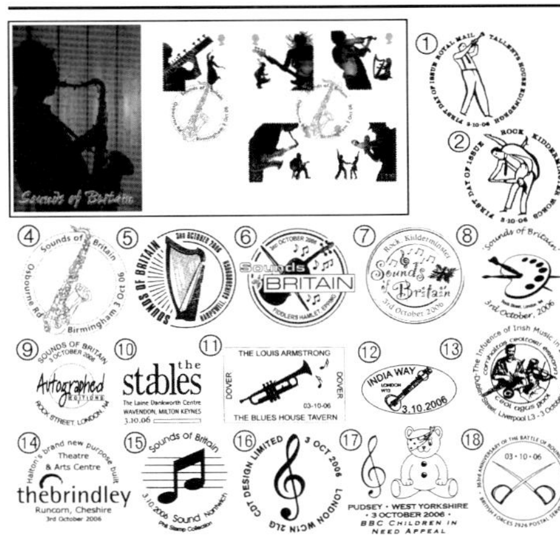

17th Oct 2006 - SPECIAL MOMENTS

1st New Baby; 1st Best Wishes; 1st Thank You; 1st Balloons; 1st Fireworks; 1st Champagne

SPECIAL HANDSTAMPS SPONSOR
Price Guide Ordinary Covers £3-£5 / Sponsored Covers:

(1) FDI - Tallents House .... *Royal Mail (n.s.c.)*
(2) FDI - Grinshill, Shrewsbury .... *Royal Mail (n.s.c.)*
(3) -do- non pictorial version .... *Royal Mail (n.s.c.)*
(4) Love Lane, Birmingham .... *Royal Mail (n.s.c.)*
(5) Kittywell, Braunton ....£10 *Benham*
(6) Bangor ....£10 *Benham*
(7) Glass, Huntly ....£10 *Benham*
(8) Soar, Brecon ....£10 *Benham*

C.D.S. POSTMARKS Price Guide £7-£10
(9) *details to follow in next edition*

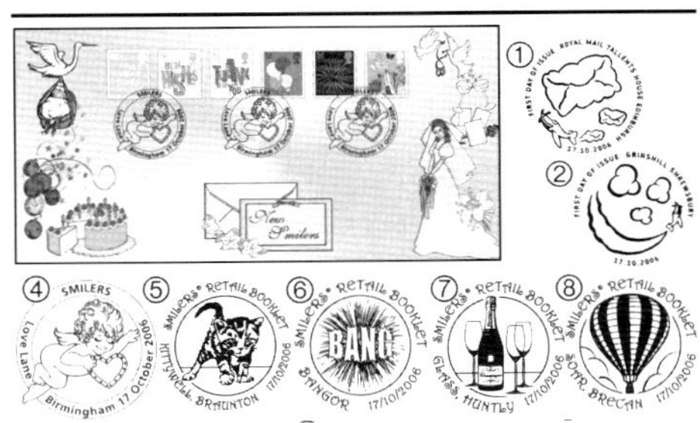

7th Nov 2006 - CHRISTMAS

2nd Snowman; 2nd (Large) Snowman; 1st Santa; 1st (Large) Santa; 72p Reindeer; £1.19 Christmas Tree

SPECIAL HANDSTAMPS **SPONSOR**

Price Guide Ordinary Covers £3-£5 / Sponsored Covers:

(1)	FDI - Tallents House	*Royal Mail (n.s.c.)*
(2)	FDI - Bethlehem	*Royal Mail (n.s.c.)*
(3)	-do- non pictorial version	*Royal Mail (n.s.c.)*
(4)	St. Nicholas Gdns, Birmingham	*Royal Mail (n.s.c.)*
(5)	Rudolph Road, E13	*Benham*
(6)	Snowhill, Enniskillen	*Benham*
(7)	St. Nicholas, Goodwick	*Benham*
(8)	Yuletide Close, NW10	*Benham*

9th Nov 2006 - LEST WE FORGET

1st Poppy; 4 x 72p Country Pictorials

SPECIAL HANDSTAMPS **SPONSOR**

Price Guide Ordinary Covers £3-£5 / Sponsored Covers:

(1)	FDI - Tallents House	*Royal Mail (n.s.c.)*
(2)	FDI - London SW1	*Royal Mail (n.s.c.)*
(3)	-do- non pictorial version	*Royal Mail (n.s.c.)*
(4)	Poppy Lane, Birmingham	*Royal Mail (n.s.c.*

14th Nov 2006 - BELGICA

30th Nov 2006 - CELEBRATING SCOTLAND

2007 Royal Mail Stamp Programme

9th January	The Beatles (6 stamps + Mini Sheet)
1st February	Sea Life (10 stamps)
13th February	The Sky at Night (6 stamps)
1st March	Inventions (6 + Mini Sheet + PSB)
22nd March	Abolition of the Slave Trade (6 stamps)
23rd April	Celebrating England (Mini Sheet)
15th May	Beside the Seaside (6 stamps)
17th May (tbc)	Wembley (Miniature Sheet)
5th June	Machin 40th Anniv (Mini Sheet + PSB)
3rd July	Grand Prix (6 stamps + Mini Sheet)
26th July	Scouts (6)
4th September	Birds (10 stamps)
20th September	British Army Uniforms (6 + PSB)
16th October	Queen's 60th Wedding (6 + MS)
6th November	Christmas (6 stamps + Mini Sheet)
8th November	Lest We Forget (Mini Sheet)

Dates may be subject to change

DEFINITIVE ISSUES

Including Booklet Panes, Coils, Postage Dues, Framas and Regionals

GENERAL NOTES

Please also read the General Notes at the beginning of this catalogue.

Prices and Condition

1839-1936 Prices vary considerably, according to condition, for all early definitives on first day covers. **The prices quoted are for good covers with clear postmarks. Unless otherwise stated prices are for plain covers.** Superb examples may realise a better price whilst covers in poor condition will fetch less

1936-1970 Prices are given for both plain and illustrated covers, with any postmark. Where relevant postmarks are known to exist these have been listed. **The prices quoted are for good covers with clear postmarks.**

1970 to date Covers are usually available for this period unaddressed (or with small printed labels etc.) and the prices reflect this. Prices are given for the more sought after Windsor postmarks and for covers with any other type of postmark. Where relevant special handstamps were sponsored for specific issues, these have also been listed as have any *official/sponsored* covers (see General Notes at the beginning of this catalogue).

Format

This Section has been sub-divided as follows for ease of reference:

(1) New Stamps, (2) Commemorative Labels, (3) Prestige Stamp Book Panes, (4) Stamp Book Panes, (5) Varieties - changes to phosphor, perfs, gum, paper etc., (6) Self Adhesives, (7) Channel Islands Occupation issues, (8) Regionals, (9) Country Pictorial Definitives, (10) Retail Book Panes, (11) Stamp Coils, (12) To Pay and Frama Labels, (13) New Services

Scope

Where the first day of issue is known, all new definitive stamps have been listed. With effect from the new *Machin* definitives issued in 1967 the Post Office provided first day of issue facilities for most **new values** and **colour changes**. Varieties in perforations, phosphors, papers etc are also listed where known. However these are not recognised as new stamps by Royal Mail and are therefore only available with permanent pictorial handstamps (see page 12) or CDS postmarks.

Changes in Postal Rates since two-tier postage was introduced in 1968:

16 SEP 1968: 1st Class 5d, 2nd Class 4d
15 FEB 1971: 1st Class 3p, 2nd Class $2\frac{1}{2}$p
10 SEPT 1973: 1st Class $3\frac{1}{2}$p, 2nd Class 3p
24 JUNE 1974: 1st Class $4\frac{1}{2}$p, 2nd Class $3\frac{1}{2}$p
29 SEPT 1975: 1st Class $8\frac{1}{2}$p, 2nd Class $6\frac{1}{2}$p
13 JUNE 1977: 1st Class 9p, 2nd Class 7p
20 AUG 1979: 1st Class 10p, 2nd Class 8p
4 FEB 1980: 1st Class 12p, 2nd Class 10p
26 JAN 1981: 1st Class 14p, 2nd Class $11\frac{1}{2}$p
1 FEB 1982: 1st Class $15\frac{1}{2}$p, 2nd Class $12\frac{1}{2}$p
5 APR 1983: 1st Class 16p, 2nd Class $12\frac{1}{2}$p
3 SEP 1984: 1st Class 17p, 2nd Class 13p
4 NOV 1985: 1st Class 17p, 2nd Class 12p
20 OCT 1986: 1st Class 18p, 2nd Class 13p
5 SEP 1988: 1st Class 19p, 2nd Class 14p
2 OCT 1989: 1st Class 20p, 2nd Class 15p
17 SEP 1990: 1st Class 22p, 2nd Class 17p
16 SEP 1991: 1st Class 24p, 2nd Class 18p
1 NOV 1993: 1st Class 25p, 2nd Class 19p
8 JULY 1996: 1st Class 26p, 2nd Class 20p
26 APR 1999: 1st Class 26p, 2nd Class 19p
27 APR 2000: 1st Class 27p, 2nd Class 19p
8 MAY 2003: 1st Class 28p, 2nd Class 20p
1 APR 2004: 1st Class 28p, 2nd Class 21p
7 APR 2005: 1st Class 30p, 2nd Class 21p
3 APR 2006: 1st Class 32p, 2nd Class 23p

Prices (1839-1936) are for plain covers except where stated.

Queen Victoria (1837-1901)

		£
5 Dec 1839	Uniform 4d Post	350
10 Jan 1840	First DayUniversal Penny Post	450
6 May 1840	The Mulready 1d Stationery	2,500
6 May 1840	1d Black (imperf.)	20,000
8 May 1840	2d Blue (imperf.)	25,000
22 Feb 1855	2d Blue (perforated, Plate 4)	2,500
7 Mar 1865	6d Deep Lilac	1,800
1 Oct 1870	½d Rose Red (small format)	
	on Asylum cover	1,000
	printed on postcard	600
12 Apr 1872	6d Deep Chestnut	1,500
1 Sep 1873	1s Green	2,500
1 Jan 1880	1d Venetian Red	1,750
24 May 1881	1s Orange Brown (Imp Crown)	4,500

Jubilee Issues

24 May 1887	½d Orange	2,500
	5d Dull Purple & Blue	1,250
15 Sep 1892	4½d Green & Carmine	3,000
17 Apr 1900	½d Blue-green	900

Uniform Penny Postage Jubilee – official envelopes

16 May 1890	Guildhall handstamp (No. 1)	50
2 Jul 1890	South Kensington (No. 6)	30
	-do- (Nos. 4 or 5)	70
	-do- (Nos. 2 or 3)	50
	All five h/s on one cover	125

King Edward VII (1901-1910)

1 Jan 1902	½d Blue-green	75
	1d Red	75
	2½d Blue	250
	6d Purple	350
	The above 4 values on one cover	1,000
	-do- with Parliament Street C.D.S.	1,250
1 Nov 1909	4d Brown-orange (on postcard)	600
12 Jul 1911	4d Orange	1,200

King George V (1910-1936)

Downey Head (Imperial Crown Watermark)

22 Jun 1911	½d Green	75
	-do- Junior Philatelic Soc. cover	325
	½d Green – printed on postcard	75
	1d Red	60
	½d & 1d on one cover	150
	-do- Westminster Abbey C.D.S.	2,500
	-do- Windsor C.D.S.	2,500
1 Jan 1912	Redrawn ½d and 1d	1,200

Profile Head (Royal Cypher Watermark)

		£
17 Jan 1913	½d Green	1,200
8 Oct 1912	1d Red	950
15 Oct 1912	1½d Red-brown	650
	-do- Int. Stamp Exhib. h/s	800
20 Aug 1912	2d Orange	600
18 Oct 1912	2½d Blue	500
	-do- Int. Stamp Exhib. h/s	950
9 Oct 1912	3d Violet	1,500
15 Jan 1913	4d Grey-green	1,500
30 Jun 1913	5d Brown & 9d Agate	3,000
1 Aug 1913	6d Purple **or** 7d Olive	2,600
	8d Black-yellow	2,800
	10d Turquoise	2,800
	1s Bistre	2,800
8 Mar 1934	½d,1d,1½d ....Harrison Printing	750

Profile Head (Block Cypher Watermark)

14 Feb 1935	½d Green	1,500
30 Apr 1935	1d Red (sideways wmk)	2,000
7 Feb 1935	1½d Red-brown	1,500
30 Apr 1935	2d Orange (sideways wmk)	2,500
10 Oct 1924	2½d Blue & 3d Violet	2,500
23 Oct 1924	4d Grey-green	3,000
17 Oct 1924	5d Brown	4,000
11 Nov 1924	9d Olive-green	4,500
28 Nov 1924	10d Blue	5,500

High values – 'Sea Horses'

30 Jun 1913	2s 6d Brown	2,400
16 Oct 1934	2s 6d Brown re-engraved issue	3,500

Photogravure (Block Cypher Watermark)

19 Nov 1934	½d Green ....(illust. cvr £40)	15
24 Sep 1934	1d Scarlet ....(illust. cvr £40)	15
20 Aug 1934	1½d Red-brown ....(illust. cvr £50)	15
21 Jan 1935	2d Orange ....(illust. cvr £90)	40
18 Mar 1935	2½d Blue	30
	3d Violet	40
	2½d & 3d - one cover	95
2 Dec 1935	4d Grey-green	80
	9d Olive-green	100
	4d & 9d - one cover	250
22 Feb 1936	5d Yellow-brown	700
	covers exist with 17th Feb pmk	
24 Feb 1936	10d Turquoise-blue	800
26 Feb 1936	1s Bistre-brown	600
	Set of 9 or 11 covers	1,800
	All 11 values on one cover	3,500

Prices now are for plain or illustrated covers where known. ('n.k.' = not known)

King Edward VIII (1936)

		plain covers £	illus. covers £
1 Sep 1936	½d, 1½d & 2½d	15	125
	-do- King Edward, Banff C.D.S.	125	n.k.
	-do- Windsor C.D.S.	160	500
	-do- Kingstanding C.D.S.	n.k.	150
	-do- Buckingham Gate C.D.S.	100	n.k.
14 Sep 1936	1d	20	150
	-do- King Edward, Banff C.D.S.	120	n.k.
	-do- Windsor C.D.S.	120	n.k.
	All 4 values on one cover	100	n.k.

King George VI (1936-1952)

Low values – original issue

10 May 1937	½d, 1d & 2½d	10	35
	-do- Windsor pmk	n.k.	100
	-do- Kingstanding, B'ham pmk	40	100
30 Jul 1937	1½d Red-brown	10	50
31 Jan 1938	2d Orange	15	35
	3d Violet	15	35
	2d & 3d - on one cover	30	80
21 Nov 1938	4d Grey-green	20	n.k.
	5d Brown	20	n.k.
	4d & 5d - on one cover	50	n.k.
	-do- Windsor pmk	200	n.k.
30 Jan 1939	6d Purple	40	n.k.
27 Feb 1939	7d Emerald-green	25	n.k.
	8d Carmine	25	n.k.
	7d & 8d - on one cover	55	n.k.
	-do- Windsor pmk	220	n.k.

King George VI (1936-1952) contd.

		plain covers £	illus cvrs £.
1 May 1939	9d Olive-green	80	n.k.
	10d Turquoise-blue	90	n.k.
	1s Bistre-brown	90	n.k.
	9d, 10d, & 1s - on one cover	275	n.k.
29 Dec 1947	11d Plum	35	100
	Set of 15 values	500	n.k.
High values - 'Arms' Design			
4 Sep 1939	2s 6d Brown	950	n.k.
9 Mar 1942	2s 6d Yellow-green	950	n.k.
21 Aug 1939	5s Red	350	n.k.
30 Oct 1939	10s Dark blue	1,500	n.k.
30 Nov 1942	10s Ultramarine	2,150	n.k.
1 Oct 1948	£1 Brown	175	n.k.
Low values - change to pale colours			
1 Sep 1941	½d Pale green	25	n.k.
11 Aug 1941	1d Pale scarlet	20	n.k.
28 Sep 1942	1½d Pale red-brown	45	n.k.
6 Oct 1941	2d Pale orange	50	n.k.
21 Jul 1941	2½d Pale ultramarine	35	125
3 Nov 1941	3d Pale violet	85	n.k.
	Set of six covers	225	n.k.
2 Oct 1950	4d Light ultramarine	20	75
3 May 1951	**Low values - colour changes:**		
	½d, 1d, 1½d, 2d, 2½d	10	40
	ditto Battersea C.D.S. pmk	20	80
	'Festival' High values:		
	2s 6d, 5s, 10s, £1*	150	675
	ditto Battersea pmk*	n.k.	900
	** (on one cover or set of four covers)*		

Queen Elizabeth II £.s.d. issues (1952-1970)

Low values			
5 Dec 1952	**1½d, 2½d**	5	20
	-do- with Windsor postmark	25	60
	-do- with Buckingham Palace pmk	125	175
6 Jul 1953	**5d, 8d, 1s**	10	40
31 Aug 1953	**½d, 1d, 2d**	10	40
2 Nov 1953	**4d, 1s 3d, 1s 6d**	25	125
18 Jan 1954	**3d, 6d, 7d**	25	75
8 Feb 1954	**9d, 10d, 11d**	40	150
	Set on matching covers	150	600
9 Feb 1959	**4½d new value**	15	200
'Castles' High values			
1 Sep 1955	**10s, £1** - on one or two covers	200	450
	10s, £1 - Edinburgh C.D.S.	-	625
	10s only - Edinburgh C.D.S.	200	-
	£1 only - Windsor Castle C.D.S.	250	-
23 Sep 1955	**2s 6d, 5s** - on one or two covers	75	400
	2s 6d only - Carrickfergus C.D.S.	75	250
	5s only - Caernarfon C.D.S	100	-
	Set of 4 on matching covers	275	1500
New Style (Machin Head) Definitives			
5 Jun 1967	**4d, 1s, 1s 9d** *(Windsor Illus. £10)*	1	5
8 Aug 1967	**3d, 9d, 1s 6d** *(Windsor Illus. £10)*	1	5
5 Feb 1968	**½d, 1d, 2d, 6d** *(Windsor Illus. £10)*	1	5
1 Jul 1968	**5d, 7d, 8d, 10d** *(Windsor Illus. £10)*	1	5
6 Jan 1969	**4d Red & 8d Turq.** *(Windsor Illus. £10)*	1	5
5 Mar 1969	**2s 6d, 5s, 10s, £1**	8	15
	-do- Stampex special handstamp	-	25
	-do- Stampex official cover	-	35

All prices now are for illustrated covers

Queen Elizabeth II £.p. issues (1970 to date)

		Windsor postmark £	other pmk £
17 Jun 1970	**10p, 20p, & 50p**	10	5
	(1) Decimal Stamps Windsor h/s	20	-
15 Feb 1971	**½p to 9p Low values** (12 values)		
	F.D.I. + GPO Strike cachets	15	5
	C.D.S. - open during strike	-	15
	Field Post Offices -do-	-	15
	Decimal Currency in PO slogan	-	200
11 Aug 1971	**10p small design**	8	3
6 Dec 1972	**£1 - redrawn '£'**: F.D.I. pmks	15	4
	(2) -do- Large Windsor F.D.I.	25	-
24 Oct 1973	**4½p, 5½p, 8p**	10	3
4 Sep 1974	**6½p**	8	3
15 Jan 1975	**7p**	8	3
24 Sep 1975	**8½p**	8	3
25 Feb 1976	**9p, 9½p, 10p, 10½p, 11p, 20p**	15	5
	(3) -do- Stampex spec h/s	-	25
	-do- on Stampex cover	-	35
2 Feb 1977	**50p, £1, £2 & £5**	20	8
26 Apr 1978	**10½p colour change**	8	3
15 Aug 1979	**11½p, 13p & 15p**	10	3
30 Jan 1980	**4p, 12p, 13½p, 17p, 17½p, 75p**	10	3
22 Oct 1980	**3p & 22p**	8	3
14 Jan 1981	**2½p, 11½p, 14p, 15½p, 18p, 25p**	10	3
27 Jan 1982	**5p, 12½p, 16½p, 19½p, 26p, 29p**	10	3
30 Mar 1983	**3½p, 16p, 17p, 20½p, 23p, 28p, 31p.**	10	3
3 Aug 1983	**£1.30 Parcel Post**	10	2
	(4) Philatelic Bureau h/s	-	8
	(5) London E16 h/s	-	10
	(6) Parcel, Centenary Salisbury h/s	-	15
	-do- Hampstead C.D.S.	-	25
	1st Aug pmk (actual centenary date)	-	45
28 Aug 1984	**13p, 18p, 22p, 24p, 34p**	10	3
28 Aug 1984	**£1.33 Parcel Post**	10	3
	(7) N.Eastern Parcel Centre h/s	-	35
	-do- Hampstead C.D.S. pmk	-	20
17 Sep 1985	**£1.41 Parcel Post**	10	3
	(7) N.Eastern Parcel Centre h/s	-	20
	-do- Parcel Post pmk	-	20
	-do- Hampstead C.D.S. pmk	-	20
29 Oct 1985	**7p & 12p**	6	2
	Bureau h/s + 'ITALIA' cachet	-	4
2 Sep 1986	**£1.50 Parcel Post**	10	4
	(7) N.Eastern Parcel Centre h/s	-	20
	-do- Parcel Post pmk	-	20
	-do- Hampstead C.D.S. pmk	-	20
15 Sep 1987	**£1.60 Parcel Post**	10	3
	-do- Parcel Post pmk	-	20
	-do- Hampstead C.D.S. pmk	-	20
23 Aug 1988	**14p, 19p, 20p, 23p, 27p, 28p, 32p, 35p**	10	3

		Ordinary covers £	Sponsored covers £
18 Oct 1988	**£1, £1.50, £2, £5 'Castles' High Values**		
	(8) FDI, Bureau special h/s	20	– *Royal Mail*
	(9) FDI, Windsor special h/s	25	– *Royal Mail*
	(10) Carrickfergus h/s	30	60 *Benham*
	(11) Caernarfon h/s	30	60 *Benham*
	(12) Edinburgh h/s	30	60 *Benham*
	(13) Windsor h/s	30	60 *Benham*
	Set of 4 with appropriate h/s	25	
	Windsor Castle C.D.S.	220	
	Carrickfergus C.D.S.	250	
	Windsor C.D.S.	150	
	Caernarfon or Edinburgh C.D.S.	150	
	Set of 4 with appropriate CDS	200	
22 Aug 1989	**Non-Value Indicators:** 1st, 2nd	15	(*Windsor pmk*)
26 Sep 1989	**15p, 20p, 24p, 29p, 30p, 34p & 37p**	10	(*Windsor pmk*)
10 Jan 1990	**Penny Black Anniversary** *See commemorative issues (10 Jan 1990) & booklet panes (30 Jan & 3 May 1990).*		
7 Aug 1990	**Non-Value Indicators:** 1st, 2nd	10	(*Windsor pmk*)
4 Sep 1990	**10p, 17p, 22p, 26p, 27p, 31p & 33p**	10	(*Windsor pmk*)
10 Sep 1991	**6p, 18p, 24p, 28p, 34p, 35p & 39p**	10	(*Windsor pmk*)
	-do- 'New Postage Rates' slogan	20	
24 Mar 1992	**Security Printing 'Castles': £1, £1.50, £2 & £5**		
	(14) FDI, Bureau h/s	20	– *Royal Mail*
	(15) FDI, Windsor h/s	20	– *Royal Mail*
	(16) Carrickfergus h/s	25	35 *Benham*
	(17) Caernarfon h/s	25	35 *Benham*
	(18) Edinburgh h/s	25	35 *Benham*
	(19) Windsor h/s	25	35 *Benham*
	(20) 'Security Printing' Windsor	35	75 *Bradbury*
	Windsor CDS	35	
	Windsor Castle CDS	150	
	Other relevant CDS	35	
	Set of 4 with relevant CDS	35	
2 Mar 1993	**£10 Britannia:**		
	(21) FDI, Bureau h/s	18	– *Royal Mail*
	(22) FDI, Windsor	20	– *Royal Mail*
	(23) FDI, London	25	– *Royal Mail*
	(24) Windsor h/s (Britannia)	25	45 *Bradbury*
	(25) £10 Britannia, Porth h/s	25	45 *Benham*
	(26) £10 Dover h/s	25	45 *Benham*
	(27) Britannia Way h/s	25	45 *Benham*
	(28) Spring Stampex h/s	40	
	(29) National Postal Museum h/s	50	
	Britannia, Pounds or Brailes CDS	45	
	Maritime Mail or Paquebot CDS	35	
	Windsor CDS	40	
	Windsor Castle CDS	150	
26 Oct 1993	**19p, 25p, 29p, 36p, 38p & 41p**	4	(*Windsor pmk*)
	-do- 'New Postage Rates' slogan	5	
9 Aug 1994	**60p Airmail (new value in bkt)**	4	(*Windsor pmk*)
22 Aug 1995	**£1 (small format) & £3 Carrickfergus Castle**		
	(30) FDI, Bureau h/s	5	– *Royal Mail*
	(31) FDI, Bureau (lions) h/s	5	– *Royal Mail*
	(32) FDI, Windsor h/s	5	– *Royal Mail*
	(33) FDI, London h/s	5	– *Royal Mail*
	(34) FDI, Carrickfergus h/s	5	– *Royal Mail*
	(35) Carrickfergus (harp) h/s	5	10 *Benham*
	(36) Carrickfergus (heraldic) h/s	5	10 *Benham*
	(35) Carrickfergus CDS	15	–
25 Jun 1996	**20p, 26p, 31p, 37p, 39p, 43p, 63p**	5	(*Windsor pmk*)
	New Postage Rates slogan	8	–
21 Apr 1997	**Golden Definitives 1st & 26p** *See commemorative issues. See also booklet pane section.*		
10 Mar 1998	**'Wilding' reprints 20p, 26p, 37p**	5	(*Windsor pmk*)
	Windsor (National Emblems) h/s	5	10 *Bradbury*
	See Prestige Booklets (Definitive Portrait) section.		
19 Jan 1999	**European NVI 'E'**	3	(*Windsor pmk*)
	(37) Waterloo h/s	3	8 *Benham*
	(38) Ashford h/s	3	8 *Benham*

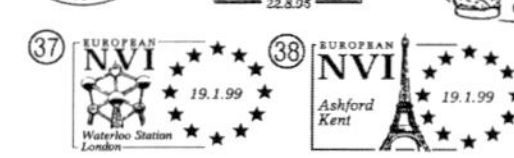

24 March 1992 **Security Printing 'Castles'**

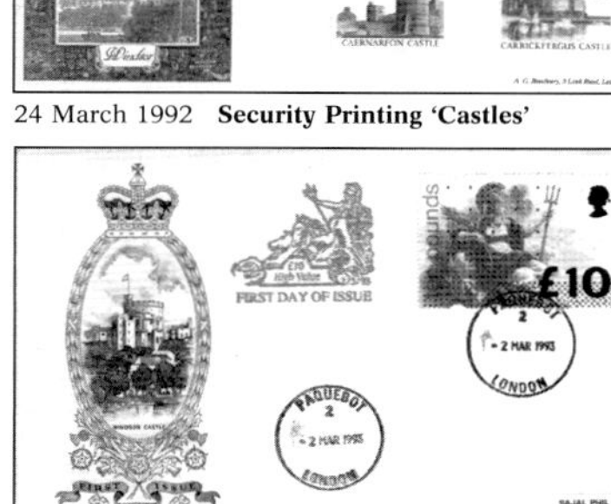

2 March 1993 **£10 Britannia**

Date		Ordinary covers £	Sponsored covers £
16 Feb 1999	**Large Style Machin 1st NVIs x 3**	5	*(Windsor pmk)*
	Windsor (Gateway) h/s	5	10 *Bradbury*
	See Prestige Booklets (Profile on Print) section.		
9 Mar 1999	**£1.50, £2, £3, £5 Small Format**	15	*(Windsor pmk)*
	(39) King Edward Street h/s	15	28 *Benham*
	(40) London SW1 (lions) h/s	15	23 *Benham*
	(41) London W1 (lions) h/s	15	25 *Benham*
	(42) Edinburgh (Scottish lion) h/s	15	28 *Benham*
	(43) Balmoral (Scottish lion) h/s	15	23 *Benham*
	(44) Cardiff (Welsh Dragon) h/s	15	28 *Benham*
	(45) Conwy (Welsh Dragon) h/s	15	23 *Benham*
	(46) Belfast (Hand) h/s	15	28 *Benham*
	(47) William Shakespeare h/s	15	28)*Benham*
	(48) Dylan Thomas h/s	15	) *Set of*
	(49) Robert Burns h/s	15	) *Four*
	(50) Jonathan Swift h/s	15	) *Covers*
20 Apr 1999	**7p, 38p, 44p, 64p**	4	*(Windsor pmk)*
	(51) London SW (Beefeater) h/s	4	10 *Bradbury*
6 Jan 2000	**Millennium Definitive 1st Class**		
	See commemorative issues & booklet pane section.		
25 Apr 2000	**8p, 33p, 40p, 41p, 45p, 65p**	4	*(Windsor pmk)*
	(52) London (Buckingham Pal) h/s.	4	10 *Bradbury*
22 May 2000	**Stamp Show Exhibition Souvenir Miniature Sheet**		
	(53) Philatelic Bureau	6	
	(54) Earl's Court	6	
	(55) Stamp Capital of the World	7	12 *Bradbury*
	(56) Westminster Abbey	7	12 *Westminster*
	(57) Earl's Court Security Print	7	12 *CoverCraft*
	(58) Stamp Show 2000	7	12 *T Hurlstone*
	(59) Dr Who/Stamp Show 2000	7	12 *Steven Scott*
	(60) Lyceum Post Office	7	12 *P Sheridan*
	(61) Artist's Palette, Picadilly	7	12 *Benham*
	(62) Artist's Palette, Earl's Court	7	12 *Benham*
	(63) Artist's Palette, Strand	7	12 *Benham*
	(64) Artist's Palette, Kidderminster	7	12 *Benham*
	(65) Earl's Court cds pmk	10	
6 Feb 2002	**'Wilding' reprints 2nd & 1st Class**		
	(66) A Gracious Accession	7	12 *Bradbury*
	Various special handstamps	5	
	See commemorative issues of same date for full details of postmarks & Prestige Stamp Book section.		
5 Jun 2002	**Gold Definitive 1st Class Self Adhesive**		
	Various special handstamps......from	5	
	See commemorative issues for postmark details.		
4 Jul 2002	**37p, 42p, 47p, 68p**		
	(67) Tallents House (Arms) h/s	4	- *Royal Mail*
	(68) Windsor (Coat of Arms) h/s	4	- *Royal Mail*
	(69) Windsor (Castle) h/s	4	12 *Bradbury*
4 Jul 2002	**E, 42p, 68p Self Adhesives**		
	(70) Hampton Wick h/s	4	12 *Bradbury*
5 Dec 2002	**'Wilding' reprints Miniature Sheet No.1**		
	Various special handstamps......from	8	
	See commemorative issues for postmark details.		
27 Mar 2003	**52p, £1.12 Universal Rates NVIs Self Adhesive**		
	(71) Tallents House (Arms) h/s	5	- *Royal Mail*
	(72) Windsor (Coat of Arms) h/s	5	- *Royal Mail*
	(73) Universal Rates Birmingham	4	- *Royal Mail*
	(74) Europe & Worldwide London	4	12 *Bradbury*
	(75) New NVI definitives London	4	12 *MachinColl*
	(76) RMS Titanic, Belfast	4	12 *Benham*
	(77) SS Great Britain, Southampton	4	12 *Benham*
	(78) SS Great Britain, Bristol	4	12 *Benham*
	(79) English Channel, Dover	4	12 *Benham*
	(80) Aviation, Southampton	4	12 *Benham*
	(81) Universal Airmail, Send	4	12 *Phil Stamp*
6 May 2003	**34p New Postage Rate**		
	(as 71) Tallents House (Arms) h/s	2	- *Royal Mail*
	(as 72) Windsor (Arms) h/s	2	- *Royal Mail*
	(82) Stoke on Trent (Crown) h/s	3	10 *Phil Stamp*
20 May 2003	**'Wilding' reprints Miniature Sheet No.2**		
	Various special handstamps......from	8	
	See commemorative issues for postmark details.		

20 April 1999 **New Values 7p, 38p, 44p, 64p**

27 March 2003 **Universal Rates - NVIs**

		Ordinary covers £	Sponsored covers £	
1 Jul 2003	**£1.50, £2, £3, £5 Iriodin Ink**			
	(1) Tallents House (Arms) h/s	15	–	*Royal Mail*
	(2) Windsor (Arms) h/s	16	–	*Royal Mail*
	(3) Great Britons Portsmouth h/s	17	20	*Benham*
	(4) Great Britons Althorp h/s	17	20	*Benham*
	(5) Great Britons Blenheim h/s	17	20	*Benham*
	(6) Great Britons Downe h/s	17	20	*Benham*
	(7) High Values Hastings h/s	17	20	*Benham*
	(8) London Transport h/s	17	20	*Benham*
	(9) High Values Stoke on Trent h/s	17	20	*Phil Stamp*
1 Apr 2004	**7p, 35p, 39p, 40p, 43p**			
	(10) Tallents House (Arms) h/s*	3	–	*Royal Mail*
	(11) Windsor (Arms) h/s*	4	–	*Royal Mail*
	(12) Stoke-on-Trent	5	10	*Phil Stamp*
1 Apr 2004	**43p Universal Postcard Rate**			
	(13) Tallents House (Arms) h/s*	3	–	*Royal Mail*
	(14) Windsor (Arms) h/s*	4	–	*Royal Mail*
	(15) Birmingham h/s	5	–	*Royal Mail*
	(16) London h/s	5	12	*Bradbury*
	(17) Croydon h/s	5	12	*Benham*
	(18) Southampton h/s	5	12	*Benham*
	(19) Falmouth h/s	5	12	*Benham*
	(20) Woking h/s	5	12	*Phil Stamp*
5 Apr 2005	**9p, 35p, 46p**			
	(21) Tallents House (Arms) h/s*	3	–	*Royal Mail*
	(22) Windsor (Arms) h/s*	4	–	*Royal Mail*
	(23) Stoke-on-Trent	5	10	*Phil Stamp*
28 Mar 2006	**37p, 44p, 49p, 72p**			
	(24) Tallents House (Arms) h/s*	3	–	*Royal Mail*
	(25) Windsor (Arms) h/s*	4	–	*Royal Mail*
	(26) Stoke-on-Trent	5	10	*Phil Stamp*
	(27) Machin Road Birmingham	5	–	*Royal Mail*
1 Aug 2006	**Pricing in Proportion: 2nd Small, 2nd Large, 1st Small, 1st Large; Make-up Values 12p, 14p**			
	(28) Tallents House (Arms) h/s*	3	–	*Royal Mail*
	(29) Windsor (Arms) h/s*	4	–	*Royal Mail*
	(30) Birmingham	5	–	*Royal Mail*
	(31) The Strand	5	12	*Bradbury*
	(32) London EC	5	12	*Benham*
	(33) Mailcoach Bristol	5	12	*Benham*
	(34) Stoke-on-Trent	5	12	*Phil Stamp*
	(35) Bird Stamp Society, Swansea	5	–	*n.o.c.*

* *Same postmark designs as Nos. (1) and (2)*

15 Aug 2006	**PiP: 2nd Small, 1st Small ~ Self Adhesives**			
	Windsor or other running h/s	6		
12 Sep 2006	**PiP: 2nd Large, 1st Large ~ Self Adhesives**			
	Windsor or other running h/s	6		

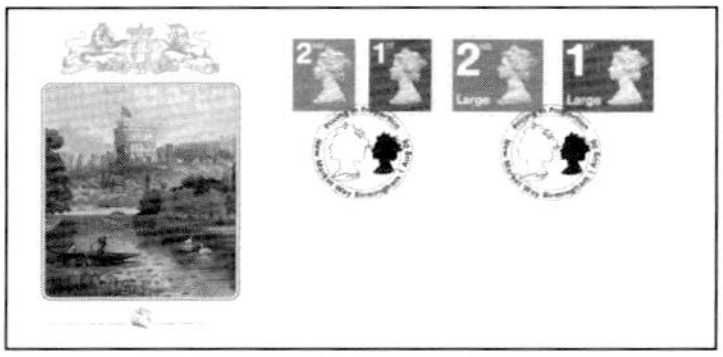

1st Aug 2006 **Pricing in Proportion**

STAMP COILS

Prices quoted for single value coils are for covers with at least two adjoining stamps. Covers only bearing a single stamp from the coil are worth approximately half catalogue price. All prices are for illustrated covers. Single value coils are issued in two formats: Sideways or Horizontally (H) and End-on or Vertically (V)

All Prices for illustrated covers		Windsor Postmark £	Other Pmks £
Se-tenant (multi-value) coils:			
27 Aug 1969	**1s Coil:** (2 x 2d, 3d, 1d, 4d)	10	3
15 Feb 1971	**5p Coil:** (2 x ½p; 2 x 1p; 1 x 2p)		
	With 'Posting Delayed by Strike' cachet	10	3
	Without 'Strike' cachet	n.k.	10
11 Mar 1971	**5p Coil:** *alternative issue date*	n.k.	12
3 Dec 1975	**10p Coil:** (2 x ½p, 1p, 2p, 6p)	8	3
14 Dec 1977	**10p Coil:** (2 x ½p; 2 x 1p; + 7p)	8	3
16 Jan 1980	**10p Coil:** (2 x 1p, 8p + 2 labels)	8	3
Readers' Digest (multi-value) coils:			
2 Sep 1981	**11½p Coil:** (1 x 2½p + 3 x 3p)	5	2
	-do- with early June/July dates *..from*	n.k.	20
30 Dec 1981	**12½p Coil:** (1 x ½p + 3 x 4p)	5	2
14 Aug 1984	**13p Coil:** (1 x 1p, 3 x 4p)	5	2
18 Mar 1988	**13p Coil:** (1 x 1p; 3 x 4p) ACP	25	10
5 Sep 1988	**14p Coil:** (1 x 2p; 3 x 4p)	5	2
10 Oct 1989	**15p Coil:** (1 x 3p; 3 x 4p)	5	2
27 Nov 1990	**17p Coil:** (1 x 5p; 3 x 4p)	5	2
1 Oct 1991	**18p Coil:** (2 x 5p; 2 x 4p)	5	2
31 Jan 1995	**19p Coil:** (1 x 4p; 3 x 5p)	5	2
	-do- Reader's Digest Swindon pmk	–	10
Single value coils:			
16 Sep 1968	**4d Coil** Horizontal	300	–
15 Feb 1971	**1p Coil:** Vertical	–	600
	2½p or 3p Coils: Vertical *each*	600	500
	2½p or 3p Coils: Horizontal *each*	600	500
28 Jan 1976	**6½p & 8½p Coils:** Vertical	n.k.	150
13 Oct 1976	**6½p & 8½p Coils:** Horizontal	250	80
13 Jun 1977	**7p & 9p Coils:** Vertical	125	45
16 Nov 1977	**7p & 9p Coils:** Horizontal	250	45
14 Nov 1979	**8p & 10p Coils:** Vertical	60	10
11 Jun 1980	**10p & 12p Coils:** Vertical	50	40
11 Mar 1981	**11½p & 14p Coils:** Vertical	50	35
1 Feb 1982	**12½p & 15½p Coils:** Vertical	50	25

		Windsor Postmark £	Other Pmks £
Single value coils (contd):			
20 Apr 1983	**16p Coil:** Vertical	20	3
3 Sep 1984	**13p & 17p Coils:** Vertical	40	3
12 Nov 1985	**12p Coil:** Vertical (centre band)	8	2
23 Sep 1986	**12p Coil:** Horizontal	5	2
20 Oct 1986	**18p Coil:** Vertical (official date)	15	–
21 Oct 1986	**13p (H) & 18p (V) Coils:**	30	7
23 Jun 1987	**1p (H) Readers' Digest Coil**	5	2
	-do- on 'Readers Digest' envelope	10	–
3 May 1988	**18p Coil:** Vertical	5	2
26 Jul 1988	**1p Coil:** Vertical	5	2
5 Sep 1988	**14p Coil:** Horizontal	8	3
	14p & 19p Coils: Vertical	8	3
16 Oct 1989	**15p & 20p Coils:** Horizontal	6	2
	15p & 20p Coils: Vertical	6	2
17 Sep 1990	**17p & 22p Coils:** Vertical	5	4
16 Sep 1991	**18p & 24p Coils:** Vertical	5	4
	-do- 'New Postage rates' slogan	–	9
11 Feb 1992	**33p & 39p Coils:** Vertical	5	3
1 Nov 1993	**19p, 25p, 35p & 41p Coils:** Vertical	8	4
16 May 1995	**25p Coil: (V)** two phosphor bands	5	2
6 Feb 1996	**25p Coil: (H)** Blue Fluor	5	–
8 Jul 1996	**1st & 2nd NVIs (V) Coils**	5	3
	37p & 43p (V) Coils Blue Fluor	6	4
	1st, 37p & 43p (V) 8mm 2B Phos	30	–
12 Dec 1996	**63p Coil (V)** for Airmail rate	5	2
	-do- Heathrow permanent spec h/s	–	5
	63p Coil 8mm & 9mm Phos	12	–
29 Apr 1997	**1st & 2nd NVIs (V)** lay flat gum	6	3
26 Aug 1997	**37p & 43p Coils (V):** Harrisons	8	4
4 Jul 2001	**1st & 2nd NVIs (H)**	4	3
15 Oct 2002	**1st (Gold) & 2nd NVIs (V)**	4	3
21 Jan 2003	**1st (Gold) & 2nd NVIs (V)**	4	3
28 May 2003	**1st (Gold) De La Rue NVIs (V)**	4	3

To Pay & Frama Labels

POSTAGE DUES (plain envelopes)		£
20 Apr 14	½d Green (postcard)	650
	1d Red (cover or postcard)	450
	2d Black	500
	5d Brown	850
23 Dec 20	4d Dull grey-green	1,000
1 Oct 24	1½d Chestnut	500
7 Jun 56	1d Violet-blue	800
1 Oct 68	8d Red	475
	Prices from 1970 are for illustrated covers.	
17 Jun 70	**TO PAY LABELS: 10p, 20p, 50p, £1**	475
	TO PAY LABELS: ½p, 1p, 2p, 3p, 4p, 5p	
15 Feb 71	Authentic C.D.S. postmarks	750
11 Mar 71	Official issue date C.D.S. pmks	125
2 Apr 73	**£5 TO PAY LABEL**	450
21 Aug 74	**7p TO PAY LABEL**	50
18 Jun 75	**11p TO PAY LABEL**	40

9 Jun 82	**1p-£5 TO PAY LABELS:**	
	Stratford permanent h/s	350
	Any CDS on one or two covers	30
1 May 84	**'FRAMA' LABELS: ½p-16p**	£
	(32 values) on six covers:	
	Philatelic Bureau spec h/s	20
	Cambridge special h/s	25
	London EC special h/s	25
	Southampton special h/s	25
	Windsor special h/s	20
	Set: 6 covers with related C.D.S.	100
28 Aug 84	**'FRAMA' LABELS: 16½p & 17p**	
	Philatelic Counter handstamps	2
15 Feb 94	**TO PAY LABELS: 1p-£5** (9 values)	
	First Day of Issue – London EC3	25
	Tower of London special h/s	25
	-do- Benham official cover	35
	To Pay Labels, Windsor special h/s	25
	-do- Bradbury official cover	50
	Authentic Surcharge/C.O.D. pmk	125

COMMEMORATIVE LABELS

		Ordinary covers £	Sponsored covers £	
27 Jul 94	**£1 Bank of England**			
	(1) Bank of Eng 1694–1994	10	25	*Royal Mail*
	(2) Bank of Eng (Britannia)	10	25	*Bradbury*
	(3) 300 Years Bank of Eng	10	20	*Benham*
	Stock Exch or Britannia CDS	35	–	
16 May 95	**£1 Spitfire**			
	(4) Stoke on Trent	5	15	*Royal Mail*
	(5) Southampton (signature)	5	20	*Bradbury*
	(6) Southampton Spitfire	5	10	*Benham*
	(7) Stoke Mitchell Designer	5	10	*Benham*
	(8) Mitchell BF 2465 PS	5	–	
	(9) VE Day BBMF, SW1	5	20	*CoverCraft*
	Biggin Hill or Eastleigh CDS	10	–	
	Butt Lane, Stoke CDS	10	–	
16 Apr 96	**£1 Queen's Birthday**			
	(10) Westminster Abbey	5	10	*Benham*
	(11) Bruton Street, SW1	5	10	*Benham*
	(12) Queen Street, W1	5	10	*Benham*
	(13) Windsor spec h/s	5	10	*Benham*
	(14) London SW1	5	20	*Bradbury*
	(15) Balmoral	5	20	*Bradbury*
	(16) Windsor (Castle)	5	20	*Bradbury*
	Windsor CDS	8	–	
12 Feb 97	**£1.04 Hong Kong**			
	(17) Farewell Chinatown	6	15	*Benham*
	(18) Parliament Square	6	10	*Benham*
	(19) London SW1	6	10	*Benham*
	(20) Chinatown W1 (junk)	6	15	*Bradbury*
	BFPO Hong Kong CDS	25	–	
	Any relevant CDS	10	–	
21 Oct 97	**£1.04 Commonwealth**			
	(21) Edinburgh (circ. text)	5	10	*Benham*
	(22) Edinburgh (rect. text)	5	10	*Benham*
	(23) Edinburgh (building)	5	10	*Benham*
	(24) Edinburgh (thistle)	5	12	*Bradbury*
	Any Edinburgh CDS	8	–	
14 Nov 98	**£1.04 Prince of Wales**			
	(25) 50th Birthday Tetbury	5	15	*Royal Mail*
	(26) Tetbury, Glos	5	10	*Benham*
	(27) Balmoral	5	10	*Benham*
	(28) Windsor	5	10	*Benham*
	(29) Caernarfon	5	10	*Benham*
	(30) Balmoral	5	12	*Bradbury*
	(31) The Mall, SW1	5	12	*Westminster*
	(32) St. Pauls	5	12	*Westminster*
	(33) RN Covers	5	20	*RN CvrsGp*
	Any relevant CDS pmk	8	–	
12 May 99	**£1.04 Berlin Airlift**			
	(34) Brize Norton Carterton	5	15	*Royal Mail*
	(35) Watford	5	10	*Benham*
	(36) Oakington, Cambridge	5	10	*Benham*
	(37) Lyneham RAF Station	5	10	*Benham*
	(38) Brize Norton, Oxford	5	10	*Benham*
	(39) RAF Lyneham	5	12	*Bradbury*
	(40) Oakington, Cambs	5	10	*RN CvrsGp*
	(41) HMS Glasgow	5	10	*RN CvrsGp*
	(42) RAF Abingdon	5	10	*Cam.SC*
	(43) RAF Museum, NW9	5	10	*Westminster*
	(44) Settle Rd, E13	5	12	*PM Payne*
	Any relevant CDS pmk	8	–	
1 Oct 99	**£1.04 Rugby World Cup**			
	(45) Caerdydd, Cardiff	5	15	*Royal Mail*
	(46) Rugby 1999, Twickenham	5	10	*Benham*
	(47) Rugby 1999, Cardiff	5	10	*Benham*
	(48) Rugby 1999, Edinburgh	5	10	*Benham,*
	(49) Rugby 1999, Belfast	5	10	*Benham*
	(50) Birthplace of Rugby	5	12	*Bradbury*

27 July 1994 **Bank of England**

		Ordinary covers £	Sponsored covers £	
	(51) Rugby, the Cup	5	12	*PM Payne*
	(52) Cardiff, Wales	5	10	*Westminster*
	(53) Widnes Vikings RLFC	5	10	*P Sheridan*
	(54) Rugby Street	5	20	*GBFDC*
	(55) Royal Naval Rugby	5	10	*RN CvrsGp*
21 Mar 00	**£1.04 Postman Pat**			
	(56) Keswick	5	10	*Benham*
	(57) London SW13	5	10	*Benham*
	(58) Leeds	5	10	*Benham*
	(59) Colne	5	10	*Benham*
	(60) Children's Favourite	5	12	*Bradbury*
	(61) Pattishall Post Office	5	12	*M Brazier*
4 Apr 00	**£1.04 Botanical**			
	(62) Llanarthne	5	10	*Benham*
	(63) Llanarthne (bee)	5	10	*Benham*
	(64) Kew, Richmond	5	10	*Benham*
	(65) Westonbirt, Tetbury	5	10	*Benham*
	(66) Llanarthne	5	10	*Benham*
	(67) Kew, Richmond	5	12	*Bradbury*
	(68) Llanarthney	5	12	*Royal Mail*
29 Jan 01	**£1.62 Queen Victoria - prices for complete label and six stamps**			
	(69) Victoria Centenary	6	12	*Bradbury*
	(70) The Strand	6	10	*Westminster*
	(71) Kensington	6	10	*Westminster*
	(72) Autographed Editions	6	10	*Westminster*
	(73) 1st Ever Self Adhesive	6	–	*Internetstamps*
	(74) East Cowes (circle)	6	–	*Benham*
	(75) Windsor	6	–	*Benham*
	(76) East Cowes	6	–	*Benham*
	(77) East Cowes (oval)	6	–	*Benham*
	(78) London SW1	6	–	*Benham*
	(79) Self Adhesive Stamp Bks.	6	–	*n.o.c.*
	(80) Battle of Assaye	6	–	*Benham*

Retail Book Panes

Special Retail Books contain two panes of stamps, viz: one pane of eight 1st Class definitives and one pane of two special stamps. Prices are for covers with the special stamp pane only.

12th May 1999 Special Retail Book No.1

26p Pilgrim Fathers & 26p Mill Towns

Price Guide Ordinary Covers £2-£3/Official Covers £8-£10

(1) Millennium Bklt Edinburgh *Benham*
(2) Millennium Bklt Bolton *Benham*
(3) Millennium Bklt Greenwich *Benham*
(4) Millennium Bklt Plymouth *Benham*
(5) Windsor Berks *Bradbury*

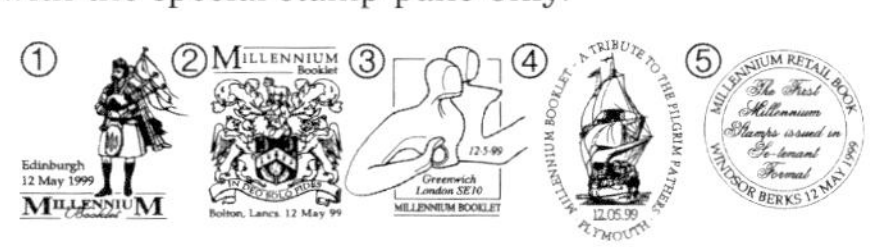

21st Sept 1999 Special Retail Book No.2

2 x 26p Farmers' Tale

Price Guide Ordinary Covers £2-£3/Official Covers £8-£10

(1) Millennium Bklt Detling *Benham*
(2) Millennium Bklt Belfast *Benham*
(3) Millennium Bklt Cardiff *Benham*
(4) Millennium Bklt Stoneleigh *Benham*
(5) Windsor Berks *Bradbury*

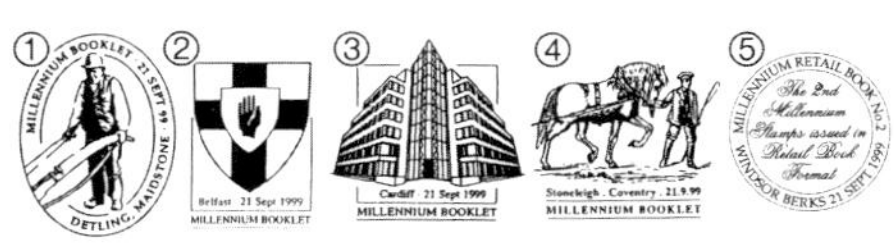

26th May 2000 Special Retail Book No.3

1 x 1st Space Centre & 1x 1st Web of life (As the Space Centre stamp was a new issue, i.e. a 1st Class NVI, please see Commemorative Section for details of this issue)

5th Sept 2000 Special Retail Book No.4

1 x 1st Trans Pennine Trail & 1 x 1st Eden Project

Price Guide Ordinary Covers £2-£3/Official Covers £8-£10

(1) Millennium Bklt, St. Austell *Benham*
(2) Millennium Bklt, St. Austell *Benham*
(3) Millennium Bklt, St. Austell *Benham*
(4) Millennium Bklt, Liverpool *Benham*
(5) Pennine Trail, Barnsley *Bradbury*
(6) Garden of Eden, St. Austell *Bradbury*
(7) Eden Project, St. Austell *Mill. Comm. Covers*

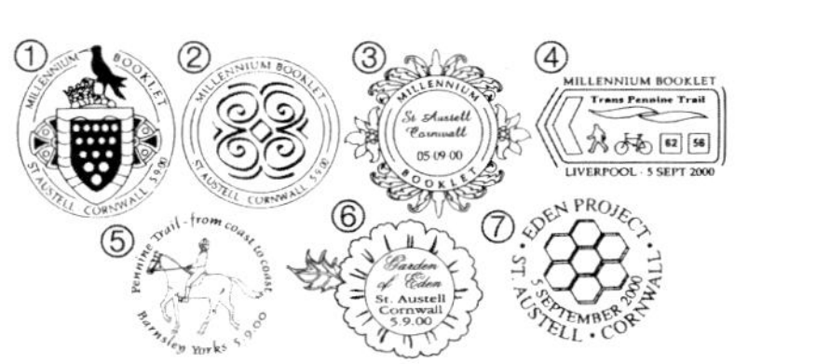

PRESTIGE STAMP BOOK PANES

Prices are for the set of four covers with the complete pane of stamps plus descriptive/pictorial panel. Covers serviced with the stamps only are worth considerably less. Sponsored covers exist for most issues - these are worth at least a 50% premium, often more.

***1 Dec 1969* £1 Stamps for Cooks**	£
(1) Milk Marketing special h/s	95
***24 May 1972* £1 Wedgwood**	
(2) Bureau special h/s	75
(3) Barlaston special h/s	110
***16 Apr 1980* £3 Wedgwood**	
(4) Bureau special h/s	30
(5) Barlaston special h/s	40
Burslem CDS	150
***19 May 1982* £4 Stanley Gibbons**	
(6) Bureau special h/s	25
(7) London WC FDI h/s	35
(8) Plymouth special h/s	45
London WC special h/s	45
***14 Sep 1983* £4 Royal Mint**	
(9) Bureau special h/s	35
(10) Llantrisant special h/s	50
***4 Sep 1984* £4 Christian Heritage**	
(11) Bureau special h/s	25
(12) Canterbury special h/s	30
(13) St. Mary le Strand h/s	50
(14) St. James Piccadilly h/s	50
Christian Heritage slogan	75
Holy Island CDS or similar	55
***8 Jan 1985* £5 The Times**	
(15) Bureau special h/s	25
(16) London WC special h/s	30
Times 1785-1985 slogan pmk	80
Fleet Street CDS	80
***18 Mar 1986* £5 British Rail**	
(17) Crewe special h/s	35
(18) Bureau special h/s	25
T.P.O. pmks	60
Railway slogans or CDS	50
***3 Mar 1987* £5 P & O**	
(19) Bureau special h/s	35
(20) Falmouth special h/s	45
(21) Spring Stampex h/s	75
Maritime Mail CDS	85
Appropriate CDS	55
Clydebank slogan	95
***9 Feb 1988* £5 Financial Times**	
(22) Bureau special h/s	30
(23) London EC4 special h/s	40
Fleet Street C.D.S.	80
***21 Mar 1989* £5 Scots Connection**	
(24) Bureau special h/s	15
(25) Inverness special h/s	30
Appropriate CDS pmks	45
Visit Isle of Skye slogan	45
***20 Mar 1990* £5 London Life**	
(26) Bureau special h/s	15
(27) Tower Hill special h/s	25
(28) Stamp World special h/s	35
(29) Victorian Heritage h/s	35
Set of four different handstamps	40
Relevant CDS or slogans	50
***19 Mar 1991* £6 Agatha Christie**	
(30) Bureau special h/s	20
(31) Marple special h/s	45
(32) Orient Express h/s	45
(33) Sunningdale special h/s	45
Set of four different handstamps	45
Torquay CDS	60
Bite out of Crime slogan	35
***25 Feb 1992* £6 Wales**	
(34) Bureau special h/s	15
(35) Cardiff special h/s	30

(36) Stampex special h/s	35
(37) Snowdon special h/s	35
Set of four different handstamps	40
relevant C.D.S. pmks	40
***27 Oct 1992* £6 Tolkien**	
(38) Bureau special h/s	50
(39) Oxford special h/s	55
(40) Rings End, March h/s	65
(41) Bagendonspecial h/s	65
(42) Meriden special h/s	75
Set of four different handstamps	65
relevant CDS or slogans	50
***10 Aug 1993* £5.64 Beatrix Potter**	
(43) Bureau special h/s	40
(44) Keswick special h/s	40
(45) London special h/s	60
(46) Near Sawrey special h/s	60
(47) Frederick Warne h/s	60
(48) Tom Kitten special h/s	60
(49) The Tailor Gloster h/s	60
Set of four different handstamps	60
relevant CDS postmarks	60
***26 Jul 1994* £6.04 Northern Ireland**	
(50) Bureau FDI special h/s	15
(51) Belfast FDI special h/s	30
(52) London special h/s	30
(53) Belfast special h/s	40
(54) Belfast special h/s	40
(55) Mourne special h/s	40
(56) Giant's Causeway h/s	40
Set of four different handstamps	45
relevant CDS postmarks	45
Northern Ireland Booklet slogan	55
***25 Apr 1995* £6 National Trust**	
(57) Bureau FDI special h/s	15
(58) Tintagel FDI special h/s	15
(59) London special h/s	30
(60) This England special h/s	35
(61) Bodiam Castle special h/s	35
(62) Windermere special h/s	40
(63) Biddulph Grange special h/s	35
(64) Erddig House special h/s	35
Set of four different handstamps	40
relevant CDS postmarks	45
***14 May 1996* £6.48 Football**	
Set of four different handstamps*	45
relevant CDS & slogan pmks*	50

**All Football pmks are illustrated in the commemorative section for the same date -* *please see page 116.*

***23 Sep 1997* £6.04 BBC**	
(65) Bureau FDI special h/s	15
(66) London W1 FDI h/s	30
(67) Birmingham FDI h/s	35
(68) London FDI special h/s	35
(69) Belfast special h/s	40
(70) Glasgow special h/s	40
(71) Cardiff special h/s	40
(72) London W1 special h/s	40
(73) London W12 special h/s	40
(74) The Archers special h/s	40
(75) BBC special h/s	40
(76) Autographed special h/s	20
Shepherd's Bush CDS	35
Set of four different handstamps	40
***10 Mar 1998* £7.49 Definitive Portrait**	
(77) Bureau special h/s	20
(78) London SW1 special h/s	20
(79) Stamp Show 2000 h/s	30

(80) Westminster Abbey h/s........... 30
(81) Windsor special h/s................. 30
(82) Queen Alice special h/s.......... 35
(83) Bond Street special h/s.......... 30
(84) Earl's Court special h/s.......... 30
(85) Portman Square h/s................. 30
(86) King Edward Street h/s 30
(87) Longford special h/s................ 30
Set of four different handstamps 35

***13 Oct 1998* £6.16 Speed**

(88) FDI - Bureau h/s...................... 15
(89) FDI - Chislehurst h/s 20
(90) FDI - London h/s..................... 30
(91) Pendine special h/s.................. 30
(92) Pendine (flags) h/s 30
(93) Beaulieu special h/s.................. 30
(94) Duxford special h/s 30
(95) Coniston special h/s 30
(96) Chislehurst special h/s............. 30
Set of four different handstamps 30

***16 Feb 1999* £7.49 Profile on Print**

NB Five panes/covers in this set

(97) FDI - Bureau h/s...................... 20
(98) FDI - London SW1 h/s........... 20
(99) Windsor h/s.............................. 35
(1) Self Adhesive, Windsor h/s 35
(2) Machin Portrait h/s................. 35
(3) Piccadilly W1 h/s..................... 35
(4) Millbank, SW1 h/s 35
(5) High Wycombe h/s 35
(6) Stoke on Trent h/s 35
(7) Walsall h/s 35
(8) Parkhouse Street SE5 h/s 35
Set of five different handstamps 35

***21 Sept 1999* £6.99 World Changers**

NB Five panes/covers in this set

(9) FDI - Bureau h/s........................ 20
(10) FDI - Downe h/s...................... 20
(11) Exhibition Road, SW7 h/s 30
(12) Birmingham New Age h/s 30
(13) Charles Darwin h/s 30
(14) Michael Faraday h/s 30
(15) Alan Turing h/s........................ 30
(16) Edward Jenner h/s................... 30
(17) Moon Street, N1 h/s 30
Set of five different handstamps 30

***15 Feb 2000* £7.70 Special by Design**

(18) FDI - Bureau h/s...................... 15
(19) FDI - London SW5 h/s........... 15
(20) Buckingham Palace Rd h/s..... 25
(21) Nat Postal Musuem h/s 25
(22) Belfast special h/s 25
(23) Edinburgh special h/s 25
(24) Cardiff special h/s 25
(25) Earl's Court special h/s........... 25
(26) London EC4 special h/s 25
(27) Westminster Abbey h/s........... 25
(28) Earl's Court h/s 25
Set of four different handstamps 25

***4 Aug 2000* £7.03 Queen Mother**

Set of four different handstamps* .. 25

**All Queen Mother pmks are illustrated in the commemorative section for the same date - please see page 143.*

***18 Sept 2000* £7 A Treasury of Trees**

(29) FDI - Bureau h/s...................... 15
(30) FDI - Llangernyw h/s.............. 15
(31) Kew Gardens h/s 30
(32) Sherwood Forest h/s 25
(33) London SW7 h/s...................... 25
(34) Cardiff h/s................................ 25
(35) Glasgow h/s.............................. 25
(36) Ardingly h/s............................. 25
(37) London SW7 h/s...................... 25
(38) Birmingham h/s....................... 25

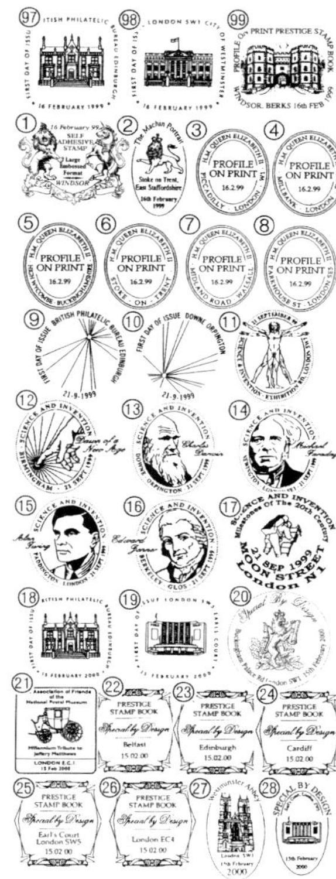

***22 Oct 2001* £6.76 Unseen & Unheard** *
***6 Feb 2002* £7.29 Gracious Accession** *
***24 Sep 2002* £6.83 Across the Universe** *
***25 Feb 2003* £6.99 Microcosmos** *
***2 June 2003* £7.46 Perfect Coronation** *
***16 Mar 2004* £7.44 Letters by Night** *
***25 May 2004* £7.23 Glory of the Garden** *
***24 Feb 2005* £7.43 The Bronte Sisters** *
***21 Oct 2005* £7.26 Trafalgar** *
***23 Feb 2006* £7.40 Brunel** *
***21 Sept 2006* £7.44 Victoria Cross** *

**See commemorative section for same dates for full details of postmarks for these issues.*

STAMP BOOK PANES

Book panes are included if some or all of the stamps are new or different (e.g. se-tenant formats, perfs, phosphors, gums, papers etc) to those previously issued. Prices are for the complete panes.

		plain covers £	illus. cvrs £
3 May51	**1s Book:** (4 x ½d; 4 x 1d; 4 x 1½d)	-	200
15 July 63	**2s Holiday Book:** 4 x 2½d	40	100
	Se-tenant 3 x ½d + 2½d	30	90
6 Sep 63	**2s Book reprint:** 2 panes as above	50	90
1 Jul 64	**2s Holiday Book:** Se-tenant 2 x 2½d + 2 x ½d		
	Se-tenant pane tourist pmks *each*	n.k.	10
	Holiday resort slogan pmks	10	25
21 Jun 65	**6s Book:** 6 x 4d	100	175
16 Aug 65	**2s Book:** 2 panes:		
	(2 x 1d + 2 x 3d) + (4 x 4d)	50	150
	Se-tenant pane only	15	70
6 Dec 65	**2s Christmas Book:** 4 x 3d	100	250
21 Sep 67	**6s Machin Book:** 6 x 4d	5	100
25 Mar 68	**10s Livingstone Book:** 3 panes Stampex pmk:		
	(6 x 4d; 6 x 3d; 6 x 1d)	10	90
6 Apr 68	**2s Machin Book:** 2 panes:		
	(2 x 1d + 2 x 3d)+(4 x 4d)	20	70
10 Jul 68	**4s 6d Cutty Sark Book:** 2 panes:		
	(6 x 4d)+(6 x 1d)	20	100
16 Sep 68	**2s Book:** 2 panes:		
	(4 x 4d)+(2 x 4d + 2 L)	5	20
	-do- Windsor postmark	8	30
	4s 6d Golden Hind Book: 3 panes:		
	2 @ (6 x 4d)+(6 x 1d)	10	60
	10s Scott Book: 3 panes:		
	(6 x 4d)+(6 x 5d)+(4 x 1d + 2 x 4d)	15	85
16 Oct 68	**6s Woodpecker Book:** 6 x 4d	15	95
27 Nov68	**5s Ightham Mote Book:** 6 x 5d	15	90
8 Jan 69	**4s 6d QE2 Bklt:** two panes*	15	80
	10s Mary Kingsley Book: three panes*	20	80
	10s known with 6 January date		
28 Feb 69	**6s Barn Owl Book:** 6 x 4d	10	70
3 Mar69	**2s Book:** two panes*	5	80
	**As 16 Sep 1968 but 4d colour change to red.*		
3 Mar70	**5s Philympia Book:**		
	6 x 5d Stampex pmk	5	50

L = Label; CB = Centre Band Phos
SB = Side Band Phos

		Windsor Postmark £	Other Pmks £
15 Feb 71	**New Decimal Books:**		
	10p Pillar Boxes (2 x 2p + 2 x ½p) +(2 x 1p + 2 x 1½p) Vertical format		
	25p Omnibus (5 x 2½p + L)+(4 x 2½p + 2 L) +(5 x ½p + L)		
	30p Curlew (5 x 3p + L)		
	50p Bindweed (6 x 3p)+(4 x 3p + 2 x 2½p SB) +(5 x 2½p CB + L)+(5 x ½p + L)		
	Set of 10 panes	100	50
	Set of 3 se-tenant panes	40	15
14 Jul 71	**10p Book:** (2 x 2p + 2 x ½p)		
	+(2 x 1p + 2 x 1½p) Horizontal	450	375
23 Jul 71	**30p Bk:** (5 x 3p + L imperf in margin*)	250	200
17 Sep 71	**25p Book:** (5 x 2½p + L)+(4 x 2½p + 2 L) +(5 x ½p + L)		
	Labels imperf in margin* – 3 panes	n.k.	150
	50p Book: (5 x 2½p CB + L)+(5 x ½p + L)		
	Labels imperf in margin* – 2 panes	180	125
	**Changes introduced as an aid to the blind.*		
24 Dec71	**25p & 50p Christmas Books:**		
	25p (5 x ½p + L)+(5 x 2½p + L)+(4 x 2½p + 2 L)		
	50p (5 x 2½p + L) – *different to 25p booklet*		
	Four panes with Southampton pmk	n.k.	95

		Windsor Postmark £	Other Pmks £
14 Nov73	**50p Book:** Two panes:	140	80
	(5 x 3½p + L)+(5 x 3p CB + L)		
30 Jan 74	**30p Book:** 5 x 3 CB p + L	n.k.	50
9 Oct 74	**45p Book:** 5 x 4½p + L	150	70
23 Oct 74	**35p Book:** 5 x 3½p phos + L	100	60
10 Mar76	**10p Book:** 2 x ½p; 3 x 1p; 1 x 6p	3	1
	-do- Telecom h/s (official cover)	–	15
14 Jul 76	**65p, 85p** (10 x 6½p)+(10 x 8½p)	100	45
26 Jan 77	**50p Books:** 2 @		
	(2 x ½p; 2 x 1p; 2 x 6½p; 4 x 8½p)		
	Pair of mirror image panes	12	4
13 Jun 77	**50p Books:** 2 @ (2 x 1p; 3 x 7p; 3 x 9p)		
	Pair of mirror image panes	8	4
	70p & 90p Books: (10 x 7p)+(10 x 9p)	20	9
	30p & 60p Sachet Books	150	–
13 Oct 77	**10p Book:** Reprint:narrow selvedge	–	60
8 Feb 78	**10p Bk:** (2 x ½p; 2 x 1p; 1 x 7p + L)	2	1
15 Nov78	**£1.60 Xmas Book:** (10 x 9p; 10 x 7p)	5	2
5 Feb 79	**70p Book:** (10 x 7p) Kedleston Hall;		
	90p Book: (10 x 9p) Tramway Museum, Crich.		
	Derby CDS **or** Postcode slogan (pair)	–	150
	Kedlestone CDS & Crich CDS (pair)	–	125
	Issued in conjunction with the opening of Derby Mechanised Letter Office.		
28 Aug79	**50p Books:** (2 x 2p; 2 x 8p; 3 x 10p + L)		
	Pair of mirror image panes	5	2
3 Oct 79	**80p & £1 Books:** (10 x 8p)+(10 x 10p)	6	3
17 Oct 79	**10p 'London 1980'**(2 x 1p; 1 x 8p + L)	2	1
	-do- 'London 1980' slogan pmk	–	3
14 Nov79	**£1.80 Xmas Book:** (10 x 10p; 10 x 8p).	3	2
	BPE Wembley special h/s	–	6
4 Feb 80	**50p Books:** (3 x 2p; 2 x 10p; 2 x 12p + L)		
	Pair of mirror image panes	8	3
4 Feb 80	**£1 & £1.20:** (10 x 10p)+(10 x 12p)	10	4
25 Jun 80	**50p Chambon:** (as 4th February)		
	Pair of mirror image panes	80	70
27 Aug80	**10p Chambon: 'London 1980'**	2	1
12 Nov80	**£2.20 Xmas Bk:** (10 x 12p; 10 x 10p)	4	3
26 Jan 81	**50p Books:** (1 x ½p;1 x 1p; 3 x 11½p; 1 x 14p)		
	Pair of mirror image panes	5	2
26 Jan 81	**£1.15 & £1.40:** (10x11½p)+(10x14p)	6	3
6 May81	**£1.30 National Stamp Day Book:**	3	1
	Birmingham special h/s	–	3
	British Library special h/s	–	3
	Cameo Stamp Centre special h/s	–	3
	London EC special h/s	–	3
	Pair of mirror image panes	7	2
26 Aug81	**50p Books:** (3 x 2½p; 2 x 4p; 3 x 11½p)		
	Pair of mirror image panes	7	2
11 Nov81	**£2.55 Xmas:** (10 x 11½p; 10 x 14p)	7	3
1 Feb 82	**50p Books:** (1 x ½p; 4 x 3p; 3 x 12½p)		
	Pair of mirror image panes	4	1
1 Feb 82	**£1.25 & £1.55 Books:**		
	(10 x 12½p)+(10 x 15½p)	6	3
	£1.43 Book: (4 x 12½p + 6 x 15½p)		
	Pair of mirror image panes	8	2
10 Nov82	**£2.55 Xmas Book:**		
	(10 x 12½p; 10 x 15½p)	6	3
	Star, Glenrothes CDS	–	15
	Sold at 30p discount. Star printed on reverse.		
5 Apr 83	**50p Glos 'Old Spot' Book:**	2	1
	(2 x 1p; 3 x 3½p; 3 x 12½p)		
	Cotswold Farm Park special h/s	–	5
	-do- Benham official cvr	–	10
	£1.60 Book: (10 x 16p)	5	3
	£1.46 Books: (4 x 12½p; 6 x 16p)		
	Pair of mirror image panes	10	4
10 Aug83	**£1.45 Discount Book:** (10 x 16p)	7	3
	Sold at 15p discount + printed 'D' on reverse.		

Date		Windsor Postmark £	Other Pmks £
9 Nov83	**£2.20 Christmas Book:** (20 x 12½p)	5	2
	-do- Aladdin WC2 special handstamp	–	15
	30p discount with star printed on reverse.		
3 Sep 84	**£1.54 Books:** (4 x 13p; 6 x 17p)		
	Pair of mirror image panes	5	3
	50p Books: (3 x 1p; 2 x 4p; 3 x 13p)	3	1
	£1.30 & £1.70: (10 x 13p)+(10 x 17p)	15	6
5 Mar85	**£1.55 Discount Book:** (10 x 17p)	7	3
	Sold at 15p discount + printed 'D' on reverse.		
4 Nov85	**50p Discount Book:** (3 x 17p + L)	3	1
	Sold at a 1p discount with star printed on reverse.		
14 Jan 86	**£1.20 Book:** (10 x 12p)	6	2
	£1.50 Books: (4 x 12p; 6 x 17p)		
	Pair of mirror image panes	10	4
29 Jul 86	**50p Book: (**2 x 1p; 4 x 12p)	2	1
	£1 Book: (6 x 17p) *2p discount*	7	3
12 Aug 86	**50p Book:** (3 x 17p + label) *1p discount*	2	1
	Different to 4 Nov 1985 issue – no Star underprint		
20 Oct 86	**50p 'Roman Britain' Book:**		
	(1p + 13p; 2 x 18p)	2	1
	St. Albans h/s or Porchester CDS	–	4
	50p 'Pond Life' Book:		
	(1p + 2 x 5p; 3 x 13p)	2	1
	Pond CDS	–	4
	£1 (1 x 13p; 5 x 18p) *3p discount*	3	2
	£1.30 & £1.80: (10 x 13p)+(10 x 18p)	12	5
2 Dec 86	**£1.20 Xmas Book:** (10 x 13p)	5	3
	10p discount with Star printed on reverse		
	Glastonbury special handstamps	–	6
27 Jan 87	**2 x 50p, £1, £1.30 Books:** – set of 4	35	25
	As 20 Oct 1986 but with new phosphor ink.		
14 Apr 87	**£1.80 Book:** (10 x 18p) ACP	5	2
4 Aug 87	**52p** (4 x 13p); **72p** (4 x 18p); **£1.04** (4 x 26p);		
	£1.30 (10 x 13p); **£1.80** (10 x 18p)	30	20
	Printed with a selvedge around all four sides. giving the appearance of small 'sheetlets'. Issued on trial at Bristol, Nottingham, Preston & York.		
	Set of five with any of these pmks	–	30
29 Sep 87	**50p Mount Stewart Book:**		
	(1 x 1p, 2 x 5p, 3 x 13p)	2	1
	Belfast pmk. (Mount Stewart)	–	3
	£1 Sherlock Holmes Book:		
	(1 x 13p; 5 x 18p) *3p discount*	3	2
	Baker St. C.D.S.	–	25
	Produced with straight edges (i.e. outer long edges had no perforations).		
23 Aug88	**56p** (4 x 14p); **76p** (4 x 19p); **£1.08** (4 x 27p);		
	£1.40 (10 x 14p); **£1.90** (10 x 19p)	25	15
	Issued on trial at Bristol, Nottingham, Preston & York.		
	Set of five with any of these pmks	–	30
5 Sep 88	**50p** (1 x 14p; 2 x 19p + L) *2p disc.*	2	1
	£1 (2 x 14p; 4 x 19p) *4p discount*	3	2
	£1.40 & £1.90 (10 x 14p)+(10 x 19p)	10	7
11 Oct 88	**56p, 76p, £1.08, £1.40, £1.90** Set	30	10
	As 23 Aug issue, but selvedge replaced by straight edges at top and bottom of stamp panes.		
	Bklts: £1.40, £1.90 Pair	15	8
	Questa – the first 14p and 19p litho printings.		
24 Jan 89	**Bklts: 56p, 76p**	4	2
	As 23 Aug 1988 but with three straight edges.		
25 Apr 89	**£1** (2 x 14p; 4 x 19p) *4p discount*	4	2
	-do- Walsall Security Printers spec h/s	–	6
	-do- Walsall C.D.S. pmk	–	30
	Walsall Security Printers with straight edges		
26 Jun 89	**£1.90** (10 x 19p) Jumelle Press	5	2
10 Jul 89	**£1.40** (10 x 14p) Jumelle Press	4	2
22 Aug89	**Non-Value Indicator Books:** Set of 4	20	15
	56p (4 x 2nd) & **76p** (4 x 1st) Walsall		
	£1.40 (10 x 2nd) **£1.90** (10 x 1st) Harrison		

BF = Blue Fluor
PB = Phosphor Band

Date		Windsor Postmark £	Other Pmks £
19 Sep 89	**Non-Value Indicator Books:**		
	£1.40(10 x 2nd),**£1.90**(10 x 1st)Questa	10	7
2 Oct 89	**50p Book:** (2 x 15p; 1 x 20p + label)	2	1
	£1 Book: (5 x 20p + label)	3	2
	£1.16 Airmail Book: (4 x 29p)	3	2
28 Nov89	**60p Book:** (4 x 2nd) – Harrison*	15	–
5 Dec 89	**80p Book:** (4 x 1st) – Harrison*	25	–
	**Three straight edges (top, right and bottom).*		
30 Jan 90	**Penny Black Anniv. Books:** Set of 4	20	8
	60p (4 x 15p); **80p** (4 x 20p);		
	£1.50 (10 x 15p); **£2** (10 x 20p)		
	Penny Black Anniv. Books: Set of 3	16	7
	50p (2 x 15p; 1 x 20p + L) – Harrison Printers		
	£1 (5 x 20p + L) – Harrison Printers		
	£1 (5 x 20p + L) – Walsall Printers		
17 Apr 90	**Penny Black Anniv. Books:** Set of 3	20	12
	80p (4 x 20p) Harrison 3 straight edges		
	£1.50 (10 x 15p) Questa full perfs		
	£2 (10 x 20p) Questa full perfs		
	Standard definitives:		
	£1.16 (4 x 29p) 3 straight edges	4	2
12 Jun 90	**Penny Black Anniv. Books:** Pair	10	4
	£1.50 (10 x 15p) Walsall – 3 straight edges		
	£2 (10 x 20p) Walsall – 3 straight edges		
7 Aug 90	**Non-Value Indicator Books:** Set of 8	40	25
	60p (4 x 2nd); **80p** (4 x 1st); Walsall Printers		
	£1.50 (10 x 2nd); **£2** (10 x 1st) Walsall Printers		
	£1.50 (10 x 2nd); **£2** (10 x 1st) Harrison Printers		
	£1.50 (10 x 2nd); **£2** (10 x 1st) Questa Printers		
4 Sep 90	**50p Book:** (3 x 17p) *1p discount*	2	1
	£1 Book: (2 x 17p; 3 x 22p)	3	1
17 Sep 90	**£1.24 Book:** (4 x 31p) Walsall	3	2
6 Aug 91	**Non-Value Indicator Book:** Set of 7	25	12
	68p (4 x 2nd); **88p** (4 x 1st) Walsall		
	£1.70 (10 x 2nd); **£2.20** (10 x 1st) Walsall		
	£1.70 (10 x 2nd); **£2.20** (10 x 1st) Questa		
	£2.20 (10 x 1st) Harrison		
10 Sep 91	**50p & £1 Book:**		
	(2 x 24p; 2 x 1p);(4 x 24p; 2 x 2p)	4	3
	-do- 'New Postage Rates' slogan	–	6
16 Sep 91	**£1.32,£1.56**(4 x 33p);(4 x 39p) Walsall.	7	3
	-do- with 'New Postage Rates' slogan	–	10
28 Jul 92	**78p Kelloggs Book:** 2 x 39p	10	3
8 Sep 92	**£1.32 Book:** (4 x 33p) Dextrin Gum	4	2
22 Sep 92	**£1.80 NVI Book:** (10 x 2nd Class)	6	3
	Harrison: straight edges at the top & bottom.		
9 Feb 93	**£2.40 NVI Book:** (10 x 1st Class)	6	3
	Walsall: straight edges at the top & bottom.		
	£1 Book: (4 x 24p; 2 x 2p)	4	2
	Walsall ACP with straight edges at left & right.		
16 Mar 93	**£1.80 NVI Book:** (10 x 2nd Class)	6	3
	Walsall ACP straight edges at the top & bottom.		
6 Apr 93	**Non-Value Indicator Books:** Set of 5	18	10
	96p (4 x 1st); **£2.40** (10 x 1st) Harrison		
	72p (4 x 2nd); **£2.40** (10 x 1st)* Walsall		
	£1.80 (10 x 2nd) Questa		
	Perfs all round with elliptical perfs.		
	**Walsall £2.40 – two phos. bands.*		
17 Aug 93	**96p NVI Book:** (4 x 1st) Walsall	4	2
7 Sep 93	**72p NVI Book:** (4 x 2nd) Harrison	4	2
1 Nov 93	**50p** (2 x 25p) Harrisons; **£1** (4 x 25p) Walsall;		
	£2 (8 x 25p) Harrisons Set of 3	10	5
	£2.50 NVI Book: (10 x 1st Class)	6	3
	Questa with elliptical perfs		
	Overseas Rates Books: Walsall		
	£1.40 (4 x 35p); **£1.64** (4 x 41p)	8	4
25 Jan 94	**50p** (2 x 25p) Harrisons;		
	£1 (4 x 25p) Walsall	10	3
22 Feb 94	**£1.90, £2.50 NVI:** (10 x 2nd);(10 x 1st)	8	5
	Walsall Printers with elliptical perfs		

Stamp Books (contd.)

Date	Item	Windsor Postmark £	Other Pmks £
26 Apr 94	**£1 Book:** (4 x 25p) Harrison	5	3
9 Aug 94	**60p Airmail Rate Book:**	6	3
	Any Airport postmark	–	6
4 Apr 95	**£2.50 NVI Book:** (10 x 1st) Harrison	7	3
16 May 95	**£1 R J Mitchell Book:** (4 x 25p 2 PB)	3	2
	Any Spitfire/VE Day special h/s	–	3
	Any relevant CDS postmark	–	6
6 Jun 95	**50p, £2** (2 x 25p); (8 x 25p 2 PB)	6	4
5 Oct 95	**£1.40** (4 x 35p) - Walsall (BF)	6	–
12 Dec 95	**76p** (4 x 2nd) - Walsall (BF)	5	–
	£1.90 (10 x 2nd) - Harrison (BF)	6	–
16 Jan 96	**£1, £2**(4 x 25p);(8 x 25p) Questa (BF)	8	–
19 Feb 96	**£2.50 Walt Disney Book:**		
	10 x 1st *(First Scratch Card Bklt)*	5	–
20 Feb 96	**£2 Book:** (8 x 25p) - Harrison (BF)	5	–
19 Mar 96	**£1.64 Book:** (4 x 41p) Walsall (BF)	–	5
	£2.40 Book: (4 x 60p) Walsall (BF)	5	–
8 Jul 96	**£1** (3 x 26p; 20p; 2 x 1p) & **£2** (7 x 26p; 20p)		
	£1.48 (4 x 37p) & **£2.52** (4 x 63p)	10	8
	-do- New Booklets Windsor spec h/s	15	–
21 Apr 97	**Gold Definitives Books:**		
	£2.60 (10 x 1st Class) – Harrison		
	£2.60 (10 x 1st Class) – Walsall.......pair	10	5
	-do- special golden wedding pmks*	10	10
	**See commemorative section for full details of pmks*		
29 Apr 97	**£2 Book:** (10 x 2nd) Harrison	5	2
26 Aug 97	**£1.04** (4 x 1st); **80p** (4 x 2nd);		
	£1.48 (4 x 37p); **£2.52** (4 x 63p) ....set	15	10
18 Nov 97	**£2.60** (10 x 1st) Harrison-lay flat gum	6	3
	£2.60 (10 x 1st) Harrison	5	2
	£2.60 (10 x 1st) Walsall	5	2
5 May 98	**£1.20 Book:** (4 x 30p) Walsall	5	2
1 Dec 98	**Change to gravure printing process:**		
	£2 (10 x 2nd) & **£2.60** (10 x 1st)	10	4
	£1 (3 x 26p; 1 x 20p; 2 x 1p + 2 L)	5	2
	£2 (7 x 26p; 1 x 20p)	6	2
19 Jan 99	**European NVI 'E'** (4 x E)	6	2
26 Apr 99	**£1** (3 x 26p; 1 x 19p; 1 x 1p, 1 x 2p + L)	3	2
	£1.52 (4 x 38p)	4	2
	£2 (7 x 26p; 1 x 19p)	6	3
	£2.56 (4 x 64p)	6	3
6 Jan 00	**£2.60** (10 x 1st Millennium) Walsall	6	4
	£2.60 (10 x 1st Millennium) Questa	6	4
27 Apr 00	**£1** (3 x 1st; 1 x 2nd)	3	2
	£2 (6 x 1st; 2 x 2nd)	4	2
	£1.60 (4 x 40p)	5	3
	£2.60 (4 x 65p)	6	3
29 Jan 01	**Set of 7 Self Adhesive Stamp Books**	30	25
	£3.24 (12 x 1st) Walsall; **£3.24** (12 x 1st) Questa; **£2.28** (12 x 2nd) Questa; **£2.70** (10 x 1st) Questa; **£1.90** (10 x 2nd) Questa; **£1.14** (6 x 1st) Walsall; **£1.90** (6 x 2nd) Walsall		
17 Apr 01	**£1** (Text change on label)	3	2

N.B. With effect from July 2002, stamp books contained self-adhesive stamps with the matrix (or selvedge) stripped away from the backing paper. It is therefore impossible to affix a complete pane of stamps to covers other than by using glue.

Varieties

This section includes changes of watermark, paper, perforations, phosphor, gum etc. where the dates of issue are known.

Similar changes to stamps from stamp book panes are included in the Prestige Stamp Book Panes and Stamp Book Panes Sections.

Date	Item	plain covers £	illus. covers £
17 Jul 1956	**3d** St. Edward Crown wmk	275	–
19 Nov 1957	**½d, 1d, 1½d, 2d, 2½d, 3d**	40	80
	Graphite lines *printed under the gum as an experiment in automatic letter sorting at Southampton.*		
4 Dec 1958	**2d** Multiple Crowns wmk	125	–
23 Dec 1958	**6d** Multiple Crowns wmk	125	–
24 Mar 1959	**9d** Multiple Crowns wmk	175	–
18 Nov 1959	**½d,1d,1½d,2d,2½d,3d,4d,4½d**	40	100
	Phos-Graphite: *Similar to above with the addition of phosphor bands on the front - Southampton pmk.*		
27 Jun 1960	**6d** Phosphor	–	350
6 Jul 1960	**½d, 1d, 1½d, 2d, 2½d, 3d, 4d, 6d, 1s3d** Phosphor	–	135
	Phosphor Sorting Machine - Southampton pmk.		
17 May 1965	**4d** Deep Ultramarine	30	75
	3d Deep Lilac Phosphor	30	75
	Covers are known with earlier dates: 28th April (4d) and 29th April (3d).		
30 Dec 1966	**10d** Phosphor	150	–
15 Feb 1967	**7d** Phosphor	400	–
9 Jun 1967	**5d** Phosphor	175	–
28 Jun 1967	**8d, 1s** Phosphor	225	–
	'CASTLES' HIGH VALUES: Unwatermarked Paper		
6 Dec 1967	**£1** London Underground cover	–	900
	£1 Plain cover with CDS pmk	200	–
16 Apr 1968	**5s and 10s**	575	–
4 Jun 1968	**2s 6d** Chalky Paper	150	350
3 Jul 1968	**2s 6d**	n.k.	600
28 Aug 1968	**1s 6d** PVA Gum	–	175
16 Sep 1968	**4d** Phosphor	10	25
29 Nov 1968	**9d** PVA Gum	–	175
10 Dec 1969	**1s 6d** Phosphor	1	5

Date	Item	Windsor Postmark £	Other Pmks £
17 Jun 1970	**10p, 20p, 50p & £1** (Recess printed in sheets of 100)	750	600
16 Nov 1970	**1s 9d** PVA Gum	–	175
23 Aug 1972	**3p** Gum Arabic	–	60
13 Sep 1972	**2½p** Gum Arabic	–	60
22 Sep 1972	**½p** Gum Arabic	–	40
31 Oct 1972	**4p** Gum Arabic	–	70
1 Feb 1973	**50p** Phosphor Southampton C.D.S.	–	80
6 Jun 1973	**6p** Gum Arabic	–	120
8 Aug 1973	**2½p** PVA/Dextrin Gum	–	25
22 Aug 1973	**3½p** PVA/Dextrin Gum	–	60
10 Sep 1973	**3p** Phosphor: Centre Band	15	5
10 Sep 1973	**3p** Gum Arabic + **1p, 2p, 3p** PVA/Dextrin Gum	80	30
27 Sep 1973	**£1** Bradbury Contractors Paper	–	675
9 Oct 1973	**½p** PVA/Dextrin Gum	–	60
30 Oct 1973	**6p** PVA/Dextrin Gum	–	125
12 Nov 1973	**4p, 10p** PVA/Dextrin Gum	–	125
30 Nov 1973	**20p** Bradbury Contractors Paper	–	400
20 Feb 1974	**50p** Bradbury Contractors Paper	–	400
22 Mar 1974	**9p** PVA/Dextrin Gum	–	150
5 Jun 1974	**1½p, 5p** PVA/Dextrin Gum	–	40

Varieties (contd.)

Date	Postmark:	Windsor £	Other £
24 Jun 1974	**3½p** Phosphor: Centre Band	30	6
13 Nov 1974	**4½p** Experimental Phosphor	25	3
	Cambridge, Aberdeen or Norwich pmks *each*	–	30
	(Stamps on sale at these Post Offices)		
15 Jan 1975	**7p** Phosphor: Two Bands	2	1
	-do- with phosphor omitted	20	8
17 Mar 1975	**5½p** Phosphor: Centre Band	4	1
21 May 1975	**2½p** Phosphor: Two Bands	10	4
24 Sep 1975	**6½p** Cent. Band, **8½p** Two Bands	2	1
24 Mar 1976	**8½p** Experimental Phosphor	2	1
26 Jan 1977	**9p** All Over Phosphor	–	75
31 Oct 1977	**6p, 7p, 9p, 10p** Halley Press	250	175
20 Aug 1979	**8p** Phosphor: Centre Band	2	1
20 Aug 1979	**10p** Phos Coated Paper + 2 Bands)	2	1
10 Oct 1979	**1p, 2p, 5p, 20p** New Phos Paper	2	1
12 Dec 1979	**1p, 2p** PCP + **8p** Enschedé	2	1
4 Feb 1980	**10p** Phosphor: Centre Band	2	1
4 Feb 1980	**10p** Phosphor Coated Paper	75	25
21 May 1980	**2p, 5p** Questa, **20p** Waddington, **50p** non-phos	2	1
27 Aug 1980	**11p** Phosphor Coated Paper	3	2
22 Oct 1980	**3p + 22p** PCP1 & PCP2	10	5
10 Dec 1980	**½p** Phosphor Coated Paper	2	1
7 Dec 1981	**4p, 20p** PCP Waddington printing	15	5
14 Dec 1983	**10p** Phosphor Coated Paper	2	1
21 Feb 1984	**5p, 75p** Perforation change	2	1
19 Jun 1984	**17p** Advanced Coated Paper	2	1
19 Jun 1984	**26p** Advanced Coated Paper	75	–
10 Jul 1984	**2p** Perforation change	2	1
19 Feb 1985	**75p** New Paper	150	–
16 Jul 1985	**10p** Advanced Coated Paper	2	1
17 Sep 1985	**31p** Advanced Coated Paper	2	1
29 Oct 1985	**12p** Star underprint	2	1
7 Jan 1986	**1p** Advanced Coated Paper	2	1
25 Feb 1986	**2p, 5p** Advanced Coated Paper	2	1
13 May 1986	**4p, 20p** Adv. Coated Paper - Questa	2	1
24 Jun 1986	**26p, 34p** Advanced Coated Paper	2	1
11 Jul 1986	**12p** New phosphor ink	40	25
7 Oct 1986	**75p** New Paper, **28p** ACP	5	2
27 Jan 1987	**13p** Experimental phosphor	4	–
5 May 1987	**3p** Advanced Coated Paper	2	1
4 Aug 1987	**26p** Redrawn value	20	6
23 Feb 1988	**2p & 75p** Redrawn values	2	1
26 Jul 1988	**2p, 4p, 5p, 75p** Harrison printing	2	1
13 Mar 1990	**50p** Colour variation	5	1
19 Nov 1991	**18p** Enschedé printing	2	1
21 Jan 1992	**3p** Redrawn value, **50p** ACP	2	1
27 Apr 1993	**6p** Enschedé printing	2	1
8 Jun 1993	**1p, 5p, 10p** Enschedé printings	2	1
27 Jul 1993	**30p** Enschedé printing	2	1
17 Aug 1993	**35p** Enschedé printing	2	1
5 Oct 1993	**1st, 2nd NVIs** in Sheet Format	2	1
	Windsor – Tudor Rose h/s	3	–
14 Dec 1993	**4p, 20p, 50p** Enschedé printings	3	2
16 Jun 1994	*FDCs exist with 2nd Class NVI stamps. It is understood that these experimental stamps were obtained under dubious circumstances and as such are outside the scope of this catalogue.*		
19 Jul 1994	**19p** PVA Gum/Harrison	3	2
17 Aug 1994	**1st NVI 'Boots'** Promotional Label	2	1
	Nottingham 'B' spec h/s	–	3
	-do- Bradbury official cover	–	15
	Nottingham 'NVI' spec h/s	–	3
	Benham official cover	–	8
26 Oct 1994	**£1.50** Re-engraved	100	–
15 Nov 1994	**£2** Re-engraved	100	–
2 Dec 1994	**£1** Re-engraved	100	–
20 Dec 1994	**25p** Phos: Two Bands Harrison	2	1

Date	Postmark:	Windsor £	Other £
11 Apr 1995	**2p** Enschedé printing	2	1
11 Sep 1995	**1st NVI** Promotional Label	2	1
	Windsor 'G' spec h/s	3	–
	-do- Bradbury official cover	10	–
	Card for Grandparents Day slogan	–	5
25 Sep 1995	**1st NVI** 'Boots' Blue Fluor	5	3
10 Oct 1995	**25p** Enschede/changed gum	–	5
24 Oct 1995	**4p** Enschede Blue Fluor	5	–
14 Nov 1995	**1st, 2nd** NVIs Blue Fluor	6	–
16 Nov 1995	**2p** Enschede printing Blue Fluor	5	–
10 Jan 1996	**10p, 35p, 38p** Enschede Blue Fluor	6	–
6 Feb 1996	**25p** Harrison printing Blue Fluor	5	–
14 Feb 1996	**29p** Enschede printing Blue Fluor	5	–
5 Mar 1996	**1p & 50p** Blue Fluor	5	–
5 Mar 1996	**£1.50** PVA 'Lay-Flat' Gum	–	5
26 Mar 1996	**6p** Enschede printing Blue Fluor	5	–
26 Mar 1996	**30p** Enschede printing Blue Fluor	5	–
26 Mar 1996	**5p, 20p** Enschede Blue Fluor	5	–
2 May 1996	**£2** PVA 'Lay-Flat' Gum	25	–
17 Sep 1996	**£5** PVA 'Lay-Flat' Gum	15	–
3 Dec 1996	**2nd NVI** extended phos	2	1
27 Feb 1997	**£3** PVA Gum	85	–
1 Apr 1997	**1p, 6p, 43p, 50p £1** Gravure	5	3
29 Apr 1997	**20p** Gravure	4	2
27 May 1997	**2p, 4p, 5p, 10p, 30p, 39p** Gravure	4	2
27 May 1997	**1st NVI** Promotional Label Gravure	4	2
26 Aug 1997	**31p, 37p, 63p** Gravure	4	2
29 Jul 1997	**£1.50, £2, £3 & £5 Castles** Enschedé		
	Windsor permanent special h/s	15	–
	Windsor h/s *(Benham official £20)*	15	–
	Edinburgh *(Benham official £20)*	–	15
	Caernarfon *(Benham official £20)*	–	15
	Carrickfergus *(Benham official £20)*	–	15
	Appropriate CDS pmks	25	25
18 Nov 1997	**1st NVIs** Sheet Format/Walsall	2	1
	26p Harrison 'Lay-Flat' Gum	2	1
20 Apr 1999	**19p** De La Rue	2	1
	20p 2 Phos De La Rue	2	1
5 Oct 1999	**'E' NVI** Sheet Format/DeLaRue	2	1
11 Apr 2000	**£1.50, £2, £3 & £5** DeLaRue		
	Windsor permanent special h/s	15	–
	Cardiff *(Benham official £20)*	–	15
	Edinburgh *(Benham official £20)*	–	15
	Belfast *(Benham official £20)*	–	15
	London EC1 *(Benham official £20)*	–	15
	High Wycombe *(Benham off. £20)*	–	15
	Appropriate CDS pmks	20	20
9 May 2002	**1st & 2nd** Enschede	5	1
4 Jul 2002	**Gold 1st Class** Enschede	5	1
18 Mar 2003	**1st & 2nd** Walsall	5	1
1 Jul 2003	**Gold 1st Class** DeLaRue	5	1
10 May 2005	**35p** DeLaRue	5	1
	Pricing In Proportion:		
15 Aug 2006	**2nd, 1st Large** Self Adhesives	5	1
12 Sep 2006	**2nd, 1st Small** Self Adhesives	5	1

1 Jul 2003 **Gold 1st Class** DeLaRue

SELF ADHESIVES (Experimental Issues)

		ordinary covers	official covers	
		£	£	
10 Feb 1974	**Self Adhesive Labels:** ½p, 1p, 1½p, (3p + 5p), (½p + 5p)	275		
19 Jun 1974	**Self Adhesive Labels:** 3p, 3½p	50		
19 Oct 1993	**Self Adhesive Stamps: 1st Class NVI**			
	FDI – Philatelic Bureau (1)	5	-	*Royal Mail*
	FDI – Newcastle (2)	5	-	*Royal Mail*
	FDI – 1st London (3)	5	-	*Royal Mail*
	Windsor (Britannia) (4)	10	15	*Bradbury*
	Windsor (Arms) (5)	10	15	*Bradbury*
	Newcastle (Cathedral) (6)	10	15	*Benham*
	Walsall Security h/s (7)	10	20	*Walsall*
	Lickey End Bromsgrove (8)	10	-	*Royal Mail*
	New Postage Rates slogan	10	-	
	Complete pane on cover	20	-	
18 Mar 1997	**Self Adhesive Stamps: 1st & 2nd NVIs Horizontal**			
	FDI – Philatelic Bureau (9)	3	-	*Royal Mail*
	FDI – Glasgow (10)	3	-	*Royal Mail*
	FDI – London (11)	3	-	*Royal Mail*
	Windsor (Arms) (12)	5	10	*Bradbury*
	Windsor (Castle) (13)	5	8	*Benham*
6 Apr 1998	**1st & 2nd Class NVIs Vertical (rolls of 200) - Enschede**			
	Windsor (Arms) (14)	5	10	*Bradbury*
	Windsor special h/s (15)	5	8	*Benham*
	Glasgow special h/s (16)	5	8	*Benham*
	Clydebank special h/s (17)	5	8	*RN Cvrs Gp*
22 Jun 1998	**1st & 2nd Class NVIs Vertical (sheets of 100) - Walsall**			
	Windsor (Arms)	5	10	*Bradbury*
	-do- with 'dagger' perfs	75	-	
16 Feb 1999	**1st Class NVI Large White ex *Profile on Print* PSBklt**			
	Windsor (Arms)	5	10	*Bradbury*
4 Sep 2000	**1st & 2nd Class NVIs New style business sheets of 100**			
	Windsor (Castle) h/s	5		

N.B. For later self-adhesive definitive issues please refer to: main definitive section (new values, colours etc), or varieties section (different printers etc).

19 Oct 1993 **The First Royal Mail NVI self adhesive Double postmarked on last day of sale**

6 Apr 1998 **1st & 2nd Self Adhesives (rolls of 200)**

Channel Islands Occupation Issues

		plain covers	illus cvrs
Guernsey Bisects		£	£
27 Dec 1940	2d Orange George V (Profile)	125	–
	2d Orange George V (Gravure)	90	–
	2d Orange George VI	35	–
	2d Orange Centenary	25	–
Guernsey 'ARMS' issues			
7 Apr 1941	½d green	6	40
11 Mar 1942	-do- on Bluish French Banknote paper	300	–
18 Feb 1941	1d scarlet	6	40
9 Apr 1942	-do- on Bluish French Banknote paper	100	–
12 Apr 1944	2½d blue	20	65
	All 3 values on one cover with correct dates	100	–

		plain covers	illus cvrs
Jersey 'VIEWS' issues		£	£
1 Jun 1943	½d green	6	20
1 Jun 1943	1d scarlet	6	20
1 Jun 1943	½d & 1d on one cover	15	40
8 Jun 1943	1½d brown	15	30
8 Jun 1943	2d orange-yellow	15	30
8 Jun 1943	1½d & 2d on one cover	25	50
29 Jun 1943	2½d blue	15	30
29 Jun 1943	3d violet	15	30
29 Jun 1943	2½d & 3d on one cover	25	50
	All 6 values on one cover with correct dates for each pair	45	–
Jersey 'ARMS' issues			
29 Jan 1942	½d green	5	40
1 Apr 1941	1d red	5	40
	Both stamps on one cover with correct dates	80	–

REGIONALS

The first regionals were issued in 1958 - these were for Scotland, Wales, Northern Ireland, Isle of Man, Jersey and Guernsey. By the early 1970s all three small islands were independent stamp producers. With effect from 1971 there were pictorial regional special handstamps provided by Royal Mail for **new values** or **colour changes**. Philatelic Bureau handstamps are worth approximately half catalogue value.

Prices are for illustrated covers with regional postmarks

Set of 6 = Wales, Scotland, Northern Ireland, Guernsey, Jersey & Isle of Man
Set of 3 = Wales, Scotland & Northern Ireland

NEW STAMPS

		£
18 Aug 1958	**3d** Wales or Scotland	20
	Northern Ireland or Isle of Man	35
	Guernsey or Jersey	25
	Set of 6	125
29 Sep 1958	**6d & 1s 3d** Wales or Scotland	30
	Northern Ireland	40
	Set of 3	110
8 Jun 1964	**2½d** Isle of Man	35
	Guernsey or Jersey	30
7 Feb 1966	**4d Blue** Set of 6	40
1 Mar 1967	**9d & 1s 6d** Set of three	30
	Wales special slogan pmk	25
	N.I. special slogan pmk	25
4 Sep 1968	**4d Brown & 5d Blue** Set of 6	30
	Wales special slogan pmk	25
	N.I. special slogan pmk	40
	Scotland special slogan pmk	35
26 Feb 1969	**4d Red** Set of 6	25
7 Jul 1971	**2½p, 3p, 5p, 7½p** Set of 3 + I.o.M.	25
23 Jan 1974	**3p phos, 3½p, 5½p, 8p** Set of 3	25
6 Nov 1974	**3½p phos, 4½p** Set of 3	20
14 Jan 1976	**6½p, 8½p** Set of 3	20
20 Oct 1976	**10p, 11p** Set of 3	20
18 Jan 1978	**7p, 9p, 10½p** Set of 3	20
23 Jul 1980	**10p phos, 12p, 13½p, 15p** Set of 3	20
23 Jul 1980	**12p, 13½p, 15p** Set of 3	20
8 Apr 1981	**11½p, 14p, 18p, 22p** Set of 3	20
24 Feb 1982	**12½p, 15½p, 19½p & 26p** Set of 3	20
	Stampex spec h/s Set of 3	50
27 Apr 1983	**16p, 20½p, 28p** Set of 3	20
23 Oct 1984	**13p, 17p, 22p 31p,** Set of 3	20
7 Jan 1986	**12p** Set of 3	15
6 Jan 1987	**18p** Set of 3	15
8 Nov 1988	**14p, 19p, 23p & 32p** Set of 3	25
28 Nov 1989	**15p, 20p, 24p & 34p** Set of 3	25
4 Dec 1990	**17p, 22p, 26p & 37p** Set of 3	25
3 Dec 1991	**18p, 24p, 28p & 39p** Set of 3	25
7 Dec 1993	**19p, 25p, 30p, 41p** Set of 3	25
23 Jul 1996	**20p 26p 37p & 63p** Set of 3	25
1 Jul 1997	**20, 26, 37, 63** (Wales dropped 'p')	8
8 Jun 1999	**19p (gravure) 38p & 64p** (N.Ireland)	15
25 Apr 2000	**1st 40p & 65p** (N.Ireland)	10

Paper, Perf, Phosphor, Gum, Printer Varieties etc.

		£
29 Jan 1963	**3d, 6d, 1s 3d** Scotland (phos)	100
15 Jul 1963	**3d** Isle of Man chalky paper	250
7 Feb 1966	**4d Blue** Scotland - phosphor	8
9 Jun 1967	**3d Lilac** Jersey - phosphor	200
5 Sep 1967	**4d Blue** Jeresy - phosphor	200
28 Sep 1970	**9d** Scotland unwatermarked paper	20
22 Sep 1972	**2½p** Scottish Gum Arabic	60
22 Sep 1972	**2½p** Welsh Gum Arabic	60
14 Dec 1972	**3p** Scottish Gum Arabic	60
6 Jun 1973	**3p** Welsh Gum Arabic	60
21 May 1975	**5½p phos** Set of 3	10
2 Nov 1983	**16p** Scotland ACP	1
10 Jan 1984	**12½p, 16p** Wales Perf change	2
28 Feb 1984	**12½p, 16p** N.I. Perf change	4
25 Jun 1985	**17p** Scotland PCP/PVA	2
4 Dec 1985	**31p** Scotland Re-drawn lion	250
25 Feb 1986	**17p** Wales ACP	2
25 Feb 1986	**17p** N.I. ACP	2
29 Apr 1986	**12p, 17p, 31p** Scot: perf & paper change	2
9 Sep 1986	**17p** N.I. Redrawn Crown	150
4 Nov 1986	**13p** Scotland 'Questa' printing	1
28 Nov 1986	**13p** N.I. Redrawn Crown	75
27 Jan 1987	**Advanced Coated Paper, Questa:**	
	Scotland: 22p, 26p, 28p	
	Wales 26p, 28p, 31p & N.I. 26p, 28p	6
14 Apr 1987	**13p** Coated Papers Ltd. Set of 3	5
	31p N.I. ACP	2
14 Apr 1987	**13p** Wales Dextrim gum	12
29 Mar 1988	**18p Scotland & Wales**	
	Henry & Leigh Slater paper - pair	2
25 Apr 1989	**19p** Scotland Coated Papers Ltd	2
20 Jun 1989	**19p** Wales Coated Papers Ltd	2
14 May 1991	**22p, 26p, 37p** Scot: Coated Papers	3
	22p Wales Coated Papers Ltd	2
18 Feb 1993	**28p** Scottish Perf Error 13½ x 14	45
3 Oct 1995	**19p** Scottish Blue Fluor	5
19 Oct 1995	**19p** Welsh Blue Fluor	5
1 Feb 1996	**19p** N.Ireland Blue Fluor	5
5 Mar 1996	**25p** N.Ireland Blue Fluor	5
30 Apr 1996	**41p** Welsh Blue Fluor	5
1 Jul 1997	**20p, 26p, 37p, 63p** Walsall: Scot & NI	4

Royal Mail special handstamps:
top row: 7th July 1971
bottom row: 23rd January 1974

England Pictorials

		Ordinary covers	Sponsored	
23 Apr 01	**2nd, 1st, E, 65p**	£	£	
	(1) Philatelic Bureau	3	–	*Royal Mail*
	(2) Cry God for Harry	3	–	*Royal Mail*
	(3) St George & Dragon	3	40	*RM Ingot cvr*
	(4) Shakespeare Country	3	–	*Royal Mail*
	(5) First Pictorials Windsor	3	12	*Bradbury*
	(6) St George's Day	3	12	*Bradbury*
	(7) Eng. Pictorials London	3	10	*Westminster*
	(8) -do-	3	10	*Westminster*
	(9) -do-	3	10	*Westminster*
	(10) -do-	3	10	*Westminster*
	(11) London (flag)	3	10	*Westminster*
	(12) Cardiff (flag)	3	10	*Westminster*
	(13) Edinburgh (flag)	3	10	*Westminster*
	(14) Belfast (flag)	3	10	*Westminster*
	(15) St George's Day	3	10	*P Sheridan*
	(16) Westminster	3	10	*Benham*
	(17) Windsor	3	10	*Benham*
	(18) Bishopswood	3	10	*Benham*
	(19) Lancaster	3	10	*Benham*
	(20) Bond Street W1	3	10	*Benham*
	(21) William Shakespeare	3	10	*Benham*
	(22) Windsor Berks	3	10	*Benham*
	(23) Buckingham Palace Rd	3	10	*Benham*
	(24) Battle of Waterloo	3	10	*Benham*
	(25) Blockading Zeebrugge	3	10	*RNCoversGp*
4 Jul 02	**68p**			
	(26) Tallents House	3	–	*Royal Mail*
	(27) Cry God for Harry*	3	–	*Royal Mail*
14 Oct 03	**2nd, 1st, E, 68p White Borders**			
	(28) Tallents House	3	–	*Royal Mail*
	(29) Cry God for Harry*	5	–	*Royal Mail*
	(30) London (3 Lions)	3	10	*PhilStamps*
	(31) Bakewell	3	10	*Benham*
	(32) Castlerigg	3	10	*Benham*
	(33) London	3	10	*Benham*
	(34) Newport	3	10	*Benham*
	(35) London (Map)	3	10	*Westminster*
11 May 04	**40p**			
	(36) Tallents House	2	–	*Royal Mail*
	(37) Cry God for Harry*	3	–	*Royal Mail*
	(38) London (Oak Leaves)	3	8	*PhilStamps*
5 Apr 05	**42p**			
	(39) Tallents House	2	–	*Royal Mail*
	(40) Cry God for Harry*	3	–	*Royal Mail*
	(41) Macduff	3	8	*PhilStamps*
10 May 05	**42p** De La Rue	4		
28 Mar 06	**44p, 72p**			
	(42) Tallents House	2	–	*Royal Mail*
	(43) Cry God for Harry*	3	–	*Royal Mail*
	(44) Windsor	3	8	*PhilStamps*

** Same design postmark as No. (2)*

23 Apr 2001 **The first English Pictorial issue.**

Scotland Pictorials

Date	Issue	Ordinary covers £	Sponsored £	
8 Jun 99	**2nd, 1st, E, 64p**			
	(1) Philatelic Bureau	3	–	*Royal Mail*
	(2) People of the Country	3	–	*Royal Mail*
	(3) First Scottish Defins	3	20	*Bradbury*
	(4) Lochawe (Lion)	3	10	*Benham*
	(5) Glencoe (Thistle)	3	10	*Benham*
	(6) Glasgow (Flag)	3	10	*Benham*
	(7) Ballater (Tartan)	3	10	*Benham*
	(8) Edinburgh (Celtic pattern)	3	10	*Benham*
	(9) Braemar (Celtic border)	3	10	*Benham*
	(10) Edinburgh (Thistle)	3	10	*Westminster*
	(11) Walsall	3	–	
	(12) Cricket World Cup	3	10	*SPublicity*
	Scottish Parliament cds	25	–	
25 Apr 00	**65p**			
	(13) Philatelic Bureau	3	–	*Royal Mail*
	(14) People of the Country*	3	–	*Royal Mail*
	(15) New 65p Edinburgh	3	10	*Bradbury*
5 Jun 02	**2nd, 1st** De La Rue	3		
4 Jul 02	**68p**			
	(16) Tallents House	3	–	*Royal Mail*
	(17) People of the Country*	3	–	*Royal Mail*
14 Oct 03	**2nd, 1st, E, 68p White Borders**			
	(18) Tallents House	3	–	*Royal Mail*
	(19) People of the Country*	5	–	*Royal Mail*
	(20) Edinburgh (Sporran)	3	10	*PhilStamps*
	(21) Glencoe (Stag)	3	10	*Benham*
	(22) Edinburgh (Lion)	3	10	*Benham*
	(23) Isle of Skye (Thistle)	3	10	*Benham*
	(24) Isle of Lewis (Stones)	3	10	*Benham*
	(25) Edinburgh (Map)	3	10	*Westminster*
11 May 04	**40p**			
	(26) Tallents House	3	–	*Royal Mail*
	(27) People of the Country*	3	–	*Royal Mail*
	(28) Edinburgh (Thistle)	3	8	*PhilStamps*
5 Apr 05	**42p**			
	(29) Tallents House	3	–	*Royal Mail*
	(30) People of the Country*	3	–	*Royal Mail*
	(31) Macduff	3	8	*PhilStamps*
10 May 05	**42p** De La Rue	4		
28 May 06	**44p, 72p**			
	(32) Tallents House	3	–	*Royal Mail*
	(33) People of the Country*	3	–	*Royal Mail*
	(34) Windsor	3	8	*PhilStamps*

* *Same design postmark as No. (2)*

8 June 1999 **The first Scottish Pictorial stamp issue.**

8 Jun 99	**2nd, 1st, E, 64p**			
	(1) Philatelic Bureau	3	–	*Royal Mail*
	(2) The Red Dragon	3	–	*Royal Mail*
	(3) First Welsh Defins	3	20	*Bradbury*
	(4) Pormeirion (Dragon)	3	10	*Benham*
	(5) Builth Wells (Daffodils)	3	10	*Benham*
	(6) Caerphilly (Leeks)	3	10	*Benham*
	(7) Caernarvon (P of Wales)	3	10	*Benham*
	(8) Cardiff (Celtic border)	3	10	*Benham*
	(9) Cardiff (Dragon)	3	10	*Westminster*
	(10) Walsall	3	–	
	(11) Cricket World Cup	3	10	*SPublicity*
25 Apr 00	**65p**			
	(12) Philatelic Bureau	3	–	*Royal Mail*
	(13) The Red Dragon*	3	–	*Royal Mail*
	(14) New 65p Cardiff	3	10	*Bradbury*
4 Jul 02	**68p**			
	(15) Tallents House	3	–	*Royal Mail*
	(16) The Red Dragon*	3	–	*Royal Mail*
4 Mar 03	**1st** De La Rue	3		
28 May 03	**2nd** De La Rue	3		
14 Oct 03	**2nd, 1st, E, 68p White Borders**			
	(17) Tallents House	3	–	*Royal Mail*
	(18) The Red Dragon*	5	–	*Royal Mail*
	(19) Cardiff (Dragon)	3	10	*PhilStamps*
	(20) Llanrwst (Leek)	3	10	*Benham*
	(21) Cardigan	3	10	*Benham*
	(22) Llanberis (Daffoldil)	3	10	*Benham*
	(23) Cardiff (Dragon)	3	10	*Benham*
	(24) Cardiff (Map)	3	10	*Westminster*
11 May 04	**40p**			
	(25) Tallents House	3	–	*Royal Mail*
	(26) The Red Dragon*	3	–	*Royal Mail*
	(27) Cardiff (Dragon)	3	10	*PhilStamps*
5 Apr 05	**42p**			
	(28) Tallents House	3	–	*Royal Mail*
	(29) The Red Dragon*	3	–	*Royal Mail*
	(30) Macduff	3	8	*PhilStamps*
10 May 05	**42p** De La Rue	4		
28 Mar 06	**44p, 72p**			
	(31) Tallents House	3	–	*Royal Mail*
	(32) The Red Dragon*	3	–	*Royal Mail*
	(33) Windsor	3	8	*PhilStamps*

* *Same design postmark as No. (2)*

8 June 1999 **The first Welsh Pictorial stamp issue.**

Northern Ireland Pictorials

Date	Issue	Ordinary covers £	Sponsored £	
6 Mar 01	**2nd, 1st, E, 65p**			
	(1) Philatelic Bureau	3	–	*Royal Mail*
	(2) At Dusk Horizons	3	–	*Royal Mail*
	(3) NI Pictorial Stamps	3	12	*Bradbury*
	(4) Bushmills (rectangle)	3	10	*Benham*
	(5) Bushmills (oval)	3	10	*Benham*
	(6) Belleek Enniskillen	3	10	*Benham*
	(7) Bushmills (circle)	3	10	*Benham*
	(8) Lisburn	3	10	*Benham*
	(9) Belfast	3	10	*Benham*
	(10) Newcastle	3	10	*Benham*
	(11) Battle of Trafalgar	3	10	*Benham*
4 Jul 02	**68p**			
	(12) Tallents House	3	–	*Royal Mail*
	(13) At Dusk Horizons*	3	–	*Royal Mail*
15 Oct 02	**'E'** De La Rue	3		
14 Oct 03	**2nd, 1st, E, 68p White Borders**			
	(14) Tallents House	3	–	*Royal Mail*
	(15) At Dusk Horizons*	5	–	*Royal Mail*
	(16) Belfast (Leprechaun)	3	10	*PhilStamps*
	(17) Belfast (Harp)	3	10	*Benham*
	(18) Cookstown (Flax)	3	10	*Benham*
	(19) Portrush (Cross)	3	10	*Benham*
	(20) Londonderry (Hand)	3	10	*Benham*
	(21) Belfast (Map)	3	10	*Westminster*
11 May 04	**40p**			
	(22) Tallents House	3	–	*Royal Mail*
	(23) At Dusk Horizons*	3	–	*Royal Mail*
	(24) Belfast (Flower)	3	8	*PhilStamps*
5 Apr 05	**42p**			
	(25) Tallents House	3	–	*Royal Mail*
	(26) At Dusk Horizons*	3	–	*Royal Mail*
	(27) Macduff	3	8	*PhilStamps*
26 Jul 05	**42p** De La Rue	4		
28 Mar 06	**44p, 72p**			
	(28) Tallents House	3	–	*Royal Mail*
	(29) At Dusk Horizons*	3	–	*Royal Mail*
	(30) Windsor	3	8	*PhilStamps*

* *Same design postmark as No. (2)*

6 Mar 2001 **The first Northern Ireland Pictorial issue.**

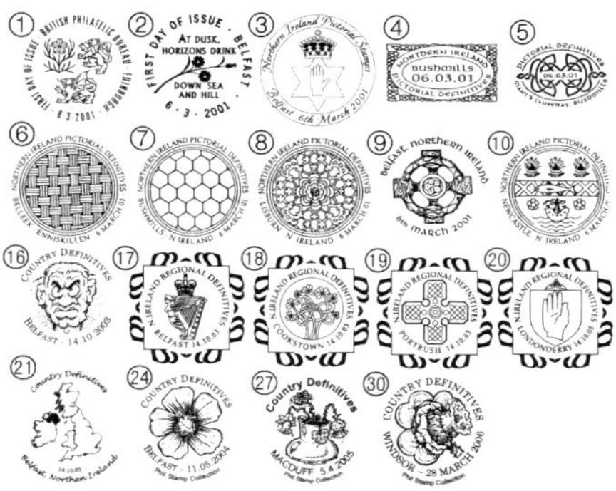

New Services

Date	Service	£
1 Aug 1883	**6d Parcel Service**	750
9 Sep 1911	**Coronation UK First Aerial Post**	
	½d Green (Postcard)	55
	½d -do- Privilege card in violet	250
	1d Red (Envelope)	80
	1d -do- Privilege envelope in violet	350
25 Jan 1912	**Wilkinson Meter Mail**	300
1 Feb 1961	**Recorded Delivery**	60
16 Sep 1968	**Two Tier Post** pair of covers	10
	-do- Windsor postmark	30
24 Nov 1975	**SpeedPost** Brighton or Bexhill pmks	25
24 Jan 1977	**SpeedPost** Extension of service	150
12 Oct 1998	**Special Delivery**	15
14 Feb 2002	**New labels** Set of six	50
15 Jan 2004	**SmartStamp Service**	30

Index for Commemorative Issues

D

E

F